Social Scientific Models for
Interpreting the Bible

Biblical Interpretation Series

VOLUME 53

SOCIAL SCIENTIFIC MODELS FOR INTERPRETING THE BIBLE

Social Scientific Models for Interpreting the Bible

Essays by the Context Group in Honor of Bruce J. Malina

EDITED BY

John J. Pilch

Society of Biblical Literature
Atlanta

Library of Congress Cataloging-in-Publication Data

Social scientific models for interpreting the Bible : essays by the Context Group in
honor of Bruce J. Malina / edited by John J. Pilch.
    p. cm. – (Biblical interpretation series ; v. 53)
   Includes bibliographical references and index.
   ISBN 978-1-58983-287-9 (pbk. : alk. paper)
  1. Bible–Social scientific critcism. I. Malina, Bruce J. II. Pilch, John J. III.
Context Group (1986?–)

BS521.88.S63 2007
220.6'7–dc22   2007035223

Printed in the United States of America
on acid-free paper

Contents

The Honoree: Bruce John Malina

This collection of fresh, social-scientific analyses of biblical text-segments is presented by the authors to Bruce John Malina on the occasion of his sixty-fifth birthday. The Editor and all members of the Context Group join colleagues and friends in thanking Bruce for his pioneering efforts and ground-breaking contributions to this approach in interpreting the Bible and other ancient documents. All have drawn inspiration from his work and benefited from his advice and encouragement in their own areas of interest and publication projects.

Bruce was born on October 9th, 1933 to Mary and Joseph Malina, Sr., in Brooklyn, NY, the oldest of nine children. His early education was taken at Our Lady of Consolation Parish School, in the Williamsburgh section of Brooklyn, and St. Bonaventure High School, Sturtevant, WI, where he won the *Optime merenti* award, among others, for maintaining the highest scholastic average in his class for all four years. Bruce was so committed to his studies that as a senior, he resigned from the first string Varsity Basketball team when he felt that this activity was taking valuable time from his studies.

His brothers, Joseph, Jr., and Robert, attended St. Anthony of Padua Prep School, Watkins Glen, NY, approximately during the same years that Bruce attended the sister school, St. Bonaventure's. The three brothers engaged in friendly sibling competition since each of them were on the honor roll each quarter. More significantly, already in these years Bruce demonstrated with his siblings a trait that would characterize his life and career even to the present. He regularly prodded each of his brothers to greater achievements by recommending books to read, or films to see, or by proposing some challenge they might consider undertaking. Indeed, all three brothers have had successful academic careers in their respective fields of study.

From 1953 to 1969, Bruce was a member of the Franciscan Order completing his BA at St. Francis College, Burlington, WI *summa cum laude* (1956) and earning certification in social ministry with studies at Christ the King School of Theology, West Chicago, IL (1960). He pursued graduate religious studies at St. Anthony University, Rome,

Italy (STL *cum laude*, 1964) and graduate biblical studies at the Pontifical Biblical Institute, Rome, Italy (SSL *summa cum laude*, 1966) and at the Department of Biblical Studies in the Jerusalem, Israel campus of St. Anthony University (STD *summa cum laude*, 1967).

A pivotal experience in Bruce's life and career was living in the Philippine Islands (1960-63; 67-69). In addition to teaching biblical studies to Filipino students, he studied anthropology and linguistics (the language of Samar) and did field work with two very competent colleagues: Rev. Neal Kaminski, OFM, and Rev. Julian Arent, OFM. This experience and the encouragement of these two colleagues inspired and eventually prompted him to write his world-renowned book: *The New Testament World: Insights from Cultural Anthropology* (1981; rev. ed. 1993; translated into German, 1993, and Spanish, 1995).

Bruce returned to the United States in 1969 to accept a teaching position at Creighton University where he continues as Professor of Biblical Studies to the present time. His career has been spent with undergraduate students, and he has won awards for teaching at Creighton. In recent years he has been an outside reader for doctoral dissertations at Drew University, Southern Baptist University, Northwestern University, the University of South Africa, Augustana Hochschule in Neuendettelsau, Germany, and a co-director of doctoral dissertations successfully defended at the University of Salamanca, Spain.

He was a Fulbright Scholar at the Bibelvitenskap, University of Oslo, Norway (Fall, 1986), a visiting Professor at the University of Naples, Italy (Fall, 1990), a visiting scholar at the Consejo Superior de Investigaciones Cientificas, Madrid, Spain (Spring 1991), and a visiting professor at the University of Stellenbosch, South Africa (Winter, 1994). In 1995, The University of St. Andrews, Scotland, awarded him an honorary doctorate in Sacred Theology in recognition of his singular contributions to biblical scholarship.

Bruce has held editorial positions in the Society of Biblical Literature and the Catholic Biblical Association of America, serving as Vice-President (1986-87) and President (1987-1988) of the latter organization. He has also convened and chaired task forces and other groups in both organizations.

Central to Bruce's research and publication activity has been the friendship and collaboration with members of the *Context Group: A Project on the Bible in its Cultural Context*.

In 1977, Bruce attended a National Endowment Humanities Summer Seminar facilitated by Wayne Meeks at Yale University. His research report at that seminar creatively integrated the social scientific theories of Talcott Parsons, Mary Douglas, and Michael Polanyi into a model that would be helpful in understanding early Christianity. Later that summer, he shared these insights in a Task Force on Healing at the annual meeting of the Catholic Biblical Association of America in Detroit, MI (see *CBQ* 39 [1977] 543). Further reflection upon and refinement of that research would eventually result in two books: *The New Testament World: Insights from Cultural Anthropology* (1977) and *Christian Origins and Cultural Anthropology* (1986).

In 1979, Malina struck up a working relationship with John Elliott at the Catholic Biblical Association meeting. They and other colleagues who had been exploring the use of social scientific approaches to interpreting the Bible banded together to shape the new direction of the Social Scientific Task Force at the CBA meetings. This collaborative approach to scholarship and research eventually flowered into the Context Group (for a history, see Douglas M. Oakman, "After Ten Years: A Draft History of the Context Group: Project on the Bible in its Cultural Context," unpublished manuscript, 1996).

Even before they became the Context Group, the scholar-members had been collaborating in annual meetings of Continuing Seminars and Task Forces at the Catholic Biblical Association, of various sections at the Society of Biblical Literature, and for a brief while in the Social Facets Seminar of the Westar Institute. Since 1990, the Context Group has been meeting annually in the Franciscan Renewal Center, Portland, Oregon, and periodically in Europe for international meetings (Medina del Campo, Spain; St. Andrews, Scotland; Prague, Czech Republic; Tutzing, Germany). David Bossman has observed that at their meetings, "these scholars are explorers not inventors, seekers not protagonists, pathfinders not preachers" (*BTB* 22 [1992] 51). The primary purpose of the Context Group is to facilitate publication by sharing insights, bibliography, a wide variety of primary sources, and a wide array of research tools. All participants and observers at the meetings whether in the US or abroad have been impressed by the collegiality, fellowship, and positive mutual encouragement in comments shared by Context Group members. As a key inspirational figure in these meetings, Bruce Malina continues the same kind of gentle yet challenging encouragement he tended earlier in his life to his siblings. Indeed, Context Group members strike others as so remarkably bonded that they appear to constitute a fictive kinship group!

The thirteen Context Group contributors to this volume honoring Professor Malina present the kind of exciting new research with which the Group has become identified. They adopt models from the social sciences and use them both as tools for gathering data-sets and interpreting data-sets. They draw on Mediterranean "informants" (e.g. Seneca) to provide information that might fill in gaps in biblical materials. Such information was assumed by biblical authors to be so familiar to original readers as not to require presentation or explanation.

The first two essays are particularly significant in this volume. None of the contributors knew what others were preparing. Still, it is typical of the group that members frequently adopt different positions and draw different conclusions on the same topic. The ensuing discussions are friendly and productive with no need for closure or declaring winners or losers. Professor Elliott has long championed the use of sociology in his own research, and in particular he has argued that Bryan Wilson's "sect" model is applicable in the analysis of the Jesus group. While Elliott has argued this point most often with Bruce Malina who does not agree with that position, the young South African scholar, Professor Pieter Craffert produced an essay that further develops Malina's position and serves as a fitting contrast to Elliott's shedding fresh light on an ongoing discussion. There could be no better way to open this volume. Nor could there be any more appropriate tribute to Professor Malina who stimulates and encourages this kind of fruitful and friendly exchange of ideas.

Unanticipated personal difficulties prevented other members of the Context Group from contributing to this volume. Had these not occurred, it would have been necessary to plan a companion volume. Nevertheless, all members of the Context Group are pleased to have shared in scholarly collaborations over the years that have helped these contributors to honor our esteemed colleague, Bruce, with excellent scholarly essays. Testimony to the inspiration of Bruce and all of us to each other can be found in the personal bibliographies listed on The Context Group web-page: http://www.serv.net/~oakmande/index.htm, click on "Context Group Publications".

We present this book to Bruce with gratitude for his inspiration and leadership and with heartfelt good wishes for many long productive years with us.

Ad multos annos! Sto lat!

John J. Pilch, Editor
Georgetown University, Washington, DC

1

On Wooing Crocodiles for Fun and Profit: Confessions of an Intact Admirer

John H. Elliott, *University of San Francisco*

Introduction

I have been collaborating with my dear friend Bruce since we first met in 1979. Because this has been an intensely personal as well as professional form of collaboration, I offer to our honoree some reflections on my own personal journey, on the eventual merging of our paths, and on the nature of the exegetical enterprise that has brought us together. Bruce may recognize a portion of these remarks as an echo of a paper I delivered at the annual meeting of the American Academy of Religion and Society of Biblical Literature held at San Francisco in 1992 as part of the Society's series of invited lectures on "Biblical Scholarship in the Twenty-First Century." In that 1992 lecture, a precursor of my book of the following year, *What is Social-scientific Criticism?* (Minneapolis: Fortress, 1993), I discussed the rise of social-scientific criticism as a valuable enhancement of our exegetical study of the New Testament and its social-cultural context and key figures in the formation of this approach. Our honoree has figured prominently in the construction and advance of this interdisciplinary method uniting the methods and perspectives of exegesis and the social sciences, and most of our research since 1980 has been the product of ongoing dialogue and collaboration.

Exegetes conventionally have been reluctant to comment on, or reveal, their own "social location" and the personal experiences that have shaped the interests, values, and agendas that inform their research. Analysts committed to a social scientific criticism of the Bible such as Malina and myself, however, realize that aspects of one's own social location are as important to consider as are the factors shaping the social location and perspectives of the biblical authors and their literary productions. It is this concern that accounts for the autobiographical nature of the remarks that follow. Since crocodile wooers and fellow travelers will inevitably debate, as well as agree on, aspects of technique and tracking along the way (read: method and models), this reflection would be incomplete without a word or two concerning a topic on which Bruce and I continue to have spirited discussion and debate; namely, the appropriateness and utility of analyzing the Jesus movement as a development from faction to sect.

I offer these reflections as an homage to a dear friend and in gratitude for all he has taught us about the everyday reality and vision of our ancestors in the faith and about the delight of wooing crocodiles for fun and profit.

On Wooing Crocodiles

Since the reader may be wondering what place crocodiles have in an homage to a resident of Omaha, Nebraska, let us turn immediately to the concept of "wooing crocodiles." In a 1984 survey of the "relationship between Sociology and New Testament studies," Derek Tidball, a British theologian, compared the growing exegetical interest in the social sciences to the "wooing of a crocodile." Tidball adopted the analogy from Winston Churchill who first used it in the Cold War period following World War II, with reference to maintaining good relations with the Soviets. In Churchill's words, "You do not know whether to tickle it [that is, the Soviet crocodile] under the chin or beat it over the head. When it opens its mouth you cannot tell whether it is trying to smile or preparing to eat you up" (Tidball 1985:106). With this analogy Tidball was not so much suggesting an odious comparison between sociology and the Soviet Union as he was issuing a warning that exegetical dalliance with the social sciences was a dangerous business and that crocodile wooers needed to keep their wits about them at all times.

The warning is indeed not groundless. See the recent study on raising crocodiles for fun and profit by former crocodile trainer Lefty one-armed McGraw. The comparison of the social sciences to a crocodile is especially interesting given the fact that sociologists themselves are fond of citing Thomas Hobbes' description of the raging beast of societal chaos, "Leviathan," as that daunting phenomenon upon which the science of sociology seeks to gain some handle. Tidball's comparison takes us from sociology as Leviathan tamer to the danger of the enterprise itself, and the uneasiness of innocent exegetes courting the menacing crocodile. Is there cause for caution and wariness? If the lion is invited to lay down with the lamb, is it likely, as philosopher Woody Allen has observed, that "the lamb won't get much sleep." In the ruminations that follow, I shall be speaking as a yet intact admirer who has discovered some decidedly positive payoffs of the marriage of exegesis and the social sciences.

Social-Scientific Criticism and a Personal Journey

The method under discussion I first labeled "sociological exegesis" in my 1981 study on 1 Peter, A *Home for the Homeless*. Bruce, however, convinced me that a more appropriate label for an analysis that included anthropology as well as sociology was "social-scientific criticism" and that has been the label I subsequently employed in the subtitle of the second edition of *Home for the Homeless* (1990) and in the title of the volume in the Guides to Biblical Scholarship series of Fortress Press, *What is Social-Scientific Criticism?* (1993). Since this volume contains an extensive account of the emergence of this method, its practitioners and their work, its presuppositions and operations, and a discussion of critical assessments, I will limit myself here to only a few cursory remarks concerning the main features of what we call Social-Scientific Criticism, that is, a method resulting from a merger of exegesis and historical research with the resources of the social sciences.

Since this approach operates with the assumption that all communicators and interpreters past and present are conditioned in their perspectives by time, place, and circumstances, and that such perspectives are determined by one's social location, I begin with some autobiographical detail about my own social location and the personal process which eventually led me to see the need for supplementing a conventional historical-critical method with the research, theory and methods of the social sciences.

In 1963 I completed a dissertation on 1 Peter at the Wilhelms-Universität in Münster, Westfalen, Germany. This work appeared in the Supplements to Novum Testamentum series in 1966 under the title, *The Elect and the Holy*. It comprised a traditional-redactional study of the use made in the second chapter of this letter of the covenant formula of Exod 19:5-6 and of 1 Peter's theology of election and holiness. However, it included minimal attention to questions of social and cultural context, a serious lacuna as I latter came to realize. Upon my return from Germany in 1963, I taught exegesis at Concordia Seminary in St. Louis, Missouri, from 1963-1967. There in St. Louis, a turbulent battleground of the Civil Rights movement then underway, I first came to realize my limited conceptual resources for comprehending and confronting the racial war that was raging in America in the mid-sixties. Imagining nevertheless that the Church and theology had a vital role to play in any possible social reconciliation, I agreed in 1965 to serve on a city-wide commission on religion and race that was trying to come to grips with the racial turmoil confronting St. Louis. At that time, I, along with other members of the commission, received a late night call from Martin Luther King Jr. and his team in Selma, Alabama, to join them in the confrontation taking place in that city. Within the hour I had to decide whether my participating in this political event should take precedence over my teaching responsibilities at the seminary the next day.

Could I reconcile my job as an exegete and seminary teacher with my political convictions? What should I do? I did join others in the flight to Selma and it was on the dusty streets of Selma that I lost my political innocence. On our return to St. Louis, there was a massive outcry from church people and others. We theologians, priests, nuns, ministers and rabbis who participated in the Selma stand-off, our critics said, had profaned our holy calling, our collars and sacred habits. We had made an invalid and unacceptable link between church and politics and had participated in an affair that was none of our concern. The persistent criticism and my vulnerable situation at Concordia seminary made my continuation there difficult, and in 1967 I accepted a position at the University of San Francisco where I have been teaching ever since.

There in the Bay Area, as elsewhere in the country, people were beginning to see the connection between racial conflict and the growing police action in Viet Nam. This undeclared war, however, presented a different set of problems more complex in nature. Those of us who were speaking out in protest, blocking draft boards, and assisting our youth in applying for conscientious objector status at the same time were being called upon to help parishioners with enlisted children come to grips with the overwhelming complexity of the political, economic, social, and religious issues over which so many well-meaning Americans were divided. At this point it became clear to me, as to many other theologians and clergy, that sorting through this maze of issues required a far more sophisticated analysis and framework of thought than we had been equipped with in our previous training. As I turned to the social sciences for developing this larger perspective, it gradually occurred to me that in my analysis of biblical texts many of these same embracing social issues were implied. Their analysis, too, required a much broader perspective than was provided by the conventional historical critical method. As I continued to ponder this connection between my current political experience and my analysis of biblical texts, I discovered several other theologians and exegetes in the Bay Area doing the same thing. Eventually we decided to meet together on a regular basis and formed a group called the BASTARDS: the Bay Area Seminar for Theology and Related Disciplines. Norman Gottwald and I served as conveners and in the early 70s it was this collaboration that stimulated my returning to the letter of 1 Peter for a second look from a social-scientific perspective as it did Gottwald's work on *The Tribes of Yahweh*. His volume was published in 1979. Mine was submitted this same year and appeared in 1981 under the title, A *Home for the Homeless. A Sociological Exegesis of 1 Peter, its Situation and Strategy.*

It was in 1979 that I first met our honoree. Earlier in the 1970s each of us served at the annual meetings of the Catholic Biblical Association of America as conveners of study groups focusing on the New Testament in its social and cultural contexts, but we had made no personal contact. In 1978 I had lectured at the Pontifical Biblical Institute in Rome and had completed the manuscript of A *Home for the Homeless*. At the 1979 meeting of the CBA I delivered a paper on the method of sociological exegesis, which subsequently appeared as the Introduction to A *Home for the Homeless*. Bruce was present at that paper and indicated that we were kindred spirits who needed to put our heads together. We have been doing so ever since. A ground-breaking study of his, written at the same time as mine, likewise appeared in 1981 as *The New Testament: Insights from cultural Anthropology* (followed by a revised edition in 1993). With my study group of the CBA concluded, I joined Bruce's group and down to the present this three-day summer meeting served as an occasion for focusing attention on specific aspects of the social and cultural world of the New Testament and introducing new visitors to the practice of social scientific criticism.

In reflecting on my experience and social location, I think it quite likely that my multi-year stints in Germany and Italy as a resident alien, my marriage to a German resident alien, my 6 month alien residence in Rome in a Jesuit community, and my work with Central American resident aliens at my church in Berkeley, California, Lutheran University Chapel, all had a role in sensitizing me to the issue and social condition of resident aliens in early Christianity as well and to the likelihood that the term *paroikoi* in 1 Peter had profound social as well as symbolical connotations, as I proposed in A *Home for the Homeless*. In addition, living abroad in Italy and Israel introduced me to Mediterranean culture and provided that personal experience which would then resonate with research into Mediterranean anthropology and its utility for studying Old and New Testament cultural environments.

The method of biblical interpretation that gradually began to take shape in my research and writings and conversations with colleagues has involved an expansion of the conventional historical-critical method with the research, theory, and models of the social sciences. In terms of definition, Social Scientific Criticism is that phase of the exegetical task which analyzes the social and cultural dimensions of texts and their environmental contexts through the use of the perspectives, theory, models and research of the social sciences. As a component of the historical-critical method of exegesis, social scientific criticism investigates biblical texts as meaningful configurations of language intended to communicate between composers and audiences. With this method we set out to examine (1) the social features of the form and content of texts and the conditioning factors and intended consequences of the communication process; (2) the correlation of the text's linguistic, literary, rhetorical, theological-ideological, and social dimensions; and (3) the manner in which this textual communication was both a reflection of and response to a specific social and cultural situation--that is, how it was designed to serve as an effective vehicle of social interaction and an instrument of social as well as literary and theological consequence. Inasmuch as these texts encode information about, and derive their plausibility, meaning, and persuasive power from, the social and cultural systems in which they are produced, this method also requires examination of the salient and interrelated properties of the society and culture, the institutions and cultural codes, that governed ancient thought, institutionalized behavior and conventional modes of interaction.

This operation of the exegetical enterprise, therefore, is closely related to other disciplines with a broader focus not on specific texts but on ancient social and cultural systems in general as investigated by historians, sociologists, anthropologists, and archaeologists. The disciplines, like the materials investigated, obviously overlap and complement each other. The social-scientific analysis of texts is constantly carried out in conjunction with study of the social and cultural systems in which these texts were produced and which provided their frameworks of meaning. On the other hand, examination of the latter is constantly nourished by the research of the former. This is an approach, in other words, that focuses on both texts and contexts and which seeks to understand how texts in given social and cultural contexts are designed to communicate meaning, narrate plausible and persuasive stories and move their audiences to concerted social action.

In this task, the empirical research, theory, and models of the social sciences play an essential role. In the first place, the cross-cultural research of ethnographers, anthropologists, and sociologists provides us with the necessary material and models for distinguishing ancient patterns of social, economic, and political organization and cultural scripts typical of pre-industrial, agrarian societies from those of the modern-day interpreter. Sensitivity to this fundamental distinction helps us to avoid the anachronistic and ethnocentric errors, for instance, of imagining in the ancient world the existence of a middle class, or the possibility of societal revolution or an egalitarianism like that sponsored by the American and French revolutions or a post-enlightenment notion of individuality.

Secondly, we learn to make valid distinctions between "emic" and "etic" perspectives; that is, differentiations between the perspectives and construals of human organization and behavior from the vantage point of the native, on the one hand, and the modern researcher, on the other, the persons populating the texts of the Bible, on the one hand, and modern Bible readers, on the other. This allows us to validly gather, organize, and ultimately explain raw material in terms of concepts and theories that are different from those of our biblical informers.

Thirdly, social science perspectives assist us in conceptualizing entire social systems and the interrelation of natural environment, climate, material resources, economic, social, and political activity. With these interlocking features of the entire social system in view, we are then more ably prepared to examine and explain, for instance, how Roman taxation, combined with the expropriation of peasant lands, the policies of the Temple aristocracy, and then famine together placed an unbearable burden on the Palestinian peasantry and collectively set the stage for the first Judean-Roman war.

Fourthly, with knowledge of the pivotal values and cultural codes of ancient Mediterranean and Near Eastern society in view, honor and shame, kinship loyalty, patronage and clientelism, hospitality and generosity, male/female behavioral codes, group oriented personality, perception of limited good and the like, we are equipped for a culturally sensitive reading and understanding of the social dramas presented to us on the pages of the New Testament.

In sum, models of social organization and cultural codes provided by the social sciences equip us with a heretofore lacking set of lenses for seeing the big social picture and for cueing in to the cultural scripts and latent meanings conveyed by the biblical documents. This in turn, then, puts us in a more advantageous position for assessing both the manner and limits for appropriating these biblical writings and applying them to the urgencies of our own day.

This social-scientific perspective is essential if we are to grasp and explain the social dimensions of the early Christian movement and the social and cultural implications of the communications produced by this and other social groups of antiquity. Moreover, it is a natural outgrowth of the historical critical method itself, which has always raised, if not satisfactorily answered, the crucial question of social setting or *Sitz im Leben*. Thus social-scientific criticism is an expansion of the exegetical tool-kit and a complement, not an alternative, to social history and so-called social description. Of course it is important to gather information on individual persons, unusual events, and specific periods and localities. Such distinctive and uncommon properties, however, only become evident, as Max Weber has reminded us, when the common, recurrent and typical features of a society are first known. Moreover, whereas historians and social describers generally work with unacknowledged and implicit models, social-scientific critics insist on exposing conceptual models at the outset so that hypotheses are clarified and then exposed to verification on the basis of the fit of data and model and their capacity for explanation. Ultimately only such a procedure can lead to the testing of hypotheses and emulation by others and thus to a genuine advance beyond guesswork and hunches, however inspired. For social-scientific criticism seeks to advance beyond mere description to explanation of human behavior, of social organization, and social change, and, in Wayne Meeks's felicitous phrasing, of the correlation of patterns of belief and patterns of behavior.

My own exegetical work along social-scientific lines, stimulated by my political and pastoral activities, had led me to return to the letter of 1 Peter in the early 1970s and to a nagging question I had never been able to put to rest. Did early Christianity offer its adherents little more than a "pie-in-the-sky-by-and-by" compensation in the future for resolute endurance of hostility and suffering in the present? Generations of readers of 1 Peter have assumed as much with an assurance only strengthened by centuries of pietistic theology and hymnody singing plaintively of a pilgrimage of earth and a desire for a heavenly home. As I began to analyze this letter from a social scientific point of view, however, quite a different picture of 1 Peter's situation and strategy began to emerge.

Analysis of key designations of the letter's addressees and their situation (*paroikoi, parepidemoi,* 2:11; *paroikia,* 1:17), on the basis of the sense of these terms in Greek inscriptional evidence and the Greek Old Testament, shows that these terms identified actual "resident aliens" and "visiting strangers" living in lands removed from their original homes, with limits on their social and legal rights in the places they inhabited. In the Septuagint, it is Abraham, Sarah and their progeny, the House of Israel, who are constantly identified as "resident aliens" living in foreign territories (Canaan, Egypt, Babylon etc.) and subject to the usual vicissitudes experienced by all strangers and aliens in the ancient world. Since the phrase "resident aliens and visiting strangers" of 1 Pet 2:11 appears derived from Abraham's description of himself in Gen 23:4 LXX, and since the Christian wives addressed in 1 Pet 3:1-6 are called Sarah's "children" (3:6), it is apparent that the Petrine author sees his audience as linked inseparably not only with Israel and its forebears, Abraham and Sarah, but also with Israel's repeated plight of alien residence in strange and hostile environments. This situation of social alienation then appears consistent with, and explanatory of, the harassment, slander, and suffering that the addressees experienced at the hands of their hostile and abusive neighbors (2:12, 15, 20; 3:9, 13-17; 4:1, 4, 6, 12-19; 5:8-9, 10).

A comparison of the diagnosis of the situation and the response presented in 1 Peter with the typical situation and strategies of sectarian movements in pre-industrial societies led me to see that the sectarian model of the conversionist sect as elaborated by Bryan Wilson (1973) provided a useful model for detecting the predicament faced by the addressees of this letter. Suspicion, slander and abuse as typical native responses to strangers and aliens had resulted in innocent Christian suffering. This suffering, unless provided with a positive rationale, would have led to discouragement, despair, and even defection. The communities addressed found themselves in a typical sectarian dilemma. Abuse from outsiders could be eliminated if the sect were to conform to conventional expectations and social standards. But if social conformity were adopted as a solution, the sect would soon sacrifice its distinctive identity and thus lose its basis for attracting new members. For the members constituted a distinctive community called into being by God and to loyalty to Jesus as the Christ, a calling which entailed conversion through baptism and disengagement from previous allegiances and alliances (1:3–2:10; 3:21; 4:1-4, 15; 5:10). Their appeal for conversion would only be plausible and effective if their social differentiation were maintained.

The sectarian model also provided a means for appreciating the major social concerns and sectarian strategy of this letter: an affirmation of the distinctive communal identity of the Christian brotherhood as a messianic sect of Israel, a call for internal social cohesion and an exemplary morality that would attract recruits, and a explanatory and legitimating ideology that would provide a positive rationale for suffering and a persuasive motive for continued emotional commitment to God, Jesus Christ, and one another.

In this light it then became evident that in the ideological portrayal of the Christian movement as a "brotherhood" (2:17; 5:9), a "household" of God (2:5; 4:17) and a fictive kin group, the collective metaphor of *oikos tou theou* served as a social correlate and contrast to the condition of the Christians as *paroikoi* in society. *Paroikoi* they were and should remain, 1 Peter insists, because in the household of God strangers in society had found a home for the homeless. *Paroikia* existence, with all its vulnerability and social estrangement, was for the Christian movement, as it was for their Hebrew forebears in Canaan, Egypt, Babylon and the Diaspora, an unavoidable concomitant of a people on the move, of a social movement coupled with geographical movement. 1 Peter reflects that fact and attests the attraction which early Christianity held for both the geographically and culturally displaced as well as the rootless and socially marginalized of society while simultaneously demonstrating the key role which the family and household played as a material and social basis of the Church's recruitment and as an ideological symbol of Christian identity, cohesion, and commitment.

Wooing Crocodiles Together

Following the publication of this study on 1 Peter in 1981, and under our honoree's prompting, I began to direct more focused attention to the use of social-scientific models in the exegetical enterprise in general. The nature and role of models and the need for their explication and testing was the subject of my 1986 essay on "Models and Method," which included a critique of Gerd Theissen's work on *The Sociology of Early Palestinian Christianity* (1978). This piece was included

in the essays I collected and edited in the thirty-fifth volume of Semeia, *Social-Scientific Criticism of the New Testament and its Social World*
(1986), a collection also including Bruce's provocative piece on challenging "received views."

In the Spring of 1986 yet another form of collaboration came into
being, one that led to the happy formation of the Context Group in
1990. The circumstances are carefully chronicled in the account of
Douglas Oakman, After *Ten Years. A Draft History of the Context Group:
Project on the Bible in its Cultural Context* (1996). Under the aegis of
Robert Funk's Westar Institute, Oakman recalls,

> a group of established scholars and graduate students, noted for their
> study of the social history of early Christianity or social inquiry into the
> Bible, gathered in Redlands, CA. The stated agenda of the meeting was
> to explore possibilities of rapprochement between members of the Social
> History of Early Christianity and the Social Sciences and New Testa-
> ment Sections of the Society of Biblical Literature.

From the persons present, enlisted from a wide variety of social
networks, a group called the "Social Facets Seminar" was born in a
process of "forming, storming, norming, and adjourning," to borrow a
model of group formation familiar to members of this group. Meeting
twice yearly in tandem with the Jesus Seminar and other groups of the
Westar Institute, the Social Facets Seminar soon generated a series of
articles (initially published in the Institute journal *Forum* and subsequently in *Biblical Theology Bulletin*) and several significant collaborative
volumes including *Calling Jesus Names* by Bruce Malina and Jerome H.
Neyrey (1988); *The Social World of Luke-Acts,* edited by Jerome H.
Neyrey (1991); *Introducing the Cultural Context of the Old Testament* and
Introducing the Cultural Context of the New Testament by John J. Pilch
(1991a and b); *Biblical Social Values and Their Meaning* edited by John J.
Pilch and Bruce Malina (1993; updated edition 1998); and a series of
"Readers Guides" to social-scientific research on the New Testament
and its world compiled and edited by Richard L. Rohrbaugh, *The
Social Sciences and New Testament Interpretation* (1996). Numerous other
publications of the Seminar members from 1988 to 1992 are listed in
my *What is Social-Scientific Criticism?* (1993:151-162).

The eventual disengagement of the Social Facets Seminar from the
Westar Institute in the Fall 1989, while somewhat tumultuous (Oak-
man, *After Ten Years,* 5-6), was in retrospect decidedly fortuitous.
Rather than disbanding, its members, aware of the immense benefit of
collaboration in an atmosphere of mutual respect, reorganized as The
Context Group and held the first of its annual meetings in the Spring

of 1990 at the Franciscan Renewal Center adjacent to Lewis and Clark College in Portland, Oregon. Jerome Neyrey was elected Executive Secretary; Douglas Oakman, chief of Communications (receiving and distributing papers before the annual meeting); John J. Pilch, chief of Public Relations; Richard L. Rohrbaugh, head of Local Arrangements, and I, the previous Chair of the Social Facets Seminar, as Program .Chair. Expanded by scholars from Australia, Europe, and South Africa, and aimed at providing positive feedback and assistance in the preparation of manuscripts for publication, The Context Group has produced a remarkable number of influential publications and is an eloquent witness to the benefit of collaborative research. Beyond annual meetings at Portland, international conferences involving the Context Group have taken place at Medina del Campo, Spain (1991), St. Andrews, Scotland (1994), and the International Baptist Theological Seminary in Prague (1997). Papers from these meetings have appeared in various journals, including *Biblical Theology Bulletin* and *Listening: Journal of Religion and Culture,* and essay collections (Esler 1994, 1995; Malina 1996c). For my part, the stimulation and support I have enjoyed in the company of these scholars and friends has been the highlight of my academic career, a feeling that I am confident is shared throughout the Group. In all these meetings, our honoree has played a major role as teacher, mentor, international conference organizer, and general gadfly par excellence.

Are practitioners of social-scientific criticism all of one mind? Of course they're not. Are there points of disagreement within the company of the Context Group? Of course there are. Consider one such disagreement between our honoree and myself. I have proposed on several occasions that the sociological model of the sect is a valuable tool for analyzing and understanding the strategies and ideological/ theological positions of the Jesus movement as it transmogrifies from Jesus faction to sect within the House of Israel (see esp. Elliott 1981/ 1990; 1996). Our honoree, on the other hand, while always on the lookout for useful heuristic models, has expressed reservations about the appropriateness of this model since it was developed by Ernst Troeltsch as a model for identifying and explaining collective forms of Christianity that arose as counterparts to and often in protest against an organized, institutionalized "church" as dominant institution of Western society. Applying this model to an examination of formative Christianity in the first and second centuries, when no such dominant institution existed, he has maintained, would be a misapplication of an anachronistic model (see Seland 1987, expressing Malina's view). In response, I have argued, and continue to argue, that research on sectarian phenomena has not stood still since the work of Troeltsch and Max Weber in the first decades of this century. One significant advance in this area is the work of Bryan Wilson, one of our foremost students of sectarian phenomena. "The sect," he insists in his important 1973 study, *Magic and the Millennium*, "is a phenomenon that transcends Christendom, and it is a term which has been more widely and more appropriately employed, in common usage as well as in sociology, for separate minority religious movements within the context of various dominant religious traditions" (1973:11). As the subtitle of this work announces, "A Sociological Study of Religious Movements of Protest among Tribal and Third-World Peoples," Wilson shows how the concept of sect can be dissociated from the institutional church of the West as its only appropriate counterpart and instead be used to identify and analyze social movements of reform and protest in pre-industrial, traditional societies beyond the fringe of orthodox Christianity. In such environments, "the principle criterion of classification is in terms of the movement's *response* to *the world*" (1973:19). A principle feature of sectarian movements is the tension in which they exist with the macro society and the world "and it is the type of tension and the ways in which its is contained or maintained that are of particular importance." (1973:19). "Sectarians necessarily seek ... salvation in some other way than by the acceptance of the secular culture and the institutional facilities that it provides men [sic] to attain social and cultural goals" (1973:19). In this study Wilson presents a taxonomy of eight basic "supernaturalist responses to the world" ranging from an acceptance of the world and the goals and values society offers to seven differing responses that in varying ways reject prevailing cultural values, goals, and norms and that construct alternative visions of the world, evil, theodicy, humanity, and salvation, and alternative strategies governing social and moral conduct. Some sects, termed "conversionist," place a primary emphasis on personal conversion ("God will change us"). Others look for God's overturning of the world ("revolutionist"). A third type, "introversionist" sects, hear a call from God to abandon the world; a fourth type, "reformist," seeks to amend the world with God's help; a fifth, "utopianist, aims at reconstructing the world; a sixth, "manipulationist," seeks a change in the perception of its members and a transformed method of their coping with evil; and a seventh, "thaumaturgical," looks for relief from present and specific ills by special dispensations and the working of

miracles and wondrous cures. These ideal types will vary, of course, in
their collective features from one actual situation to another and on
occasion may even overlap. Several, if not all, of these sectarian types,
as outlined by Wilson, contain features strikingly similar to various
social and ideological expressions of the Jesus movement (see, inter
alia, Wilde 1974, 1978; Elliott 1981/1990, 1995). Hence, I would
argue, they, as types of sectarian movements rooted in *pre-industrial and
traditional societies*, provide useful models for analyzing and understanding strategies and ideologies of Jesus movement in the
Mediterranean world of the first century and the circumstances of its
transformation from inner-Israel faction to inner-Israel sect. This includes the movement's self-identification as the continuation or
fulfillment of Israel's history and hopes (e.g. as children of Abraham
and Sarah [Gal 3:29; 1 Pet 3:6] or as Israel's "remnant" [Rom 9:27;
11:5]), while at the same time its expropriation of essential identifying
features of Israel ("Israel of God," people of the covenant, elect and
holiness etc.), its boundary-marking vis-à-vis outsiders, and its tactics
for maintaining internal social cohesion and ideological commitment—all under conditions of a gradual dissociation of the sect,
ideologically and socially, from mainstream Israel. (For a fuller list of
features, their documentation and discussion, see Elliott 1995; and for
another appropriation of the sect model by a member of the Context
Group see Esler 1987). It is, by the way, this clinging to the identity,
tradition, and many of the self-defining tactics of Israel that requires
our conceptualization of the Jesus movement as a *messianic sect of* Israel
even after the death of Jesus. This must be stressed in opposition to the
recent claim of sociologist Rodney Stark that, beginning with its belief
in the resurrection of Jesus, the Jesus sect movement suddenly became
a "cult" and its members, "participants in a new religion" (Stark 1996:
44-45). To the contrary, the messianic sect continued to declare its
continuity with Israel, despite its embrace of Gentiles, and continued
to see itself as the fulfillment of Israel's hope.

While our honoree may still question the appropriateness of the sect
model, I would maintain that this model as *developed by Wilson with
respect to traditional societies* cannot be summarily dismissed as an anachronistic model, given the fit I believe others and I have established
between typical features and social conditions of these pre-industrial
sects and the similar social conditions and numerous aspects of the
Jesus movement in the early stages of its formation and expansion. At
the very least, more sustained testing of the model is in order.

In regard to biblical interpretation in general, analysis along social-scientific lines is advancing throughout the exegetical guild and across the globe, as the discussion and bibliography in Elliott 1993 makes clear. Social-scientific criticism of biblical texts, identification of social institutions and how they work, and examination of pervasive cultural beliefs, values, and behavioral scripts are now the focus of an increasing number of studies worldwide. The contribution of this addition to the exegetical toolbox and the future of the subdiscipline of exegesis will be measured by the degree to which this method provides a fresh conceptual framework for advancing beyond old exegetical cruxes, how it acquaints the ordinary Bible reader with the "strange old world" of the Bible, and how it provides for all modern readers of the Bible the necessary scenarios for reading and appreciating its content with social sophistication and cultural sensitivity. The ultimate payoff of this method theologically, I would suggest, is the means it provides for detecting the continuities and changes in values, social institutions, and constructions of reality that link us to and separate us from the biblical past. In so doing, it affords us a more precise means for respecting the Word of God as inscribed in the words of humans and a more reliable basis for deriving from that Word inspiration and guidance in our own time.

Questions and a Shift in Metaphor

Of course there are questions occasionally put to our honoree and other practitioners of Social-Scientific Criticism. I shall mention just two. Some of our colleagues and students ask whether the identification and use of theory and models is essential to the exegetical enterprise? Insofar as our visiting the strange ancient world of the Bible is comparable to Western anthropologists investigating traditional cultures, let me offer as a response some advice given to an earlier generation of budding anthropologists by one of the giants of our time, anthropologist E. E. Evans Pritchard (1976:240-243):

> In science as in life, one finds only what one seeks. One cannot have the answers without knowing what the questions are. Consequently, the first imperative [of research] is a rigorous training in general theory before attempting field-research so that one many know how and what to observe, what is significant in the light of theory. It is essential to realize that facts are in themselves meaningless. To be meaningful, they must have a degree of generality. It is useless going into a field blind. One must know precisely what one wants to know and that can only be acquired by a systematic training in academic social anthropology ... of

course the anthropologist's observations are biased by his theoretical dispositions, which merely means that he [or she] is aware of various hypotheses derived from existing knowledge and deductions from it, and, if his field data permit, he tests these hypotheses. How could it be otherwise? One cannot study anything without a theory about its nature. theory about its nature... Anyone who is not a complete idiot can do fieldwork, and if the people he is working among have not been studied before, he cannot help making an original contribution to knowledge. But will it be theoretical, or just factual knowledge? Anyone can produce a new fact; the thing is to produce a new idea.

A second question concerns the wooing of the social sciences in general. Must we exegetes not exercise caution in adopting the premises, theories, and research of the social sciences? Of course we must, as must social scientists in their appropriation of the diverse theories, methods and models of exegetes. But does mutual caution and critical judgment cast our disciplines as opposed herds of crocodiles preparing for dinner? Instead of dreading our social science colleagues as crocodiles intent on devouring us, what about following the venerable tribal adage: "They are our enemies, we marry them." Or better yet, as we move toward the twenty-first century and face the need for an integrated approach to the study of human communities past and present, is it not time for dropping the notion of academic hostility and aggression altogether, time for regarding putative enemies as colleagues, and time for shifting the metaphor from fear to the fun and profit of cooperation, collaboration, and cross-fertilization?

About the answer of our intrepid, fun-loving colleague to this question I have no doubt. Hail to you, O peerless and fearless crocodile-wooer and ardent collaborator! *Ad multos annos!*

2

An Exercise in the Critical Use of Models:
The "Goodness of Fit" of Wilson's Sect Model

Pieter F. Craffert, *UNISA, Pretoria, South Africa*

The lifelong research program of Professor Bruce Malina can be char-acterized by a very legitimate problem: how to become a considerate reader of first-century Christian documents. In his own words: "I set as my task to lay out the meanings that emerge from reading pieces of a document, with an awareness of the cultural perspective that gener-ated those meanings" (1996b:73). From his earlier publications (e.g., 1981) until his most recent ones (1996b), he has emphasized the need for twentieth-century people to become considerate readers of New Testament texts if they wish to learn what first-century persons said and meant to say. A central assumption of his research is that meanings are derived from social systems and that present-day readers, in order to become considerate first-century readers, have to learn the scenarios of the documents' original readers (Malina 1996b:79–81). In doing that, he has contributed to a wide field of topics constantly pointing out ethnocentrism and anachronism in the reading scenarios employed by modern readers. This he has done on hospitality (1986a), group formation (1995) and sacrifice (1996a), to mention only a few topics.

That sect models are quite anachronistic for understanding the Jesus movement group (1988:15) as well as the early Christian associations (1995:113 n 8), has also been on his agenda.[1] However, despite these

---

[1] Malina rejects both sect and cult models for describing the development and ex-pansion of early Christianity as inappropriate "since both these designations come from contemporary society in which religion is conceived as separate from and independent of other social institutions" (1988ª:15; and see 1986b:94). In his view there is no fit between the model and the data set. Seland (1987:198) closely follows Malina in arguing that the "first century world did not have our religious structures of denomi-nations and churches which are the background for the common use today of the category 'sect'". Thus, the category *sect* 'is dysfunctional both for investigations of

efforts of discouraging the use of sect models, they have persisted and are still employed in current research.

Since he has done so much to create an awareness of the ethnocentric and anachronistic scenarios (or models) by means of which first-century documents are read according to the received view, and to replace them with considerate historical and cultural models, it seems appropriate to offer, in recognition of his achievements, a further contribution to the same task. It will be done by picking up on a theme I have explored in an earlier publication (Craffert 1992) but which, to my mind, remains neglected by many social-scientific critics. A model's "goodness of fit," to use Carney's phrase (1975:11), will be demonstrated by discussing the case of a specific sectarian model employed in New Testament studies: the model of Bryan Wilson. A fine tuning of the criticism against the employment of Wilson's sect model will not only be an acknowledgment of Malina's efforts in this regard but also of his contribution to New Testament science in general.

The Validity Dilemma in the Use of Social-Scientific Models

The conscious and explicit use of models
In the circle of social-scientific critics of the New Testament it is no longer debated whether social-scientific models should be used or not. The dictum, expressed by Carney (1975:5) that the choice is not whether models will be used, but whether they will be used consciously and explicitly, has long been accepted. However, the supplementary principle of the "goodness of fit" of models, has generally speaking been neglected. Models just have no special magical qualities in ensuring their usefulness. Esler (1994:13), for example, argues that it is inappropriate to debate whether a model is 'true' or "false" or "valid" or "invalid". What matters, he says, is whether it is useful or not. Certain (anthropological) models just have a close fit to the biblical data, and what they contribute is a fresh set of questions to put to the texts (Esler 1994:23).

> In theory, however, it is often admitted that there should be some fit between model and data. Esler admits that the usefulness of models is almost unlikely without a fair degree of comparability between the model and the data under consideration. This raises the question of how comparability can be assessed. Is the mere use of anthropological models sufficient warranty in this regard? Is a confession about comparability

many non-Western societies of today, and for studies of religion in the 1st century Mediterranean world".

sufficient or is it necessary to demonstrate such comparability? These are important questions which also often occupy the minds of other social scientists. Gumerman and Phillips (1978:187) for example, have pointed out that simply because there is a good fit of archaeological data with a specific model does not necessarily signify confirmation of that model. It will be demonstrated that a fit between a data set and a model is not necessarily a confirmation that it is either a good model or an appropriate model for that set. Just as important as the application of a model to the interpretive process, if ethnocentrism and anachronism are to be avoided, is the critical evaluation thereof.

A critical and self-critical use of models

Since the conscious and explicit use of models aims at the prevention of selective perception, Carney warns that we should not selectively perceive only the advantages one gets from the use of models. These very handy tools have a downside in that certain limitations accompany them. Carney (1975:34-37) discusses some such shortcomings.

The most obvious limitation is that models impose an "iron law of perspective". Once within the framework of a particular model, it is difficult, if not impossible, to consider viewpoints which do not belong to that framework. Another problem is constituted by the question of how to know that a problem has correctly been simplified in order to arrive at the model's outline. The fact that a model is readily applicable does not necessarily mean much. Carney (1975:37) furthermore discusses the "theology of models" which refers to the tendency of using a specific model in and out of season. Together with the "drunkard's search", which refers to the tendency of simplifying the data in order to apply a model, it captures the typical pathologies of model builders and users.

My own objections to the use of models is more informed by theoretical arguments (Craffert 1992) and can be summarized in a number of points. The first is that any use of models is embedded in a philosophy of history and theory of science. One's use of models is predetermined by the philosophical choice referred to as one's *aim of interpretation*. On a continuum this refers to the alternatives, on the one hand, of acknowledging the contingency of interpreters and models and on the other hand a disregard for their meaning system. In the case of cross-cultural comparisons, my point in short is that compatibility and commensurability cannot be assumed, but rather a fit between model and evidence has to be demonstrated and argued. The problem of parallelomania in the use of models (the assumption that institutions in different cultures resemble each other) is a serious one in both sociological and anthropological research. A solution to the "cookie cutter approach" and its twin brother, "tunnel vision", is neither a retreat into more data nor a tailoring of evidence to fit the model or of the model to fit the data, but the application of higher standards to the testing and choice of models. The application of models not only leads to eternal vigilance, as Carney (1975:37) says, but to continuous criticism and self-criticism.

Once it is realized that a text or data set can sponsor almost any reading or interpretation (it can be fitted into almost any model), the importance of testing models is no longer optional (Craffert 1992:233). At least this much should be admitted: if interpreters' ethnocentric and anachronistic common sense models can be applied to ancient texts (as is often done in New Testament studies), most other non-fitting models (whether anthropological or sociological) can be applied with similar ease. If one's expectation is that models should be useful in showing up questions and possibilities not asked before, then most (ethnocentric and anachronistic) models will pass the test.

It should be apparent that I fully share Holmberg's (1990:108) sentiment that it is a scholar's duty to immerse himself or herself in the critical discussion of the model he or she has chosen as analytical instrument, instead of simply taking it over on trust, just because it comes from a sociologist or an anthropologist.

These general limitations regarding the use of models can be captured in two specific rules: models must be used with caution and in a self-critical way, and secondly, one must expect constant refinements and updating of the models available (Carney 1975:37). In short, the explicit and conscious use of models should always be accompanied by the critical and self-critical use thereof.

I assume that these arguments can easily be brushed aside by the defense that obviously models are not used as iron matrixes but are indeed used cautiously. An evaluation of the goodness of fit of Wilson's sect model can verify such a defense and simultaneously serve as test case for demonstrating the "goodness of fit" principle.

Wilson's model is taken for two reasons. Firstly, the current consensus remains that sect models throw important light on the phases of development and expansion of the early Christian movement. Elliott (1990:7), for example, maintains that social-scientific and cross-cultural studies of sectarian movements in pre-industrial as well as industrial societies have now produced a valuable body of research and set of models for analyzing the early Christian movement as a sectarian phenomenon. He suggests that much more work needs to be done in the examination of the sectarian nature and development of early Christianity (Elliott 1995:92). Secondly, its use for this and other purposes in New Testament studies is enough evidence of its popularity and of its importance in constructing the historical realities of early Christianity. Any model with such a wide and pervasive appeal and with the potential of shaping perceptions of historical realities should be critically evaluated.

In evaluating the goodness of fit of a model, at least two different kinds of evaluation are possible. The one focuses on the origin and characteristics of a particular model while the other zooms in on the employment of that particular model in New Testament studies. Before that is done, a glimpse at the use of Wilson's model in New Testament studies will give an indication of the importance and necessity of this enterprise.

Wilson's Sectarian Typology in New Testament Studies

Wilson's sect typology is employed by New Testament scholars for a variety of purposes.[2] At least four such purposes can be identified.

It is used for describing the organizational development and expansion of early Christian groups
In a number of studies Wilson's typology is used for describing the organizational development and expansion of early Christian communities or groups. Esler, for example, uses it to describe the expansion of both the Pauline communities and the Lucan community.[3] He reads Luke-Acts as the carefully formulated text by an author who wanted to help his community cope with the pressures as a result of their sectarian status in relation to Judaism and the Hellenistic world (1987:47). Furthermore, in some of the Pauline communities, "Paul advocated a

---

[2] A number of studies are consciously excluded from this overview for the simple reason that they do not exclusively operate with Wilson's typology. Scroggs (1975) comes close to be included, but in my view, his seven-featured definition owes more to Stark than to Wilson. The same applies to Meeks (1986:98-99) and White (1988:14) who operate with modified versions of Wilson's typology. Since I do not claim to have consulted all studies employing a sect typology, a number of studies could have been overlooked.

[3] In Esler's view (see 1987:51) it is unfortunate that modern sectarian investigation has paid very little attention to the process by which a reform or renewal group within a church manages to continue to exist within the church and later after being expelled, acquires the status of a sect. In my view the answer to this problem is obvious. Modern sect investigations, and especially that of Wilson, do not deal with the phenomenon of organizational development.

type of Christianity inevitably sectarian in relation to Judaism" (Esler 1994:69). He claims that the proper setting for applying the sect model is in the stages of the development of the earliest Jesus movement from a reform movement internal to Judaism to a sect outside of Judaism (1994:13-15).[4]

Watson, following Esler, argues that the historical development of the Pauline movement groups can in sociological terms be described as "*the transformation of a reform-movement into a sect*" (1986:38). The Jesus movement was a movement to reform Judaism but was changed by Paul into a sect of Judaism more or less separate from the Jewish community (Watson 1986:38-39). In his view, "the church" is the sect which separates itself from the parent community, "the Jewish community" (1986:61).[5]

According to MacDonald, the Pauline communities are in a process of separating themselves from those who do not accept their view of salvation. Because of their self-identity, they distinguished themselves from the outside society (MacDonald 1988:34) because, after all, they existed outside and in opposition to Judaism (1988:37). She claims that Wilson's conversionist response best suits this condition and should therefore be applied for describing the expansion of the Pauline groups.

It is used for a typification of specific early Christian groups

Closely connected to the above usage is another favorite one, the utilization of Wilson's model for typifying specific early Christian groups. It should come as no surprise that Wilson's conversionist response is the most popular category for this purpose.

The community behind 1 Peter, Elliott (1981:74-76) claims, can be seen as a conversionist sect. By using the generic sect definition of Wilson, he claims that a comparison of the data in 1 Peter with this model leaves no doubt about the sectarian character of this community. More specifically, this community most closely conforms to a conversionist sect, as described by Wilson. Pauline Christianity, in MacDonald's view (1988:34), also conforms to Wilson's conversionist category.

---

[4] Without explicitly pointing out that Wilson advocates a sect definition which operates with the sect versus parent body notion, Esler (see 1994:13) claims that his sectarian model draws on that of Wilson.

[5] Although Watson does not refer to Wilson (he merely refers to Esler), the latter claims that Watson indeed follows his version of Wilson's definition (see Esler 1994:13).

The conversionist and revolutionist responses are self-evident, Esler claims, when categorizing Luke-Acts' sectarian relationship with Judaism (1987:58-59). On the basis of the Johannine view that Abraham is irrelevant to the Christian community, Esler concludes that they have turned their back on a central aspect of Jewish tradition. In this respect "their response to the world is a powerfully introversionist one" (1994:89).[6]

It is used for compiling the salient features of "the" sect
The way in which Elliott (1995:80-84), amongst others, uses Wilson's typology for compiling the salient features of "the" sect adds an additional feature to the utilization of this sect typology. He is concerned with a description of a typical sect, and he goes a long way in listing all the possible features of "the" sect. In so doing, Elliott combines descriptions, definitions and characteristics from a variety of sect typologies.

Elliott (1995:80-84, 93-95 n 6-27) first expands the seven featured definition of Scroggs (who basically relies on Stark's sect model), then adds his own version of Wilson's model plus Meeks's revised version of Wilson plus a number of other sect typologies in order to compile a list of salient features of the sect. In the end he lists 21 salient sectarian features, all in the format, "the sect...".

The same is true with Stanley's use of Wilson. He adds insights from a number of other sect typologies in order to arrive at the features of what he calls an "ideal sect" (1986:412).[7]

It is used for identifying possible responses within specific documents
Esler (1987:50, 1994:72) claims that any given religious movement may be comparable to more than one of the seven types identified by Wilson. Therefore he finds traces of both conversionist and revolutionist responses in Luke-Acts. In a single chapter from a Pauline letter (1 Cor 9), Robbins (see 1996a:176-178) finds signs of at least four responses to the world: conversionist, revolutionist, utopian and gnostic manipulationist. Wilde (see 1974:61) claims that the Gospel of Mark approximates more the revolutionist type of response but identi-

---

[6] Not only the Johannine community but also the Qumran community can be described as introversionist. Esler claims that the introversionist nature of the Qumran and the Johannine communities "was manifested in a profound separation between the members and non-members, the community and the world" (1994:90).

[7] It should be noted that contrary to Wilson who claims that the seven responses correspond to the ideal type (see 1982:100), Stanley maintains that every actual sect "does not need to embody the eight traits of an ideal sect" (1986:413).

fies at least two other responses which rank high on a scale: thauma-
turgy and conversionist (see 1978:61).

At this point we can turn to Wilson's sect typology in order to establish its potential for being used by New Testament scholars.

Wilson's Sect Model as a Test Case

In order to understand and appreciate Wilson's sect definition, it is
essential to do three things: first to grasp something about the trends in
sect definitions as such, secondly, to determine what Wilson is interested in and thirdly, to establish how his typology is received by the
experts.

Some trends in sect definitions
The first trend is rather obvious on any artificial scanning of the field.

Not one category, but several
Beckford points out that the term *sect* is used with widely differing
meanings. In the words of Holmberg (1990:114), it "is not one category, but several". This is the case not only in sociological and
anthropological studies, but also in New Testament studies.

The term sect is used with a variety of connotations not only within
the field of the sociology of religion but also in non-religious contexts,
such as the political field. Stark and Bainbridge point out that since
empirical cases did not fit the church-sect typology of Weber and
Troeltsch, "new users created new church-sect typologies" (1979:122).
A second, but related trend is that once confronted with the shortcomings of the church-sect typology, researchers realized that it was
necessary to develop definitions which apply to specific circumstances
(Berger 1954:477; Johnson 1963:544). Together these two factors
introduce an important variable to sect definitions: the environment
within which a specific model or typology is used becomes the basic
reference point determining the category being investigated. One example will illustrate this point.

Johnson (1963:542) suggests the following specific considerations in
distinguishing between church and sect. "A church is a religious group
that accepts the social environment in which it exists. A sect is a religious group that rejects the social environment in which it exists".
Given the American religious environment, he argues that the vast
majority of religious bodies seem to accept the dominant value system.
Therefore, they should be placed towards the church end of the

church-sect continuum (Johnson 1963:544). The impact of this kind
of definition is that all religious groups are now evaluated in terms of
their relation to the social environment. It is, for example, obvious in
terms of this model that the Catholic Church in the USA is more
sect-like than the Catholic Church in Ireland (Stark & Bainbridge
1979:124). With this Johnson has created a definition which is context
specific and which specifically does not carry all the baggage of former
definitions. This description introduces a second feature: sect definitions tend to have developed over time.

From the church-sect typology to sect classificatory systems

The term *sect* is used nowadays in at least three clearly identifiable
scholarly traditions (O'Toole 1976:146). The first is the traditional
sociology of religion field where, following Weber and Troeltsch, it is
concerned with typologizing religious organizations. The second is
represented by sociologists of religion who are dissatisfied with the
constrictions of the church-sect typology and who seek to locate their
analyzes of sectarianism within a broader framework. They tend to
develop definitions which are context specific. In these theories the
sect concept is employed to formulate a classificatory system for religious organizations. Thirdly, explorations with the concept *sect* outside
the field of the sociology of religion reveal its usage in the context of
political studies. Following some of the steps of the history of sectarian
studies in the sociology of religion will be illuminating.[8]

The church-sect typology has its origin in the work of first Weber
and then Troeltsch. Weber was trying to understand the processes by
which Christianity and the larger social system interacted to bring
about the pluralizing and secularizing of the Western world. *Church*
and *sect* were introduced "as two idealized types of arrangement of a
single element in the organization of the religious institution: that is,
the mode of membership" (Swatos 1976:132). By means of this distinction, Weber drew some conclusions about the movement of
certain currents within Christianity. In short, he described specific
social-religious groupings in society.

The antitheses between church and sect were introduced at their in-
ception (Berger 1954:468-469). The church is related to political
institutions and is a hierocratic establishment. The sect is a voluntary

---

[8] Many of the New Testament studies do contain an overview of the development
of the church-sect typology from Weber and Troeltsch to the present (see e.g. Wilde
1974:27-38; Elliott 1990). It is, however, significant that they all assume that since the
same terms are used, the historical overview covers the same categories.

association restricted to those who are religiously and ethically qualified. In the church, charisma is attached to the office and in the sect it
is attached to the religious leader. One is born into a church but joins
a sect. These are some of the typifications which characterize each type
of organization.

Troeltsch departed from this aim in using the church-sect typology
for describing people's religious behavior. He identified churchly,
sectarian and mystical behaviors (subsequently the latter was dropped)
and used the concepts *accommodation* and *compromise* to describe people's behavior. The church came to be described as accommodative
and compromising and sects as the opposite (Swatos 1976:133-134). In
short, he "conceived of church and sect as independent sociological
expressions of two variant interpretations of Christian tradition"
(Johnson 1963:540).[9]

Closely connected to this definition is the one proposed by Berger
(1954:474): "The sect, then, may be defined as a religious grouping
based on the belief that *the spirit is immediately present*. And the church,
on the other hand, may be defined as a religious grouping based on the
belief that *the spirit is remote*." On the basis of this definition a typology
of church and sect is then introduced. This wide definition leaves open
the possibility of including many sociological aspects in a specific description, without introducing them into the definition. By focusing
on the concept of religious motif in religious experience, Berger is able
to identify an enthusiastic, a prophetic and a gnostic experience and
each with several possible motifs and attitudes attached (1954:478). He
then adds that it goes without saying that types are often mixed. As in
other sect typologies with so many variables, an almost impossible
number of options become available which at the end defeats the purpose of the typology.[10] It is important to note that Berger already uses
the narrow definition (what a sect is) with the wider typology (what all
the sociological features of a sect are).

As we have seen above, Johnson brought a new dimension to
church-sect typologies when he introduced a single attribute to distinguish between church and sect. His definition deals with church and

---

[9] According to this typology the church accepts the world, is conservative, supports
the values of the ruling classes and includes people from cradle to grave in its salvific
system. A sect, on the other hand, is a small group which one enters by means of
conversion and it is often critical of the world and its values (see Holmberg 1990:87).

[10] Some sects which are supposed to be spiritual turn out to be very legalistic while
others which are supposed to reject conversion because of their avoidance of the
world (according to the model) stress conversion (see Berger 1954:479).

sect in terms of a single variable which takes seriously the setting within which it is employed.

When all religious groups are categorized in relation to their social environment, an important element is lost, according to Stark and Bainbridge. They maintain that prior definitions of deviant religious movements have focused on schismatic movements. However, not all deviant movements are schismatic in that they originate from existing parent groups. Therefore, they distinguish between sects, which are in a state of high tension with their environment but have prior ties with another religious organization and cults, which are in a state of high tension with their environment but have no such prior ties (Stark & Bainbridge 1979:125). A sect is thus constituted as a reestablished version of an existing group while a cult represents an independent religious tradition in a specific environment. They therefore state: "To be a sect a religious movement must have been founded by persons *who left* another religious body *for the purpose* of founding the sect. The term sect, therefore, applies only to schismatic movements" (1979: 125).

A significant trend can be identified in these definitions: they vary from a concern with religious organizations and a concern with religious experience to a description of schismatic groups and finally attitudes towards the broader environment. In short, it confirms that the same term is used for different categories and that new users simply create new church-sect typologies in order to fit their empirical cases. The same term covers different phenomena.

What these different typologies furthermore introduce are a variety of social and cultural conditions under which each exists. From Troeltsch's concern with specific historical and cultural conditions for describing the features of both church and sect to Johnson's description of the experience of the outside world, specific conditions stamp each typology.

The trouble, as Johnson (1963:541) points out, is that most new typologies suffer from the same defects as those that they replace, namely, a large number of features exist within both sect and church categories. Stark and Bainbridge (1979:123) add that it is impossible to rank groups as more or less church-like. The more difficult it becomes to determine what is meant by "church", the more difficult it becomes not only to know what "sect" is, but to employ a church-sect typology as such. The church-sect typology, it seems, breaks down as soon as it is applied to circumstances different to what Troeltsch experienced (Miller 1979:164).

Within this context it is important to ask what exactly Wilson has in mind when he talks about sects.

Sects as responses to the world

In order to evaluate the potential of Wilson's project for understanding early Christian groups and texts, it is extremely important to ask what he is interested in. His project can be summarized by means of five main points:

Sects are new religious movements among less-developed peoples following contact with westerners

Wilson states that he has examined new third-world religious movements within the context of wide, evolutionary processes by employing analytical procedures that have previously been applied to sects (1973:4). More specifically, he looked at new religious movements among less-developed peoples following contact with westerners (see 1973:1). These movements are then described by means of the central concepts drawn from the sociology of religion, particularly the concept *sect*.[11]

To be sure, Wilson did not investigate sects as such but employed post-Reformation sect models for understanding new religious movements in third-world countries which have been in contact with westerners. In spite of significant differences, new religious movements among less-developed peoples, he claims, have much in common with the sects that have arisen in Christendom since the Reformation (1973:4). Wilson is very clear about the phenomenon that he is investigating:

> first, to provide examples of the types of movements that arise at various stages of cultural contact; second, to indicate what types of movement arise at the many different points in the balance of subordination and domination of indigenous and invading peoples; and third, to indicate the correspondence of varying levels of cultural development and consciousness and specific modes of religious response to a disrupted and evil world (1973:5)

Sects as the experience of evil and the need for salvation

Wilson is particularly interested in understanding the wider social processes (1973:1) and specifically the interpretation of evil in particular

---

[11] There can be little doubt that Wilson is aware of the limitations of the term *sect* in the ideal-type construct. He admits that "the concept *sect* is usable in other cultures only with considerable circumspection" (1982:102).

movements and the course of action prescribed to deal with it. Members of new religions experience contemporary evils and the need for salvation from them (1973:3). In his own words, it is "the nature of the salvation men seek that has been my primary focus of interest, and the general cultural conditions in which specific soteriological conceptions are attractive and successfully capture the minds of men" (1973:4).

Evil and salvation are central to these responses. Wilson claims:

> Men seek salvation in a world in which they feel the need for supernatural help... Men apprehend evil in many different ways, and thus look for relief from it in different forms of supernatural action. The various responses to the world embrace different conceptions of the source of evil and the ways in which it will be overcome (1973:19, 21).

Evil takes different forms. It might be seen as the work of supernatural beings (devil, spirits) or persons with supernatural powers (witches or sorcerers) or simply as illness, poverty or barrenness (1973:21). Salvation follows the pattern of any of eight responses to evil.

A total of eight responses to the world

In order to avoid, in his view, the outdated church-sect typology, Wilson (1973:15, 34; 1982:103) constructed seven sub-typifications of the sect which conform to the broader ideal-type construct (1982: 100).[12] However, there are actually eight soteriological categories, the dominant position being that of acceptance of the world. More precisely, dominant, base-line or orthodox response (whether secular or religious) is the position 'of acceptance of the world, the facilities it offers, and the goals and values that a given culture enjoins upon men' (Wilson 1973:21; and see Miller 1979:165).

To be sure, there are eight basic supernaturalist responses to the experience of evil in the world and the search for salvation, seven of which are rejections of the cultural arrangement and consequently described as sects. The sub-types are designated on the basis of their responses to evil in the world (see 1973:18-26),[13] and are seven ways in

---

[12] An interesting facet of his typology is the internal historical development it went through. Wilson initially started with four broad types which can be discerned 'within the framework of Protestant Christianity" (1959a:5). The essence of these categories was not altered when the additional three were added (see 1973:22-25)—they were merely stripped of their overtly Christian language.

[13] The seven soteriological solutions (see Wilson 1959a:5, 1973:22-26; Miller 1979:165) to evil are (1) the supernatural change of human nature as a response to evil

which people may respond to the cultural goals and soteriological theories and facilities of a given culture (1973:22). Wilson's main concern is with this range of orientations.

Sects are not organized groups but ranges of orientation

Wilson is not concerned with specific groups or organizations but with the specific modes of response of movements that are readily defined as religious (1973:4). As Miller (1979:163) says, Wilson's concern is with expressions of religious protest and not with concrete groups. The term *sect*, in Wilson's usage, is not to be understood in direct contrast to "the church" (1973:12; Miller 1979:164).

A sect is any self-distinguishing protest movement against the state, against any secular institution in society or against any group within society (1973:12). This point is supported by the argument that both the institutional divergence from a parent organization and the doctrinal divergence from orthodoxy too much reflect specifically Christian preoccupations in describing sects. Sects to Wilson do not designate organized groups but ranges of orientation (1973:19, 20, 31): "We are not using a term [sect] that stands in emphatic contradistinction to the more culturally bound category 'church', nor are we positing specific organizational characteristics" (Wilson 1973:34).[14]

He confirms his criticism against the traditional church-sect typology:

> We may, therefore, entirely with profit abandon both the traditional theological basis for sect classification in terms of doctrine, and the sociological attempts to distinguish new religious movements by the degree of institutionalization that they have achieved (1973:16).

In other words Wilson rejects the church-sect dichotomy as important criterion for identifying the origin and development of sects. His redefined version of sects as responses to the world avoids the demand

---

(conversionists), (2) the supernatural alteration of the social structures of an evil world (revolutionist), (3) withdrawal from the evil world (introversionist), (4) acquisition of a new knowledge of the world which aids one in dealing with evil (manipulationist), (5) personal dispensation from specific evil events (thaumaturgical), (6) reform of the social structures which perpetrate evil (reformist) and (7) total social reorganization of the world (utopian).

[14] It is apparent from his definition that he does not classify sects by the degree of institutionalization and/or by theological differences (see Miller 1979:164). He typifies them according to their response to the world or their orientation. It is significant to note that he does not classify sects, he typifies them. In other words, he admits that the seven types may be empty boxes, that is, logical alternatives that have never become historically manifest (see Miller 1979:165).

for exclusivity or the assumptions about organizational development built into the concept (1982:103).

Wilson pays relatively little attention to the origin of sects. He maintains that they can originate in a number of ways: spontaneously around a charismatic leader, through internal schism, as a result of revivalism or through attempts at revitalizing the beliefs and practices of a major religious movement (1959:7; 1973:498-499). It is, however, not without importance because with this he introduces another variable into the equation. Besides (eight) types of responses, sects can emerge in three different ways, one of which is by way of schism from a parent body.

Each of these orientations is based on a specific set of cultural conditions.

Social and cultural conditions conducive to the development of different types of sect

Wilson (see 1982:103) clearly states that his particular concern is to indicate the cultural conditions in which each of the seven responses or orientations is likely to arise and to discover something about the social and cultural consequences that follow their adoption. If it is furthermore kept in mind that all seven responses are determined by their own idiosyncratic ways of responding to evil and the search for salvation, then it comes as no surprise that different social and cultural conditions give rise to each. That is to say, specific external conditions produce the fertile ground for the development of each *sect*.

Although the importance of this point can easily be underestimated, its significance within my overall argument is considerable. The point to grasp is that Wilson's sectarian responses cannot be divorced from the external conditions within which they develop and the cultural pattern from which they emerge. The following merely gives an impression of the large number of aspects considered by Wilson to be conducive to the development of each response (Wilson 1973:31-69 for fuller discussion).

Both conversionist and manipulationist sects emerge in social circumstances in which human beings have become highly individualized. It seems unlikely that these could arise in traditional societies (1973:38, 41). Before introversionist tendencies can occur, Wilson points out that the idea of religion as a private commitment where there is freedom of choice must have been established. This can occur only in cultures where the family has acquired privacy and separation from the kinship and neighborhood groups (1973:43). In other words, not in agrarian societies. The two responses highly likely in less developed and non-literate societies, are thaumaturgical and revolutionist (1973:49, 364). Utopian responses are always concerned with colony-building (1973:26 n 18). Amongst the cultural requirements for a conversionist response are: a high degree of individuation, the atomization of social groups in a process of profound social upheaval, impairment or destruction of social structures, disruption of communities and the forcible detachment of individuals from their kinsfolk.

These remarks are illustrative rather than comprehensive. The brief summary by Miller underscores my point:

> In Third World countries the manipulationist, reformist, and utopian styles are unlikely to occur because these types require a fairly secular and culturally sophisticated public... In contrast, the revolutionist, thaumaturgical, and (somewhat less likely) the conversionist type more frequently find expression in less-developed countries (1979:166).

A complete evaluation of this model's usefulness for understanding early Christian movements will obviously have to include an analysis of the prevailing social and cultural conditions in the first-century Mediterranean world. The question to be answered is to what extent specific conditions, conducive to the origin of specific responses, prevailed in that world. Although that will not be undertaken in this study, an evaluation on a different level is equally important. That is the question of the appropriateness of Wilson's model within secular social-scientific studies.

What do the experts say about the model?
A critical interaction with any model confronts one with the evaluation of the experts. How is the model received and what is its, one might ask, life expectancy?

The model's analytical and explanatory power
The first aspect which is questioned is the analytical and explanatory power of Wilson's typology. Wilson admits that the concept *sect* is used "loosely and in general as pseudonymous with 'minority religious movements'" (1973:34). If one then takes into account his principle that models or ideal types on a very high level of generality and abstraction 'are often of very limited value in application to any one specific culture' (1982:101), the question inevitably arises whether it has any analytical and explanatory power.

The concept *responses to the world* immediately springs to mind. Koepping thinks that if

> Wilson creates such broad categories as "response to the world" *a priori* as ideal types, we end up with quasi-casual explanations of such triteness that they say that all religions are an answer to the problems in the world which people perceive as unresolved or unresolvable (1977:124).

The same can be said about the definition of sect as a *protest group*. What constitutes protest? For Wilson it is no longer the specific religious disposition of other people or the power and posture of the church but the social, cultural and political condition of the world (1982:93). However, if any group in protest against secular society (or elements in it) is designated a sect, which groups can legitimately be excluded from being sects?

What about the general and rather vague *base-line* or orthodox response of the dominant culture which is described as acceptance of the world and the facilities it offers for salvation (Wilson 1973:21)? Where on earth would one find such a "supernaturalist response" to evil and salvation? How many religions, denominations (whether established, schismatic or dominant) or churches can be categorized as accepting the evil in the world? More specifically, since the base-line response is not filled in, it can be virtually anything. It is clear that his model shares some features with Johnson's model discussed earlier. Depending on the features of the base-line response in a specific society, the supernatural responses will obviously differ.

The covert manipulation of definitions

The covert manipulation of definitions appears in sect studies in general and also in Wilson's definition in particular. This appears when one characteristic is treated as dominant while a random shift from one attribute to another takes place. With such a strategy, Beckford (1973:96) says, it is a case of "achieving analytical results purely by covert manipulation of definitions". That this is the case with Wilson's typology will be demonstrated by means of diverse examples.

The first example regards the notion of the base-line response. Since it is without any content, it can be filled in at random or be left vacant. In a sense, leaving it vacant is a precondition for identifying the other responses. The seven responses exist in a situation where the acceptance of the world is dominant. However, what happens when the conversionist response (the world is corrupt because men are corrupt) or, the revolutionist response (only the destruction of the world will suffice to save men) does in fact represent the dominant goals and values in a given culture? I suspect that many of the features of the world-view ascribed to some of the seven responses (Wilson 1973: 22-26) could easily have been a description of the dominant cultural response of not only the early Christians but even the majority of people in the first-century Mediterranean world.

The two most frequent types of responses in less-developed societies, Wilson claims, are thaumaturgical and revolutionist (1973:49). Nevertheless, the dominant cultural position in such societies is in all probability a shared magical world-view, a point accepted by Wilson (1973:25 n 17). It is likely that in such societies (e.g. agrarian) the dominant and base-line position is itself thaumaturgical. What would the features of the seven alternative responses be when the dominant cultural response assumes that the gods, powers and supernatural beings are responsible for changing this world (thaumaturgical)?

The second example refers to the different levels on which Wilson's definitions operate. It is noteworthy that he defines sects on two levels: one a broad typification of the term sectarian and two an elaboration of different types of sectarian movements (Miller 1979:163). The basic characteristics of a sect (Wilson 1959a:4; 1982:91-93) which he refers to as the "expectable features of a sect" (1982:95) represent what sociologists call an *ideal type*. He comes to refer to the responses as ideal-typifications (1973:20). The list of seven responses to the world obviously are the different types of sects while the basic characteristics represent the generic or ideal sect. Any specific case must at least be close enough to the ideal type to stand as a plausible case of a sect, he maintains (1982:95-96). In his own words, Wilson contends that the "seven sub-typifications of the sect conformed to the broader ideal-type construct of the sect taken as a generic type ... but, to this general characterization were now added specific elements which comprised each of the seven distinctive responses to the world" (1982:100).

Wilson, however, to my mind never solves the problem created by his general characterization of sects. Most of the features, such as, exclusivity, voluntarism, tests of merit, expulsion and protest against dominant cultural positions he admits, "are not always, and perhaps not usually, the attributes of the various divisions and schools that are loosely called sects in other religious traditions" (1988:226). In other words, he randomly picks which set of criteria is used for defining a sect, depending on the religious tradition. He escapes the problem by bypassing the general level of sect definition in creating categories on the sub-level to deal with the variety of sects. But why should the general sect definition apply in some instances and not in others? Put differently, can he operate with different definitions and claim that they are all sects? Furthermore, it is not only possible to jump between the generic and the distinctive features, it is also possible to decide in each instance which of the generic and/or distinctive features are to be applied. Why treat only one characteristic as dominant and how can only one feature account for a group's distinctiveness? Are a minimum number of features from either the generic and/or the distinctive set required before a protest group can be considered a sect? Wilson does not escape the general failure of sect definitions explicated by Beckford (1973:96): "Definitions of church and sect may be composed of several dimensions of opposed attributes, but explanation of collective processes and structures may be covertly framed in terms of only one particular set of oppositions."

As seen earlier, this gap between the general and specific levels was already present in Berger's definition and the tendency to jump between them without proper justification is one of the main reasons why Beckford (1973:96ff) calls for a moratorium on church-sect typologies subsequent to that of the founding fathers. The criticism added in this study, to my mind, confirms such a judgment and furthermore makes Wilson's typology doubtful outside the very broad and very vague contribution it can make.

The Goodness of Fit of Wilson's Model

Since the above discussion contains an evaluation of the model as such, it is important to turn to the second aspect of the goodness of fit of models: whether justice is being done to the specific model employed. Before we look at some of the strategies employed by New Testament scholars when using Wilson's typology, a brief summary of the above discussion will be given.

The main features of Wilson's model

Wilson does not describe the dynamics or interaction between deviant and parent religious groups. In fact, his sect model says virtually nothing about the interaction, development or organization within and between different religious groups. He describes different orientations which minority religious groups can take in society, and does not address the stages or phases of development of religious groups vis-à-vis other groups.

The sect typology is explicitly no longer used by Wilson in opposition to the church concept since it is historically confining and religiously specific. Sect, to Wilson, does not describe the dynamics between parent group and deviant group but refers to the strategy employed by a deviant group which does not share the culture's dominant way of dealing with evil and salvation.

The fact that Wilson has lumped together groups from a variety of geographical areas and claims to make use of anthropological studies, does not make his sect typology cross-cultural as such.[15] Given the lack of a clear cross-cultural theoretical base, it is an open question whether it can live up to the claims that it provides a cross-cultural model for understanding early Christianity (Elliott 1995:76; Esler 1994:71).

Since this typology is very low in analytical and explanatory power it is to be expected that it will be applied to a great variety of phenomena. Since nothing is left outside the definition, one cannot expect it to illuminate much on the inside.

Compared to the definitions of Berger, Johnson and Stark, Wilson's is no simplification of the church-sect typology. If anything he has multiplied the variables. At least three sets of variables are included in his sect typology: eight responses to the world, three ways in which sects can originate and a number of features which belong either to the generic or to the distinctive sect categories. With such an all-inclusive definition nothing is excluded and obviously very little can be illuminated. If this number of variables is connected to the tendency to covertly manipulate definitions, it becomes possible to include every single group within the typology.

The goodness of fit in New Testament studies:
strategies and characteristics
The evaluation of the goodness of fit of Wilson's typology in New Testament studies will focus on five strategies which characterize the employment of that typology in New Testament studies.

---

[15] Beckford (1973:98) points out that the changing scene of religion in a modern world requires new conceptualizations, not just modifications of old ones. Very little can be explained about the dynamics of religious organizations by focusing exclusively on the dimensions provided by the church-sect typologies. This point seems to me extremely important when we come to the New Testament groups. What is needed are new conceptualizations of the early Christian groups.

The invention of a Jewish parent body

A common feature of most New Testament sectarian studies is the invention of a Jewish parent body from which the specific Christian group has been separated. In many instances it is merely referred to as Judaism (Esler 1994:52, 71, 79, 84) while in other instances the Jewish parent becomes a corporate body.

To Watson (1986:19-20) "the Jewish community" constitutes the parent body in the traditional church-sect typology while *Judaism* in Esler's view, is a parent body which consists of a number of elements all of which make up Judaism. It can either have the synagogue as its primary institution (1987:58, 66) or the temple as one of its institutions (1987:65). This is also the case with Elliott who maintains that early Christianity as such can be seen as a Jewish sect (see 1995:76). The nation of Israel (the *ethnos* Israel) rooted in the Torah and Temple, functioning as a corporate body, constitutes the parent group. One finds this corporate body specifically embodied in the Temple aristocracy and the control they claimed over the social and cultural life of Jewish Palestine (Elliott 1995:77-78, 90).

In echoing the criticism against the traditional typology, Holmberg (1990:109-110) is certainly on target when he points out that it is not a suitable cross-cultural model because of its strong ties with the Christian tradition. The application of its main feature, the schism of a deviant group from the parent group, is nothing more than reflecting the early church in the mirror of the church history. It is significant that this feature keeps on recurring in New Testament studies which employ typologies no longer sharing that feature.

A problem connected to this is the assumption of some kind of normative Judaism in the first century. If one accepts the growing consensus of a variety of Judaisms in the beginning of the Christian era, any such notion of a parent Jewish body becomes problematic (Craffert 1993:245-256; also White 1988:10). Neither the Temple religiosity nor the different synagogue communities constituted a normative or corporate body for all Jews. Not only were the majority of Judeans and Galileans in the first century excluded from the Herodian Temple sacrality, but symbols such as Temple and Torah were open for debate.[16] In my view the most appropriate description of

---

[16] Although some Jews in the Diaspora venerated the Temple (for example sending their yearly taxes), they remained outside its concentric circles of order (Lightstone 1984:54). Kraabel argues that Jerusalem remained the center of their worlds, but "not necessarily the Palestine of their own times, but the biblical Israel elevated to mythical status" (Kraabel 1987:55). First-century Judaisms did not react in a monolithic way to

first-century Judaism is that it was constituted by a variety of groups who claimed Israel's traditions and symbols, coupled with varying interpretations thereof.

Wilson's typology is often combined with other church-sect typologies
It is apparent that Wilson's typology is often combined with other church-sect typologies in at least two different ways. The first is its assimilation with traditional church-sect typologies, especially that of Troeltsch.

Fully aware of the criticism against Troeltsch's church-sect typology, Esler claims that such criticism does not preclude application of the typology to the beginnings of Christianity "which did originate from within Judaism and did constitute, at least in part, a protest against various features of that 'church'" (Esler 1987:48-49). Troeltsch's typology can be enriched, he says, by bringing to bear on the data in the text Wilson's sectarian typology. In his words: "We are now equipped with a typological apparatus for instituting precise comparisons with the data in Luke-Acts: a combination of Troeltsch's typology for the broad church-sect questions and Wilson's typology for a more detailed and precise examination of the variety of sectarian responses in the text" (Esler 1987:50).[17]

The second trend has already been mentioned. Not only Wilson's but a variety of other sect typologies are assimilated in the activity of compiling lists of salient sectarian features. In the case of Elliott often explicitly hostile typologies (such as those of Stark and Wilson) are combined.

At this stage it should be obvious that the same term is used for different categories. In fact, Wilson (like others such as Johnson, Berger and Stark) makes no secret of the fact that he uses the concept for describing very specific social phenomena. He furthermore strongly dissociates himself from Troeltsch's typology specifically on the basis

the Temple. Some, like the Pharisees, had no need for the actual Temple while other Judaisms erected either their own temples or their own priesthoods.

[17] Esler (see 1987:53) does ask the "fit" question with regard to Troeltsch's church-sect typology. The way in which he establishes such a fit is by comparing a number of features of Luke's community with the typology: it was small, essentially autonomous, and lacking a rigid hierarchy, it had a separate identity and was organizationally separated from the synagogue community (see 1987:54-58). A number of features suggest to Esler that Luke's community did not have dual membership of the church and the synagogue. Since the sectarian nature of the Lucan community is established in this way, the second step is to determine which kind of sectarian responses are displayed by this sectarian group.

that his responses to evil in the world do not assume a separation from a parent body (1982:101-102).

Except for the haphazard assimilations, it should also be clear from the brief overview presented above, that within the field of sectarian studies, the same term which is used for different categories and concepts cannot that easily be hijacked in order to compile all the features of "the sect". In fact, in terms of the various meanings of the term, there does not exist something like "the sect". If it is taken into account that in each typology the sect is an ideal type, and given the problems which have already been pointed out in claims that such constructs have analytical power, it becomes even more problematic to assume that taken together these typologies can give a picture of the ideal sect.

Wilson's responses are divorced from their socio-cultural conditions

To my mind, one of the most serious shortcomings of the use of Wilson's typology is the insufficient attention paid to the socio-cultural conditions in which sects emerge. Part of the criticism against his typology is that it runs on such a high level of abstraction (divorced from specific socio-cultural conditions) that it loses any explanatory power. In New Testament studies this tendency is taken to its extreme when found in the following two different versions. The first is when a single text or Christian group displays features of more than one sectarian response simultaneously. The second instance is when elements of sectarian responses are identified in groups or texts but it is not argued that such texts or groups are themselves sectarian (see the many examples in Elliott 1995:84-87).

It is only when sectarian responses are divorced from any socio-cultural conditions that it becomes possible to state that the same text (e.g. Luke-Acts) or group (e.g. the Lucan community) displays features of more than one response. In most instances the socio-cultural conditions identified by Wilson are rather specific and particular to specific responses. How then is it possible that the same group can experience all of these conditions at once? The second instance perfectly displays the tendency that a single element can be used for characterizing the whole.

Disregarding the social and cultural conditions of Wilson's typologies becomes most evident when his responses are adapted to describe ways of argumentation (Robbins 1996a:147-150). Instead of the seven responses to the world, one now finds seven ways of argumentation. For example, *utopian argumentation* asserts that people should inaugurate a new social system free from evil and corruption and it encourages partly withdrawing from the world and partly wishing to remake it into a better place. To be sure, the content of the argument is used for describing the kind of argumentation. From this point it is a short step to state that it would be rare for a long text (such as the Gospel of Mark) "to contain only one kind of social response to the world" (Robbins 1996a:150).

The part represents the whole

As is the case in sectarian studies in general, it often happens that when the features within a category are multiplied, they are simply added as alternative features to identify the whole. Part of Beckford's criticism (see above the section on the covert manipulation of definitions) includes that analyses can shift from one attribute to the next as the analysis proceeds or that only one characteristic becomes dominant, depending on the analytical needs. The same thing happens in New Testament sectarian studies making use of Wilson's typology.

Revolutionist responses, according to Esler (1987:59), are found all over the New Testament where a possible destruction of the political system is mentioned (e.g., in Revelation and Mk 13) or where reference to the restoration of the kingdom of God (e.g. Acts 1:6) is referred to. This same community (Lucan) is, however, preoccupied with individual penance and is therefore also conversionist. The same applies to Esler's description of the Qumran and Johannine communities as introversionist since they promoted profound separation between members and non-members (Esler 1994:90).

It has already been indicated that the typologies of Troeltsch, Wilson and others are often combined in order to establish the dynamics of "the sect's" response against a parent body. All possible features from Wilson's seven sectarian responses are added to elements from other sect definition in order to construct the features of "the sect". With such a definition, everything can be a sect since almost any group will display at least one or some of the features.

Wilson's vague concepts are filled in as demands arise

The broad scope of Wilson's terms has already been indicated. It is therefore not surprising that such words as *the world* and *protest* are filled with meanings that happen to be in demand at the moment. MacDonald (1988:38) admits that it is impossible to determine against what, if anything, members of the Pauline sect were protesting with respect to the world. Therefore, it can be filled in by such vague descriptions as "they perceived their ideas and values to be at variance with society at large". The same applies to the content of "the world" which can mean almost anything, and in this case means what traditional theology has always insisted it to mean (MacDonald 1988:39).

In Esler's case, the appropriateness of Wilson's phrase "response to the world" in Luke-Acts is established by pointing towards three features. Luke utilizes a Hellenistic prose style, he presents Christianity as a historical phenomenon within the setting of the Roman imperium and he is aware of the status of Christians in the eyes of the Roman political, military and judicial authorities (1987:58-59). These elements give an indication of Luke's perception of the relationship between Christianity and "the outside world." The question arises, whether on the basis of such features, it is not possible to identify the response to the world of every single document or group in the New Testament.

Holmberg notes that Wilson's description of the different responses still has a rather theological character (Holmberg 1990:110 n 86). Add to that that the salient features of traditional church-sect typologies (sect versus parent group) continue to inform current New Testament sect definitions. Is it surprising that New Testament studies, using Wilson's typology, often claim that there is an apparent correspondence between the data and a specific response?[18] Given the theological jargon and the prominent church-sect features which reflect the early church in the mirror of the church history, one wonders whether the use of the conversionist category does not suffer from the same amount of circular reasoning Holmberg has pointed out with regard to the use of a millenarian model for describing the Thessalonian Christians. He asks: "How could the Thessalonian Christians *not* fit into the millenarian model? They practically created it!" (1990:86).

Some Concluding Remarks

Questions which inevitably arise are whether Wilson's model is used against its grain and whether the shortcomings inherent in his typology just become magnified when used in New Testament studies. In other words, is it treated fairly in its own right or is the model perhaps

[18] A single feature of the conversionist response, for example, makes it obvious to Esler that this response fits New Testament material (see 1987:59) while the comparability of Wilson's introversionist response to the Qumran group is readily apparent to him (see 1994:80). This comes despite the fact that introversionists regard salvation as a present reality and that the Qumran group tended to expect an immanent end. Esler allows for this by maintaining that they exhibit certain beliefs which appear more akin˙ to the revolutionist response.

pushed into directions it would not want to go? To my mind, it is a matter of both.

Despite the shortcomings which have been identified, it seems to me as if New Testament scholars are indeed taking advantage of a typology which cannot sponsor this application. A model which is primarily designed for describing strategies for dealing with evil in the world, is used for describing the dynamics of the organizational development and expansion of early Christian groups. Against the grain of the model, it is assimilated with other sect typologies which use the same term but do not deal with the same categories. On the historical side, the continuous use of any form of normative Judaism remains one of the biggest obstacles in New Testament studies. More important than the application of such inappropriate sect models is the demand for establishing the dynamics and sociology of group formation in the first-century world. The first steps in this regard have been taken by Bruce Malina (1995).

It should be obvious that the above argument does not prevent the use of sect models if the avoidance of ethnocentrism and anachronism is not important. Such a model can indeed throw new light on early Christian groups and their stages of development if they are treated anachronistically and ethnocentrically. In fact, the possibilities are legion if sect models are used for creative interpretive purposes. However, in light of the above shortcomings inherent in Wilson's typology as well as the problems involved in its application in New Testament studies, it seems to me better to abandon it on attempting historical interpretation of the New Testament.

Finally, "goodness of fit" of models is not a luxury, it is an essential first step in any social-scientific interpretation if the above mentioned pitfalls are to be avoided. Admittedly, it complicates the interpretive process in that the evaluation of models' appropriateness becomes a goal in itself. The use of social-scientific models turns into a multiple process where interpretation takes place on a variety of levels. The application of social-scientific models, it seems, indeed not only leads to eternal vigilance but to a process of continuous criticism and self-criticism.

3

Coming to Terms with a Neglected Aspect of Ancient Mediterranean Reciprocity:
Seneca's views on benefit-exchange in *De beneficiis* as the framework for a model of social exchange

Stephan Joubert, *UNISA, Pretoria, South Africa*

Man is a reciprocal being, *homo reciprocus* whether in so-called "primitive societies" where the exchange of gifts leads to the establishment of long-term relations between the transactors, or in modern economic transactions where commodity-exchange establishes a relation between the goods transacted. Even in advanced societies there is still no such thing as a free meal, or, for that matter, a free-gift coupon, as Mary Douglas (1990:viiff.) tells us.

In this essay the emphasis will be on reciprocity in the socially stratified Mediterranean world of the first century where the exchange of services was never voluntary but reciprocal. More specifically, ancient benefaction, as a particular form of *social exchange*, will demand our attention.

Social exchange, which refers to the reciprocal relationships which are established and/or, maintained between the parties involved in an exchange of services, has been of particular interest to scholars within the social-scientific field of research. Advancing from the theoretical perspective that the social-scientific paradigm presents us with its own agenda of problems that need to be solved, this study is intended as an exercise in addressing and, hopefully, refining the present state of research on benefit exchange by means of a study of Seneca's *De beneficiis*. Finally, a basic model of exchange for the interpretation of reciprocal interaction will also be offered. In terms of the Kuhnian concept of "normal science" (Kuhn 1970:23-42), my aim is not to invent any new theories in this regard, but rather to articulate one of the phenomena under discussion.

The Contours of the Social-Scientific Paradigm

Ground-breaking research on the ancient Mediterranean cultural scripts by Bruce Malina and a number of other scholars were constitutive in the formation of the social-scientific approach (Joubert 1994). The failure of traditional exegetical methods to solve existing scientific problems, facilitated the formation of this new paradigm with its own distinctive methodological apparatus and epistemology. Social-scientific criticism soon moved beyond the description of social data, to a comprehensive method of social scientific interpretation in order to facilitate culturally sensitive readings of biblical texts. In this regard the modes of analysis and processes of explanation of the ancient Mediterranean world in general, and the early Messianist movement/groups in particular, were (and still are) guided by cross-cultural models from a broad spectrum of social-sciences in order to address the new set of problems that presented themselves as objects of research.

In their attempts to come to terms with the social systems within which early Messianist groups were rooted, biblical scholars, working within the parameters of the social-scientific approach, have during the last few years followed the route of general science. They generally use the same type of explanatory models, agree on basic standard solutions to scientific issues, occupy themselves collectively with solving the remaining issues and the refinement of present knowledge. Important new areas of research relevant to the social-scientific approach are still being explored in this regard (cf. e.g. the analysis of the Graeco-Roman *encomium* or speech of praise, in Malina & Neyrey 1996:23ff.), while on the other hand, overviews of the present state of research on topics such as honor and shame, kinship, ancient economies, patronage, etc., as well as some further refinements of existing knowledge, are also offered (Rohrbaugh 1996).

"Benefactorism" as a Form of Social Exchange in the Ancient Mediterranean World

After these preliminary theoretical remarks we shall now move our attention to a topic of research which is of interest to biblical scholars in general and to adherents of the social-scientific approach in particular, namely *ancient Mediterranean benefaction*. In terms of the above-mentioned remarks, the following investigation is intended as a small contribution to and the further refinement of present knowledge on ancient benefaction.

Reciprocity was basic to all forms of social interaction in ancient societies. Cicero (*De officiis* 1.47), for example, tells us that if obligations are incurred between two parties, an adequate response is required, for no duty is more imperative than that of proving one's gratitude. Seneca (*De beneficiis* I.4.2), in turn, does not hesitate to point out that reciprocal interchange constitutes the chief bond that holds people together in society. According to the late first century magnate, Dio Chrysostom of Prusa (*Oratio* 75.6), at least the following three distinct social relationships were marked by reciprocal obligations: children and parents; beneficiaries and private benefactors, and cities and their public benefactors. On his part Aristotle in his *Nichomachean Ethics,* when sketching the profile of the so-called magnificent man (μεγαλο-πρεπής—IV.2.5) and the great-souled man (μεγαλόψυχος—IV.3.1ff.), presents us with the profile of the two basic types of benefactors in the Hellenistic world, namely: (a) the noble figure who engaged in collective undertakings for the common good of all his fellow citizens, and (b) the individual in the upper social strata of society who engaged in reciprocal interchanges of a more personal nature with status-equals or near-equals. Spicq (1994:107-113) also confirms this dual meaning of the term εὐεργέτης in the Hellenistic period. He maintains that this word always retained its banal sense, "benefactor", but it also became a technical term for the "benefactor-protector of a city or a people, and, in the case of the gods, the whole world". *Benefactorism* therefore refers to both these forms of social exchange in the Graeco-Roman world. Firstly, we shall briefly look at civic benefaction, or "euergetism" as Paul Veyne (1990:10) calls it, before turning our attention to interpersonal benefaction as reflected in Seneca's *De beneficiis*.

Euergetism

Our most important sources of information on euergetism are *honorific decrees*, those stereotyped public expressions of gratitude on the part of beneficiaries for the efforts of the nobles who assisted them in various ways, such as providing military and monetary support, games, cheap or free grain, buildings, banquets, etc. (cf. in this regard the standard works on Graeco-Roman benefaction by Gauthier 1985; Veyne 1990, and Quass 1993). According to Winter (1994:27) the Greek epigraphic benefactor genre conveyed the following information: "Whereas A did X and Y for our city, it is therefore resolved to honor A as follows...in order that all may see that the People appropriately honor benefactors commensurate with their benefaction." As a matter of fact, civic benefaction went hand in hand with what researchers refer to as the "epigraphic habit" since it was advantageous to donors "to put their donations on public record, while, from the other side, honors could be made meaningful by being perpetuated in stone by a grateful recipient community or its representatives" (Rajak 1996:308).

Honorific decrees confirmed the elevated status of benefactors as belonging to the category of the nobles, the καλοὶ καὶ ἀγαθοὶ ἄνδρες their outstanding moral character traits such as καλοκἀγαθια and φιλοτιμία and for the excellence and prestige that were already manifested by their ancestors. Honorary inscriptions and/or the erection of statues in prominent places, such as market-places or sanctuaries was therefore due recognition for every person involved in the "noble search" (more correctly: in the agonistic competition) for honor. Apart from being awarded eloquent titles such as σωτήρ, φιλότιμος, and εὐεργέτης, other tangible honors did not remain behind: special seats at public games, golden crowns, public eulogies, honorary positions in temples, even for their families and offspring.

Individuals who were elected to public positions such as magistracies were expected to direct their expenditure on behalf of the community to pleasures and public works, *voluptates* and *opera publica* (Veyne 1990:10ff.). But these benefits were always to be conferred on the community as a whole, not only on a few fortunate individuals. This also held true for private benefactors who bestowed benefits on fellow citizens. All inhabitants of a town or city had to benefit from it, not only friends or family members. Benefactions were definitely not intended by the Greeks and the Romans as a form of public charity (Hands 1968:20ff.; Prell 1997:296). In spite of some munificent forms of assistance by nobles to their communities, in general most of them used their benefactions to increase their own honor and not so much to alleviate the want of others. Therefore, they frequently indulged in the more popular and glamorous benefits such as games, monetary handouts, and festivals.

The picture presented to us by the honorary inscriptions is that of a socially stratified society with the notables conferring benefits in exchange for the bestowals of honor by the masses, which at the same time also served as expressions of the latter's social and political allegiance. In this regard, the bestowal of benefits could actually be understood as a form of "tax" on the elites, limiting the uncontrolled accumulation of wealth by inducing them to spend some of it on their communities (Kidd 1990:114).

Although bestowal of benefits were in principle voluntary, immense pressure was brought to bear on benefactors to part with their possessions. The placing of inscriptions in prominent public places such as busy market-places or sanctuaries, or even better offering benefactors the choice where they wanted their statues to be erected (cf. Pliny, *Ep.* VIII.6.14) as well as the phraseology of the inscriptions functioned as "payments for services rendered." It also encouraged the agonistic attitude prevalent among benefactors (cf. Plutarch's criticism of this practice in his *Moralia* 820B). Honorary decrees often ended with an exhortatory formula introduced by the phrase ὅπως ἅπαντες εἰδῶσιν "in order that all could see" that the inhabitants of a specific city appropriately honor their benefactors (e.g., the inscriptions for doctors from Kos approximately 241-200 BCE in Danker 1982:62ff.). By making it clear that they were fulfilling their reciprocal responsibilities towards their "great sons", the beneficiaries also, in terms of the reciprocity ethic, provided an incentive for the same person, and also for other would-be benefactors to bestow further benefits upon them. In the words of Rajak (1996:307): "The honours were a not-too-subtle statement to the donor that he had a reputation which could only be kept up by further benefaction."

Seneca on Interpersonal Benefit–Exchange
The aim of *De beneficiis*

Lucius Annaeus Seneca, the well-known first century CE Stoic philosopher wrote his *De beneficiis*, an ethical treatise on benefits, somewhere between 56-64 CE but most likely during his service in Nero's court (cf. the good overview of Seneca's life and work in Klauck 1996:79-85). Although not his best-known work, *De beneficiis* is the most detailed material available on benefit-exchange in the ancient Graeco-Roman world.

Seneca in this long treatise deals with the responsibilities (*officia*) of people involved in reciprocal relations. In this regard he is of the opinion that a benefit forms a common bond which binds two people together (VI.41.2). Therefore, from his point of departure that every obligation involving any two people makes an equal demand on both (II.1.18), he addresses the question on how to furnish and receive benefits on *interpersonal level* (I.1.1; V.1.1). The ever present problem inherent to social-exchange, namely debtors' reluctance to return benefits forms the framework against which Seneca's instruction should be understood. He expresses his disapproval of this practice in strong terms: ingratitude is accentuated as the greatest sin (I.1.13) and also as the most common of the vices (I.1.2).

Aware of the threat that ingratitude holds for the practice of bene-faction and for the *concordiam humani generis* (IV.18.1), Seneca presents an idealistic reinterpretation of the basic tenets of this system in terms of Stoic ethical perspectives by providing a *lex vitae*, a law of conduct, in this regard (I.4.2). But this is not done along the usual lines. Se-neca's aim is to replace the generally accepted perception in the ancient Graeco-Roman world, namely that one is to give with a view to receiving something back (Hands 1968:26-48) with an ethic of giving as an intrinsically rewarding experience in itself. In typical Stoic fashion emphasis is placed on the reason and intentions (*animus*) of the individual which should be used in order to make the right selections (II.31.1- cf. also Sørensen 1985:194). Apart from relating his views to the inner freedom of the individual and in this process turning the giving of benefits into a virtue in itself, Seneca's reinterpretation of the basic tenets of reciprocity is also related to the conduct of the gods as ultimate examples of selfless behavior. According to Seneca only the good man (*vir bonus*) is able to achieve these lofty ideals, since he is able to give, receive and return benefits in spite of ingratitude on the part of the recipients. This theme actually forms an *inclusio* which en-compasses this entire treatise (cf. I.1-13; VII.26-32).

In order to assist the *vir bonus* to give concrete expression to the ideal of imitating the Fatherly God, he has to learn the correct princi-ples underlying reciprocal relations as well as the necessary diplomacy in daily interchanges (Maurach 1991:107). In this process Seneca, the idealist, also becomes the practical philosopher who often resorts to casuistic reasoning on a wide spectrum of daily situations in which reciprocal interactions take place, thus creating a dialectic tension be-tween ideals and reality; between the possibility of viewing the bestowal of a benefit and gratitude as virtues in themselves to the harsh reality that benefits eventually have to be reciprocated.

The True Nature of a Benefit

For Seneca a true benefit is a virtue (*virtus*). It is to be desired because of itself, not for any external advantages it may hold (IV.20.1). At the same time Seneca distinguishes between the form in which a benefit is bestowed and the benefit itself of which the provenance is in the mind (*res animo geritur*—I.5.2). He also emphasizes the latter as being the most important and enduring. Typical of Stoic dualistic thought,

Seneca in his understanding of benefits thus deals with corporeally observable objects as well as with the inner disposition of the benefactor and that of the recipient without, however, relinquishing his idea of corporealism (Inwood 1995:259; cf. also Sharples 1996).

At the same time Seneca accentuates the *inalienability* of giver and gift. Using the distinction between the outward form of a benefit and the "true benefit", he states that the latter remains unaltered in the process of giving and receiving material gifts (VI.2-3). Thus, even though a recipient may lose all outward benefits he possesses such as his money or property, his benefit still stays intact. Any benefactor could therefore echo Mark Anthony's ironic words: *hoc habeo, quodcumque dedi* ("Whatever I have given, that I still possess!"). As a matter of fact, the only way in which one can make one's material possessions one's own, is to give them away as gifts. The moment a gift is given away, it turns into a benefit (*cum donasti, beneficium est*).

The Role of the Benefactor

1. Benefits are Gifts, not Loans

From the perspective of the benefactor, a benefit is described by Seneca as the act of a person who derives joy from the bestowal of gifts thus making *the intention of the giver* more important than what is given (I.6.1). Benefits are also to be viewed by the giver as *gifts* not as investments (I.1.9) or loans (II.34.1). Shameful self-centered motives such as the wealth or exalted social position of the recipient (IV.3,1-2) should be very far removed from the benefactor's mind. Not even ungratefulness on the side of the recipient should deter him from continuing with the conferral of benefits on the same unthankful person! (VII.32.1). At the same time personal comfort and safety as well as material means should also be sacrificed for the sake of others without looking for any return (IV.13.5). But, on the other hand, the benefactor should be careful not to bring financial ruin upon himself in the process of conferring benefits (II.15.1-2).

2. Benefit-Exchanges are not Agonistic Contests

The *agonistic* ancient Mediterranean culture turned most forms of social interaction from invitations, meals, public debates, recitals, business transactions, right up to gift-exchanges into agonistic contests for honor (Malina 1993a:37). As a matter of fact, the great Greek athletic contests as well as local sports competitions provided the metaphoric framework for the agonistic Hellenistic attitude towards life (Schwankl

1997:174ff.). These motifs were also related to the context of social exchange often turning it into a competition for honor among benefactors as well as for goods and services among prospective beneficiaries. However, Seneca would not have anything of this. at least not in terms of misusing bestowal of gifts as a means to insult or humiliate others (I.1.8). For example, his disgust at Gaius' shocking reaction to Pompeius Pennus' gratitude after he spared his life by extending his left foot to be kissed (II.12) makes this very clear. Nevertheless, Seneca's sensitivity to the social circumstances of the recipient should also be mentioned in the same breath. The person who experiences humiliating circumstances should be helped in private (II.9.1), while "glorious" benefits such as military decorations should be conferred publicly (II.9.1). Furthermore, a benefactor should promptly deliver the benefits he had promised. The recipients should not be kept in suspense or forced to ask a second time (II.5.1-5). Benefits should also not be misused as opportunities to offer advice or level reprimands at the recipients (II.5.6).

3. Choose Worthy Recipients
Benefits should not be bestowed thoughtlessly. Therefore those who are "worthy" of receiving gifts should be carefully sought out (I.1.2; cf also Peterman 1997:67). In this regard Seneca offers us a profile of the "ideal recipient": somebody who is upright, sincere, mindful, grateful, who does not steal, who is not greedily attached to his own possessions, and who is kind to others (IV.11.1). If a person matching these character traits is not in a position to return a benefit, this should not disqualify him (IV.10.3-4). However, the contingent needs of everyday life forces Seneca to make a few adjustments as to the "proper" recipients (IV.11.2-3). For example, one should avoid giving benefits to somebody who is on the point of emigrating to some distant country or to a sick person who has no chance of getting better. On the other hand, benefits are to bestowed upon the stranger who is putting into the harbor, and one who is about to embark again, or to a shipwrecked stranger.

4. Internalised Reciprocity and Social Approval
In the ancient Mediterranean world social interactions outside the family were based on the scheme of giving and returning the equivalence received. But in practice, the principle of *balanced reciprocity* (cf. e.g. Malina 1988a) which assumes that the parties involved were to benefit equally from their social interaction was often ignored, since

those in debt did not always reciprocate, or at least not with benefits of equal value. This brought the beneficial system which, according to Seneca, formed the chief bond of society into jeopardy

Seneca responds to this problem by turning the bestowal of benefits into a virtue as such thus making it an intrinsically rewarding experience. "The man who, when he gives, has any thought of repayment deserves to be deceived" (I.1,9). But would this altruistic behavior on the part of the giver actually encourage benevolent behavior along the lines suggested by Seneca? Would any relationship that was conceptualized as an exchange of rewards not come to an abrupt end when these expected reactions were not forthcoming? In any society based upon the notion that the advantageous consequences of people's good deeds are important inducements for doing them, at least some incentives are needed for encouraging unselfish behavior of this kind. The principle of *social approval* is one such an incentive, since it is one of the basic rewards sought by individuals in exchange-relations. Seneca also utilizes this principle by "adding" to his basic conception of benefits the joy which a giver receives on account of bestowing a benefit upon a grateful recipient. This is clear from his criteria for worthy (' grateful) recipients, and his description of a benefit as something which does good and brings joy (*gaudium*—I.6.1; II.31.2-4; V.20.4).

Although the approval or gratitude of the recipients cannot be coerced from them, Seneca is of the opinion that a person who has no desire to heap any burdens upon his recipients usually reaps a grateful return because others gladly return benefits to him (V.1.4). In other words, it leads to social approval and also to the necessary reward for the "basic costs" invested by the benefactor. Blau (1964:101) refers to three basic "costs" that individuals usually incur in providing social rewards for others, namely: "investment cost"—that is, the time and effort needed to acquire the skills required for furnishing instrumental services; "direct cost"—that is the subordination involved in expressing respect or manifesting compliance; and "opportunity cost"—that is the alternatives foregone by devoting time to a given exchange relation.

5. What Kind of Benefits should be Conferred?

Seneca identifies three hierarchical categories of benefits to be bestowed: the necessary, the useful, and the pleasurable (I.11.6). The first category includes things without which people cannot live (such as being saved from a wrath of a tyrant); secondly, those without which they ought not live (liberty, chastity and a good conscience); and thirdly, those without which they are not willing to live (family, household gods). Among the useful benefits are included money to provide for a reasonable living, public office, and assistance of those with high political aspirations. The third category of pleasurable benefits are the superfluities which tend to pamper a man.

6. Should the Benefactor Ask for a Return?

"No. One should rather lose a benefit than ask for a repayment" (I.1.13). In view of Seneca's perspectives on the nature of benefits, this view is not surprising. But he places even more restrictions on the giver by stating that the recipient should not be constantly reminded of the benefits bestowed upon him. He should remember it on his own accord. To recall these in his presence is in fact a reminder that he should repay it (II.11.1-2).

On the other hand, in terms of everyday realities Seneca also makes a few exceptions to his basic rule by stating that one should ask for a return in a time of crisis (V.20.7), but then only if the recipient is in the position to make a return (V.21.3). Seneca offers an interesting motivation in this regard: by reminding the forgetful, a second benefit is actually bestowed upon them since they are kept from doing wrong by not returning a benefit. In other instances a person could be reminded of his obligations by the bestowal of a second benefit on him (II.11.2; VII.32.1).

Benefits and the Recipient

1. Choose the Right Benefactor

According to Seneca it requires even more discernment to choose a benefactor than a recipient because it is nothing less than grievous torture to be under obligation to somebody one objects to (II.18.3-8). Since exchange of services in ancient societies implied the commencement of a long-term relationship between the parties involved, Seneca's admonition should not be passed over too lightly. Once an individual accepted a gift, he was placed under obligation to the benefactor which implied the start of a long-term relationship marked by mutual exchanges of gifts and counter-gifts.

To emphasize the necessity of making the right choice on the part of the recipient, Seneca draws a comparison of the roles of a creditor and a benefactor. He points out that when one has returned the money he borrowed from a creditor, he is under no further obligation to him (II.18.5; VI.14.4). But in the case of a benefactor the repayment of a debt of gratitude does not dissolve the bond. As a matter of fact, the whole exchange process then starts all over again since a lasting bond of friendship (*amicitia*) based upon the bestowal of these benefits has taken shape. Seneca thus draws a distinction between economical and social exchange. In the first instance, a relationship is formed between the objects exchanged which is clearly specified in terms of a single quantitative medium of exchange and also brought to an abrupt end at the date set for the repayment (III.10.1). But in the second instance a lasting relationship between the persons involved in the exchange of goods is formed which is usually based on unspecific obligations and without any set dates for the repayment of benefits.

The commencement of any social exchange relation was dependent upon the acceptance of the benefactor's gift. Seneca is well aware of this rule (VII.19.1). Therefore he advises that one should outrightly reject an unwanted gift (more correctly: an unwanted relationship) and also verbally state one's position in this regard (I.11.1). This humiliation to the benefactor would bring an abrupt end to the relationship (VI.42.1). Another alternative is to immediately send back a gift in return so as to wipe out a gift with a gift which is nothing less than a repulse (IV.40.5).

When circumstances prevent the recipient to exercise his right of choice, and he is forced to receive a gift from a bad person, such as a tyrant, then he is under no obligation to him (II.19.2). The principle of *free choice* thus determines the nature of a relationship either as an "economical exchange" or a "social exchange". Therefore, when one's life is saved by a bad man or when he receives money from him, it should be understood in monetary terms as a loan which should be repaid in like manner. As a "business transaction", the services received should then be returned.

How should one go about to actually bring one's needs to the attention of a benefactor? Seneca refers to Socrates who once tactfully said within hearing range of his friends that he would have bought himself a coat if he had the money. A rivalry then broke out among the friends as to who would be the first to give it to him (VII.24.1).

2. Ingratitude and Obligations

Social exchange leads to differentiation in power all the more so if a person commands certain services others need while at the same time being independent of any services which they command. This imbalance of power usually establishes reciprocity in the exchange, since nobody wants to be in the inferior position as Aristotle (*NE* IV.3.24) tells us. Thucydides shares the same view. According to him, the one who takes the initiative in an exchange is in the stronger position. The recipient who has now lost the edge in the relationship has to repay this kindness not as a favor bestowed but as debt repaid (cf. Marshall 1987:10). Seneca addresses this predicament on the part of the recipient warning him that the hasty return of a benefit is a sign of ingratitude. It points to a person who wants to get rid of the burden of being under obligation to a benefactor (VI.35.3-5).

Instead of looking for every possible opportunity to rid oneself of one's debts, one should rather adjust oneself to the convenience of the benefactor and wait for a suitable chance to make the return (VII.19.3). The recipient should view any service that was offered to him as a gift from a friend, not as a heavy burden from which he must free himself at the first possible opportunity.

Seneca's aim is to create a balanced reciprocal situation where the duties and responses of both benefactor and recipient are viewed as of equal importance. In other words, over against imbalanced or unilateral bestowals of gifts that entrench power differentials and often lead to exploitation, the "normal context of exchange" should consist of an exchange of obligations where each in turn renders to the other the services that he requires (II.18.2).

3. Gratitude is Sufficient Reward, but the Debt must still be Repaid

In terms of the well-known "Stoic paradoxes" Seneca states that benefit bestowed upon a recipient is fully repaid by his gratitude, since the actual exchange takes place in the minds of the giver and receiver, with the latter meeting the good will of the benefactor with his own good will (II.31-32). *Gratitude* is actually the only legitimate response on the part of the recipient in the exchange relationship in which two levels of activity take place, the intentional as well as the material (II.34-35). This implies that a return may have been made on the first level (= gratitude), but not yet on the material level (= the debt). In this regard, true to his idea of benefits a benefactor thus bestows two things on a recipient: property and good will. Therefore the latter owes two things (VII.15.3- cf. also Inwood 1995:261-2). Some similar gift to the one the recipient received should still be returned. Also gratitude should be expressed publicly (II.23-25). Those who refuse to express it in the open are not discreet but ungrateful (cf. also Peterman 1997:69-70). A benefit should also never be accepted in a submissive manner, nor in a spirit of indifference. Verbal expressions of gratitude in public are a fitting response (II.24.4; cf. also Mott 1975:61-2).

4. The Agonistic Contest of Benefit-Return

According to Levi-Strauss (1957:85), bestowals of gifts often function as a deliberate means of establishing domination. In the agonistic contests of gift-giving which characterize social interaction in ancient societies, the person who cannot match the gifts bestowed upon him becomes obliged to the giver thus losing his own prestige, rank, authority, and privileges to the giver. Although Seneca rejects this agonistic attitude on the part of the benefactor, he does in fact use the image of an athletic contest albeit in a reinterpreted manner when dealing with the responsibilities of the recipient. In this most honorable contest (*contentio*) of conquering benefits with benefits, the debtor should not only equal the gift bestowed upon him; his ideal should be to surpass it in deed and spirit (I.4.3-4). But at the same time Seneca also relates these agonistic images to the correct inner orientation of the recipient which will enable him to match his benefactor's *animus* (V.4.1-4). In the ensuing "battle", the person who has learnt how to owe a debt, cannot be outdone in benefits. The strong desire to give proof of his inner gratitude is actually more important than making big returns or matching the extrinsic benefits bestowed upon him. Therefore from this perspective, people of lesser means and lower social status can bestow benefits upon those who of high status; slaves can bestow benefits upon their masters, sons upon their fathers, subjects upon kings, etc (cf. also Stevenson 1992).

5. What Kind of Benefits have to be Returned?

Benefit-exchange in the ancient Mediterranean world was not legally regulated in terms of the value of the goods that had to be returned and in terms of the time span that was allowed to elapse between the bestowal and return of benefits, although it was generally believed that benefits of equal value had to be returned within a short period of time. Conflicts often erupted between benefactors and recipients with regards to aspects such as the value of the gifts offered and returned. Seneca (III.8-10) rejects the possibility that a court of law could settle these problems because the measure of gratitude involved in an interchange cannot be determined by a judge. At the same time, the external value of benefits or the grandeur with which they are given could also not be used as a means to determine their value. To give people Roman citizenship or to escort an aristocrat to the seats of honor at a public game might be impressive, but is it really more important than bestowing less glamorous benefits such as offering a person advice which prevents him for committing a crime or sitting at the bedside of a sick person?

Seneca in this regard also refers to disputes between benefactors and recipients over the value of their gifts and return-gifts. The unhappy benefactor for example tells his recipient that he gave him a house, upon which the latter responds: "Yes, but I warned you that yours was tumbling down upon your head!" Seneca amply captures the gist of these dilemmas as follows: "Since benefits may be given in some form and repaid in another, it is difficult to establish their quality. Besides, for the repayment of a benefit no date is set..." (III.9.3-10.1). The ideal situation wherein benefactor and recipient carefully selected each other would be Seneca's solution to these conflicts, that is, where the benefactor knows that a benefit (although not specified) will eventually be returned to him. And even if it is not, he has already received the gratitude of the recipient as sufficient reward. On his part, the recipient will return a benefit cheerfully when the benefactor wishes it (VI.43.1-3).

The Social Embeddedness of Benefit-Exchanges

Apart from interpersonal benefit exchanges between individuals of the same or different social statuses which is his main concern, Seneca in *De beneficiis* also focuses on social-exchanges among family members, friends as well as among patrons and clients (cf. in this regard Elliott 1996). But neither friendship nor *patrocinium* form the basic interpretative framework against which benefit-exchange is understood by Seneca (so also Bormann 1995:171-2). Admittedly he himself "swam in the sea of patron-client relations. He used it to further his career and to define his position in Roman society. He knew the system of giving *beneficia* and repaying *gratia* as well as anyone living in Rome" (Inwood 1995:244). Many examples used by Seneca in *De beneficiis* are therefore typical of patron-client interactions such as his references to the imperial benefactions bestowed on individuals and the *populus Romanum* (II.7.2; 25.2; III.27.4; VI.19.1-5), "client-friendships" (VI.34-35), typical benefits bestowed by patrons (II.21.5; III.9.1-2), etc. But this does not mean that Seneca approved of these patron-client interchanges. As a matter of fact, he offers strong criticism against the misuse of power which often went hand in hand with patron-client relations such as the "client friendships" (VI.34-35) between powerful Roman patrons and their large clienteles who flocked to their doors every morning during the customary morning salutations (cf. Saller

1982). The relationship between the Emperor and the *populus Romanum* as well as that between other public figures and the citizens which included public bestowals of benefits, does not qualify as "legitimate" forms of benefit exchange either, even though they are undertaken for the common good of all (VI.19.1-5). *For a service to qualify as a benefit it must have been undertaken because of a specific individual, and not just bestowed on him as one of the crowd.*

Scholars who do not take Seneca's benefit exchange to be a social relationship proper usually interpret his views in terms of relationships such as *amicitia* (e.g., Marshall 1987; White 1990). But they do not leave enough room for Seneca's own perspectives on benefit exchange as Bormann (1995:171) correctly points out. In this regard he states that

> Seneca behandelt im wesentlichen die Bedeutung des *beneficium* außerhalb der Freundschaft, in der Hauptsache zwischen einander unverbundenen Personen, aber dann auch im Rahmen bestehenden Bindungen wie zwischen Söhnen und Vätern, den Göttern und Menschen, Sklaven und ihren Herren, Ärtzten und deren Patienten u.a.

Seneca clearly understood the exchange of benefits in terms of an independent social relationship brought about by the exchange of services between individuals.

A Basic Model of Social-Exchange

Seneca provides us with a basic conceptual framework for the understanding of reciprocal relations between individuals and groups on personal level in ancient Mediterranean societies. In this regard the following *basic processes* could be inferred from his views of benefit exchange:

a. An individual renders a rewarding service to another person.
b. The person to whom the service is rendered, accepts the service.
c. The recipient is obliged to the person who rendered the service.
d. The recipient discharges his obligation by rendering a service to the first in turn.
e. The original benefactor is placed under obligation by the return service to return a second service.

Although concern in exchange relations is often with the exchange of extrinsic benefits, the significance of the "extrinsic" services rendered and returned cannot be understood in isolation from the *social relationship* that is formed and/or maintained through benefit exchange. From this perspective the following *basic model of social exchange*, also based on the information from Seneca, can be constructed:

Phase 1. Scenario A: A person (or group) in need of specific services makes his needs known to another person/group who is perceived as being in the position to provide the services required. The latter (i) either responds negatively, thereby ending the relationship, or (ii) responds positively, thereby confirming the expectations about his ability to deliver the services in question. In terms of status demarcations, the superiority of the benefactor in the exchange-relationship is also confirmed.

Scenario B: A person makes a claim (that is, without any prior requests from a person/group in need of specific services) in terms of the establishment of a relationship with another person (or group) through an offering of particular services.

Phase 2: The extrinsic service is delivered. In terms of Phase 1 Scenario A, this serves as a visible confirmation of the benefactor's honor, and confirms his superiority in the exchange relationship. In terms of Phase 1 Scenario B, the giver makes a claim to superiority in a subsequent relationship.

Phase 3: The recipient (i) either refuses the services offered, thereby abruptly ending the relationship, or (ii) accepts it, thereby establishing a hierarchical interpersonal relationship characterized by stereotypical role-expectations and *officia*.

Phase 4: When the service is accepted, the recipient becomes obliged to the benefactor for the durance of this phase of the relationship. This phase is characterized by a distinct power differential between the benefactor and recipient.

Phase 5: The recipient (i) either refuses to return a service, which leads to further submission, hostilities, or a total break-off in the relationship, or (ii) returns a service.

Phase 6: The return service is offered to the benefactor, thus confirming the recipient's honorable fulfilment of his *officia*.

Phase 7: The benefactor (i) either rejects the service offered, which leads to conflict or a break-off in the relationship, or (ii) accepts the service, thus reversing the hierarchical positions of the interlocutors: the benefactor is now placed under the obligation to respond with a new service to the recipient, who attains the superior position.

Phase 8 etc.: The whole process from Phase 2 forward is repeated.

Conclusion

Any exchange of services in the ancient Mediterranean world produced mutual obligations as well as unequal relationships of domination between the parties involved, specifically in terms of the giver who had some kind of superiority. In this regard benefactors were not so much concerned with maximizing their net income but rather then net giving. In other words, they wanted to acquire a large following of people (gift-debtors) outside their families who were obliged to them. The latter had to reciprocate the benefits they had received so as to fulfill the stereotype roles associated with the principle of balanced reciprocity (that is, returning the same sort of gifts, or gifts of equal value for those received). Any failure in this regard distorted the basic fiber of society. It led to loss of credit, honor and trust; and ultimately, exclusion from further exchanges and a decline in social status, particularly as the person's reputation as one who did not honor his obligations spread in the community (cf. also Blau 1966: 108).

Seneca was well aware of the various problems facing benefactors and beneficiaries in reciprocal exchanges. In *De beneficiis* he endeavors to offer a balanced, more "humane" form of social interaction by shifting the emphasis from the services being exchanged to the social bond which is established between the interlocutors. In this regard he presents us with the ideal picture of the benefit exchange:

The ideal benefactor is the person "who gives readily, never demands any return, rejoices if a return is made, who in all sincerity forgets what he has bestowed, and accepts a return in the spirit of one accepting a benefit" (II.17.7).

The ideal beneficiary is a person who takes seriously the following important advice from Seneca: "Do you want to return a benefit? Accept it with pleasure; you have paid it with gratitude—not so fully that you may feel that you have freed yourself from debt, yet so that you may be less concerned about what you still owe!" (II.25.5).

And *the ideal exchange situation*? Well, that is when "in the exchange of obligations, each in turn renders to the other the services he requires" (II.18.2).

Finally, in the spirit of benefit exchange, a word of gratitude to a modern-day benefactor, Bruce Malina: *nescis, quid mihi praestiteris, sed scire te oportet, quanto plus sit, quam existimas.*

4

"By the Hand of a Woman":
Culture, Story and Theology in the Book of Judith[1]

Philip F. Esler, *St Mary's College, University of St Andrews, Scotland*

Addressing the dilemma of Judith

The book of Judith poses a short and sharp dilemma. What are we to make of a biblical text[2] which, although originating in a notably androcentric culture, tells of a *woman* who acts as God's agent to save her people and does so by first deceiving and then decapitating the leader of the enemy host? The shock of this text lies in the fact that it describes how Israel is saved when God strikes down the foe "by the hand of a woman" (*en cheiri thêleias*), a phrase used on three occasions in the work—in Judith's prayer for success (9:10), when she informs the Bethulians she has slain Holofernes (13:15), and in the concluding prayer (16:6).

Not surprisingly a book as provocative as this has attracted considerable attention from scholars. Older interest on the part of Catholic critics lay especially in the question of possible historical foundations for Judith and her actions,[3] although that interest now seems misplaced

---

[1] I wish gratefully to acknowledge the assistance Dr John Pilch has given me with this essay, both in discussing aspects of it and in providing a number of references. It goes without saying that he is not responsible for its contents.

[2] I will refer to the Book of Judith as 'biblical' on the basis of its deutero-canonical status from the time of Jerome onwards, a status it still enjoys among Roman Catholics, even though it was never accepted into the Hebrew canon (indeed not a fragment of the ancient Hebrew text usually supposed to lie behind the Greek versions which are extant from antiquity has survived) and is, accordingly, an apocryphal text for Protestants. The fact that it was included in Christian Bibles from the time of Jerome onwards justified the enormous interest shown in the text by Western artists and writers. See Moore 1992b for a discussion of why the book of Judith was not included in the canon.

[3] See Brown *et al.* 1968:xvii for a discussion of this perspective which largely disappeared under the influence of the Papal Encyclical *Divino afflante Spiritu* (30 September

and has largely disappeared in favor of the view—accepted here—that Judith is a fictional character. In recent years we observe a concern with the inherent literary qualities of the book (Alonso-Schökel 1974; Craven 1983), its intertextual links to Israelite (Skehan 1963; Merideth 1989; White 1992) or even Greek (Caponigro 1992) writings, its portrayal of its central character (Hellmann 1992), its influence on later Jewish and Christian tradition (Dubarle 1959), its potential for feminist interpretations (Levine 1995; van Henten 1995), and its huge impact on the European visual arts tradition (Hellmann 1992; Bal 1995). Essays in the last three of these areas frequently take up the ethical dimensions of Judith's actions.

In the present essay I have a rather different aim. While undertaking doctoral research in Oxford in the early 1980's I came across Bruce J. Malina's *The New Testament World*, first published in 1981. I learned to appreciate from it, from the reading in anthropological literature which it provoked, and from discussions with members of the Context Group (many of whom are represented in this volume), how necessary it is for understanding biblical texts to take into account the distinctive nature of Mediterranean culture which formed an important part of the context in which they were written and first interpreted.[4] Accordingly, as a contribution to this collection in honor of Bruce Malina, my aim is to read the story of Judith within the framework of a Mediterranean culture quite remote from the culture of modern Northern European and North American individualism.[5] That is to say, although I concur with the central point of narrative criticism that we should always be alive to the total literary form of a biblical text, I am concerned to see how the story would have worked *as a story*, but within a Mediterranean cultural context quite alien to our own.[6] I

1943), although Bruns (1954 and 1956) continued to argue that Judith was a real person.

[4] Dominick LaCapra has rightly pointed out that there are many dimensions to the 'context' of a text (1983:35-71). He identifies (although in a different order): (a) society, (b) culture, modes of discourse, (d) the author's intentions, (e) the author's corpus and (f) the author's life. Although other taxonomies are possible, LaCapra's discussion does highlight many important features of context. In the present essay the two elements of context emphasized are (Mediterranean) culture and the modes of discourse which comprise Israelite scriptural traditions.

[5] I do not deny that individuality existed in the ancient Mediterranean world, only that individualism did not. For the meaning of individualism in this context, see Hofstede 1980 and 1994 and Esler 1998a:13-14.

[6] In speaking of 'Mediterranean culture' I am admittedly speaking at a certain (and convenient) level of abstraction and I do not deny that there was a great amount of variety in the ancient Mediterranean region, both regionally and diachronically.

hope to show how many features of the text, especially some of those which have troubled commentators for one reason or another, can be interpreted afresh using this perspective.

At the same time, however, we cannot avoid the frequent notices in the text that Judith was working God's purposes in her mission, so that we must consider how the way the story is told in its context carried a theological message for its original audience. Indeed, I will seek to go further and suggest that it is difficult to get the theological point of the book without undertaking this process. To this extent, I hope that the present essay will illustrate how social-scientific approaches to biblical texts are not inimical to theological ones (which is a common misunderstanding) but can actually facilitate a new appreciation of the theological point of biblical works.

In recent writings elsewhere I have similarly sought to interpret certain other Old Testament narratives, namely those concerning Saul in 1 Samuel 8–31 (Esler 1998b) and David and Goliath in 1 Samuel 17 (Esler 1998c), as stories whose original force and impact can only be understood within the cultural context in which they were crafted. Although Bruce Malina can certainly not be held responsible for the results of this type of interpretative exercise in relation to Judith, I trust that my debt to him extending over many years will be apparent throughout. While I would certainly not claim that this approach exhausts the dilemma posed by the book of Judith with which I began, I hope it might be regarded as at least throwing some light on it.

Although the issue of the date of composition of the book of Judith will not feature much in what follows, I agree with commentators who consider that the work was written in the Hasmonean period (Cowley 1913:245; Moore 1985:67-70; 1992:1123). Apart from the signs in the text of Hellenistic provenance (Delcor 1967), a particular reason for this dating is the similarity between the presentation of the Israelite government in the text, by a high priest and council of Israelite elders (*gerousia*; 4:8; 15:8), and the epigraphs on Hasmonean coinage, probably first minted about 103 BCE by Alexander Jannaeus (who reigned 103-76 BCE),[7] which regularly refer to a (named) high priest and a *heber* of *yehudîm*, a council of Judeans (Kindler 1974:9-21; Hendin 1976:13-17; Meshorer 1982:74-87). I actually favor a date in the first half of the first century BCE, rather than in the second century BCE in the time of Hyrcanus (so Moore 1992a:1123), but I must leave for another place an exposition of the basis for my view.

---

[7] Meshorer (1982:75) argues against suggestions that John Hyrcanus 1 (reigned 135-104 BCE) minted his own coinage.

Challenge-and-response in the Structure of Judith

Encountering the Book of Judith as an Ancient Mediterranean Story
There are sixteen chapters in the book of Judith and Judith herself does not appear until ch. 8. To some critics this feature represents a problem with the structure of the work. Thus A. E. Cowley, having suggested that the work fell naturally into two parts, 'the introduction' (chs. 1–7) and 'the story of Judith' (chs. 8–16), went on to observe:

The book is thus almost equally divided between the introduction and the story proper. The former is no doubt somewhat out of proportion, and the author dwells at rather unnecessary length on the military details (1913:242-243).

Other critics share this estimation (Alonso-Schökel 1974:3; Dancy 1972:67). More recently, however, commentators, including Craven (1977; 1983), Moore (1985; 1992a) and van Henten (1995), have asserted the unity of the work and have tended to reject the notion that it is unbalanced.

Craven, who has been especially influential, has argued that chs. 1–7 serve as a foil for chs. 8-16 in a number of ways, such as in developing a detailed contrast between Nebuchadnezzar and Holofernes with their huge military force on the one hand and Judith, with her beauty, faith and astuteness on the other. She describes the focus of her interest as 'the compositional architecture of the text' (1983:45) or its "structure", by which she means "something akin to a narrative x-ray of the architectural or compositional pattern that undergirds the story" (1983:20). In practice, inspired by Robert Lowth's pioneering explorations into the nature of Hebrew poetry in the eighteen century and Muilenburg's call to critics to attend to the structure of Hebrew texts (1969), Craven seeks out and finds patterns of parallels and antitheses in the work, both at the level of features of the plot and also of linguistic expression. For example, she argues that chs. 1–7 and 8–16 form two balanced sets of chiastic structures (1983:47-64), a phenomenon she describes, rather oddly, as "the *external* (my emphasis) design" of the text, meaning that the pattern she has discovered should be susceptible of "external verification" (1983:45).

Although Craven finds these patterns aesthetically pleasing, it is clear that this judgment would not be shared by everyone today who agreed that they were to be found in the text, since some of us might wish to suggest that this level of symmetry (and contrived asymmetry) in a

literary text is simply monotonous.[8] In any event, Craven's interpretation is certainly a specialist one, born of long and patient work on the
book's architecture, and seems rather a long way from the response of
a non-specialist reader, whose experience of how the text works *as a
story* will depend more on an encounter with its overt features in their
narrative order as the text unfolds than with any sense of what an
"x-ray" of its structure might reveal. In other words, ordinary readers
encounter literary texts, just like persons, with respect to their external
presentation and movement, not their bone-structure, so that radiog-
raphy seems an inappropriate metaphor for a non-specialist reading.

The same considerations apply *a fortiori* to ancient readers, although
now we need to bring their very different cultural context into the
picture. I wish to propose that *ancient readers,* engaging with the overt
features of the text as the narrative unfolded, would have found the
work a satisfying and socially engrossing artistic unity for the particular
reason that it embodies a central social dynamic of ancient Mediterranean culture—the pattern of challenge and response. First formulated
by Pierre Bourdieu (1965) and developed by Malina (1993a:34-45),
challenge and response refers to the myriad examples of social interaction—in a culture oriented around achieving honor—where one
person "challenges" another, that is, makes a claim to enter his (rarely
her[9]) social space and this claim is met by a vigorous response, frequently eliciting a counter-challenge from the original challenger, then
another response and so on until some final resolution is reached, often
the disgrace and sometimes even the death of one of the parties. Since
Malina has set out the pattern very clearly diagrammatically (1993a:36)
and since I have discussed its elements elsewhere (Esler 1994:27-29), I
will not rehearse the details here but will refer to appropriate aspects
where relevant below. Malina himself has drawn attention to the extent to which the controversies Jesus has with his opponents in the
Gospels may be interpreted within the conventions of challenge and
response (1993a:59), while I have recently analyzed John 8:31-59 as an

---

[8] If, for example, the world is divided into those who find chiastic structures noteworthy and significant and those who do not, I confess to finding myself in the latter
group.

[9] Since the focus in ancient texts is most commonly on interactions between males,
with the book of Judith constituting a rare exception, usually both the challenger and
the person challenged are males. However, one interesting arena of the pattern involving women occurs in households where the dominant male has two wives, or a
wife and another woman, in competition with one another. A good instance is that of
Hannah and Peninnah in 1 Samuel 1.

extremely developed version of the pattern, with numerous challenges and counter-challenges (Esler 1994:84-90).

I am proposing, then, that ancient readers (or listeners) would have derived a sense of the work operating as an effective story, carrying them along briskly from its beginning through its middle to its end, not so much from the factors to which Craven has valuably drawn our attention, nor indeed from others which van Henten has argued render Judith 7–13 cohesive (1995:225-232), but from experiencing the exciting succession of challenge and counter-challenge, which flows remorselessly from Nebuchadnezzar's initial attack on Arphaxad (1:5) and his request for help from the western countries (1:7-10) to Israel's final expression of victory and self-exultation (16:1-24). I will now set out the details of this proposal.

Challenge and Response in the Book of Judith

The Initial Stages

The work begins with the (historically impossible)[10] reference to the twelfth year of Nebuchadnezzar's reign over the Assyrians in Nineveh (1:1) before immediately mentioning that Arphaxad was then reigning over the Medes in Ecbatana, a city which he had surrounded with huge stone walls (seventy cubits in height), towers and gates (1:2-4). This description of the huge fortifications of Ecbatana serves to set the scene for the scale of Nebuchadnezzar's daring in initiating war against Arphaxad and the scale of his ultimate triumph, but it is also the first challenge in the work, since fortifications on this scale enter the social space of other kings in the region, such as Nebuchadnezzar, both simply through the virtuosity of their architecture ("No-one can build more magnificently than I!") but more importantly as a military threat ("With these fortifications no-one can defeat me!").

An ancient reader, accordingly, would not be surprised by the very next action described in the text: "Now at this time King Nebuchadnezzar gave battle to the King Arphaxad in the great plain lying in the territory of Ragae" (1:5). This constitutes a likely response by a neighboring king, with the initial focus on the military aspect of the challenge, although the eventual (and necessary) destruction of Arphaxad's capital was presumably a goal of the campaign.

All the peoples from adjacent regions (in the east) came to the aid of Nebuchadnezzar (1:6). Yet when Nebuchadnezzar sent to all the in-

---

[10] The extraordinary, indeed ludic, treatment of history in the work is an important feature which is beyond the scope of this essay but which I hope to discuss elsewhere.

habitants (*pantas tous katoikountas*) of Persia and the western lands, (that is) to those inhabiting (*tous katoikountas*) Cilicia, Damascus, Lebanon and Anti-Lebanon and to all those along the coast, Carmel, Gilead, Upper Galilee and the great plain of Esdraelon, to all those in Samaria and its cities, to those beyond the Jordan as far as Jerusalem, Bethany, Chelous, Kadesh, and even as far as Egypt (1:7-10), the result was very different. In terms of challenge-and-response, his message (presumably a request that they come to his assistance) constituted a positive challenge, to which a positive response would have been to march quickly to his side.

One can sense the gasp of horror which would have been voiced among an ancient audience listening to this story by the actual response of these peoples:

All those who dwelled in all the land derided (*ephaulisan*)[11] the message of Nebuchadnezzar king of the Assyrians and they did not rally to him for the purpose of war, because they were not afraid of him and as far as they were concerned he was a single man. So they sent his ambassadors home empty, with their faces covered in shame (*en atimia prosôpou autôn*; 1:11).

The uniformity of the response is worth noting. The people in this list of those who scorned Nebuchadnezzar, someone with the status of "a single man" (presumably meaning someone without allies) and therefore liable to be destroyed easily (6:3), and shamed his ambassadors including several whom the text will later identity as Israelites inhabiting Judea (1:12; 3:2; 4:1, 13; 8:21; 11:19),[12] from Galilee in the north, through Samaria and as least as far as Jerusalem in the south. In other words, the Judeans engage in prevailing cultural patterns relating to honor and shame just as surely as do the other peoples mentioned. As the story develops, the extent to which the Israelites are deeply embedded in the ambient culture and, at least in some quarters, highly adept at playing its central game of challenge-and-response will emerge as important themes.

In this culture such a negative response to Nebuchadnezzar's positive challenge inevitably leads to the sort of reaction the king exhibits:

---

[11] Note that the point of the verb, that the recipients consciously dishonor the message, is missed in the translation of the Jerusalem Bible ('JB' hereafter) which has 'ignored'. In this essay, translations from the Greek text of Judith or other sections of the Septuagint (such as 1 Samuel 17) are mine unless otherwise stated.

[12] The word *Ioudaios*, 'Judean', does not appear in the book of Judith although it is very common in other literature from the Maccabean period, including 1 and 2 Maccabees.

> Nebuchadnezzar was grievously angry with all this land and swore by his throne and his kingdom to take revenge on all the regions of Cilicia, Damascene and Syria and to destroy with his sword all those who dwelled in Moab, the children of Ammon, all those of Judea and all those in Egypt as far as the regions of the two seas. (1:12)

This is the typical reaction in this culture if a request for help is rejected, since such a response shames him who sought the help. The desire for vengeance to restore one's besmirched honor (which the Judeans and the Israelites will themselves express later) motivates each of the latter stages of challenge-and-response. There are other cases in the Old Testament very similar to Nebuchadnezzar's reaction. Gideon, for example, asks the towns Succoth and Penuel to help him, but they refuse since he has not yet defeated his enemies, and when he is victorious he wreaks a harsh vengeance upon them (Judges 8:4-17). Secondly, when David's messengers are refused provisions from Nabal, he is only prevented from taking vengeance in the form of killing every male in Nabal's household by the timely intervention of Abigail (1 Sam 25:2-35). Thirdly, when the envoys David sends to greet the new king of Ammon are sent home in complete disgrace, the insult leads to war (2 Sam 10:1-7).

In due course, when Nebuchadnezzar and his forces have defeated Arphaxad's army, captured Ecbatana, effectively responded to the original challenge by turning its magnificence (*kosmos*) into a disgrace (*oneidos*), killed Arphaxad himself and then feasted for 120 days (1:13-16), Nebuchadnezzar plans 'to take vengeance on the whole land, just as he had threatened' (2:1). An ancient reader, probably expecting something rather special from Nebuchadnezzar at this point, would not be disappointed with his counter-challenge to those who scorned him. The king informs a council of his staff that he wants everyone who did not answer his appeal to be destroyed (2:2-3). He chooses the leader of his armies, Holofernes, as his agent for this plan, aided by 120,000 infantry and 12,000 cavalry. They are to conquer the region, holding those who surrender to await the arrival of the king and killing all those who resist (2:4-13). Holofernes then begins the campaign, putting the counter-challenge into effect, as directed (2:14-20).

Further Developments
The rest of the book, including the actions of Judith and Israelites right through to chapter 16, is naturally interpreted as consisting of various types of responses to the challenge posed to the western na-

tions by Holofernes' invasion. The dynamic of challenge-and-response provides the unifying structure for the work. After his initial successes (2:21-27), the terror-stricken coastal towns such as Sidon and Tyre, Jamnia, Azotus and Ascelon, send envoys to sue for peace, laying themselves open to his advance (2:28–3:5). They welcome him with garlands and dancing (3:7), yet he demolishes their shrines, destroys all local gods and compels the people to worship Nebuchadnezzar alone and to hail him as god (3:8). This is, in fact, the first time that this dimension of Holofernes' campaign has been mentioned and it considerably augments the nature of the challenge to the peoples of the west, especially, as will soon emerge, to monotheistic Israel.

At this point Holofernes stops for a month to muster supplies, camping on the edge of Esdraelon, near Dothan, a village facing the great ridge of Judea. Thus is Nebuchadnezzar's counter-challenge brought home to "the sons of Israel living in Judea" (*hoi huioi Israēl hoi katoikountes en tē Ioudaia*; 4:1). They tremble for the threat posed to their own recently rebuilt Temple (no doubt because Holofernes has just destroyed the shrines of neighboring peoples), alert the people in various parts of the country, occupy the summits and prepare for war (4:1-5). Joakim the high priest in Jerusalem orders the inhabitants of Bethulia and another village facing Esdraelon to occupy the mountain passes and prevent an enemy advance (4:6-7), which they do (4:8). Thus the counter-challenge of Holofernes on behalf of his master Nebuchadnezzar is met with a courageous response, not a capitulation as with the coastal towns. With prayer and fasting all the children of Israel beseech God to save them and their Temple from profanation and ridicule (chapter 4). An early sign that God will rescue them comes at 4:13: "The Lord heard their voice and looked with favor upon their affliction".

In Chapter 5 Holofernes seeks intelligence concerning the Israelites who alone of all the western peoples are opposing him and receives from Achior, leader of the Ammonites, a brief history of the Israel and a warning that if their God is against them Holofernes should attack, but that if their God is with them, they are best left well alone:

But if there is no lawlessness (*anomia*) among their nation, let my lord leave them alone, lest their lord and their God shield them and we become a laughing-stock (*oneidismos*) before all the earth (5:21)

Within the context of challenge-and-response Achior's words constitute a warning to the Assyrians only to respond to the initial insult to Nebuchadnezzar on the condition that Israel's God is against them. In quite predictable fashion Holofernes' men take these words as a challenge to their honor—why should they be frightened of a puny people like the sons of Israel? After threatening to tear Achior apart, they urge Holofernes into battle so as to remove this slur on their valour: "Therefore, we will go up, and they will become provisions for your whole army, Lord Holofernes" (5:22-24).[13]

In Chapter 6 Holofernes continues rebuking Achior, but goes beyond merely criticizing him for his views on when and when not to fight the race of Israel (*genos Israêl*) to utter what will prove to be *verba mortifera*:

(You say) that their God will protect them. But who is their God if not Nebuchadnezzar? He will send forth his power and wipe them from the face of the earth, and their God will not save them (6:2).

In terms of the model, Holofernes has made the terrible mistake of directly challenging Israel's God. He has insulted him, both by suggesting that he will not protect his people, but also by asserting that he is not really their God at all, for that role is filled by Nebuchadnezzar. Although invading Judea and threatening Israel had also constituted a challenge, now we have Holofernes putting God's honor directly on the line. Although the pattern of challenge-and-response was played between social equals, in the present case Holofernes is really speaking as the agent of Nebuchadnezzar, so that one (purported) god is challenging another God. Ancient Israelite readers of this story would have surely expected that Holofernes would come to a terrible end by reason of such hubris and folly. Part of the dynamic of the story would thereafter have been the expectation of the divine vengeance which would inevitably flow from this effrontery.

There is a close parallel to Holofernes' challenge and its consequences in 2 Chronicles 32. During the course of his campaign against Judah, the Assyrian king Sennacherib sent to King Hezekiah in Jerusalem to persuade him to stop his resistance. Part of the message was this:

Do you not know what I have done, I and my ancestors, to all the peoples of other countries? Have the gods of any single nation in those countries ever been able to save them from me? ... So how could your god save you (2 Chron 32:13-14; JB)?

Yahweh's response to this impudence, or possibly challenge if we interpret the king as the agent of his gods, was firm:

Yahweh sent an angel who massacred all the mighty warriors, commanders and officers in the camp of the king of Assyria. Covered with disgrace he retired to his own country. He went into the temple

---

[13] On the role of Achior in the text, see Roitman 1992.

of his god, and there some of his own children struck him down with
the sword (2 Chron 32:21; JB).

Having predicted complete victory against Israel, Holofernes arranges for Achior to be handed over to the Israelites of Bethulia, to die
with them in due course (6:10-13). The Bethulians take him to their
town, where he tells them what transpired before Holofernes
(6:14-17). Not surprisingly, Achior interprets what Holofernes had to
say as "boasting ("talking big") over the house of Israel" (6:17) and at
this the people (*laos*) fall on their faces in worship and ask God to
"look upon their arrogance (*hyperêphania*) and take pity upon the humiliation (*tapeinôsis*) of our race (*genos*) (6:19)". This expression
unequivocally reveals the honor/shame dimension to the challenge
and the Israelite desire for God to bring about an appropriate response.

On the following day, Holofernes orders his army to begin the
campaign against the Israelites (7:1-5). On the next day they take the
wells at the foot of Bethulia, to force the town to succumb through
thirst, rather than taking it by force—which could result in a loss of
considerable numbers of their own men (7:6-18). After thirty four
more days the Bethulians have run out of water and beseech Uzziah
(previously identified as belonging to the tribe of Simeon; 6:15) and
the chief men of the town to surrender (7:19-29). Uzziah suggests
giving God five more days to save them and sends them home
(7:30-32). Within the framework of the model, their imminent capitulation (after a robust start to their resistance) constitutes a very
feeble response to the Assyrian challenge. The people are in favor of
complete surrender and the abject and utter dishonor that would involve; they would be enslaved but at least would live.

At this juncture Judith enters the narrative. The extent to which
patterns of challenge-and-response figure in the course of chs. 8–16
will appear in the next section of this essay, where they are given a
particular character by virtue of intertextual linkages with other parts
of Israelite tradition. To round off the current section of this essay,
however, it is enough to say that by the end of the work the challenge
thrown down by Holofernes and the Assyrians to Israel and Israel's God
will have been subjected to a decisive, indeed triumphant response.

Judith as a New David?

Intertextual Approaches to the Book of Judith
There have been many attempts to relate the book of Judith to other
parts of the Old Testament. These are based on what Van Henten has

plausibly described as "the intricate palette of intertextual relations" which exists between Judith and (other) biblical writings, a factor he reasonably cites against any tendency to interpret the text only in relation to one other Old Testament tradition (1995:224).

Several intertextual explorations have related Judith to decisive female characters. One comparison often cited is to Jael, the wife of Heber the Kenite who slew the Canaanite Sisera, as described in Judges 4:17-22 and 5:24-27. Thus J. Edgar Bruns argued in 1954 (and 1956) that the book of Judith was composed by one of the Jews of Elephantine on the model of Jael (whom he regarded as historical) when his people were facing a threat from the growing independence of their Egyptian neighbors. "In both cases a heroine slays a national enemy singlehanded, and in both cases she does so by attacking the victim's head" (Bruns 1954:12). On this thesis, which seems too implausibly localized to have won support, Judith becomes "a symbol of Jewish resistance to foreign tyranny based on the truly historical character of Jael, whose memory lived among the Jews of the dispersion in this way" (Bruns 1954:2).

A more plausible use of the Jael story has been offered recently by Sidnie Ann White. Her thesis is not historical but literary in nature: she argues that "the author of Judith had the story of Jael and Deborah in the front of his mind as he wrote his story" (1992:5).[14] She sets out a number of parallels, beginning with two fairly general observations.

First, in each story "a heroine slays an enemy of Israel singlehandedly, by attacking his head" (1992:5). This is similar to Bruns, whom she does not cite. Secondly, as far as the structure of the two stories is concerned, each starts with a political struggle (which has religious implications) between the Israelites and a foreign power, moves to a climax in a private scene between the heroine and the male opponent that ends in his death and culminates in a victory song.

White next sets out a number of similarities at the level of plot and character, some of which are more convincing than others:

a. Both Judith and Jael enter the story at a late point in the plot. Once they have entered (that is, been mentioned) they are identified in relation to husbands who are, although for different reasons, absent. Both are childless. Since Judith is a widow,

---

[14] White notes that in spite of this way of putting it, she does not assume the author is male (1992:14, fn. 2). Van Henten (1995:225, 245-252) squarely raises the intriguing (and, for many reasons, attractive) possibility of a female author for the book of Judith, but also the presence of 'female voices' within the text.

and Jael a member of a non-Israelite clan, both are somewhat anomalous in relation to Israelite society.

b.   Both Judith and Jael deceive the men they kill.

c.   In both cases the scene of the action is a tent.

d.   Both men are encouraged to drink something which lulls them to sleep, milk in Sisera's case and wine for Holofernes.

e.   The heads of both men are the target of the attacks.

f.   Judith pulls down Holofernes' bed-canopy and takes it with her and Jael covers Sisera with something like a rug.

Her other points are not so noteworthy as these.[15] Moreover, a number of factors not taken into account by White weigh against her thesis. First of all, the scale of the action is very different. Israel is threatened by Holofernes and his host, but not by Sisera, whose army has already been annihilated to the last man by Barak (4:12-16) before Jael kills him. While the issue of the campaign actually turns on what Judith does, Jael is engaged in little more than a handy mopping-up

---

[15] (a) Although, as she notes, both Judith and Deborah (not Jael) regard themselves as knowing God's will and give men orders accordingly, this is inherent in the situation of a woman who acts decisively.

(b) While there are two references to the hand of Jael (Judges 4:21 and 5:26) and Judith says the Lord will deliver Israel by her hand (8.33) and deliverance 'by a woman's hand' (9:10; 13:15; 16:6) is an important motif, the hand is such a common theme in Israelite literature (see Skehan 1963) that this feature does not create an obvious link between the two stories.

(c) Following Mieke Bal, she suggests that just as there is a sexual theme in the encounter of Judith and Holofernes, is it also possible to imply one between Jael and Sisera. But this is rather far-fetched.

(d) To claim that Achior is a foil for Judith like Barak is for Deborah produces a rather strained comparison.

(e) Just as there is a victory hymn in the book of Judith (chapter 16), a victory hymn features in Judges 5. Yet even White notes that Judith's hymn is also indebted to Miriam's in Exodus 15, and this case has been powerfully argued by Skehan (1963), whom she cites.

(f) Judith displays the head of Holofernes after she has killed him, just as Jael shows the body of Sisera to Barak. 'These events confirm Yahweh's use of a weak, marginalized member of society in order to save it' (1992:10). This is a standard method of dishonoring an enemy in ancient Israel (it happened to Saul—1 Samuel 31:9) and while Judith is a widow she is also a person of property, honor and influence.

(g) Although White proposes that both Jael and Judith bring peace to the land for a generation, Barak had already slain Sisera's army to the last man (Judges 4:12-16) before Jael killed the fleeing Sisera in what was really just a mopping-up operation.

(h) Her suggestions that both texts seem to share a Deuteronomist theology or that Jabin stands behind Sisera, just as Nebuchadnezzar stands behind Holofernes, are too generalized to be convincing. Moreover, there are unmistakable Isaianic elements in the book of Judith.

operation. Thus, Judith is a heroine who saves Israel, Jael is not. Secondly, Judith's intervention is planned by her in advance and authorized by the local representatives of Israel, whereas Jael's action is a piece of *post eventum* opportunism. Thirdly, Judith's conquest occurs in a situation where her victim had been seeking to get the better of her; it was a contest, a further pattern of challenge-and-response, a version of single combat in fact, which she won. There was no contest between Jael and Sisera; she simply offered a fugitive hospitality and then slew him.

We are left then in the position that although it is possible to agree—on the basis of the more persuasive points of similarity proposed in White's careful comparison—that there might be allusions to the story of Jael and Sisera and that ancient readers or listeners might have derived a sense of some intertextual affinity to Jael in Judith's actions (thus supporting van Henten's insistence on the intertextual richness of the book of Judith), there are good reasons for proposing that significant disparities between the two narratives prevent us regarding Jael as a central model for Judith. I will argue in the next section of this essay that there is a far more persuasive comparison available, but before doing so I will note two other commentators who have sought to compare Judith with male figures in Israelite tradition.

Firstly, Toni Craven has suggested a resemblance to 1 Kings 18, which records the contest between Elijah and the prophets of Baal on Mount Carmel, since "the book of Judith tells a story in which the enemy of Israel takes the lead in the contest" (1983:47). More particularly, she notes, one character stands against the many, Elijah stands against 450 prophets of Baal and the mute community of Israel; Judith stands against the hoard of Nebuchadnezzar, and the cowardice of her community (saying in her prayer that she knows Yahweh's power does not depend on numbers (9:11); Both stories contain"'delightful mocking scenes (1 Kgs 18:27-29 and Jdt 10:11-13.10a); and in both stories the objective is to have all know that Yahweh is God (1983:47-48). On the other hand, the facts that 1 Kings 18 does not involve a military confrontation between Israel and a powerful and threatening external enemy and that the outcome of the contest does not result in any immediate improvement in the position of Israel (which retains Ahab as its king) and Elijah (who must soon flee to the wilderness) both count against seeing this narrative as particularly close to that concerning Judith.

Secondly, van Henten has proposed that the narratives concerning Moses in Exodus 17, Numbers 20 and Deut 33:8-11 have served as a model for important features of Judith 7–13 (1995). Van Henten points to features in the book of Judith such as thirst (of which the Bethulians complain to their leaders) and drinking, a forty day framework for the predicament and salvation of Bethulia and several other features. Van Henten's reading:

focuses on the testing of the leader in a situation of an impending catastrophe for the people; and suggests a comparison with the role of Judith, grandfather of Levi according to Jdt 8:1, with that of Moses, another descendant of Levi (Exod 21) (1995:240).

While it is reasonable to discover such allusions in a work as rich as the book of Judith, it is submitted that certain fundamental differences between the position of Moses and that of Judith prevent us seeing in any connection between the traditions the principal intertextual resonance. The main differences are the fact that in the book of Judith Israel faces a powerful, external military threat, that the people remain faithful to Yahweh (even if tempted to surrender) and that the Israelite leader saves the people by killing the leader of their foes.

Nevertheless, while there are difficulties with according a privileged place to either of their proposals, both Craven and van Henten have taken an important step in putting forward male models for Judith. As such, they have established a precedent for the proposal which I will now develop, that it is actually in the story of David and Goliath in 1 Samuel 17 that we have the most extensive material available for intertextual comparison with the book of Judith in the Israelite tradition.

The Connection with David and Goliath in 1 Samuel 17 (LXX)

As far as I know, this is the first extended attempt in the field of biblical scholarship to relate Judith to David, although on rare occasions commentators have pointed out some aspects of comparison.[16] Yet the connection between the two narratives has long been made by artists and civic leaders in the West. Thus, Judith is portrayed on Ghiberti's Gates of the Garden of Eden in Florence (constructed in 1450) with a sword in her right hand next to a panel describing David's war against the Philistines (Stone 1992:81). After the expulsion of the Medicis from Florence, Donatello's statue of Judith and another he had done of David with Goliath's head at his feet were moved to the main square of the city as symbols of Florentine independence and freedom (Stone

---

[16] Thus van Henten cites 1 Sam 17:16 as a case where biblical salvation comes after forty days, but without developing the comparison between David and Judith (1995:230).

1992:81-82). The killings of Goliath and Holofernes are depicted together on a fresco on the ceiling of the San Ignazio church in Rome (van Henten 1995:230).[17]

In an investigation into the David and Goliath story presented elsewhere (Esler 1998c) I have isolated twenty two distinct elements in the Septuagintal version of the encounter between David and Goliath in 1 Samuel 17, which I consider to represent the oldest form of this narrative.[18] While there may be other ways to subdivide this narrative, the use of these elements, here slightly modified to twenty separate aspects—in the order in which they appear in the LXX of 1 Samuel 17—will facilitate a detailed comparison between the David and Goliath story and Judith.

1. The Setting: Between Two Armies
The Septuagint describes the setting as follows:

> [1]The Philistines (*allophyloi*) gathered their armies to battle, and gathered together at Socchoth of Judea, and encamped between Socchoth and Azeca in Ephermen. [2]And Saul and the warriors of Israel gathered together, and they encamped in the valley, and arranged themselves for battle against the foreigners. [3]The Philistines stood on the mountain (*oros*) on one side, and Israel stood on the mountain (*oros*) on the other side, and the valley (*aulôn*) was between them.

Bethulia was located in the mountains (*ta orea*) and the Assyrians occupied the slopes (*anabaseis*) leading up to the town (7:7, 10-11), then took control of the valley (*aulôn*) and its wells on which the Bethulians relied for water (7:17) and camped in the plain (*pedion*) (7:18). Thus, we have recognizably similar topography, although the rough parity of forces and position which characterized Philistines and Israelites is not replicated in the book of Judith, where the Bethulians face a huge opposing force which has compelled them to rely on the safety of their town walls and the mountainous terrain. The situation is also different in that Judith will go right into the enemy camp for her confrontation with Holofernes, and not like David to a space between the two armies.

2. A Huge Enemy Comes Forward
Goliath was physically huge and a champion, although he was not the leader of the Philistines:

---

[17] It is interesting that this valuable observation did not prompt van Henten to develop the comparison himself (see previous footnote).

[18] I am unable to set out the reasons for this view within the ambit of the present paper, but see the reasons offered by Tov (1985 and 1986).

> [4]And there came forth a mighty warrior out of the Philistine army, Goliath by name, of Geth; his height was four cubits and a span.

Yet we learn nothing of Holofernes' physique and he is the leader of the enemy. Nevertheless, both accounts have in common that the Israelite engages with the most prominent member of the enemy host. Each contest represents a form of single combat, *monomachia*, which was a phenomenon known in the eastern (de Vaux 1972) and western (Oakley 1985) Mediterranean.

3. His Armor and Weapons

Goliath had fearsome equipment:

> [5]And he had a helmet upon his head, and he wore a breastplate of chain armor; and the weight of his breastplate was five thousand shekels of brass and iron. [6]Greaves of brass were upon his legs, and a brazen shield was between his shoulders. [7]The staff of his spear was like a weavers' beam, and the spear's head weighed six hundred shekels of iron; and his armor-bearer went before him.

There is no description of Holofernes to match these details of Goliath's armor and weapons. On the other hand, there are several references—before and after the actions of Judith—to the huge size and power of the Assyrian army which, in effect, she defeats (2:5-17; 7:2, 18; 9:7; 16:3), acting with the agreement of the leaders of only one town in Israel. In both cases victory is achieved against highly unfavorable odds. Bagoas may be regarded as fulfilling a role analogous to Goliath's armor-bearer.

4. Challenge

The challenge of Goliath is of the negative type, that is, an insult (in contrast to a positive challenge which takes the form of a gift, praise or a request for help):

> [8]He stood and cried to the army of Israel, and said to them, Why are you coming out to arrange yourselves for battle against us? Am not I a Philistine, and are you not Hebrews of Saul? Choose a warrior for yourselves, and let him come down to me.

The (negative) challenge posed by Holofernes comes most immediately from his having brought up his forces against the Bethulians with hostile intent and cut off their access to water. In addition, however, there is the challenge offered to Israel's God at 6:2-3, as previously discussed.

5. Proposed Result of the Combat for the Rival peoples

There is nothing in the book of Judith to match the direct arrangement which Goliath offers Saul's Israelites:

> [9]And if he will be able to fight against me and to defeat me, then will
> we be your servants: but if I should prevail and defeat him, you will be
> our servants and serve us.

Nevertheless, Judith certainly regards what she is about to do
(which will only involve Holofernes) as leading to complete victory
for her people, as she tells Uzziah:

> Listen to me. I intend to do something, the memory of which will be
> handed down to the children of our race from age to age ... Before the
> time fixed by you for surrendering the town to our enemies, the Lord
> will make use of me to rescue Israel (8:33).

6. Repetition of Challenge

There is nothing in the book of Judith directly parallel to Goliath's
repeated challenge, the word for which (ôneidisa) underlines that he has
dishonored Israel:

> [10]And the Philistine said, Behold, today, this very day, I have challenged
> (ôneidisa) the army of Israel: give me a warrior, and we will both fight in
> single combat.

On the other hand, as just noted, Holofernes does make two challenges, one to God and one to Israel in the form of his assault on
Bethulia.

7. Shameful Response by Challenged Army

The response of the Israelites to Holofernes is very similar to the response of Israel to Goliath:

> [11]Saul and all Israel heard these words of the Philistine, and they were
> dismayed, and greatly terrified.

The Bethulians are described as faint-hearted or dispirited (*to pneuma
autôn ôligopsychêsen*) as soon as the Assyrians have surrounded them
(7:19). After a siege of thirty four days which leaves them without
water they are in favor of complete capitulation even though that will
mean enslavement; at least that way they and their wives and children
will live (7:26-29). Uzziah persuades them to wait five more days before taking this step. Within the local cultural norms, their imminent
surrender entails gross dishonor for the Bethulians—as stated in the
text, the people in the city were in a state of great humiliation (*pollê*

tapeinôsis; 7:32). While Saul's Israelites did not go so far as to contemplate capitulation, just like the Bethulians they had no response to the enemy other than the dishonorable one of inaction.

8. The Hero Steps Forward

It is at this critical juncture that the one man of honor among Saul's Israelites steps forward:

> [32]And David said to Saul, 'Let not the heart of my lord sink within him: your servant will go and he will fight with this Philistine. [33]And Saul said to David, 'You will not be able to go against this Philistine to fight with him, since you are a mere youth, and he is a warrior adept at war from his youth.

But whereas readers of 1 Sam 17:32 are already familiar with David from his anointing as king of Israel by the prophet Samuel in 1 Samuel 16, the author of the book of Judith needs to introduce her before describing the very similar way in which she offered herself to assist Israel out of its dilemma. Accordingly, we learn details of her lineage, always of major interest in the group-oriented culture of Israel (8:1), her husband and the circumstances of his death (8:2-3), the seriousness of her widowhood (8:4-6), her beauty and resources (8:7) and, last but certainly not least, her good repute and devotion to God (8:8). Having heard that the townsfolk have become dispirited (*ôligopsychêsan*) with lack of water and wish to surrender to the Assyrians, Judith steps forward just like David. She summons two of the elders and, in a rather long speech (which contrasts with David's brief words to Saul), Judith rebukes them for having, in effect, put God to the test, when the proper attitude is simply to pray to him for help (8:9-20). She is extremely sensitive to the shame which will result from their surrender, and the inevitable defeat of the rest of Israel thereafter (8:21-22):

> ... our new masters will look down on us as an outrage (*proskomma*) and a disgrace (*oneidos*); for our surrender will not reinstate us in their favor; no, the Lord our God will establish it as something shameful (*atimia*) (8:22-23).

She urges them to be steadfast and pray to God (8:24-27). Since up to this point, Judith has not actually offered to do anything herself in relation to the Assyrians, it is not surprising that Uzziah should assume something of Saul's mantle by suggesting that although she is a wise and a devout woman the best thing would be for her to go off and pray for rain (8:28-31)! Perhaps provoked by this courteous dismissal,

Judith now at last steps forth, like David, to offer herself as the agent of salvation for Israel:

> Listen to me. I intend to do something, the memory of which will be handed down to the children of our race from age to age ... Before the time fixed by you surrendering the town to our enemies, the Lord will make use of me to rescue Israel. You must not ask what I intend to do; I will not tell you until I have done it (8:34; JB).

9. The Hero Makes an Honor Claim to Establish his Credentials to Fight

David needs to convince Saul he is adequate for the task and does so like this:

> [34]And David said to Saul, 'Your servant was tending the flock for his father; and when a lion came and a she-bear, and took a sheep out of the flock, [35]then I went out after him and defeated him, and snatched it out of his mouth: and as he rose up against me, I caught hold of his throat, and defeated him, and slew him. [36]Your servant smote both the lion and the bear, and the uncircumcised Philistine shall be as one of them; shall I not go and defeat him, and remove this day this insult from Israel? For who is this uncircumcised one, who has challenged the army of the living God? [37]The Lord who delivered me out of the paw of the lion and out of the paw of the bear, he will deliver me out of the hand of this uncircumcised Philistine.'

Judith makes no honor claims of this sort, but the issue of her credentials does arise, since Uzziah has already conceded she is wise and devout before she announces she herself will take the initiative (8:28-31). Moreover, just as in 1 Sam 17:36 David reveals how greatly he resents the shame Goliath has inflicted upon Israel, so too does Judith exhibit a strong sense of affront.

10. The Leader Gives Permission, invoking Divine Help

Saul's next statement to David, "Go, and the Lord will be with you" (1 Sam 17:37), is closely matched by Uzziah's words to Judith:

> Go in peace. May the Lord show you a way to take revenge (*ekdikêsis*) on our enemies (8:35).

Both men have the wit (or inspiration) to realize that God is at work in the improbable warrior before them. At the same time, Uzziah's indication that revenge is necessary at a time when not a single Israelite has died at Assyrian hands indicates the extent to which in this

culture the mere suffering of a challenge incites the need for vengeance to redeem the honor of those who have been challenged.

11. Arming of the Hero

In 1 Samuel the traditional motif of arming of the hero takes an almost
comic term when David at first unsuccessfully tries on Saul's armor
before settling on his usual (and humble) shepherd's weaponry:

> [38]Saul clothed David with a military coat, and put his brazen helmet on
> his head. [39]And he equipped David with his sword over his coat: and
> David was exhausted having walked about with them once or twice and
> said to Saul, 'I will not be able to go forward with these, for I am not
> experienced with them.' So they took them off him. [40]And he took his
> staff in his hand, and he chose for himself five smooth stones out of the
> wadi, and put them in the shepherd's bag which he used for his supplies,
> and his sling was in his hand ...

Judith also prepares herself to "fight". She begins by repeating the
rituals of mourning, throwing herself to the ground, scattering ashes
on her head and uncovering the sackcloth she was wearing (9:1), before saying a long prayer to God at the same time as the afternoon
sacrifice was being offered in the Temple in Jerusalem (9:2-14). Although I will return to the terms of her prayer below, it is useful to
note that it climaxes in her imprecation that God would give her deceptive speech (*logos mou kai apatê*) to wound and kill those who have
plotted evil against his covenant in order to show that Israel has him as
its sole protector (9:13-14). At the conclusion of this prayer, Judith
"arms" herself for the mission. At this point ancient readers would
have encountered a comic dimension to the story, analogous to the
comedy surrounding David's arming to meet Goliath, in the fact that
Judith prepares for her contest by making as beautiful as possible. She
washes, anoints herself, arranges her hair, puts on a turban and her best
dress, and then dons sandals, necklaces, bracelets, rings, earrings and all
her jewelry. "She made herself very beautiful to deceive (*eis apatêsin*)
the eyes of the men who saw her" (10:4).

12. The Hero Approaches Challenger

Just as "David advanced against the Philistine warrior" (1 Sam 17:40),
so too Judith, accompanied by her maid, went down the mountain
and across the valley (10:10), seeking Holofernes (10:12-13) and
eventually being brought to him in his tent (10:20-23).

13. Verbal Exchange between Challenger and Israelite

Prior to the physical contest between David and Goliath, they engage in an exchange of insults. Goliath begins this rather ritualized interaction (called "flyting" in medieval European contexts) which forms part of their total pattern of challenge-and-response by disdaining David as an unworthy opponent:

> [42]Goliath saw David, and despised him; for he was a lad, and ruddy, with attractive features. [43]And the Philistine said to David, "Am I as a dog, that you come against me with a staff and stones?"

David responds briefly, "No, but worse than a dog." This elicits a curse and a threat from Goliath:

> And the Philistine cursed David by his gods. [44]The Philistine said to David, "Come to me, and I will give your flesh to the birds of heaven, and to the beasts of the earth."

Which elicits this reply:

> [45]And David said to the Philistine, "You come against me with sword, and with spear, and with shield; but I come against you in the name of the Lord God of hosts of the army of Israel, which you have challenged this day. [46]And today the Lord will deliver you into my hand; and I will kill you, I will cut off your head and I will give your limbs and the limbs of the army of the Philistines this day to the birds of heaven, and to the wild beasts of the earth. Then all the earth shall know that there is a God in Israel. [47]And all this assembly shall know that the Lord delivers not by sword or spear, for war is the Lord's, and the Lord will deliver you into our hands."

David's is a much more involved insult, so that he might be regarded as having bested Goliath in this area before defeating him in physical combat. David matches the invocation by Goliath of his gods by drawing the Israelite God into his response. He makes clear, for example, that Goliath has challenged God in challenging the Israelite army.

The extensive material in the book of Judith detailing the conversations between Judith and Holofernes that precede his death provides a reasonably close parallel to this trading of insults. Since, Judith needs to win her way into his confidence, she does not insult him so much as deceive him with flattery (11:8) and with lies about how the Israelites are sinning and will incur God's wrath at Holofernes' hand (11:9-19). At the same time, he greatly flatters her (11:20-23) and wants to seduce her, since not to do so would sound to the Assyrians' dishonor in a culture where the men of one group are honor-bound to have sex with the women of other groups:

He said to Bagoas, the eunuch in charge of his personal affairs, "Go and persuade that Hebrew woman you are looking after to come and join us and eat and drink in our company. We shall be disgraced (*aischron tô prosôpô hêmôn*) if we let a woman like this go without knowing her better. If we do not seduce her (*epispasômetha*), everyone will laugh at us!" (12:11-12; JB)

Each is trying to get the better of the other by the arts of discourse. Indeed Judith's use of the word "deceive" (*êpatêsen*; 13:16) in relation to her having gulled Holofernes is also used to describe how he had hoped to get the better of her (*apatêsai*; 12:16). In other words, we have here an oral contest which precedes the physical one which, *mutatis mutandis*, is similar to that of David and Goliath.

14. Combat begun by Challenger

The fact that it is Goliath who initiates the combat—"And the Philistine arose and went to meet David" (1 Sam 17:48)—finds an echo in Holofernes' invitation to Judith (via Bagoas) to come and occupy the seat of honor opposite him in a drinking-party (12:13). Judith readily agrees, adding that doing so will give her joy to her dying day (12:14).

15. Hero kills Challenger By Superior Technique

David is successful against Goliath by means of his superior military technique, even though the fact he has God with him is suggested by the improbable feature that his stone actually penetrates the Philistine's helmet into his forehead:

> [49]And David stretched out his hand to his bag, and took out a stone, and slung it, and struck the Philistine on his forehead, and the stone penetrated through the helmet into his forehead, and he fell on his face upon the ground. [51]And David ran, and stood over him, and took his sword, and killed him ...

Judith also manifests a superior technique, first by making herself beautiful ("dressing to kill", as it were) in a way which incites in Holofernes a powerful desire to sleep with her and then to drink more than he had ever drunk before, so that he passes out on his bed, leaving no-one in the tent except Judith (12:15–13:3). Although the scene is not played out before the rival armies, there is a congruence of situations in that what will prove the fatal space is shared only by the contestants in the *monomachia*.[19] Thus, Judith, like David with his sling, manages to render her enemy prostrate and defenseless. And just like David, Judith uses Holofernes' own sword to cut off his head.

16. Treatment of Challenger's Body

The fact that Judith employs decapitation, as David had done (1 Sam 17:51), is a noteworthy detail common to the two narratives. Both these Israelites could have applied the sword to their opponent's body in some other fashion to deliver the quietus. That they both chose to decapitate their foe testifies to the status of the head as the most honorable part of the body in this culture and the importance of grossly mistreating it in this way to maximize the disgrace inflicted on the enemy. This consideration explains why the Philistines cut Saul's head from his corpse (1 Sam 31:9) and why John the Baptist would later suffer death by beheading (Mark 6:17-29).

17. Response by Enemy Army

Since the combat between David and Goliath is played out before the two armies, the reaction of the Philistines is immediate:

> The Philistines saw that their champion was dead, and they fled (1 Sam 17:51).

The secrecy with which Judith effects her defeat of Holofernes results in the narrative developing in a different direction. Judith and her maid must first return to Bethulia (13:10-15), where she displays Holofernes' head triumphantly to the townsfolk and emphasizes that she dishonored Holofernes, not he her:

> My face deceived (*êpatêsen*; 13:16) him to his own destruction; he committed no sin with me to pollute and disgrace (*eis miasma kai aischynên*) me (13:16).

In accordance with Judith's instructions, the next morning the Bethulians hang Holofernes' head on the town walls and charge down upon the Assyrians (14:1-4; 11). At this point Bagoas discovers what has happened to his master, accurately summing up the situation as follows:

> One Hebrew woman has brought dishonor (*aischynên*) on the house of king Nebuchadnezzar. Look, Holofernes is lying dead on the ground and his head is not on him (14:18).

---

[19] Goliath's shield bearer is mentioned at 1 Sam 17:7. But he is not mentioned in the confrontation, just as Judith's maid stays outside the tent (13:3).

The result is that consternation strikes the Assyrian army (14:19). Just like the Philistines, they flee (15:1-3).

18. Response by the Hero's Army
Saul's army pursued the Philistines:

> [52]And the warriors of Israel and Judah arose, and shouted and pursued them as far as the entrance to Geth, and as far as the gate of Ascalon: and the slain among the Philistines fell in the way of the gates, both to Geth, and to Accaron (1 Sam 17:52).

So too did the Israelites set off after the Assyrians. "As soon as the Israelites heard the news, they fell on them as one man and massacred them all the way to Choba" (15:5).

In due course, moreover, "the warriors of Israel returned from pursuing the Philistines and they destroyed their camp" (1 Sam 17:53). The same fate befell the Assyrians' camp in the book of Judith:

> The rest, who had stayed in Bethulia, fell upon the Assyrian camp and looted it to their great profit. The Israelites returning from the slaughter seized what was left (15:6-7)

19. Further Dishonor of the Challenger
In 1 Samuel 17 David compounds the dishonor he metes out to Goliath in this way:

> [54]And David took the head of the Philistine, and brought it to Jerusalem; but he put his armor in his tent (1 Sam 17:54).

In the book of Judith Holofernes' head has already been subjected to public ridicule by being hung on the battlements of Bethulia; thus, the element is common to both narratives but in a slightly different order. Nevertheless, one other point of similarity to David's bringing Goliath's head to Jerusalem is that Judith dedicates her share of the booty as an offering in the Temple (16:19).

20. Praise for Hero
The next section in the Septuagintal version of the story[20] is the description of women coming out with dancing and musical instruments to greet David (1 Sam 18:6), and saying:

> Saul has struck his thousands, but David his tens of thousands (1 Sam 18:7).

---

[20] The Massoretic texts contains the additional details of Saul's enquiry about David's identity (1 Sam 17:55-58), the friendship between David and Jonathan (1 Sam 18:1-4) and the fact that Saul gave David command of the army (1 Sam 18:5).

This public response to David's contest with Goliath and other Philistines (not hitherto mentioned in the text) makes Saul very angry (1 Sam 18:6-7).

In the book of Judith there are two expressions of praise for the heroine. The first enunciated by Uzziah when she has returned with Holofernes' head (13:18-20) and the second, after the total defeat of the Assyrians, by the high priest Joakim and the council of the elders of Israel (15:9-10). Both statements refer to Judith's honor and invoke God's blessings on her. Uzziah prays that she may be blessed beyond all women on earth (13:19) and Joakim and the council assert that she is the great foundation for the honor (*mega kauchêma*) of their race (15:9).

Yet there is one particular feature of the praise which Judith receives which is very reminiscent of David. For just as the women came out from all the towns on Israel to meet David and Saul, singing and dancing to the sound of the tambourine and lyre and singing the song just cited, so too in the book of Judith, "all the women of Israel, hurrying to see her, formed choirs of dancers in her honor" (15:12). She then led the women as they danced.[21]

The Point of the Comparison with David

I have elsewhere argued that lying at the heart of the story of David and Goliath is the profound social upheaval involved in David's emerging as victor (Esler 1998c) and I will now mention a few of the factors which would have made his victory surprising to an ancient Mediterranean audience. First, David does not enjoy the ascribed honor which comes from belonging to an aristocratic family. In fact, he tells Saul's servants that he is a man who is humble (*tapeinos*) and not honorable (*endoxos*; 1 Sam 18:23). Secondly, in a culture which honors age, David is a mere youth (*paidarion*—1 Sam 17:33), inexperienced in war. Thirdly, he is the youngest member of his family in a culture which tended to give precedence to elder sons over younger (see Greenspahn 1994:27-29), so that it was a sign of social disorder for youths to be pre-eminent (Isa 3:4). On this basis, if any of the sons of Jesse was to volunteer to fight Goliath it should have been the oldest

[21] It should be noted that in chapter 16 there is a long hymn of praise to God, sung by Judith with all Israel around her, which goes beyond anything in 1 Samuel 17-18 at this point and which has echoes of the song of triumph in Exodus 15 (Skehan 1963). This is a sign of the intertextual richness of this work, which has been mentioned already.

one. Fourthly, David was a shepherd, a difficult and despised occupation (Jeremias 1968), associated with various forms of dishonor (such as thievery), and naturally relegated to the male in the family of lowest status. On the other hand, David does enjoy the ascribed honor of being Saul's lyre-player and armor-bearer and also has something of a reputation for being intelligent, a fighter, prudent in speech, handsome and of having the Lord with him (1 Sam 16:18), although the extent of his fighting abilities is not specified and the real significance of the last feature was not appreciated until he had defeated Goliath.

Thus we have the youngest brother, a lowly shepherd in fact, from a non-elite family, yet secretly anointed by God to be his king (1 Sam 16:1-13) and destined to become a famous warrior. It is this juxtaposition of David's very different status with respect to the divine and human levels which would have struck ancient Israelites as perhaps the most arresting aspect of the narrative and of the facts of Israel's past which they would have thought it represented. In choosing someone like David as his anointed, a person of lowly status and little honor, God had overturned central cultural norms in Israel. Even Samuel himself had to learn this lesson, since when he went out to anoint one of the sons of Jesse as king he naturally assumed it would be the eldest, Eliab, but soon discovered that God judges not by appearance, but looks into the heart (1 Sam 16:6-13).

The portrayal of Judith is readily explicable in the light of such a presentation of David. For Judith, too, is an utterly improbable savior of Israel, not because of the features just mentioned in relation to David, but simply because in a society which assigned most public roles to men, especially those of waging warfare, she is a woman. For although she is a woman of wealth and respected in the community in way David was not (even if being an attractive widow outside male control rendered her somewhat anomalous),[22] it is her status as woman and the active role she takes in the male world of war, even to the extent of cutting off Holofernes' head, that renders her achievements as surprising as those of David. Her victory is noteworthy for the same reason as David's, since it is only the nature of their initial apparent inability to succeed which differs. Her story is really David's played in a different key.

Fully to assess the significance of the similarity between these two Israelites requires a consideration of the theology operative in the two texts and this will be taken up in the last section of this essay. Prior to doing so, however, we must consider one last aspect of the text in its

[22] See Malina 1993a: 50.

cultural context, namely, the role of deceit in Judith's victory, since this feature is important in reading the story and in understanding the nature of its theological significance.

The Function and Value of Judith's Deceit

The Issue

It is by deception that Judith contrives the situation that she is left alone with a dead drunk Holofernes and is thereby able to remove his head. This deception, as we will see in a moment, covers two forms: first, Judith's outright lies and cleverly ambiguous statements and, secondly, the allure of her physical appearance. Both features contribute to her success and the text openly celebrates them.

Our overall aim of seeking to understand the dynamics of the story within its original cultural framework requires that we pay some attention to the function and value of Judith's deceit as it emerges in the text. This is especially important given that many commentators in modern times have expressed unfavorable views of Judith in precisely this area. H. M. Hughes is a good example from earlier in this century:

> The writer is at pains to make clear that Judith violated none of the ceremonial laws of diet ... This scrupulous regard for ceremonial purity stands in striking contrast with the deliberate pursuit of lying and deceit (12:1-4). The end is held to justify the means. Judith even prays that her deceit may be used as a weapon of divine chastisement of the enemies of Israel (9:10, 13). In the very act of her deceit she protests the truth of her utterances (9:5). The moral standard is low ... (Hughes 1909:85-86).[23]

The point is a critical one and brings out very sharply the issue of the cultural difference between our world and the ancient Mediterranean, the importance of which, as I mentioned at the start of this essay, Bruce Malina has been tirelessly emphasising since the early 1980s. I will begin by developing this aspect of Malina's model and then explore the textual data in the light of it.

The Model in Brief

Our starting point is that aspect of Malina's model which outlines how in a group-oriented and honor-obsessed culture like that of the ancient

---

[23] Hughes continues this passage by saying 'and an unfavourable light is cast by the book upon the moral (as distinct from ceremonial) standard of Pharisaism' (1909: 86). The idea that Judith represents a Pharisaic position is a fairly common one. Like some others (including Raven 1983: 120-121), I consider this suggestion erroneous, but the focus of the present essay renders a detailed consideration of the issue inappropriate.

Mediterranean "moral commitment in telling the truth unambiguously ... derives from the social commitment or loyalty to persons to whom such commitment is due." In this context "there is no such thing as universal social commitment ... Lying and deception are or can be honorable and legitimate. To lie in order to deceive an outsider, one who has no right to the truth, is honorable." For "to deceive by making something ambiguous or to lie to an outgroup person is to deprive the other of respect, to refuse to show honor, to humiliate another" (Malina 1993:43).

There is a reasonably large body of anthropological literature discussing the modern Mediterranean region which provide support for this specific aspect of the model, including du Boulay (1976) and Gilsenan (1976). Further support can be found in Bailey (1991) and in the literature on cross-cultural approaches to secrecy (Tefft 1980), secrecy in religions (Bolle 1987) and deception in biblical and post-biblical Judaic tradition itself (Freund 1991). John Pilch has brought much of this work together in two pioneering articles (1992; 1994). I will develop certain aspects of the model in the discussion of the text, to which I now proceed.

It is worth noting here that a model is not a description of empirical reality but a simplification, at a particular level of abstraction, used for heuristic purposes. Thus, for Malina to include the manner in which deception functions in a strongly group-oriented culture like that of the ancient Mediterranean does not mean that different attitudes were not possible, especially in philosophical circles which were less tied to loyalty to *polis* or *ethnos*. Thus it is worthwhile noting that Freund has argued that Philo considerably watered down the numerous lies in Genesis, although Josephus did not go nearly so far in this direction (1991). Nevertheless, the book of Judith probably predates the first century CE and the extent to which it provides data consonant with this aspect of Malina's model amply justifies the use of the model to interpret it.

Deceit in the Book of Judith

The Story of Dinah (Genesis 34)
The theme of deceit enters the text in way which is both unexpected and provocative. Once the elders of Bethulia have departed having heard Judith's announcement that the Lord will use her to rescue Israel and avenge themselves on their enemies, she begins her prayer like this:

Lord, God of my father Simeon, you armed him with a sword to take vengeance (*edikêsis*) on the foreigners who loosed a virgin's womb (*mêtra*)[24] to defile her (*eis miasma*), stripped her thigh to her disgrace (*aischynê*), polluted her womb (*mêtra*) to her dishonor (*oneidos*), since you said, "This shall not be", yet they did it. For this you delivered their leaders to slaughter, and in relation to their bed, which was ashamed by their deceit (*apatê*), they were deceived (*apatêtheisan*) into the shedding of blood (9:2-3).

She then recounts how they struck down the slaves with the masters, carried off their wives and children, and shared out their spoils "among the sons you loved, who had been so zealous for you, had loathed the stain put on their blood and called on you for help" (9:4).

All of this refers to the events of Genesis 34. There we learn how Shechem, the son of Hamor the Hivite took Dinah, the daughter of Jacob and Leah, lay with her, and, the Septuagint adds, humiliated (*etapeinôsen*) her. But Shechem, whom we discover later had actually carried Dinah off to his house (34:26), loved her and asked his father to arrange a marriage. Jacob heard that his daughter had been defiled (*emianen*) when his sons were away and kept silent until they returned. They were deeply disturbed when they found out. Faced with a marriage proposal from Shechem, Jacob's sons agreed on the basis that all the Hivites first be circumcised. But this was an arrangement made falsely (*meta dolou*), since their sister had been defiled. The Hivites were circumcised and two days later, while they were still in pain, two of Jacob's sons, Simeon and Levi, full brothers of Dinah, armed themselves with swords, broke into the town and killed every male. They retrieved their sister, and carried off all the Hivites' women, children and possessions. When Jacob remonstrated with them for the danger into which they had brought him by these actions, they replied "Is our sister to be treated as a prostitute?"

Judith celebrates this bloody incident at the start of her prayer, which begins with an invocation to God revealing that Simeon was actually her ancestor, whose trickery and homicide she completely endorses. Judith's version is fairly close to the Genesis narrative, except for the mention of "their deceit", that is, the deceit of the Hivites. This is noteworthy, since there is no deceit in the source, merely Shechem's forcible ravishing and abduction of Dinah. The author of the book of Judith has interpreted these actions as "deceit" (*apatê*; 9.3) to provide a balance, or rather a contrast, to the successful deception of Simeon and Levi. The idea is sharpened by the role of (Shechem's)

---

[24] This word is frequently translated as 'girdle'.

bed both in experiencing shame at the violation of Dinah and also in playing a role in the bloody act of revenge, presumably because Shechem was in bed recovering from circumcision when Simeon and Levi killed him.

That Judith should begin her prayer with this incident immediately brings us into the group-oriented ethics described by Malina. What matters is not adherence to some absolute standards of truth such as those familiar to modern readers, but rather the tactical use of lying and deception to advance the interests of a particular group—in the case of Simeon and Levi, those of their immediate family, and in Judith's case, the interests of Israel vis-à-vis those of the Assyrians.

This means that there is, in effect, an institutionalized form of double standard in this context presupposed in the text. It is perfectly acceptable to rail against the lies and deceit of other people, even while you do exactly the same thing yourself. The point is to be the final winner, to promote one's honor by obtaining revenge (*edikêsis*) in the action which brings the exchange to its close, thus conclusively settling the score for previous dishonors suffered, such as those of Dinah (*aischynê; oneidos; miasma*) or of the Israelites before Judith's intervention. Thus, the detailed description of the vengeance of Simeon and Levi in Judith 9:2-4 sets the tone for all the many subsequent references to deception in the text. Moreover, to condemn Judith's actions with reference to modern canons of morality misses this aspect of their contextualisation in ancient Mediterranean culture.

There is other data which falls to be understood within this framework. When Judith says in this same prayer, "by the deception of my lips (*ek cheileôn apatês*) strike slave down with master" (9:10) and "give me a deceitful discourse (*logos mou kai apatê*) to wound and kill" (9:13), she is speaking from this moral universe where the abiding responsibility is to defend one's group and its honor.

Judith's Lies, Charms and Ambiguities

This attitude is then manifested in thirteen direct lies which Judith tells to Holofernes and other Assyrians and five cleverly ambiguous statements which further promote her scheme. I will now run through both categories.

First for the lies. She tells the Assyrian scouts that she is fleeing from the Hebrews, since they will soon be their prey (10:12), that she has trustworthy information (*hrêmata alêtheias!*) for Holofernes and that she will show him the road to take if he wants to capture all the highlands without losing a single life (10:13). She offers a wish for long life to

Nebuchadnezzar (11:7). She says that death is about to fall on her people (11:11), offering the imaginative fiction that this will happen since they are about to eat animals, corn, wine and oil dedicated to God (11:12-15). Her seventh lie is that she fled from the Bethulians when she heard of this plan (11:16). She seeks permission to go out each evening to pray to God to let her know when they had committed her sin (11:17), whereas she actually intended going out to bathe. Her ninth lie is that she will tell Holofernes when God has so informed her, so he can march out against them (11:18). She foretells that she will enthrone him in the middle of Jerusalem (11:19), that he will lead the Israelites like sheep (11:19) and that she has foreknowledge of all these events for the purpose of telling him (11:19). Her thirteenth lie is to Bagoas prior to joining Holofernes in his tent, that she would be going out to her prayers (13:3).

Next there are her cleverly ambiguous statements. She tells Holofernes that she will speak no lie (*pseudos*) in "to my lord tonight" (11:5), where he would think she was referring to him, whereas she means the Lord God. She further informs him that God will bring his work to a successful conclusion (11:6), which is similar to the Pythian oracle telling Croesus of Lydia that if he invaded Persian he would destroy a great kingdom (Herodotus, *Histories* 1.53). God has sent her to do things with Holofernes which the world would marvel to hear (11:16). Before she ran out of her own provisions, the Lord would have used her to accomplish his plan (12:4). Lastly, she is happy to drink with Holofernes since she had never felt her life more worthwhile than on this day (12:18).

The second broad aspect to Judith's deception, in addition to her discourse, is her beauty. After her success she states that her face deceived (*épatêsen*) Holofernes leading to his destruction, although he committed no sin with her to defile (*eis miasma*) or disgrace (*eis aischynên*) her (13:16), thus avoiding the fate (described in the same terms) which had befallen Dinah (cf. 9:2). In the hymn at the end it is said that 'she disarmed him with the beauty of her face' (*en kallei prosôpou autês parelusen auton*; 16:6). Finally, the same hymn contains a section describing how various aspects of her appearance helped to fool Holofernes:

> She anointed her face with perfume,
> bound her hair under a turban,
> put on a linen gown to deceive him (*eis apatên autou*).
> Her sandal seized (*hêrpasen*) his eye,
> her beauty captured (*êchmalôtisen*) his life,

and the scimitar ran though this neck (16:8-9).

There is grim humor here in military language (*hêrpasen*; *êchmalô-tisen*) being applied metaphorically to the effect of "weapons" which consist of women's clothing and cosmetics, but in a passage which climaxes with the woman so clothed and perfumed using an actual weapon to achieve a very literal result.

Irony in Context

According to C. A. Moore, while a number of biblical books make effective use of irony, "few, if any, are as quintessentially ironic as Judith" (1985:78). Basing himself on a dictionary definition of irony (rather than, say, the understandings of irony to be found in ancient rhetoric and in modern literary theory) and on E. M. Good's *Irony in the Old Testament* (1965), Moore sets out a large amount of data in the text which he finds "ironic". Some of this data includes features discussed above in connection with the lies and ambiguities crafted by Judith to gull Holofernes, for example her statement that she would say nothing false to her lord this night (11:5) or that the lord would accomplish through him things which would astonish the whole world (11:16).

There is no doubt that these, and many other features of this type, are ironic as suggested by Moore (and by Good before him), since they do illustrate in various ways how characters in the narrative, Holofernes and his Assyrians, are ignorant of what is well known to the audience. Israel's enemies are excluded from knowledge of the actual state of affairs until it is too late. Through most of the narrative they exist in a dangerous fog of incomprehension. I will add to Moore's discussion that this type of irony had been brought to a high pitch of perfection in the ancient Mediterranean world long before the book of Judith was written—in Athenian tragedy, in plays such as Aeschylus' *Agamemnon*[25] and Sophocles' *Oedipus Rex*.

The difficulty with Moore's approach to irony is that it is essentially a pigeon-holing exercise; he is concerned to establish certain categories of irony and then to show that data capable of inclusion within each can be found in the text:

The total effect of all the preceding passages ... is to create a work which contains Good's three categories: punctual, episodic, and the-

---

[25] Note the very poignant irony in this play which consists in the fact that the Trojan prophetess Cassandra prophesies truly the slaying of Agamemnon by Clytemnestra to the chorus, but nothing is done to save him.

matic irony. Thus, the book is a perfect example of what Northrop Frye (*Anatomy of Criticism*, p. 162) has characterized as the last of the four categories of narrative literature, namely. the tragic, the comic, the romantic, and the ironic (1985:83-84).

Although it is of some help to have textual data characterized in this way, it is difficult to see how simply lining the text up against a conceptual grid like this contributes significantly to understanding how it works as a story, in particular a story told in an ancient Mediterranean context. We need to move beyond merely *describing* instances of irony in order to offer an *explanation* of what function they serve in the narrative. To achieve this result we must ask what role the irony stemming from the persistent ignorance of the Assyrians on matters understood in quite another sense by the audience plays in the unfolding narrative—but always in the light of group-orientation and honor focused in the pattern of challenge-and-response which, as we have already seen, structures the text from beginning to end.

In this perspective the critical feature of the text comes immediately after Bagoas has discovered the headless corpse of Holofernes:

> He gave a great shout, wept, sobbed, shrieked and rent his clothes. He then went into the tent which Judith had occupied and could not find her either. Then, rushing out to the men, he shouted, "Those slaves have duped us! One Hebrew woman has brought shame on the House of Nebuchadnezzar. Holofernes is lying dead on the ground, with his head cut off!" When they heard this, the leaders of the Assyrian army tore their tunics in consternation, and the camp rang with their wild cries and their shouting. When the men who were still in their tents heard the news they were appalled. They were so gripped with panic and dread that no two men could keep together; the rout was complete. They fled along every track across the plain or through the mountains (14:16–15:2; JB).

In the terms of ancient rhetoric these events constitute an *anagnorisis*, a sudden recognition, when the scales fall from the eyes of some of the characters.[26] Here the author has depicted in sharp relief the moment when the Assyrians discover that they have been defeated and that all is lost. This is the very point at which the veil of ignorance is torn away, when at last they see the whole situation in the bitter light of reality and react in the usual fashion in an honor-culture like this. We might compare this with the scene in Sophocles' *Oedipus Rex* when Oedipus at last discovers as an undeniable fact that he has killed

---

[26] See Aristotle, *Ars Poetica*, 11 and Esler 1995: 1 for *anagnorisis* in the Emmaus story (Luke 24.30-32).

his father and married his mother (1182-1185), an *anagnorisis* to which
the play has been pressing with remorseless insistence, or with the
moment in Aeschylus' *Agamemnon* when Agamemnon cries out in
death at the hand of his wife Clytemnestra (1343-1345), a death ironically hinted at earlier by Clytemnestra herself (906-913)[27] and which
Cassandra had predicted to the chorus but to no effect (1246). In the
book of Judith, however, the tone is very different, being mordantly
comic rather than tragic.

Triggering the Assyrians' collapse leading to their total defeat in the
book of Judith is the realization that slaves (*douloi*) have duped
(*êthetêsan*) them, that one Hebrew woman (*mia gynê tôn Hebraiôn*) has
brought shame (*aischynê*) upon the House of Nebuchadnezzar. This is
the significance of the death of the Holofernes—that all of them have
been disgraced by decisively losing the contest. In a context where
individual selves were closely aligned with significant groups, the
shameful death of the group leader is the death of their honor as well.

How an ancient Israelite audience must have savored this picture,
with its imaginative evocation of the greatest success in a challenge-and-response interaction possible in their experience! Yet we
can go further than this, for throughout the course of the narrative to
this point such an audience would have appreciated every reference to
Judith's successfully lying to the Assyrians, or employing cunning ambiguity, or flaunting her many charms at him, as part of her stratagem
of drawing the enemy deeper and deeper into a state of compliant
ignorance until she had finally reduced Holofernes (and his army) to
utter helplessness. Thus, the extensive irony in the text, that is the way
in which the Assyrians operate on one, very defective level of knowledge—to their cost—while (Israelite) readers have access to the full
picture, operates within the challenge-and-response structure of the
work both to underline the brilliant way in which Judith takes control
of the situation as soon as she encounters her first Assyrians and also to
enhance Israelite appreciation of the scene when the Assyrians recognize to their horror and utter shame how they have been tricked.

---

[27] Especially note 910-911, where Clytemnestra gives this direction to her atten-
dants as Agamemnon alights from his chariot on returning from Troy: 'Immediately
strew his path with purple, so justice (*dikê*) may receive him into a house he never
hoped to see', with its veiled prophecy of Agamemnon's death.

The Theology of the Book of Judith[28]

As suggested at the start of this essay, we cannot read the book of Judith without noting its high level of theological seriousness. That is to say, although Judith is a fictional character, her story conveys a profound message concerning how the God of the ancient Israelites dealt with his people. We may be confident that the first Israelite readers of the book of Judith (just like the readers of 1 Samuel 16–18 before them) did not merely regard it as a fine tale, but learned from it about the God whom they worshiped and on whom they rested their identity as a people. The author of the story of Judith provides a fictional parallel to the story of David and Goliath by recounting one of the most stunning interactions of God with his people, and one of the most momentous instances of challenge-and-response, which could possibly be imagined. With Judith, as with David, the core of the message is that God will not be restrained by established social roles and institutions in effecting his purposes, especially in that he means to raise the lowly to positions of pre-eminence and to bring down the mighty.

Yet to understand the nature of the divine initiative as far as Judith and David were concerned, to comprehend their truly radical nature, we must conceptualize their stories within the usual and everyday patterns of ancient Mediterranean social life. Indeed, unless we make a real effort to appreciate the power of the social conventions at work in these narratives, we cannot begin to understand what an ancient Israelite reader would have made of the God who so thoroughly overturned them for his purposes.

Both Judith and David represent Israel as a whole in being small, inferior and frequently despised compared with surrounding nations, and often facing apparently insuperable odds, but nevertheless with God on their side, a God who comes to the aid of the weak and socially marginal and rescues them from dangerous predicaments. This is a storyline which in Israelite tradition reaches from Abraham to the Maccabees.[29]

Throughout the Bible, Israel's God exalts the lowly and crushes the arrogant who oppress them. He leads the Israelites from slavery in Egypt to the promised land. He helps them to conquer the powerful peoples of Canaan. He brings them home from exile. He takes the side

[28] I gratefully acknowledge my debt to John H. Elliott in this section, since a detailed response he offered to an essay of mine on David and Goliath (Esler 1998c) has stimulated the line of thought I develop here.

[29] I reiterate my indebtedness to John Elliott in this area.

of the widow and orphan against rich and corrupt judges and merchants. He reverses the shame of initially barren women (like Sarah,
Rebekah and Hannah). He regularly prefers younger sons over their
brothers (Abel over Cain, Isaac over Ishmael, Joseph and his son
Ephraim over their brothers, Jacob over Esau, and Moses and David
over their elder brothers and so on). He even gives victory to women
(like Deborah, Jael, Esther and Susanna), an unusual phenomenon in
the ancient Mediterranean. One of the great expressions of this theme
is the song of Hannah (1 Sam 2:1-10), which is echoed in Mary's
Magnificat (Luke 1:46-55). It is fair to say that the book of Judith is a
powerful expression of a characteristically Israelite theology which is
central to the meaning of the Bible, in both its Testaments.[30]

There is one notably unambiguous expression of this theology in
the work. In the prayer she makes before departing for the Assyrian
camp, after referring to the actions of Simeon and Levi (9:2-4) and
expatiating upon the need to smite the arrogant Assyrians, to break
their pride with a woman's hand (9:7-10), Judith says:

> For your strength does not lie in numbers,
> nor your might in strong men;
> but you are the God of the humble (*tapeinôn*),
> the help of the lowly (*elattonôn*),
> the support of the weak (*asthenountôn*),
> the refuge of the despairing (*apegnôsmenôn*),
> the savior of those who have lost hope (*apélpismenôn*) (9:11).

Yet a similar message emerges elsewhere, for example in the long
passage in the concluding hymn which describes how apparently
all-powerful Assyria—sweeping down from the mountains in the north,
to burn the land, kill the young men and children and carry off the
women—was improbably thwarted by a woman:

> For their hero did not fall at the young men's hands,
> it was not the sons of Titans who struck him down,
> no proud giants made that attack,
> but Judith, the daughter of Merari,
> who disarmed him with the beauty of her face (16:6; JB).

After a description of how Judith deceived him (16:7-9), discussed
above, the hymn continues with an account of the humble (described
in a way which echoes the language of 9:11) overthrowing the
mighty:

---

[30] Also see Walsh 1987.

The Persians trembled at her boldness,
the Medes were daunted by her daring.
These were struck with fear when my humble ones (*hoi tapeinoi*) shouted,
these were seized with terror when my weak ones (*hoi asthenountes*) shouted
  louder,
and when they shouted loudest, these gave ground.
The children of mere girls ran them through,
pierced them like the offspring of deserters.
They perished in the battle of my Lord (16:10-12; JB, slightly modified)

Yet even here the celebration of Judith's deceit (16:7-9), by which—with God's complete blessing—she secures a victory for her people, serves to reinforce the extent to which this message comes to us embedded in a cultural perspective which is quite alien to our modern sensibilities. For we have moved far away from the profound group-orientation of this text, with its adamant insistent on God's partiality for a lowly and humble Israel and opposition to her enemies, and the accompanying ethic that virtually anything is permissible to defeat them.

So, in the end, we must face up to this cultural distance if we wish to continue to find in the story of Judith resources for the enrichment of contemporary Christian identity, thought and action. This is not an unreasonable goal when we consider how the understanding of God as the protector and liberator of the humble of the earth has fueled various liberation theologies in the last few decades. It is an exciting challenge, and one for which Professor Malina laid the foundation by his introduction of Mediterranean anthropology into biblical research two decades ago.

5

Models and Archaeology in the Social Interpretation of Jesus

Douglas E. Oakman, *Pacific Lutheran University, Tacoma, WA*

> The conflict between Jesus and his Jewish opponents was thus an intra-Jewish conflict (with the elite who represented the dominant ethos) about how to interpret the tradition. It was a hermeneutical struggle with sociopolitical consequences (Borg 1991:13).

> It was only when the implied challenge of the full ministry in Galilee was recognized for what it was, first by the scribes, but then also by the priestly aristocracy, that plans had to be made to have him removed, predictably in the Jerusalem setting, not the Galilean (Freyne 1988:238).

Historical Jesus studies today, no longer preoccupied with the existentialist theological questions of mid-century, pursue a more refined tradition criticism, seek enlightenment through the excavations of Palestinian archaeology, and search for the most appropriate conceptual frameworks for understanding. Effective social interpretation depends not only upon the textual and artifactual information available but also upon conceptual resources that condition our questions and amplify our perceptions. This essay, working with social-systems models, urges a more comprehensive and integrated approach to the social world of Jesus and the interpretation of his historical activity.

Systems Models in the Social Interpretation of Jesus

All historians are conditioned by their contemporary social experience. This conditioning makes the social understanding of the past difficult. Inappropriate assumptions and analogies all too easily distort perceptions. The very different depictions of Galilee in Sanders 1993 and

Horsley 1987 offer a case in point. Sanders sees no real basis for conflict under "the good Herods," while Horsley perceives a "spiral of violence." Since both scholars draw upon virtually the same source material, their disagreement resides largely in their conceptual frameworks. Sanders' picture of a Galilee ruled by benevolent despots with enlightened tax policies seems influenced by unwarranted political assumptions. Horsley's use of peasant studies and sensitivity to the political realities of a colonial situation provide him with a very distinctive perspective on conditions under client rulers.

Historians too often promote generalizations based on anecdotal "evidence" without reaching clarity about larger social issues or contexts. Such inductive positivism, masquerading as an objective "social description," masks ideological bias and obscures conceptual basis for interpretation. Clear models help to overcome bias and social obfuscation by permitting critical examination of the conceptual frameworks into which historical data are summoned as evidence. Critically selected models allow data to speak in relationship to a larger picture, transforming it into compelling evidence. Further, potent models provide selectivity, aiding the interpreter in seeing what is most important or by highlighting social information that might otherwise be overlooked (Elliott 1993:40-48).

An inductive positivist method in historical Jesus studies can be improved upon, therefore, through abductive procedures (Malina 1991b; Elliott 1993:48). Abduction synthesizes both theoretical consciousness informed by the social sciences and historical data. A more sophisticated sociological imagination thus can inform social inquiry centered on the historical Jesus or Roman Galilee.

This is coming to be appreciated in recent scholarship. The cultural anthropology of the Mediterranean world (e.g. Gilmore 1987a) highlights key values and social arrangements in the largest socio-cultural environment of Jesus and Galilee studies. Malina and Rohrbaugh (1992) appropriately urge the ubiquitous importance of Mediterranean institutions like patronage for understanding the synoptic tradition.

Likewise, the macrosociologies of Gerhard Lenski and John Kautsky offer important sounding boards (Horsley 1987; Saldarini 1988a, 1988b; Fiensy 1991; Duling 1993:649-52). Lenski (1984; 1987) identifies key features in the social stratification of agrarian societies. His theory also highlights the importance of power and privilege in relation to social structure. Despite his claim to mediate and move beyond functionalism and conflict theories, Lenski's schema is rather static and of somewhat limited significance in understanding historical dynamics in the social picture. His theory needs supplementation. Kautsky (1982) shows the prominence of politics in ancient societies, especially in the face of low productivity economies (where redistributive mechanisms are more significant than productive mechanisms).

Macrocultural and sociological perspectives can be enhanced by systems perspectives. While systems theories are weak in the analysis of causation and in some forms hinder conflict analysis, they help to elucidate the interrelationship of social phenomena. The theoretical perspectives of Talcott Parsons (1937; 1969; 1971) can be of use in the model-building of this essay. While Parsons' theories were developed largely with "modern societies" in mind, their abstraction lends them cross-societal value (Collins 1988:57). Bellah (1970) shows the power of such a theoretical approach for understanding religious evolution in relation to social function. Malina (1986a:68-97; 1987) demonstrates the utility of Parsons' conceptions of generalized symbolic media for discussing early Christian developments. For critical assessments of functionalist sociology, see Elliott (1986) and Horsley (1989).

Parsons' four-function model of the social system employed strictly as an analytical framework generates insight especially into how Mediterranean values were made operational in the political institutions of early Roman Palestine. A simplified version of the model looks like this (Collins 1988: 58):

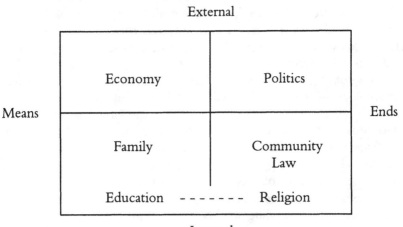

In real societies, the "quadrants" of the model usually do not exist discretely. Social domains interpenetrate one another; otherwise said, social domains can be embedded one within another. It is important to understand how one domain governs those that are inset.

The key social domain in Mediterranean societies permeating all other institutional arrangements is the family (Malina 1993a:84, 119-26; Pilch and Malina 1998:75, 158). The most likely explanation for the preeminence of this social domain lies in the environmental adaptation demanded of peoples living in the circum-Mediterranean world. Life in a climate where rainfall is unpredictable, as well as life threatened repeatedly by encroaching mountain tribes, has socialized Mediterraneans to trust only those in firm interpersonal relationship (Crossan 1991:12).

Whatever the comprehensive causes of the primacy of family, even a cursory investigation of ancient literature will show how significant family was in autobiographical or biographical considerations. For instance, the first words of Josephus' *Life* are "my family" (*emoi de genos*). Likewise, Matthew's Gospel presents what the early church considered (from its placement in first rank) the authoritative story of Jesus. Matthew begins the story by reference to the putative genealogy of Jesus, tracing his lineage back to glorious ancestors of Israel.

As the first paragraphs of Josephus' *Life* also demonstrate, a first-century Judean stands within an extended family whose interests and values supply a basic point of reference for the social action of the individual.

The ancient family had its internal politics, with males over females, fathers over children and slaves, older over younger, etc. There would be a religious life of the clan, and its activities to feed, clothe, and provide amenities for its members could be labeled economic. The Greek word *oikonomia*, of course, means "household management." To understand the dominance of family-structure and the interpenetration of institutions, we talk about *domestic politics*, *domestic religion*, and *domestic economy*. The adjective underscores the linking of social dimensions.

What is often ignored in scholarly discussions of ancient societies is the primacy of power and prevalence of power-structured relationships throughout ancient institutions. When one clan or family deals with another, it does not do so on the basis of kinship but on the basis of power. As Marshall Sahlins has shown for tribal societies (1966), family or quasi-familial relations are governed by reciprocity exchanges of one kind or another. However, relations with strangers or enemies exhibit negative reciprocal characteristics. To do the stranger or enemy harm is the ordinary thing. Therefore, all social institutions of a public character in the ancient world have a political dimension that needs to be recognized and taken into account. Illustrious families strove to dominate others. To understand the peculiarities of ancient politics—patronage and enforcement, temples, and estates—we must speak of *political kinship, political religion,* and *political economy.* Again, the adjective underscores the linking of social dimensions.

Political kinship appears in faction members, clients, slaves, tenants, tax collectors, and the like. *Political religion* appears with the temple state (with its own political kin organization), which is religiously rationalized into being "God's estate." The focus of political religion is the majesty and honor of the deity, i.e., worship. This worship demands appointments, so religious taxation (a rationalized political reality) is a necessity. *Political economy* identifies taxes, debts, forced extraction of goods and labor, production for redistribution (redistributive economy), and production for trade. Power relations govern all of these phenomena.

We need to be clear from the start, therefore, about the ranking of the socio-cultural (value) domains of Jesus' Mediterranean context: Kinship—Politics—Economy. Otherwise, we approach that social world inappropriately out of our own where economy structures all other social institutions (even families) and where social institutions appear discrete and self-governing.

The comprehensive model for the work of this paper grows out of the preceding reflections and building blocks (compare Oakman 1993:204). The arrows in the following "Systems Model for the Social Interpretation of Jesus" attempt to indicate feedback and feedforward loops through attached pluses and minuses. A feedback loop indicates resistive or diminishing action; a feedforward loop indicates amplifying action.

The model highlights major values and interests involved in the social action of elites and non-elites. A macrosociological focus on power relations addresses concerns of conflict theory (social interests divide). However, a focus on the social system elucidates structural-functionalism's interest in operative social structures (which seek an integral system). Attention paid to values and symbols that motivate action brings in the emphasis of symbolic interactionists. The model attempts to integrate concerns of major theoretical camps.

The model does not focus directly on the domestic politics, religion, or economy. Domestic religion in the Jewish regions of Roman Palestine would perennially emphasize election motifs and intimacy with God. For elite Judeans, torah and temple symbolized election. The model, however, urges us to examine how institutions controlled

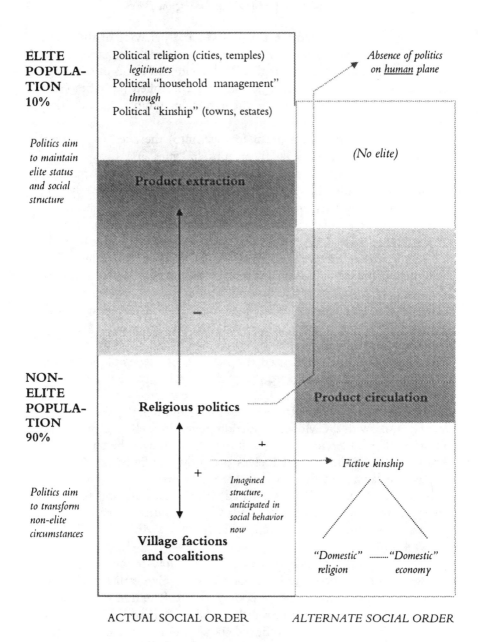

ELITE
POPULA-
TION
10%

Politics aim
to maintain
elite status
and social
structure

Political religion (cities, temples)
   legitimates
Political "household management"
   through
Political "kinship" (towns, estates)

Absence of politics
on __human__ plane

(No elite)

Product extraction

−

NON-
ELITE
POPULA-
TION
90%

Politics aim
to transform
non-elite
circumstances

Religious politics

Product circulation

+

+

Imagined
structure,
anticipated in
social behavior
now

Fictive kinship

Village factions
and coalitions

"Domestic" .... *"Domestic"*
religion   *economy*

ACTUAL SOCIAL ORDER   *ALTERNATE SOCIAL ORDER*

Systems Model for the Social Interpretation of Jesus

by the upper 10% shaped the perspectives and behavior of the lower 90%. Elite religion serves political functions when legitimating social order and mandating taxes that flow to the elite. In terms of the actual society of Jesus, the Herodian-Judean elite controlled the cities (Sepphoris, Tiberias, Jerusalem) and the Jerusalem temple, i.e., the key political(-religious) institutions.

Political religion implies (feeds forward into) the need for political kinship, represented strongly by groups in cities and towns. These "political kin" are responsible for the "political household management." They are the enforcers and collectors for the system, responsible for actually entering the pressing installation to ensure the purity of oil and wine or going into the village to remove grain from the threshing floor. They are also the accountants for the system.

The Pharisees offer an interesting case study in this light. They emerged under John Hyrcanus when the Hasmonean dynast realigned himself politically with the Sadducees. Outright war between Pharisees and Hasmoneans ensued under Jannaeus. The Pharisees apparently represented a protest group from within the political kinship structure. Primarily lay, they formed fictive kingroups called *havûrôth*; members were *havêrîm*. They emphasized the keeping of the whole law, even for laity. Thus, they embraced the purity regulations of the priests in daily life. Why did they do this? They were retainers of elite priests (Saldarini 1988a; 1988b). In their service of the temple, they became very familiar with the Mosaic legislation governing religious purity and taxation. They, therefore, came to know the laws even better than the priests and to distinguish themselves as a group by living according to the whole law, even though they were not priests. Throughout the first-century BCE, the Pharisees dared to criticize king and priest for their failure to adhere strictly to the law. The political repercussions of resistance or rebellion were predictable (Josephus *Ant.* 13 §§ 288-91; 17 §§ 41-46).

From the non-elite side, a basic issue in a low-productivity, low-energy, semi-arid ecological adaptation (with elite structures as described) is whether there will be enough to eat. The non-elite provide the productive labor, only to see the produce carried off by tax collectors. When not much is produced anyway, hunger is a close relative (Oakman 1986; Crossan 1991:43-46). The model indicates that *human political institutions* are a source of difficulty for the non-elite. Their strategies of resistance understandably tend to organize around the primary variable of kinship. Because of the need for concerted action, *fictive kinship* emerges, undergirded by religious warrant. The formation of fictive kin ties in villages and within coalitions represents a form of power; the politics of these groups tends to be sanctioned by deeply-held religious views. Therefore, non-elite politics tend to become *religious politics*. Non-elite leaders come to envision alternate social orders with two primary characteristics: the absence of politics or of religiously sanctioned violence on a human plane *and* the organization of society through fictive kinship with concomitant domestic religion and domestic economy.

How can the model help to understand first-century Galilee? Were Galilean Jews Torah- and temple-loyal? Was there a distinctive Galilean theology bound up with specifiable social interests? A consideration of such questions especially in reference to Jesus of Nazareth must be deferred until we examine how archaeology can contribute to social understanding.

Social models, then, are not reality. They are symbolic simplifications of reality to aid in understanding strategic social features or processes (De Raadt 1991:9; Carney 1975:10). The conceptual frameworks of this paper attempt to provide interpretive depth, like an old stereoscope, by linking several important perspectives, especially informed by macrocultural, macrosociological, and social-systems studies. The gain is an augmented understanding of politics as a key institutional and cultural variable and of struggles over social goals in the environment of Jesus. Herodian and Judean elite families dealt with non-elites through social institutions characterized by power and resource inequities. Non-elite politics and social action, conversely, were underwritten by culturally informed values that envisioned alternate institutions. Contemporary realities of power would shape non-elite imagination of a familial community without political economy.

Galilean Archaeology in the Social Interpretation of Jesus

Archaeological materials and interpretation are playing an increasingly important role in discussions of the social world of Jesus. For more precise understanding of first-century Galilee, archaeology needs to distinguish between cultural and social indices. Cultural indices ostensibly reflect the prevalent values of a people ("the Jews"), but are often urged or enforced by powerful elites (Jerusalem). These values may be shared formally by different social classes though not necessarily understood in the same way. For first-century Judaism, such phenomena as aniconic coins and architecture could be viewed as "cultural" artifacts. In the now somewhat dated summary of Meyers and Strange

(1981), cultural discussion predominates. The authors refer to "cultural indicators" (33), "cultural factors" (35), the pluralism of Galilean culture (38), etc., and generally treat linguistic and "religious" indices. That these indices tend to reflect the interests of elites does not receive discussion. Again, Strange's recent article (1992: 31-32) focuses on Rome's "urban overlay" upon "Jewish culture." There is no suggestion of similar "overlays" within Jewish culture.

Archaeological social indices, however, must be of such a character that they can reliably identify social differentiation within a cultural group. The identification of social indices implies recognition of social "fault lines" introduced into material culture by inequities of power. Sometimes cultural indices can play a socio-interpretive role, for instance, when select Jewish groups might adopt Hellenistic coins embossed with pagan motifs. The archaeologist will want to shed light, so far as this is possible from the material record, upon where such coins were handled or how they were perceived by different social strata. The following reflections, therefore, are intended to be suggestive of the kinds of social information archaeologists might be seeking or examining to clarify the issues central to this paper.

Settlements

Most archaeology in Palestine up until recently was based upon work in ancient cities. This made sense in terms of historical investigations. "Biblical archaeology" correlated urban stratigraphic records with the literary record. Typological sequences of pottery were needed for determining archaeological periods. Coins aided in developing the basic chronologies required for future work. Moorey 1991 chronicles the rise and decline of biblical archaeology, characterizing its basic weakness as "simplistic explanation" (175).

Even standard tools are limited by prevailing paradigms of interpretation. The regional articles in the *New Encyclopedia of Archaeological Excavations in the Holy Land* or the coverage of sites in the *Anchor Bible Dictionary*, for instance, more often provide perspectives on historical and cultural developments than information useful for sociological interpretation. However, as interest has grown in the social interpretation of the literary and archaeological records, a more extensive and comprehensive assessment of archaeological remains is needed. What seems called for are in-depth surveys of a wide variety of sites in Galilee, with special attention devoted to non-elite contexts. Only in this way will powerful social indices be identified.

Archaeological method, of course, is also a critical factor. The Israeli method, often intent on exposing architecture, has seemed most useful for ascertaining cultural information. The American stratigraphic method, influenced as it is by general anthropology and concerns for total societal reconstruction, is best suited for refinement toward using the material culture for social interpretation. Shanks indicates some of the issues at stake (1987; see Gottwald 1985:59, 63).

The following areas of archaeological inquiry might contribute further to the social interpretation of Galilee.

Buildings

Some preliminary work is available for illustrating how settlement patterns and spatial organization can help us do social interpretation. David Fiensy provides a synthesis for supporting further work on the archaeology of the lower classes. He demonstrates how building remains—isolated farms, houses, courtyards, alleys, villages—might provide significant social information. He thinks the early Roman *insulae* at Capernaum contribute evidence for an extended family organization of labor (1990:131-32). Could they also suggest the provision of housing by fishing contractors?

Social interpretation needs not only information from the cultural-political centers, the cities, but also now from towns and villages. Most of Jesus' contemporaries lived in villages; towns like Jotapata and Cana, Capernaum and Magdala, represented the domiciles of the "political kin" (see above on conceptual models) of the Herods and Judean elites. These sites will fill out our understanding of political economy in Galilee.

Monumental Structures, Waterworks, Roads

Archaeologists need to begin asking about the labor requirements involved in archaeological remains. Work of Dar and others, for instance, showed that each of the 962 stone towers in Samaria, weighing about 150 tons apiece and probably serving as artificial caves for estate wine production under the Ptolemies, were the result of 300-400 days of coordinated labor (Applebaum 1978; Dar 1986; Fiensy 1991: 32). These nearly 1000 years worth of petrified labor, extracted by Hellenistic overlords in less than a century's span, attest to the real political costs of the Greco-Roman period. What can be learned similarly from temples, roads, fortresses, and aqueducts? To what extent do these projects represent the accumulation of forced labor (Horsley 1987:6; Seeman 1993)?

Coins

As coins are excavated, archaeologists need to give more sustained attention to the social context of coin finds: Where are silver coins "contextualized"? Where are bronzes discovered? What types of hoards are found in cities, towns, or villages? Did these accumulations originate in commerce, taxation, loans, or rent extraction? A *desideratum* for social interpretation in Galilee would be a specialist publication that provided detailed coin profiles and maps detailing locations of discovery for all excavated and surveyed sites.

It is known that the temple tax was to be paid in Tyrian money (*m. Bek.* 8:7). Probably Herodian rents and taxes were paid in this currency as well, since the prevalence of Tyrian coins in towns of Lower Galilee and the Golan (Gamala, Chorazin, Bethsaida, Jotapata) is notable. It may reasonably be asked, therefore, how the presence of Tyrian coinage relates to political economy. Would the coin record bear out the thesis: Silver coinage, especially the Hellenistic types established at Tyre and Acco, supplied the basic money of the political economy— both in terms of taxation (Herodian realm, temple) and commerce (Tyre connection)? My suggestion is that Tyrian coinage reflects the political influence of Tyre, even in the domains of the Herodians and high priests. The text of Acts 12:20 is suggestive of the economic grounds for conflict between the Herods and Tyre. Since both taxation and commerce were elite pursuits, this conflict provides only an indirect index for village attitudes.

Would archaeological work also bear out the thesis of Polanyi that bronzes were token money intended only for rudimentary commodity exchanges or for conversion—with commissions (another form of taxation)—into silver by money-changers (Polanyi 1977:116-119 and especially 258-264)? Consider the results of a concordance study of the New Testament: The silver *denarius* is strikingly associated with political economy, especially debt (Matt 18:28), estate payment (Matt 20:2, 10), taxation (Mark 12:15), and commerce (Luke 10:35; Rev 6:6). The non-elite are most likely familiar only with bronze coins: The two *lepta* of the widow (Mark 12:42); Jesus asking, probably not disingenuously, about the inscription and image on a silver coin (Mark 12:15).

The coins of the first revolt offer equally suggestive social information. Silver shekels of the first Jewish-Roman War have been discovered in connection with priestly effects (Yadin 1966: 108). These typically have the inscription "Jerusalem the Holy" (holiness a priestly interest) and were probably used to pay the temple tax. Bronze coins found elsewhere at Masada bear inscriptions "For the freedom of Zion" or "For the redemption of Zion," while a unique bronze type at Gamala is inscribed "For the redemption of Holy Jerusalem." Yadin remarks, "[The silver coins] must have been hidden by the defenders of Masada to prevent their falling into the hands of the Roman conquerors, unlike the bronze coins which were scattered all over the place" (108).

Of the bronzes Hengel observes, "It is a remarkable fact that 'freedom' does not, as it does in the case of the coins of the second revolt, refer predominantly to Israel, but is applied fundamentally to Zion" (1989a:118; see Betlyon 1992:1087). The clear association of bronzes with a concern for Zion's freedom likely indicate a concern about temple taxation. The bronze revolt coins possibly mark as much a revolt against the temple establishment as against the Romans. The hidden silver coins at Masada indicate even there the conflicting ideologies and aims of the revolt. For a good discussion of these, see Price 1992.

Archaeological work, it can be seen, needs to become precise enough to identify in the coin record differing circulation patterns and economic systems with quite different purposes. The vertical system of taxation and elite-commerce was by far the most significant. Thus, MacMullen's comment that local trade involved about "seventy-five percent" of total economic exchange value in the Roman empire is a meaningless social statistic without some assessment of how much was controlled by elites (MacMullen 1970:333). Edwards (1992:55) thinks MacMullen's views permit the inference that Galilean cities were not parasitic. This view ignores the political nature of Galilean economy. A social interpretation alert to politics needs to suspect that regional commerce was not conducted on a level playing field and that perhaps up to seventy-five percent of system goods were moving vertically.

Bath Complexes

Up until now, *miqva'oth*, or ritual bath complexes, have been thought to be significant cultural indicators for a Jewish presence in the Galilee. For first and second-century Sepphoris (Meyers 1992b:88), the excavations on the western side of the acropolis have uncovered significant evidence for a "Jewish quarter." The presence there of private ritual baths, utility mosaic floors, and burials outside of the city precincts would show, in this interpretation, both a concern for ritual purity (baths) and aniconic sensitivities demonstrated through non–depiction of plants, animals, or humans on mosaic floors (Meyers 1992a:325).

A consideration of where *miqva'oth* appear in towns and outside cities gives pause to a simplistic cultural interpretation. As is well-known from the Mazar excavations at the temple mount and from Avigad's work in the Jewish Quarter of the Old City of Jerusalem, *miqva'oth* are clearly associated with concern for the purity of the temple and with the likely pre-70 CE domiciles of the high priestly families (Avigad 1976; Mazar 1980). The Judean Essenes at Qumran clearly had concern for ritual bathing, attested both in the Scrolls and in the archaeological remains (La Sor 1987). The bath complexes in the western palace of Herod at Masada may also indicate that monarch's concern to abide by Judean purity regulations. The wealthy and powerful could have these in domestic contexts.

What is striking about the *miqva'oth* in rural Judea is their association with agricultural installations, mostly pressing installations. These installations were provided by the estate owner for the workers to insure the ritual purity of the product. Ronny Reich's 1993 ASOR presentation (Annual Meeting), "*Miqva'ot*' (Jewish Ritual Baths) in Rural Regions in the Second Temple Period," showed that purity baths were often part of Judean estate pressing installations.

In Galilee, the same pattern seems to hold outside the cities. At Gamala, a *miqveh* appears beside the oil press. At Chorazin, although probably from a much-later period, one finds *miqva'oth* near economic installations. Jotapata seems to show a similar configuration. Interestingly, pools at Nazareth do not seem associated with the oil/wine presses (Bagatti 1969:52-57, 119-23, 219-33; Bagatti and Tzaferis 1993:1104). Plastered basins discovered under the Churches of the Annunciation and St. Joseph seem unrelated to the presses. The basins likely come from a time later than the early first century and show evidence of cultic functions. Could they be installations associated with the removal of the high priestly course to Nazareth after 70 CE? Otherwise, they might have been *loci* for Jewish Christian baptisms (however, see Meyers and Strange 1981:132, 136). Their absence at installations associated with other Galilean Jewish villages would be a significant social index. Presses from this period in western Galilee appear to lack *miqva'oth* as well, but this is perhaps related to the dominance there of Acco (Frankel 1992).

I suggest that for Jewish villagers in Lower Galilee *miqva'oth* were associated with political economy, and thus with *political* religion. Therefore, Galilean peasants had ample reason to detest purity concerns, along with the product extraction linked to them. Peasant anger compromised village loyalty to the temple, since it was the temple and levitical law that mandated such arrangements.

Pottery

The work of Adan-Bayewitz is noteworthy in pointing toward new ways of gleaning social information from the artifactual record. His tracing of pottery origins and distribution by detailed analysis of chemical profiles of pottery clay is a real step forward from simple morphological identifications. We accept Adan-Bayewitz's basic conclusions that Kefar Hananyah and Kefar Shikhin manufactured the basic cooking wares and storage vessels respectively for Lower Galilee in the early Roman period (Adan-Bayewitz and Perlman 1990).

The discoveries of Adan-Bayewitz have seemed to support the notion that Lower Galilean society was well-integrated (low level of conflictual relations) and thoroughly commercialized, so that villagers could buy or trade pottery much as we would visit the store for dishware. It is at this point that the lack of an explicit model of agrarian societies in Adan-Bayewitz's work leads to an unlikely conclusion. For it is much more likely, given what we have looked at in this paper, that powerful interests controlled the two pottery villages—especially when Shikhin was very close to Sepphoris and manufactured the basic vessel of liquid commerce—and that the distribution of these products reflects rather the outcome of monopoly than of a free market. Furthermore, one might ask whether other pottery manufacturing outlets could have existed *de facto* (given the necessary supplies of local clay), but did not *de jure* because of the prevailing socio-political arrangements. This is a matter that requires further inquiry. Furthermore, to speak of markets, as Adan-Bayewitz and Edwards do, is to ignore the results of comparative studies like Polanyi's that indicate "market" as we understand that word did not exist in antiquity; ancient markets were not price-markets; politics and "kinship" governed the dynamics of exchanges, distorting the purely economic rationality that modern people associate with markets (Polanyi *et al.* 1957; Polanyi 1977:42-43, 126-42).

Archaeologists should give attention, in addition to formal pottery typologies and quantitative studies of pottery remains, to what types of vessels appear where. In towns, for instance, one might expect to find many storage jars and *pithoi* precisely because towns were the enforcement or collection points for rent and tax extraction. What kinds of volume do extant storage jar remains indicate? We will look below at the Unjust Steward parable of Jesus with precisely this question in mind.

Stone vessels, finally, like *miqva'oth*, are thought to be cultural indices of ritual purity concern (e.g. *m. Kel.* 10:1). These, not surprisingly, have been found in the wealthy area (Upper City) of ancient Jerusalem, at Qumran, and at Masada. They become social indices for political economy and political kinship contexts, i.e., they correlate well with the domiciles of the powerful or their agents.

Archaeology will have much to offer in the future for the social interpretation of Galilee. The interpretation of material artifacts is not exempt from the problems of textual interpretation. The interpreter has to have "some idea" of what is going on while approaching the material record. Social-systems modeling urges that archaeologists look for social indices that map social and economic structures and relations. As James F. Strange has noted, such modeling and interpretation will go hand in hand with work on the literary traditions (Strange 1992:25).

A Proposal for the Social Interpretation of Jesus

Conceptual models and archaeology can help to control the present discussion about the Jewishness (better: the Judean orientation) of Galilee and the meaning of the earliest Jesus movement. To this task we turn.

Burton Mack's recent analysis of Q (1993) provides a baseline for the ideas developed here. He sees the earliest collection of Jesus' sayings in Galilee (Q1, 40s CE) projecting an image of a cynic teacher. The Q tradents celebrate an ever-present kingdom of God through a playful, freedom-loving lifestyle. With the second stratum of Q (60s CE), clear marks of disappointment enter the picture. Besides the addition of material appealing to the "epic" tradition of Israel (Jonah, Solomon), Q2 condemns "this generation" for rejecting the messages of John and Jesus, who are now envisioned in the line of Wisdom's emissaries. In Q2, Jesus is understood in relationship to an imminent apocalyptic visit from the Son of Man. Q3 completes the tradition before its assumption into the canonical Gospels of Luke and Matthew. In Q3, Jesus quotes scripture to Satan and grieves over Jerusalem. Mack sees this stratum reflecting the aftermath of the Jewish-Roman war.

These results presuppose that Galilee, culturally speaking, was a highly Hellenized place and minimize the Judean orientation of Jesus.

Mack indeed characterizes Galilee as a cosmopolitan area strongly permeated by Hellenistic culture (1993: ch. 4). He is also at pains to argue that "Judaism" in Galilee is like Samaritanism or Hellenized Judaism elsewhere. Only weak ties to Jerusalem or the temple are imagined.

This proposal can be evaluated as follows: It seems reasonable to say that some literate group, early on in urbanized northern Palestine, understood Jesus as a cynic sage. Mack and others have advanced arguments to make this perspective plausible (cf. Crossan 1991:72-88, 287-302; Vaage 1994). However, this characterization has not shown that the historical Jesus is best understood in this way. Scholars like Freyne, Sanders, and Vermes raise important questions for Mack's portrait because they see the historical Jesus in some definite relationship to the traditions of Israel. A further difficulty with Mack's theory: How could a so-thoroughly Hellenized Jesus and sayings-gospel be brought back so quickly into a certifiably Jewish domain in Q2? What sociologically is going on? Why did not the Q tradition continue in its original "purely Hellenized" trajectory, so that Gospel of Thomas was its only legacy? This problem remains unresolved in Mack's presentation.

Mack rightly underscores, though, how difficult it may be to characterize the relationship between Jesus and Judaism. Jesus is not purely and simply a Judean, the way the Pharisees, Essenes, and Sadducees are Judeans. These three Judean groups known to us from Josephus, the Dead Sea Scrolls, and rabbinic traditions are all identifiable because of their intimate relationship to the temple. All three have measurable concerns for purity and for interpreting levitical traditions in Moses. The Jesus tradition shows uneasiness about simply fitting Jesus into temple and purity concerns without qualification. Crossan (1991:322) and Borg (1984; 1987; 1991) depict a Jesus in programmatic conflict with the temple system. The approach of Vermes is less persuasive in saying, e.g., that after the temple incident Jesus "calmed down" and remained temple-loyal (1993:14), or that Jesus did not violate sabbath, food laws (1993:22-26).

As Mack observes, the Samaritans could give equal attention to Moses and no scholar today would call them "Jews." Should this designation be given to Galileans without further ado? Freyne and others have shown that *some* Galileans at least were devoted to the temple, if not overly to purity concerns. Freyne has also suggested that some Galileans were descendants of Israelites (Freyne 1980:38). Gary Rendsburg has proposed that "Israelians" continued in Galilee from

722 BCE through the time of the Mishnah, since there are clear linguistic contacts between Israelian Hebrew and Mishnaic Hebrew
(1992:227, 235). 2 Chronicles 30 makes this suggestion quite persuasive, and it is an especially important text for the recognition of
Israelians by Judeans at the time of Passover—a point we shall develop
further.

We shall continue to call these Galileans "Jews," because of some
measurable concern for both Jerusalem temple and Mosaic torah, with
the proviso that we understand "Palestinian Judaism" in the first-
century as a very broad and pluralistic designation and that we specify
Jesus' Judaism in a way that does not fit neatly with Phariseeism, Es-
senism, or Sadduceeism. It is to a sketch of this relationship, and an
attempt to account for why a Galilean Jew ends up crucified in Jerusalem, that we finally turn in this paper.

Jesus and the Kingdom of God
Most recent Jesus studies have acknowledged Jesus' focus on "kingdom of God." For most of the twentieth century, the expression
"kingdom of God" has been read against an apocalyptic Jewish background; in recent times that judgment has been contested. Borg
(1991:1-2), Crossan (1991:284, 292), Mack (1993:124), and Evans
(1993) all see a wisdom background. Sanders (1993:448) continues to
hold out for the older Schweitzer view.

It seems remarkable in the light of our previously developed model
that Jesus would pick a political metaphor to be central to his preaching (Horsley 1987:170). As Jesus' articulation of non-elite Jewish
aspirations in Galilee, it is our thesis that his central symbol signifies
the removal of politics from the human plane, i.e., the elimination of
political society entirely. The rule of God confers power to act differently, here and now, for the one who "enters it."

Crossan is surely correct in identifying healing and eating as central
motifs of the Jesus movement. The exorcism of demons or the healing
of bodies makes the kingdom real and present for the degraded, the
unclean, and the expendables (Lenski's bottom classes). These actions
of Jesus represent not only healing of bodies but restoration of people
to the community (Horsley 1987:170).

Jesus' "open commensality," his eating with tax collectors, "sinners," and strangers, is surely one of the central metaphors for what
kingdom means. The beautiful quote by Peter Brown sums up this
connection to kingdom: "In the straitened Mediterranean, the kingdom of Heaven had to have something to do with food and drink"

(qtd. in Crossan 1991:366). As with the healing of bodies, so the feeding of people has to do centrally with community.

Commensality was, rather, a strategy for building or rebuilding peasant community on radically different principles from those of honor and shame, patronage and clientage (Crossan 1991:344).

However scholars may evaluate the last phrases—Bruce Malina (1988a) would disagree on the "radically different principles"—the emphasis on a communal outcome to feeding is very important. On these basic points, Crossan has offered very powerful arguments.

Concern for community in the historical Jesus undercuts the Mack approach in a fundamental way. For he (and those who would go along with him) sees "community formation" at a later point. Indeed, if Jesus was a cynic individualist, community formation was far from his aim. Mack's early Q stratum, then, offers support in his mind for a group of social dropouts. Crossan's instincts seem more to be correct, especially given that a Jewish Jesus will always imagine a community in response to God's reign.

We see in terms of our elaborated model that Jesus as an advocate of non-elite interests in Galilee envisions the emergence of an alternative social order under God's reign; this reign implies a community of fictive kinship. Its emergence, however, is hindered as long as the prevailing political order remains. There are indications in very ancient Jesus material of a critique of that political order.

Jesus' Critique of the Herodian-Judean Political Order

In the analysis by Crossan, Luke 9:57-58 is the only one of the so-called Son of Man sayings with multiple independent attestation. Crossan argues that the saying recollects an original Jesuanic idiom, when he occasionally used the semitic phrase to refer to humanity generally (Crossan 1991:255-56). Crossan makes the prescient remark, "its meaning will demand much further context for final interpretation" (1991:256).

This saying, in fact, makes eminent sense in a Galilean context. Its meaning within the formative stratum of Q could be used to support a cynic appreciation for natural living. In such a reading, foxes and birds would have their natural homes, but human beings have to build "unnatural dwellings." This gives a rather general sense to the *logion*, but one that might have been compelling to those who thought nonconformity meant a rejection of all social life.

A different reading emerges through familiarity with Jesus' old neighborhood. Nazareth stands near the location of ancient Sepphoris,

Herod's capital city. Jesus is said to refer to Herod as "that fox" (Luke 13:31-33); Sepphoris derives from the Hebrew word for bird. The natural image now receives a natural political referent: The "birds of the air," the Sepphoreans, control the villages and the product of the land. Such a reference to the elite receives support when one considers a saying of Tiberius Gracchus (Plutarch *Tiberius Gracchus* 9.1)—a point first noticed by Arnold Toynbee (Brown 1991:113).

The large oil and wine presses, perhaps with their accompanying ritual baths, serve the elites. They are signs of the extraction of product, of its removal from profane or local use, and of its transfer far away. The tentacles of commercial Tyre and the temple system reach across the land. The Phoenician, Herodian, and Judean elites alike benefit from the Roman peace. The Herodian and Judean-oriented elite at Sepphoris have everything they need, but the ordinary person has nothing! The ordinary person meanwhile goes away hungry. "For to him who has will more be given; and from him who has not, even what he has will be taken away" (Mark 4:25 and pars.). The *Foxes Have Holes* saying is critical of society, as the Q tradents thought, but its original concern was blame of political society and not praise of nature.

A similar picture emerges from a study of Luke 16:1-7 (8). The steward (*oikonomos*) is situated somewhere within the political kinship structure of Jesus' Galilee. Perhaps the rich man lives in Sepphoris, while the steward oversees an estate in the fertile Beth Netofa Valley to the north. What hermeneutical possibilities does the systems perspective suggest for Luke 16:1-7 (8)?

Here as in other parables of Jesus, the kingdom of God hovers behind the narrative. Does Jesus tell the story: 1) with sympathy for the master's interests and values? 2) to hold up the behavior of the steward as a negative or a positive example? 3) out of sympathy for the debtors?

Verse 8a, which is not considered by Jeremias (1963:45-46) to be a part of the original parable of Jesus, would perhaps support hermeneutical Option 1 if included. One possible reading of the parable in this form identifies the *kyrios* ("master," "lord") of verse 8 with the steward's master (verse 3). Scott advances literary arguments in favor of this identification (Scott 1986:38-41). Though the steward is labeled "dishonest" (*oikonomos tēs adikias*), the master finds the steward's shrewdness admirable. What the master particularly admires, we are probably to understand, is the steward's political wisdom; for by utilizing the master's resources yet once more to acquire a brood of clients, the steward's "benefactions" set him up royally for the near future.

This interpretation would overlook, however, the injury of the master's interests by the steward's behavior (Kloppenborg 1989:486). The following social consideration might urge that Jeremias is correct in rejecting verse 8 as a part of the original parable: The master typically would not have appreciated the steward's continuation of the ripoff. Columella (mid-first century) relates the advice of Cornelius Celsus (early first century):

> [Celsus] says that an [illiterate] overseer ... brings money to his master oftener than he does his book, because, being illiterate, he is either less able to falsify accounts or is afraid to do so through a second party ... (qtd. from Lewis and Reinhold 1955: 171).

Matt 24:45-51//Luke 12:42-46 graphically depicts penalties for impropriety or malfeasance in a stewardship: The offending slave is cut in two (*dichotomê*). Was the steward's meditation (Luke 16:3), therefore, designed to provoke laughter from Jesus' audience (Scott 1989:263)? Kloppenborg sees rather the master on trial in the court of public opinion (1989:489).

It does not seem likely (at least to this writer) that Jesus' original intent was simply to evoke the audience's outrage or delight at the injury of the master's interests. Furthermore, it seems unlikely, on the basis of the previous considerations of this paper, that Jesus told a simplistic morality story to justify the interests of the landlord class. Option 1, therefore, appears to be ruled out. In a similar vein, Jesus probably did not tell this parable strictly to hold the steward's action up for censure or blame (option 2a). Such a reading would only make sense from the master's point of view.

In favor of the view that Jesus portrays the steward as a hero (option 2b), Jeremias holds that verse 8a reflects a change of subject in the earliest Jesus tradition to bring out Jesus' own attitude toward the steward's behavior. In this reading, the Lord (Jesus) praises the shrewd action of the steward. The question then arises, what is praiseworthy about the steward's deed? Jeremias concludes simply that the steward acts resolutely in a crisis and that Jesus held this behavior up as exemplary in his eschatological message. Besides the objection that Jeremias' eschatological reading is outmoded, the trouble with this interpretation is that the hearer/reader of the parable is expected to suspend moral judgment on what transpires and to grasp simply that the "end" (the eschatological times) justifies the means (radical and apparently selfish behavior). The parable rather seems to invite moral judgment (in first-century terms) to come into play; the original hearers were un-doubtedly captivated with the moral implications of such a story (see Danker 1972:173).

Proceeding to option 3, we might expect Jesus to be sympathetic to the victims of this story, namely, the people who were under both the master's and the steward's power. Jesus, of peasant origins, shared the values and outlook of the Palestinian peasantry to some extent. He took interest in the plight of victims (Oakman 1992). The two central characters in Luke 16:1-8 are beneficiaries of the Galilean political economy that disenfranchised and disinherited so many small peasants. What does the parable mean when viewed from the underside of Jesus' society?

The nature and value of the debts involved in the story need to be discussed. The significance of the debt remission also requires consid-eration.

Jeremias offers the following suggestion about the nature of the debts:

> The debtors ... are either tenants who have to deliver a specified portion (a half, a third, or a quarter) of the yield of their land in lieu of rent, or wholesale merchants, who have given promissory notes for goods re-ceived (1963:181).

Jeremias correctly sees private debts here. We are not to think of a public debt; the parable presents a different social situation from the one envisioned in Matt 18:23-34. On the other hand, it is probably unlikely that wholesale merchants are involved; the items in the Lukan text would more likely be "exported" from the estate by merchant middlemen in exchange for silver coinage.

That the debtors are tenants seems the most likely scenario. Are these then individual tenants? Examining the value of the debts may help to decide here. Jeremias, on the basis of the work of Dalman and others, thinks that 100 cors of wheat is the yield of 100 acres or 550 cwt. (= 27 short tons or 25 metric tons). An independent calculation, using the computer program in Oakman 1986, finds that 100 cors is 30 metric tons, over 1000 bushels of wheat, and the yield of 99.5 acres. The Mishnah attests rents in the 10 cor per annum range (*m. B. Mes.* 9:7-10). The likelihood is that few small cultivators, who un-doubtedly comprised the majority of tenants in early first-century Palestine, could have been responsible for the rent of 100 acres. Most tenants (and their families) farmed between 5 to 10 acres—a fact sug-gested by the late first-century report about the land holdings of Jesus' relatives: When summoned before Domitian, these relatives claimed

39 *plethra* (1 *plethron* = either 0.5 or 1 *iugerum* ' either 0.3 or 0.6 acre; 39 *plethra* = either 6 or 12 acres) between two families (Oakman 1986:61; Fiensy 1991:93-95). Similarly, Jeremias notes that 100 baths of oil were the product of 146 olive trees or nearly 4000 liters of oil. Based upon the measurements in Adan-Bayewitz and Perlman (1990:165), a typical Galilean storage jar held about 15 liters. 100 baths would amount to 267 jars of oil. A typical peasant family probably could not care for so many trees or have so many jars of oil, but a village certainly could.

Hence, these debtors are representatives of tenant villages paying the (annual?) rent assessed against former village lands now part of a large estate somewhere in Galilee. The representatives, like the *kômogram-mateis* in early Hellenistic Palestine (Zenon Papyri), were the village tax accountants responsible to the landlord for the entire village obligation. As the story clearly indicates, these persons were literate (Luke 16:7).

How much were the debts worth? Jeremias calculates that the 100 cors of wheat were worth 2500 *denarii* and the 100 baths of oil, 1000 *denarii*, but since "oil was dearer than wheat" he sees a rough equality between the debt remissions (1963:181). In Galilee, the presumed original setting for Jesus' parable, the price of oil was extremely variable, because of the prevalence of olive orchards. The evidence for oil prices in Josephus and in rabbinic material indicates a fairly large range between the times oil was plentiful and the times oil was dear. A *denarius* might buy anything between 2 and 40 liters of oil (Heichelheim 1959:184-85). Hence, Jeremias cannot be so sure that oil was dearer than wheat in the Galilean context. He is correct in saying that for both cases large debts were involved.

If this reading of the type of debt is correct, these debts were a heavy burden upon the local villages and representative of the changing social situation under the Romans. Not only were the debts burdensome, but their nature implies significant loss of local control over the product of the land. The reduction of the peasants' ties to the overlord to a relationship of economic exploitation would produce a great deal of resentment (Mark 12:1-12).

Does the steward's strategy of debt remission lead to a tactical power gain or is a fundamental change of relationship between the steward-enforcer of the political economy and the debtors envisioned? These two interpretive sub-options of hermeneutical Option 3 need to be explored for a moment.

There does not seem to be any indication within Jesus' narrative that the steward is in fact repentant of his former behaviors and that now a truly new behavior is in view. This consideration speaks against Fitzmyer's interpretation (1974:176-77). He follows Derrett in thinking that the steward has simply foregone usury. Kloppenborg (1989:481-86) provides additional arguments against these views. The steward continues in his former behavior of embezzlement and acts in his own interests with the two debt remissions. Furthermore, as has been suggested already, the steward's self-interested benefactions put the debtors in his debt. Gift-giving in the ancient Mediterranean world brought with it the expectation of reciprocity; to give to someone else obligated them (Malina 1993a:101, 103, and hint on 115). Surely the meaning of Jesus' similitude preserved by Luke at 11:5-8 hangs upon the same social assumption: A villager may not get up at midnight to provide for someone because he is a friend, but to keep the other in debt he certainly will. The meaning of the word *anaideian*, upon which this interpretation is hinged, is disputed, but the Egyptian papyri strongly urge the meaning "shameless desire for personal gain." The "friend" will make a loan at midnight on this basis.

The steward obviously counts on certain effects to follow his debt remission scheme. He is sure that his new friends will "welcome me into their houses" (v. 4). His tactics carefully demonstrate his new-found affections. He does not tell the debtors what they owe the master, as might be expected from the master's plenipotentiary, but asks each debtor what they owe. These presumably give a "low estimate." Then, the steward underbids even that low estimate. Finally, the debtors themselves are told to write their own contract. Would this be the normal course, or another opportunity for further reductions? The debtors are in his power, albeit a different kind of power than formerly. Malina and Rohrbaugh (1992:373-75) see the master also within the power of the steward, because the master's honor is also increased within the community by the steward's actions. The master cannot but praise the steward. Hence, Malina and Rohrbaugh find a good cultural reason to retain v. 8 as part of the original parable. Their interpretation, however, deflects attention slightly from the socio-political implications of the story.

It is not easy to see how this message coalesces with Jesus' overall message of the kingdom of God. Perhaps the key to a genuinely new option within the situation lies in seeing the core element of debt forgiveness. The peasantry view the debt collection as "theft" and unjust. Rigorous enforcement of debt collection led to violence (again

Mark 12:1-12). The story suggests that if folks can lower the debts even a little bit, and can live as friends—even if not under strictly mutual obligation—then the Galilean situation can improve, if only infinitesimally.

In reference to the kingdom, there is implied here a "lesser to the greater" moral argument. If the steward's dishonest personal machinations can have beneficial social effects, how much more will the debt forgiveness accomplish that is practiced under the conviction of the imminence of God's reign? Jesus is fascinated with the community-building possibilities of debt remission (Oakman 1986:149-56; Herzog 1994). The story of Zacchaeus (Luke 19:1-10) also recalls this fascination. Kloppenborg considers the "swerve" in v. 8 to signify that the master is "laughing" at his own honour and at the honour-shame codes with which the story has operated" (1989:492). This interpretation is striking, but like Malina and Rohrbaugh's only indirectly offers critique of social-structural dynamics.

Jesus' story contains humor, irony, social critique, and the suggestion of new possibilities all rolled into one. While the original meaning remains uncertain, a combination of steward as hero and debt remission as a moral good gives the most satisfying result, since the parable focuses on the behavior of the steward but has implications for the debtors as well. Jesus' parable envisions the "conversion" of the political enforcers of the Galilean economy to the alternate social order of fictive kinship under God's rule. With the undermining of enforcement or attraction of members of the enforcer (political kinship) class to his movement, Jesus was certainly going to come to the attention of the authorities and become a marked man.

The Galilean Life of Jesus and His Judean Death
Important suggestions have been offered recently about the relationship between Jesus' Galilean life and Judean death (Mack 1988; Evans 1989; 1993; Richardson 1992). Mack (1988), Miller (1991), Seeley (1993), and Crossan (1993) see the canonical passion narratives as substantially literary fictions, though Jesus' death in Jerusalem is accepted as fact. Yet Mack's and Crossan's general views seem unable to account persuasively for the Judean interest of a Galilean "cynic" or for his death at the hands of the Jerusalem elite. Why would a cynic Jesus go to Jerusalem or be killed by the elite? Evans (1993), rejecting Mack's "accidental" view, sees in Jesus' execution as "King of the Jews" a move to stop his proclamation of God's kingdom.

While claims about historical fiction writing deserve serious consideration (the presence of creative elements in the passion narrative is indubitable), there are discernable weaknesses in them also. Refined tradition critical inquiries should be done, of course. But is it reasonable to see wholesale creation of crucial details, entirely unconstrained by communal memory? Crossan's insight into the general character of such creative work—that creative process and event are generally and substantively interrelated—can restrict radically deconstructive readings and help to recover the essential meaning of Jesus' death in relation to Passover.

Furthermore, important assumptions are made in specific arguments about historical fiction that deserve careful scrutiny. For instance, Miller's claim (1991:248) that Jesus' temple action is "implausible" rests upon the assumption that immediate arrest should have ensued. Josephus recounts, though, that Jesus, son of Ananias, cried woe against the temple for seven years and five months, despite occasional arrest and opposition (*Bell.* 6 §§ 302, 308; cf. Acts 4-5). Theissen's observation (1976:149) still retains force: The elites' concern over popular sentiment protected Jesus of Nazareth from immediate arrest (cf. Mark 14:2). Horsley has a variant of this view (1987:298). On another issue, Seeley (1993:265) simply assumes with E. P. Sanders and Jacob Neusner that all Jews in Jesus' day looked upon the Jerusalem temple as an "indispensable" and legitimate institution. In light of the Elephantine papyri, the Egyptian temple of Onias IV (Jos. *Ant.* 13 § 63), or even Qumran (Temple Scroll), this is clearly false for the Second Temple period.

Manifestly, Passover could become the focal point for alternative visions. In late Israelite times, observance of Passover clearly had political significance. Josiah's reform emphasized a centrally observed Passover service, probably as a potent symbol of liberation from Assyrian power (2 Kgs 23:21-23). During the Persian period, Passover was seen as an important time of pilgrimage in support of Judean interests (2 Chr 30). Passover had clearly political overtones during the Hellenistic period (Ezekiel the Tragedian), but liberation themes were coopted by elite interests (Finkelstein 1938; 1942; 1943).

For the early Roman period, it is instructive to work through Josephus' explicit references to the Passover feast in order to make a judgment about his understanding of it. His usual habit is to characterize Passover by "the feast of unleavened bread" (*Bell.* 2 §§ 10, 224, 244; 4 § 402; *not* 6 § 423; *Ant.* 18 § 90 or 20 § 106). It is at this feast that Archelaus slaughters those protesting Herod's murder of the men who had torn down the golden eagle (*Bell.* 2 § 10; *Ant.* 17 § 213). Under Cumanus, a soldier's unseemly gesture leads to a riot (*Bell.* 2 § 224; *Ant.* 20 § 106). Crossan notes that this event nearly provokes the Jewish-Roman war twenty years prematurely. Quadratus the Syrian Legate has to visit Jerusalem (Crossan 1991:184). Likewise, Vitellius (*Ant.* 18 § 90) and Gallus visit Jerusalem at this feast (*Bell.* 2 § 280). The Sicarii act at this time to raid Engeddi (*Bell.* 4 § 402). John murders the partisans of Eleazar at the feast (*Bell.* 5 § 99). It was at this time that omens appeared in the temple (*Bell.* 6 § 290). And it is at this time that the catastrophic war against Rome broke out (*Bell.* 6 § 421). Josephus makes it clear that Passover was a volatile time of year in Jerusalem.

Antiquities 3 describes the institution of the *Pascha* sacrifice, "seeing that in this month we were delivered from bondage to the Egyptians" (§ 248). This is as much as Josephus ever says about its meaning; he never explicitly links Passover with contemporary aspirations. Both *Jewish War* and *Antiquities* emphasize that the people participate in the sacrifice *in groups* (*Bell.* 6 § 423; *Ant.* 3 § 248).

The Samaritans desecrate the temple at Passover time (*Ant.* 18 § 30). This act is not simply a hostile jab against Judaism but occurs after Judea (and Samaria in train) has become a Roman province (in the governorship of Coponius, 6-9 CE). Here the Samaritans perform a symbolic action in response to the perceived betrayal of the Mosaic tradition. A chapel of the Emperor is no better than a chapel of Pharaoh!

Passover is not mentioned at all in *Against Apion*. Here Josephus is content to counter the slanders of Manetho about the Exodus, the purpose of which in Josephus' mind was to found Jerusalem and the temple (*Ag. Ap.* 1 § 228). This probably states the normative meaning for the Jerusalem elite. Liberation readings of the Exodus are downplayed. Though it is a difficult fact to document directly, non-elites understand the liberation implications in the light of their own situation (just as African slaves in America). With the help of Josephus, Crossan (1991:160-67) can point to the several magicians or prophet figures who led people into the wilderness to relive the conquest of the land. Josephus, of course, downplays their significance and popularity. Nevertheless, these figures are important signs of liberation readings of Moses among the non-elites in Judea.

Surprisingly therefore, Brandon and Hengel make little of a Passover concern among the Zealots (Brandon 1967; Hengel 1989a). Hengel's statement:

> One can look in vain in the Old Testament, in the book of Ecclesiasticus and in the Qumran documents for an equivalent to the Greek term *eleutheria* in its purely political meaning. ... The first appearance of the Hebrew concept for 'freedom' that can be precisely dated occurs significantly enough at the time of the Jewish War, when we find the word *hêrûth* [on coins of the Jewish War] (1989a:116)

is too narrowly focused on the linguistic evidence, ignoring important information about Passover disturbances in Josephus. Besides, the appearance of the word *hôrín* in the Aramaic introduction to the Passover Haggadah is likely in a pre-70 tradition (see below). Hengel is nevertheless aware of what is at stake: "As soon as Israel's freedom came to be based, in the Haggadah, on the liberation from Egypt, the political question came to the surface ..." (1989a:119).

The Fourth Philosophy "founded" by Judas of Gamala at the time of Judea's incorporation into the Roman provincial system (and of the census of Quirinius) had a simple tenet: God is the only Lord, and to pay Roman taxes was to admit to slavery. This was a radical reading of the implications of Exodus 20:1-3 for the Galilean-Golan Jewish situation under the early empire. Later, Gamala was to make a desperate last stand against Titus (*Bell.* 4 §§ 70-83). Horsley gives some account of the relationship between Judas and Exodus (1987:82-83).

And Horsley alone of our interpreters sees Jesus in relationship to Passover. He makes this connection several times without drawing the conclusion we are drawing (Horsley 1987:45, 50, 82, 93, 155, especially 189 [discussion of allusion to Exodus 8:19 in Luke 11:20], and 300). He explicitly denies, though, that Jesus' frequent festive meals can be explained by the once-a-year Jewish Passover meal (1987:179).

Jesus' Death (however it occurred) and Passover
Our model and previous discussion prompt us at last to explore how Jesus' non-elite vision coheres with the basic tradition of Israel. After benedictions, the Passover Seder begins:

> This is the bread of poverty which our forefathers ate in the land of Egypt. Let all who are hungry enter and eat; let all who are needy come to our Passover feast. This year we are here; next year may we be in the Land of Israel. This year we are slaves; next year may we be free men (Glatzer 1979:20-21).

Segal (1963:241) makes no firm judgment on the antiquity of this part of the Haggadah, though he refers to Finkelstein's views that portions of the Haggadah are pre-70. Finkelstein makes no explicit statement about the Aramaic introduction, but sees pre-Maccabean material in the sections immediately following (1938; 1942; 1943). These, he stresses, make political accommodations to Ptolemaic or Seleucid sensitivities. Bokser, uninterested in political understandings of Passover, sees a great deal of anachronistic retrojection in the Seder (1992:764).

Glatzer regards the Aramaic introduction as beginning "one of the oldest parts of the Haggadah" (1979:20). In light of a well known liturgical principle, the switch from Hebrew to Aramaic conservatively repristinates the ordinary speech of the Second Temple period. Especially important is the late-Hebrew word *hôr*. It referred originally to the elite of Judah (1 Kgs 21:8, 11; Jer 27:20; Neh 2:16; 4:8, 13; 5:7; 6:17; 7:5; 13:17). *Pace* Hengel, the Hebrew or Aramaic plural of the word following *bên* can represent the abstract noun (GKC § 124 d, e; BDB s. v. *bên* 8, p. 121). It is assumed in the following, therefore, that the Aramaic introduction to the Passover Seder was known in similar (if not identical) form to the Jewish Jesus.

Crossan takes pains to show that Jesus' message, like cynicism, urges voluntary poverty, freedom, and kingdom. The freedom of the cynic philosopher grows out of his self-sufficiency. In this, the cynic finds freedom from social convention. As a free individualist, the cynic is his own king "Notice, in the flow of that passage [in Epictetus], the sequence from 'nothing' to 'free' to 'king,' the logic of poverty leading to freedom leading to royalty" (Crossan 1991:79). This is highly suggestive for the interpretation of Jesus with his proclamation of kingdom, but Crossan (and Mack) decontextualize a Jewish Jesus in order to make the cynic philosophical connection.

The Aramaic introduction to the Passover Haggadah, as the more likely basis for making these points, shows that poverty (and its alleviation!), rule (over land), and freedom are equally hallmarks of Israelite-Jewish consciousness. Jesus leaves the issue of rule to God. He and his followers practice domestic economy (eating) and religion (healing, "sons," "freedom") in response. Horsley (1987) thus appropriately links God's "politics" with feasting (170, 178), healing (181), and freedom (188). Central in Jesus' strategy is fictive kinship, which Horsley calls "Renewal of Local Community" (chs. 8-9).

Furthermore, the Beatitudes, among the oldest and best Jesus traditions are concerned with just these matters. Consider the following table:

Passover Haggadah	*Beatitudes*
The bread of poverty	Blessed are you poor
Let all who are hungry	Blessed are the hungry
This year we are here	Blessed are those who mourn

The last element of the Aramaic introduction holds the words, "next year may we be free men" (*benê hôrîn*, lit. "sons of freedom"). In Matt 17:25-26 Jesus tells Peter, in relation to the temple tax, that "sons are free." In terms of Jesus' program of domestic religion, the alternate social order ("kingdom") of God does not involve political taxation as the Judean temple does. Horsley comes close to saying this (1987:288, 300): Jesus' temple action and words announce God's judgment against the Herodian temple-system. Jesus' vision grows out of the foundation story of Israel.

In discussing Jesus' meal practices, Crossan claims:

> We have moved from, first, open commensality during the lifetime of Jesus through, second, general eucharistic meal without and then with a bread and wine (cup) emphasis and on, third, to specific passion remembrance, celebration, and participation (1991:365).

This judgment needs reconsideration. Crossan reaches it in a series of steps (1991:360-64) by asserting that Jesus' "open eating": (1) followed the standard Greco-Roman meal pattern of food/drink, (2) was not a distinctive sort of meal, (3) is still reflected apart from a Last Supper/Passover connection in Didache 10, and (4) only later was ritualized as such by Paul (1 Cor 11) and Mark (14).

Crossan's case hinges on separating Didache 9-10. Kept together, these sections contain elements of a Jewish Passover meal with cup and blessings before and after the meal (Behm 1965:732-37; Jeremias 1966). The cup was the first element blessed (Greek: *eucharisteô*) in the Passover rite (Did. 9:1-2). The blessing of bread preceded the Passover meal proper (Did. 9:3; 10:1). Another blessing followed the meal, in conjunction with the third cup of wine, i.e., the "cup of blessing." This thanksgiving would properly dwell upon God's creative power and the gift of food and drink for humanity (Did. 10:3). Jeremias discussed Did. 9-10 (1966:117-18), but missed its real significance. He thought it showed the separation of Lord's Supper from an Agape meal.

What it really shows is the consistent practice (Paul, Mark, Didache) of eating Jesus' meal as a Passover meal whenever (1 Cor. 11:26) it was eaten! Crossan, downplaying Jesus' Jewishness as he does, has neglected to consider that Jesus' open table was founded upon the Passover meal and understood in that light even in Galilee. Saldarini

1984:32 and Behm 1965:734 insist that the Passover meal had to be eaten in Jerusalem. They do not consider the political nature of this requirement: Exod 12:46 presumes household rites. Deut 16:2 is understood in later tradition, e.g. Tob 1:6, to refer to Jerusalem; Exod 23:15, 17 had not been so specific. Segal's discussion (1963: 20-25) shows that Jubilees (49:16, 21) stresses the requirement to eat in Jerusalem, while Ezekiel the Tragedian (Charlesworth *OTP* 2.815-16) does not mention it. Thus, Mark 14 can be "true" as "process to event," recollecting Jesus' customary practice of (daily) Passover remembrance.

We are now in a position to summarize our proposal: If, as Evans argues and Crossan seems to accept, the death of Jesus was contingent upon his Galilean activity, we can now say that Jesus' Galilean table practices also included Passover bread and wine celebrations. That is, Jesus' meal-sharing was shaped at every point during his Galilean life by his understanding of the root tradition of Israel; therefore, even if early Christian process has shaped the passion narrative especially at the point of Last Supper, that process had to have included Jesus' understanding of his own tradition. This makes great sense if other northern Jews, like Judas of Gamala, understood their tradition as a liberation tradition. Therefore, the interpretations of Passover attributed to Jesus ("this bread is my body," "this wine is my blood of the covenant") should preeminently be understood as significations of the inner meaning of his Galilean activity. His healing as a social symbolization as well as his eating as a reconstitution of peasant community were both contributions to the covenant community that the Moses tradition evoked.

Jesus, therefore, is best not read against Judean levitical traditions. He was not as Schweitzer thought an apocalyptic prophet or a messianic futurist. Messiahs and apocalyptic prophets were Judean preoccupations. Samaritanism, the Fourth Philosophy, and Jesus' own Galilean Judaism found their fullest theological context within Exodus, not within Leviticus.

Systems thinking, a concern for archaeological social indices, and criticism of the Jesus traditions converge on the same interpretive result: The non-elite, Galilean Jesus made sense within broader Israelite tradition, was opposed to Herodianism and priestly Judeanism in Galilee on a principled basis, and finally went to his death for the sake of Passover freedom. Jesus' brief but enormously influential career might reasonably be understood as a non-elite midrash upon Israel's foundational story.

6

Recruitment to the Jesus Movement
in Social-Scientific Perspective

Dennis C. Duling, *Canisius College, Buffalo, NY*

Rarely does a scholar offer such distinctive contributions to a field that (s)he changes the way other scholars *really* think. Such a scholar is Bruce Malina. Malina has taught us all to re-conceptualize our work in terms of social-scientific models about the past developed from Mediterranean cultural anthropology. Among the many proposals that have emerged from his creative mind is the suggestion that we consider ancient groups in terms of what the Mediterranean anthropologist Jeremy Boissevain called "coalitions," especially the "faction" (Boissevain 1973; 1974; see Malina 1986a; 1988a; 1988b). It was also Malina who made us more aware of certain recent trends in social movement theory (Morris and Mueller 1992; see Appendix 1). As will become abundantly clear, both of these proposals have greatly informed this study. Thus, it is my great honor—we have it, too!—to dedicate it to Bruce—scholar, colleague, and friend.

★ ★ ★ ★ ★ ★ ★ ★

Recruitment to groups and movements in Mediterranean antiquity has received much attention from historians, literary critics, and exegetes interested in "charismatic leadership," political movements, teacher and pupil contacts, and "call scenes" (Hengel (1981 [=1968]; 1992; Droge 1983; Robbins 1982; 1984 [=1992]). In this paper I explore ancient recruitment stories with the aid of social-scientific studies. First, I draw on networking theory in Mediterranean anthropology, specifically the "faction" model with its focus on personal recruitment, and offer appropriate modifications for the ancient Mediterranean. Second, I explore "social movement" (SM) theory and especially "new religious movement" (NRM) theory to gain further perspective, arrive at a definition of recruitment, and develop a working model of recruitment; again, I suggest modifications for the ancient Mediterranean. Third, I briefly survey select recruitment accounts in the Hebrew Scriptures, Josephus, 1 Maccabees, and the Greek and Roman philosophers, and make observations about these witnesses based on the faction and recruitment models. Fourth, I examine the recruitment stories in the Jesus Movement as represented by the New Testament, with the same object in view. Finally, in an Addendum, I explore the question of the origins of recruitment in relation to the historical Jesus. My aim is to discover how social scientific studies of recruitment help to raise questions and suggest perspectives for interpreting the ancient recruitment stories.

Recruitment in the "Faction" Coalition

The Mediterranean cultural anthropologist Jeremy Boissevain is one of several network analysts interested in understanding *informal* personal relationships that fall on a spectrum, the poles of which are individuals and formalized groups called "corporations" (Boissevain 1968; 1974; 1985:557; see Mitchell 1973:15-18; 1974:279-283; Johnson 1994).[1] These informal "coalitions" appear especially in times of social unrest and change, sometimes reflecting it, sometimes contributing to it, or both. They are temporary, unstable *ad hoc* alliances whose members join together for a limited time and draw upon each other's resources in order to achieve some limited purpose; thus, by definition, individual identities and commitments are not totally lost in group identity (Boissevain 1974:170).

---

[1] Credit for transforming what had been a "social network" metaphor into an empirical, fieldwork-based analysis is usually given to J. A. Barnes' study of the Norwegian island parish of Bremnes (1954). He argued that personal relationships, in contrast to formalized groups, have an independent structure of their own. Subsequent field work expanded Barnes' views to different cross-cultural social contexts. See further, Barnes 1969; Whitten and Wolf 1973; Mitchell 1974; Boissevain 1979; Marsden 1992; Scott 1996). The image of points connected with lines in network analysis is taken from mathematical "graph theory," see Ore 1990; for the model applied to early Christianity, see Atkins 1991; Clark 1992.

Boissevain concentrates on four types of coalitions (Boissevain 1974: 170-205). I focus only on one, the "faction" (see Duling 1992a:104-107):[2]

> [A] faction is a coalition of persons (followers) recruited personally, according to structurally diverse principles by or on behalf of a person in conflict with a person or other persons, with whom they were formerly united over honor and/or control of resources. (Boissevain 1974:192)

In this definition there are *three major emphases.*

First, *the context is agonistic; it is one of social conflict.* Factions compete with rival factions for access to scarce resources such as honor or the truth, a form of power. They are ideological, inherently political, and usually opposed to the established authorities (194-95; 201).

Second, *the faction centers around a strong leader* ("Ego") who is considered to have more honor and "resources" than his or her followers ("alters"); (s)he has the "propensity to coordinate," to maneuver followers in order to achieve desired ends (196). If a core group develops around the leader, there is potential for a longer life, but also for internal rival leaders (factions within factions).

Third, *the leader personally recruits followers.* There are "no clear-cut recruitment rules" (200). Recruitment principles are "structurally diverse," that is, followers, each of whom has distinct networks of his or her own (192), are drawn from different, often unrelated, "activity fields," such as family, work, and friendships. Factions are "qualitatively diverse," that is, relationships between Ego and alters vary in intensity (see below). Thus, factions have "low density": while all members are related to the leader and/or core members, not all have close, personal relations with each other. Network relations are therefore "asymmetrical" (200, 202).

The centrality of Ego means that *the faction is also an Ego-centered network.* The image is that of a center ("Ego") with lines radiating outward (links) to points ("alters"), that is, a star subgraph. Around the center is a series of concentric circles or "zones" of intensity. The "first order zone" consists of Ego's *intimate network.* In this zone alters are "adjacent" to Ego; they interact closely with Ego. The "second order zone" is Ego's *effective network.* In this zone alters are not as adjacent to Ego; they interact less closely with Ego. The "third order zone" consists of unknown, distant, potentially knowable "friends of friends," who form an *extended network.* In theory such zones can be extended

---

[2] Boissevain's other types of coalitions are "cliques," "gangs," and "action sets" (Boissevain 1974:170-205).

to the whole world. In theory it is possible to have a "total" network that is infinite and unbounded. In practice it is more common to focus on a "partial" network that is finite and bounded, that is, persons who are linked in specific ways. These are normally the first and second order zones. These persons are known, whether intimately or effectively; they are more dedicated to Ego; and they attempt to meet honorably Ego's demands.

I conceptualize the Ego–centered network faction like this:

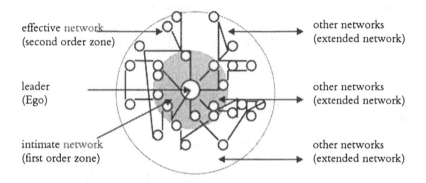

effective network
(second order zone)

leader
(Ego)

intimate network
(first order zone)

other networks
(extended network)

other networks
(extended network)

other networks
(extended network)

Figure 1: Faction Model

The Faction Model in Mediterranean Antiquity

Network analysts' interest in informal coalitions developed in part from the recognition that in complex, large-scale societies individuals have many independent, unconnected relationships in a variety of "activity fields." Often Ego has no direct personal relationship with alter's kin, neighborhood friends, or fellow or sister workers. Such networks have "low density." Analysts term these single stranded relationships "uniplex" (as contrasted with "multiplex," typical of simple, small scale societies). Such networks might be thought to have fit only with modern (weak group/high grid) societies rather than (strong group/low grid) societies characteristic of the ancient Mediterranean world (Malina 1986a:37–44).

While ancient Mediterranean society was indeed characterized by a higher degree of "groupism," two additional qualifications need to be made. First, the ancient Mediterranean is an advanced agrarian and commercial society (Kautsky 1982; Turner 1984; Lenski and Lenski 1987). Thus, while it has remnants of simple, small-scale societies, especially in rural, peasant contexts, it has also developed more complex social arrangements, especially in urban contexts (Kautsky 1982; Duling 1995b:160-61). In such contexts, single stranded, uniplex relationships can occur. Second, Malina argues that though religion (as well as economics and education) did not exist as a separate, differentiated, and distinct social institution, he allows that it could have existed in "fictive kin" arrangements (Malina 1986a:86). Neyrey also holds that while males are embedded in both political and kinship groups, these include *fictive kinship groups* (1997; see note 13 below). These qualifications are important for what follows. In advanced agrarian societies, there is room for what Boissevain describes as an Ego-centered network, that is, a person-centered, person-recruiting faction that removes persons from their traditional family and work-centered social connections.

Recruitment in New Social Movement (NSM) and New Religious Movement (NRM) Research

The main body of social scientific theory about recruitment comes from sociological research about conversion to modern Euro-American "New" Religious Movements (NRMs), that is, "sects" and "cults."[3] The word "conversion" usually means that a person is—better, claims to be[4]—a passive recipient of powerful external forces without rational free choice (Richardson 1985; Snow and Machalek 1984:180;

---

[3] Though these terms are much debated, "sects" here refers to deviant religious movements that retain more traditional beliefs and practices, and thus are not "new" in the strictest sense. "Cults," in contrast, are deviant religious movements that develop relatively novel beliefs and practices, but which may have historical antecedents in an alternative historical tradition (Stark and Bainbridge 1987:121-94). Sects appeal more often to less educated, less privileged, lower social strata; cults appeal more often to more educated, more privileged, upper social strata (Stark 1996: 36-47). See further, Lofland and Stark 1965; Lofland 1977; Stark and Bainbridge 1979; 1980; Snow and Phillips 1980; Snow, Zurcher, and Ekland-Olson 1980; Snow and Machalek 1980; Ellwood 1988; Robbins 1988; Stark 1996. A well known attempt to give a more cross-cultural view of "sect" with subtypes is found in Bryan Wilson (1973). For New Testament applications, see Elliott 1995.

[4] The testimonies of "converts" typically turn out to be creative retrospective narratives constructed to appeal and convince others; they are filtered through a particular NRM's ideology, understanding of organizational structure, and norms for "true conversion," and they often change over time (Beckford 1978; Snow and Machalek 1984:175-78). There is no consensus about the degree of transformation required to be called "conversion." Indeed, some who join NRMs claim not to have been converted (Bromley and Shupe 1979; Balch 1980). Greil and Rudy go so far as to state: "What purport to be studies of converts to religious ideologies are actually studies of recruits to religious groups" (Greil and Rudy 1984:311).

Stark and Bainbridge 1987:195-196; Robbins 1988:64-67). Conversion has been interpreted most often by means of *psychological stress theory*, that is, "converts" have "predisposing traits" that are activated during periods of extreme personal stress (Robbins 1988:72-79). In contrast, "recruitment" usually means the process by which one becomes attracted to, and affiliates with, a coalition, movement, or group (Robbins 1988:64, 81). It has more affinities with *sociological deprivation theory*.

In this paper, I shall use the term recruitment, a choice which has several advantages. First, it dodges controversial issues about conversion and psychological interpretations of it. Second, it sidesteps disputed interpretations about the apostle Paul's so-called "conversion experience" (discussion in Stendahl 1963), often seen as the basis of contemporary conversion conceptions (Richardson 1985). Third, it avoids the objection that psychoanalytic analysis cannot analyze persons from non-Western cultures, especially in the past (e.g., Johnson 1977:1-6; Pilch 1997). Fourth, "recruitment" is a common term in the literature about broader "social movements" (SMs) or "new social movements" (NSMs) and "social movement organizations" (SMOs).[5] Therefore, fifth, recruitment language and conceptuality are useful where there is little or no separation between politics and religion, as is typical of Mediterranean antiquity (Malina 1986b). Thus, sixth, it can be used at a higher level of abstraction. Seventh, recruitment strategies for both "sects" and "cults," while not precisely the same (see below), are similar (Stark and Bainbridge 1979; 1980:1377). Eighth, it has the advantage of usefulness in contexts where the recruit undergoes, or considers herself or himself to undergo, little or no radical change in perspective (Greil 1977: 115-17). Finally, ninth, it is a central term in Mediterranean anthropological analysis of "coalitions" discussed above.

Towards a NRM Recruitment Model

Though I have just distinguished between conversion and recruitment, influential social-scientific discussions of recruitment are most often found in the so-called "conversion literature," that is, sociological

---

[5]A social *movement* (SM) is "a set of opinions and beliefs in a population which represents preferences" about whether or not there should be social change; a social movement *organization* (SMO) is "a complex, or formal, organization which identifies its goals with the preferences of a social movement or a counter-movement and attempts to implement those goals" (McCarthy and Zald 1973:1217-1219). For SM/NSM theory, see Morris and Mueller 1992, especially Zald 1992; Appendix 1. There is an increasing tendency to wed NSM *theory* with NRM *theory* (Hannigan 1990, 1991).

analyses of free-standing RMs and NRMs in the modern Euro-
American society.[6] The most influential recruitment model in NRM
research has been John Lofland and Rodney Stark's (L-S's) seven-step
"value added" model of "conversion to a deviant perspective" origi-
nally based on participant observation of the Unification Church
(Lofland and Stark 1965). It is a "causal process model," that is, each
successive step increasingly leads the recruit toward commitment to a
NRM (Robbins 1988:66, 79). The model is divided into two parts,
(A) "predisposing factors" (3 steps) and (B) "situational factors" (4 steps).
One of L-S's own summaries reads as follows:

... a person must

[Predisposing factors]
    1.   Experience enduring, acutely-felt tensions
    2.   Within a religious problem-solving perspective,
    3.   Which leads him to define himself as a religious seeker;
[Situational factors]
    4.   Encountering the (NRM) at a turning point in his (or her) life,
    5.   Wherein an affective bond must be formed (or pre-exist) with one or more converts,
    6.   Where extra-cult attachments are absent or neutralized;
    7.   And, where, if he (she) is to become a deployable agent [total convert], he is exposed to intensive interaction (Lo-
fland and Stark 1965:874; cf. 862; Stark and Bainbridge 1987:200).

Another general conclusion of L-S was that while there were instances of recruiting strangers "off the street," many of whom were
social isolates, *growth in a movement occurred when recruitment was based on
pre-existing networks*, that is, when new recruits were drawn from previously recruited members' families, relatives, and friends.

In the rest of this section I attempt to synthesize the main points of
the much discussed L-S model. I also place in brackets Greil and
Rudy's judgment about whether ten well studied NRMs contain each
of L-S's seven steps (e.g. [7/3] = 7 "contains," 3 "does not contain";
see Appendix 2; Greil and Rudy 1984:313).

It should be emphasized that L-S 5, L-S 7, and the above general
conclusion have been generally accepted by other NRM scholars

---

[6] For some ancient Mediterranean modifications, see the following section.

(Lofland 1977:815; Bainbridge 1978; Snow and Phillips 1980:444; Snow, Zurcher, and Ekland-Olson 1980; Snow and Machalek 1984: 182-83; Greil and Rudy 1984). Accordingly, L-S 7 (intensive interaction leading to commitment) has the highest statistical incidence [9/10; 1 no evidence]). L-S 5, also statistically high [8/10], was L-S's most innovative step. Research prior to L-S had generally emphasized that the key to recruitment was "deprivation-ideological appeal," that is, the experience of real or relative deprivation in a context where traditional norms and values have become weakened or are in conflict (Durkheim's social *anomie*) becomes more bearable from the perspective of an attractive new ideology (Linton 1943; Hobsbawn 1959; Cohn 1961; Wilson 1959b). L-S accepted this variable, but argued that *at the initial stages of recruitment people were attracted to the ideology because of their ties to the group ("affective bonds" or "interpersonal bonds") rather than being attracted to the group because of its ideology* (Stark and Bainbridge 1980: 1378-79; also Lofland 1977:806).[7] Their conclusion that *pre-existing networks are also critical for movement growth* has been generally confirmed. The strength of L-S 5 and of the general conclusion is also supported by sociologists of broader SMs/NSMs. As Gamson writes: "The argument that recruitment to a movement follows lines of pre-existing social relationships and that recruitment networks are a critical part of the mobilization process has become part of our shared knowledge" (1992:61).

The other five steps (1-4, 6) have received a mixed reception. L-S 1 ("acute and enduring tensions"), though often mentioned by "converts" [7.5/10], implies the often contested *psychological stress theory* (Lofland 1977:817) and is subject to the problematics of "convert's" retrospective narration, lack of a control group by which to measure stress, and the meaning of "acute" and "enduring" (Greil 1977; Snow and Phillips 1980:433-35; Greil and Rudy 1984:314). L-S 2 ("religious problem-solving perspective" [7/10]) is not always present, even though it is agreed that people naturally affiliate with those who have a similar "prior socialization" or "cognitive style," or are "ideologically congruent" (Lofland 1977:806; Greil 1977:121-24; Snow and Phillips 1980:436; Barker 1981; Greil and Rudy 1984:315; Robbins 1988:81-82). L-S 3 ("seekership") is also sometimes missing [6.5/10]: some recruits claimed to have no religion; others were only mildly curious about the new religion; and still others seemed to find it *fashionable* to

---

[7] As a concrete illustration, the most successful of modern religious recruiters, the Mormons, have a 13-step set of guidelines that suggest "teach them in your home" as the *final* step (Stark and Bainbridge 1980:1389).

think of themselves as "seekers," suggesting, again, retrospective creativity (Lofland 1977:815; Snow and Phillips 1980:438; Greil and Rudy 1984:315). L-S 4 ("turning point") [6/10, 1 no evidence], is vague, subject to all the weaknesses of L-S 1 (Grail and Rudy 1984:315-16), and could apply to anyone anywhere and anytime (Lofland 1977:815), especially after initial contact (Snow and Phillips 1980:439-40). Finally, L-S 6 ("absent or weak extracult affective bonds") is less widespread [6/10] and tends to be in tension with the important general principle that a movement grows on the basis of pre-existing networks with family, co-workers, and friends (Snow and Phillips 1980:441).

In general, these critiques suggest that *psychological* "predisposing factors" emphasized in stress theory need to be at least counterbalanced by more *sociological* factors, especially social deprivation theory. Furthermore, L-S's distinctive insight about affective bonds at the initial stages of recruitment (L-S 5) should not lead to the diminution of deprivation/ideological appeal (Stark and Bainbridge 1980:1382; 1987:204, 207-14; Ebaugh and Vaughn 1984:155).

Snow and Phillips argued that the five debated steps of L-S do not fit less isolated, less exclusivist, less "communal," more "respectable" NRMs such as *Nichiren Shoshu* (Snow and Phillips 1980:431). Greil and Rudy then distinguished two group types: (a) "communal" NRMs stigmatized by society whose recruits undergo a radical discontinuity of social roles and consider themselves "converted," and (b) "respectable," "non-communal" NRMs whose recruits do not (Greil and Rudy 1984:309; Appendix 2). Ebaugh and Vaughn also related the same schema to ideology and recruitment strategies: "less isolated," "denominationalist" groups more typically recruit by close personal bonds; "conversionist" groups more typically recruit by "casual acquaintance-type friendships" (Ebaugh and Vaughn 1984: 155; see also Lofland 1977). Lofland's retrospective review of his work made a similar contrast but developed a different process for the "conversionist" type: (1) casual acquaintance recruitment in public places ("picking up"); (2) recruitment at invitational meals and lectures ("hooking"); (3) aggressive unfolding of ideology, often in a controlled environment that uses chanting, singing, and lectures at a week-end retreat, and the like ("encapsulating"); (4) intimate personal relations ("love bombing"); and, finally, (5) total involvement ("committing") (Lofland 1977:806-814).

In another important study, Lofland and Skonovd specified six types of "conversion motifs" (Lofland and Skonovd 1981; Robbins 1988:67-

71).[8] Though they can be criticized as vague and they overlap some-what (Robbins 1988:73), I offer them as suggestive of *recruitment strategies* and, motivated by Stark and Roberts' later comments about so-called "charismatic" founders of NSMs and NRMs (Stark and Roberts 1987:356-58), add a seventh motif, "attractional."[9]

1. *Attractional*: the founder/leader's ability to attract and recruit followers, whether by a new ideology or simply unusual social skills, or both.

2. *Intellectual*: "activist" *self-recruitment* by means of "disembodied media" (e.g., books, lectures, and meditation on statues, icons, etc.).

3. *"Mystical"*: traditional, individual conversion by means of auditory and visionary experiences.

4. *Experimental*: conscious decision to participate in a movement's rituals and organization activities but with a "wait-and-see" approach about its ideology, world view, and thus about total commitment.

5. *Affectional*: focus on L-S's affective bonds (L-S 5), that is, attraction to the group as a new social support system.

6. *Revivalist*: managed or manipulated ecstatic arousal in a group context (see Lofland's "encapsulating" and "love bombing" above).

7. *Coercive*: so-called "brainwashing" (see Lifton 1961: ch. 22).

Set out overleaf is Lofland and Skonovd's chart of six conversion motifs plus my seventh. Each is related to five major variations.

Finally, using a synthesis of data and two primary sources (*Nichiren Shoshu*; *Hare Krishna*), Snow, Zurcher, and Ekland-Olson expanded the original L-S model by analyzing the contrast between public recruitment of strangers and networked recruitment of familiars

---

[8] Lofland and Skonovd consciously blurred Beckford's distinction (1978) between the "objective" phenomenological event, which they called "first level reality," and the recruit's socially constructed "subjective" account of it, which they called "second level reality"; they then added the analyst's interpretation or explanation as " third level reality." "Second level reality" and "third level reality" are equivalent to the anthropologist's "emic" and "etic"; see Pike 1966; Headland, Pike, and Hams 1990.

[9] Stark seems to hedge on the word *charisma*: he says ". . . *[founders] are uncommonly skilled at recruiting.* . . . In a sense, then, they deserve to be called *charismatic*" (Stark and Roberts 1987:356-57 [italics mine]); yet, *"[charisma]* is unscientific because it implies that the charismatic person actually possesses superhuman powers to lead and persuade" (Stark and Bainbridge 1987:195). I have chosen the expression "attractional." Malina prefers "reputational" (Malina 1984).

	1 Attractional	2 Intellectual	3 Mystical	4 Experiential	5 Affectional	6 Revivalist	7 Coercive
1. Degree of Social Pressure	medium to high	low or none	none or little	low	medium	high	high
2. Temporal Duration	short	medium	short	long	long	short	long
3. Level of Affective Behavior	high	medium	high	low	medium	high	high
4. Affective Content	love (& fear)	illumination	awe, love, fear	curiosity	affection	love (& fear)	fear (& love)
5. Belief-Participation Sequence	participation-belief	belief-participation	belief-participation	participation-belief	participation-belief	participation-belief	participation-belief

MAJOR VARIATIONS

(acquaintances, friends, relatives) as they relate to "structured availability" and recruitment success. I summarize their general propositions which are *not* wed to "pre-disposing" psychological factors and are somewhat more generalizable:

Proposition 1: Those outsiders who are linked to one or more movement members through *preexisting extra-movement networks* will have a greater probability of being contacted and recruited into that particular movement than will those individuals who are outside of members' extra-movement networks.

Proposition 2A: The fewer and the weaker the social ties to alternative networks, the greater the structural availability for movement participation.

Proposition 2B: The greater the structural availability for participation, the greater the probability of accepting the recruitment "invitation." Persons whose ties with family and friends are weaker are more open to recruitment.

Proposition 3A: Movements requiring exclusive participation by their members in movement activities will attract members primarily from public places rather than from among extra-movement interpersonal associations and networks.[10]

Proposition 3B: Movements which do not require exclusive participation by their members in movement activities[11] will attract members primarily from among extra-movement interpersonal associations and networks, rather than from public places.

Proposition 4A: The success of movement recruitment efforts, measured by the numbers of outsiders actually recruited, will vary with the extent to which movements are linked to other groups and networks via members' extra-movement interpersonal ties, such that:

Proposition 4B: Movements that are linked to other groups and networks will normally grow at a more rapid rate and normally attain a larger membership than will movements which are structurally more isolated and closed. (Snow, Zurcher, and Ekland-Olson 1980:792, 794, 796, 797).[12]

---

[10] From the above critique, these are most often NRMs that are more deviant, isolated, socially stigmatized, communal, and/or "revolutionary." See Lofland's "picking up" in public places and "hooking" by meals and lectures (Lofland 1977).

[11] From the above critique, these are most often NRMs that are less deviant, isolated, socially stigmatized, communal, and/or "revolutionary."

[12] See the application of this proposition to the rise of early Christianity by Stark in the last section of this paper.

Drawing on the above critiques of L-S, I add the following three propositions:

Proposition 5. NRMs and accompanying recruitment practices are more likely to surface in contexts of social *anomie* brought about by real and/or relative deprivation, rather than in contexts of social harmony.

Proposition 6. Even though potential recruits have "ideological congruence" with NRM members, they will have a greater probability of being recruited if they perceive the NRM to hold an attractive "new" ideology in which to "believe."

Proposition 7. NRM recruitment strategies can vary with the emphases in movement types, though they may overlap: attractional, intellectual, mystical, experimental, affectional, revivalist, or coercive.

The NRM Recruitment Model and Ancient Mediterranean Society

As noted at the beginning of the previous section, the above model is based on NSMs/NRMs in modern Euro-American society. It is important to modify it with respect to at least the following generalizations about the ancient Mediterranean.

First, NRM analysis is based on religion as a "free standing" institution in modern Euro-American society; in antiquity religion was normally embedded in kinship and politics (Malina 1986b; Osiek and Balch 1997:41-43).

Second, however, "religious" groups could serve as *surrogate* families, especially in urban contexts (Malina 1986a:86; Duling 1995b:160-61). While it was common to "voluntarily" affiliate with more than one such group at a time, for example, Greco-Roman mystery cults, such a possibility hardly existed for strict monotheists.

Third, the Roman state did not normally consider Greco-Roman associations (which were in varying degrees "religious") to be subversive. Yet, Roman legal restrictions on voluntary associations show that some were of the political type (Duling 1995b:162-63; Cotter 1996). While the risk of affiliation was usually minimal, it was not always so. In this respect, most come closest to the non-communal, "acceptable" NRMs in modern society, though the exceptions come closest to RMs of the political type.

Fourth, those ancients who affiliated with a deviant movement, especially one considered by the state to be subversive, experienced a much greater break with trusted family, friends, and work associates, thus a more immediate social, not to mention political, risk than in modern Western society.

Fifth, because of geographical climate there is much more open, public living space in the ancient Mediterranean world; this is represented in architectural design of houses, from peasants to elite.

Sixth, there is a distinction between public male space and private female space. Yet, architecturally the distinction is more descriptive of Greece and the East than of Rome (Osiek and Balch 1997: ch. 1). It is also clear from many ancient texts that males had private as well as public space.[13]

Summarizing to this point, I have attempted to develop the contours of a recruitment model. A major locus for recruitment is the faction type of coalition which is also an Ego-centered network. In this type of coalition, an attractional leader in an agonistic context personally recruits followers. When total commitment is demanded, it is more likely that recruitment involves stranger or casual acquaintances and takes place directly and publicly. However, eventually followers, especially in more socially acceptable movements, can be recruited from wider social networks: kinship, neighborhood, work, friendship, personal association, and casual acquaintances. These sorts of contacts will more often occur in private places and are indirect, that is, mediated through social network contacts. Thus, recruitment strategies may vary at different stages of group development. Initially, the leader forms an intimate network, a core, which, in the competition for resources, can eventually challenge the leader's authority. The leader also has an effective network. Such networks enhance the possibility of growth. Attraction to the leader may include ideology—this is more common in relation to direct, public recruitment—but at the initial stages interpersonal relationships with faction members will be crucial. It will be important to attempt to take account of the dimensions of public and private space and the ways in which these may interact with direct and networked recruitment.

Researchers in NRMs have developed a related model that classifies "general outreach and engagement possibilities for movement information dissemination, promotion, and recruitment." Since the *mediated*

---

[13] Jerome Neyrey (1997) has assembled a number of texts from Greek and Latin writers showing that 1) males are embedded in both political and kinship groups, but these include *fictive kinship groups*; 2) males have a *polis* life *and* a non-*polis* life *not* synonymous with household, that is, *a life with other males*, such as in symposia; and 3) while males are always embedded in some group, this can be expressed as *an individual in private space* (see, e.g., Aristotle, *Rhet* I.3.3; Plutarch, *Tranquillity* 465C).

form of recruitment in the model stresses modern forms of communication (television, telephone, etc.), it must be modified for antiquity to include networking forms such as rumor and gossip. It is also important to keep in mind the ancient Mediterranean qualifications noted above. Modified, the model looks like this:

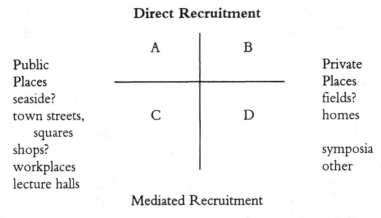

Direct Recruitment

Figure 2

Recruitment in Ancient Mediterranean Society[14]

Recruitment in ancient Mediterranean society is found in ancient texts that inhibit direct access not only to "objective" historical, phenomenological events ("first level reality"), but even the recruit's socially constructed "subjective" account of them ("second level reality").[15] They are narrative interpretations that follow ancient literary conventions (Aune 1987). They are also narratives that embed assumed, unspoken communication typical of "high context" societies (Hall 1976:74–112; 1983:55–72). The difficulties of accurate "thick description" (Geertz 1973:3–30) are obvious. Nonetheless, by being sensitive to these issues, some headway about recruitment in a general way can be made ("third level reality").[16]

[14] Not included is literature on Graeco-Roman peasant revolts and "Jewish" proselytes; see Dyson 1971; Stuehrenberg 1992; Fiensy 1994.

[15] For these distinctions, see footnote 8 above.

[16] For a suggestion about "first level reality" related to the historical Jesus, see Addendum.

As mentioned at the beginning, recruitment in ancient Mediterranean texts is captured especially by terms of "call" and "response" (Hengel 1981 [=1968]; 1992; Droge (1983); Robbins 1982; 1992 [=1984]). On the one side is a direct, personal "call" by an attractional leader to carry out a task (implied ideology and usually public), which implies "a new relationship to the one who does the calling" (interpersonal bonds) (Louw and Nida 33.312-14 [καλεῖν; see also ἐκκαλεῖν, ἀνακαλεῖν, "to summon"]). On the other side is the appropriate response, "to follow" (ἀκολουθεῖν) or "to accompany" (ἕπεσθαι), which implies total commitment. I have noted such language in the following examples.

The "Hebrew Bible"/LXX. In the Hebrew Bible/LXX recruitment of humans by other humans becomes a model for the way the Deity recruits human beings for special tasks. Thus, Yahweh directly calls Israel or individual Israelites to carry out his purpose.[17] Often God summons his chosen agents, the prophet-leaders, through ecstatic visions, a common ancient near eastern motif (Huffmon 1992:477-82). In the typology of Lofland and Skonovd, these are "mystical" conversion motifs. Prophets often resist the call or, having accepted, "turn back," another common theme. In response Yahweh is said to offer his help or to touch the prophet's lips, which results in the gift of prophetic speech. Such scenes often happen in public places, but seem nonetheless to be private. Again, commitment must be total. Examples of such accounts are the divine recruitment of Abraham (Gen 12:1-9), of Moses on Mt. Horeb (Exod 3:1-12; 4:10-17; 6:2-13; Deut 18:15-22), of Isaiah in the Jerusalem Temple (Isaiah: Isa 6:1-13; 49:1-5), and of Jeremiah at Anathoth (Jer 1:4-10; 15:19; see Robbins 1984 [1992]: 115). In the latter two examples recruitment of a leader is divinely "predestined."[18]

Conversely, divine-to-human recruitment lurks in the shadows of the accounts of human-to-human recruitment. One common type is located in a typical Deuteronomic pattern: the people's idolatry, Yahweh's punishment of the people by foreign oppression, the people's crying out, *the call of a leader*, the defeat of the oppressors, and the people's lapse into idolatry again. In this cycle the leaders are "judges"— Ehud,

---

[17] E.g., Isa 42:6 of covenanted Israel as a light to the nations, being called in righteousness and taken by the hand (ἐκάλεσά σε); 41:9 of Abraham and his descendants as "servant" (ἐκάλεσά σε... ἐξελεξάμην σε). See also Isa 46:11; 48:12; 50:2; 51:2; K. L. Schmidt *TDNT* 490-9 (καλέω). One can also find examples of individual recruitment by Yahweh, e.g. Isa 41:2, 25 of Cyrus as "servant" (ἐκάλεσεν; κληθήσονται).

[18] The predestination theme has influenced Paul's interpretation of his call from God (Gal 1:15-17), after which Paul retreated to the wilderness (see below).

Barak, Gideon, and Abimelech—and "king" Saul. Recruited by Yahweh, they in turn recruit the Israelites "to follow" (καταβαίνειν ὀπίσω πορευϑῆναι ὀπίσω) them into battle against their foreign oppressors.[19] These leaders are attractional; they possess a higher degree of honor and resources. Themes in the accounts often overlap and most motifs look more like recruitment to political NSMs than to deviant NRMs. The prophet Deborah "calls" (ἐκάλεσεν) the judge Barak (Judg 4:6 LXX A, B) who then publicly calls the Israelites to battle. An angel of Yahweh recruits the prophet Gideon while he is engaged in a mundane task, beating wheat in a wine press. Like Moses, Isaiah, and Jeremiah, Gideon initially resists (Judg 6:11-24). While the prophet-to-judge recruitment seems to be private, the judge-to-Israelites recruitment is clearly public. The context is agonistic, that is, political conflict.

The clearest example of RM-type direct person-to-person recruitment is Elijah's call of Elisha (1 Kgs 19:19-21), which contains themes that echo Yahweh's treatment of Elijah himself ("pass by"; "return"; Robbins 1982; 1984 [1992]:99-101).[20] Heeding Yahweh's command to appoint a successor (1 Kgs 19:16b), Elijah finds Elisha, like Gideon, engaged in his ordinary work, plowing a field with twelve yoke of oxen. As Elijah "passes by" he casts his mantle on Elisha. Elisha initially runs after Elijah and—note a typical theme—requests a delay: "Let me kiss my father [MT: and my mother], and then I will follow you" (LXX: ἀκολουϑήσω ὀπίσω σου). Elisha wants to honor his father and mother as a dutiful son. At first, Elijah denies Elisha's request—total commitment is implied—so he tells him to "return." However, when Elisha "returns," he slays his oxen, boils them with the yoke, and feeds them to the people, apparently to show that his commitment is total. Thus, he is willing to make a break with his family, village, and work, and he is affiliating with Elijah, a deviant prophet, and the prophetic guild, the fifty "sons of the prophets" at Jericho (2 Kgs 2:15).[21] Then he is accepted. Elisha arises and follows (LXX: ἐπορεύϑη ὀπίσω) Elijah and ministers (ἐλειτούργει) to him. This comes closest

---

[19] Ehud (Judg 3:28: καταβαίνετε ὀπίσω μοῦ); Barak (Judg 4:14: δέκα χιλιάδες ἀνδρῶν ὀπίσω αὐτοῦ); Gideon (Judg 6:34-35: ἐβόησεν Αβιεζερ ὀπίσω αὐτοῦ ἐβόησεν καὶ αὐτὸς ὀπίσω αὐτοῦ); Abimelech (Judg 9:4: ἐπορεύϑησαν ὀπίσω αὐτοῦ; 9:49: ἐπορεύϑησαν ὀπίσω); Saul (1 Sam 17:13-14: ἐπορεύϑησαν ὀπίσω Σαοὺλ εἰς πόλεμον). On Saul, see Jos.*Ant.* 6.5.3 (77): ἀκολουϑήσουσιν.

[20] "Pass by": 1 Kgs 19:11 (LXX: παρελεύσεται) = 19:19 (ἐπῆλϑεν); "(Go,) return": 1 Kgs 19:15 (LXX: πορεύου ἀνάστρεφε) = 19:20 (ἀνάστρεφε).

[21] For prophets and prophetic guilds ("sons of the prophets") in relation to Elisha, see 2 Kgs 2:3, 5, 15; 4:1-2, 38; 5:22; 6:1; 9:1.

to direct recruitment of a stranger "off the street" ("in the field") by an attractional leader. It might be called a "succession recruitment"— Elisha will be Elijah's successor—which implies knowledge of ideology and perhaps some "affective bonds" between the two prophets.

In summary, the Old Testament texts emphasize *four types of recruitment*: a direct divine summons to Israel for salvation; a direct divine call to prophets in a vision; a mixed two-stage type in which "judges" divinely recruited, sometimes through a prophet, carry out a divine command to recruit Israelites for battle; and the direct "succession recruitment" of the prophet Elisha by the attractional leader/prophet Elijah. The first is in private space; the second and fourth can occur in public space (Temple; field) but are still essentially private; the third is mixed private/public, but mainly public. Prior networks are not always clear or well developed, but seem to be implied. Totalism is explicit. The most explicitly agonistic, political contexts are the stories of the judges who issue calls to battle.

The Philosophers. Examples of recruitment are also found in the literature about the philosophers (Hengel 1981:25-28; Droge 1983: 246, n. 10; Robbins 1984 [1992]:88-108; Jordan 1986). Due to space limitations I must be selective.

I note initially the *logoi protreptikoi*, lectures or tracts supposedly spoken or written by members of all philosophical schools (Marrou 1956:206-207; Jordan 1986; Aune 1991; Mason 1996:39-41). Unfortunately, there is no theoretical discussion of them in the rhetorical manuals (*progymnasmata*) and the chief example, Aristotle's *Protreptikos*, survives only in fragments. Jordan (1986) has attempted to piece together the *logos protreptikos* from four fragmentary examples and indirect references. Steve Mason paraphrases Jordan's view of the genre: "writers of protreptic try to persuade interested parties, who are still vulnerable to persuasion by others, of a higher level of commitment to their own schools" (Mason 1996:40; see Jordan 1986:330). In short, the *logos protreptikos* was a recruiting genre, sometimes addressed to crowds, sometimes written to individuals, in which a philosopher argued for the superiority of his particular philosophical school. The *logos protreptikos* also seems to have contained a direct personal appeal to the hearer/reader to have a "change of heart" (e.g. Lucian's *Wisdom of Nigrinus* 35-37). Perhaps the *logos protreptikos* lies in the background of some of the recruitment scenes that follow.

One type of scene stresses an "attractional" philosopher who attempts to "hook" large crowds. Pythagoras' public lecture at Croton was said to have immediately won him 2,000 disciples who, with their wives and children, did not return home, but remained to establish the Pythagorean school (Porph. *Vita Pyth.* 19-20; Iamb. *Vita Phth.* 6.30). Emphasizing his teaching and healing, Empedocles wrote: "Whenever I enter into their flourishing cities, *they follow (ἕπονται) me by the thousands*, some seeking oracles, while others beg to hear a word of healing for their various diseases" (Empedocles, *Katharmoi* fr.B.112 [Diels-Kranz]). Large crowds were attracted in public places to Apollonius' deviant life-style; a core group (intimate network) followed him. In this case, the accounts stress that the initiative lies with the prospective follower, suggesting intellectual, "activist" self-recruitment, though the account has a divine-human-human sequence. Thus, Damis says, "Let us depart, Apollonius, you following (ἑπόμενος) God, and I you" (Philostratus *Apollonius* 1.19).

A second type speaks of indirect recruitment of individuals by reading a philosopher's work. Such accounts are clearly examples of intellectual, activist, self-recruitment, and even a woman and literate peasant could be so recruited! The Arcadian Axiothea, after reading Plato's *Republic* (at home?), hurried to hear Plato's public lecture and "forgot from then on that she was a woman!" It is said that Nerinthos, a Corinthian peasant, upon reading Plato's *Gorgias*, "immediately left the fields and the vineyards, entrusted his soul (Πλάτωνι ὑπέθηκε τὴν ψυχήν) to Plato, and sowed Plato's (teachings) and planted them out" (*Norinthus* 1.8.64 [=Themistius *orat.* 33 p. 356]). A similar story from a third-century CE account of Zeno's decision to follow Crates combines a stranger's *reading* (alone?) about Socrates in a public place, a shop, which involves a mediator, the bookseller.

> Zeno went up to Athens and sat down in a bookseller's shop, being then a man of thirty. As he was reading the second book of Xenophon's *Memorabilia*, he was so pleased that he inquired where men like Socrates were to be found. Just then Crates *passed by* and the bookseller pointed to him and said, "*follow* (παρακολούθησον) that man." From that day on he became Crates' disciple. (Diogenes Laertius, *Biogr. Vit* 7.2-3).

Affiliation with Epicureanism, a philosophy that by its nature does *not* aggressively recruit, but nonetheless had no small number of recruits, is another case of intellectual self-recruitment, this time in relation to a disembodied medium. This medium is the magnetic attraction of the numinous statue of Epicurus portrayed as a perfected self in the form of God, divine healer, and culture bringer (Frischer 1982).[22]

These examples suggest that ideology was more significant than personal ties to the leader or his networks, though the latter are not to be ruled out.

A third type is more specific about the philosopher's ability to attract disciples. Usually a network of friends or acquaintances is involved. Plato says that Socrates first heard about Theaetetus from Theaetetus' teacher, the geometrician Theodorus. So Socrates asks Theodorus to summon him in order to talk to him. Theodorus responds with, "Theaetetus, *come to Socrates* (δεῦρο παρὰ Σωκράτη)" and they talk, at first with Theodorus present, then Socrates and Theaetetus alone. After encouraging him, Socrates says to Theaetetus, "*Come then to me* (προσφέρου οὖν πρός με), remembering that I am the son of a midwife and have myself a midwife's gifts, and do your best to answer the questions I ask as I ask them" (Plato *Theaet.*144D, 151B-C; Robbins 1984 [1992] :89). Theaetetus accepts. There is no *literal* "following" in this account, but then Socrates is not itinerant. This example clearly involves an acquaintance network and is primarily private, not public and "off the street."

Similarly, Socrates learns about Charmides through Critias and suggests that Critias call (κάλεσας δεῦρο) the young man. Critias agrees (καὶ καλοῦμεν αὐτόν) and has his attendant call Charmides (κάλει Χαρμίδην). After some persuasion by Socrates Charmides accepts Socrates as "the physician of his body and soul." In the background are members of Socrates' intimate network (Plato *Charm.* 155A). Plato devotes one whole dialogue to Socrates' recruitment of Alcibiades for the purpose of teaching him virtue in order to govern the Athenians; while a network seems to be implied, the process is private (*Alcib. Maj.;* see Robbins 1984 [1992]: 90-91).

Recruitment to follow *itinerants* comes into view when Plato remarks that certain Sophists traveled from city to city persuading young men to break their usual ties, to join them, to pay them, and to be duly appreciative in addition (Plato *Apology* 19E)! This illustrates an-

---

[22] Frischer writes: "Religious, political, and philosophical movements have two basic sources of new membership: persons in the existing social and familial network of their current members, and strangers outside such networks. Potential members in the first category are easier to reach and persuade than those in the second, and recent sociological research has shown that contemporary cults and sects are most successful in recruiting and retaining new members known or related to old members" (1982:46). His source for this statement is the study of Stark and Bainbridge (1980), discussed above, and he cites their key example, the Mormons (see above, footnote 7).

cient "picking up" by attractional leaders. Recruitment of this type is caricatured in Aristophanes' play *The Clouds*. Socrates, portrayed as a Sophist, says to Strepsiades, "Don't chatter there, but *follow me* (ἀκολ-ουθήσεις ἐμοί). *Make haste now* (δευρί), quicker, here" (Aristophanes *Nub.* 505). Like the prophets, Strepsiades delays. He asks for a honied cake. Yet, the chorus implies that he follows (Robbins 1984 [1992]: 92-93).

Examples of direct personal recruitment combined with following are found in the third-century CE biographer Diogenes Laertius (see Robbins 1984 [1992]:93-94). The following *chreia* recalling Socrates' recruitment of Xenophon sets the scene in a public place, but the call nonetheless looks private:

> The story goes that Socrates met ... [Xenophon] ... in a narrow passage, and that he stretched out his stick to bar the way, while he inquired where every kind of food was sold. Upon receiving a reply, he put another question, "And where do men become good and honorable?" Xenophon was fairly puzzled; "Then follow me (ἕπου τοίνυν)," said Socrates, "and learn (μάνθανε)." From that time onward he was a disciple of Socrates. (Diogenes Laertius *Biogr. Vit* 2.48).

The following account of recruitment at a private banquet in a home illustrates the Cynic Diogenes' crudity. Presumably some sort of network involving invitations is in the background, but nothing explicit is related.

> (4) ... And indeed, once when I went to the house of a lad, the son of extremely prosperous parents, I reclined in a banquet hall adorned all about with inscriptions and gold, so that there was no place where you could spit. (5) Therefore, when something lodged in my throat, I coughed and glanced around me. Since I had no place to spit, I spit at the lad himself. When he rebuked me for this, I retorted, "Well then, So-and-So (speaking to him by name), do you blame me for what happened and not yourself? It was you who decorated the walls and pavement of the banquet hall, leaving only yourself unadorned, as a place fit to spit onto!"
>
> He answered, "You appear to be criticizing my lack of education, but you won't be able to say this anymore. I don't intend to be one step behind you."
>
> From the next day, after he distributed his property to his relatives, he took up the wallet, doubled his coarse cloak, and *followed me* (εἵπετο) ... (Diog. *To Monimus* 138 4b-5 [Malherbe 1977:163]).

In this example, the break with family and wealth to take up the Cynic's strict, itinerant lifestyle is clear.

Summarizing, the accounts about philosophers and their followers is very useful "close comparison" material[23] for personal recruitment by an attractional leader/philosopher, though there are a number of variations. In the background may have been the *logos protreptikos*, a lecture or pamphlet designed to recruit "seekers" who have not made up their minds. Some recruitment accounts suggest a combined attractional leader and intellectual self-recruitment, that is, large crowds are attracted to, and a core "follows," an itinerant philosopher due to contact in public places, the initiative apparently being with the prospective pupil (Apollonius). Some accounts stress that large numbers are "hooked" by a stationary philosopher in public (Pythagoras; Empedocles). There are accounts of intellectual recruitment by private reading a work by Plato (the woman Axiothea; the slave Nerinthos) or by gazing upon a numinous statue (Epicurus). Another intellectual example combines Zeno's reading about Socrates in a public shop with a bookseller who mediates following a Socrates-type leader, Crates. There are also accounts of recruitment implying networks of friends and acquaintances combined with philosophical instruction, with no mention of itinerancy, thus no "following" (Socrates' recruitment of Charmides, Theaetetus, and Alcibiades). Finally, there are "picking up" type personal recruitment accounts combined with "following" an itinerant (the Sophists) and among them is direct, personal recruitment (Socrates of Xenophon). The Cynic Diogenes is especially interesting. He is itinerant, and both public/stranger and private, networked cases seem to be involved. Commitment to the Cynic lifestyle involves a break with one's usual lifestyle, and perhaps one's family and friends. One fact thus far not mentioned stands out: recruitment by the philosophers does not take place in an obviously agonistic context, that is, it *is not explicitly political,* as are many of the New Testament accounts. The next category offers a contrast.

1 Maccabees and Josephus. In 1 Maccabees and Josephus the social context for recruitment is one of political conflict and relative deprivation, and there is clearly dramatic ideological appeal. Thus, aspects of the model related to NSMs rather than NRMs are more obvious.

At the outbreak of the Maccabean Revolt Mattathias is said to cry, "Every one who is zealous for the law and supports the covenant, *let him come out with me*" (ἐξελθέτω ὀπίσω μου) (1 Macc 2:27)! The narrative continues, "... many who were seeking righteousness and justice

[23] For the distinction between "close comparisons" (here, the Mediterranean region as cultural arena) and "distant comparisons" (cross-cultural in the broadest sense), see Esler 1989.

went down to the wilderness (κατέβησαν ... εἰς τὴν ἔρημον) to live there, they, their sons, their wives, and their livestock, because troubles pressed heavily upon them" (1 Macc 2:29-30). Here, the attractional leader makes a direct appeal in a public arena. There is no break with families: they take their families with them! Striking is the theme of *following a leader into the wilderness as a place of refuge.*[24] In this connection, one may note that the Essenes also saw the wilderness as a place of refuge, but their purpose for going there was to study Torah in preparation for the End. Perhaps the Teacher of Righteousness recruited disaffected priests to follow him, but unfortunately one can only speculate.[25]

Josephus *warns against* "impostors and deceivers" who recruit people "to follow" (ἔπεσθαι; ἀκολουθεῖν) them into the wilderness, usually to work signs and wonders (Jos. *Ant.* 20.8.6 [167]; Jos. *Bell.* 2.13.4 [259]; see Brandon 1967; Horsley and Hanson 1985). In this respect Josephus is like New Testament and the Qumran writers.[26] Here is a representative list of such recruiters:

1) a popular prophet, "the Egyptian," got together 30,000 men whom he led about *from* the wilderness (περιαγαγὼν δὲ αὐτοὺς ἐκ τῆς ἐρημίας; Jos. *Ant.* 20.8.6 [167]; Jos. *Bell.* 2.13.5 [261-63]; cf. Acts 21:38: he "led out" [ἐξαγαγών] 4,000 Sicarii *into* the wilderness);

2) the Sicarius Jonathan the Weaver, claiming to be Moses, "led" (ἡγεῖτο) the poor of Crete—men, women, and children!—into the wilderness, promising them signs and apparitions, and they "followed" (ἠκολούθουν [Socrates, *Hist.Eccl.* 7.38]; see Jos. *Bell.* 7:11.1 [437-442]);

---

[24] Two prototypes come to mind. First, Moses led the Yahweh's "chosen people" Israel through the wilderness. Literature approximately contemporary with the New Testament compares following the "prophet like Moses" (Deut 18:15, 18) with following God himself (MekEx 12.39; 14.15, 31; 15:22; see Hengel 1981:21, n. 20). Second, David, at this time considered to be a prophet (Jos.*Ant.* 6.8.2 [249]; Fitzmyer 1972), led his band of six hundred followers from hideout to hideout in the Judean wilderness (1 Sam 23:13-14).

[25] If "the Prophet" (1QS 9:11) or "The Prophet like Moses" (4Q175 [4QTest] 1.5) can be identified with the "Teacher of the Community" (CD 19:34; cf. 1QpHab 7:3-5), and if he is in turn identified with the Teacher of Righteousness, perhaps the Teacher of Righteousness personally recruited a faction of disaffected priests and led them there to study Torah in preparation for the End in fulfillment of Isaiah 40:3: "Prepare in the desert the way of [the Lord], make straight in the desert a path for our God" (CD 8:12-16). See further, Brooke 1994.

[26] Matt 24:26: μὴ ἐξέλθητε = Luke 21:8; see further, Funk 1959. 1QH 4:7 warns "the builders of the wall" (Ezek 13:11) not to "follow after" (הַהֹלְכִים) "Precept" who is a "spouter" (Mic 2:6), whom Hengel speculates might have been a revolutionary Pharisee like Simeon ben Shetaih (Hengel 1981: 20).

3) a Sicarius, a "certain impostor," who promised the villagers salvation (σωτηρίαν) and freedom from their miseries if they would "follow" (ἔπεσθαι) him into the wilderness, gathered "followers" (τοὺς ἀκολουθήσαντας) who were pursued and destroyed there (Jos. *Ant.* 20.9.10 [188]);

4) Theudas' retinue "followed" (ἔπεσθαι; ἀκολουθήσαντας) him into the wilderness to the River Jordan which was supposed to part like Moses' miracle at the Red Sea (Jos.*Ant*.20.5.1; 20.8.6 [167] = Jos. *Bell.* 2.13.4 [259]; cf. Acts 5:36: 400 men "were joined" (προσεκλίθη) to Theudas and "followed" [ἐπείθοντο] him).

There are similar accounts of others without the wilderness motif:

5) Judas the Galilean, a "teacher" gathered people who "followed" him, "drew [them] away" (ἀπέστησεν) (see Jos. *Bell.* 2.117-119, 433; 7.253; *Ant.* 18.2-10, 23-25; 20.102; Acts 5:37: ἐπείθοντο); and

6) a popular prophet, the Samaritan, "commanded" some of his countrymen "to gather to him" (κελεύων ... αὐτῷ συνελθεῖν) on Mt. Gerizim with the result that Pontius Pilate took military action (Jos. *Ant.* 18.4.1 [85]).

At the unrest that followed the death of Herod in 4 BCE there arose self-styled "strong men," believed to have superior size or ability, whose followers accepted them as kings or "messiahs"—clearly attractional leaders.

7) Judas, son of the bandit-chief Hezekiah, in attempting to become king, "got together a multitude of men" (συστησάμενος πλῆθος ἀνδρῶν) and seized weapons and booty from the palace in Sepphoris of Galilee (Jos. *Ant.* 17.10.5 [271-72]);

8) Simon of Perea, "of a tall and powerful body," donned the royal diadem, was "declared to be a king" (αὐτὸς βασιλεὺς ἀναγγελθείς) by recruits "who stood by him" (τίνος πλήθους συστάντος), and after plundering Herod's royal palace in Jericho, was finally caught and beheaded (Jos. *Ant.* 17.10.6 [273-77]);

9) the shepherd Athronges, "a tall man" "excelled in the strength of his hands," donned the diadem and claimed to be "king," supported by four brothers, also tall and strong-handed, each of whom was in charge of a band of men (Jos. *Ant.* 17.10.7 [278-84]; *Bell.* 2.4.3 [60-65]); and

10) each brother was a "commander" who "ruled over an armed band (λόχος)"; together those whom they "gathered together to them" (συλλέγεται ... πρὸς αὐτούς) were "a great multitude" (μεγάλη πληθύς) that went about attacking both Roman and Herodian troops (Jos. *Ant.* 17.10.7 [278-84]).

During the wars with Rome from 66–70 CE, other leaders who recruited followers arose.

11) Manahem "won over some notables" (ἀναλαβὼν τοὺς γνωρίμους, Jos. *Bell.* 2.17.8 [433]), took Masada, and entered the Jerusalem Temple robed as a king along with his armed "Zealots" (τοὺς ζηλωτάς, Jos. *Bell.* 2.9 [444]);

12) John of Gischala, a "social bandit," "welded together" (συνεκρότησεν) four hundred strong, courageous, militarily skilled villagers, mainly from the region of Tyre, and in opposition to Josephus sought to gain control of all Galilee (Jos. *Bell.* 2.21.1-2 [585-94]);[27] and

13) Simon bar Giora, "superior in strength and courage," proclaimed liberty to those in slavery, ravaged the wilderness villages of Judea and Idumea, "mustered a set of wicked men from all quarters" (τοὺς πανταχόθεν πονηροὺς συνήθροιζεν, Jos. *Bell.* 4.9.3 [508]), eventually influenced powerful men in the cities, developed an army no longer composed of slaves and robbers, but "a great many of the peasants" who "were obedient to him as their king" (δημοτικῶν οὐκ ὀλίγων ὡς πρὸς βασιλέα πειθαρχεῖν, Jos. *Bell.* 4.9.3-5), and joined the Sicarii in Jerusalem; at the end of the war, Simon appeared in royal robes and was taken to Rome where he was executed.

Josephus retells the story of Elijah's recruitment of Elisha. He claims that when Elijah's (magical?) mantle caused Elisha to prophesy, only then did Elisha "follow" (ἠκολούθησεν; Jos. *Ant.* 8.13.7 [354]) Elijah. He became Elijah's "disciple" (μαθητής) and lifelong "servant" (διάκονος), typical philosophical motifs. Hengel notes that in the Rabbinic literature Elisha's recruitment is compared to the selection of the

---

[27] In an as yet unpublished chart K.C. Hanson lists Josephus' other references to "social bandits" as: Hezekiah (*Bell.* 1.10.5 [204]; *Ant.* 14.9.2 [159-60]); cave bandits (*Bell.* 1.16.2-4 [304-13]; *Ant.* 14.15.4-5 [413-30]); unnamed bandits (*Bell.* 1.16.5 [314-16]; *Ant.* 14.15.6 [431-33]); unnamed bandits (*Bell.* 1.20.4 [398-400]; *Ant.* 15.10.1 [344-48]); Judas ben Hezekiah (*Bell.* 2.4.1 [56]; *Ant.* 17.10.5 [271-72]); Asinaios and Anilaios (*Ant.* 18.9.1-9); Tholomaeus (*Ant.* 20.1.1 [5]); unnamed bandits (*Bell.* 2.12.2 [228-29]; *Ant.* 20.5.4 [113-14]); Eleazar ben Dinai and Alexander (*Bell.* 2.12.4 [235]; *Ant.* 20.6.1 [121]); unnamed bandits (*Bell.* 2.21.1-2 [595-98]; *Life* 26 [126-31]); Jesus ben Shaphat (*Bell.* 3.9.7 [449-52]; *Life* 22 [104-11]); Josephus' hired bandits (*Bell.* 2.20.7 [581-82]; *Life* 14 [77-79]); bandit coalition of Zealots (*Bell.* 4.3.3 [135-39]; *Bell.* 4.3.9 [160-61]); bandit crucifixions (*Bell.* 2.13.2 [253]; *Ant.* 20.8.5 [160-61]); bandit-led peasant revolt and looting/burning (*Bell.* 1.13.6 [264-65]; *Ant.* 20.8.6 [172]); bandit executions (*Bell.* 2.14.1 [271]; *Ant.* 20.8.10 [185]); ransomed bandits (*Bell.* 2.14.1 [272-72]; *Ant.* 20.9.5 [215]). There are other examples of mainly unsuccessful native peasant rebellions in the Mediterranean world (cf. Dyson 1971; Fiensy 1994). In these cases, attractional leaders of the peasants were mainly from the upper strata of society.

revolutionary Phinehas of Haphta by lot during the Jewish Revolt in 66 CE (T. Yoma 1.6; Sifra Lev 21.10; Hengel 1981:17).

In short, a major theme stands out in 1 Maccabees, Josephus, and Rabbinic texts that is not characteristic of the philosophers: attractional leaders rooted in the biblical tradition of conflict, relative deprivation, and ideological appeal (Moses, the "judges," and king David) directly and personally recruit in public places. These accounts represent political SMs. Josephus transforms the recruitment of Elisha by means of various philosophical themes.

Personal Recruitment in the Jesus Movement: Gospel Traditions

A full analysis of personal recruitment to the Jesus Movement would consider minimally the Jesus' geographical context in Galilee, his ideological appeal, and links to his own kin, friends, and work associates. Here I restrict myself to a few observations about specific recruitment scenes. [28]

In the Gospel of Mark Jesus recruits two fishermen, brothers Simon and Andrew, along the Sea of Galilee (apparently a public place) near Capernaum. His words are, "Come after me (Δεῦτε ὀπίσω μου) and I will make you become fishers of human beings." The brothers "immediately" (εὐθύς) leave their nets and "follow" (ἠκολούθησαν) him. The story implies the attractional leader's direct appeal to strangers in a public place and the brothers' total commitment. Preexisting bonds are not mentioned. Yet, the subsequent account of Peter's mother-in-law (Mark 1:29-30) may imply a family network (cp. 1 Cor . 9:5).

Going on a little farther, Jesus "immediately called" (εὐθὺς ἐκάλεσεν) two more fishermen, brothers James and John, as they were mending their nets. Leaving behind their father Zebedee, they also immediately "went after him" (ἀπῆλθον ὀπίσω αὐτοῦ) (Mark 1:16-20). In this case, recruitment by an attractional leader suggests a sharp break with traditional family practices, and thus deviant behavior.

Jesus next "summons" (προσκαλεῖται) "those he desires" and appoints twelve men to be with him in order that he might send them out to preach and exorcise demons (3:13-14). Other passages contain the rhetoric of recruitment (6:1 [ἀκολουθοῦσιν]) in relation to his

---

[28] I omit the "conversion" of Paul, which is of the "mystical" type; see Stendahl 1963; Richardson 1985.

"summoning" (προσκαλεῖται) a core group to be his disciples (Mark 6:7; cf. 4:10-12).

In general Peter, James, and John, and perhaps Andrew, as well, are portrayed as Jesus' inner circle (Mark 5:37; 9:2; 14:33), but there are eight others chosen (cf. 3:16-18; 13:3). They are Ego's intimate network, a first order zone. If these disciples are thought to be friends, there would be greater multiplexity. However, there are some hints at rivalry within Jesus' intimate network (Mark 8:27–9:1; 10:35-45).

There are recruits who represent the effective network. In the Markan version, Jesus summons the toll gatherer Levi at the Capernaum toll office with "(Come,) follow me" (ἀκολούθει μοι) and Levi immediately gets up and "follows" (ἠκολούθησεν) him (2:14). There are also others who "follow": a cured blind man (10:52 [ἠκολούθει]), the young man at Gethsemane (14:51 [συνηκολούθει]), and three named women (15:41 [ἠκολούθουν]). Certain statements about those who "follow after" Jesus—"crowds" (ὄχλοι [5:24; 8:34]), the "multitude" (πολὺ πλῆθος [3:7]), and others (10:32; 11:9)—are similar to recruitment of large crowds in the Greek literature, though some would dispute their being directly affiliated with Jesus (so Hengel 1981: 63); nonetheless, they add to the impression that Jesus attracted a wide group of followers with an extended network and selected from them an effective network and his intimate network. Indeed, Mark 4:10 clearly mirrors the concentric circle model of Egocentered faction— Ego, intimate network, and effective network. The members of the intimate network are usually portrayed as leaving, or being requested to leave, their kin, friends, and worker groups. The resulting faction is a surrogate family, a fictive family. Though the context is not urban, neither is it fixed in a single location or totally "rural."

An excellent illustration of this totalism is found in the story of the rich man and the following verses (Mark 10:17-31) . Jesus tells him to sell his possessions, give to the poor, and "come, follow me" (10:21: δεῦρο ἀκολούθει μοι). The rich man is not able and in the following exchange, Peter exclaims, "Lo, we have left everything and *followed you* (10:28: ἠκολουθήκαμέν σοι)." The prospective follower must "deny oneself," "bear one's cross" (8:34), give up one's possessions (10:21), and leave "everything," including home, brothers, sisters, mother, father, children, or lands (10:28-30). "Following" is not *only* a metaphor for discipleship. It demands total commitment to the extent of actually breaking (at least partially) with one's customary family, friends, and work associates and forming new ones. It is total. There is no hesitation, no turning back. The echo of the Elijah/Elisha story can be heard. Yet, networking is implied by the sets of brothers, by Peter's family at Capernaum, and by fishing contacts around the Sea of Galilee. It is also implied in relation to disciples of disciples (9:38 [ἠκολούθει]) and to specific persons who "follow" but are not in the intimate network.

Matthew and Luke accept and interpret Mark's general picture of recruitment; so these gospels need not delay us.[29] It should not be forgotten that in the First Gospel the name Matthew replaces the name Levi and this Matthew is now part of Jesus' intimate network (Matt 9:9; 10:3; Duling 1992b). Though the Third Gospel transforms the recruitment of Jesus' first followers so that they respond to a miracle (5:1-11), the language of recruitment is generally retained (5:11: ἀφέντες πάντα ἠκολούθησαν). Luke also states that James and John were work partners with Peter (Luke 5:10), and that the twelve disciples were selected from a larger group (Luke 6:13) to which he elsewhere adds followers (Cleopas, 24:18, 22; Joseph Barsabbas or Justus and Matthias, Acts 1:23).

Before leaving the synoptic gospels, a word should be said about Q, which has an "itinerant" social setting (Vaage 1994:17-39). An obvious reference is the Q warning not to follow false Christs and false prophets into the wilderness (Matt 24:26: μὴ ἐξέλθητε = Luke 21:8: μὴ πορευθῆτε ὀπίσω αὐτῶν), which recalls similar warnings in Josephus (see above).[30] Q also emphasizes the difficulty of following Jesus with total commitment. This theme is found in Q's "three followers of Jesus" (Q 9:57-60, [61-62]):[31]

> 57 As they were going along the road, a man said to him, "I will follow you (ἀκολουθήσω σοι) wherever you go." 58 And Jesus said to him, "Foxes have holes, and birds of the air have nests; but the Son of man has nowhere to lay his head." 59 To another he said, "Follow me (ἀκολούθει μοι)." But he said, "Lord, let me first go and bury my father."

---

[29] Mark 1:16-20=Matt 4:18-22; Mark 2:14=Matt 9:9=Luke 5:27; Mark 8:34=Matt 16:24=Luke 9:23; Mark 10:21=Matt 19:21=Luke 18:22). Matthew 11:28 (Δεῦτε πρός με ...) in reference to those who labor is not a typical recruitment scene. It may be a Matthean composition based on .Sir 51:23-27 and Jer 6:16 (but see also "rest" in GTh 86). On the importance of "following" in Matthew, see Kingsbury 1978.

[30] There are hints of recruitment in the invitation of the supper parable in Q 14:16-17 ("those invited") and the *Gospel of Thomas* 64 ("My lord invites you" [4x]), but the references are very general. See footnote 30.

[31] Kloppenborg (1988:64), says of Luke 9:61-62: "Of all the Lukan *Sondergut*, this has the strongest probability of deriving from Q since it is found in a Q context, the saying coheres with the preceding sayings formally, and it evinces the same theology of discipleship typical of other Q sayings."

> 60 But he said to him, "Leave the dead to bury their own dead; but as for you, go and proclaim the kingdom of God." 61 Another said, "I will follow you, Lord (ἀκολουθήσω σοι, κύριε); but let me first say farewell to those at my home." 61 Jesus said to him, "No one who puts his hand to the plow and looks back is fit for the kingdom of God." [32]

Clearly Q emphasizes a sharp break with the family (Robbins 1989; Patterson 1993; Neyrey 1995).

The Gospel of John has a different approach to recruitment. The verb "to call" is absent but the response "to follow" is present (see 1:35-50). Striking in contrast to the synoptics is overt networking with kin and friends in the villages. Jesus summons Philip of Bethsaida with "Follow me" (1:43: ἀκολούθει μοι). Philip then seeks out Nathanael of Cana (21:2). When the Cananean responds, "Can anything good come out of Nazareth?", Philip replies, "Come and see" (1:46), the same words that Jesus used when he summoned Andrew who "followed" (ἀκολουθησάντων) John the Baptist (1:39-40). Moreover, Andrew recruits his brother Simon Peter (1:40-42) and both are from *Bethsaida* (1:44; contrast Mark 1:21, 29). Thus, in the Gospel of John preexisting kinship and village networks are much clearer than in the synoptic accounts (cf. John 10:27, 4-5).

Based on the above analysis, I shall now fill out the public/private and political dimensions of the model found above at the end of the initial social-scientific discussion about recruitment.

Summary

I have attempted to demonstrate how faction and NSM/NRM recruitment research can offer some valuable modeling insights for Mediterranean antiquity in general and to the gospel stories in particular. Personal recruitment by a leader is a major feature of the "faction coalition" model which is also an Ego-centered network. In an agonistic context a faction leader personally recruits followers. In cases where the leader recruits publicly and demands total commitment, the followers will more likely be strangers "off the street" or casual acquaintances. In cases where the leader recruits privately and total commitment is less obvious, the followers will more likely be

---

[32] There is a well known parallel to the "foxes have homes" passage of Q 9:58 in *GTh* 86. Though the "following" verse in Q 9:57 is missing in *Thomas*, it is quite possible that something like it is implied since *Thomas* is often thought to have an itinerant social setting like Q (Patterson 1993:134).

networked from family, friends, neighborhood acquaintances, work partners, and the like. In more deviant NRMs recruitment is often facilitated by weak ties to such persons. In more socially acceptable NRMs recruitment is usually accompanied by continuing ties to such persons—indeed, members are usually recruited from wider social networks. This suggests that recruitment strategies may vary somewhat at different stages of group development. Initially, the leader forms an intimate network, a core. The leader also develops an effective network which enhances potential for growth. Ideology may be an important factor in attraction to the leader—this is more common in relation to direct, public recruitment to deviant, "communal" movements—but at the initial stages interpersonal relationships with faction members will be important, sometimes determinative. It is important to attempt to account for the dimensions of public and private space and the ways in which these may interact with both direct and networked recruitment. It is also important to take account of modifications necessary for ancient Mediterranean society.

In the background of the accounts about philosophers and their followers may have been the *logos protreptikos*, a lecture or pamphlet designed to recruit undecided "seekers." Some philosophical accounts combine attractional leader and intellectual self-recruitment. Also a philosopher attracts large crowds and a core "follows," or an itinerant philosopher recruits in a public place, though the initiative seems to lies with the prospective pupil (e.g., Apollonius). Occasionally large numbers are "hooked" in public by a stationary philosopher (Pythagoras; Empedocles). "Intellectual" self-recruitment" can occur by private reading a philosopher's (Plato's) work (the woman Axiothea; the slave Nerinthos), by gazing upon a numinous statue (Epicurus), by (Zeno's) reading about Socrates in a public shop with a mediating bookseller. Recruitment by networks of friends and acquaintances yoked with philosophical instruction also happens (Socrates' recruitment of Charmides, Theaetetus, and Alcibiades). Lastly, there are instances of "picking up" combined with "following" an itinerant (the Sophists), including direct, personal recruitment (Socrates of Xenophon). The itinerant Cynic Diogenes engages in both public/stranger and private, networked recruitment. In these philosophical cases, recruitment is not explicitly political.

Political contexts and direct recruitment in public places are more prominent in the Old Testament, 1 Maccabees, and Josephus. Given the Old Testament Holy War ideology and "conquest" stories, the Maccabean Revolt, and Josephan accounts of prophets, bandits, and messiahs,

RECRUITMENT PATTERNS[33]

(Italics = itinerant leader; boldface = political; ! = wilderness)

	Quadrant A Direct Public Places	Quadrant B Direct Private Places	Quadrant C Network Public Places	Quadrant D Network Private Places
	(Yahweh→) prophets→Israel	**(Yahweh)→Moses**		
	Moses→Israel !	(Yahweh)→Isaiah		
B	**Ehud→Israel**	(Yahweh)→Jeremiah		
I	**Gideon→Israel**			
B	**Israel←Barak←**	**←Barak ←Deborah**		
L	**Abimelek→Israel**			
E	**Saul→Israel**		Elijah→Elisha	
S	**David→band of 600 !**			
	Axiothea ←—————		Plato's lecture←(reading Plato)	Socrates→Theodorus→ Theaetetus
G	*??(Apollonius→crowd)??*			*??(Apollonius→core)??*
R	Pythagora→crowd		(reading Plato)→Nerinthos	Socrates→Critias→ Charmides
E	Empedocles→1000's	Socrates→Xenophon		Socrates→Alcibiades
K			(reading about Socrates +) bookseller of Crates→Zeno	Socrates?→Alcibiades
S	*Sophists→followers*		*Diogenes→party youths*	*Diogenes→someone*
	Socrates/Sophist→Strepsiades			*Diogenes→young man*
	Pythagoras→2000 followers			

[33] Excludes Graeco-Roman peasant revolts (Dyson 1971; Fiensy 1994) and "Jewish" proselyte movements (Stuehrenberg 1992).

??(Teach. Right.→priests)??

Mattathias→rebels
Egyptian→Sicarii !

Josephus' Elijah→Elisha

Sicar. Jonathan W.→ poor !

1   **Imposter→ villagers !**
M   **Theudas→rebels !**
A   **Judas Gal.→Galileans**
C   **Samaritan→countrymen**
C   **Judas bandit→Galileans**
    Simon Perea→Judeans
J   **Athronges→Judeans**
O   **Manahem→Zealots**
S   **John Gischala→Tyrians**
E   **Simon Giora→peasants !**

Rabbinic Elijah→Elisha
Hillel→Jerusalem workers

2ⁿᵈ   *Mark's Jesus→Simon & Andrew*
T   *Mark's Jesus→James & John*
E   ***Mark's Jesus→ crowds***
S   *Mk J.→Levi/periph. group*
T
A   *John's Jesus→Philip→ Nathaniel*
M   *John's Jesus→Andrew→ Simon Peter*
E
N   *Q's Jesus→3 followers*
T   *GTh's Jesus→followers*

these factors are to be expected. The accounts deal mainly with political oppression and social deprivation by foreign powers, key elements in the agonistic context. Attractional leaders are on the move and total commitment to the group—the people—is expected. NSM theory is thus somewhat more relevant to this context. A major exception, of course, is the Elijah/Elisha story and its implicit and explicit prophetic guild context. Here total commitment is also expected. Josephus' retelling of the Elijah/Elisha narrative transforms it with philosophical recruitment themes; only the Talmudic retelling gives it a political flavor. On the other hand, preexisting networks and private spaces are more frequent in the philosophical recruitment stories, even though there is much variety. Less obviously political, these accounts are also closer to NRM recruitment, often of more socially acceptable groups, though there were also deviant philosophies, especially Cynicism.

It is striking from the "recruitment patterns" chart that direct, public, non-networked recruitment "off the street" seems more obvious in the synoptic gospels than in the Gospel of John where family and town networks are clearer. From the perspective of NRM research, the synoptics point to a form of recruitment more typical of deviant "communal" groups. It may be true that these accounts, as Robbins and Droge argue, have been conformed to philosophical, especially Cynic, patterns. Yet, the Cynics were, as just noted, deviants. From the same perspective, the Gospel of John's stress on networks comes closer to recruitment to more "acceptable" groups. That is somewhat surprising, given the usual view of conflict and "sectarianism" in the Johannine gospel.

Finally, from the perspective of NSM recruitment, one may ask the developmental question: has political SM recruitment been progressively defused by NRM recruitment, whether deviant or not? One should be cautious since these forms of recruitment share much in common and, as noted above, the Talmud does the reverse: it transforms the Elijah/Elisha narrative into a more explicitly political-revolutionary account. Transformations can go in both directions. In any case, that question can be best answered by a broader, total perspective on the historical Jesus.

Addendum:
Recruitment to the Historical Jesus Movement Faction

In *The Rise of Christianity* sociologist Rodney Stark argues that post-crucifixion Christianity was a *cult* that rapidly expanded (40% per decade from 40 CE to 350 CE) through preexisting networks among the more privileged classes, but the pre-crucifixion Jesus Movement was a Jewish *sect* composed of members from the less educated, lower classes (Stark 1996:17-21; see Stark 1987; Stark and Roberts 1987).[34] In contrast, John Elliott argues that early Christianity can be described as a *sect*, but the pre-crucifixion Jesus Movement should be seen as a *faction*, as was also the Baptizer movement (Elliott 1995:76-78). The main reasons for this definition contrast are twofold. First, Stark operates with generalized models developed from sociological data about contemporary North American sects and cults; Elliott, in contrast, operates with a view of sect developed from Bryan Wilson's cross-cultural studies (Wilson 1973) and, following Malina (1988a:20; 1988b:14-16) and Seland (1987), a view of faction coalition developed from Boissevain's cultural anthropology (Boissevain 1974). Second, and perhaps more important, Stark accepts the "new consensus" of social historians developed since E. A. Judge (Judge 1960; see Malherbe 1983:31) that early Christianity was not a proletarian movement, as A. Deissmann had argued (1965 [originally 1908]); rather, it was a movement dominated by upper class converts who became its patrons. The primary sources for this "new consensus" are the letters of Paul. Elliott, however, has in mind a Jesus Movement which is the sectarian "child" of parent "Israel." Its major sources are the synoptic gospels.

While I have benefitted greatly from Stark's analysis with respect to *recruitment*, I would agree that cross-cultural and social anthropological models are suggestive for antiquity. More important, the "new consensus" accepted by Stark works better for the larger Greco-Roman world represented by the Pauline letters than for the Palestinian Jesus Movement represented by the synoptic gospels. This point was well stated by Robin Scroggs (Scroggs 1980:169-70). To be sure, the current views that Palestine was Hellenized and that the gospels are strati-

---

[34] See the definitions in the section "Recruitment in New Social Movement (NSM) and New Religious Movement (NRM) Research" above. When in an oral response Ronald Hock points out that ancient networks were more complex because ancient households were more complex and urban life was more public, Stark agrees, but claims to be "unrepentant" (1996:21), stressing that social historians dealing with texts tend to resist general explanatory theories that are not locked into time and space (1996:21-27). Thus, he says, "*[h]owever* people constitute structures of direct interpersonal attachments, those structures will define the lines through which conversion will most readily proceed" (1996:22 [italics his]). However, it is important to recall a point parallel to that of Hock, namely, the strength of kinship and friendship ties in Mediterranean antiquity would affect the potential strength of preexisting networks on the one hand and dramatically highlight breaks with the family on the other (also Seland 1987:204).

fied complicate matters. Yet, if Stark were to deal more directly with the earliest stages of the synoptic gospels, he would probably have little difficulty in accepting the earliest stage of the Christian movement as a "faction." Indeed, it might be possible to extend Elliott's development from faction-sect to faction-sect-cult.[35]

I have sometimes blurred distinctions between faction coalitions, SMs, and NRMs ("sects" and "cults") in the synthetic recruitment model above because their recruitment strategies are similar. Yet, there are some differences between more "acceptable" and less "acceptable" NRMs, and the faction is somewhat closer to a SM. In this section, I shall restrict my language and conceptuality to "faction" because of its emphasis on the importance of ideology in an agonistic political context typical of ancient agrarian empires and because of its appropriateness for the beginning of the Jesus Movement. This approach also has more in common with (N)SM analysis and the possibility that the synoptic gospels reflect an evolution from recruitment from a more political to a less political group. This is not the place for an extended discussion of literary "criteria of authenticity," but I shall note them in passing (see further, Boring 1985; Duling 1990; Duling and Perrin 1994:1-31, 507-49).

It is generally accepted that all the gospel recruitment accounts are "idealized scenes" (Bultmann 1968:28). Droge argues that they are modeled on Cynic *chreiai* and tell us little about Jesus' actual historical context (Droge 1982). Robbins does not deal directly with the historical Jesus, but argues in an analogous fashion that the Markan author combined Hellenistic and Jewish rhetoric and then altered it by viewing Jesus as one who takes over the functions of Yahweh, for Jesus has no prior call (Robbins 1984 [1992]:117 [1992!]).[36] These arguments are powerful. However, there are equally convincing formal parallels with the Elijah/Elisha story: the appearance of leader "passing by," the prospective recruit engaged in daily work, the summons, and the "following." The fact that Josephus turns the story into private recruitment by a teacher on the philosophical model is suggestive for the gospels, especially when it is remembered that the Mekilta transforms it into a public recruitment by a revolutionary! Clearly, there are tendencies in Christian tradition to see Jesus as a prophet/teacher who recruits his most intimate followers in a form understood in the cul-

---

[35] However, Malina, who accepts Boissevain, prefers to avoid the language of "sect" as too Weberian; see Malina 1984.

[36] The position that Jesus did not have a prophetic "call" from God—the "mystical" form of "conversion" noted above—is not universal; see, e.g., Borg 1987:32.

tural environment ("criteria of authenticity": tendencies developing in the tradition; modification of tradition; language and style; cultural environment).

While the arguments in favor of contextual communication and typical scenes in the recruitment stories are strong, there are also strong arguments for a historical core. First, recruitment accounts are found in Mark, John, and Q, and they are implied in the *Gospel of Thomas* (criterion: multiple attestation), even though the names of the recruits and the emphasis on networking vary. Second, there is nothing *quite* like the directness of the recruitment initiative and the immediate, unhesitating following response (criterion: distinctiveness). Even Droge states, "The distinguishing feature of these narratives ... is that each is marked by the initiative of Jesus and the demand for an immediate response" (Droge 1983:245). Third, such recruitment coheres with the sort of "radical" picture painted in much current Jesus research (criterion: coherence). It is consistent with elements of itinerancy and break with traditional ties of family, home, and village so much discussed since Theissen's influential essay (1978). It is especially characteristic of Q and the *Gospel of Thomas*, lynch pins for some current "Third Quest" research. At the same time, it seems clear that Jesus had, at least for a time, a "local" headquarters at Capernaum, perhaps even a house (Mark 2:15). Certainly his activity centered around the Sea of Galilee where there was thriving fishing activity (Wuellner 1967:26-63; Kant 1994; Rousseau and Arav 1995; Hanson 1997).

What, then, might be a plausible tradition history? The "fishers of human beings" saying in Mark 1:17 and Luke 5:10 is a strong candidate for the beginning. Mark 1:17 states: καὶ εἶπεν αὐτοῖς ὁ Ἰησοῦς, Δεῦτε ὀπίσω μου, καὶ ποιήσω ὑμᾶς γενέσθαι ἁλιεῖς ἀνθρώπων. Luke 5:10 states: Μὴ φοβοῦ· ἀπὸ τοῦ νῦν ἀνθρώπους ἔσῃ ζωγρῶν. Already Dibelius, seconded by Bultmann, suggested that this odd saying was the core of the tradition (Dibelius 1934:111-12; Bultmann 1968:386), and that the "ideal scene" was a later expansion. As Hengel has demonstrated, Mark's "fishers of human beings" and Luke's "you will be catching human beings" represent translation variants of a Semitic original such as צַיָּדִים, "hunters," "fowlers," "fishers" (Hengel 1981: 76). The imagery is already captured by Jeremiah 16:16: "I am now sending for many fishermen [Egyptians?], says the LORD, and they shall catch them; and afterward I will send for many hunters [Babylonians?], and they shall hunt them from every mountain and every hill, and out of the clefts of the rocks." The metaphor is suggestive: Yahweh sends foreign powers to judge unfaithful Israelites; thus, the meaning is more like "ensnaring," or a "man hunt." However, when 1QH alludes to this same Jeremiah saying, it interprets: "And Thou hast set me in a place of exile among many fishers that stretch a net upon the face of the waters, and (among) hunters (sent) against the sons of perversity." (1QH 5:7-8), a reference to exile and trial. Wuellner writes:

> That his [the Teacher of Righteousness'] commission to fish men was essentially a constructive, positive, or soteriological function, and not exclusively judgmental, has been emphasized among others by G. Jeremias. As Priestly teacher, in the tradition of his Old Testament counterparts, the Qumran leader and the community that followed him (the "many fishermen" of 1QH 5:7f.) represented the true Israel, true Torah obedience, true covenant loyalty, and all the other symbols traditionally used of the eschatological community. This makes him and his followers seemingly indistinguishable from the Baptist and his followers, and from Jesus and his disciples. (Wuellner 1967:129)

Wuellner's theological language is heavy, but the point is clear: the image of fishing for human beings could take on a variety of positive meanings associated with a leader recruiting persons for a faction or movement dedicated to an alternative ideology. I ask with Hengel: given the Sea of Galilee as the context for Jesus' activity (Hanson 1997), what could the gospel saying mean without some such recruitment scene as that found in Mark 1:16-20 (Hengel 1981:80-83)?

Appendix 1: Social Movement Theory in Morris and Mueller

Sociological theory about social movements (SMs), social movement organizations (SMOs), or simply "new social movements" (NSMs), has gone through several phases (Zald 1992; see Morris and Mueller 1992 *passim*). Prior to the 1950s three types were common: (1) social psychological "mass society" explanations (LeBon), that is, people are attracted to irrational, extremist social movements when there is loss of traditional "community" beliefs and values in modern urban society (Durkheim's *anomie*; Tönnies' *Gemeinschaft/Gesellschaft*); (2) political geographical sociology explanations, that is, political power is related to region and social class; and (3) Weberian explanations, that is, the evolution of charismatic leader/follower movements into bureaucratic institutions.

In the wake of the many new social and political movements of the 1960s, the social psychological orientation gave way to "resource mobilization" (RM) which is concerned with the construction and maintenance of collective identity. It asks *where* resources for new collective movements are available, *how* the movements are organized and maintained, *how* the state supports or opposes them, and *what* are their outcomes (Mueller 1992:3-4). The dominant theoretical perspective became "rational choice theory," which is closely related to economic exchange theory. It says that rational, self-interested persons will carefully weigh the costs and benefits of becoming activists in SMs or SMOs; indeed, joiners who chose *not* to be activist, called "free riders," are a major preoccupation.

A very recent shift with respect to RM charges that "rational choice theory" is too individualistic, utilitarian, and instrumental, too indebted to natural science (Morris and Mueller 1992: *passim*). Ferree, for example, claims that rational choice theory is Western, white, male, bourgeois, and capitalist (Ferree 1992). Some RM theorists have returned to social psychology, but with a new slant, one that includes semiotics and the meaning-interpreting sciences. One hears again about grievances, values, collective identities, and ideologies, but the agenda is set by gendered, class, and racial inequalities, beliefs about injustice, goals and ideologies shaped in locally based communities, "collective action frames" (interpretative frameworks created by SMOs, rather than formal ideologies), "micromobilization," sources of *ressentiment* found in traditional rural societies, and conflict and violence (Mueller 1992:5-22). Thus, there is a return to "stress"/"deprivation" theory similar to Durkheim's *anomie*, but from a less psychological or psychiatric and more social scientific perspective.

Stark calls himself a rational choice theorist (Stark and Bainbridge 1987; Stark 1996). Yet, William Garrett says that Stark has "mellowed," especially in his study of early Christianity (Garrett 1990). Stark denies it (Stark 1990).

Appendix 2: Greil and Rudy's Case Studies

The following is based on ethnographic information supplied by those who have studied the various groups. The Table is an oversimplification; the classification is based on the majority at the time the study was made. There are variables between the initial phase of the recruit's entering a movement and later phases; the initial phase of the group and later phases; the core group and more peripheral members; and sometimes between emic and etic descriptions. I have omitted footnotes to some of these variables in the original Table (see Greil and Rudy 1984: 309).

Table 1: Variation among the Conversion Cases

1.1   Does the group in question advocate for its members a communal lifestyle?

Communal	Non-Communal
Christ Communal Organization	Church of the Sun
Hare Krishna	Crusade House
UFO Cult	Divine Light Mission
	Levites
	Nichiren Shoshu

1.2   Does membership in the group in question involve a radical discontinuity in social roles?

Radical Discontinuity	More Moderate Change
Christ communal Organization	Church of the Sun
Divine Light Mission	Crusade House
Hare Krishna	Levites
UFO Cult	Mormons
Unification Church	Nichiren Shoshu

1.3   Are members of the group regarded as "deviant" by the "general public"?

Stigmatized	Non-Stigmatized
Christ Communal Organization	Church of the Sun
Divine Light Mission	Crusade House
Hare Krishna	Levites
UVO Cult	Mormons
Unification Church	Nichiren Shoshu

1.4   Do the members of the group in question see themselves as having moved from one universe of discourse to another?

Conversion	Alternation
Church of the Sun	Christ Communal Organization
Divine Light Mission	Crusade House
Hare Krishna	Levites
Nichiren Shoshu	Mormons
Unification Church	UFO Cult

Table 2: Do the Cases Fit the Lofland-Stark Model? (see Greil and Rudy 1984: 313)

	Tensions	Previous Dispositions	Seekership	Turning Point	Affective Bonds	Neutralized Extra-Cult Attachments	Intensive Interaction
Church of the Sun	Yes	Yes	Yes	½	Yes	Yes	Yes
Christ Communal Organization	Yes	Yes	Yes	no evidence	Yes	Yes	Yes
Crusade House	½	½	No	½	Yes	No	Yes
Divine Light Mission	Yes	Yes	Yes	Yes	Yes	Yes	Yes
Unification Church	Yes	½	Yes	Yes	Yes	Yes	Yes
Hare Krishna	Yes	Yes	Yes	Yes	Yes	Yes	Yes
Levites	Yes	Yes	No	no evidence	Yes	No	Yes
Mormons	No	No	No	No	No	No	no evidence
Nichiren	Yes	No	No	Yes	Yes	No	Yes
Shoshu	Yes	No	No	Yes	Yes	No	Yes
UFO Cult	No	Yes	Yes	Yes	No	Yes	Yes
TOTALS	8.5	6.5	6	6	9	6	10

Appendix 3

Snow, Zurcher, and Ekland-Olson (1980): 791

Studies with Data Specifying Mode of Recruitment to Various Movements (Percentage)

| Investigator | Movement | N | Recruited through Social Networks | | | | Total % Recruited Outside Networks[b] |
			% by relatives	% by Friends, Acquaintances[a]	Tot. % Rec. thr. Ntwks.		
Sills (1957)	March of Dimes	234	[c]	90	90		10
Murata (1969)	Sokagakkai	100	16	76	92		9
Dator (1969)	Sokagakkai	120	65	35	100		[d]
White (1970)	Sokagakkai	[e]	24	86	96		4
Gerlach/Hine (1970)	Pentecostal	77[f]	47	32	79		21
Harrison (1974)	Catholic Pentecostal	169	[g]	59	59		[g]
Bibby/Binkerhoff	Evangelist. Protestant	132	45	29	74		26
Leahy (1975)	Anti-Abortion	31	26	65	91		9
Judah (1974)	Hari Krishna	63	0	3	3		97

a Includes all individuals recruited through networks other than familial or kinship (e.g., occupational, neighborhood).

b Includes all individuals recruited by strangers in the street or at mass meetings, or who sought out the movement after learning about it through the public media, or who joined on their own initiative.

c Percent recruited by relatives, if any, not reported. Of the 90% recruited through networks, 52% were recruited by friends, 20% through community networks, and 18% through organizational and occupational networks.

d Data derived from 200 testimonials of American members in a Sokagakkai newspaper. Of the 60% (120) indicating mode of recruitment, none was recruited by strangers or through the media. The reason for the large percentage recruited by relatives is that the majority of the individuals in the sample were American GI's stationed in Japan who were married to Japanese members.

e Sample size not given. Percent figures based on the average of three to five different surveys. Percent figure for friends and acquaintances based on the average of three surveys; percent figure for relatives and the last two columns based on the average of five surveys.

f Figures based on the compilation of Gerlach and Hine's (1970:79–80) reported findings regarding two separate Pentecostal churches.

g Percent recruited by relatives or strangers, if any, not reported. Therefore the actual percentage recruited through networks may have been greater than the 59% reported.

Appendix 4: Jesus Research

My approach to synoptic texts in this paper presupposes a synthetic research model that can be imagined as concentric circles.

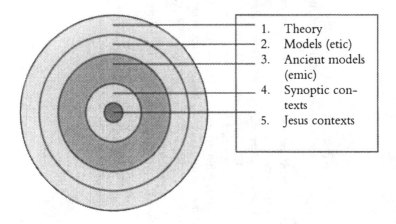

1. Theory
2. Models (etic)
3. Ancient models (emic)
4. Synoptic contexts
5. Jesus contexts

Figure 3: Research Model

In the outermost circle (1) lies consideration of social-scientific theory at both macro- and micro-social levels,[37] the building blocks for constructing modern models of structure and function ("etic" models), the second circle (2). In the middle circle (3) lie native ("emic") models of structure and function from antiquity. The fourth circle (4) narrows the focus to models in early Christianity, specifically, the synoptic gospels or their sources/traditions; finally, in the center (5) lies the "Jesus Group." The ultimate aim is to arrive at "a reasonable degree of contiguity between emic and etic perspectives" (Esler 1995: 6), thus developing a coherence between theoretically based models (1, 2) and ancient models and their actual social contexts (3, 4, 5). In analyzing the synoptic gospels it is possible to deal with "literary stratigraphy," and in dealing with the historical Jesus, it is necessary; thus, the last two concentric circles should be seen from a three-dimensional perspective:

[37] Macro-social: politics and economics in relation to macro-social distribution of power, privilege, and honor as it relates to social stratification. Micro-social: group formation; stage of group development; structure [formal and informal]; function [relation to macrosocial structures; interaction and process]; task and socio-emotive dimensions; roles [leaders and followers]; beliefs [ideology]; norms [rules]; values; boundaries; external and internal conflict; and deviance and social control. See Elliott 1993 ""Appendix"; Duling 1995a.

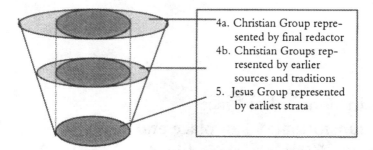

4a. Christian Group represented by final redactor
4b. Christian Groups rep-
   resented by earlier
   sources and traditions
5. Jesus Group represented
   by earliest strata

Figure 4: Literary Stratification

The methods used to arrive at level five include the historical critical methods of the "Second Quest" (Boring 1985; Duling 1990; Duling and Perrin 1994:1-31, 520-23), though two "Third Quest" modifications are required. The first is the "Hellenization" of Palestine (Hengel 1974) especially with reference to lower Galilee (Meyers 1985; Freyne 1992; Oakman 1994), resulting in the possibility of more varieties of pre-70 "Judaism" and "Christianity." This modification affects "criteria of authenticity" such as tendencies developing in the tradition, tradition modification, plausible tradition history, cultural environment, and language and style. The second is the continuing reevaluation of extra-canonical Christian sources, especially impact of the *Gospel of Thomas* on Jesus research. This modification affects multiple-source and multiple-form criteria. Both of these modifications will also affect—but in my view not invalidate—the criteria of distinctiveness and embarrassment.

7

Kingdom Takes Place:
Transformations of place and power
in the Kingdom of God in the Gospel of Luke

Halvor Moxnes, *University of Oslo, Norway*

"The Kingdom of God is about the transformation of social structure."
This is a typical statement from Bruce Malina: it is pointed, unambiguous, even to the point of oversimplification, and it locates Jesus, his
life and message within a cultural context that must be studied as a
social structure. This does not mean that there is only one way to do
this or only one method that can be utilized. On the contrary, Bruce
may vigorously suggest one approach one day, another one the next,
but both will be based on a lot of reading in other disciplines and
bring up unexpected perspectives. His energy and intellectual vitality is
amazing, his loyalty and generosity to friends are no less so, so it is no
wonder that he creates such enthusiasm and co-operation around him.
It is with deep gratitude for friendship and important intellectual
stimulation that I shall attempt to follow up on Bruce's suggestion that
"the Kingdom of God is about the transformation of social structure."
It is part of a section on Malina's discussion of whether Jesus can be
understood as a "charismatic leader" in Weberian terms (1996c:138).
Malina rejects this possibility, as created too much in the image of a
strong individual, whereas Malina suggests that we see Jesus as an expression of Jewish values. Among these were also values of politics and
power in the Mediterranean in the first century. Consequently, Malina
says, "the proclamation of the Kingdom of Heaven and of the rule of
God and talk of Sadducees, Herodians and Romans were all concreti-
zations of the selfsame focus, political power." Therefore, Malina says
that "any discussion of the Kingdom of God (or Heaven) presupposes
contemporary forms of political power as its opposing realities"
(1996:137).

To say that the Kingdom of God is about "the transformation of social structure" is a suggestion that makes one start questioning
commonly held views. However, I am reluctant to say that the Kingdom of God *is* about one particular thing, as a symbol it can have
many and different meanings. But I am willing to test this perspective
in a small study of Luke's Gospel. It can only be an attempt, without
going into detail, to sketch out *how* one could study the Kingdom of
God as "transformation of social structure." I suggest that recent sociological and geographical studies of "place" and "social relations" can
be of help to organize Luke's presentation of "given" social structures
as well as the structure of the Kingdom that he envisages.

The Gospel of Luke: Kingdom as "place" and "structure"

To choose the perspective "transformation of structure" for a study of
the Kingdom of God seems to go against the grain of most studies.
The Kingdom of God in the message of Jesus has most often been
discussed in terms of time and *eschatology:* is it present or future? Traditionally, positions have been divided into "consistent" or "future
eschatology", and "realized eschatology", as well as a position that is a
combination of the two. The most recent discussion within the historical Jesus debate has been whether his message was eschatological or
non-eschatological (Chilton). As a consequence, studies of the meaning of "kingdom" has focused on the "when" question, and almost
exclusively seen *basileia* within the context of *time*. One result has been
constructions based on understandings of "time" in modern cultures
that are oriented towards the future and towards change. These presuppositions have been questioned by Bruce Malina (1996c:179-204)
who argues that this modern concept of "time was not in the same
way present in ancient, Mediterranean societies.

In Luke in particular the discussion of *basileia* was for a generation
dominated by H. Conzelmann's landmark study *Die Mitte der Zeit*
(1954) and his thesis that Luke's gospel was characterized by a delay of
parousia expectations. Taking Luke 16:16 as his starting point he divided the Gospel into three time-periods: before John the Baptist, after
him the time of Jesus, and finally the time of the church. This division
and the hypothesis about Luke's de-eschatologisation of Jesus message
have been questioned but not the focus on time itself.

There have not been many longer studies of the Kingdom of God
in Luke. Apart from a number of articles (recently by Weiser,
O'Toole, see 148 for literature until 1987) the first major study is the

recent dissertation by Alexander Prieur, *Die Verkündigung der Got-
tesherrshaft.* Prieur studies both Luke's Gospel and Acts. He is primarily
interested in the special Lukan usage of *basileia*, and his focus is on
passages that combine *verba dicendi* (especially *euangelizesthai)* with
basileia tou theou. The result is a strictly redaction-critical study of Luke
in which the larger compositional structures are neglected as well as
the social context of Luke and his audience. An interest in the social
and political context is strikingly lacking in many other contributions,
for instance in a collection of essays titled *The Kingdom of God in 20*[th]
Century Interpretation (Willis). This prompted Amos Wilder to urge his
colleagues in the foreword to that collection not to forget the "political dimensions" in the Gospels. Wilder explicates: "These had to do
not only with God's sovereignty but with power-status, social roles,
and liberation, at least in an underground way, vis-à-vis the structural
authorities of the time, whether in Palestine or in the provinces" (ix).
It is some of these dimensions that I shall attempt to trace.

Structure and Geography

When Malina says that the Kingdom of God is about transformation of
"social structure", he speaks of a structure that ruled a geographic area,
Palestine, within the Roman Empire. Thus, "the Kingdom of God" is
about a different structure, a different organization of relations that are
in some ways related to this area. Joel B. Green has a similar perspective in *The Theology of The Gospel of Luke,* although he does not use
the term "Kingdom" but speaks rather about "world". Green distinguishes between three different meanings of "world". The first is the
world that Luke assumes, i.e. the world of Jesus in Palestine. This is a
broader picture than the world as Luke portrays it. Finally, there is the
world as Luke wants it to be. This, Green says, is that which "represents and challenges the world of 1st century Mediterranean." It is
obvious that "world" here does not just refer to a physical space, it
bears the connotation of a geographic and social space that is organised
and structured in a certain way. Only thus can it present a challenge.

Whether we speak of "kingdom" (the emic term which was used
by Luke) or of "world" (the etic term employed by modern authors)
these expressions are clearly cultural representations of geographic
space, a space that has a certain structure. This has often been neglected by social science studies that have focused on social structures
and neglected "place". However, this perspective has now become
increasingly important in a broad range of disciplines, e.g., sociology,

cultural geography, social anthropology and cultural studies (e.g. Duncan and Ley). David Harvey's discussion of "place" in *The Condition of Postmodernity* represents such a combination of perspectives. One of Harvey's main concerns in the book is to investigate the relations between space and social relations. He says that "command over space is a fundamental and all pervasive source of social power in and over everyday life" (226).

Harvey's "grid of spatial practices" is a detailed and complicated construction, but it gives a good grasp of the many aspects of social practice and the ways in which they are related to space. Inspired by Henri Lefebvre he speaks of three dimensions that form the vertical side of the grid. The first dimension is represented by "material spatial practice" (experiences), they refer to physical and material flows in and across space to assure production and social reproduction. The second dimension moves from the concrete experience to the way in which it is perceived and understood: "Representation of space (perception) encompass all the signs and significations, codes and knowledge, that allow such material practices to be talked about and understood...." Finally, the third dimension is represented by an alternative vision: "Spaces of representation (imagination) are mental inventions (codes, signs, 'spatial discourses,' utopian plans, imaginary landscapes, and even material constructs such as symbolic spaces, particular built environments, paintings, museums and the like) that imagine new meanings or possibilities for spatial practices" (218-19).

The third dimension that Harvey mentions, "spaces of representation" or "imagination" is especially important in that it goes beyond the strictly empirical discussion. Instead it indicates ways in which new meanings, e.g. in the form of utopian plans can be imagined. Lefebvre and Harvey see these three dimensions as standing in a dialectical relation to each other, and the third dimension, "spaces of representation" may act as a "challenge" to the others. Harvey says that : "The spaces of representation, therefore, have the potential not only to affect representation of space but also to act as a material productive force with respect to spatial practices" (219).

The complexity of Harvey's "grid" becomes visible when Harvey introduces, in a horizontal line of his grid, four aspects of spatial practice that correlate to the three dimensions above. For our purpose two of them are especially relevant, "appropriation and use of space" versus "domination and control of space". The first refers to activities on local or small group level not controlled from the outside. The category "appropriation and use of space" deals with "the way in which space is occupied by objects, ... activities, ... individuals, classes and other social groupings." The second term indicates an hierarchical power relation: "the domination of space reflects how individuals and powerful groups dominate the organization and production of space ..." (222).

It is the combination of these aspects with representation of space as a set of codes or as mental inventions that gives Harvey's grid such a comprehensiveness in an analysis of a specific context. This type of approach, combining space and social structure, has bearing for studies of the Kingdom of God in Biblical texts as well. This combination of perspectives may help overcome a division in studies of Kingdom between those who say that Kingdom "means" a space (e.g. a house) and those who say that it "means" God's reign. I think that it can best be interpreted as a combination of both, place and structure as an integrated whole. Moreover, in terms of approach, I see Harvey's ideas as running along parallel lines with those of Malina and Green. For Harvey the "representations of spaces" in the forms of utopia, codes, imaginary landscapes draw on the existing "spatial practices" and their ideological justifications, but represent a challenge, aiming at a reordering of these practices and their power relations. For Malina, the proclamation of the Kingdom of God must be understood in its relation to "contemporary relations of power," with a goal to affect "the transformation of social structure". Therefore, I find that Harvey's three "dimensions" represent three ways in which to look at Luke's material about "kingdom" within a Palestinian context: First, what are the relevant "material practices" which he describes? Second, what are the shared codes and knowledge about "kingdom" that make communication possible between Luke and his audience? And thirdly, how does Luke imagine new structures and new spatial practices when he speaks of the "Kingdom of God"?

Luke's "Kingdom of God" and his location in the Roman Empire

Luke's rendering of Jesus' proclamation of *basileia* must be seen against the context of the political institutions of his day and against known traditions about "kings" and "kingdoms". For the time of Jesus that meant the client "kingships" of his time in Palestine, with Herod and his sons as "princes" with kingly aspirations. As far as Luke is concerned, according to the most common view he lived within an Hellenistic context; most scholars suggest a city in the Eastern part of the Mediterranean (Esler 1987:27-30) maybe Ephesus or Antioch in

Syria. Consequently, the Roman empire with the emperor in Rome and the system of Roman administrators as well as local elite were known to him, as well as the history of Hellenistic kings and rulers.

But Luke also knew Jewish traditions of the kingdom of David, and the expectations of how God would act as "king" to liberate and to rule his people, Israel. These Jewish expectations were part and parcel of his stock of material that makes him in many ways come across as a writer who writes out from a Jewish tradition (Jervell 1972). This means that we will find a double perspective in Luke. He writes about Jesus in Palestine, i.e. within the structures of that society with its particular rule, and with heavy use of the Jewish religious tradition concerning righteous relations and social structures. On the other hand, he stands within a more Hellenised context, probably in a Greek city-state in Asia minor, and was influenced by the particular political and social situations in these cities, especially concerning rich and poor (Esler 1987:171-87).

These simple observations have consequences for our construction of "Kingdom of God" in Luke and for what we consider to be relevant material for such a construction. Often studies of the "kingdom of God" in Luke focuses only on passages that show the term *basileia tou theou*. The most recent study by Alexander Prieur list 11 (or 12) instances in which the term comes from Mark (Luke 4:43; 8:10; 9:2, 11, 27; 18:16, 17, 24, 25, 29; 21:31 (23:51)). In 10 instances the term occurs in passages shared with Matthew (Luke 6:20; 7:28; 10:9; 11:2, 20; 12:31; 13:18, 20, 29; 16:16). Finally, there are 13 instances that are unique to Luke (8:1; 9:60, 62; 10:11; 12:32; 13:28; 14:15; 17:20a,b, 21; 19:11; 22:16, 18). In addition there are passages where the term *basileia* does not occur, but that from the context clearly speak about "the Kingdom of God". Furthermore, the context must include the extra-textual evidence about "kingdom", "kings", "rule", etc. in the world that Luke describes, i.e. Palestine at the time of Jesus, and in the world that Luke inhabits, i.e. the Eastern Mediterranean within the Roman empire in the latter part of the first century. This means that Jewish ideology about God as King is relevant but so too the daily experience of being ruled, of living under an empire. Moreover, we should not forget more popular views and cosmologies about how the world was ruled, what adverse or positive powers were at work to effect people's lives.

Having laid out a theoretical approach, we shall now proceed to a brief attempt to present the material. First, the "spatial practice" relevant for "kingdom" as Luke narrates it, then the "representation of space", i.e. the commonly held views and ideologies that made communication possible, and finally, Luke's own "spaces of representation" as he presents the "Kingdom of God."

"Spatial Practice": Roman Empire and Herodian Kingdom

What are the "material spatial practices" recorded in Luke's gospel that are relevant for a study of the "meaning" of the "kingdom of God"? I would say that it includes all activities like production, exchange of resources and reproduction as well as restrictions or control from others concerning these activities. Most of these activities are related to life in specific *locations* and are described in spatial categories. The horizon for the gospel narratives that Luke shares with other authors is made up by household and village, with city and the world beyond situated at a distance. The social and economic activities of the household and between households are central to Luke's description of the "village scene" (Moxnes 1988:48-98). But Luke prepares his readers for a broader, "political" understanding of the Kingdom by the way in which he frames the Jesus story with kingdom and empire as the larger contexts of "house and village".

It is well known that Luke appears to be vague in his knowledge of the specifics of Palestinian geography. However, he is more clear about the structures of rule over this geographic area and makes frequent references to the political powers of Palestine and the Roman Empire at the time of Jesus. He places the story of Jesus within this political setting , so that "kingdom and power" becomes the context of Jesus proclamation of *basileia* in Luke. The story of the birth of John the Baptist is introduced with a reference to "the days of Herod, king of Judea" (1:5), and the birth of Jesus with references to the rulers of his time, the emperor Augustus and the governor of Syria, Quirinius (2:1-2). Likewise, the calling of John the Baptist is given a very lengthy introduction that places him on the political scene of the region (3:1-2). This political context is an important element in the Jesus narrative, it is taken for granted and sometimes it becomes visible.

That can happen in terms of brief Lukan references to the rule of Pontius Pilate (13:1) or Herod Antipas (13:31-33). In some instances Jesus is directly confronted with the Roman presence, for example in the confrontation over tribute to Caesar (20:20-26 par). This "material practice" of paying tribute had signal importance, represented by the way in which Jesus was portrayed as confronted with conflicting claims of loyalty, the power of Caesar versus "national interests". The accusers of Jesus bring the same issue up again in their accusation against him before Pilate (23:1-2). In Luke this topic is more pronounced than in the other synoptic gospels, precisely because the political context is introduced already in the infancy narrative. A similar element is introduced in the passion narrative itself, in the story of Jesus before Pilate and the following story, special to Luke, of Jesus before Herod. Pilate's question to Jesus is phrased in the same way in all the synoptic gospels: "are you the king of the Jews?" But Luke introduces his question with a rendering of the accusation from the Jewish leaders that makes explicit the political context of the issue: "We found this man perverting our nation and forbidding us to give tribute to Caesar, and saying that he himself is Christ a king" (23:2). Thus, the claim to be "king of the Jews" is in Luke's gospel not understood as a "local" issue, nor merely an issue that was concerned with internal Jewish questions about Davidic claims, it was set in direct confrontation with the power of the emperor himself. Finally, with the Herod scene, Luke deftly set up a scheme of competition and political alliances between the Roman governor Pilate and Herod Antipas, the tetrarch over Galilee, against which the mocking scene of Jesus as "king" is played out (23:6-12). Thus, there can be no doubt that Luke has situated Jesus "in place", within the context of the Roman empire and the vassal kingdom of Herod the Great and the tetrarchy of Herod Antipas.

"Representation of Space"

But what is Luke's understanding of these "places" and the "practices" that are played out within them? This question refers to Harvey's second category: what is the "representation of (this) space" in Luke, what are the codes and the (implicit) knowledge with which he communicates his view of this space and participates in a common discourse about it? We shall look at three ways in which "space" is ideologically presented: in terms of kingdom and rule, in terms of God's rule over the land and in terms of cosmology.

How does Luke speak of "kingdom"?

We find some clues about Luke's understanding of the "politics of place" in his additions to Synoptic material showing an awareness of the structures of power. We mentioned above the list of political rulers in Luke's introduction to John the Baptist (3:1-2): "In the fifteenth year of the reign of Tiberius Caesar, Pontius Pilate being governor of Judea, and Herod being tetrarch of Galilee, and his brother Philip tetrarch of the region of Ituraea and Trachonitis, and Lysanias tetrarch of Abilene, in the high priesthood of Annas and Caiaphas ..." This is more than just any list. It marks the relation between two social realms in terms of an hierarchical relation: Judea, Galilee and the other regions ruled by sons of Herod the Great are all under the dominion of Rome (Kato 1997:93). So are the high priests of the Jerusalem temple at the end of the list. This reading of the list is supported by another example, the temptation story where Luke makes a slight alteration in terminology. When the devil shows Jesus "all the kingdoms (*basileis*) of the world", Luke's term for "world" is not *kosmos* (Matt 4:8), but *oikoumene* (Luke 4:5). In Luke's usage *oikoumene* is a political term, it means not just "world" in a "geographical" sense, but carries the political meaning of "empire" and indicates a social and political order. Luke T. Johnson translates the phrase with "all the kingdoms in the empire"and suggests that "the vision is of an empire with suzerainty over kingdoms, which in turn controls cities, exactly Luke's perception of imperial arrangements" (74).

This is only implicitly present in Luke's text here, but it is explicitly brought out in his version of the parable of the talents (11:11-27). In Matthew this parable shows a domestic scene of responsibility and accountability in a hierarchical household. In Luke's version the setting of the parable is one of political power and of control over space. The scene depicts a local "nobleman" may be an allusion to Herod or one of his sons who went to a "far away country" to receive "kingdom" (*basileia*) and to return with it. This ambition to become "king" is controversial. We hear of "citizens" (*politai*) who send an embassy to protest, but in vain. The nobleman "receives" his kingdom, and returns to deal with his "servants" in his household. Those who are found faithful are entrusted with authority over "cities". But he also deals with his political enemies, who protested against his rule, by executing them (19:27).

This political setting shows Luke's awareness of the structures of power and domination over Mediterranean space: the absolute power sits in Rome, that is where local pretenders must go to "receive" a confirmation of their vassal power. That is also where citizens from around the Roman empire and dependent areas send their embassies to argue their cases. Within the areas granted to vassal princes, they rule their lands as an extended household: their trusted men or local noblemen are represented as their "servants" and are granted dominion of "cities", i.e. a town with its surrounding rural villages. Here we have in a narrative form a good description of political structure of domination in the Mediterranean, an "emic" description that would make sense among Luke's contemporaries and that provides clues to modern etic descriptions of benefactor (patron) and clients' forms of political rule.

"Benefactor" is not a modern category only; it was well known in the Eastern Mediterranean world of Luke's time (Danker). Luke uses this term in his rendering of Jesus' rebuke of the discussion among his disciples of "who is greatest?": "The kings of the Gentiles exercise lordship (kyrieuousin) over them; and those in authority over them are called benefactors (euergetai)" (22:25). Only Luke provides the technical term that the rulers were called "benefactors", euergetes. It is obvious that Luke here introduces the benefactor/client relationship as a well known type of relationship for the domination of space and material practices. In its form it was more an expression of Hellenistic city life than a Roman form (Johnson: 344). It expressed a form of *reciprocity* between ruler and people in which the flow of beneficence was made dependant upon loyalty from the recipients. However, the context indicates that Luke is sceptical to this common practice, it suggests that there is something about the claim to be called "benefactor" and the subsequent relationship between benefactor and recipient that is being criticized (Moxnes 1991:261).

Luke's version of the story of the centurion of Capernaum (7:1-10) is another example of his fitting a story into the framework of Hellenistic descriptions of social structures, in this case of benefactions and response on a local scene, between the centurion and the village elders (Moxnes 1991:252-53). This provides a new setting also for the centurion's description of his position within a hierarchy of dominance: "I am a man set under authority (exousia), with soldiers under me " (7:8). This represents an "understanding of exousia held by those higher on the social pyramid" (Johnson 1991:118).

Luke appears to be consistent in his "representation of space" concerning the setting of Jesus' life. His text is "coded" in such a way that an audience that was integrated into the politics of the Roman empire and the Hellenistic culture of his time would be able to pick up the cues. Even readers in Asia Minor without knowledge of the history and changing administrative arrangements of Palestine in the beginning of the century would recognize the system of domination and the hierarchy of power from Rome downwards. And the implications of being recognized as "benefactor" and the expectations that came with that were well known to all who lived in a Hellenistic city state. That Luke uses these "codes" does not necessarily imply that he always agrees with them, but they represent a shared knowledge that, in the words of Harvey "allow such material practices to be talked about and understood" (218).

Structures of ancient societies: Conceptual models

We must try to fit the information that Luke gives explicitly or implicitly into a conceptual model of the socio-political structure of the Roman empire. A interesting, but ultimately flawed attempt to do that is a recent study by Takashi Kato, *La Pensée Social de Luc-Actes*. She analyses the social thought of Luke-Acts with the help of sociology and anthropology looking at the social function of motifs in Luke-Acts. The main part of the book falls into three parts: one outlines the picture of the Jewish society in Luke-Acts, another that of Greco-Roman society, and a third the social perspective on the Christian group. In the first part of book she outlines different types of "ideal societies" that can be used in to interpret the social information in Luke-Acts. Kato criticizes a "Western" perspective that imports individualism in its interpretation of ancient texts. This criticism is rather similar to that Bruce Malina has voiced in many instance (e.g. 1981:51-70; 1996:35-66) but from a different basis. She builds on Japanese sociology that emphasizes that the individual is always part of social relations, so that *relationism* becomes an alternative to *individualism*. Kato outlines various forms of "ideal social structures" exemplified by Japanese, Chinese, Indian and Western societies respectively. These outlines provide good examples of how differently societies can be organized, structurally and ideologically. However, her suggestion for an "ideal type" for Western societies, applicable to the Roman Empire as well, is unsatisfactory. Her "type" for classical antiquity appears to be modelled on the Athenian city state in the classical period: Society was divided into two levels. The inferior level was composed by *household groups* (*oikos*) with an hierarchical structure. The relational model is prevalent and obedience towards the head of the household is demanded from the group members. The superior level consists of the household heads who· make up the *city* (*polis*). This level is characterized by freedom and individualism. There are several problems with Kato's "ideal type" for Western societies applied to the world of the Roman empire. The term "individualism" is not qualified and thus gives wrong connotations about the role of the superiors in this period. Moreover, this "ideal type" consisting of hierarchical household and equal heads of households does not really fit the more complicated structure of the Roman Empire or Jewish society in Palestine in 1st century. For instance, it does not take into account the role of the emperor within the Roman Empire.

Thus, it seems more appropriate to divide society conceptually into *household* and kinship as the smaller unit and *politics* as the macro perspective. The following is a quick reference to a model that has informed many studies in history of Antiquity represented by many works of Moses Finley and in biblical studies by members of the Context group and others (see e.g. Neyrey ed. 1991). *Household* was the basic small group in peasant communities . It consisted of a group of people most often bound together by close kinship who lived together and worked together. The group performed various tasks: production and sharing of resources, reproduction through childbearing and -raising, transmission of resources to next generation. The household was the basic group for its members. It provided a place of belonging and also provided the basis for contact with the outside world, the local village and beyond. Households were linked to a larger kinship group, a source of support and also of belonging to a history with their ancestors, illustrated by genealogies.

Palestine in the Roman period can be understood as part of an "advanced agrarian society", or in terms of political structure, an "aristocratic empire" (Herzog 1994:53-73). The structure of domination, the type of hierarchies and patterns of relationships were very much the same whether the political rule was in the form of a governor of an imperial province, a client kingdom or a temple hegemony. There was a strong division between a small elite with a retainer class of "bureaucrats", and the large mass of villagers, peasants, with a group of "expendables", pure, impure and unclean at the very bottom.. Relationships, also what we would term "political" ones, e.g. between emperor and people, were understood in "personal" terms. The most prevalent such relationship in the Roman world was the patron-client relationship, between a powerful person and his clients, people who were dependant upon him but who also contributed towards his power by their loyalty (Malina 1996c:143-78; Saller 1982). The Greek form of this type of relationship was the benefactor-city relationship. Persons with high status and wealth contributed to the welfare of the city, and their beneficence was transformed into political power and status through public offices and honors.

Economy was not a separate sector of society, but part of the activities of politics and household (kinship) and structured by their concern for power and prestige. The economic and social relations can be explained in terms of redistribution, reciprocities, and patron (benefactor)

/client relationships. In political terms we might speak of the economy as based on distribution: there was a collection of resources to a center, followed by a redistribution, but often a use of the resources in the centre for the benefit of the small elite. In personal terms and on a local scale there was an economy of *reciprocities*. Reciprocity could take three forms: generalized reciprocity, i.e. giving without (immediate) expectation of a return, a balanced reciprocity, based on a secured return, and negative reciprocity, i.e. taking without giving anything in return.

Religion likewise did not make up a separate sector but was part of the activities of politics and household, e.g. so that "God" was part of a "political" vocabulary. That there was no separation between "religion" and "society" is accepted by most scholars. The main issue was not separation between "religion" and "state" but rather what gods should be honoured, as for instance in clashes between Jews (and later Christians) and Roman authorities over the emperor cult. For the Jews it was extremely important to hold onto the claim of Yahweh's supremacy. But there was also another side to religion, a side that has often been obscured and given less attention in scholarship, and that is magic and superstition. That may partly be because these activities have not been part of a literary canon in the same way as "official" religion and that they have been hidden from public view, more related to the individual and small group than to the "nation". Magic, superstition and the miraculous are above all associated with the well-being of life, for instance concerned with health, success in love, and the question of *power* over this life.

I have given this brief outline of a conceptual model here to provide a context for interpretation of Luke's "representation of space", first for his views of "kingdom" and "rule" in a political and social context. But its inclusive nature makes it useful also when we look at other representations of power in space.

God as king over Israel

I have suggested that the actual political rule in Palestine and the Roman empire forms the most important "extratext" to Luke's construction of "Kingdom of God", and that the political ideology of his day was part of his "intertext". Another part of that "intertext" to the "Kingdom of God" was made up of Jewish traditions about "reign" and "God's reign" in Israel (see Chilton). It becomes visible especially in Luke's extensive use of the Septuagint particularly in the way he prefaces his gospel with an introductory section (Luke 1-2) that appears as a continuation of biblical writing. We find here an ideology that puts emphasis on the exclusive relation between God and Israel, in which the *land* has an all-important place (Davies; Wilken 1992:1-45). The history of the people was a history of their relation to the land, of its conquest, and of exile from the land into foreign lands. The center of the land was the temple in Jerusalem, and eventually both the city and the land was called "holy". The importance of "the land" is so pervasive that in references to "Israel", "Jerusalem", the promise to Abraham, "house of Jacob", "Throne of David" we must always presuppose the relation to the land.

Luke begins with a message about Jesus reviving the Davidic Kingdom with a combination of references to space and to the people described in kinship terms: "God will give him the throne of his father David, and he will reign (*basilevsei*) over the house of Jacob for ever, and of his kingdom there will be no end" (1:32-33). This statement stands within a Jewish spatial tradition. The Gospel ends on a similar note about the disciples sitting on twelve thrones as judges of Israel (22:29), but now the statement is qualified by the context (see below) . Luke presents Jesus as coming into a socio-political situation of power and domination. Magnificat (1:46-55) speaks in the manner of the classical prophets about the way in which God acts against unjust structures of domination by the rich and powerful. One of the concepts of God is of one who brings about a reversal of roles and casts the powerful from their thrones (1:52). The horizon is in this first chapter limited to "Israel", "his people", "Abraham and his children's children", that is, it does not appear to go further than the Jewish people. However, the perspective is broadened in the birth narrative in Luke 2. The Davidic descent and the national expectations are emphasized and Jesus is spoken of as "the Lord's Messiah" (2:26). At the same time the perspective is broadened to include "all nations" and "the Gentiles" (2:31-32).

Luke clearly knows the "national" expectations about God's rule over "the land", and the way he brings them into his text indicates that they were present among at least some of his audience, at the same time as some explanation of its content was needed (for other sections of the audience?) as for instance in the redactional comment in 19:11. Clearly, here is a set of shared assumptions and "codes" that had to be taken into account in any discussion of the Kingdom. However, as we shall see, the way in which he brings them explicitly into his text in the main part of his gospel signifies a strong degree of modification of an idea of an exclusive rule of God over "Israel" in the land.

The Devil and "challenged space"

There is a third "inter-text" for the Kingdom of God that must be brought in, and that is the way in which illness and evil were conceptualised as *powers* over space, both physical, bodily space and cosmological space. In think we have underestimated the role that illness and the fear of illness played in the ancient world, both physically and in terms of its place in cosmology. One way to view illness was to see it as a *challenge* to one's life posed by somebody. It always had a source: it could be caused by magic, by somebody's envy ("evil eye", see Elliott 1991a), or one could talk of it in terms of larger cosmic powers. Illness played a large role in ordinary people's lives in 1st century Mediterranean. No wonder that "healing" was such an important issue in religions in Antiquity. We notice for instance the important cult places for Asclepius (Epidaurus, Pergamon) and the descriptions of holy and powerful men. Magic, medicine and miracle were closely connected.

That Luke belongs within this cultural context is born out by studies by Susan Garrett and John J. Pilch. Pilch has studied the meaning of sickness and healing in Luke-Acts. He found that Luke shares a common world view in the "common, popular sector" (as opposed to the professional sector) in which influences of spirits and demons were important as sources of illness. The view that illness could be caused by spirits and demons was shared by all Gospels, but it is particularly prominent in Luke. Garrett has studied the place of magic and the demonic in Luke's writings and has found that the remarks about Satan are of great significance. Even if they are few, they are very important for Luke's plot. Jesus and Satan stand over one another in a fight for authority. Moreover, this image of the Devil as a cosmic challenge to God's rule is not new or unique to Luke or the other Gospels. Behind the references to the Devil in Luke's Gospel and Acts Garrett suggests that there is an apocalyptic story of the conflict between God and Satan. Various aspects of the story can be found in Jewish or Jewish-Christian documents from about the same period, ca. 100 BCE to 100 CE, for instance in the Book of Revelation or the Martyrdom of Isaiah (Garrett 1989:58-60).

We might therefore say that the plight of people in ancient Mediterranean and their suffering under illnesses formed a social and cultural context for Luke. And there was a commonly shared view of demons as sources of evil as well as of the power of healers. Furthermore, Luke knew Jewish traditions of cosmological conflicts between God and Satan.

Conclusion

What is the function of these "representation of spaces" in terms of political power, God's rule over the land, a cosmology and anthropology with devils and demons? Henri Lefebvre (1991:32-33) argues that "representation of space" is the ideological underpinning of the power behind the existing spatial practice and represents this practice as "the order of things", as the "natural". His is one of the major explanations of the ways in which ideology works. Thus these "representations" serve to maintain social relations in a state of coexistence and with cohesion. In this view, Luke's vignettes that introduced the political context for the lives of John the Baptist and Jesus serve to present the Roman domination as a "given" order, as "natural". Luke also presents the position that the rule of God was inextricably linked to the "land" as a "given" position, that is, from a Jewish point of view. The difficulty, of course, is that Luke's text combines elements of "representation of spaces", that is, commonly shared codes and knowledge, and "spaces of representation", an alternative structure and order of space that interact with and challenge the first one. It is to this activity of Luke we shall now turn and ask: how does he present the Kingdom of God?

Kingdom as "Spaces of Representation"

I suggest that Luke's narratives about the Kingdom of God be understood as "spaces of representation", i.e. parables, sayings, visions, acts etc. that present a different way to structure "material practices". Lefebvre places these "spaces of representation" (in his terminology "representational spaces") in a different social location. They are "linked to the clandestine or underground side of social life" (1991:33) The social location of Luke has been much discussed (see Robbins 1991a). With the education that he most likely had, he did not himself belong to "the underground side of social life", but maybe to city non-elite with some means and some social standing. However, he may have chosen to view the world from the view point of the peasants and the poor (Moxnes 1988:162-70). Moreover, there is no question that the Christian groups represented some sort of "clandestine" movement within the Roman empire and thus were outside the positions of power. One of Luke's goals may have been to integrate Christians in the public space of the city milieu of the Roman empire (Moxnes 1995). This may have limited the areas of conflict with the ideology found in the "representation of spaces." His confrontations with this ideology may have been selective, so we must pay attention to *what are the spaces* and *what are the types of social interaction* that Luke brings up in his picture of the Kingdom of God.

Kingdom as liberated space and new boundaries: Luke 4:16–43

Luke 4:16-30 is commonly regarded as the thematic introduction to Luke's gospel. It represents a programmatic speech of Jesus for his ministry and takes the place of the introduction in Matthew or Mark of Jesus' proclamation of the Kingdom of God (Mark 1:15; Matt 4:17). There are many studies of this passage (see Sanders), so I need not present here a substantial interpretation of the text but only point to what seems significant from the point of view of the spatial representation of Kingdom. The first direct reference to *basileia tou theou* in Luke is in 4:43, but it refers back to Luke's version of Jesus first proclamation of the kingdom: his speech in 4:16-18. The passage from Second Isaiah that Jesus reads in the Synagogue in Nazareth represents in Luke's rewriting a "space of representation", a vision of a liberated space that challenges the socio-political structure of society. However, this "space of representation" is contrasted with the space in which Jesus makes this speech: Nazareth, Jesus' "hometown" (4:16, 23, 24) and the "representation of space" in terms of "keeping one's place" that is reflected in the exchange with his fellow villagers.

This speech is programmatic for Luke's presentation of Jesus and of his proclamation of *basileia*. Luke combines "kingdom" (the terminology is *euangelizasthai ten basileian* 4:43; 8:1; 16:16; Acts 8:12) with "proclamation for the poor" (4:18; 7:22) and "release of the captives". Thus, much more directly than in Matt and Mark there is in Luke a definition of "kingdom" in terms of "for the poor". The extra-text is the socio-economic situation and structures of Palestine and of peasant population elsewhere in the Mediterranean. The inter-text of Jesus' reading from Second Isaiah opens up for a way to look at statements and narratives about the "poor" not as a matter of isolated instances but as part of a larger system of use of and control of the land. The reading from Isaiah is a conflation of Isa 61:1-2 and Isa 58:6. There are strong spatial allusions in this passage. It speaks of people who are confined to debt prison, secluded in a space that is controlled by others, and who suffer illness. With the concluding term: "to proclaim the acceptable year of the Lord", the Sabbath and the Jubilee traditions are brought in as Intertext. The basic component of the Jubilee tradition was a theology of the land based on the household and kinship struc-ture (Wright).The most important text was Lev 25 that gave the provisions for the Jubilee and the rules for the releasing of debts. The main purpose was to keep the equal distribution of possessions and land among the Israelites and to preserve the land for the use of the household. The justification for these provisions was that God was the owner of all land (Lev 25:23). Thus, Leviticus 25 reflects a perspective upon the household and the clan as the central and constituent groups of people. Their right to the land was the central concern. This legis-lation was therefore a protection against exploitation by external or internal forces that could gain control over the land and resources that were meant for the local household or clan.

The underlying mentality was the idea of "*limited good*": if some are poor or thrown into (debt) prison, it is because somebody has ex-ploited them, haz taken away from them what was rightly theirs. But "poor" was not just an economic category, as Malina has pointed out (1981:84-85). In an honour-shame society, "poor" indicates those who cannot maintain their *status*. And they are often listed together with other groups that explain the import of poor: in Luke 4:16-18, they are "the captives," "the blind", "the oppressed". Elsewhere in Luke they are "the hungry", "the mournful", "the persecuted" (6:20) or "blind", "lame", "leper", "deaf", "dead" (7:22). Such status based on *ascription* determined status in the community, For instance, this would exclude persons from priestly status or even from membership in the community (Green 1997:76-84).

The use of Isaiah 61:1-2 in the Cambrian community is instructive for this point (Sanders). The Cambrian community applied the passage about the year of the lord to themselves, they were the "liberated" community living at the end of time. However, their own under-standing of themselves as recipients of the "favourable year of the Lord" was contrasted with those outside the boundaries of the com-munity, who experienced "the vengeance of the Lord". Thus, the message of Isaiah 61 was used as a *boundary mechanism* to divide into ingroup and outgroup. The omission of "the day of vengeance of our God" in the quotation for Isaiah 61:2 therefore is highly significant in that it breaks with such divisions.

This vision of a "new" order or a "return" of an old, "ideal" order for social relations within the land is contrasted with Jesus' conflict with his fellow villagers in the form of a challenge-riposte exchange over honors as Richard L. Rohrbaugh has recently pointed out. Luke emphasizes that this is a conflict with Jesus' *home-place,* where he was brought up. And it is a confrontation with the "representation of place", i.e. the implicit codes of homeplace and village that starts the exchange: "Is not this Joseph's son?" (4:22). This question pointed to Jesus' "social place", as it was known to everybody in the village, and implied a village boundary mechanism that demanded that one should "keep to one's place". The challenge in the question was that Jesus had gone beyond "his place" in extravagant honour claims. The response pushes the boundaries even further to the point of breaking them. When Jesus gives examples of God's help to persons in need, persons who would illustrate the distress from the Isaiah quotation, he picks non-Jews from outside the boundaries of Israel (4:25-27).

Thus the Nazareth scene draws up a conflict not only with forces of economic and social oppression but also with the maintenance of the boundaries of the village and of the villagers' concept of Israel. Moreover, the rest of this section shows Jesus healing the ill and exorcising demons (4:31-42) before this first presentation of him is summed up by his purpose to "proclaim the good news of the Kingdom of God to the other towns also" (4:43). Thus, the kingdom is associated with a special set of activities in space (release, liberation, healing) which are related to special groups of people (poor, blind, captives, oppressed, possessed). And finally, as "spaces of representation" these visions of kingdom challenge traditional organizations of space and the perceived order, where everybody and everything has its "place".

The presentation of Jesus in Luke 4 has introduced the main conflict areas related to the organization of space: the question of domination of space, the question of boundaries, and the question of cosmology. Next we can try to discuss each of these in turn.

Spaces of representation: Table as reversed space

What are the structures associated with the Kingdom? In Harvey's grid of spatial practice two aspects referred to the power over space, one was "domination and control of space", the other "appropriation and use of space". "Domination" reflects how individuals or powerful groups dominate the organization of space, and thereby control also others in their use of space. "Appropriation" refers to the use of space by individuals or groups and may produce "territorially bounded forms of social solidarity: (Harvey 220). These categories provide a perspective to look at practice *in space,* for instance, practice concerning the production, collection and distribution of resources from the land but also the creation and maintenance of social space, as a source of communal and individual identity. Thus, we may see the structural similarities between activities that we would describe in (economic) categories of *production and exchange* and activities that we would describe in (social) categories as *honour and shame, hospitality*.

If we look at the "blessings and woes" in Luke 6:20-26 from a spatial perspective, they are built around the contrast between "domination of space" versus "appropriation of space". This passage is directed to the "disciples", so Luke is here probably addressing the situation of Christian groups (Neyrey 1995 against Roth). The first saying, addressed to the poor, ascribes to them "the kingdom of God" (6:20), and the following sayings bring out the characteristics of life in the kingdom in contrast to the structures of their present life. Now they experience hunger, they weep, they are hated and rejected. These terms describe loss of control over their "space": they do not have control over what they produce or access to food from the land. Not only do they lack the resources necessary for life, they are also shamed, ostracised, spoken of with scorn. This is typical of Luke's combination of elements of description. "Poverty" is almost always combined with other human situations of deprivation, illness, shame, impurity or a position of marginality. This is because "poverty" was not just an economic condition but a total situation. Thus, the descriptions that are added here bring together a combination of aspects that all express that the poor are not in control of their situation, they do not have power over their own "place", rather they are put in a place defined by others: a place of shame, scorn, derision.

Their situation is put in contrast to that of the "rich". These groups are not just two opposite groups but are rather interlocked in an adversarial relationship. Within a "limited good economy" "rich" and "poor" are linked in a relationship of exploited and exploiters, of negative reciprocity in which the rich take advantage of the poor. There is no absolute rejection of property in Luke but rather a critical attitude to the rich. Their riches may be badly got, for instance by extortion and pressure, by domination and control based on power of wealth and status. Thus, the place of status they receive in the form of honors is false. Therefore, the reversal of the fortunes of the poor do not make them "rich" but rather takes them out of a place in which they were under domination into a space they could appropriate and enjoy. Moreover, the control of the rich was substituted by structures that were the opposites of control, viz. reward (6:23). The reversal of the status of the rich, however, puts them in the position of the "poor" now they end up in a position of being under domination.

Within Greco-Roman societies there was a strong emphasis on hierarchies between rich and poor, master and slaves, superiors and inferiors, and subsequently of "keeping one's place". Read against an Hellenistic conception of society, this type of reversal in Luke 6:20-26 would express overturning of that type of hierarchies, of creating a re-ordering of place. In the context of Jewish mentality, the terminology of "rich" and "poor" had in some instances been manipulated , so that for instance "poor" could be used as an honorary term for "pious", and the "rich" were extrapolated as external enemies. Thus, "rich" and "poor" could be used as codes not just for social locations but for locations along the boundaries of "Jews" and "non-Jews". The closest intertext for Luke, however, is the use of "poor" in the LXX, where in many instances "poor" becomes a "type" of a person who is vulnerable, an object of human evil but also of divine salvation (Roth 1997:132-34). But even a "character type" belongs within the context of a social world and presuppositions of how the world works. Thus, the juxtaposition of the two groups in 6:20-26 point to "real" social positions as their field of reference.

What is the relation between the order of *physical space* and the order of *social space*? And how do "material practices" show themselves as indicators of "symbolic practice", i.e. related to definitions of social location? These are issues that arise from the narrative in Luke 14 (Moxnes 1988:127-38). The scene of Jesus at a meal in the house of a rich Pharisee starts with a healing story (14:1-6) followed by Jesus' parable directed at the guests (14:7-11) and his advice to his host (14:12-14). Finally follows Jesus' parable of the great banquet (14:16-24). A comment (unique for Luke) in 14:15 introduces this as a discourse dealing with "kingdom": "when one of those who sat at table with him heard this, he said to him: 'Blessed is he who shall eat bread in the kingdom of God.'" In this perspective the whole sequence might be read as a description of the Kingdom. Luke applies the well known image of "meal" of the kingdom, but whereas the meal often is just a code word, here Luke turns the story into a discussion of the meal itself. It takes the form of a *re-ordering of space* around the *dining table*. It is well known that Luke puts great emphasis upon the importance of meals, and meal scenes are prominent settings for discussions (Neyrey 1991b). But in several instances they are more than "settings". For example, in this instance the table itself and the ordering of guests has an independent importance. Since the host is identified as a "ruler", he obviously belonged to the prominent members of the village or town with other "rich neighbours" present (14:12). From Jesus' comments we gather that the guests come from this group of friends, brothers, kinsmen and neighbours and that the hospitality that takes place is characterized as one where the guests compete for "the places of honors" (14:7). Both the host and the guests are criticized, and it is this criticism that prompts the macarism of those who will eat in the kingdom. Consequently, the behaviour that is criticized by Jesus represent an anti-type to that expected in the kingdom.

We can identify the ideology behind this behaviour. Luke displays his knowledge of his cultural context by phrasing the criticism by Jesus in the terminology of *reciprocity* as it was used in an Hellenistic context: "When you give a dinner ... do not invite your friends etc., lest they also invite you in return and you be repaid (*antapodoma*)" (14:12). The relationship between host and guests is structured according to *balanced reciprocity*. Luke views this negatively, he shows in the description of the behaviour of the guests that it creates distance and competition for honors, that is, for a superior location in the hierarchy of place (14:7). Moreover, it establishes a *closed group* in that those who cannot participate in this form of exchange are excluded from this *space* altogether. Thus, the table symbolizes the social structure of the society that Luke addresses as well as the social interaction in terms of an exchange that is "economic". Although the persons involved are friends and brothers and kinsfolk, their relationship is based on a quick return, something that is typical of more distant relations.

The alternative posed by Jesus takes the form of a different *structure of relations*: "But when you give a feast, invite the poor, the maimed, the lame, the blind, and you will be blessed, because they cannot repay you. You will be repaid at the resurrection of the just" (14:13-14). The ideal is *generalized reciprocity*, an invitation that does not expect a return.. This is not quite true, since the word of Jesus speaks of being repaid at the resurrection of the dead, i.e. by God. However, the main aspect is that the expectation of return is taken away from the relationship itself. This implied a break with the patron-client or benefactor-recipient structure that always expected a return in one form or the other. Instead there is the pattern from the close group, the household or family, that practised generalized reciprocity without expectations of a quick return. In this way the impure outsiders were included on the basis of a type of relations that was otherwise an attribute of the close group. Likewise, there was an end to competition for honour—when it was recognized that honour was *attributed by*

God, not something that could be *claimed* for oneself and used to secure a position vis-a-vis others.

"Table" is a "space of representation" as an utopian organisation of
space. Luke describes the situation that he criticizes as one of domination of space, the alternative is one of use of space without
domination. With the discussion of "table etiquette" Luke has effectively broached a number of subjects concerning social order and social
relations. A table at meals is a well organized space, and by means of
this narrative Luke has addressed the hierarchical ordering of social
place, the economic structures of relations, that partly create competition for the highest place among the insiders and partly exclude some
from the field altogether. The "table" thus functions as a microcosmos
of a society, and Luke argues for a reorganization in terms of *boundaries*
(who are inside and who are outside) of *hierarchies* and of *power* of
structuring practices in space.

"Table" and "meals" as utopian organization of space are part of a
longstanding tradition about the "heavenly banquet". It is Luke's emphasis on the socio-economic organization of this banquet that makes
it so special, to the point that the practices he denounces are given
cosmological importance. That is illustrated by Luke 16, with two
parables placed on either side of the famous statement about the
preaching of the kingdom of God (16:16) which was the basis for
Conzelmann's theory of time in Luke. In the parable of the rich man
and Lazarus (16:19-30) the spatial elements signal social and economic
divisions and hierarchy: the rich man is inside his house feasting with
his rich friends, the poor man lies outside at the gate of the house. The
reversal of their position which brings to mind Luke 6:20-26 is also
expressed in spatial terms: the poor man ends up in the bosom of
Abraham, a version of the traditional theme of the banquet in the
Kingdom of God with the patriarchs (13:28-30), whereas the rich man
is placed in Hades.

The much debated parable of "the dishonest steward" (16:1-9) is
also about hierarchies. Its setting is spatial practices concerned with the
land with the steward as middleman between the absentee landlord
and the peasants. The steward is commended because he used "the
unrighteous Mammon" shrewdly. I take that to mean against the
structure and purpose of "Mammon". For Mammon is contrasted with
"true riches" (16:11) and takes its meaning from the illustrations of the
behaviour of the rich in Luke. Ultimately the conflict takes on cosmological dimensions. "Money" is not neutral, it is "Mammon" and is
contrasted with God in a statement that sums up Luke's construction

of two economic systems: "You cannot serve God and Mammon" (16:13). Thus "Mammon" receives a symbolic and cosmological dimension that appears to run parallel to that of the Devil: as a force behind the structures of domination and exploitation of human space.

Spaces of Representation: Kingdom as "new" household

We saw that Luke could use "table" and the exchange associated with meals as a symbol for two opposing structures of social and economic exchange and power hierarchies. Not explicitly directed against Roman rule, it was clearly directed against the power of the elites over society and thus not just against individuals. Luke sets up a similar form of contrast of two systems of relations and power in his presentation of two significant institutions: "temple" and "house, household". John H. Elliott has found that they are more important in Luke-Acts than in any other New Testament writing. In terms of structural arrangements and themes, Elliott argues that "temple and household constitute key elements in Luke's Gospel of the reign of God in human history" (Elliott 1991:212). The localization of events to one or the other of these institutions has structural importance. The Gospel begins and ends with stories located in the temple. In the first part of Acts the location shifts back and forth between temple and household, whereas in the latter part the emphasis is upon the house. This shift in localization implies a shift in activities, in groups and in their allegiances, attitudes and values as well.

Each institution is associated with specific structures. The temple has an ambiguous character in Luke. In the first part of the Gospel, the temple appears as a positive symbol of Jewish national identity, as the central place of God's presence. However, criticism mounts as Luke continues his story: the temple, the temple personnel and other leaders associated with the temple system come under attack. The purity system upheld by the temple works to keep people under control, the leaders of the temple exploit people, so that the temple instead of functioning as a place of *redistribution* instead becomes a place of *exploitation*. Most significant the temple and temple leaders rejected and persecuted Jesus. Thus, in the Gospel the temple becomes a location that is is false, it pretends to be a place of God, but it is a place that persecutes Jesus and his followers. The ambiguous character of the temple becomes visible in Acts as well, the followers of Jesus loyally come to the temple, but they are rejected by the temple leaders.

Instead of the temple, the *house* and *household* becomes the significant place for of Jesus and his followers. Especially in Acts the household structure of the community becomes visible as an alternative to a society organized around the temple or the synagogue. But this transfer is prepared in Luke's Gospel. Elliott points out how much Jesus' parables are filled with examples from domestic life and how large blocks of his teaching in Luke are organized around domestic setting. But most importantly, household serves as an important symbol of the kingdom of God. Elliott points how this institution based on consanguinity "provides a model for a community of fictive kin united by the bonds of mercy, faith and filial obedience" (227). Moreover, the boundaries are expanded to include the marginalised and outcasts. And above all, in this household, God is depicted as a generous "father".

In this general picture I will emphasize the significance of the *shift* that Luke makes in the picture of "house" and "household" in light of Harvey's discussion of the importance of "spaces of representation" or "imagination". The temple served as a "code" or symbol for an oppressive structure and for the power relations held in place by that structure. But the alternative was not just the household as it existed. We notice a distinction between the "ideal" household and household practice that did not reflect that ideal. Luke's focus is upon the household as a social unit in the village and upon the social resources that are pooled in the household: sharing of work, food, other possessions, protection. This emphasis upon sharing of resources within the household is an expression of the *ideal* of the household with the expectations of a high degree of solidarity. This ideal household is not only contrasted with the temple but also with records of "spatial practice" within households, especially conflicts between siblings over household resources (12:13; 15:11-32).

What made it possible for Luke to turn "household" into a "space of representation", i.e. that gave "household" its power of "utopian plan", "imaginary landscape"? I find the emphasis Luke puts on the father figure in the household significant, especially his language about God as "father" of the household. This of course is found in all gospels, but it has an added emphasis in Luke. "Household" becomes a model structure from "top" down , with the father as an ideal figure as for instance in 15:11-32. In 11:2-13, Luke has combined Jesus' teaching about prayer, starting with the address "God our Father", followed by a petition for the advent of the Kingdom, and with the petition for daily bread followed up by two parables of the gift of bread, one with God like the "father". Also in the admonition not to worry, Luke has strengthened the identification of God as "father" who gives his Kingdom (12:32). That means that God is portrayed as "father" of the Kingdom, not as "king" (Müller). This juxtaposition of "father" and "kingdom" suggests that "kingdom" should be understood as "household", i.e. that the Kingdom should follow the ideal household structures.

But this "ideal" household was not identical with the "given" household. Place theory has also emphasized the pivotal importance of "house" as place, expressed in terms like "home-place", or in a phrase coined long before political correctness was a norm, but particularly well suited for Luke: "Father place is the beginning of place" (Smith). Place is a fundamental expression of *identity*. Therefore there is such emphasis on "birthplace" and "homeplace" in Luke, we notice the importance of Bethlehem (2:4-5) and of Nazareth (2:39, 51; 4:16, 23) a place that Jesus "outgrows". But the house of Jesus' parents, Mary and Joseph, is inferior as "father place" for Jesus compared to "my father's house" (2:49). This childhood story about Jesus that contrasts two "house" spaces, prepares the reader for a similar contrast between "leaving home" and "going (home) to my father" (cf. Luke 15:13, 18). It is the "Father" who actually creates a space called "home", characterized by the "ideal behaviour" of the father towards his sons.

The contrast between households as "imaginations, spaces of representation" and actual households is emphasized by the exhortation to *leave* households *"for the sake of the kingdom"* (9:60, 62: 18:29) a terminology that is uniquely Lukan. A conversion experience is necessary in order to become part of the "new" house. No wonder that it is children who are closest to the Kingdom (18:16-17). Does Luke think in terms similar to John 3: 1-8, that it is through a new birth that one becomes the children of God? That would make the demand to a husband to leave his "wife" to follow Jesus intelligible (18:29). Luke is the only Gospel writer who makes asceticism "in this life" a demand with the justification that it is "for the Kingdom's sake" (18:29; 20:34-36, see Seim 1994:213-29). Without marriage and sexual relations there can be no children born to a house, thus, the household as a socially given place for identity and social relations will come to an end. However, the implication must be that the household of God does not depend upon procreation. Members are "born" into it as a place of identity and as a community of sharing by "following Jesus".

Thus, it is in many ways a "new" household that Luke presents as his vision, as an "imagined space", a challenge not only to the temple but also to "politics" as a structuring of society by the social hierarchy and economic exchange of the elite. Moreover, it also represented a

challenge to the existing households. In terms of functions and responsibilities it built on the ideal of a household, but in terms of
identity it was a new structure.

Spaces of representation: opening up of "national" space

The question of Luke's view of the "land" and of God's relations to
Israel is a huge and much discussed issue that it is impossible to go
into, for two representative and diverging views see J. Jervell (1972,
1991) and S. G. Wilson . We can here only look at some passages in
which Luke explicitly refers to "national" expectations of the Kingdom of God.

In the main section of the gospel and in Acts we find several explicit
references to the "national" and spatial character of God's reign as part
of Luke's intertext. It is possible that Luke here refers to expectations
of "the Kingdom" as liberation from Roman supremacy over the land,
a widespread hope in the first century. However, it seems that Luke
actually distances himself from them. He provides a redactional comment in 19:11: "he proceeded to tell a parable, because he was near to
Jerusalem, and because they supposed that the kingdom of God was to
appear immediately". We notice that this expectation is attributed to
Jesus' listeners, so that Luke keeps a distance from this position.
"Kingdom of God" is here associated with Jerusalem, i.e. it is conceived of in geographical terms with Jerusalem, the temple city, as its
center. But the parable itself does nothing to support the idea of a
Kingdom of God based in Jerusalem as a unified Jewish state: Luke's
version of the parable of the talent presents a picture of a society that is
conflict with itself and under the dominion of Rome. Another statement that has a "nationalist" ring to it is found at the close of the
gospel. It is voiced by two disciples who encounter the risen Jesus on
their way to Emmaus and who spoke of their hopes in him that he
was "the one to redeem Israel" (24:21). Jesus' response to them might
be seen as a rebuke of the expectation about Messiah as a "national
redeemer", it focuses on the necessity of the *suffering* of the Messiah.
Finally, in the introduction to Acts, Luke tells that after his resurrection Jesus spoke to his disciples for forty days about "the Kingdom of
God" (1:3). But then Luke sets up almost as an ironic example of misunderstanding the disciples' question that interprets the "kingdom" in
"nationalist" terms: "will you at this time restore the kingdom to Israel?" (Acts 1:6). This question places Jesus within a set of national
expectations related to the land of Israel and to the people of Israel.
But Jesus' response shifts the focus towards the receiving of the Holy

Spirit and the subsequent mission not just to Jerusalem, Judea, and Samaria but to "the farthest corners of the world" (1:8).

It seems that Luke does reject a "political" expectation of a Kingdom for the people of Israel with its center in Jerusalem, that does not, however, mean that the spatial aspect disappears. There is a widening of perspective to the "world", but more importantly there is a new definition of what "Kingdom" means. The forms of rule and power structures found in this Kingdom are characterised by suffering and the Holy Spirit.

"Spaces of Representation": Cosmic space regained

It was part of the cosmology shared by Luke that there was a conflict between God and the devil, demons etc., and that people suffered from the attacks of these evil powers. Luke's proclamation of Jesus and the Kingdom of God had to confront this cosmology. This was a matter of control of space, both cosmic space and human space and the placing of magic within a larger cosmological context. Among the synoptic gospels, Mark is regularly interpreted as the one in which Jesus is described most in terms of a magician. But it is Luke who most clearly exposes a cosmology in which magic, healing and miracles become part of a conflict between Jesus and the devil over control of the world (Garrett). The temptation story (4:1-13) is an example of how conflict over power and rule over kingdoms is put within a wider cosmological framework. The spatial elements in this story are important. First, its setting is in the wilderness, a place which has been interpreted in different ways either as the place for God's acts with his people, or as a place for the temptations of the devil and for Israel's rejection of God. More importantly, the second temptation revolves around the control of the world. The devil shows Jesus "all the kingdoms of the world (*oikumene*)" and promises to give him the power (*exousia*) over them if Jesus will show him obeisance. In a statement unique to Luke, the Devil claims that he has been given the power over them (i.e. by God), and that he can give it to whomever he wishes (Lk 4:6). Thus, Luke represents the Devil as one who claims domination and control of "the kingdoms of the world". This claim is refuted throughout the gospel, starting with Jesus response that only God is to be worshipped as the one who has the power of the world (4:8).

This power over the world becomes visible in the close linkage between Kingdom of God and healing of illness and exorcisms in Luke's gospel. That is a prominent feature in the first presentation of

Jesus following directly after the temptation story, 4:31-42. Further-more, the technical term "proclaiming the kingdom" is in many instances combined with summary statements of healings and exor-cisms (8:1-2; 9:1-2, 11; 10:9). In his study of Luke-Acts, Pilch emphasizes the importance of Jesus healings as expressions of power, the only power that he has in his social world. He suggests that his exorcism can be identified as "political actions performed for the pur-pose of restoring correct order to society". Presupposing that ancient societies had only two types of institutions, kinship and politics, Pilch suggests that "the political dimensions of Jesus' healing activity would be self-evident to all witnesses". And "since Jesus has effective power against demons, he has the power to maintain order in society as it should be. By keeping demons in their place, Jesus maintains good order in society" (198). I want to qualify this evaluation and will try to show that Luke presents the matter as a conflict over what constitutes "good order."

It was Conzelmann's thesis that the "time of Jesus" was the time without the devil, after the temptation the devil left Jesus "until an opportune time" (4:13) which, according to Conzelmann, was the moment when "Satan entered into Judas Iscariot" at the time when the plot against Jesus was nearing its climax (22:1-3). In this way the Devil was kept away from Jesus during his ministry and also away from the *basileia* which was to appear later. But in this way one of the major elements of conflict in Luke's description of the Kingdom disappears. This is a conflict that is related to the *domination of space,* first intro-duced in the temptation story.

The central passage for this question is 11:14-26. Jesus is accused of driving out demons by "Beelzebul, the prince of demons". The accu-sation is one of *magic,* of working through the power of Beelzebul. This is actually an accusation that Jesus is upsetting the "world order", rather similar to the accusation directed against him by the villagers in Nazareth: Jesus is "out of place", he is a deviant. The accusations de-construct Jesus' exorcisms and attempt to show that they instead of containing the devil actually conceals his involvement in Jesus' activi-ties. In his response to this accusation Jesus situates the conflict in space and in spatial metaphors. He points to a characteristics of the *politics of space*: a kingdom (*basileia*) or a house (*oikos*) can have only one ruler, otherwise the result is divisions and eventually collapse (11:17-18). The same presupposition as in 4:5-6 is implied: evil powers want to control a space, their influence over people is envisaged as power ex-pressed in space. Consequently, if Beelzebul both sent demons and was the force behind the expulsion of them, his rule was divided and his kingdom could not stand. The implications are that also the Kingdom of God should be understood as related to "space": if the Kingdom of God has arrived it means that is God who controls space.

This spatial language about control and domination of space is continued in the following parables. The first (11:22-23) about a "strong man" who guards his palace and has control over his possessions. Then an even stronger man comes, and attacks him and takes away his armour, i.e., the signs of his control of his house, and plunder his goods. This is a parable of the fight between Satan and Jesus: when Jesus exorcises demons, he wrests people out from the domain of Satan. Thus, each exorcism is part of the fight between Jesus and Satan and consequently an expression of the "kingdom of God".

But it might not fit Luke's perspective to say that Jesus is maintaining "good order" in society by keeping the demons in their place. Luke suggests that exorcisms create conflict, he points out how Jesus is accused of breaking with the "good order" maintained by the authorities. But in return Jesus argues that the good order as perceived by the authorities actually oppresses people who suffer and thereby support the domination of Satan (13:10-17). And Jesus' power to heal and to exorcise is put in direct confrontation with Herod, the political ruler of Galilee (13:32).

In most instances "proclaiming the kingdom of God" and healing and exorcisms are joined without any further explanations, but in 11:14-26 (and 10:17-20) Luke presents an interpretation in terms of metaphors about *control over space*. The "space" that is fought over is not just human bodies in their spaces of village and wilderness, but cosmic space spanning heaven and earth (10:17-20). Illness and possession by demons were important aspects of people's life, and relief and healing were therefore significant events. Luke has given them a cosmic dimension in that he has integrated them into two "world orders": illness into Satan's attempted rule over the world, healing and exorcism into the Kingdom.

Spaces of representation: Summing up the Kingdom in Luke 22:14-38

Luke 4:16-43 served as an introduction to "the Kingdom" in Luke, Jesus' farewell speech in the passion narrative (22: 14-38) has a similar function in summing up the Gospel in this respect (see Neyrey 1985:5-48). In this passage all the threads that made up Luke's presentation of the Kingdom of God in terms of "space" are combined.

There are three specially Lukan references to "Kingdom (of God)", 22:16, 18, 30). The context is characterized by the return of *Satan* (22:1-3, 31). The setting is Jerusalem at Passover, a focal time for Jewish "nationalist" expectations. Jesus and his disciples gather in a guest room, the "upper room" of a house in the city. They form a *household group* for the Passover meal around a table. The meal forms the setting for Jesus' farewell discourse to his disciples. This discourse is a Lukan construction and it brings up crucial issues concerning legitimate power in the Kingdom of God, forms of authority and its relations to Israel.

Although Jerusalem and the Passover form the setting for Luke's narrative and thus serve as a frame for interpretation, the "spotlight" is on the table with Jesus and his disciples in a house setting. One of the functions of meals in Luke is to serve as a mechanism to establish and sustain a social group, to make up a household group of fictive kin (Moxnes 1986). The Passover meal has this special function with the disciples sharing this meal with Jesus. It is this fellowship with his disciples and Jesus' impending death that represent the preparation for the Kingdom of God and serve as a reinterpretation of the Passover tradition. There is a similarity between the present meal and the future meal in the Kingdom (22:15-18, 30).

It is at this point that the question of *table* and *hierarchy* returns. The "map" of a table was a sure replication of social structure, and Luke explicitly refers to this well known "social map" with his distinction between "master" and "servant" (17:7-10; 22:27). This type of "map" served as a "representation of space", i.e., codes and implicitly shared knowledge which made interpretation of a social situation possible. In Luke 22 this social map is taken from the political realm about kings who rule over their subjects and who claim the title of Benefactor. In Luke's "space of representation" these roles are challenged: rulers who claim to be benefactors bind people to themselves in servitude, but the disciples are urged to be masters who act as servants (22:26-27). The places at table are indicators of status, master and servant take positions that are spatially as well as hierarchically different. In Luke's alterative it is not so much a matter of *reversal*, of positions being overturned, as of a confusion of the role structures. Within Luke's social world political relations were expressed as "personal", the emperor was "father", and patron-client relations were expressed in terms of friendship. But if Jesus is among them "like one who serves", the system is radically challenged.

It is in this light we must read the next section of the farewell address, 22:20-30, which presents the leadership in the kingdom. Again Luke has expanded on a Q-saying of the promise that the disciples will sit on thrones and judge the twelve tribes of Israel (Matt 19:28) and transferred it to the farewell speech. Jerome H. Neyrey (1985:23-28) has pointed out how Luke has edited the saying for his purpose in this context. The saying in Matthew 19:28 has an almost triumphalist ring to it, and is clearly placed in the future, in "the new world". In Luke, the picture of the disciples in the farewell speech is less positive, their weaknesses are clearly shown. Nevertheless, they are not just promised, but actually now entrusted with the Kingdom, on the basis of their fidelity to Jesus in his trials. Thus, while Luke retains that they shall be rulers over the twelve tribes of Israel, this "national" concept is reinterpreted by the premise that the Kingdom shall have rulers who have followed Jesus in his trials. The space indicated by the "twelve tribes of Israel" is redefined into a path in which Jesus is followed (cf. Acts 1:21; 9:2).

The final conflict with Satan is also related to kingdom and power. In the passion narrative Satan has entered the space of Jerusalem. Luke is the only author to ascribe to Satan the betrayal by Judas (22:3), and also the temptation to Peter to deny Jesus (22:31). There is probably also a reference to the Devil in the expression "power of darkness" in 22:53. In light of the conflict with the Devil throughout Luke's gospel, Jesus' claim gets a special significance when he says to his disciples: "now I entrust to you the kingdom which my Father entrusted to me" (22:29). The Devil claimed that he was given the "kingdom", i.e. by God, and that he could give to anyone he wished (4:6). But Luke has shown that claim to be false, and now presents Jesus as the one who had received the Kingdom as "son" who therefore could legitimately give it away.

Holy space, Jerusalem, is contrasted with the household-group around Jesus; table places as indicators of hierarchies are contrasted with the head of the household performing the tasks of a servant. And the claim of the Devil for control over space is contrasted with the confident claim of Jesus to be in possession of "his father's" Kingdom. As darkness closes in on the group and Jesus' free movement in space will be curtailed and he will be executed at a place called the Skull, Luke's focus on "the Kingdom" in the farewell meal and speech is a dramatic and defiant production of a visionary space. Although spoken of with claims to *power*, it is a space that is ultimately defined through service and suffering.

Conclusion

Is the kingdom of God in Luke about transformation of social structure? Speaking to "an advanced agrarian society" Luke addressed the very structure of that society: the power relations at work in the economic exchange, the social hierarchies as well as the boundaries that were created. Likewise, Luke was concerned with health and illness, dangers that threatened people's lives, and that were interpreted within a cosmological space with the Devil as a powerful source. In consequence, the "envisaged space" of the Kingdom takes the form of new structures of exchange, a challenge to hierarchies and a liberation from the devil. Moreover, as Elliott has pointed out, the household becomes an important setting as well as symbol for the Kingdom. Ideal forms of household economy of use and appropriation of space in terms of sharing and giving provide models for the Kingdom, and an ideal father role becomes a role model for reign in the Kingdom, together with the servant role.

The setting in Luke's Gospel for the presentation of the Kingdom is more directly related to the power structures of the Roman Empire and client princedoms in Palestine than in the other gospels. However, the alternative vision comes more in the forms of a different structure of social and economic relations than in open attacks upon the source of power in the Roman empire. This observation may lead into a final question: what were the relations between the "spaces of representations" in Luke's vision of the "Kingdom of God" and the "representations of space" in the forms of the ideology of the reigning order? We recall that Lefebvre located the "spaces of representation" in the "clandestine or underground side of social life" (33). This points to the enormous difference in *power* between this location and the location of the reigning order. This makes Lefebvre's suggestion that the relations are "dialectical" less than helpful. Harvey (219) appears to be more realistic when he argues that the power of the imagined over the experienced is constrained. One effect of that may be that Luke withdrew from confrontation. In significant ways the Kingdom is removed from the political order. There is a challenge to social and political structures, but at the same time a removal from them when household is redefined as a group of fictive kin, or the "national space" of Israel is reinterpreted in light of the suffering of Jesus.

What makes Luke's position so difficult to evaluate is that "representations of space", especially the ideology behind the Roman rule and hierarchy, are so closely linked to his alternative "spaces of representation". But I do think that just this juxtaposition shows both the challenge involved in his presentation of the Kingdom of God as "visionary" space and the serious constraints upon him. These constraints were not just imposed by external powers upon his social location but also integrated within his construction of his world (Robbins 1991a:328-30). Thus, Luke's presentation of the Kingdom of God illustrates both the possibilities of producing new "spaces of representation" but also the severe limitations imposed upon such productions. It is a small comfort that this location of possibilities and constraints is shared with present day interpreters. But we, too, need to be reminded that our attempts at reconstructions of the Kingdom of God always takes place within the context and constraints of the present-day powers and structures.

Note: Earlier versions of this paper were given as lectures at the Aristotle University of Thessaloniki, 1996, and Aarhus University, 1997. It was finished in the summer of 1998 while I enjoyed the hospitality of the Department of Religion, Duke University.

8

Kingdom and Family in Conflict:
A Contribution to the Study of the Historical Jesus

Santiago Guijarro Oporto, *Universidad Pontificia de Salamanca*

The Synoptic gospels have preserved some sayings and pronounce-ments (Bultmannian apophthegms) in which Jesus asks his followers to neglect important family obligations (Luke 9:57-62 par. and 14:26 par.). In other cases, following Jesus means leaving home (Mark 1:16-20 par. and 10:28-30 par.), while fidelity to him provokes strong tensions among members of the same family (Mark 13:12 par. and Luke 12:51-53 par.).

These saying and pronouncements which reflect a conflict between the disciples and their families have not received the attention they deserve in the research of recent years (Barton 1994:220; Jacobson 1995:376). Doubtless the most comprehensive study is the monograph by S. Barton on Mark and Matthew (Barton 1994). In a brief article A. Jacobson has studied the sayings in Q, suggesting leads to follow in subsequent research (Jacobson 1995). P. Kristen has published (1995) a monograph in which he studies the relationships between discipleship and family in Mark and Q, and J. Neyrey an article (1995) which situ-ates the original macarisms of Q in the context of the disruption of the family to which the texts quoted above refer.

These publications and older ones which had addressed this subject in the context of a wider research (Schüssler Fiorenza 1989; Theissen 1979) have studied these passages at the level of the redaction of the gospels (Barton; Kristen), of Q (Jacobson; Kristen) or in the Jesus movement (Schüssler Fiorenza; Theissen), but not in the context of Jesus and his disciples, which is where most of them had their origin. The recent studies on the historical Jesus deal with these passages in a brief and incomplete way (Crossan 1991:299-302; Theissen and Mertz

1996: 202-203). The one study which tackles one of the quoted passages from the perspective of the historical Jesus continues to be the monograph of M. Hengel (1981b), in which however the problem of the relationships between discipleship and family ties is not central.

The purpose of this essay is to ascertain what can be attributed to the historical Jesus from these sayings and pronouncements and to situate them in the context of the Mediterranean culture of the first century in order to understand properly the meaning they had for the disciples of Jesus and their contemporaries.

The sayings of Jesus about breaking with family

The passages quoted above contain eleven small units which probably were transmitted independently in the oral tradition: five sayings (Q 12:52, 53; 14:26 and Mark 13:12) and six pronouncements (Q 9:57-58, 59-60, 61-62; Mark 1:16-18, 19-20 and 10:28-30). From this initial data base we have to discard one of the sayings and one pronouncement story, both of which can only be attributed to Jesus with great difficulty (Mark 13:12 and Q 9:61-62) and another pronouncement story which referred originally not to discipleship but to Jesus' own lifestyle (Q 9:57-58).

Mark 13:12

A comparison among the three synoptic versions of this saying reveals that Mark was the source for the other two. There are no traces of redactional activity in it and because of this it is commonly thought that we are dealing with an Israelite saying of an apocalyptic character in which the split between members of the family appears as one of the signs of the coming of the end (Mich 7:6; Isa 19:12; Zech 13:3: Jub 23:16; 1 En 100:1; 4QTest 15-17). Its insertion in Mark is somewhat artificial, given that it is formulated in the third person singular, while the second person plural is being used in the context (Kühschelm 1983:110-113). On the other hand, the description it gives of the trials of the disciples in the synagogues and the law courts corresponds better to the experience of the later followers of Jesus than to the experience of the disciples of the historical Jesus. It is probable that this saying reflects the situation in which the community of Mark was living (Van Iersel 1996:257-258).

Q 9:61-62

The pronouncement story of the man who asks permission of Jesus to say farewell to his family is only found in Luke. A comparison with the two preceding pronouncements (Q 9:57-58, 59-60) reveals that many expressions here are taken from those previous statements. In the pronouncement story itself the style and theology of Luke are very much present (Fleddermann 1992:549-552). J. Kloppenborg thinks however that this pronouncement story was in Q (1988:64). In any case, these data and the similarity between this episode and 1 Kings 19:20 lead us to think that Q 9:61-62 was composed among the first generation of Jesus group members on the basis of the preceding pronouncements and an agrarian proverb, according to the story line of 1 Kings 19:20 (Steinhauser 1989:155-158). This means that we cannot consider this episode as historical, nor the saying as coming from Jesus.

Q9:57-58

We also have to discard from our database the pronouncement story about the homelessness of the Son of man, although it is highly probable that the saying of this pronouncement story was uttered by Jesus. The pronouncement story comes from Q where it probably has a form close to that of Luke 9:57b-58, but this was not its oldest form. In Gos. Thom. 86 we find an almost identical saying, but without the narrative framework. Now, if we consider that a sixth of the logia of Gos. Thom. are pronouncements, it is not reasonable to think that its author has extracted the saying from the original pronouncement story; it is more reasonable to think that the pronouncement story was composed on the basis of the saying (Kloppenborg 1987:191). This saying probably comes from Jesus since it meets the criteria of dissimilarity, multiple attestation and being consistent with other sayings on his style of life (Vaage 1989:166-167), but its relationship with discipleship is indirect. Originally the saying spoke about the lifestyle of Jesus, although we may suppose that those who followed him for a long time adopted the same lifestyle.

Once we have discarded Mark 13:12; Q 9:57 and Q 9:61-62, we have to consider the rest of the sayings and pronouncements to find out which form they had before they were reworked in the process of oral transmission and redaction of the gospels and to see if they contain a pre-Easter tradition. Of them all, the pronouncement story on the burial of the father (Q 9:59-60) and the saying about hatred between family members (Q 14:26) are the ones we can attribute to Jesus with most probability.

Q 9:59-60

The pronouncement story about the burial of the father has a different formulation in Matthew and in Luke. In Mt 8:21-22 "one of his disciples" seeks Jesus' permission to go to bury his father and Jesus answers him with an enigmatic saying which clearly puts following him before this obligation. In Luke 9:59-60, an invitation from Jesus precedes this dialogue: "Jesus said to him: Follow me"; and at the end follows a motivation which justifies this renunciation because of the urgency of the mission: "Go and announce the Kingdom of God". Matthew has probably kept more closely to the form which the pronouncement story had in Q, adding only the identification of Jesus' questioner as "another of his disciples", which was not in Q (Hengel 1981b:14-15; Fleddermann 1992:547). Luke has changed the pronouncement story into a vocation story in view of the mission, thus making the demand of Jesus more reasonable.

This pronouncement story is related to the passage of the vocation of Elisha (1 Kings 19:20). The formal similarities are easy to spot, but the differences are much more evident. Elisha's request is very different from the one made by Jesus' anonymous interlocutor, since he only wishes to say farewell to his parents, while the other feels himself bound to perform the sacred duty to bury his father. The replies of Elijah and of Jesus are also quite different: while Elijah poses no serious objection to Elisha's request, Jesus proposes to the man who wants to bury his father that he should not carry out this filial obligation but rather follow him. In this sense, the pronouncement story of Q is much more radical than the story of 1 Kings 19. Very probably the first Jesus group members related both passages, underlining the strong contrasts that existed between them, and this contrast enabled them to understand the newness of the call of Jesus (Pesch 1969:11-12; Hengel 1981b:31-32).

There is no other extant independent witness to this pronouncement story that might help us to trace the history of its formation. It is difficult to believe that the saying contained in it had an existence independent of the narrative framework because without it one cannot understand the relationship between the invitation to follow Jesus and the words about the dead burying the dead. Further, it is quite improbable that the first Jesus group members had created the narrative framework because this would suppose a radicalization of the saying of Jesus (Sanders 1985:254), while what we observe in the Lukan redaction is rather a tendency to soften the radical edge of the words of

Jesus. Thus, the form which this pronouncement story could have had in the oral tradition is the following:

> One of them said to him:
> "Let me go and bury my father first."
> And Jesus replied to him:
> "Follow me and leave the dead to bury the dead."

The arguments for attributing this pronouncement story to the circle of the first followers of Jesus before Easter are very powerful. M. Hengel has shown that this is the saying of Jesus which contravenes most radically the norms of the law, of moral conduct and of standard religious practice (Hengel 1981b:17-30). It would have been difficult for the Jesus groups to invent a saying like this. It is too scandalous to attribute it to Jesus without foundation. On the other hand, the attitude which Jesus demands from one who wishes to follow him must have been so embarrassing for the first Jesus groups that it is conceivable that this pronouncement story was preserved because it reflects a historical event.

Q 14:26

In this case also the versions of Matthew and Luke are different. The verb "hate" used by Luke probably reflects the original wording of the saying. Perhaps Matthew introduced the expression "he who loves ... more than me" to stress the explicit reference to Jesus as the motivation for breaking with the family (Luz 1990:140). This Christological motivation would also explain the repetition of this same formula in Mt 10:37b and the triple repetition of the expression "is not worthy of me", which means that Luke has best preserved the final clause: "cannot be my disciple" (Stein 1989:109-192). Nevertheless, in the listing of family members the version of Matthew is preferable. Luke, perhaps with the intention of relativizing the rupture between parents and children, has added wife and brothers and sisters to the list of family members. Luke's final phrase: "and even his own life" is probably a duplicate of Luke 9:24 taken from Mark 8:34. The form of the saying in Q would therefore be the following: "Anyone who does not hate his father and his mother and his son and his daughter cannot be my disciple".

We find two parallels to this saying in the Gospel of Thomas (Gos. Thom. 55 and 101). The first of these goes as follows: "Jesus said: anyone who does not hate his father and his mother and who does [not] hate his brothers and his sisters and who does [not] take up his cross as I do, is not worthy of me". This saying consists of two parts which begin with the expression "he who does not hate...." The first coincides with the beginning of Luke's version. The second however has its own formulation (repetition of "he who does not hate") with an element from the Lukan version (brothers and sisters), plus the Matthean version of the saying about taking up the cross (Matt 10:38). These similarities with Luke and Matthew may suggest that Gos. Thom. 55 depends on both gospels (Fleddermann 1992:480). Nevertheless, we observe that between the two parts of the saying there exist notable differences. In the second we find elements of both synoptic versions and leaving brothers and sisters is mixed in with the necessity of taking on the cross. On the contrary, in the first part not only are there not these mixtures, but rather its formulation coincides with that of Q, with the only difference being that mention is made in Q of leaving sons and daughters, and this is not found in Gos. Thom. These observations allow us to venture the hypothesis that Gos. Thom. 55a contains the oldest form of this saying, while Gos. Thom. 55b is a later amplification dependent on the Synoptics.

Gos. Thom 101 affords us some confirmation of this hypothesis. It is an enigmatic logion, whose second part is not very well preserved. The first part, however, contains a saying almost identical to that of Gos. Thom. 55a, which might also witness to the form this saying had in the oral tradition. It runs thus: ["Jesus said:] He who does not hate his father and mother as I do will not be able to be my disciple; and he who does [not] love his father and his mother as I do will not be able to be my disciple because my mother has [borne] me but [my] true [mother] has given me life." This logion too has two parts: the first contains a double affirmation of antithetical character (hate-love); while the second adds a motive or explanation. In the first, the affirmation "he who does not love ..." is an antithetical development of the first, so that the logion could have been formed out of the saying: "He who does not hate his father and mother as I do will not be able to be my disciple", which coincides literally with Gos. Thom. 55a, with the exception of the expression "as I do" which must be attributed to the redactor, because it does not appear in any of the other parallels.

The difference between the saying which is the basis for these two logia from Gos. Thom. and that from Q is significant. The first was only directed at children because it only mentioned "hatred" towards parents. The one from Q however was directed as much to children as to parents. It is highly probable that Gos. Thom. has preserved the older form of the saying, and that Q represents the first stage of the tendency to widen the number of family members which we have clearly detected in Luke's version. The oldest form of the saying, therefore, would be the following:

> [Jesus said:]
> "He who does not hate father and mother cannot be my disciple."

There are very compelling reasons to hold, against R. Bultmann (1963:160-163), that this saying was spoken by Jesus. First, we are dealing with a saying without parallel in Israelite writings of the time. A statement like that of Q 9:59-60 involved an outrage against the family, the firmest pillar of Israelite society. It is very difficult to imagine that the first Jesus group members invented this saying and attributed it to Jesus. The very fact that Matthew and Luke have softened it in different ways suggest that this demand was embarrassing for them. The multiple and independent attestation (in Q and Gos. Thom.) is another argument in favor of its authenticity (Stein 1989:188-189). Finally, this saying is consistent with others which are recognized as authentic in which Jesus practices or proposes a highly counter cultural behavior (Vaage 1989:72).

The pronouncement story about the burial of the father and the saying about hatred towards family members, as we have reconstructed them, coincide in three features which are relevant to our study. First, they talk about the relativizing of family ties because of discipleship. Second, in them mention is made only of a split between parents and children. And third, the division is caused by the children, not the parents, because it is to the children that the words of Jesus are directed.

Now we have to consider the three pronouncements of Mark (Mark 1:16-18, 19-20; 10:28-30) and the two sayings of Q (Q 12:52. 53) to see whether in their original form these saying and pronouncements contained any of these three features.

Mark 1:16-20
Mark contains the oldest version of these two pronouncement stories. Matthew clearly depends on Mark despite the redactional changes he has introduced. Luke's redaction is much deeper because he has transferred the story to another place in his narrative, has completely suppressed the call of Andrew, James and John, and has inserted this call in the context of the miraculous drought of fishes which was originally an independent story (John 21:1-11). All these modifications are due to Luke's specific intention (Marshall 1978:199-201). It can be

said therefore that the three synoptic stories represent a single tradition, whose oldest version is that of Mark.

E. Best (1981:167-168) has identified in 1:16-20 the following phrases as dependent of the Markan redaction: "Passing by the Sea of Galilee he saw ... because they were fishermen ... and going on a little further ... at once". Most of them are found in the introductions of both pronouncements, frame them geographically and establish a time link between them. This means that in the tradition before Mark the two stories lacked the geographical framework which they now have, the explanation of Simon and Andrew's occupation, and the adverb *euthys* which underlines in Mark the immediate answer to Jesus call. Its form may have been the following:

> Simon and his brother Andrew were casting their nets in the sea. Jesus said to them: "Come follow me and I will make you fishers of men". And they, leaving the nets, followed him.
>
> James, the son of Zebedee, and his brother John were in the boat, preparing the nets. Jesus called them. And they, leaving their father Zebedee in the boat with the day laborers, went after him.

It is probable that the story of Elisha's call (1 Kgs 19:19-20a) has influenced these two stories in their final form, but there exist notable differences between them. First, the fact that two persons are called and not one; second, Jesus calls Simon and Andrew not only to follow him but also for a task: "I will make you fishers of men"; and third, the insistence on the quick answer of the disciples leaving their father (Pesch 1969:9-13). It is probable that these three elements, which have been introduced by squeezing the literary mold a little, come from the pre-Easter tradition.

The saying about the disciples as fishers of men very probably goes back to Jesus, because it contains an image that had never been used before to describe a positive mission (Wuellner 1978:88-107); and afterwards it was not used to refer to the task of Jesus group missionaries unlike what happened to the image of the shepherd. It is moreover an image linked to the historical context in which the activity of Jesus was carried out and to the previous occupation of his first disciples. Furthermore, the description of how to fish is perfectly in tune with fishing practices on the Sea of Galilee before the introduction of more modern techniques (Nun 1990:16-21, 23-27 and 28-36). On the other hand, the news about leaving the father, which does not fit too well in the literary pattern, is consistent with the other passages which speak about the relationship between family and discipleship in which leaving one's father or breaking family ties have an important place.

The apparent contradiction between these data and the version of Jesus' meeting with his first disciples in the gospel of John (John 1:35-51) can be solved by positing the first meeting of Jesus with some of his Galilean followers in the Baptist's circle in Judea. The fact would make the immediate reply of the disciples more likely (Schnackenburg 1980:344-364). All these elements allow us to conjecture a background of historicity behind a formulation which tends to make the disciples an example of how to answer to Jesus' call.

Mark 10:28-30

Despite the difficulties for the priority of Mark posed by the existence of some minor agreements between Matthew and Luke against Mark, the fact is that Mark alone has a second listing of family members (Mark 10:30b). Here, too, Matthew and Luke depend on Mark. On the one hand, Matthew agrees with Mark against Luke, in the words of Peter (Mark 10:28b par.); in the listing of family members who are left (Mark 10:29b par.); and in the reward (Mark 10:29c). On the other, Luke agrees with Mark against Matthew in two important details of the formulation of the saying of Jesus: the beginning of the statement and the distinction between the two stages of the reward.

E. Best (1981:112-114) and H. Fürst (1977:22-29) have suggested that the introduction of the pronouncement story could be the work of Mark because the terminology of the vocation stories is repeated in it and because there exists a certain disconnection between the question of Peter and the reply of Jesus which is not directed at Peter but rather at all the disciples. The expressions "for the sake of the gospel" and "with persecutions" also come from Mark (Marxsen 1981: 115-119). Finally, the mention of eternal life can be considered redactional, as it would have been of use to Mark in relating this episode with the first scene of the triptych which deals with the search for eternal life (Mark 10:17).

Stripping Mark's version of all these redactional additions we recover the form which this pronouncement story had in the oral tradition. In it Jesus instructs his disciples about the reward which awaits them. In this case it is easy to separate the saying from its narrative framework, and it is highly probable that the pronouncement story has been elaborated on the basis of a saying of Jesus. The most probable hypothesis is that the saying originally ended with the phrase, "a hundred times more." The reason for this is that as the distinction between a single and a double reward reflects the situation of the first Jesus groups rather than that of Jesus' activity (Best 1981:113-114; Fusco 1991:120). The expression with which the saying begins would also belong to the original saying: *"oudeis estin hos ... ean me ..."* It is unusual in Greek and has been corrected by both Matthew and Luke. Finally, it is highly probable that the list of what is left has been expanded to reach the number seven. From what we see in the other saying about discipleship and family, the mention of father and mother could be considered as the oldest part of the statement (Gnilka 1986:106). According to these clues the original saying may be reconstructed thus:

> [Jesus said:]
> "There is no one who has left father and mother for my sake, who will not receive a hundred times more".

V. Fusco (1991:119-120) thinks that the saying in Mark 10:29-30 reflects the "prolonged missionary experience of the primitive church". This is true when we argue the authenticity of the saying on the basis of the form it has in Mark. If however we consider the saying in the form in which we have reconstructed it, and if we compare it with the sayings about the disruption of the family that we have studied previously now, we observe a significant coincidence. Even the mention of a reward could be understood in the context of the Kingdom of God which Jesus proclaimed. Moreover, this saying reflects a situation of homelessness which was common in Palestine in the first century (Theissen 1985) and belongs to the lifestyle of Jesus and some of his disciples.

Q 12:51-53

We turn now to the two sayings which refer to division among members of the family as a consequence of the coming of Jesus. The relationship between family divisions and discipleship does not appear explicitly in the sayings, but it can be easily inferred that these divisions above all affected those who followed Jesus.

The first of them (Q 12:52) is only in Luke and it is difficult to know if it was in Q. The second is in Matthew and Luke and lists the divisions to which the activity of Jesus gives rise (Q 12:53). It is probable that in this case it is Luke who has best preserved the form it had in Q, because in the version of Matthew there is an obvious interest in approximating the words of Jesus to those of Mic 7:6 (Selew 1987:646-652; Patterson 1989:122-125; Jacobson 1995:365). A feature of Israel's apocalyptic tradition saw in family divisions a sign of the arrival of the end. It is worth asking whether this feature influenced this statement in its previous form. However to find an answer we have to compare the version of Q with that of Gos. Thom. 16 which states: "Jesus said: Perhaps men think that I have come to bring peace to the world and they do not know that I have come to bring divisions on the earth, fire, sword, war. Because there will be five in one house; three will be against two and two against three: the father against the son and the son against the father and among themselves, and they will stand solitary."

If we exclude the list "fire, sword and war" and the final "among themselves, and they will stand solitary" which can be attributed to the redactor of the Gospel of Thomas, it is evident that this logion has more similarities with the version of Luke than with that of Matthew. The more probable hypothesis however is that Gos. Thom. 16 represents an independent version of the Synoptics and prior to Q (Patterson 1989:126-130).

H. Koester (1990:94 and 154) has shown that Gos. Thom. 16c has not the apocalyptic aspects that were introduced in the second redaction of Q. In this case the apocalyptic reworking would consist of the expansion of the list of confrontations, an expansion that would bring it closer to the apocalyptic tradition represented by Mic 7:6. It is highly probable therefore that Mic 7:6 influenced the expansion of the saying about the split between father and son, and that this broadening of the categories is an apocalyptic feature which Matthew makes more explicit. According to this, the oldest form of the sayings would be:

> [Jesus said:]
> "There will be five in a house; three against two and two against three."
> [Jesus said;]
> "I have come to divide son against father and father against son."

The main difficulty in attributing the second of these sayings to Jesus comes from its form. Bultmann (1963:162-163) considers the "sayings in the first person about coming" a creation of the community because they presuppose an elaborated reflection on the origin and mission of Jesus. Such a blanket assertion, however, needs to be nuanced. It is certain that we observe a tendency to multiply this type of saying in the post-Easter tradition, but this does not mean that they have all been composed by Jesus group prophets. Many of the sayings could well be a reworking of already existing sayings in which Jesus was not talking about his coming, and the one we are currently studying could well be one of them.

It is reasonable to think that these sayings were spoken by Jesus. In favor of this hypothesis we can point to the fact that they referred originally to the consequences of Jesus activity. Further, they are consistent with other statements of his about the renunciation of family (above all Q 9:59-60), and also with the relationship between these teachings and his own experience (Mark 3:21-22. 31-35 and parallels). These two sayings reflect a generational conflict within the family, which is perfectly feasible during the activity of Jesus. It is, therefore, unnecessary to have recourse to the later experience of Jesus group members to explain its origin.

Having studied the pronouncement stories in Mark and the two sayings in Q we see now to what extent the three features which we have identified in Q 9: 59-60 and Q 14: 26 appear in them.

The first feature was the relationship between following Jesus and the disruption of the family. This feature is central to the first two pronouncements of Mark (Mark 1:16-18, 19-20). Although only in the second is it clearly stated that they left their father, we have to bear in mind that in the first century the family was a unit of production, and so leaving one's job implied leaving one's family; then we may conclude that the first pronouncement story too spoke implicitly about the renunciation of the family. The same can be said of the third pronouncement story (Mark 10:28-30), where the cause of leaving parents is Jesus. Only in the second of the two sayings in Q is the cause of the family division explained (Q 12:53): the lifestyle of Jesus. It is not too risky to suppose that such a division affected those who followed him.

Secondly, we had observed that the family conflict was mainly between parents and children. This feature also appears in the oral tradition which underlies all of the passages we have considered. In Mark 1:16-18 leaving one's job implies leaving one's father. In Mark 1:19-20 explicit mention is made of leaving Zebedee. In Mark 10:28-30 the original saying probably referred to the division between son and parents. In Q 12:52 we hear of a confrontation within a patriarchal family between the adult generation (two: the father and the mother, who in a patriarchal family is at the same time the mother-in-law) and the younger generation (three: the son, the daughter and the son's wife). Finally, Q 12:53 only mentions the confrontation between the father and the son.

Thirdly, we had noted that the division happens in the ascending direction: the son against the father (or parents). We find this in the three pronouncements of Mark, but it is not clear in the sayings of Q. These latter sayings speak of family division between the two generations but do not specify which of the generations causes the division. Nevertheless, the agreement of the other sayings and pronouncements in this aspect seems to indicate that this family division had its origin in the attitude of the children, and that these sayings could have been directed to the younger generation.

The Father-Son Relationship in the Mediterranean Family of the First Century: A Reading Scenario

The sayings we have studied were produced in a social system which was very different from the social systems of the industrialized West. Social and cultural distance condition our understanding of the ancient documents in a telling way because language, insofar as it is an objectifying instrument, is the representation of a socially interpreted reality. It is only when we know the clues of this socially interpreted reality that it is possible to understand in its own terms the language in which it is objectified. To say this another way, the meaning of words comes from the social system which is shared by those who participate in the communication in which these words are used; only through knowing this social system is it possible to understand their meaning adequately (Malina 1991a). For this reason, in order to understand written documents produced in another culture, we need a reading scenario which makes explicit the social system in which the documents saw the light of day.

A reading scenario is a hypothetical reconstruction of a relatively complete and consistent segment of some phase of a social system, which includes among other things the values and symbols which determine the world view which a social group has, the patterns of behavior accepted within that world view, the institutions and relationships through which interaction among group members is channeled, the consequences of such behavior, as well as other non-explicit elements which are intuitively perceived by those who have been socialized in the culture in question. A scenario is the framework within which human action and the language which describes it acquire a definite meaning. Without such a scenario it is impossible to evaluate the behavior of a person or understand its meaning (Malina and Rohrbaugh 1992:9-14; Elliott 1993:40-48).

In order to reconstruct the social settings of written documents and traditions born in the Mediterranean society of the first century we have two kinds of instruments. First there is the literary, epigraphical and archaeological evidence of that period which have come down to us in a fragmentary way. Second, there are a range of studies on traditional Mediterranean cultures. These latter provide us with models with which we can adequately contextualize literary and archeological data, which in turn allows us to refine the models taken from comparative studies on traditional Mediterranean societies (Malina 1993a).

In order to understand the father-son relationships which are the context of the sayings of Jesus about the disruption of the family, I am going to use an explanatory model proposed by F. Barth (1971) on the basis of different studies of traditional Mediterranean societies. According to Barth, behavior in a relationship is determined by the intrinsic attributes of such a relationship and by the setting in which such behavior takes place. The intrinsic attributes of the relationship depend in their turn on the values of a society, and in the case of the Middle Eastern societies studied by Barth, "these values are such as to give a prominence to the father-son relationship that may legitimately be characterized as dominance, while other relationships, such as that between husband and wife, become recessive, so that behavior in them is strongly modified and in part suppressed" (Barth 1971:88).

Two theoretical aspects of this model are relevant to this study: the definition of intrinsic attributes and characterization of dominant relationships. The first of these is defined by Barth in the following way:

Intrinsic attributes are the basic specifications of the relationship which no party to that relationship can deny in his behavior without repudiating the relationship as a whole: that is, they are the minimum specifications of the statuses involved in the relationship (Barth 1971:88).

These intrinsic attributes define the roles which become incarnate in a relationship. The exercise of these roles is constrained in part by the situation in which those who incarnate them operate, so that "regularities in behavior... can be understood in part from the constraints that status specifications impose, in part from external or 'ecological' constraints in the context where the behavior takes place and the role thus has to be consummated" (Barth 1971:89).

In order to determine which are the dominant relationships in the kinship system Barth proposes the following keys:

They are important and clear enough to take precedence over other relations and to block the use of certain idioms and the expression of certain qualities in those relations which would challenge or repudiate the 'intrinsic attributes' or status-defining characteristics of the 'dominant' relationship (Barth 1971:90).

On the basis of these theoretical principles and of several studies of the field, Barth argues that the intrinsic attributes which determine the father-son relationship make it the dominant relationship in the majority of Middle Eastern cultures, due principally to a series of characteristics of the family in these cultures. "Especially ... where political life is structured by patrilineal descent groups and productive resources are held collectively be patrilineal groups, the importance of the father-son relationship is overwhelming: and throughout the area the system can be characterized as patrilocal and patriarchal" (Barth 1971:90).

The dominant character of this relationship can be verified when other members of the family are present. In this case, problems arise for the actor in composing his behavior, his role, in such a way that activity in one relationship does not repudiate obligations or qualities important in the relationship to others who are present. Here, one relationship may emerge as dominant over others; it takes precedence and is little modified, whereas other relationships become latent and/or behavior in them is strongly modified... Thus substantial sectors of the interaction appropriate between parties in non-dominant relationships may become suppressed ... such dilemmas may go to the extent of imposing latency on the whole relationship (Barth 1971:94).

According to Barth, the type of family in which the father-son relationship is dominant is characterized by (1) having patrilineal descent groups, (2) with productive resources held collectively; and at the same time (3) it is patrilocal and (4) it is patriarchal. Now these four features are also characteristic of the family in the Hellenistic society of the first-century Mediterranean.

The most characteristic element of the traditional Mediterranean family was its patriarchal structure. The importance and centrality of the paterfamilias in the house appears in the so-called domestic codes (Aristotle, *Politics*, 1:1253b; Didimus, *Strobaeus*, 148:5-8, 15-19, 21; 149:1-5; Cicero, *De Officiis*, 1:54; Sir 7:18-28). The consistency and continuity of the family was based on submission to the authority of the *paterfamilias*, and this contributed to the fulfilment of the household role in society as a whole. Patriarchalism was central to the social organization of the different peoples of the Eastern Mediterranean from very early times and was so rooted in that culture that its thinkers justified the exercise of paternal authority saying that it belonged to human nature (Aristotle, *Politics* 1259b, Didimus, *Strobaeus* 149:5-10; Josephus, *C. Ap.* 2:201).

The existence of patrilineal descent groups is also a characteristic feature of the ancient Mediterranean family. In ancient Israel such a group was called the *mishpahah*. The *mishpahah* was a self-sufficient and self-protecting social organism formed by the bloodline descendants of a common ancestor, that is to say, by the sons of the male descendants of a common ancestor and by the people dependent on them. The unity of this wide group of relatives was expressed sometimes in the common residence (Judg 18:11; Neh 11:4-8). Within the fold of this kinship group, the resources were passed on (by inheritance and by marriage). Belonging to the group produced cohesion and solidarity among family members, Furthermore, all group members were the trustees of the honor accumulated by the ancestors; this honor was passed on—as was the land—by inheritance (Goody 1968:401; Wright 1990:48-53).

The patrilocal character is also characteristic of the Mediterranean family of the first century and was evident in the case of marriage. From the social, religious and juridical point of view, marriage consisted in the transfer of a woman from her house of origin to a new house in which she would fulfil the role of wife and mother. The young woman who got married stopped belonging to her original house; she was no longer under the authority of her father, brother or tutor, but rather under the authority of her husband or of his father (Ps 45:11, 17; Mark 4:5).

Finally, the property was also held in common in the Hellenistic family. This is what we see in the laws about the members of the extended family. The relatives had the right to claim family property (above all, land) in the case where some member of the kinship group was obliged to sell it or where he died without an heir (Num 27:8-11). This means that family property was not linked to the "house" but rather to the extended family; it was not supposed to pass out of their control (Lev 25:48-49).

Another characteristic feature of the Mediterranean family in the first century, mentioned only in passing by Barth, is the existence of a common honor. Honor, as with material possessions belonged to the extended family. For this reason, the same people who could claim an inheritance or who had the right to buy the land, were those who had the obligation to protect and avenge the honor of those who belonged to the same kinship group. The most complete expression of honor was not individual honor but family honor. All members of the family contributed towards it and all shared in it. This also meant that the dishonor or shame of any member affected the whole family (Malina and Neyrey 1991a:32-33).

These features of the family in the Hellenistic society reflect the ideal of elite families, but there were few of them. The situation in Galilee where the tradition of the sayings of Jesus has its origin was little different from the rest of the non-elites of the Roman Empire. I have argued elsewhere (Guijarro 1997:57-61) how domestic archeology, interpreted with the stratification of agrarian societies, reveals the existence of at least four different family types. The features we have just mentioned were present in different ways in these categories: extended families, multiple families, nucleated families and scattered families. Only extended families, which were approximately 1% of the population) fully possessed the features quoted above, but the rest always tended towards the ideal which they represented. In all of them the authority of the paterfamilias was the axis which underpinned and gave unity to the family group; in all of them descent was by the male line (agnatic), and residence was patrilocal; possessions and honor, although in short supply, were held in common, and although most families were very small and did not have many relatives to call on, the bonding to the kinship group and to the extended family were the ideal.

The basic traits of the Hellenistic family coincide with those which F. Barth identifies in the Mediterranean kinship systems in which the father-son relationship is dominant. We have now to show whether the intrinsic attributes of this relationship, as they appear in the textual and epigraphic evidence of that time, reveal the fact that such a relationship was dominant. Before doing this however, two clarifications are in order.

The first is about the nature of family roles in the ancient world. These roles were highly determined by life expectancy and by the development of the life-cycle within the family. In the Roman world life expectancy at birth was twenty one years, marriages on average did not last more than ten or fifteen years, many children never knew their mothers, were reared by foster-mothers and wet-nurses, and the majority of men no longer had a father by the time they got married (Dixon 1992:30-34). This meant that changes in the life cycle happened very quickly, and that there was little time left to invent the roles of husband, wife, son, slave, or master creatively. The behavior of those who had to incarnate these roles was regulated by law and custom, because the adequate functioning of society depended on the family.

The second clarification has to do with the region in which the sayings of Jesus were produced. Although it is true that the family in Galilee was little different from the family in other regions of the Empire, especially in the cities and among the upper classes, when we go down the social scale and get away from the cities, we begin to find some differences. For this reason, when describing the intrinsic attributes of the father-son relationship, I shall use when possible data from Israelite authors; these probably better represent the ideals of the families of the followers of Jesus to whom the sayings we are studying were addressed.

Having made these clarifications, I turn now to some intrinsic attributes of the father-son relationship which are reflected in the rights and obligations attached to this relationship. I begin by examining the rights and obligations of the father towards the son.

The father exercised his authority over his son throughout his life. At birth it was the father who decided if the newly born child was accepted as a member of the family and it was the father who later welcomed him into the family by giving him a name (Suetonius, *Nero* 6:1-2; Matt 1:18-21). Everything the son did required the consent and approval of his father, be it his own marriage, an economic transaction or accepting a public office. Such was the authority of the father that he could even legally sell his own son or condemn him to death (Philo, *Spec.* 2:232, 243-248; Josephus, *Ant.* 4:260-264; 16:365; *m. Sanh.* 7:4).

Along with this authority, law and custom placed a series of obligations on the father towards his son. The most elementary of these consisted of feeding him, educating him, protecting him, helping him economically and giving him a job (Yarbrough 1993:41-49; Reinhartz 1993:69-77). The obligation on the father to educate and instruct his son was of particular importance (Prov 4:1-4; Tob 4; Philo, *Spec.* 2:228). According to a Talmudic tradition, it was Joshua Ben Gamala, a contemporary and friend of Flavius Josephus, who began to recruit teachers in Jerusalem, and then in other districts to teach the Law to young people, but "in other times, when a child had his father, it was he who used to instruct him, and, if he had no father, he did not receive instruction" (*b. b. Bat* 21a). An important aspect of domestic education consisted in telling and learning the great deeds of the ancestors, those deeds which had brought prestige and honor to the house. The illustrious ancestors' example was used to model the character and lifestyle of those who would one day have the responsibility of continuing the house's name (Josephus, *C. Ap.* 2:204). The father was also in charge of teaching his sons how to run the house and family properties, and, in the case of a more humble family, of teaching him a trade (*m. Qidd.* 4:14).

During the years of education the father had to treat his son with severity, imposing his authority on him by means of punishments. In this way, the order of the house was assured, and the future paterfamilias learned how to exercise his authority (Sir 30:1-13; Prov 13:24; 22:15; 23:13-14; Philo, *Spec.* 2:240). This educational model is characteristic of agrarian societies, in which the authority of the father is a key element in preserving family lands (Pilch 1993a:101-107).

The father also had the important obligation of handing on the religious tradition to his son. In various passages of the OT (Exod 12:26-27; 13:14-15; Deut 6:20-24; Josh 4:6-7.21-23) the explanation of an event, institution or memorial is entrusted to the father. The father-son relationship was also the privileged channel to transmit religious attitudes and behavior in the Hellenistic cultures of the Roman world. Israelite fathers handed on to their sons the religious tradition of a people which was symbolized in the great events of their common history: the exodus, the conquest and the gift of the land, the handing over of the law etc (Tob 4; 4 Macc 18:10-19; Philo, *Legat.* 115; *Spec.* 4:150; Josephus, *C. Ap.* 1:60; *m. Pes.* 10:4).

The duties of a father towards his son had their counterparts in the obligations which the son had towards him (Yarbrough 1993:49-53; Reinhartz 1993:77-81). These obligations had great social relevance, because the continuity of the house depended on then. The son was obliged to honor and obey his father as long as he lived, to assist and care for him in his old age and to give him burial and carry out the funeral rites when he died.

To honor and obey one's father was a grave obligation of sons in ancient Israel. We find it in the Decalogue (Exod 20:12; Deut 5:16), in the wisdom literature and later in Hellenistic Israelite writings. The son had to respect his father, to listen attentively to his instruction, to obey his directives; he had not to maltreat him, speak ill of him or make a fool of him; he had to be his support in old age and help him when his strength was failing (Prov 1:8; 4:1; 23:22; 19:26; 20:20; 30:17. Sir 3:3-16; Ps 126:3-5; Philo, *Decal.* 111-120, 165-167; *Spec.* 2:223-262). In consequence, he who despised his father called a curse down on himself and cut himself off from a blessing; he who did not take care of his father in old age was a blasphemer; and he who disobeyed him deserved death (Deut 27:16; Sir 3:8-9. 16; Deut 21:18-21; Josephus, *C. Ap.* 2:206). The law concerning the rebellious son (Deut

21:18-21), which was still in force in the Hellenistic-roman period (Philo, *Spec.* 2:232, 243-248; Josephus, *Ant.* 4:260-264; 16:365), bears witness to the importance that the ancient Israelites attributed to these obligations.

The fathers' death was the moment in which the son showed respect towards him in the most visible way, giving him burial according to the established rites (Gen 25:9-11; 35:29). By means of these funeral rites the deceased father passed on to become a family ancestor, but at the same time his death put the continuity of the house in danger because the person who had held it together with his authority was disappearing from the scene. At this juncture the importance of the heir was apparent because he prevented the house from disintegrating or disappearing.

In the burial rite the heir was presented and recognized as the new paterfamilias and from then on one of his principal functions would be to venerate the remains of the ancestors to whom the living still felt themselves bound as members of the same family. This obligation was one of the most sacred that a son had towards his father, and it did not finish on the day of burial but was prolonged in a series of funeral ceremonies after the burial and in the annual commemorations whose celebration was also entrusted to the son (Gen 49:29-32; 50:25; Josh 24:32; Tob 4:3-4; 6:15; 14:9, 11-12; Jub 23:7; 36:1-2, 18; 2 Macc 5:10; Josephus, *Bell.* 5:545; T. Reu 7:1; T. Levi 19:5).

The intrinsic attributes of the father-son relationship go much further than the rights and obligations implied in it, but these are a clue as to the importance which was accorded to this relationship. In antiquity the relationship between father and his male offspring was the closest and most lasting of all relationships because the whole continuity of the family was based on it. From his father the son inherited the house with its properties, its honor and its worship, and in order to preserve this heritage he received authority over all those persons who formed part of the household. The value attributed to this continuity shows that what mattered was not individuals but the household. It was the household which perpetuated itself in time; the head of a family was only its representative and guardian at any specific time. Because of this, fathers saw in their sons another "I", one more link in the chain of succession who would guarantee the continuity of the household and who would honor them as ancestors (Sir 30:4; 44:10-11; 46:12).

The Meaning of the Sayings of Jesus about the Disruption of the Family

In the first part of this study I concluded that the sayings of Jesus about the disruption of the family reflected the fact that some children had broken off from their parents, and that the cause of this family conflict was that they had followed Jesus. In the second part I attempted to show that breaking with the family and the renunciation of family ties had connotations in the first century which no longer resonate in today's industrialized West. The reading scenario I have proposed helps to discover some of the connotations which this generational conflict had in each one of the sayings and pronouncements mentioned.

In Q 9:59-60, Jesus asks one of his followers to leave undone the gravest obligation that a son had in antiquity: to bury his father. The saying probably referred not only to the burial but also to the obligation to feed and take care of the aged father (Bailey 1983:26-27), which makes the reply of Jesus more likely and, at the same time, more dramatic. Not to look after an aged father and not to bury him when he died was an act of impiety (Hengel 1981b:29) which stained the family honor (Vaage 1989:169-171), but it also had economic consequences and affected the continuity of the family itself. If the obligation to bury the father fell on the son, this was because the burial was linked to the passing on of the inheritance to assure the continuity of the house. We are dealing here with a conflict of loyalties, and Jesus states that following him is more important than fulfilling family obligations, even though this involves dishonor and jeopardizes the continuity of the house.

The saying in Q 14:26 was probably spoken by Jesus in a very similar situation. We can deduce this from the meaning that the verb *misein*. In the culture in which Jesus lived, to love (*agapan*) and to hate (*misein*) were not simply internalized sentiments confined to the realm of the psychological. Rather they were attitudes coupled with behavior which expressed group, rather than individual, values and were related to belonging and fidelity (love) or division and infidelity (hate). This is the sense which both verbs have in Q 16,13 and in some passages from the LXX (Gen 29:31-32; Deut 21:15-17; Mal 1:2, quoted in this sense in Rom 9:13) and Josephus (*Ant.* 6:255-256, 324; 7:254). In this case too it seems we have to deal with a conflict of loyalties in which it was necessary to chose between one's own parents and following Jesus.

In Mark 1:16-18 we are told that Peter and Andrew left their trade in order to help Jesus in his task. We have seen that one of the obligations of fathers in that society was to teach a trade to their sons, and that this fact was related to the obligation of sons to care for and feed their fathers in their old age (*m. Qidd* 4:14, commentated on in this sense in *b. Qidd* 30b, 31b; Philo, *Spec.* 2:228-230; *Decal.* 117). This means that abandoning one's trade involved not attending to the obligation to feed and care for an aged father.

An explicit mention of this relationship between trade and father appears in Mark 1:19-20, given that James and John do not only abandon their boat and their nets, but also their father, Zebedee. The most dramatic element in the scene however is the fact that Zebedee is left alone in the boat with the hired laborers. This means that James and John were his only male offspring, and that their act of following Jesus put the continuity of the family in danger.

The most significant factor of the saying which served as a basis for the pronouncement story in Mark 10:28 is the reference to a reward for those who have to leave their parents. This brings out an element implicit in the preceding sayings: the consequences which the fact of breaking with the family brought upon the followers of Jesus. These consequences were so harsh, that in some cases it was necessary to motivate the decision with a promise.

In the remaining sayings (Q 12:52, 53) we hear of internal divisions, and one gets the impression that the split has not yet happened. This could mean that the disruption of the family referred to in the preceding sayings was the result of a process which perhaps began with these kind of divisions. In any case, in the ancient world divisions were a very negative element which impeded the smooth running of the family, and, because of this, great insistence was placed on the virtues which contributed to maintaining the unity and bonding between the members of the family; there were even religious ceremonies whose goal was to restore broken unity (Ovid, *Fasti* 2:623-626).

All these sayings show that in some cases Jesus asked his disciples to abandon their parents and their filial obligations. The sayings however do not say in what concrete circumstances such a demand was made, nor what sense Jesus gave to it. In the majority of them however we observe that the reason to abandon the family was to follow him (Q 9:60; 12:52-53; 14:26; Mark 10:29). This suggests that, in order to know the reasons of the disruption of the family caused by Jesus, we have to place these sayings in the context of his lifestyle and his relationship with his followers.

In these sayings, to be a disciple (Q 14:26: *einai mou mathetes*) is equivalent to "following" Jesus (Q 9:60; Mark 1:18; 10:28: *akolouthein*), or "going behind" him (Mark 1:17. 20: *opiso mou*). These expressions have a double meaning. They refer to physically following, to going physically behind Jesus in order to learn from his words and from his way of acting, but they refer also to imitating his life-style (Kittel 1964:213-214). Following Jesus then supposes identifying oneself with his life-style, with living as he lived. And it is here that we find the reason why some of his followers entered into conflict with their families and had to separate themselves from them.

The gospels have preserved some traces of the counter cultural behavior of Jesus which provoked scandal and rejection by his contemporaries. The passages which refer to this life-style have a solid historical foundation. The majority of them reflect a line of behavior which would have been embarrassing for later Jesus groups. The behavior does not respond to the conventions of the Israelite custom of the time (dissimilarity). Further, many of these sayings are not only found in independent sources (multiple attestation), but also in different literary genres (pronouncement stories, sayings). Finally, the different reports cohere among themselves to form a scenario of a consistent life-style.

In the first chapters of the Gospel of Mark we find some of them: his itinerant style of life, without fixed abode (Mark 1:14-39), his meals with publicans and sinners (Mark 2:15-17), his disrespectful attitude towards some norms and religious practices, such as the observance of the fast (Mark 2:18-20), Sabbath rest (Mark 2:23-28), or to certain norms of ritual purity (Mark 7:1-15); his claim to declare God's forgiveness of sins (Mark 2:7).

This life-style to which Mark gives witness in narrative form is also reflected in some of the insults which his enemies directed at Jesus. These insults tried to discredit him in front of his disciples and in the forum of public opinion, distorting and ridiculing the meaning of his life-style. He did not have a fixed abode (Q 9:58); they called him Beelzebub and said that he was possessed by the prince of demons, because he performed exorcisms (Matt 10:25; Mark 3:22; Q 11:15; John 8:48); they also called him *anthropos phagos kai oinopotes* because he did not keep the fast (Q 7:34a); *philos telonon kai hamartolon*, because he used to eat with people on the social and religious fringes (Q 7,34b); and *eunouchos* because he did not have a wife and children (Matt 19:12).

For Jesus, however, this behavior was related to the coming of the Kingdom of God. His itinerant life-style reflected his dependence on God (Q 12:6-7, 22-23); his exorcisms were an evident sign that the mighty one had been beaten and that the Kingdom of God had started to come (Mark 2:23-27; Q 11:20); his meals with publicans and sinners showed that it was not reserved for a few, but rather it was offered to all, especially to those most in need (Mark 2:17; Q 14:21-24); finally, his renunciation of family expressed the absolute priority of the Kingdom of God (Matt 19:12). Consequently, these features which characterize the behavior of Jesus were not only signs of the coming of the Kingdom, but rather an expression of it. The Kingdom of God was being accomplished in Jesus' way of acting, and this is why it was so important that his disciples should live as he lived.

Because he lived in this way, Jesus had to stand up to rejection and social ostracism. The nicknames mentioned above were in antiquity, as they are even today in traditional Mediterranean culture, a way of stigmatizing social deviants who cut themselves off from the established social order (Malina and Neyrey 1991b:99-110). This social stigmatization of Jesus appears in a saying which, in its oldest form, spoke of Jesus as a prophet who had lost his honor (Mark 6:4 and Matt 13:57: *atimos*; John 4:44: *timen ouk echei*; Luke 4:24 and Gos. Thom. 31: *ouk estin dektos*) in his native village (Barton 1994:86-92). This reaction of his countrymen has its origin in the counter cultural behavior of Jesus which they effectively reject by attacking his prestige and good name. They rejected him because they did not want the disrepute and comments which his way of behaving provoked to affect them. To declare Jesus *atimos* was equal to expelling him from the community to which he belonged (Fustel de Coulanges 1984:210).

This social stigmatizing of Jesus affected his family, and it is in this context that we must understand the passages that reflect the opposition from his own family. This opposition appears most clearly in the Gospel of Mark (Mark 3:20-21, 31-35 par.) His relatives come in search of Jesus not because they thought that he was "out of his mind" but because the people were saying this about him (the imperfect *elegon* must be understood as impersonal: "it was said", "people were saying"; a similar case to Diogenes Laertius, 6:88). The same opposition appears in the Gospel of John (John 7:2-5) and in the saying Q 7:34 which we have quoted above. In this latter saying, Jesus is accused of being a glutton and a drunkard, an accusation which referred in Israelite tradition to the rebellious son who dishonored the family by his behavior (Deut 21:18-21); it is possible that this connotation was intended by those who accused Jesus in this way (Bosetti and Nicacci 1993; Philo, *Ebr.* 15; 27-28; 95). These passages indicate that the conflict between Jesus and the members of his family had its origin in the bad name which his behavior was earning them. The sayings which speak about breaking with the family because of discipleship are a reflection of the experience of Jesus himself; the root of this conflict is to be found in his life-style which brought into question the values on which that society was based, contravened its purity laws and assaulted the honor and the social hierarchy which was based on it.

Jesus' way of acting and the reactions his life-style aroused among his adversaries, his countrymen and, above all, among his own relatives is the background against which we must understand the implications involved with being his follower. Those who followed him not only listened to his teachings and were witnesses of his signs, but also adopted his life-style. During the eastern Mediterranean dry season, they led an itinerant life with him (Mark 1:18.20; 2:14), and they accompanied him in his meals with publicans and sinners (Mark 2:15). Their attitude toward Israelite religious norms was the same as that of Jesus: they did not keep the fast (Mark 2:18), they did not observe the Sabbath (Mark 2:23-24) nor keep the norms of ritual purity at mealtimes (Mark 7:2-5) They also carried out exorcisms and expelled demons (Q 11:19; Mark 6:13; 9:49). It is not hazardous to suppose that Jesus' adversaries had a similar attitude towards Jesus' followers they had towards Jesus himself, and that they used the same denigrating epithets of the disciples as they used of him (Matt 10:25).

To follow Jesus, imitating his life-style, meant for his disciples acquiring this bad name which not only affected those who had decided to follow him, but also the rest of the family. A saying preserved in the Q tradition could reflect this situation. The parents of some of these disciples accused him of casting out demons by the power of Beelzebub in order to discredit him publicly and thus stop their children following him (Q 11:19-20). Jesus replies to them with an *ad hominem* argument which could refer to a real situation: "And if I cast out demons in (the name) of Beelzebub, in whose (name) do your sons cast them out?" His answer presupposes that the sons of those who were accusing Jesus were doing the same thing he was doing: casting out demons; so, the accusation of the parents is turned against their own children and, ultimately, against themselves.

It is very probable that in situations like these some of the disciples felt constrained to leave their families, thus losing what the family had to offer: support, solidarity, honor etc. What we know about the first disciples of Jesus suggests that some of them belonged to relatively extended families with moderate access to wealth. The family of James and John, that of Levi and, perhaps to a lesser degree, that of Peter and Andrew belonged to this category (Guijarro 1997:59-63). For disciples who held this social ranking, leaving one's own family meant a significant renunciation, for, in that society, he who did not have the backing of his family was exposed to absolute helplessness (Epictetus, *Disc* 3:12:3-4).

The Greek word which best defines the situation of those who at that time lacked family support was *ptochos*. As opposed to the poor who needed to work in order to live (the *penes*), the *ptochos* was a poor person who could not survive without begging. Now, in Hellenistic society poverty was not defined principally by economic criteria but rather by kinship because kinship was the main way of accessing economic resources and all other goods (Malina 1987:355-356, 360-361). Read in this context, some words of Jesus which mention the *ptochoi* could refer not only to those who were poor but also to those who had become poor as a consequence of the rejection by their families.

This could be the case of the first macarism (Q 6:20) which declares the poor blessed and also of the other three which were in Q. The fourth, which is the most explicit and rhetorically has a more important place, describes the social ostracism of the disciples in terms which remind the family sanctions against the rebellious son. As Neyrey has suggested (1995:145-147), the four macarisms do not refer to different types of people, but rather to those whose situation is described with more detail in the last one: the disciples who had been repudiated by their parents The majority of the peasants who listened to Jesus were probably not beggars (*ptochoi*) but rather people who had to work for a living (*penetes*) Those who had lost all link with their families however could be counted among the *ptochoi*.

Some sayings of Jesus directed to his disciples in Q fit this context; these exhortations recommend attitudes which are proper to beggars. In them, one is encouraged to make requests with confidence (Q 11:9-13), not to be worried about material things (Q 12:22-32) and not to store up treasure in this world (Q 12:33-34). The foundation for this confidence is a God who is father, not the family, which was then the social institution that supplied all these things (clothing, food, wealth etc.). The recipients could be the poor of whom the beatitudes speak, and, among them, those who had been cast off by their families as rebel children because they had become disciples of Jesus.

The disruption of the family experienced by the first followers of Jesus has to be understood in the context of discipleship. Another question implied in these sayings is what attitude did Jesus have towards the family. We have seen that the confrontation between father and son is prominent in them, and that the relationship between them formed the basic axis of the family in that society. It was through the father-son relationship that property, religion and honor were handed on; it was upon this relationship that the continuity of the family rested. The fact that the words of Jesus were an invitation to break this relationship suggest that he had a hostile attitude towards the patriarchal family.

Theissen (1979:13-20) thinks that the wandering charismatics of the first generation had an anti-family ethos. Schüssler Fiorenza (1989: 188-200) takes up and completes Theissen's thesis, insisting on the abolition of patriarchal structures. The first generation of Jesus group members shaped their communities according to the model of brotherly family relationships, but the father-figure and all that it represented did not exist in them (196). Crossan, in a very quick and somewhat superficial analysis which does not take into consideration the most relevant passage on this theme (Q 9: 59-60), concludes that Jesus was against the patriarchal family (1991:299-302).

Other sayings of Jesus however suggest that these statements need to be nuanced. One of them is the saying about divorce which we find in three independent traditions (Q 16:18; 1 Cor 7:10; Mark 10:11-12). In order to understand this saying, we have to bear in mind the consequences which divorce had for a woman in that culture. At that time, divorce was not a matter between husband and wife, but rather between their families, and it took place in a society whose central value was honor. A rejected wife had to leave her husband's family and go back to her father bringing with her the shame or not having lived up to what was expected of her. The saying about divorce, read in this context, attempts, above all, to defend the woman, and contains a criticism of the excessive authority that the husband had over her. At the same time however, it reveals that the disintegration of the family as such was not an aim of Jesus' program.

On the other hand, different gospel traditions suggest that some of Jesus' closest followers did not abandon their families to follow him. Having left his nets, Peter goes to his home with Jesus (Mark 1:29); the same thing happens with Levi (Mark 2:15) and perhaps also in the case of James and John (Matt 20:20; 27:56). In the same way, the references to the boat which Jesus and his disciples used to get about the lake (Mark 4:36; 5:18; 6:32.45) could be an indication that not all of his disciples had abandoned their trade.

Mention is made in other passages of the houses in which Jesus and the disciples were received by families in which following Jesus has not caused division (Pesce 1984:365, 370-371). A family lived in Bethany who supported Jesus and his disciples with their hospitality (Mark 11:11; 14:3; Luke 10:38-42; John 11:1-54), and even in Jerusalem there was a family who could offer them a large room in which to celebrate the Passover (Mark 14:12-16).

To these data we have to add the oldest tradition of the sending out of the disciples which has reached us in two independent versions. In both Mark 6:10 and Q 10:5-7a, the disciples are sent to houses. In both accounts, but above all in Q, the proclamation of the Kingdom of God is not addressed principally to individuals but to families. Conversion, which requires welcoming the coming Kingdom of God, does not seek to abolish the family as such, but rather to transform the relationships which exist within it.

These passages reveal that Jesus' plan did not have the disintegration of the family as its object and, consequently, renouncing one's family was not a basic demand of discipleship. This affirmation and the evidence on which it is based seem to contradict the sayings about breaking away from one's family, because in them it is evident that both he and some of his disciples were in conflict with their families and were rejected by them.

In order to understand this apparent contradiction it is necessary to bear in mind that the proclamation and activity of Jesus did not take place within the framework of "domestic" religion, but rather within that of "political" religion (Malina 1986b:92-94). His proclamation did not involve the attempt, as did that of the Pharisees later on, to regulate the religious practices of the home, but rather it announced the coming Kingdom of God which would transform this world. This means that Jesus did not have a specific program with regards to the family, and that in his sayings there was no hostile attitude towards the household as such.

The coming Kingdom of God, which Jesus announced, intended a radical transformation of the values on which that society was built. This transformation implied, among other things, the abolition of purity norms and the redefinition of honor, which were the two basic pillars of that society. The patriarchal household exercised a fundamental role in the preservation and transmission of these values. Within the household, the concern for honor was cultivated and passed on; within it, the patriarchal structures, which were afterwards reproduced in the remaining social relationships, were constantly re-inforced. The household was therefore the guardian and tradent of those values which Jesus questioned in his preaching. This explains the second aspect: the conflict that Jesus and some of his disciples had with their families.

This conflict did not inevitably arise. When all the family accepted the message of Jesus, there were no divisions created because of him. In those cases, the disciples continued living in their houses with their relatives but they formed a fictive kinship group with Jesus and his disciples, while those who had to abandon their homes and family found hospitality, support and solidarity in these households which had accepted the message of Jesus. The sayings in Mark speak of this fictive kinship (Mark 3:34; 10:30).

This attitude of Jesus towards the family explains the existence of two types of disciples: those who renounced their families in order to follow Jesus and those who remained at home. Theissen identifies these two types of disciples as "wandering charismatics" and "sympa-thizers of the local communities", respectively. This distinction of Theissen's, which refers to post-Easter Jesus movement groups, has been applied to the period of Jesus' ministry, distinguishing two types of call. Jesus would have called some disciples to a closer following and would have asked them to abandon their homes and their families; others he would have permitted to remain in their own homes which would serve as bases for the itinerant disciples. This would mean in fact that there was a double ethos in following Jesus (Lohfink 1996:41-45, 49-51),

The study of the passages about the disruption of the family allows us however to propose a different interpretation. The origin of these two forms of discipleship is not to be found in two different calls from Jesus but rather in the different attitudes of families towards those who had decided to become followers of Jesus. When the whole household welcomed the message of Jesus, or when it did not reject those mem-bers who welcomed it, then there was no family conflict and the disciples could continue living at home, although they left home tem-porarily to help Jesus. When the opposite happened, when there was a family conflict because of Jesus, the disciples were disowned by their families and were forced to live, like Jesus, without a family and a home.

9

Gossip in the New Testament

Richard L. Rohrbaugh, *Lewis and Clark College, Portland, OR*

According to Ogden Nash,

> There are two kinds of people
> who blow through life like a breeze,
> one kind is gossipers,
> and the other is gossipees.
> *I'm a Stranger Here Myself*

The writer of James had a somewhat less whimsical view. "But no human being can tame the tongue—an unruly evil, full of death-dealing poison. With it we honor the Lord and Father, and with it we curse human beings, the ones in the likeness of God. Out of the same mouth come blessing and cursing. My brothers, it ought not to be" (3:8-10). A few verses later he warns his readers, "Do not slander (καταλαλέω) each other, brothers. He who slanders a brother or judges his brother, slanders the law and judges the law" (4:11). Or as the proverbialist puts it, "A scoundrel rakes up evil (רעע) and his speech is like a scorching fire upon his lips. A perverse man stirs up dissension and a gossip (נרגן) separates close friends." (Prov 16:27-28).

While gossip has been enjoyed by virtually all who have participated in it—and roundly condemned by all who imagine themselves the keepers of the civil discourse—it has not always been the subject of thoughtful inquiry. Yet Max Gluckman kicked off a flurry of debate among cultural anthropologists in an insightful article in which he argued that gossip is among the most important social phenomena we can study (307). He made the case that it is much a more complex and far-reaching phenomenon than is usually suspected, and is indeed a significant means of informal social formation and control. Moreover, given the unique role gossip plays in oral cultures like that in first-century Palestine, we suggest it should be of special interest to those studying the cultural world of the New Testament.

Before looking at specific studies of gossip in Mediterranean village life, however, a cautionary note is in order. We must recognize that gossip is a nearly universal phenomenon and thus it cannot be claimed that there is something uniquely Mediterranean about its existence—at least nothing like that has been identified to date. Nonetheless two things may be said in this regard. First, the claim does appear to be justified that gossip plays a different role in non-literate societies than in literate ones, not only in scope and impact, but also in shape and social function.[1] There is justification therefore in looking at studies of gossip in all non-literate settings in order to gain an understanding of its complexity.[2] Second, as we shall see below, it may also be true that there are things about Mediterranean societies which make the study of gossip there a special case. Of course gossip has not been the same in all Mediterranean societies at all times in history, and therefore we cannot assume that gossip in Greek villages today is the exact equiva-lent of gossip in the Greek villages of antiquity. But ethnographers argue that several lasting features of Mediterranean culture have had a marked impact on gossip there and hence these must be taken into account. And obviously if that is true the topic becomes of special interest to scholars of the New Testament.[3]

---

[1] In an early study of pre-literate societies Paul Radin made an observation that has been noticed by nearly every ethnographer since his time:

> Primitive people are indeed among the most persistent and inveterate of gossips. Contestants for the same honours, possessors of the sacred rites of the tribe, the authorized narrators of legends, all leave you in little doubt as to the character and proficiency of their colleagues. "Ignoramus," "braggart," and not infrequently "liar" are liberally bandied about" (177-78).

That this should be true in oral cultures is not surprising—we note the prevalence of complaint about gossip in the literature of antiquity—but it is important. Among those trained in the study of literate antiquity, including New Testament scholars, informal oral culture has not always been taken as seriously as it should have been.

[2] While ethnographic studies of gossip are not abundant, enough work has been done to warrant initial attempts to develop models that are cross-culturally applicable. See Daena Goldsmith, "Gossip from the Native's Point of View," *Research on Language and Social Interaction* 23:163-194.

[3] Our proposal in what follows is simply that Mediterranean ethnography offers *heuristic* aid in looking for evidence of the scope and function of gossip in the New Testament. Perhaps then we can lay to rest the frequently expressed fear that models drawn from modern ethnography are being "forced" onto the New Testament data. No claim is being made here that Mediterranean villages now are the exact equivalent of those in antiquity. Nor is there anything "necessitarian" about our use of these

Definition of Gossip

Before thinking more systematically about the social function of gossip, it is important to define it carefully. David Gilmore offers a succinct definition which will serve our purposes. Gossip, he argues, is simply "critical talk about absent third parties" (1987b:92).[4] That definition will suffice. However, two things in it are especially important to note. One is that gossip is "signed"—i.e. face-to-face—talk about people who are not present (which leads some theorists to distinguish it from "rumor" which is "unsigned"—i.e. anonymous—talk about events. Paine 1970:186). This implies that at least three parties are always part of a gossip event: the gossiper, the party listening, and the gossipee. The second important factor to note is that gossip is evaluative talk. It may be either positive or negative, but it usually implies assessment of one kind or another.[5] Given the pervasive competition for honor in Mediterranean culture we spoke of earlier, both social ranking (Bailey 1971:45) and moral evaluation (Yerkovich 1977:195) are usually involved in gossip.

Information may be as well. We shall have more to say in a moment about gossip as "information management," but gossip is often the principle means of information-exchange in non-literate villages (Arno 1980:343; Paine 1967:282). It thus overlaps with simple word-of-mouth "news" about what is going on, though simple information-sharing frequently lacks the peculiar characteristics of gossip described above. We might also note that for gossip to occur, that is, critical talk about third parties, it requires that participants (1) know each other (at least minimally), (2) understand the import of the situation, and (3) share evaluative categories (Yerkovich 1977:192ff.).

Nearly all definitions of gossip recognize the importance of "self-interest" in the matter. The theoretical debate alluded to earlier had to do with whether gossip is a purely individual phenomenon (Paine) or a group activity (Gluckman). While that debate polarized for a while, recent theorists are inclined to see it as both (Gilmore 1978, 1987b; du Boulay, Bailey 1971, Rosnow and Fine, Wilson). This seems especially clear since the interests of both individuals and groups are often served.

models. They are heuristic, nothing more. They simply offer insight about what to look for and what questions to ask.

[4] Interestingly, a Talmudic sage offers an identical view: What constitutes evil speech? —Rabbah said: Whatsoever is said in the presence of the person concerned is not considered evil speech. *Arak.* 15b

[5] "Criticism and evaluation of others, which involves ranking, is the subject of gossip, said to be the chief pastime of the village" (Bailey 1971:45).

The point, then, is that in the degree to which evaluation or moral judgment is involved, gossip becomes a way of manipulating moral status (acquired honor) or other prospects in the "interests" of some person or group.

While most definitions of gossip assume it to be an oral medium, written comment about others might also qualify. When *verbal* reports come to Paul in 1 Corinthians (1:11) it is easy to see that evaluative comments about absent others are being made and that a gossip event is occurring. When *written* reports of a similar character come to Paul (7:1; 8:1; 12:1), perhaps they too should be construed as gossip.

Finally, when thinking about what constitutes gossip, we note its common association with women (1 Tim 3:11; 5:13). A Talmudic comment offers the typical stereotype: "Ten abs. of gossip descended to the world; nine were taken by women" (Caducean 49b). Juliet du Boulay observes that in her Greek mountain village gossip is an activity "indulged in pre-eminently by women" (204). She argues that while men do indeed gossip, their typical location in public space(s) tends to inhibit gossip, while the private space occupied by women is conducive to it (204). Alexander Ryman's studies suggest that the English term "gossip" developed particularly pejorative connotations only after it came to be associated with women in the nineteenth century (177). Interestingly, Ryman's studies of Chicano groups suggest that condemnations of gossip there were really condemnations of female solidarity which men feared (180).[6] Having noted the prevalent stereotype, then, we also note a certain irony in the fact that the vast majority of ancient texts which either condemn gossip as such or criticize particular instances of it refer either to male participants or make no gender reference at all.

Mediterranean Gossip Studies

A variety of studies in recent years have shown that gossip is indeed prevalent in the villages of the Mediterranean region (Campbell, du Boulay, Gilmore 1978, 1987b). Moreover, Juliet du Boulay's study of a Greek mountain village (Ambeli) convinced her that the prevalence

---

[6] David M. Guss ("The Enculturation of Makiritare Women," *Ethnology* 21/3 [1982]: 259-269), studying the Makiritare tribe in Venezuela, suggests that gossip among women there is considered a social necessity to mediate conflicts between men. Deborah Jones ("Gossip: Notes on Women's Oral Culture," *Women's Studies International Quarterly* 3/2-3 [1980]:193-198), makes the point that little is known about language use in all-female groups, a nearly irremediable problem in the study of antiquity because of the lack of sources/data.

of gossip there is not a matter of accident. In fact the peculiar character of Mediterranean village life makes it almost inevitable. She observes that the nature of gossip in Greek villages is determined by the various features of the society—the nature of the value system, the importance of a limited number of roles which express these values and which provide ideal standards of behavior, the privacy of the home, the publicity of communal life, the intense relevance of every member of the community to every other member, and the unceasing competition for reputation (204).[7]

Competition for reputation, of course, is a matter of honor, and honor is the core value in the Mediterranean world. J.K. Campbell's study of Greek shepherds in the area north of Corinth (the *Sarakatsani*) affirms this same connection. Gossip, he argues, is "closely related to the two concepts of self-regard and shame" (312). The result is that failure of any kind, but especially failure to defend honor, is the subject of taunts and even songs of ridicule. Songs are especially feared because they keep the memory of failure alive for long periods. They are never sung to the victim's face (see definitions of gossip below), but are always learned of and deeply shameful (314).

A variety of studies have also recognized that gossip "trades on" the sharp separation of the private and public domains which is characteristic of Mediterranean societies (Haviland, Gilmore 1978, 1987b, du Boulay). In theory at least, inside and outside worlds are kept apart. Family secrets are closely guarded. The result is a "continual battle between secrecy and curiosity waged between various families" in a village (du Boulay 1974: 202). Basically, then, gossip consists of "leakage from one domain into the other" (Haviland 1977a:188). Moreover, as du Boulay found out, "once a secret is let out of the family [private domain] there is little chance that it will not, sooner or later, be circulated to the entire community [public domain]" (208; also Zinovieff 121). It is always just a matter of time (Campbell 313).

Because gossip by its very nature is the telling of secrets, it is much feared for the damage it can do. In peasant communities where everyone knows everyone else so well, "people know exactly where to go to extract certain bits of information, and they know equally well the danger points of the community where a leak could be fatal" (du

---

[7] She argues that these features of village life also make gossip an activity "indulged in pre-eminently by women" (204). She suggests that while men often gossip, frequently their associations are sufficiently public that care must be taken how gossip is passed along. On why and how gossip "became a woman" in the English speaking world, see Rysman.

Boulay 207). In fact gossip is often a form of envy-aggression. Some have even seen it as the verbal equivalent of the evil eye (Zinovieff 126). Not only can words hurt, they can create actual situations which limit or destroy.

Ancient Comment

This of course accounts for the nearly universal condemnation of gossip by ancient authors. Plutarch, for example, devoted a classic essay to the topic entitled "On Being a Busybody":

> Just as cooks pray for a good crop of young animals and fishermen for a good haul of fish, in the same way busybodies pray for a good crop of calamities, a good haul of difficulties, or novelties and changes, that they, like cooks and fisherman, may always have something to fish out or butcher. *Moralia* VI:518E (7)

> He complains that gossips pass up nearly anything beautiful or worthwhile so they can spend their time digging into other men's trifling correspondence, gluing their ears to their neighbor's walls, whispering with slaves and women of the streets, and often incurring danger, and always infamy. *Moralia* VI:519F (9)[8]

In one of Plutarch's insights he offers as poignant a comment as one might ever read—from antiquity or any other time:

> Since, then, it is the searching out of troubles that the busybody desires, he is possessed by the affliction called "malignancy," a brother to envy and spite. For envy is pain at another's good, while malignancy is joy at another's sorrow." *Moralia* VI:518C (6)

The cogency of this observation in an honor-shame society is considerable.

Another ancient writer who devoted an essay to the subject of gossip was Lucian. As in the essay of Plutarch, so in this one there is a bitterness that is unmistakable:

> What I have in mind more than anything else is slanderous lying about acquaintances and friends, through which families have been rooted out, cities have utterly perished, fathers have been driven mad against their children, brothers against their own brothers, children against their parents and lovers against those they love. Many a friendship, too, has been parted and many an oath broken through belief in slander. *Slander* 1

---

[8] For other pithy comment see: *Moralia* VI:516A (2); VI:516B (2); VI:516D (3); VI:517E (5); VI:517F (6); VI:518E (7); VI:519C (9).

Were we to sample other Greco-Roman comment (which is abundant) we would find it is almost universally condemnatory.

But it is no different in the Jewish world. There is extensive comment in both Mishna and Talmud which we can only sample:

> "One who bears evil tales almost denies the foundation [of faith]" (*Arak.* 15b)
>
> "Any one who bears evil tales will be visited by the plague of leprosy" (*Arak.* 15b)
>
> "Of him who slanders, the Holy One, blessed be He, says: He and I cannot live together in the world. As it is said: Whoso slandereth his neighbor in secret, him will I destroy." (*Arak.* 15b)
>
> "Whoever relates slander, and whoever accepts slander, and whoever gives false testimony against his neighbor, deserves to be cast to dogs." (*Pesaḥ* 118a)

Once again the bitterness in the comments comes through clearly.[9]

Causes of Gossip

Ancient writers of course focus on the negative. But the fact is that gossip has many social functions, including some positive ones (see below). It also has many causes. We have already noted several of these (see du Boulay above), including the separation of private and public domains, the intense relevance of people to each other in the constant close contact of village life, and the intense competition for public reputation. In addition to these, a primary cause of gossip is the simple practical need to focus on the character of individuals with whom one might do any kind of business. In the non-literate communities of antiquity business deals, contracts, sales arrangements and the like were not written down. If oral arrangements could not be trusted, serious trouble was likely. Keeping close tabs on anything and everything which might indicate the character of others with whom one might do business was thus a basic matter of survival. As Sofka Zinovieff puts it: "Gossip can be a precious resource: people in business learn about their competitors; politicians require details about their rivals and supporters; citizens discover who are their friends and who their enemies, and so on" (124). To put it succinctly, close scrutiny of the character of others was not "mere pastime," it was a vital necessity (Goitein 1988:190).

---

[9] For additional comment see: *Qidd.* 49b; *Arak* 3; 15b, 16a.

Yet another cause of gossip has to do with the anthropomorphic worldview which sees personal causality behind nearly everything that happens. The ancient question was not the one we hear in the modern world, "W*hat?*" caused something to happen, but "W*ho?*" caused it to happen (Malina 1993a:109). As du Boulay points out, "The vivid memory and graphic mind of the villager, coupled with a natural philosophy which sees the working of superhuman forces or a supernatural law revealed continually in the doings of others, give to talk even about neutral subjects the remorseless tendency to turn into talk about personalities" (205). In other words, it was simply critical to find out not only *what* was happening but also *who* was doing it.

Zinovieff offers yet another powerful motivation for gossip: the simple need to learn from the experiences of others (121). It is part of the socialization process which provides everyone the opportunity to discuss and analyze human behavior in an informal but potent way. Because it provides a "close, oral, daily history" of a village, gossip also provides a "map" of the social environment that is constantly being updated with new experiences and new expectations. People learn from everything new or different they hear about other people. Gossip thus allows people to participate in "interpreting and constructing" their own social milieu (Zinovieff 126). To be in that game one has to talk and listen constantly.

Finally, a motivation for gossip that is not often recognized by westerners is the simple desire for entertainment. There are few organized entertainments in peasant villages, hence people enjoy simply gathering for talk (Gilmore 1978:90; Zinovieff 125). As du Boulay suggests, "it is natural that people should derive their entertainment from the human comedy around them" (205-6). Obviously the victims of this entertainment are usually not amused.

Semantic Field

One obvious way to get a sense of feel for a particular culture's attitude toward gossip is to survey the semantic field.[10] David Gilmore's studies (1987b:94-97) of an Andalusian village provide a good example. Gossip there was a much favored pastime, and Gilmore discovered eleven distinct terms being used to describe the phenomenon:

---

[10] The English word "gossip" lacks the specificity and nuance often seen in terms drawn from other languages. It developed from an earlier term "God sib," a reference to a god-parent. For an account of the development of the term and its association with women, see Rysman.

1. *Criticar:* "to criticize" (a rough equivalent of the English term "gossip")
2. *Rajar:* "to cut" (with a clear intention to harm)
3. *Darle la lengua:* "to tonguelash" (a sustained campaign of vilification)
4. *Cuchichear:* "to whisper" (uninformed talk)
5. *Murmurar:* "to murmur" (informed talk)
6. *Chismorear:* "to speak of trifles" (harmless exchange of information)
7. *Paliquear:* "to chatter or talk idly of nothing" (often with sexual undertones)
8. *Cortar el traje:* "to cut the cloth" (idle talk without malice— entertainment)
9. *Charlar:* "to chat" (a euphemism for *criticar*)
10. *Hablar occulto:* "to speak secretly" (secret talk about those in power)
11. *Contar:* "to tell" (to betray a confidence; hence the worst form of gossip)

This semantic field is of interest to biblical scholars not only because it comes from a Mediterranean society, and not only because of its scope and depth, but also because nearly all of these Andalusian terms have biblical equivalents.

Before looking at the semantic field in the Bible, however, it is worth noting that the semantic field above can be sorted into a model of gossip forms. It assumes that *criticar* and *charlar* are the more general terms and then distinguishes the other nine in light of four factors: social status of the subject, legitimacy, purposefulness and number of participants (180). By differentiating gossip forms/events in this way we avoid simply lumping all gossip activity together for indiscriminate condemnation.

Gossip Forms in an Andalusian Speech Community

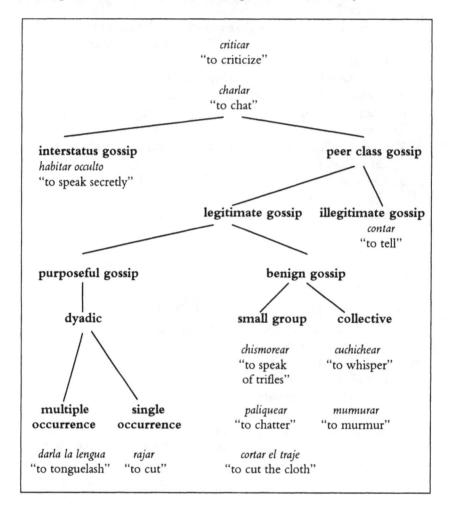

Figure 1
(Goldsmith, 180; adapted from Gilmore 1987b:94-98)

Biblical Examples

Space does not permit listing all of the instances of the following terms in the Bible. The list provided, however, will suffice to indicate that the semantic field in the biblical literature is no less rich than in Gilmore's Andalusian dialect.

Old Testament Terms

רכיל slander, gossip Lev 19:16, Ezek 22:9, Prov 20:19; דבה slander(er): Num 14:36; Ps 31:13; Prov 10:8; רכיל slandering, talebearing, gossip Jer 6:28; 9:4; רגל slander 2 Sam 19:27; Ps 15:3; לשן slander Ps 101:5; אכל slander (lit. devour) Ps 27:2; קרץ slander (lit. cut, tear apart) Ps 35:15; דפה slander (lit. ruin) Ps 50:20; רגל go around slandering, backbiting 2 Sam 19:27; לשון tongue Job 5:21, Ps 10:7; 15:3; 31:20; 64:3; 109:2; Prov 25:23; איש לשון slanderer (lit. a man of tongue) Ps 140:11; Prov 30:10; Ezek 36:3; שמעה what is heard, report 1 Sam 2:24; 1 Kgs 10:7; Prov 15:30; Isa 28:19; 53:1; שמע report: Exod 23:1; Deut 2:25; Josh 9:9; Isa 23:5; Jer 50:43; דבר word, report: 1 Kgs 10:6; Num 14:37; Josh 22:33; 1 Sam 11:4; 2 Chr 9:5; דבר speak, sometimes in sense of spreading news: 1 Kgs 13:25; or to spread gossip: Ps 41:6; אמר say, sometimes to report: Neh 6:19; to spread news: Num 14:14; 1 Sam 23:22; דבה spread slander, bring an evil report: Gen 37:2; Num 13:32, 14:36; sometimes to whisper: Jer 20:10; לחש whisper together: 2 Sam 12:19; Ps 41:7; נרגן whisperer, busybody: Prov 16:28; 18:8; 26:20, 22; שמץ whisper: Job 4:12; 26:14; נגד bring to light (hiph.), sometimes to betray or to inform against: Jer 20:10; Job 17:5; חרפה reproach, scorn (as a result of being gossiped about): Ps 15:3; 42:10; 79:12; לוץ deride, scorn: Prov 22:10; חרף scorn, reproach: Ps 69:19, 20; 89:51; לון murmur: Num 14:36; 16:11; 17:5; רגן murmur Deut 1:27; Ps 106:25. The similarity to the Spanish list is indeed striking.

New Testament Terms

φλυαρέω, φλύαρος slander, gossip, talk nonsense: 1 Tim 5:13; 3 Jn 10; κενοφωνία empty talk, foolish chatter: 1 Tim 6:20; 2 Tim 2:16; ματαιολογία, ματαιολογός idle, meaningless talk: 1 Tim 1:6, 10; μωρολογία stupid talk: Eph 5:4; λῆρος utter nonsense: Luke 24:11; σπερμολόγος information scavenger (lit. one who picks up seed; also implies passing it along): Acts 17:18; αἰσχρολογία shameful speech, slander: Col 3:8; εὐτραπελία coarse jesting, indecent speech: Eph 5:4; πρὸς τὸ οὖς λαλέω whisper, speak secretly: Matt 10:27; Luke 12:3; βαταλογέω babble, speak senselessly: Matt 6:7; λαλία talk: John 4:42; καταλαλέω, καταλαλία slander, talk against: Wis 1:11; 2 Cor 12:20; Jas 4:11; 1 Pet 2:1; κατάλαλος slanderer, gossiper: Rom 1:30; κατηχέω report, tell: Acts 21:21, 24; μηνύω inform, reveal (secretly): John 11:57; φάσις news, information, report: Acts 21:31; ἀκοή news, rumor, report, information: Matt 4:24; 14:1; Mark 1:28; 7:36; 13:7; 2

Pet 2:8; γλῶσσα tongue: Wis 1:11; Sir 5:14; 51:2; Jas 3:6, 7, 8; 1 Pet 3:10; γλῶσσα τρίτη slander, gossip (lit. third tongue): Sir 28:14, 15; φήμη news, report, information: Matt 9:26; Luke 4:14, 37; διαγημίζω spread news around: Matt 9:31; εὐαγγελίζω spread news about: Luke 1:19; Acts 8:35; δηλόω report, 1 Cor 1:11; ψσεύσης, ψεῦδος, ψευδομαι Rom 9:1; Rev 2:2; ψευδολόγος liar: 1 Tim 4:2; μαρτυρία, μαρτυρέω, report (usually to speak well of someone): Acts 10:22; 22:12; 1 Tim 3:7; Heb 11:2, 39; 3 Jn 12; καταμαρτυρέω witness against: Matt 27:13; ψευδομαρτυρία, ψευδομαρτυρέω false witness: Matt 26:59; Mark 14:56, 57; εὐλογία, praise, flattery: Rom 16:18; κατακαυχάομαι, boast against (put down another): Rom 11:18; γογγύζω, διαγογγύζω, grumble, complain: Luke 15:2; John 6:41, 61; Acts 6:1, Wis 1:10, 11; γογγυστής habitual grumbler: Jas 1:16; στενάζω Jas 5:9; ὀνειδίζω, ὀνειδισμός shame, insult, disgrace, disparage: Heb 10:13; ὑβρυστής insulter, slanderer: 1 Tim 1:13; λοιδορέω, λοιδορία, λοώδορος insult, slander: 1 Cor 4:12; 6:10; 1 Pet 2:23; 3:9; ἐκβάλλω slander, insult (lit. throw out [a name])" Luke 6:22; διάβολος slanderer: 1 Tim 3:11; Titus 2:3; Sir 19:15; 26:5; 51:2, 6; δυσφημηέω defame: 1 Cor 4:13; 2 Cor 6:8; slander in a vile manner: Matt 15:4; βλασφημηέω, βλασφημία, βλασφημος insult, defame, revile: Matt 15:19; Mark 7:22; Rom 3:8; Eph 4:31; 1 Tim 1:13; Titus 3:2; ψιθυρισμός, ψιθυριστής, ψιθυρίζω, διαψιθυρίζω habitual gossiper, whisperer: Rom 1:29; 2 Cor 12:20; Sir 12:18; 21:28: 28:31; διακρίνομαι, ἀνακρίνομαι criticize: Acts 11:2; 1 Cor 9:3; μομάομι find fault: 2 Cor 6:3; ἀκατάγνοστος above reproach: Titus 2:8; ἀναπίλημπτος above reproach: 1 Tim 6:14; ἀπελέγμος serious criticism: Acts 19:27; θρυλέθ babble: 3 Macc 3:7; διαβάλλω accuse, slander Luke 16:1; κατηγορία accusation, charge 1 Tim 5:19; μεμθίμοιρος habitual fault-finder: Jude 1:16; συκοφαντέω falsely accuse someone: Luke 3:14; ἀπαγγελλώ tell, report, spread news: Matt 8:33; 14:12; Luke 7:18; 8:36; 13:1; Acts 5:25, 2; Rom 1:8; 2 Cor 7:7; εὐφημία good report: 2 Cor 6:8; Phil 4:8; περίεργος busybody: 1 Tim 5:13; περίεργάομαι be a busybody: 1 Thess 3:11; ὀνειδισμός, ὀνειδίζω, ὀνειδος reproach, insult, disgrace: Matt 11:20; Luke 1:25; Rom 15:3; 1 Tim 3:7; 1 Pet 4:14.

We note once again the striking similarity to the Spanish list. But especially astonishing is the sheer magnitude of the field and obvious frequency of comment (even though the above is only a partial list of instances) about gossip in the Bible. Gossip, backbiting, criticism, spreading lies and the like were obviously a major concern in the world of the Old and New Testament writers.

Social Function of Gossip

We turn now to the social functions of gossip. These are more complex than is usually imagined, though any one of them is likely to be more or less prominent in a given society (or even a given village). The list that follows has been gleaned from the work of a wide variety of social theorists.

1. Clarification (consensus building), maintenance (reaffirmation) and enforcement (sanction) of group values

It should be obvious that successful gossip heavily depends on shared history and common values among at least some part of every community (du Boulay 211). Talk about values, in the form of talk about the behavior of other people, is the means by which public opinion on moral behavior first emerges and then begins to solidify. It also provides an avenue for constant updating and renewal of group norms and expectations. Each time gossip is repeated group values get re-asserted and reinforced. Moreover, whatever community consensus is built up over time becomes the norm into which all newcomers must fit and into which children are socialized. In fact, without backbiting and gossip, small-group values of all kinds would simply disappear. Roger Abrahams has summed it up nicely:

> The subjects discussed or gossiped about commonly deal with the proper maintenance of the household and the appropriate practice of interpersonal relationships within the family and among friends. Talk about such matters constantly serves to remind those involved of the importance of the norms of the community, but also rehearses the necessity of working within the decorum system by which household and friendship networks are maintained (296-7).

Clarification of values and setting moral standards via informal conversation is especially important at the level of what has been called the "Little Tradition," that is, the tradition prevalent among the non-literate, non-elite. It is a principal means by which a village takes on a cohesive identity and develops its own level of expected participation in a wider tradition. Where community consensus on moral standards is lacking, however, and where people begin to take sides on a matter of individual conduct, gossip about the "others" frequently becomes a campaign in which one side seeks social control (Suls 165).

A good example of gossip working to clarify values at the level of the Little Tradition can be seen in Matt 15:10-20. Matthew's setting is pointedly away from Jerusalem, where representatives of the Great Tradition (pharisees and scribes) have come to challenge Jesus over purity practices. After a counter-challenge in which Jesus charges his questioners with hypocrisy, he calls the crowd aside and begins clarifying his own values: "It is not what goes into the mouth that defiles a person, but it is what comes out of the mouth that defiles" (15:10). The disciples then report some gossip to him (their report is itself gossip since they are talking to Jesus about a third party), asking if he knows he has offended the pharisees. In response, Jesus tells a parable about the blind leading the blind which is clearly evaluative talk about his opponents, and Peter then asks for an insider explanation. The explanation Jesus provides is a direct insult to his rivals which charges them, among other things, with slander. In the process of talking about his opponents, therefore, that is, about others who are not like him, Jesus has clarified and defended his little-tradition behavior.

Above all, in social settings where small group interaction is pervasive, as would be true in peasant villages, gossip is an informal method of social control. As people comment on or condemn the failings of others, they reinforce behavioral norms. Conformity to the norms develops social reputation and thus competition for honor places sharp controls on individual behavior. Especially in societies with a dyadic view of personality, "conscience" is external to the individual: it is the group, the community, which monitors behavior. It is the community which "accuses," not an internal voice, and it is the community which comments. Thus nonconformity is quickly highlighted and condemned by gossipers, not only damaging reputation but also providing negative examples.

Fear of being talked about is especially effective as an informal means of control over people attempting to be part of a religious group (Suls 164; Paine 1967:278; Gluckman 1963:312). Gluckman, for example, notes that religious control of morals operates very effectively through a gossip network—or the fear of it (1963308). His argument is not that gossip creates morality, but that it creates the *appearance* of morality. It motivates people to put up defenses, to hide sins and to keep up appearances. Of course this pressure to conform in appearance creates some conformity in fact, but it also means that appearance is not quite to be trusted as reality. People work very hard at manipulating impressions (see below). Ironically, however, this very unreliability of gossip allows people margin for breaking the rules. Accusations can be dismissed as the shameless lies of a gossip because "everyone knows that only a fool believes gossip unconditionally" (Zinovieff 122).

2. Group formation and boundary maintenance

An important function of gossip is to clarify group membership. We recall that a gossip event involves at least three parties. One person is usually talking to a second person about an absent third. Usually the first is implicitly seeking solidarity with the second against the third, thus re-affirming who is "in" and who is "out." When the third party is embodied as public opinion, the gossip event serves to differentiate the two talkers and their soul mates from nearly everyone else. In this way adherents can be recruited, affirmed and reinforced (Abrahams). In fact, Gluckman argues that a critical step in gaining membership in any group is learning its gossip (1963:314).

The important point here is that gossip serves to differentiate insiders from outsiders. Obviously anyone expecting to be an insider must be trusted with the tales others in the group tell. "To be a true insider, one must know and be able to gossip about the present membership [of a group] as well as their forebears" (Rosnow and Fine 90). To tell tales you have to know the characters personally or at least know their histories (Zinovieff 123). This is one reason anonymous outsiders do not make good subjects for gossip.

The gossip circle thus marks a group off from all other groups which are not privy to its secrets (Gluckman 1963:311). It does the same with individuals who are marked as outsiders because they are not given access to the group's gossip circle (Gluckman 1963:312). Pamela Dorn quotes a Turkish (Jewish) proverb: "No one knows what is happening in the pot except for the spoon that turns." The point is that while everyone can talk about what goes on inside the house, only an insider really knows (299). In Luke 24:18 Cleopas assumes Jesus is a *paroikeis*, a resident alien, an outsider, because he seems "unaware of recent local events" (Elliott 1990:34). He appears to be an outsider; insiders always know.

One interesting twist on this is the observation by Gluckman that the more exclusive the membership of a group, the more prevalent gossip is likely to be among the members. This is so because they have to work harder to differentiate themselves from all other people. Minority groups which cannot overcome the exclusive status thrust upon them by a society provide one good example (1963:309). A second is the tendency of higher status groups to talk constantly about how they are differentiated from those beneath them. Of course gossip of this sort was endemic in the socially stratified societies of antiquity.

Group unity is also maintained by these same processes. Gossip becomes a form of boundary maintenance (Zinovieff 122). Those who push the boundaries too far are quickly sanctioned by the gossip network. Even those who gossip excessively and do not follow group protocols for gossip are subject to group sanction. Group unity is also served by a gossip network because gossip can function as an informal method of adjudicating conflict in small groups where face-to-face confrontation would do irreparable damage (Arno 343).

3. Moral assessment of individuals

The need to evaluate nearly everyone with whom a villager comes in contact has already been described as a matter of survival. It allows him/her to differentiate friends and enemies, those who are kin of heart and those who are not. All of those processes we noted above by which moral control is maintained serve in this capacity as well. Because moral assessment is the very nature of gossip, it allows gossipers to rank people in relation to others on an ongoing basis (du Boulay 211). In fact, not only do people use gossip to measure others on the scale of community values, they use it to measure themselves (Mark 8:27-30). Self-comparison with group norms often lies in the background as two people talk about others not present (Suls).

This kind of moral assessment is especially important in honor-shame societies where the give and take of challenge-riposte is the means by which gains and losses of (acquired) honor are accumulated. Since honor is always a *public* matter, the gossip network is the means by which these gains and losses are validated, and since that process is ongoing, as people gossip the relative honor status of group members is constantly being updated (Rosnow and Fine 90). Such notices that public assessment of Jesus is going on are frequent in the gospels (Mark 1:27-28; 1:45; 22; 9:15; 10:24; 10:32; 12:17; Matt 4:24; 9:31; 12:23; 14:1; 21:15-17; Luke 2:47; 4:22; 4:36; 7:17; 8:56; 18:43; 19:37; 23:47).

4. Leadership identification and competition

As the moral assessment described above proceeds, individuals begin to differentiate themselves within a group. Leaders are identified as those who embody (and can articulate) group norms (Gluckman 1963:307; Paine 278). Thus competition between leaders can often take the form of gossip. The comment of Paul Radin cited earlier (n. 1) spoke about the name-calling one leader can aim at another. As leaders talk about their rivals and as followers pass along the gossip, factions owing allegiance to particular individuals begin to emerge.

An obvious example of gossip being used in leadership competition is the long diatribe against the scribes and pharisees in Matt 23. There

Jesus directs intensely critical and insulting comment about his rivals to the crowds and his disciples. Still another example is reported by Matthew in 16:5-12. As a follower of Jesus, Matthew passes along the evaluative talk about the Pharisees and Sadducees which Jesus himself had offered to his immediate disciples. Matthew's readers are thereby warned about straying allegiance.

This competition between leaders also engenders one of the key features of gossip, what anthropologists call "impression management" (Cox). Gossip is manipulative talk. It is highly selective in terms of both audience and content. By what one says or does not say and to whom one does or does not say it, impressions can be managed for best effect. Leaders (read: politicians) often make a living doing this. They develop self-protective instincts that are finely tuned to the boundaries between insiders and outsiders, friends and enemies.

One of the key ways in which impression management is carried out is through the management of information. "The gift of the gossiper is information and the thirst for all sorts (who knows what might be useful?) is unending" (Zinovieff 124). By controlling who knows what, a gossiper can pit factions against each other, separate friends, support or undermine a cause. Because in peasant societies the spread of information depends on word of mouth, information management becomes critically important to those in power or those seeking power. An example is to be seen in Luke 7:18-23 where we are told that information about Jesus comes to John the Baptist. In response he seeks confirmation of Jesus' messianic status by sending two of his disciples to Jesus, who then offers a succinct summary of his ministry of healing and good news. Jesus concludes his comments with directions about the impression one is to get from all this: "Blessed is anyone who takes no offense at me."

Both spreading news and keeping it secret at appropriate times can play a role. It is perhaps in this light that we should understand the so-called "messianic secret" in Mark. By asking his followers to withhold information, Jesus manages information and thereby manages impressions. Of course the one form of information management which causes very special anguish is the betrayal of confidence (*contar:* see above). No doubt it is common to all societies and viewed in all societies with equal bitterness (Job 17:5; Jer 20:10).

Before leaving the notion of information management it is important to point out that gossip is a "network" phenomenon (Hannerz 39-40). People who gossip usually know each other, or know of each other. Usually they also have both mutual and exclusive friends. In turn, the same can be said of each of the friends, and so on and on. In fact most of the social functions of gossip depend on networks which can spread information in a relatively short time (stale news rarely excites the gossip instinct). Close-knit networks (kin, near-kin, close associates) circulate some kinds of gossip that would not be allowed into wider circles. Loosely-knit networks, however, can encompass an entire community and indeed what consensus on behavior and morality exists in a community does so because the gossip network is functioning properly. Of course because the spread of information cannot be completely controlled, the feeling of betrayal noted above is often the result of poorly (or maliciously) managed information that escapes the networks for which it is intended.

While the list above hits the key points, it does not exhaust the social functions of gossip or gossip networks. We have already noted that it can be a matter of simple entertainment. It can also be a form of catharsis for individuals or relate a community to its living past. Negative gossip campaigns can be a form of status degradation ritual. They can break up marriages, friendships, political alliances or business partnerships. Positive gossip can affirm values in the same way that negative gossip proscribes others. It can create intimacy between friends who develop a closeness over against the one(s) being talked about. Of course when a community begins to cease functioning properly, gossip can even accelerate its disintegration (2 John; 3 John).

New Testament Examples

In a short article it is impossible to survey all of the biblical evidence for the phenomenon of gossip. In order to provide a summary of sorts, however, we may look at three types of New Testament texts having to do with gossip. First, there are the many texts *about* the topos, that is, about gossip as a phenomenon. Like the texts cited at the beginning of this article, most of these are extremely negative.

The astonishingly frequent comment about gossip in the pastoral epistles is noteworthy in itself. It also provides typical examples. There women (wives?) are enjoined not to be "slanderers" (1 Tim 3:11, Titus 2:3; διάβολος). Widows are to be "beyond reproach" (1 Tim 5:7; ἀνατίλημπτος). It is feared that younger widows will "learn to be idle, gadding about from house to house." The writer fears "they are not merely idle, but also gossips (φλύαρος) and busybodies (περίερος), saying what they should not say" (1 Tim: 5:13. Those who are bishops are enjoined to have a "good report" (μαρτυρίαν καλήν) among outsiders lest they fall into "disgrace" (ὀνειδισμός). Many of the examples in the semantic field above are this sort of comment about the topos.

Secondly, there are a large number of texts which are reports about gossip occurring. These are more numerous than one might suspect. As representative examples we may take those texts in the synoptic gospels which report people talking evaluatively about Jesus when he is not present. There are at least twenty such instances in Mark, interestingly concentrated entirely in the Judean section of the narrative (1:28, 45; 2:1,16; 3:8, 21; 5:14, 20; 6:2-5, 14 [three references], 15, 16, 55; 7:24, 25, 36, 37; 9:14). One gets the impression that in the story-world of Mark we are very much in a word-of-mouth environment in which the gossip network functions very well.

The gossip network in Mark is widespread indeed. It includes both peasant villagers (1:28) and the royal aristocracy (6:14). Both town and country (5:14) are included. Whole regions are covered (1:28). In one of the turning points of the narrative Jesus inquires of his followers what the nature of the gossip about him is among ordinary people (8:27) and even in his own group (8:28). Here, as indeed in the other synoptics, gossip notices inform the reader that the reputation of Jesus is constantly being updated even as it spreads.

It is interesting to note that of the twenty Markan references cited above, Matthew eliminates fifteen of them. In one case he omits a Markan reference to the wider gossip network (14:1) and in another he restricts the network to the city (8:33). He adds two references to gossip that come from special M (9:26; 17:24), and another from Q, in which Jesus muses about the gossip circulating about himself (11:19). In 22:34 Matthew adds a report that the Pharisees heard Jesus had silenced the Sadducees. In general, however, one does not get the sense that we are in the same kind of oral (gossip) environment as we are in Mark.

Luke eliminates eleven of the Markan references to gossip and also changes some of the notices which he does include. In 4:37 he removes a reference to the Galilee from a rather sweeping Markan gossip notice. What Mark has as a complaint of the scribes/pharisees to the disciples about Jesus' eating habits (2:16), Luke turns into a complaint to Jesus about the eating habits of the disciples (5:30). He changes Mark's reference to gossip spreading in the Decapolis (5:20) to one about it spreading in "the whole city" (8:39).

Luke also adds a few references. In 2:17 the shepherds return and report what they had seen at the manger. In 4:14 Luke adds a classic reference to the gossip network functioning to update the reputation of Jesus in the area around Nazareth.[11] Three other new references come from special L (7:17; 23:8; 24:19). Of course how many of these added references to gossip about Jesus can be attributed to Matthew and Luke is difficult to say. The tendency of both writers to eliminate such references in texts they share with Mark suggests that most of their added references may have come from their sources rather than themselves. A noteworthy exception, however, may be the notice in 4:14. It seems to fit the Lukan rhetorical strategy in a very special way (see n. 11).

Finally there is a third type of text which should be illustrated. In addition to (1) texts about the topos itself, and (2) texts which report gossip occurring, there are (3) some texts which are themselves gossip, that is, they are actual critical talk about third parties who are not present. In Mark 2:18 a group of unidentified persons comes to Jesus with critical questions about his (absent) disciples. Presumably the parties present know each other in at least a minimal way and thus can undertake an evaluative discussion of the disciples' behavior. A similar incident is reported in Mark 7:1-15 where it occasions a long discussion about standards of behavior. In Mark 6:14 there is a report of the exact content of some gossip that was occurring about Jesus which had come to the attention of Herod. Unidentified persons ("some") had been saying that Jesus was either John the Baptist raised from the dead, or Elijah, or one of the prophets. This of course is exactly what the disciples report to Jesus in 8:28 when he inquires about how the gossip network is treating him. A third example of actual gossip (rather than a report *about* gossip) is one Paul puts in writing. In Galatians 2:11-14 Paul gossips about Cephas, evaluating his inconsistent behavior in the controversy over compelling gentile Christians to live like Jews. His complaint serves a number of the social functions noted above, but is an especially clear example of leadership identification and competition.

Conclusion

We began with the comment that gossip is especially widespread in non-literate societies. Comment about gossip by ancient authors is extremely common and represents an interesting case of written obser-

[11] This report is usually (but erroneously) labeled a "summary." For more extensive comment see Richard L. Rohrbaugh, "Legitimating Sonship: A Test of Honor: A Social Science Study of Luke 4:1-30. Pp. 183-97 in Philip F. Esler, *Modelling Early Christianity: Social Scientific Studies of the New Testament in its Context* (London: Routledge, 1995).

vations about an oral phenomenon. At a very minimum it would be accurate to say that the New Testament is in touch with this oral world; the frequency with which gossip is evaluated, reported or actually recorded is truly astonishing. The claim is also justified that the synoptic writers take the oral environment around Jesus seriously. They record his gossip about other leaders and groups and that of other groups and leaders about him. They constantly acknowledge that word is spreading orally. For the non-literate persons who heard the gospels read aloud, and who like most non-literate people shared a deep distrust of written words, these reports and records of the oral environment might well have been critical. They are a way of suggesting that the reputation of Jesus was secured first of all in that world a peasant implicitly trusts. As Papias would later put it, "I did not consider that I got so much profit from the contents of books as from the utterances of a living and abiding voice" (*Expositions of the Oracles of the Lord*, Eusebius *H.E.* III. 39).

10

"Neither *Xenoi* nor *paroikoi, sympolitai* and *oikeioi tou theou*" (Eph 2:19) Pauline Christian Communities: Defining a New Territoriality[1]

Carmen Bernabé Ubieta, *Universidad de Deusto (Bilbao), Spain*

Introduction

In the Mediterranean world of the first century, made up mainly of cities and their territories, several factors converged that brought the subject of contact and relationship with other countries increasingly more to the fore. One of them was increased mobility, favored by the spread of the Greek language, greater safety in travel, and an undeniable improvement in road links. The arrival of foreigners in big cities was becoming increasingly more frequent both for purposes of business or in search of a life that was impossible in their places of origin, often in rural areas where they had lost their lands. Another factor closely related to the previous one was the system of imperial rule and its policy of conquests.

All human groups establish a set of limits which order their world, both their physical and mental universe, which allows them to sort things out and orient themselves in space. These limits separate the inside from the outside, the familiar from the unfamiliar which is experienced as a threat to that established order that lends full meaning to human existence. The foreigner is the some one from beyond the limits. He is different for many reasons, and this difference is regarded as a threat and a sign of inferiority.

---

[1] This article is a revision of *El extranjero en la cultura Europea actual* (Bilbao: Universidad de Deusto 1997), the result of interdisciplinary research carried out in collaboration with several Faculties of the University.

It is interesting to study the theoretical and practical consideration of the Greco-Roman world towards foreigners and the specific actions taken by the cities in which they arrived. Of particular interest are the justifications given for their rejection as well as for their acceptance. Hence, the analysis of these reasons as well as the symbols and symbolic actions through which these judgements are expressed and carried ought to constitute a rich field for research It is in the area of motivation and the legitimation of xenophobic or philoxenic practices that the social function of philosophy and religion can be observed. It is also in this context that nascent Christianity will make its contribution.

This essay will specifically focus on the early Christian communities of Pauline tradition which appeared and spread across the Mediterranean Greco-Roman world, coexisting within this cultural context. It aims at offering some background to delineate and explain the social system from which a text like the epistle to the Ephesians took its meanings.

Although it is not a universal phenomenon, the attitude of hindering and rejecting a foreigner has existed at all times. In the contemporary world, this attitude has become more salient as it often manifests itself with a degree of violence. Yet even today, philosophical and religious reasons are adduced to justify the attitude, even though, obviously, they are not the only reasons.

Before considering this problem from the standpoint of the nascent Christianity—and chiefly Pauline Christianity—and in order to assess its contribution adequately in this matter, it would be helpful to know the cultural context in which the problem appears.

Common origin as a basis for benevolent behavior towards others

In the ancient world, sharing a common origin (house, clan, town) was the reason for benevolent behavior toward others. Obviously, the foreigner was excluded by definition. The notion that all human beings shared a common nature beings was not typical nor evident, since this notion took a while to evolve and develop. The foreigner had nothing in common with those within the community he was visiting. He possessed no characteristic that could justify a positive behavior towards him, nor anything that entitled him to some basic rights.

Territoriality as a way of control and its theoretical justification

One model that can help to understand this attitude and its consequences is the theory of territoriality developed by R. Sack (1986).
Establishing "territoriality" is a human strategy that has to do with the
use of land, the organization of space and the meaning given to it.
Sack defines the strategy as "the attempt by an individual or group to
affect, influence, or control people, phenomena and relationship, by
delimiting and asserting control over a geographic area. This area will
be called the territory" (Sack 1986:19). Since those relationships
change over time, it is evident that "territoriality is a historically sensitive use of space, especially since it is socially constructed and depends
on who is controlling whom and why" (Sack 1986:3).

Malina (1993b) complements Sack's theory with Geertz's definition
of religion as a cultural system. By considering territoriality from the
symbolic perspective, it can defined as "a system of symbols which acts
to establish powerful, pervasive and long lasting moods and motivations in people by formulating conceptions of geographic area and
clothing these conceptions with such an aura of factuality that the
moods and motivations seem uniquely realistic" (Malina 1993b:369).

But if it is evident that territory, according to the same author, is
"the outcome of social interpretation of space ... a social construction"
(Malina 1993b:369), it should be noted that the act of defining territoriality was always social in ancient times (Sack 1986:60). In ancient
times, people thought that they were organically related to the geographical area which had been given by some god to their ancestors
who lived in it and were buried in it. The geographical features, the
history of the place and of their ancestors, as well as the gods of those
who had chosen the place, established a connection between people
and the territory. Thus, social territoriality refers "to the delimiting of
some geographic area in terms of persons organically related to the area
which they define and delimit" (Malina 1993b:370). Therefore, "the
stranger or non-member of the group was not perceived simply in
terms of non-residence in a given territory. Rather the stranger or
non-member was one who had no social relationship to members of
the group, hence ought not be resident in a given territory because [he
has] no organic links to that territory... *Territoriality was intimately linked
with belonging*" (italics are mine) (Malina 1993b:370).

From the above, it may be deduced that if to establish territoriality
means to interpret, give social sense and meaning to space through
symbols, then, when the geographical area changes, so will the symbols
that interpret it and give it meaning also have to change. Conversely,

when these symbols change, the limits of the territory will be called into question as well as the criteria by which it had been defined.

The religious legitimization of territoriality
Religion and the worship of gods were very important factors when it came to encouraging and sustaining the feeling of belonging to a town and the link with a territory. Thus, religion was one of the legitimizing elements of the establishment of a specific territoriality with its consistent policy towards foreigners. Both Fustel de Coulanges (1984) and Sjoberg (1960) considered the importance of religion in the organization and in the self-comprehension of the pre-industrial town and its inhabitants. However, they (but especially de Coulange) seemed not to realize, that the type of society, its ways of relationship and organization, determined meaning and religious practice. The social sciences have provided us with a better knowledge of the relationship between social forms and religion in ancient towns. Malina has studied this subject in two highly enlightening articles which are a great help in establishing the cultural framework of the towns where the first communities emerged (Malina 1994a; 1996a).

Family and politics: two spheres of existence in the ancient world

In the Mediterranean world of the first century there were only two formal social institutions or spheres of life in which the inhabitants spent their lives: the family (in the broadest sense of kinship) and politics (organization and governance of the town). Neither religion nor economy constituted distinct areas of life separate from kinship or politics. Rather, religion and economy they were experienced within kinship and politics; they were absorbed and defined by them (Malina 1994a:17-18). There was a *family or domestic religion* and another *political (civic) religion*, both of which were independent, as it can be seen in the distinction made by Cicero between the *sacra privata* and *sacra publica (De Legibus* 2,8; Harmon 1978:1592). Some domestic worship ended up moving into political religion like the worship of the *genius Augusti*, which was a transposition to the State of the celebration of the *genius* of *the paterfamilias* of each home (Nilsson 1945:82; Guillen 1985:48-49; Lacey 1968:28).

The interweaving of religion within the domestic and political spheres meant that the symbols, rules and objectives of family and politics determined how to conceive and articulate the perceptions and behaviors of religion. It was the family or political roles, obligations and expectations that gave meaning and expression to religious roles, obligations and expectations (Malina 1996a:28-29). Religion reflected social organization and its imaginary context, both parts being so interrelated that a change in the ways of perceiving either part significantly influenced the perception of the other as well.

The home and domestic religion

In family life, domestic worship was highly important since it strengthened the unit and kept them together round the sacred hearth. The term *epistíon* was used in ancient Greek to designate the family. Literally it meant "what is beside the sacred hearth" (Herodotus 1,176; 5,73). The Romans had a similar and even more intense feeling (Cicero, *De Domo* 41,109; *De Officiis* 1,17,109). Family religion had its altar, its rites and its ceremonies for the benefit of the family where the ties that linked family members were expressed *par excellence* (de Coulanges 1984:65-131; Guillén 1985:49-50).

Each family home had its domestic worship and gods (*Lares, Penates, Genius* del *Pater Familias*) (Plauto, *Anularia* 1-39; cfr. Guillén 1985:50-65; Orr 1978:1562-69; Nilsson 1954:79-82). Domestic worship was focused on the hearth where a perpetual fire was burning (Orr 1978:1560-61; Rosse 1975:95-116; Malina 1996a:33-34). It involved ceremonies which celebrated and maintained the status of the various members in the family (meals, offerings, the *dies natalis*), and rites that marked the shift in position or status of the different family members (birth, adoption, marriage, death). Both types of celebrations encouraged the sense of belonging and union between the members of the family group.

In this regard, it is worth discussing the rite of admission to the family. Both in Greece and in Rome mere birth was not an entitlement to become a family member nor to be part of the descendant line. The *Paterfamilias* had to recognize the newborn baby ritually, by raising him from the ground, where he was placed after being born. The baby would be named some days later beside the domestic hearth (Suetonius, *Nero* 6,1; Tertullian *De Idolatria* 16; Harmon 1978:1596-97; Rose 1957:110-111). Illegitimate children might not have been recognized, and non-illegitimate children of others could be adopted as their own legitimate children. For this reason, adoption was a very important rite. Illegitimate children could not take part in the family sacrifice, but non-illegitimate children were obliged to leave their own natural family and join the adoptive family. After all, they were adopted for purposes of continuing that family's line. With their adoption, they were recognized as members of the *oikos*, descendants and heirs (N. Jay 1989: 41-46) and they inherited a name, possessions and worship (Cicero, *De Domo* 13,35; de Coulanges 1984:76-78).

Another focus of domestic worship was the family tomb, where the continuity and unity of the family group become evident as well as that of the living and the dead. This was also connected with the family home with its possessions and ancestors. In the tomb, the rite of death was celebrated, in which the status of the dead person became that of an ancestor. When the *Pater Familias* died, his place as a priest was taken by his son, his heir (Cicero, *De Legibus* 2,19; Fustel de Coulanges 1984:92-93; Lacey 1968:147-48).

The city and its gods: political religion

Political religion aimed at encouraging the city's political unity and welfare. The city itself was conceived as a family home made up of family homes. Each city had its temples, its altar with the perpetual fire, its ceremonies and its sacrifices (Malina 1994a:16-22; 1966:28-29).

More so for the Romans than the Greeks, the gods lived in the city (Mazzolani 1972:11), and their home was the center, the vital unit. It was around the metropolis that the city spread and the life of the citizens developed (de Coulanges 1984). These gods were, in principle, the ones that were linked to the city, to the ancestors, to the city's common history due to their belonging to some family in the city which had the right and duty to take part in the civic worship. Although the idea of the sacredness of the founding of their city was more important for the Romans (in the case of Rome) than for the Greeks, the origin of Greco-Roman cities was specially linked to their gods. It was through their oracles and prodigious signs that the founders had managed to know the founding site of the city that its protective gods had chosen. It was that moment of its past—qualitatively separate from the rest of the time—which was the origin of its history celebrated in the worship, that provided them with a common reference, identifying and defining them as a city community. The founding act had given rise to something they had to preserve and reinforce throughout the ages. This founding act from which the city developed constituted the city's tradition and gave support to its citizens (Arendt 1958). This idea was symbolized in the home-temple or city altar with a perpetual fire and a sacrifice of its own.

These were not universal gods even though some of them had the same name as universal gods. The idea of a universal god or gods only developed over time and had implications regarding attitudes towards the foreigner. Each city had its own gods who shared the same language and culture. They lived among the inhabitants and had an exclusive relationship with them. In return for worship, the gods provided protection against the enemy or in the face of adversity. They also secured fertility for the lands and the citizens. Foreign gods were often invited to leave the defeated city and to dwell in that of the victors, becoming part of their pantheon and their protective gods. In fact, this invitation involved the ritual called *evocatio* (Titus Livius V 22.3-7; Bloch 1977: 224ff). In many Greco-Roman cities, altars were erected to the unknown god (to the god or goddess of any town) because they thought that any other god of any other town could enter their lives at any time and they wanted it to be propitious to them (an example of this is can be found in Acts 17:23).

Political sacrifice and the community of citizens

There was a patronizing attitude toward the gods which was similar to the attitude citizens from the lower strata of society had toward some more powerful and wealthier citizens. As noted before, political religion reflected the social order and its relationships. This is why it is hardly surprising that customary types of social relationships and control are reflected in political religion, particularly the relationship of patronage, intermediaries and favors, which were normal and customary in that society (Malina 1994a:13-14).

The most important part of worship, that is, of the relationship that citizens had with the gods, was the ceremony of city sacrifice. Malina, following Talcott Parson's classification into four types of "generalized symbolic media of social interaction (=GSM)", locates sacrifice in the GSM he called "inducement: and defines it as "a ritual in which a deity or deities (of the household or polis) is/are offered some form of inducement, rendered humanly irretrievable, with a view to some life-effect for the offered" (Malina 1996a:37). Inducement was one of the typical forms by which subordinates tried to obtain certain things from their superiors in return for which they offered them goods and services. In the same article, and after considering the political sacrifice of Greeks, Romans and Israelites, Malina distinguishes two main types of sacrifice with different functions: first, separation-expiation (*enagismos-'olah*) and secondly, communion-celebration (*thysia-selamim*). In the first type of sacrifice, the victim is completely burnt and its blood is poured over the altar; it is a sacrifice that separates the individual and the group from defilement and danger. The second type is characterized by gathering together the participants in a community, thus creating a bond between them. Part of the victim is eaten by the offerers and part is burnt to the deity whereas the altar is sprayed with blood (Malina 1996a:31-33). Jay (1992:17ff) makes the same distinction although he names it differently (expiation-communion). While the first type "was a fellowship sacrifice joining people together in an alimentary community; it was life-enhancing and life maintaining, a celebration of the life-sustaining group"; the second type "separated the persons and group from defilement and danger; it was life-protecting" (Malina 1996a:33).

Participation in city sacrifice emphasized and validated the citizen's belonging and status. In fact, in ancient Greece it was similar to the initiation rite the young people whose status shifted from children to citizens (Humphreys 1983:15).

From this concept of sacrifice and our discussion of domestic worship, it is easy to understand how in Greco-Roman cities political sacrifice maintained the sense of belonging to the city as well as ethnic pride as descendants from the city founders. Political sacrifice also emphasized the differences from foreigners, or outsiders. The altar/temple with the sacred fire was the core, the vital center of the city that had to be kept perpetually burning. Along with the ancestors, the sacred fire was the cornerstone upon which the city and the citizens' community was built and sustained. The city was the place where the continuity and community with the ancestors was realized, since the ancestors were buried in that soil, and the gods had chosen that place. The communion sacrifices in which citizens took part created a sense of community between them and of communion with their ancestors and the gods of the city. Religion and worship of civic gods encouraged and legitimated a sense of particularism as opposed to universality. Even resident aliens could very often have their own places of worship, around which they lived (MacMullen 1974:82-84).

Neither domestic nor political religion could be considered an interior religion but rather the religious expression of the sense of belonging to a family or local group in touch with the soil and the ancestors that had founded the family or city as well as with the gods that had favored the city. It was a foundational moment that still had to be remembered and celebrated at the risk of disappearing amidst the chaos, of losing the identity that was linked to the physical place and to the history that had been experienced. Foreigners, by definition, were alien to all that. What kind of relationship existed with them?

Foreigners and hospitality

The "family house" and foreigners
The *oikos* provided a basic local, political and religious structure to distinguish the native *(oikeios)* from the foreigner *(metoikós, paroikós, that is, allótrios)*, fellow citizens from strangers, coreligionists from the "enemies" (Elliot 1981:174).

The natural way of joining the city (its government and worship) was through some *"pater familias"* or *"oikodespotês"*, that is, joining a *domus* or *oikos*. This could be done either because one belonged to it naturally or through the establishment of a *relationship of pseudo-kinship* (patronage, adoption...) as noted above, or because a bond was created by means of a ceremony such as the relationship of *hospitality*.

In order to orient himself to the community in which he arrived, a foreigner needed the protection of somebody from within to introduce him into the community and its expectation, to help him decipher the codes of meaning that guided relationships, and to vouch for him before his fellow citizens (Simmel 1908). This relationship, which was established between the foreigner and the head of the family who took charge of him, was called *hospitality* and his status shifted temporarily from one who came as a foreigner to that of a guest (Malina 1986c:181-87). For this purpose, he had to go through a ritual that would strip him of that quality that made him foreign and introduce him into the community. This ritual separated him from an "unusual" world—since he came from outside the community—that made him potentially dangerous and suspicious and would introduce him to what is known. Cultural anthropology has studied some of the rites and processes by which hospitality is established. It is effected through rites of inversion—more or less demanding and sophisticated—that symbolize social death and rebirth into a new status, in this case that of a family member, "one of the family". From some of these rites, it can be deduced that the ultimate reason for the process is the need for the "foreigner" to participate in and share with the group (family or town/city) into which he has arrived. After all, its history and origin are intensely rooted in the land, and that becomes evident in worship (Pitt-Rivers 1977:ch. 3, 5, 6; idem, 1968b).

Through hospitality and its rites it was possible, even though only temporarily, to join in the life of the townspeople's community, their history and tradition. The order of the universe, which was threatened by the alien element embodied in the foreigner, was thus re-established.

The Greco-Roman city and foreigners

Hospitality was a way of being incorporated into the city through a family household. Yet it could not always be done in this way, since both in Greece and in Rome hospitality required a certain affinity between guest and host for the language and the rites that had to be followed. Those foreigners that did not fulfill the conditions were called *allothrooi* or *barbaroi*. On the other hand, whereas in Greece hospitality was a rather private affair, in Rome this institution was more politicized, more interwoven into the city life and its relationship with other communities (Gauthier 1973).

In the Mediterranean cities of the Greco-Roman world, after the distinction between free people and slaves, the main distinction that classified their inhabitants was that of citizens and foreigners. The former were a minority of free men who had the law and rules of the city on their side and who could and had to take part in the worship of the civic gods in which the spirit of the citizen was expressed. There were different types of foreigners *(Xenoi)*, depending on whether they were just passing through *(parepidêmoi)* or whether they were habitual residents of the city *(paroikoi, metekoi)*. (On this distinction of inhabitants see MacMullen 1974:59-60.)

The attitude towards foreigners depended on whether they intended to stay in the city for a limited period of time, or whether they intended to stay permanently. There was no hospitality towards resident foreigners *(paroikoi)* who formed a distinct social group in cities and lived in different neighborhoods sometimes even with their own organizations although they faced political, legal and social limitations inherent in their status as foreigners. The foreigner was definitively incorporated into city life—with his rights and duties—only when he obtained citizenship whether for religious or political reasons. Although they could certainly gain some respect in a city especially if they were rich, resident foreigners did not have political rights nor did they take part in civic worship. Unless their country of origin had a special agreement with Rome, the rights of resident foreigners were restricted under Roman law. Both in Athens and Rome, it was the exceptional court that dealt with problems and questions regarding foreigners until they were faced with the need for some kind of justice (a *praetor peregrinus* in Rome, a *polemarca* in Athens) (Gauthier 1973:1-21).

The political religion of the Empire and the foreigners

The reason for being considered a foreigner involved being foreign to what constituted the city as a community, being alien to its origins which were considered "sacred", hence the lack of a connection with that place and with the act of foundation, of "organization" which had turned it into a community and was celebrated in the worship (Arendt 1958:81-112).

Political religion, as previously noted, played an important role in the development of the sense of community, of attachment to a common heritage that identified the citizens and distinguished them from foreigners. Being governed and controlled by political elites, it also had a clear function of organization, theorization and legitimization of the forms of government as well as the political attitudes and relations.

Roman political religion always had an integrative character, welcoming foreign worship—even nationalizing some of them—provided that they were in the interests of the State or, at least, did not threaten its unity and welfare (Chenol 1996:81). However, as the Empire moved forward, traditional political religion gradually became inadequate, mainly due to the problem of the relationship with foreigners who were being integrated into the political niche of the Empire. Nevertheless, this process did not integrate their origin, tradition, and gods with Rome although Rome would have adopted—by romanizing them—many of the gods of the towns that had been incorporated into the Empire.

Caracalla's words on granting Roman citizenship to all the inhabitants of the Empire clearly show the relationship between political religion and the immigration policy: "In order to grant the Majesty of the Very Sacred Gods the duties that are owed to them, with all required magnificence and mercy, I think I must make all foreigners in the world agree on the need for the worship of these gods, I grant them Roman citizenship, thus all Roman citizens are devoted to them, except for the dedicticii" (quoted by Chenol 1996: 86).

The development of the imperial system—which as the physical boundaries of the territory owned by the city of Rome were extended involved a change of territoriality—also entailed the development of the philosophical and religious ideological justifications for the relationship that could join the inhabitants of this new physical space with broader frontiers defined as an Empire.

Universality was not a characteristic of the Romans nor of their republican ideals. When the Empire arrived, their de facto politics was out of step with the theoretical justification for the territorial expansion. On the one hand, some considered that these politics were the result of the utopian dreams of a universal city—a community under a single rule and a single law for all men as the Greeks had thought since the third century BCE. On the other hand, others—above all the Roman nobles in the Senate—clung to the old legal order and its values (ancestral gods and moral virtues) characteristic of the Republic that better defended their privileges and dreams of ethnic superiority (in this case, curiously restricted to a city that would extend over the whole world) as well as their class distinction (Mazzolani 1972:25-33).

The expansion of the territory through conquests took place first. It was only secondarily that theoretical considerations and justifications for imperial politics arose. These were taken, on the one hand, from Greek thought that some centuries earlier had reflected on the common humanity of all humankind, on universal brotherhood and the existence of an equal natural law for everybody; and on the other hand, they were taken from a process of sublimation of their own past of conquests and assimilation (Mazzolani 1972:17-23).

In practice, imperial politics meant extending the city boundaries, redefining the territory and therefore, redefining relationships and power. It is thus understandable that the process of the effective establishment of the Empire as a universal community would be slower.

The imperial government started to imbibe the ideas of universality, with a universal community under one law, one ruler and a divine reason, redefining along with the territory the relations with those who had previously stayed outside the boundaries that lent an identity to the group, keeping it from what was alien or foreign to the common house that the city was understood as a "home of family homes".

Theoretical justification and the effective establishment of a new territoriality had a mutual influence on each other. Both Christianity and the Stoic doctrines of universal fraternity and of the common nature of all humankind had an important bearing on this process. According to Bolchazy (1977), in Rome there had previously existed a doctrine about benevolent behavior towards foreigners that made it easier to accept the new ones. It was the *"Ius hospitii, ius deii"* that was not, however, much taken into account during the whole first period of the Empire (Bolchazy 1977:65-78).

The ius hospitii-ius dei

This idea or doctrine that appeared in Roman religious thought seems to have been the only set of rules for a humane treatment of foreigners that was different from all the others. The belief that a foreigner might be a god in disguise, or in possession of a magical power that was beneficial to have in one's favor, derived from the *ius hospitii-ius dei* which claimed that it was Jupiter's will that the foreigner should be adequately welcomed. Mistreatment of foreigners was regarded as an offence to the gods of hospitality.

This type of relationship with the foreigner and its religious sanction was firmly established in the first century even though the imperial government and the official propaganda were not very fond of it. In fact, none of the more or less official writers proposed it as a model. Only Livy seemed to discover in it a spirit which was more appropriate for the new times, for the new territoriality that the imperial system was redefining. This theory gives a glimpse of a tacit acceptance that the native gods were also concerned about those who did not belong to the family or tribe. Therefore, this is the first step towards the belief in a universal god and the doctrine on the universal brotherhood of men (Bolchazy 1977:27). It was an excellent breeding ground where the Stoic and Christian doctrines would later bear fruit and on which the Empire would be based successfully.

The stoic oikeiôsis

The Stoic idea of universal brotherhood of all men along with their doctrine of a similar nature common to all human beings (*oikeiôsis*) was one of the theoretical pillars on which the Empire was based throughout this time as a norm for governance. The world was gradually becoming a single *homeland* or *oikoumene*—a big common home—led by a single "*Pater Familias*" or *oikodespotês*, the Roman emperor, who progressively became a representative of the divine Mind whose mission was to guide the whole known world. The core of these doctrines contained the seed of a universal city, although their theory about the equality of men—even of slaves—was rather more theoretical than practical due to its indifferent attitude towards earthly realities.

Stoicism provided Rome with the concept of universal love for all human beings supported by a double motivation: 1. God's will: since God loves all mankind, each man must love his fellow men. 2. The doctrine of oikeiosis: since all men "belong" to something common—they share the same nature—the duty to love oneself becomes an imperative to love other people (Bolchazy 1977). One's well-being depends on other people's well-being, like the stones in an arch (Engberg-Pedersen 1990:68-69). It is worth mentioning how this concept of belonging to a common nature becomes a term that also means a "family home".

Christianity in this city world

When the consequences of Jesus of Nazareth's message which had questioned Judaic separation/purity rules were developed, Pauline Christianity found that its beliefs and praxis had a bearing on life in the cities where the communities were being formed and developed. Its beliefs and praxis put Pauline Christianity on one side of the controversy that has been previously described, that is, on the side of universality. It shared with Stoicism the idea of a universal brotherhood which for Christianity was based on its belief in a single God who was the father of all human beings although the Christianity placed more emphasis on the community than the Stoics.

During its development in Greco-Roman cities, where it took the family home as a basic form of organization, Pauline Christianity established itself within the private sphere with regard to public and private religion. But the consequences of its doctrines and praxis—for the very characteristics of its message and assumptions even though unintended—went beyond both the sphere of family religion (well-being of the family) and that of the official civil religion (a search for the well-being of the city and the citizens) that made up public life. Each Christian family home felt linked to other domestic homes or churches—within and outside the limits of their city and country—with which they had a common faith and history: that of Jesus of Nazareth and the first disciples. That same belief and feeling triggered the main objective of civic religion.

What happened in the *oikos* inevitably had to affect the *polis;* the ideas and the practice of what was taking place in the transformed family religion eventually intruded into the political sphere since they were both interwoven. Understood as a religion "disembedded" from politics and exceeding the limits of the patriarchal family—one of its most original and critical contributions—, Christianity satisfied the condition that would allow it to influence the ideological orientations of the political and family spheres regarding the attitude towards foreigners.

Christianity was neither a civil nor a family religion. It went beyond the perceptions of both which were implicitly criticized. It was concerned neither with the welfare of a city, nor of a family but rather with the salvation of individuals that formed a community beyond ethnic or blood boundaries. It was time rather than space that defined Christian religion. The Christian God was a God that was not confined to a single place nor did that deity need one in order to be contacted (Helgeland 1980:1285-1305).

These ideas, along with the awareness of sharing a history and a tradition which were regarded as their own, which they recognized, with which they identified and, to a certain extent, which served as their very foundation were very important. They provided all Christians with a "familiarizing" reference that led them to a relative consideration of other categorizing and defensive divisions such as racial or ethnic identities. No matter whence its members came, Christianity found a quality in all human beings that "stripped" them of their status as foreigners.

It is understandable that when Christianity started to be known as an entity separate and different from Judaism, criticisms and suspicions focused precisely on that fact: it was not a religion of any nation or people in particular. It was thus logical that the Christian message had a clear social and political dimension that would later be used by Constantine to replace the ancient civil-political religion which was too limited for his new political schemes.

Mixed race group as a fundamental characteristic of Christian communities: the Epistle to the Ephesians

According to most modern scholars, the epistle to the Ephesians is addressed by one of Paul's disciples to an urban community in the Lycus valley. No reference of any kind is made to Ephesus, but it could be either this city or another one in the surroundings: Laodicea, Aphrodisias, and the like. In any case, it is a big Greco-Roman city that attracted a large number of foreigners who were settled in some of their neighborhoods or in the slum areas.

It is a community made up mainly of Christians of gentile origin, but the existence of members of Jewish origin cannot be ruled out. Although not identified as a specific problem, some authors maintain that its rhetoric indicates that the

> implied readers are not aware as they should be of some key elements of their Christian identity ... Ephesians, then, can be seen as an attempt to reinforce its implied readers' identities as those who have received salvation which makes them members of the Church and to underscore the necessity of their distinctive role and conduct in the Church and in the World. It can be inferred ... that their main problems are powerlessness, instability and a lack of resolve, and these are related to an insufficient sense of identity. A key feature of what is needed in this situation is growth". (Lincoln and Wedderburn 1993:82-83)

The epistle talks about the universal role and meaning of the Church which is referred to by means of the body of Christ metaphor, understood as something more than the combination of the different domestic communities and local churches. The epistle urges unity as an effective realization of that status and cosmic meaning of the Church where the divine "economy" (*oikonomia*) becomes effective, which is mainly characterized by the inclusion of Jewish and gentile people in one same project.

The epistle to the Ephesians is an excellent example of the social dimension of the inclusive message of Pauline tradition Christianity. Through the use of typically civil-political images and vocabulary to refer to the incorporation into the Christian group and its consequences, the author demonstrates how—by virtue of the Christian newness and its inclusive message—the discriminating distinction between the native (*oikeios*) and the foreigner (*metoikos, paroikos*, that is, *allotrios*) has been surmounted along with the consequences of privileges deriving from membership in a specific ethnic group. It is necessary to study the text with the most significant ideas and terms:

> Therefore remember that at one time you Gentiles (*ethnê*) in the flesh, called the uncircumcision by what is called the circumcision,—which is made in the flesh by hands—remember that you were at that time separated from Christ, alienated (*apêllotriômenoi*) from the commonwealth (*politeias*) of Israel, and strangers (*xenoi*) to the covenants of the promise, having no hope and without God in the world. But now in Christ Jesus you who once were far off (*makran*) have been brought near (*eggus*) in the blood of Christ. For he is our peace (*eirênê*), who has made us both one, and has broken down the dividing (*phragmou*) wall (*mesotoichon*) of hostility (*echthran*), by abolishing in his flesh the law of commandments and ordinances, that he might create in himself one new man (*kainon anthrôpon*) in place of the two, so making peace, and might reconcile us both to God in one body through the cross, thereby bringing the hostility (*echthran*) to an end. And he came and preached peace to you who were far off (*makran*) and peace to those who were near (*eggus*); for through him we both have access in one Spirit to the Father. So then you are no longer strangers (*xenoi*), and sojourners (*paroikoi*), but you are fellow citizens (*sumpolitai*) with the saints and members of the household of God (*oikeioi tou theou*), built upon (*epoikodomêthentes*) the foundation (*themeliô*) of the apostles and prophets, Christ Jesus himself being the cornerstone (*akrogônianiou*), in whom the whole structure (*oikodomê*) is joined together and grows into a holy temple (*naon agion*) in the Lord; in whom you also are built (*sunoikodomeisthe*) into it for a dwelling place (*katoikêtêrion*) of God in the Spirit (Eph 2:11-22. RSV)

As is evident, in this chapter of the epistle concepts about the home and its world predominate along with concepts about the city and ways of being integrated into it. The relationship and integration of the *oikos* and the *polis* is evident. With regard to the *polis*, the terms are grouped, on the one hand, into the semantic field of foreigner-strange, different-enemy, and feelings of hostility, separation, remoteness and exclusion; and, on the other hand, into the semantic field of city-citizen-citizenship and peace, family home, building and God's dwelling.

In the middle, which is also the center of the palistrophe in which the chapter is arranged, Christ appears making peace as the authentic conciliation (*oikeiôsis*). The social function of this affirmation is that the values and attitudes that are present in the Christian message indicate that every trace of exclusiveness is overcome. It also means that somebody who is different will not be considered dangerous or inferior, which would lead to the formation of integrated communities. We will now study this aspect more thoroughly.

This text was written by a Judaic person for a non-Judaic majority. Therefore, he has the point of view of someone who has discovered in the Christian message a way to overcome this paradigmatic division and its consequences. In order to transmit this message and its justifications, the author of Ephesians makes use of a civil-political imaginary context which is shared with his contemporaries and made up the daily social and cultural reality of the recipients of his writing. The most plausible explanation is that this would be the environment in which the recipients of the writing were living and experiencing their situation. Thus, an imaginary context could serve perfectly well to show the social consequences of the Gospel of Jesus of Nazareth, just as Pauline Christianity had developed it, the main feature of which was inclusion.

The distinction between "insiders" and "outsiders", between natives and foreigners which was made in a city by virtue of blood-line and ethnic group, was irrelevant for those who conceived their existence according to the Christian message. In Jesus, "in his blood", all human beings—recognized as brethren—have become sons, members and heirs to the House of God. The distinction between the different ethnic groups is expressed with the symbol of the dividing wall (*mesotoichon phragmou*), in reference to the wall that fenced in a physical space where a certain number of people could not enter: the city, temple, and the like. In ancient cities there were inside walls that divided and separated the different sectors in the city. Each of them was the residence of a specific type of people: citizens from the ruling classes, artisans, resident foreigners, and so on (Sjoberg 1960:97-100). In these inside walls there were doors that were locked at night which therefore controlled relations between the inhabitants of each of the areas (For good illustration of the model of pre-industrial city, cfr. Rohrbaugh 1991:135-49).

The Christian message invalidated the use of the deity to justify the exclusion of the foreigner and presented Jesus as the one whose life and death had destroyed the wall and everything that divided both nations. Jesus and his death, understood as a communion sacrifice, unites those who are ethnically different into a single community. Jesus joins people with each other and with God (v.13.14).

Since Jesus and his project were presented as authentic peace (*pax* or *eirênê*), a political declaration was being made in the sense that a new concept of authentic peace was being proposed, different from the Roman peace. The Roman Pax offered by the Emperor became blood and fire because it was in the interests of Rome that the other nations should be subordinated since they were regarded as objects rather than as subjects. The foreigner was an object of clemency, mercy or strength (Bolchazy 1977: 65-78), but he was always the means to an end: the imperial government of Rome, the increase in the power of the Emperor and of his "home", which was extending over the known world until it was made an "oikoumene" or "common home". Foreigners did not really become "one of the house" no matter how far the limits of the city were extended because Rome continued to be the reference and the rule. They were not shown the same consideration nor did they have the same rights as Roman citizens.

The Christian inclusive message presents a new type of house which is more open, a "common house" which is "more welcoming towards what is different". Once again, the civil-political imaginary context serves as an effective and transforming instrument for describing Christian comprehension. If there is a "common house" to which one belongs, it is that of God which integrates all men: Jew and non-Jew, Greek, Roman, all of whom belong to the same house of God (*oikeioi tou theou*) the Father and creator of the Universe. Consequently, the differences between and hierarchizations of foreigners according to their greater or lesser closeness to the center, Rome, lose their value and their capacity to grant honor, since the God presented by Pauline Christianity, from his foundational message and inspiration, is more than a welcoming host. He is a Father who wants to establish ties of kinship that were already initiated by Jesus of Nazareth. These bonds strip people of their status as foreigners, thus allowing them to become one more member in the house, in the family, with the same rights and duties. In view of this reality, the attachment to the soil and the ancestors fades, which creates a sense of identity and attachment in community members.

A more open, welcoming house which could integrate distinctions into its bosom posed a challenge to the very concept of city and its political religion. The gods, the traditions, the ancestors, all that gave identity and unity to the citizens also made them exclude foreigners from the full city life. In the Christian *ekklesia* (etymologically: assembly of citizens who are gathered to decide the questions of common good)̇ there are no degrees nor a hierarchy of foreigners: neither those excluded *(apêllotriômenoi)*, nor foreigners *(Xenoi)*, not even resident aliens *(paroikoi)*, living in the city community but not fully. In the Christian *ekklesia* they are all fellow citizens *(sunpolitai)*, they have all been granted full citizenship without exceptions or privileges, not even for having previously belonged to the people of Israel. Seniority accruing to the people of salvation did not grant them a higher degree of citizenship. All who believe in Jesus have become "new men" (2,15). Cicero referred to the "new men" (*homines novi*), those like himself, who were the newcomers to the Roman family and were proud of their Roman citizenship *(De Legibus* II,ii,5). However, they were despised by senior citizens like Cataline (Sallust, *De Conivratione Catilinae* XXiii,6) (Mazzolani 1972:36,40-41).

Pauline Christian communities accepted people from different ethnic origins into their midst and offered them a significant and vital history into which all could be intertwined in such a way that everybody could feel they shared the same foundations, the same cornerstone from which they could develop and a common history as a point of reference. The criteria for establishing territoriality were being changed: the landmarks, which were local and were linked to the territory before, are now "delocalized" and universalized. In the course of time, this potential would be one of the elements that the Empire would use in its own interest when it made Christianity the official religion.

The author of the epistle presents the consequences of the Christian message and his experience in the Church—understood as a supralocal body, in language filled with civil-political implications. He shows this Pauline development of the Christian message as a real pacification, the cornerstone, the pillar on which the building begins to be built. Acknowledgment of the universal paternity of the Christian God is the basis for belonging to a common family home, for sharing a common nature and origin and the same rights. The reference to Jesus and ancestors in the faith constitutes the common heritage as well as the tradition upon which they are based. In fact, it could be said that the author is proposing without realizing it, a new "spiritual" territoriality made up of the universal Church which he has presented as a cosmic reality. Even the introduction in the first chapter of a hymn in which Christ appears arranging and taking control of the heavens and the earth, space and time, stresses the awareness of a new form of community membership that is evident through out the entire epistle. This new awareness and its symbolism were later used by Constantine and his Imperial government, when he explained that "abstract territoriality" and identified it with his own territory.

On the other hand, the former universalism that integrated and respected particularities gradually became a universalism that was imposed uniformity and was imperialist and repressive of the distinctions arising from a specific particularity when elevated to universal practice. An important influence in this process was the relevance that the church of Rome began to acquire, partly as a result of being in the center of the Empire as well as by the use of Christianity as a "political religion" by Constantine and his successors.

The requisite devaluation of specific culture in the Christian message that had so characterized the Hellenistic and Roman cultures was imposed as the only way of experiencing Christianity and the norm by which other people could be judged. This gave rise to an idea of universalism that basically involved the imposition of a specific cultural development of an experience of liberation and humanization which was aimed, in principle, at being adopted by each community according to its own nature. The adoption of the way of thinking and acting peculiar to Roman imperial leaders with whom the church leaders increasingly identified once it was considered the official religion was one of the reasons for this type of imperialist development of that former universalism which welcomed distinctions much better.

The dialectics between particularism and universalism through a universalism that respects and integrates plurality and differences (Walzer 1992) is not easy to sustain. In fact, the Church failed to do it very often throughout history either because it agreed to legitimate an imposing and uniformizing universalism (imperialism)—actually, a successful particularism elevated to universal practice—, or because it supported different particularisms which equally excluded all others.

The early inclusive message and its development towards a universalism that integrated differences and respected pluralistic contexts, has a great potential which has already been developed at different times throughout the history of the Church and which today—in the light of the progress made in thinking, ethics and similar theorizing—can and must be developed to their logical conclusion. This understanding of universalism becomes a criticism of all religious legitimization—or any other kind—of imperialism as a successful particularism or of xenophobic particularisms, both of which exclude what is different. It also inspires the establishment of a supportive line of action that leaves the specific interests of the nations aside in favor of those other nations that are in subhuman situations, or of those foreigners that arrive in a country eager to take part in its social and economic life.

11

Glory, Honor and Patronage in the Fourth Gospel: Understanding the *Doxa* Given to Disciples in John 17

Ronald A. Piper, *University of St Andrews, Scotland*

As part of a volume of essays honoring the contribution made by Bruce Malina to the study of the New Testament, it is appropriate to highlight the value of social-scientific methods for tackling some traditional problems of exegesis. This applies to "theological" discourse no less than to narrative. This essay is dedicated to one such investigation, following the lead given by Bruce Malina.[1]

Statement of the Problem

The concepts of "glory" and "glorification" in the Fourth Gospel have long been considered themes of major *theological* significance within that work. This is probably most strikingly presented in Ernst Käsemann's *Testament of Jesus* (1968:20) where he develops the thesis that "John understands the incarnation as a projection of the glory of the Jesus' pre-existence and the passion as a return to that glory". The divine glory of Jesus dominates John's story.[2]

---

[1] I am indebted to Corrine Wong's paper to the British New Testament Conference in September 1997 at Leeds for highlighting the problem posed by this passage, and for members of the Context Group (and particularly Eugene Botha) for helpful suggestions at its meeting in March 1998.

[2] Käsemann (1968:18f) further declares: "The glory of Jesus is not the result of his obedience, so that, as in other New Testament writings, his glory could be defined from the perspective of his obedience. On the contrary, obedience is the result of Jesus' glory and the attestation of his glory in the situation of earthly conflict."

Other writers too have seen the Fourth Gospel's development of
the ideas of "glory" and "glorification" as related to portrayals of the
glory of God in the Hebrew Bible. R. E. Brown (1966:503) states:

> The concept of the glory of God in OT thought offers important back-
> ground for Johannine use. In the OT there are two important elements
> in the understanding of the glory of God: it is the *visible* manifestation of
> His majesty in *acts of power*.

The result is not only to interpret the use of "glory" in the Fourth
Gospel as related to the use of the Hebrew word כבוד in the Hebrew
Bible, which is frequently translated by δόξα in the LXX, but also to
associate such ideas even in the Hebrew Scriptures as fundamentally
associated with some kind of visible display of power, ostensibly a
sensory phenomenon.

Despite attempts, such as by J. M. White (1997:179-180) to contrast
the Fourth Gospel's expression of Jesus' heavenly glory (a "blaze of
light") with his earthly glory as expressed in humble acts of human
love, the latter are not always considered devoid of more powerful
manifestations in the Fourth Gospel. There are four instances in particular where the Fourth Gospel refers to "seeing" the δόξα of the
Christ, or of God through Jesus' works (1:14; 11:40; 12:41; 17:24). Jn
2:11 also refers to "manifesting" that δόξα through signs. The "hour"
of Jesus being "glorified" (δόξαζειν) as Son of Man is particularly focused on the passion and resurrection, although it applied also to Jesus
pre-incarnate state (17:5). The Fourth Gospel therefore associates the
"visible" manifestations of Jesus' δόξα around the foci of Jesus' incarnation, signs and return to the Father.[3]

The difficulty with this kind of approach to the δόξα-terminology
in the Fourth Gospel, however, is that it does not do full justice to all
occurrences of the term. In particular, it poses distinct problems when
trying to understand a passage such as John 17:22 where Jesus declares
that he has given this δόξα to his disciples. This essay will therefore be
concerned with the understanding of John 17:22. Does it make sense
to talk of those who are purportedly with him at the Last Supper having already received for themselves a visibly observable "act of divine
power"? In what sense is their δόξα comparable to that which Jesus

---

[3] The Fourth Gospel does not locate Jesus' δόξα in a particular event such as the
Transfiguration account, however. Even though it would serve in a particularly dramatic way visibly to demonstrate the divine power claimed by Jesus, the author prefers
to put the focus on other events as described above. The synoptic accounts which set
Jesus alongside Moses and Elijah may also serve to detract from the unique revelatory
role which John wishes to associate with Jesus.

possesses? Should this difficulty not alert us to other possible uses of the *doxa*-terminology in the Fourth Gospel, with nuances other than the displays of divine power described above? Indeed, is a *theological* understanding of the term dominant at all in John 17:22? Are there not both logical and theological problems to be faced in order to understand this text?

It will be argued that the primary sense of δόξα in the context of John 17:22 is that of "honor", a key value of the ancient Mediterranean world. Indeed even in the Hebrew Scriptures the meaning of "honor" may be appropriate to many texts in which the כבוד (or LXX: δόξα) terminology is present. But this is only part of the issue. The context in which "honor" is given to disciples raises other important questions which lead to a consideration of the patron–client model and its application to the disciples of Jesus in the Fourth Gospel.

Doxa as "Honor" in the Fourth Gospel

With regard to the use of the δόξα vocabulary in the Fourth Gospel, there are important examples in the gospel where the noun δόξα and the verb δοξάζειν do not refer to visible demonstrations of the divine glory, even indirectly as through signs. More generally, they do not always appear to bear a *theological* meaning in the Gospel. It is of course widely known that Greek usage of δόξα has other meanings. C. H. Dodd (1978:206) noted the Greek can signify:

> either "opinion" (which, Plato said, stands somewhere between knowledge and ignorance), or else "reputation", and in particular a good reputation, and so "honour", "distinction".

Louw and Nida (1988:734-736) take this further in their lexicon and study of semantic domains. They describe a large number of meanings in the New Testament for the term δόξα. These include the concepts of splendor, brightness and power. But one use of δόξα groups the term with a number of others in a semantic domain which refers to "honor" or "respect" in relation to status. In these cases, it serves as a way of attributing high status to someone by honoring that person.

There are clear examples in the Fourth Gospel where this meaning seems to apply. These include John 5:41, 44; 7:18; 12:43. For example, in John 5:41 Jesus declares "I do not accept δόξα from humans". It can hardly refer here to "brightness" or "divine power" or "glorious being"; it most naturally means "honor" or "good repute". The same appears again a few verses later: "How can you believe when you accept δόξα from one another and do not seek the δόξα that comes from the one who alone is God?" (John 5:44; cf. also 7:18; 12:43). The first use of δόξα in this verse must refer to competition for "honor" on a purely human level. The juxtaposition and contrast with seeking "the δόξα that comes from...God" leaves the translator and exegete with an interesting problem.

One approach is that offered by Dodd. While he accepted the presence in the Fourth Gospel of the meaning of δόξα to mean "honor", he still argues that it can sometimes be vested with theological coloring in Johannine usage. For example, Dodd wrote (1978:208):

> the evangelist plays subtly upon the varying meanings of the word δόξα suggesting that by such a death Christ both "honours" God (by complete obedience), and gains "honour" Himself; but the "honour" which He gains is no other than the "glory" with which the Father has invested Him; in other words the revelation of the eternal majesty of God in His love for mankind.

But however subtle the Evangelist may be, the parallelism in John 5:44 suggests that it is necessary to understand the second clause, referring to seeking δόξα which comes from God, in relation to that *honor* which people readily accept from one another. In other words, even if in other contexts in the Fourth Gospel the δόξα which comes from God might convey a meaning a meaning of majesty and power, the immediate context in John 5 suggests δόξα is clearly used in terms of competing sources of "honor".[4] In this sense, John 5:44 (and its near repetitions in 7:18 and 12:43) may reflect a very important argument in the Fourth Gospel. Part of the Evangelist's "problem" is to explain (i) the shame of the cross and, possibly, (ii) the shame of the expulsion of the Johannine believers from the synagogue (John 9:22; 12:42f; 16:2).[5] Thus the Evangelist frequently depicts the cross as Jesus' "glorification" and "lifting up". These too are ultimately claims to honor. By suggesting an alternative—and superior—source of honor to that operative in the world, the Evangelist has a strategy which may be employed at several points in his Gospel. He has done so with re-

---

[4] For the link between δόξα and "honor" in other texts (Hebrews, Philippians) where Christians depicted Jesus' crucifixion as exaltation, see P. F. Esler (1994:25f).

[5] The importance of such an expulsion for the Johannine adherents has been argued by J. L. Martyn (1968) and developed by, among others, R. E. Brown (1979) and W. Meeks (1972). For M. Hengel (1989b:121), however, the "immediate controversy with the Jews has long ceased to be the main theme of the school."

spect to Jesus' fate; it should not be surprising to see the same applied to Jesus' disciples.

John's gospel is noted for its deliberate plays on words by which more than one meaning for a term can be suggested for a single use. But this very phenomenon can lure scholars into fuzzy, loose and inaccurate ways of assuming that all possible meanings for a word are present on each occasion. The word δόξα can in fact be used for a number of meanings in John, which are quite distinct and which need to be assessed on the basis of context. In some contexts, "honor" is clearly the intended meaning.

This prepares for an understanding of John 17:22:

> "And I have given to them the *doxa* which you have given to me, in order that they may be one, just as we are one."
> (κἀγώ τὴν δόξαν ἣν δέδωκάς μοι δέδωκα αὐτοῖς, ἵνα ὦσιν ἓν καθώς ἡμεῖς ἕν).

In this case it is not the δόξα given to God or to Jesus which is the point of interest; it is δόξα given to the disciples. Here it is clearly more difficult for commentators to refer to visible manifestations of God's majesty. Indeed the purpose of giving disciples this glory is not particularly to "manifest" anything; it is apparently intended to promote their group identity and confidence. Here too we seem to be drawn away from "theological" ideas about God's power and towards issues of group relationships and identity.

Doxa Revealed and *Doxa* Given-Received in the Fourth Gospel

In John 17:22, reference is made to δόξα which is "given". "To give or receive δόξα" makes clear that one is dealing with a meaning which is quite distinct from seeing δόξα or displaying δόξα for others to see (as in John 1:14). This should alert one to the fact that a "revelation" is not likely to be the sense of the term in John 17:22.[6] In this verse, the author prefers the construction δόξαν δέδωκα even to the verbal form δοξάζειν.

Such constructions elsewhere in the Fourth Gospel are instructive, even if relatively rare. The use of δόξα as the object of λαμβάνεω is found interestingly in John 5:41 and 44. As has been noted, this is

---

[6] This is not to suggest that even in passages where δόξα is described as "seen" it may not refer to the public recognition involved with honor. Yet in such cases greater allowance must be made for the influence of visual manifestations of power, especially when linked to the signs of Jesus.

precisely where the contrast is made between the δόξα which the hearers accept/receive from human beings and that which they fail to seek from God. This is one of the contexts therefore in which the meaning of "honor" is present.

Instances of δόξα as the object of διδόναι are only found in two other texts in the Fourth Gospel. The first occurs in John 9:24, where the leaders in the synagogue exhort the healed blind man to "Give *doxa* to God". Again, the sense would appear to be that they wish the blind man to "honor" God for his healing *rather than honor Jesus*, who is declared to be a known "sinner". Certainly there is no sense of the blind man being able to *impart* divine glory. This would be logically as well as theologically absurd.

The other usage occurs in John 17:24, where in *heaven* the disciples will finally see the δόξα which God has given to Jesus. One has to allow that in the celestial sphere the δόξα imparted by God may be something which can indeed be observed as a kind of manifestation of power. But even here the imagery may convey a recognition of honor rather than, say, "brightness". Indeed, in ancient Mediterranean society honor was all about public recognition and display (Malina and Neyrey 1991:34-36).

Thus of the instances discussed above, John 5:41 and 44; 7:18; 9:24; 12:43 and 17:22 are the examples where other humans are explicitly cited as givers or recipients of δόξα (as opposed to being observers of it), and it is precisely here where the meaning of "honor" is clearly indicated.

Consistent with this are three other instances in which the verbal form δόξαζειν has a human subject or agent. Disciples "honor" either God (John 15:8; 21:19) or Jesus (John 17:10) by particular works: bearing much fruit, being Jesus' disciples or facing martyrdom.

When one looks at John's use of other vocabulary specifically associated with "honor"—τιμή, τιμάω—the above observations with regard to δόξα seem to be confirmed. The only occasion in which the Fourth Gospel uses τιμή is in the proverb quoted in John 4:44 ("A prophet is not without honor except in his homeland"). The verbal form τιμάω is, however, used in three passages: John 5:23 (where human honoring of the Son is equated with honoring the Father), 8:49 (where Jesus' honoring his Father is contrasted with the *Ioudaioi* dishonoring Jesus by accusing him of having a demon and being a Samaritan) and 12:26 (where it is promised that the Father will honor whoever serves Jesus). In each of these cases a human giver or recipient of honor is implicated.

It is therefore the first part of the argument of this essay that in the Fourth Gospel where the language of δόξα or τιμή is used in connection with a human giver or recipient, then it has the meaning of "honor". These are not primarily cases of perception or revelation of divine power. In particular, John 17:22 should be considered in this regard, against those many scholars who attempt to build upon the "divine" or "revelatory" significance of the term, even though perception or display is not part of the vocabulary of 17:22.

Examples of this are easy to find with regard to John 17:22. Whilst Beasley-Murray (1987:302) frankly admits "the precise nature of the 'glory' given to believers is uncertain," many scholars have offered formulations which draw upon ideas of revelation or redemption. Bultmann (1971:515) suggested that Jesus' bestowal of δόξα on the disciples employed the "language of myth" and meant revealing to them the name of God or the words of God so that they share in his work of revelation.[7] Also connecting δόξα with the theme of revelation, Carson (1991:569) argues that "Jesus has given his *glory* to them in the sense that he has brought to completion his revelatory task (if, as in vv. 4-5 and repeatedly throughout the chapter he may be permitted to speak proleptically and thus include his climactic cross-work)." Schnackenburg (1982:III.191f) adds the idea of "the glorified Christ's communication to them of divine life", the "splendor and power of divine love". Lindars (1972:530) refers to Jesus imparting to his disciples "the message of salvation" as well as "creating in them a form of life". Witherington (1995:271) writes that the "meaning seems to be that Jesus has conveyed to them the divine presence and life so that they can be spiritually united with each other and with God". On the other hand, for Barrett (1978:513) this is not any kind of crude *theologia gloriae*, but rather "the glory of Christ is acquired through, and is most clearly expressed in, the crucifixion" and the same terms of obedience and suffering apply to the church. Yet even Barrett does not see the significance of using the concept of *honor* imparted from God to counter the shame associated with their suffering.[8] Moreover, none of these scholars appears to acknowledge the general Johannine usage of δόξα with a human giver or recipient.

These observations provide the basis for applying Mediterranean concepts of honor to this text, as has also been recently done by Malina and Rohrbaugh (1998:244-245). When one does so, however, it

[7] Bultmann further relates the idea to equipping them "with the brilliance or light which he himself possesses" which "is common in the Mandaean writings" (1971:515).

[8] See P. F. Esler (1994:25f)

becomes immediately apparent that a further model is needed. Within the Fourth Gospel, and portrayed in John 17:22, one has a hierarchical pattern by which "honor" is imparted to disciples by Jesus, who effectively serves as a mediator on behalf of the Father (John 5:23, 12:26, 15:8, 17:10). This suggests a client-broker-patron model, and it is with regard to this model that "giving honor" may most fruitfully be explored for John 17:22.

The Model of Patron-Broker-Client, the Role of "Honor" and the Concept of Limited Good

Full investigation of the patron-broker-client model and its application to the Fourth Gospel in general is beyond the scope of this paper. Helpful reviews of the model can be found in J. H. Elliott (1987:39-48) and Malina and Rohrbaugh (1998:117-119). Just as Malina (1996c:143-175) and Moxnes (1991:257ff) have argued that God as benefactor-patron and Jesus as broker are central themes in the synoptic gospels, so also this theme can be developed with regard to the Fourth Gospel. Indeed, the recent social-scientific commentary on John by Malina and Rohrbaugh (1998) begins to open up such a discussion. With the accentuation of the distance between the heavenly and the earthly which one finds in the Fourth Gospel, this model and the role of broker becomes quite compelling.[9] In this essay, however, I shall sketch the broad outlines of the model and give particular attention to the significance of "honor" within it.

The range of patronage relationships is helpfully set out in Halvor Moxnes' (1991:242) quotation of A. Blok (1969:366):

> Patronage is a model or analytic construct which the social scientist applies in order to understand and explain a range of apparent different social relationships: father-son, God-man, saint-devotee, godfather-godchild, lord-vassal, landlord-tenant, politician-voter, professor-assistant, and so forth. All these different sets of social relationships can thus be considered from one particular point of view which may render them comprehensible.

The core characteristics of patronage have been set out in the social-scientific construct of S. N. Eisenstadt and L. Roniger (1980:49-51). Patronage is normally depicted as a voluntary, personal relationship existing between persons of unequal status or power. Not only are the

---

[9] For the Spirit-Paraclete as broker, see Tricia Gates Brown's recent Ph.D. thesis, University of St Andrews.

relationships normally voluntary, they also are not subject to legal sanction. Nonetheless they create a strong bond between patron and client, which (whilst not indissoluble) is portrayed as enduring and characterized by loyalty. Within such relationships is a process of reciprocal exchange, by which patron (*patronus*) and client (*cliens*) each contribute some benefit to the other. The asymmetry in the status, wealth and power of the two parties inevitably means that these benefits tend to be different in nature for patron and client. Strict accounting in such exchanges is also complex. Patrons usually possess some monopoly over access to resources of importance to the clients, whether the resources be political, social or economic. In the Roman Empire, this exchange also took place in a setting where there was no clear distinction of private and public relations.

Certain social systems are inevitably more conducive to patron-client relations than others. In contrast to Western-style democracies (Moxnes 1991:244f), patronage emerges in social systems where access to resources and influence is not free (even in principle), but concentrated in an elite. Instability, change and contest destroy trust in the social system and drive individuals to form direct relationships with those who have power at any particular time to achieve their ends (Malina 1996c:144f).

A more precise description of this relationship, the relative social standings of patron and client in the ancient Mediterranean world and the benefits which are exchanged have received considerable discussion. Terry Johnson and Christopher Dandeker (1989:219ff), for example, have questioned whether the "relationship" is a simple dyadic one, or even limited to the triad of patron-broker-client. They argue that patronage is not a particular kind of personal relationship, but rather a "system of relations" or (better) "a social system".[10] Thus they argue that one does not empirically find one-to-one exchanges of goods and services over the short term, but rather a complex network of reciprocations. Competition within the Roman elite for clients, the varying abilities of members of the aristocracy over time to provide the protection and aid sought by clients and the voluntary nature of association resulted in fluctuations of client and patron loyalties.[11]

---

[10] So also H. Moxnes (1991:244) refers to "a system of personal relations".

[11] On the likelihood of clients seeking multiple patrons in the ancient Roman world, see Richard Saller (1989:53-56). Regarding the role of change and contest in societies dominated by patron-client relationships, see also the excellent study of Halvor Moxnes (1988:45ff), based on the theoretical work of Eisenstadt and Roniger.

An important element in such a system of relationships was frequently the "broker". For example, in segmented societies where the central authorities were located in urban centers rather than the countryside, mediators or brokers were often required to provide the links between the two segments of society. A. Blok (1969:369f) further suggests that for the people in the village or rural area (the isolated segment), brokers actually perform the role of patron. Nevertheless, Boissevain (1974:147f) distinguishes first order resources dispensed by patrons from second order resources dispensed by brokers.[12] Social brokers are mainly involved in putting people in touch with each other, directly or indirectly. Obviously such a manipulator of contacts must be suitably placed socially to exercise influence in the spheres of both clients and patrons. Brokers are effective precisely because they have a foot in each camp; it is this which makes this such a powerful role in the Fourth Gospel with regard both to Jesus and the Spirit. The broker's social relations and sources of information will be his primary assets. Sometimes a broker will make use of his own kinship network in linking a client to a patron.[13] He normally exercises these contacts for profit, although this can consist of services, information or status rather than money. The "business" of the broker has further been analysed by Boissevain (1974:158ff) with regard to capital (his communication channels), tariff (the value derived, in whatever form, from the transaction), credit (what others think his capital to be), debt (the promises he makes) and interest (the flexibility to decide when and what will be offered as a return service).

The relative benefits accruing to each party in the patron-broker-client relationship are not entirely clearly defined. Wallace-Hadrill (1989:65ff) has cast doubt upon the "reality" of Dionysius of Halicarnassus' description of Romulan patronage (*Roman Antiquities* 2:9-11). Dionysius wrote:

> It is remarkable how intensely both parties competed with each other in their demonstrations of goodwill, each anxious not to be outdone in generosity by the other: clients resolved to perform every service they could for their patrons, whilst patrons were anxious to inconvenience their clients as little as possible and accepted no gifts of money.

Wallace-Hadrill argued that Dionysius' account idealizes the mutual bonds of affection in such a relationship. Other studies too have ques-

---

[12] So also B. Malina (1996c:150).

[13] J. Boissevain (1966:25) cites examples in Sicily of such "horizontal" movements by a broker.

tioned whether patronage is a mode of integration between social classes and have suggested that in fact it provides support for social inequality, dependency on the part of the laboring classes and exploitation by the elite (Gilmore 1982:193f). Yet even if patronage is a system of social control and thus to an extent exploitative, there are still perceived benefits for clients as well as patrons and brokers in such a system.

The primary benefits for clients are normally expressed as protection and access to scarce and limited resources. Patrons were seen as benefactors and protectors, and the resources which they controlled were unavailable to potential clients by other means. Members of such an elite could secure advantage for themselves by either providing or denying access to such resources. Their power extended to the political as well as social and economic spheres. As Wallace-Hadrill notes:

> The Roman political system at all times avoided any sort of direct regional representation in government. Instead, access was mediated through individuals. It was this inaccessiblity of the centre except through personal links that generated the power of patronage (1989:74).

Clients then were those who sought such access (even if mediated through brokers) through expressions of loyalty to a patron. Whilst the benefits which were sought by a client were (in the broadest sense) assistance and protection, these could take different forms. A client might seek goods, influence for obtaining certain posts, assistance in legal proceedings, or personal protection in times of need. In return, a client loyalty enabled a patron to acquire honor according to the size and significance of his group of dependants. Clients may also have contributed in some measure goods and services to their patrons, but Drummond (1989:109f) questions whether such goods and services ever made a significant contribution to the patron's material advantage. Having clients was above all "an overt expression of his power and presumably brought public esteem for his readiness to lend aid and protection to those of lower status."[14] In some contexts the support of a client for a patron was expressed through votes for public office, as for the Greek Sarakatsan shepherds and the village presidents who served as their patrons (studied by J. K. Campbell [1964]).

---

[14] Similarly, see A. Drummond (1989: 99): "The conclusion must be that if the provision of such goods or services featured in the recompense offered by a client to his patron, such assistance was normally viewed as a voluntary prestation and for the *cliens* was not usually on a scale that caused serious difficulty or jeopardized his own viability."

Competition for clients by patrons/brokers and for patrons/brokers by clients is further evidence not only of the perception of mutual advantage to be gained through such relations, but also of the way in which such advantages could be maximized by careful choice. As noted by Johnson and Dandeker (1989:230) and Wallace-Hadrill (1989:67, 82), the movement of clients from one patron to another tested loyalties to the limit, but nonetheless testified to the fact that a given patron or broker was not always well-placed to provide the assistance and resources which clients sought. Similarly, there is evidence that patrons competed for clients—especially particular clients—in ancient Roman society (see D. Braund 1989:148; A. Drummond 1989:106). J. K. Campbell (1964:231) noted the same with regard to the Greek mountain shepherds of his study:

> It is by no means certain that a President will accept any Sarakatsanos as his political client ... to accept a man as a client commits the patron to protection instead of exploitation, and to that extent it is a restriction on the free exercise of his power. A President generally prefers to assume these obligations only with Sarakatsani of some influence.

From a patron's point of view, clients are desired as a "strategic resource" (Johnson and Dandeker 1989:233), not a millstone.

These observations lead naturally to the question of honor.[15] While it has long been recognized that "honor" is one of the key benefits accruing to patrons from having clients—taking many forms including the clients being in attendance, public eulogies, or a variety of other acts of public deference and loyalty performed by clients (see H. Moxnes 1991:250)—less attention has been given to the "honor" accruing to a client in such a relationship. This may be due to several factors. Firstly, because of the inequality in access to resources separating clients and patrons, clients are often portrayed as primarily seeking material benefits or tangible forms of protection and assistance rather than honor. Secondly, it is potentially embarrassing to be seen as a client of someone else. One might seem to "lose honor" by being shown to be dependent upon another. This can perhaps explain the oft-noted reluctance during the early Roman empire to use patron-client terminology.[16] Yet the pervasive evidence for the patronage

---

[15] For the importance of "honor" more generally within the ancient Mediterranean societies, see the important discussion in B. Malina and J. Neyrey (1991:25-46); J. G. Peristiany (1965).

[16] See R. P. Saller (1982:7-11).

system in the early Roman empire, even amongst figures of power,[17] would suggest that the association of a client with someone of greater wealth and influence was not necessarily seen as dishonor. Quite the reverse; it was a potential source of honor.

This requires further analysis. With regard to the matter of terminology, Rich (1989:124) notes that: "Politeness often led Romans to use words like *amicus* ('friend') rather than *patronus* and *cliens* of what were in fact patronage relationships between individuals." The same may be detected in interstate patronage relations. He later qualifies this observation, however, by noting that "politeness" would really only apply if the social distance between patron and client was slight. "A humble man might acquiesce or even rejoice in being called the client of a great man, while someone of higher status might 'think it like death to have accepted a patron or be called a client'" (Rich 1989: 126f, also citing Cicero *de Officiis* 2.69). Here one sees the difference between protégés of the elite and more humble non-elite clients.

Whilst the language of friendship can be found even in relations characterized by substantial asymmetry (see R. Saller 1989:57-61), it must be acknowledged that the degree of asymmetry has been observed to have an effect on such language. J. K. Campbell's study (1964:232f) can again be cited. He notes that a Sarakatsan shepherd who has a "friendship" with a village president may boldly sit down at the same table as the president in a coffee shop and reciprocate in the purchasing of drinks. But although "the President will say of a villager who is similarly his client that this man is his friend, he will not say this of a shepherd. If an explanation in his presence is necessary, he may say, 'George is a good lad, I help him', but behind his back he will simply say, 'He is my man'."

Yet the Sarakatsan shepherd still acquires "honor" in the situation which Campbell describes. Even though this unequal relationship between shepherd and president may prevent the shepherd being openly called the president's "friend", Campbell notes that the asymmetrical relation of sociability "enhances the prestige of both men" (1964:232). He further notes: "What is important to the Sarakatsanos in these situations is that other shepherds who do not possess this valued link should see and envy him" (1964:233). This is in part what lies behind the above-noted contention of J. Rich that a humble man would "rejoice" at being called the client of a great man.

---

[17] As H. Moxnes (1988:47) observes, "even if one had power, one was not totally safe, since there was always some power higher up".

The source of the client's honor is significant. Within the perception of "limited good", honor—as well as wealth, land, health, power, security and all other aspects of the environment—is viewed as finite and in short supply. One individual or family can only improve its position at the expense of another (Foster 1967:304-5). "Goods", material or otherwise, are always distributed in a zero-sum pattern. How then do *both* patron and client acquire honor? Whatever value one attaches to the deference shown by a client to his patron, the patron acquires honor primarily according to his success in acquiring clients *in competition with his peers*. The client acquires honor according to the envy which he can draw from his fellows. In so far as the patron and client are of unequal status and in different segments of society, the groups from which each acquires honor are distinct.

Biblical examples of those upon whom God confers his blessings—or "favoritism", as expressed by Malina (1996c:149)—will sometimes also cite the honor which that individual acquires. The model of patronage sheds light on such instances. For example, T. R. Hobbs has recently interpreted honor-shame and patronage notions in connection with ancient Near Eastern covenant treaties (1997:501-503). He notes the central role accorded to honor in traditional Mediterranean society, and how it figures alongside protection and material benefits amongst the limited goods to which a patron-client relationship serves to provide access. The ability of a patron to sustain a large gathering of clients provides him with honor. Crucially, however, Hobbs also notes that the "clients gain honor by being associated with such a figure" (1997:502). Of course the clients seek more than honor alone from association with a great man. But "honor" nonetheless accrues to *both* parties.

God giving "honor" to a *human* servant can be found, for example, in Isaiah 22:20-24 and in Jubilees 31:11-20; 43:20.[18] In Isaiah 22, Eliakim son of Hilkiah is described as God's "servant" and invested with authority over Jerusalem. He is then described as a "throne of honor" (LXX: θρόνον δόξης) to his ancestral house, an important example of ascribed honor. Similar vocabulary is employed in the blessing of Judah in Jubilees 31:19f: "With you will be found the salvation of Israel. And on the day when you sit on your righteous throne of honor, there will be great peace for all the seed of the beloved's sons." Later in Jubilees 43:12, Joseph tells his brothers: "tell my father about all my honor and all the wealth and *honor which the Lord has given to me*".

---

[18] For Isaiah 22:20-24, see P. F. Esler (1994:26).

In each case, God's chosen servant or client is expressly afforded honor in the sight of their peers, including their kin.

From both the model of patronage and these examples, it is clear that the honor afforded a client in such a relationship is significant. With this awareness, one can return to John 17:22.

The Application of the Patron-Client Model to John 17:22

It is the contention of this paper that in John 17:22 when the Fourth Evangelist refers to the δόξα given to disciples, he is not only referring to Mediterranean concepts of honor but also is doing so in the context of patron-client relations. That such a perception of relationships should be adopted by the Evangelist in John 17 is of importance for his wider understanding of the disciples and Jesus, not least because of the significance of the John 17 discourse itself. This discourse comes at a key point within the development of the Gospel. Indeed, S. W. Theron (1987:77f) argues from a structuralist perspective that John 17 is the climax both to John 13-16 (the Farewell Discourses) and to all of John 1-16. It is also virtually the Evangelist's final word about "honor". Whilst the word δόξα is regularly used in John 1-17, it is never used in chapters 18ff.[19] Thus from a variety of perspectives, John 17 would seem to mark a significant point in the Evangelist's presentation.[20]

The Broker

In the immediate context of John 17:22, Jesus is portrayed as presenting a petition, often called his Farewell Prayer, to God on behalf of the disciples. He envisages leaving these behind when he returns to the Father. In this mediatorial role, Jesus serves clearly as a broker between the disciples and the Father.[21] Throughout the gospel Jesus has served as a communicator-broker linking human clients to their divine Patron, from whom alone the benefaction of "eternal life" can be obtained. This brokerage was inevitably competitive in view of the reliance of the Israelites upon other "brokers" such as Moses, Abraham and the temple.

[19] The term δοξάζειν only occurs once after chapter 17 (*viz.* 21:19).

[20] In addition, Theron (1987:78) suggests that the purported "prayer" of Jesus in John 17 in terms of genre marks a climax which can be paralleled to the prayer which closes the Book of Signs in John 12:20ff, which also highlights "hour" (see John 17:1) and *doxa* terminology.

[21] As noted above (n. 9), see also Tricia Gates Brown's investigation of brokerage with regard to the Spirit-Paraclete following the departure of Jesus.

The opening of the purported prayer thus goes further than just portraying Jesus as interceding for the disciples. John 17:1-5 seems to be directed to establishing Jesus' "credit" as a broker.[22] This takes the following forms:

1. his close relationship to the patron is expressed in mutual "honor" and "oneness" (17:1 "honor your Son so your Son may honor you" and 17:4f; with respect to his "oneness" with the Father, see again later in 17:11, 22);
2. his authority and ability to get the patron to work on behalf of his clients (17:2 "you have given him authority over all people to give eternal life to all whom you have given him"; 17:3 "that they may know you, the only true God, and Jesus Christ whom you have sent").

Establishing his credit (and tariff: "honor") as a broker provides the logical basis from which to launch the more precise intercession Jesus will make in John 17:6ff.

Indeed the Fourth Gospel makes a strong claim not just for God having a monopolistic control over the supreme and inaccessible benefaction (eternal life), but more particularly for the broker-Jesus exercising monopolistic control over access to the patron-God. It is likely that this accounts both for those sayings elsewhere in the gospel which depict Jesus as "the life"[23] and also the frequent attempts to show him as superior to other potential brokers.

Direct competition with other brokers is not a marked feature of John 17, but it may not be entirely absent. Suggit (1984) has argued that John 17:17 ("Sanctify them in the truth; your word (λόγος) is truth") must be seen in the light of a wider attempt on the Evangelist's part to portray the contrast between the Torah (the Word of God) and the incarnate Word (the *true* Word of God).[24] God's Word was the

---

[22] See also Malina and Rohrbaugh (1998:244) with respect to the beginning of John 17.

[23] In John 1:4 life is declared to be "in" the pre-incarnational Logos, but even here it is likely that he serves as the mediator-broker of God in creation. The Father as the ultimate source of life is affirmed in John 6:57; 12:50. Although Jesus is declared to be "the resurrection and the life" (but note variant readings) in John 11:25, later in 14:6 he is called "the way, the truth and the life". The latter draws attention to the question of "access". Even in the summary statement in John 20:31, believers are granted eternal life "in his name". Lindars (1972:618, 476) links this to the invocation of Jesus' name as in prayer in 14:13. He rejects the view that effecting a magical spell is in mind (whilst noting such practices were frequent in the ancient world!) but does note that Jesus is still depicted here as "agent of the Father's will".

[24] In this regard he cites also John 1:17; 5:36-47; 7:19 and 19:7.

means (and accordingly the "broker") of his communication with his chosen clients. By identifying God's *true* word with Jesus, the Evangelist implicitly subordinates all other such claims to serve as the patron's communicator-broker.

As indicated above, such a competition between brokers can be detected elsewhere in the Fourth Gospel. It lies behind the Fourth Gospel's relative subordination of Moses (1:17, 45; 5:46; 6:32, 49), John the Baptist (1:8, 15, 20-23, 27, 30ff: 3:28-30; 4:1; 5:36), other heavenly ascents (3:13), the angels (1:51), Abraham (8:52f, 56-58), the prophets (1:45; 8:52f) including Isaiah (12:41)[25], and the religious leaders (3:10; 10:1ff; 12:19; *passim*). Whilst these figures are not completely denigrated, their role has been restricted. Above all, they are declared to have testified in previous ages to *Jesus'* role—that is, to Jesus as "broker". This effectively neutralizes any suggestion that they established any other form of brokerage that had continuing significance. The possible exceptions are Jesus' contemporaries: John the Baptist and the religious leaders. So far as the Baptist is concerned, he also is accorded a testifying role and therefore directs his followers to Jesus (1:35-37). The religious leaders, however, are presented as regularly misinterpreting Jesus' role and misguidedly attempting to adhere to other brokers of God's patronage: the Torah of Moses, the Temple and descent from Abraham. Even in this regard their loyalty as clients is called into question by the Evangelist (see John 7:19; 8:39f).

The Fourth Evangelist's strategy in this respect seems to be so comprehensive that he even finds ways of depicting Jesus so as to "replace" the institutions and holy spaces of Judaism associated with providing access to God. It may be argued that this lies behind much of the "replacement motif" noted by D. Carson (1988:253-256) and other scholars. The images are manifold: Jesus the true temple (2:21), Jesus as Bethel the house of God (1:51);[26] Jesus as the Paschal Lamb (1:29, 36; 19:31ff); Jesus as the one who gives water and light, during the Feast of Tabernacles (John 7 and 8); Jesus as the antitype of the brazen serpent (3:14); Jesus as the true manna (6:26ff); Jesus as the vine, which may represent Israel itself (15:1); Jesus as the shepherd, an image used of Yahweh and the messiah (10:1ff). Scholars have noted that there appears to be both contrast and continuity in the use of such images.

---

[25] I would suggest that the force of John 12:40f is not simply to suggest that Isaiah prophesied about Jesus, but more importantly to show that Isaiah was subordinate to Jesus: he saw his δόξα.

[26] So interpreted by D. A. Carson (1988:255) in preference to the interpretation of Jacob's ladder.

They are both fulfilled and annulled or replaced (Suggit 1984:112f; Carson 1988:254). Yet a more appropriate description of the perspective of the Fourth Evangelist may be to suggest that their only value for brokerage was in terms of pointing to the *true* broker. This is why Jesus can declare "Your father Abraham rejoiced that he was to see my day; he saw it and was glad" (John 8:56) or "If you believed Moses, you would believe me, for he wrote of me" (John 5:46). In so doing, Jesus effectively replaces them all at a stroke. This is also why his opponents can be shown to be culpable on more than level. They not only fail to be good clients under the covenantal relationships they recognize, but they also fail to see that these arrangements are themselves ultimately inadequate for access to their desired patron and are of use only in so far as they point to one who is adequate.

There are interesting parallels here with the book of Hebrews, which also wishes to establish the superiority of Jesus as Son to other competing brokers (angels, Moses, Abraham, the Aaronic priesthood). Only Melchizedek, without ancestor and with a separate (and superior) line of priestly descendants deriving from Aaron, is allowed to be suitable predecessor for Jesus' brokerage (Heb 7:1ff). Moreover, here too Jesus' sanctuary is superior to the sacred space of the Temple (Heb 8-9), and his sacrifice surpasses any earlier form of covenantal arrangement (Heb 10).[27]

In some of the Johannine metaphors there is an ambiguity regarding whether they point to Jesus as "broker". The role of shepherd, for example, would be more appropriate to "patron". In the context of John 10, the good shepherd is contrasted to hirelings, who care not for the sheep. This too would suggest that the shepherd stands distinct from other "agents" in so far as the sheep are "his own". From the point of view of the client, however, the broker is in a sense patron.

The exclusivity of the patron–client relationship

With Jesus' departure in prospect, John 17 effectively provides Jesus' last earthly opportunity to exercise a personal intervention on behalf his clients. That intervention is based upon the loyalty which these followers have already demonstrated—to Jesus as well as to "God the patron".

As has been argued earlier, in John 17:22 Jesus is depicted as declaring that the "honor" (δόξα) which the Father has given to him is what he imparts to his disciples. Since this δόξα is described as some-

---

[27] Much of this superiority in Hebrews is explicitly depicted in "honor" language. I am indebted to P. F. Esler for this comparison.

thing which he has already given them, the Fourth Evangelist is not looking to the disciples' heavenly state in the presence of the Father. This is referred to later in John 17:24, where the hope is expressed that they will eventually be with Jesus and be partakers in the public acknowledgment of *his* honor ("see my δόξα"). In John 17:22, honor seems rather to be something which the disciples can claim already to possess.

Attempts to identify this δόξα with the disciples' receipt of the "revelation" of Jesus or "divine life" also fail adequately to account for the phrasing of the immediate context. In the following verse (17:23), the relationship between disciples, Jesus and the Father is "that they may be completely one, that *the world may know* that you have sent me and have loved them even as you have loved me". Emphasis is drawn to the purported *public recognition* of their special association with God ("that you have loved them"), the supreme patron. This is what makes the δόξα they are given even more clearly a claim to honor.

Such a claim is, however, potentially problematic. In the Fourth Gospel, recognition by the world could be interpreted as being in tension with the fact that the Evangelist also declares that the world "hates" Jesus' disciples. This appears explicitly in John 17:14 "the world has hated them because they do not belong to the world, just as I do not belong to the world". Yet there need be no fundamental inconsistency here. Within a limited good environment, the "honor" bestowed upon disciples is gained at the expense of those who lack this privileged relationship. It has previously been noted how recognition by one's peers of one's relationship as client to a patron gives rise not only to honor for the favored client but also to envy by these outsiders. It is particularly the case where clients are in competition for such patronage. Such competition may well be asserted (whether real or imputed) by the Evangelist to characterize the situation of believers *vis à vis* the synagogue. John's use of the term κόσμος (world) bears different meanings, sometimes to indicate the society of *hoi Ioudaioi* or the synagogue (compare John 7:1 and 7; also John 16:2).[28] So "the world's" hate of Jesus may well refer here quite specifically to the believers' most direct competitors, the synagogue, as in John 16. Both the community of believers and the synagogue make claims to possess God's favor. The exclusivity of the relationship to the Father claimed

---

[28] J. Ashton (1991: 136) notes that when John specifically refers to the enemies of the community, as in John 14-17, "he avoids the word 'Jews' altogether, substituting the word κόσμος (world), which obviously has a different resonance. Certainly there is no rigid distinction between the denotation of the two terms."

for disciples, and the monopolistic role which Jesus is shown to perform as broker, are clearly apparent earlier in John 17:9:

> "I am asking on their behalf; I am *not* asking on behalf of the world, but on behalf of those whom you gave me, because they are yours."

To claim therefore that the world-synagogue can "hate" disciples and yet ostensibly "know" that God "has loved them" is entirely compatible within the framework of John's language and Mediterranean values. In effect, the hate felt by disciples is portrayed as a kind of envy by outsiders.

Elsewhere in the Farewell Discourses it is also clear that "hate" is linked to intergroup competition and to that claim of "favor" which sets disciples apart from their peers in other groups. In its most extensive passage on the hate of the world, the Fourth Gospel states: "If you belonged to the world, the world would love you as its own. Because you do not belong to the world, but I have chosen you out of the world—therefore the world hates you" (John 15:19). The *selection* of the disciples by Jesus to be "out of the world"—as expressed in John 17:6 and 14—indicates an element of exclusivity, which is a basis for imputing envy to outsiders. In view of the association of "synagogue" and "world" in the Farewell discourses as representing the enemies of the disciples, perhaps there is even the suggestion that being "cast out of the synagogue" (John 16:2) is in effect being "selected out of the world" (John 15:19; 17:6). A potential badge of shame is being portrayed as an exclusive privilege.

Bruce Malina (1994b) makes the case that John's Gospel makes extensive use of "antilanguage", reflecting the "antisociety" or alternative reality which John's group created over against that of its opponents. This opposition includes "this world" and *hoi Ioudaioi*; it is reflected in the Evangelist's very use of these terms, as well as in many of his metaphors.[29] The competitive claim to honor and the exclusivity of the patron-broker-client relationship can be seen as further expressions of the "antisociety" which John reflects.

The Fourth Evangelist also connects the world's hate of the disciples with the hate directed to Jesus, based again on an argument about the exclusivity of his relationship to the patron-God. Earlier, in John 15:24 he writes: "If I had not done among them the works *that no one else did*, they would not have sin. But now they have seen and hated both me and my Father." It is often argued that (in a generalized sense) the

---

[29] See also Malina and Rohrbaugh (1998:244-245) with regard to antilanguage in John 17:9-19.

world's refusal to believe in the light of Jesus' works is the root of sin (Brown 1966:697). Yet the *uniquely* spectacular nature of Jesus' signs in the Fourth Gospel—the monopolistic claim for his brokerage—is a particular bone of contention and could hardly be other than an implicit challenge to the synagogue authorities.[30] These texts demonstrate that a claim to exclusivity was presented as an explanation for the world's hate, both with regard to Jesus the broker and with respect to the disciples as clients.[31]

Other Johannine evidence suggesting such an understanding of the world's "hate" can be found in 1 John 3:11-13. In the context of an exhortation to love one another, the story of Cain is cited. This is a classic example of envy of brother in a limited-good context, regarding a blessing or favor which can only be bestowed once. This leads Cain to murder his brother. The author of 1 John asserts that the murder was certainly due to no unrighteousness on Abel's part (3:12) and then follows the reference to Cain with words: "Do not be astonished, brothers and sisters, that the world hates you" (3:13). The implication would again seem to be that the author's people are the true and purportedly exclusive bearers of God's favoritism.

How far envy can exist in a community without being perceived as a direct threat to community stability is discussed by Foster (1967:315-17). He draws attention to the significance of "open" aspects of peasant society in which limited good is partially set aside. He notes that if the success of an individual is generated within a village, then it is almost always at the expense of someone else in the village and a variety of sanctions work against it. But if an individual's success is achieved by tapping resources outside the village system, then whilst it may be envied it is not at the expense of others in the village. Thus treasure tales, luck and *the favor of deities* are sometimes invoked to explain one's success, if an individual is forced to acknowledge that success at all. Similarly, the concern of peasants to find a patron, who is usually outside the village, is an "acceptable" (even if still envied) way of achieving progress.

In the light of these observations, does the claim to have God as patron in any way lessen the (real or imputed) antipathy of "the

---

[30] See John 11:45ff; 12:9-11.

[31] It may be argued that Jesus' exclusive role as broker is undermined, even in the Farewell Discourses, by the provision of another broker, another Paraclete, the Spirit. But the clear attempts of the Evangelist closely to tie both the sending and the functions of the Paraclete/Spirit of Truth to Jesus in John 14-16 quite deliberately avoid any suggestion of rivalry. In effect the Spirit becomes an extension of Jesus' brokerage; see also note 12 above.

world"? Is such a patron sufficiently outside the closed system in which the Johannine disciples live that his favor may not be viewed as being at the expense of others in that segment of society? In the context of monotheistic belief, it is unlikely that this is so. In a polytheistic context, the threat may indeed be lessened. The various deities may compete amongst themselves for clients, and clients may seek their patronage. The social system is not necessarily seriously upset by any one individual or group's claim to favor from any one deity. Yet if "the world" in the Fourth Gospel significantly focuses upon *hoi Ioudaioi*, and if the main competitors of believers are seen to be the synagogue, then there is only one patron for whom the Evangelist can claim both are directly competing. Limited good is operative. In the author's presentation, each group seeks an exclusive relationship with the same patron.

The benefactions sought from the Patron

That the relationship between Jesus' disciples and God is portrayed in patron-client terms, and in purported competition with other potential clients, is also displayed in another way. It emerges in the nature of what the disciples expect or seek from their patron. Early in the intercession in John 17, the gift of "eternal life" is specifically cited as a benefaction, entrusted to the Son to mediate (17:2) and linked to the clients' loyalty to "the only true God" (17:3). Eternal life is of course the supreme benefaction.

Elsewhere in John 17, however, the Patron is asked above all to dispense protection. In John 17:11 Jesus asks on their behalf: "Holy Father, protect them in your name which you have given me, so that they may be one". The protection is not just for the individual, but for them collectively. Moreover, it is noted that Jesus provided this gift on God's behalf during his earthly ministry: "While I was with them, I protected them in your name which you have given me. I guarded them, and not one of them was lost except the one destined to be lost" (John 17:12; cf. John 10:28f).

The petition is repeated later in John 17 when Jesus again asks the Father "to protect them from the evil one" (17:15). Such protective support was expected of a patron. John makes clear that it can be delivered. God's power over the world and the evil one is undisputed; Jesus' power in this respect has also been declared earlier in John 16:33 ("Take courage; I have conquered the world") and 12:33 ("now the ruler of this world will be driven out").[32] The hostility faced by disciples and the protection sought from God are the dominant themes in John 17, leading to 17:22.

Interestingly, other benefits—such as material support, hospitality or legal assistance—are not specifically highlighted in this immediate context. The hostility of the world and the evil one is generalized language rather than specific. The primary threat, however, appears to be to their unity. There is a reiterated concern that this protection is for the purpose "that they may be one" (John 17:11, 21, 22, 23).[33] Protection is associated with maintaining this group identity. The dynamic of this communal concern is itself interesting and is a subject to which we shall shortly return.

The responsibilities of the clients

One must ask, however, how far John 17 shows awareness of the responsibilities of a client towards a patron. Loyalty and honor, sometimes directed to Jesus and sometimes to the Father, are recurring themes in John 17. They are expressed in the following terms:

1. Obedience

   "they have kept your word" (17:6)

2. Showing loyalty (under testing circumstances)

   "they have received them [the words that "you gave to me" and "I have given to them"] and know in truth that I came from you; and they have believed that you sent me" (17:8)

   "I have given them your word, and the world has hated them because they do not belong to the world" (17:14)

3. Giving honor

   "All mine are yours ... I have been glorified/honored in them" (17:10)

4. Serving in designated tasks

   "I have sent them into the world" (17:18)

---

[32] G. M. Foster (1967:316) notes that among informal, unorganized group actions taken against someone attempting to better his comparative standing is the threat of witchcraft. Is the interest in protection from "the evil one" a suggestion that they will face such threats?

[33] Being scattered is associated with danger (16:32) and being lost (17:12; cf. 10:12, 16).

As is clear in John 17:18, expressions of loyalty, obedience and honor are combined with a task. It can be argued that the disciples themselves effectively become brokers of God to at least a part of the world (see John 17:20f) after Jesus' departure, but this appears to be by virtue of the fact that they already are his clients. Furthermore, however much the disciples may continue the activity of Jesus in the world, the uniqueness assigned to Jesus' role is not wholly assumed by the disciples. In other words, there appears to be a limit to the elevation of their status.

The patron-client model itself would hardly lead us to expect otherwise. The disparity in status between the disciples and God—and also between disciples and Jesus—remains great as long as Jesus' role as broker is emphasized. Thus they must remain clients.[34] It is initially obvious in the fact that they remain in the world after Jesus departs. Although they may be described (through further examples of "anti-language") as "children of God" (1:12) or "born from above" (3:3) or "one" with the Father and the Son (17:21f), the reality of their situation can hardly be overlooked, even in an idealized world-view. Expressions of fictive kinship like those noted above are not incompatible with patron-client relations and may help to portray the status of the patron in his protective role as "father" (A. Drummond 1989:102).[35] But, significantly, the terminology of kinship is rarely used in direct discourse between *Jesus* and his disciples. In the Fourth Gospel, Jesus does not call his disciples "brothers" until John 20:17, after his resurrection and with his own ascended state in view. The term "brother" never appears in the Farewell Discourses. Neither do the terms υἱοι, τέκνα or παιδές/παιδία.

More strikingly, in the Farewell Discourses the disciples are variously described as "slaves" (δοῦλοι John 13:16; 15:20) and "friends" (φίλοι John 15:15). Slaves were of course not normally viewed as clients, because the relationship was not a voluntary one.[36] Within a Jewish context, however, disciples performed many of the functions of slaves for their rabbi. It is a highly significant point therefore when Jesus declares that he does not "call you slaves any longer, because the slave does not know what the master is doing; but I have called you

---

[34] S. N. Eisenstadt and Louis Roniger (1980: 72): "While this concept [of client] entails in its very definition asymmetric hierarchical relations, it cannot be so purely interpersonal as are ritual kinship or friendship relations".

[35] See also B. Malina (1996c: 146).

[36] John also notes that slaves had no permanent place in the household (8:35).

friends" (15:15). This elevates them to potential clients, but not necessarily to any more than that.[37]

The clients as 'group'

Our final point of interest concerns the unity of these clients as a
group. It has been noted earlier how this is not simply assumed; it is a
repeated concern of the Evangelist to emphasize the need and hope for
group coherence ("that they may be one": John 17:11, 21, 22, 23).
Moreover, he employs the concepts of holiness or purity to set a
boundary around them as a group. This is partly reflected in the language about them being "given from (ἐκ) the world" in 17:6 and "not
belonging to (ἐκ) the world" in 17:14, despite their continuing presence in the world. It is also reflected in the language of sanctification.
Just as the Father is called "holy" (ἅγιε) in John 17:11, the disciples
too are said to be "guarded" (17:11, 12, 15) and "sanctified" or set
apart (ἁγιάζειν: 17:17, 19). The language of boundary maintenance is
thus strongly represented throughout this discourse.

What is the basis for their coherence as a group? Malina (1996c:44ff)
argues that the central group in the ancient Mediterranean world was
the family or kinship group. This can be configured in a variety of
ways and does not necessarily require the explicit terminology of family. It has been noted earlier how the Evangelist refers to believers as
being "born of God", "born from above", "children of God". Yet it is
striking that the "brotherhood" of disciples is not an emphasis in John
17. Their sharing of honor with Jesus and God in John 17 may be
"much like a fictive kin group" (Malina and Rohrbaugh 1998:245),
but why is it not made explicit precisely where the issue of coherence
and unity is raised? This apparent reticence is somewhat surprising, not
only in view of the synoptic tradition (which can refer to Jesus' disciples openly as his "brothers", cf. Mark 3:34f) but also in view of the
Mediterranean suspicion expressed towards all outside of family. Again
G. M. Foster makes the point with regard to peasant society that this
suspicion towards groups larger than the immediate family goes hand
in hand with the competition for resources. Those outside the immediate family represent potential threats; they are not valued as

---

[37] The image could be of a freed slave here. A. Wallace-Hadrill (1989: 76) notes
that the *patronus-libertus* relationship was significantly different from the *patronus-cliens*
relationship, particularly since the former was not voluntary and the obligations of
deference were enforceable in law. See also Roniger (1983: 70). But Malina (1996c:
146) indicates that patron-client relations can be "added to the legally sanctioned
subordination of a slave to his or her owner".

individuals. Where co-operation with others occurs, which is rare, it must clearly be of mutual value to all participants (1967:318).

This suggests strongly that we should look for the basis of cohesion of the group(s) addressed by John in the areas of mutual advantage. But in John 17 there is remarkably little suggestion of exactly how individual believers may help to support one another and therefore be better off through co-operation. The key commandment of Jesus to "love one another" in John 13:34 may well be a step in this direction.[38] But the primary security of believers seems to be expressed not so much in terms of what *the disciples will do for one another*, but rather of what *their God-patron will do for them*. They may be bound to their patron through their expressions of belief and loyalty, but this in itself may not make them a co-operative group.

The strong impression which persists therefore is that their unity, whilst seen as necessary, is expressed more as something for which to hope than as a present reality. This is true for John 17, as well as in 10:16 and 11:52 which express to desire for the creation of one flock under the one shepherd, and the gathering of the scattered children of God.[39] Does this mean that they are just loosely associated "individuals", not yet having group identity? It has been argued that the basis for Christian unity in the Fourth Gospel is each individual believer's mystical union with God. M. Pamment (1982:384) rightly criticizes this and prefers to express it as "summarizing the relationship which each has to the truth". In view of the correspondence in the Gospel between Jesus and "the Truth", one could argue in theological terms that at heart this is a common (Christological) confessional stance (cf. John 17:20), or in social-scientific terms that at heart this is reliance on a common broker.[40] But even this may in the end be too individualistic a perspective adequately to explain the author's perspective.

As already indicated, the author strives to encourage a sense of unity. He emphasizes a common and distinctive brokerage. He presents these followers as having common powerful foes. He uses language of boundary maintenance. But despite previous tradition, he holds back from *explicitly* referring to them as "brothers", fictive kin here. Even where fictive kinship is invoked elsewhere, it tends to be used "vertically" to depict the subordination of "children of God" to

---

[38] Possibly see also John 17:26.

[39] See also John 16:32.

[40] It would be possible also to see this as an implication of the vine image in John 15.

"God the father", rather than "horizontally" to depict the relationship between disciples or believers. Why?

Whilst this conundrum is not easily solved, it possible that the Evangelist adopts this approach because he has another model in mind, a kind of extension of fictive kinship. In John 11:51, the high priest "prophesies" that Jesus will die on behalf of the "nation" (ἔθνος), with which is associated the "scattered children of God". The image of the vine in John 15 was also an image for Israel (Isa 5:1-7; Jer. 2:12; Ezek 19:10-14). The flock in John 10 again draws on images relating God as the shepherd of Israel in 2 Sam 7:7f; Ezek 34:11-16 and elsewhere. Moreover, there is a significant distinction between the Fourth Evangelist's use of the term "Israel", which is rarely negative, and his use of *hoi Ioudaioi*. Although B. Lindars (1972:487) declared with respect to John 15 that the Evangelist "is not saying that the Church is to be the New Israel, and there is not the slightest indication that his thought is running along this line", one should not abandon such an idea too quickly. The wider competition which the author imputes between believers and the synagogue, and the previously-discussed attempt to show Jesus' superiority to brokers and institutions by drawing on those very images, both suggest that the category of "Israel" may indeed be in the author's mind for followers of Jesus. The believing group(s) may not be the *New* Israel, just as Jesus is not the *New* Torah-Word of God. Rather believers collectively are the *true* Israel, the true clients chosen by God, just as Jesus is the *real* broker.

Further support for this thesis of "fictive ethnicity"[41] as an extension of "fictive kinship" can be drawn from the very beginning of the Fourth Gospel, where Jesus calls his first disciples. At the climax of the call of the first four disciples, Jesus refers to Nathanael as "a genuine Israelite (ἀληθῶς Ἰσραηλίτης) in whom there is no deceit" (John 1:47). A contrast with Jacob is implicit,[42] but so also is the claim to find in these responsive new followers the true Israel.

When the Evangelist refers to the "scattered children of God" in John 11, it would appear that the Evangelist is keen to interpret as a kind of "diaspora" the phenomenon of the spread of early Christianity. The geographical spread may well reflect other differences of which he is also aware. These have been studied particularly with regard to the so-called "one-upmanship" depicted between the Beloved Disciple and Peter and the issue of how far the group(s) addressed by John can

[41] A term coined for my benefit by P. F. Esler.

[42] R. E. Brown (1966:87). Contrast B. Lindars (1972:118): "Nathanael is the devout Jew whom the Christian may hope to convert".

be considered "sectarian" *vis à vis* other believers.[43] Yet Peter appears no worse, and perhaps considerably better, in the Fourth Gospel than in Mark.[44] Whatever differences there may be between the Fourth Evangelist and other groups of believers of whom he is aware, these might be no greater than differences recognized between Palestinian and Diaspora Israelites. The bond of ethnicity can be a basis for unity amidst diversity. It is possible that the very purpose of the Fourth Gospel is to establish contact and promote the views of the Johannine group(s) more widely in the church.[45] Whilst by reason of differences of location, experience or outlook they may not find themselves easily able to call these more distant believers "brothers", they may nonetheless view them as part of the "scattered children of God", part of the "true Israel".

"Fictive ethnicity" need not be understood simply as a "model" by which to affirm unity. It can be related to a reassertion of one's ethnicity in a situation where that identity is threatened. If at some point in the history of the groups which the Evangelist addresses they belonged to the synagogue and were subsequently expelled, their "Jewishness" would have come sharply into question. The indication that they were expelled rather than that they left (16:2) would suggest no particular desire on their part to jettison their Israelite identity; it was being taken from them. Thus a reassertion of that identity is not unexpected. The point at which it becomes "fictive" ethnicity is when others are incorporated into the new group who might not have the same history. This may be precisely the likely situation from which and to which the Fourth Evangelist wrote.[46]

What remains interesting in such a theory is the relationship between the "true Israel" and *hoi Ioudaioi*. The Fourth Evangelist clearly needs a term for distinguishing the true Israel from its competition. The synagogue can hardly be called "Gentile". For this same reason it may not always be helpful to call them "the world", although the overlap between the response of the world and that of *hoi Ioudaioi* can

---

[43] See R. E. Brown (1979:83-88); K. Quast (1989).

[44] Especially if one takes into account John 21.

[45] A form of such a theory has been argued recently by Richard Bauckham (1998: esp. 26-44) for all the gospels, although one must not also lose sight of the defining influence of the experiences of the author and the specific group to which he belongs in any such wider promotional task. See also P. F. Esler (1998).

[46] The ambiguity in John 12:20 about the precise ethnicity of the "Greeks" who are going up to worship at the Passover and who seek to see Jesus may reflect such a *fictive* ethnicity—Gentiles (not just diaspora Israelites) incorporated into (even though not traditionally seen as part of) "Israel".

be considerable, as has been argued earlier. Thus the Fourth Evangelist has chosen a term, *hoi Ioudaioi*, which may well not be intended to be descriptive in any technical sense except to distinguish those who falsely claim the heritage which the Evangelist claims. In this way one finds an explanation for his distinction in vocabulary between "Israel" and *Ioudaioi*.

Conclusion

Consideration of the place of honor in ancient Mediterranean values, and analysis of how such honor is conveyed in a competitive system of patron-broker-client relationships, shed light not only on John 17 but on the whole of the Fourth Gospel. Rather than treat the discourse in John 17 simply as a set of theological themes, divorced from both cultural and social context, it has been shown how attention to such contexts adds considerably to understanding the Evangelist's argument.

It has been shown that throughout John 17, the main responsibilities which one would expect of a client towards his patron are depicted, intermixed with the petitions for protection and the gift of "eternal life" from God as patron. Together they make a powerful case for interpreting these verses in the light of patron-client relations and exchange. In such a context the δόξα given to disciples in John 17:22 can be best understood as the "honor" bestowed upon the disciples-clients as a result of association with their God-patron. In the competitive environment of the ancient Mediterranean, such honor claims associated with God's patronage could be employed by the Evangelist to balance the apparent shame of the crucifixion of Jesus as well as the expulsion from the synagogue of the group(s) addressed by the Fourth Evangelist. The continuing claim to God's patronage through the exclusive brokerage of Jesus helps maintain their group boundaries and reinforce their understanding of reality in a competitive environment against others who also claim God's favor.

12

Sacrifice as Metaphor

Wolfgang Stegemann
Augustana Evangelische Hochschule, Neuendettelsau, Germany

It gives me great joy to honor my friend and colleague, Bruce J. Malina, on his 65th birthday, by contributing this essay to this collection. In the course of a person's scholarly career, there are but few people of whom one case say: "They changed my mind." This is the significance of Bruce J. Malina for me. With his wide-ranging scholarly work, he opened entirely new mental horizons to me. For this I am grateful to him, but also for the ties of friendship that bind us.

Modern Discourse about Sacrifice

Everyday language gives witness to an almost inflationary usage of the word-field of sacrifice. This word-field includes the activity (to sacrifice), the entity sacrificed (a victim) as well as the process (a sacrifice) (see Schenk 1995:3). There are traffic victims, war victims, victims of fires. Parents sacrifice for their children; professors sacrifice valuable time for committees; physicians deal with sicknesses that demand their sacrifice; politicians appeal to the self-sacrificing devotedness of taxpayers. Thus at bottom, the term vocabulary of sacrifice connotes loss and deprivation. A person gives something up or gives it away; a person experiences a loss of some material goods, of a quality of life, of physical integrity, or even of life itself. Furthermore, the (usually defenseless) object of a power relationship can be labeled as a victim (that is, an entity sacrificed). People can be victims of a crime, a relationship that contrasts the victim (entity sacrificed) with the perpetrator of the crime (the one doing the sacrifice).

The English terminology contrasts with German usage. For the single German word, *Opfer,* is used to signify both the offering of a sacrifice (Lat. *sacrificium, immolatio*) as well as the entity sacrificed, the victim (Lat. *victima, hostia*). This lexical imprecision can further clarify contemporary German usage. For in everyday speech, the German word "Opfer" is, for the most part, a semantic equivalent of the Latin term *victima* (or *hostia*). As such, it is used to label the passive object of the sacrificial process (the entity sacrificed). Even the reflexive usage of the verb, "to sacrifice oneself," implies taking on a passive role in some event. This aspect is rendered in Latin likewise with *victima*, but not with *sacrificium*. Thus Cicero can say that a person sacrificed himself for the state (*se victimam rei publicae praebuisset* ...). Is it a coincidence that both Latin words for sacrificial animal are of the grammatical feminine gender—*victima* and *hostia*? After all, ancient Mediterraneans associated passivity above all with female gender roles (see Malina 1990). However in the modern usage of sacrificial terms both in English and in German, what predominates is the sacrificial logic of the victim's loss, endurance of suffering, subjection to force, identification with the victim rather than the sacrificial logic of active offering or self-giving (Spämann 1995:12). English is heir to the Latin rooted terms *sacrifice* and *victim*, and the spectrum of meanings covered by the German *Opfer* largely covers the same ground. However what is noteworthy of English is the use of the vocabulary of sacrifice in the sphere of economics, e.g. "to sell at a sacrifice."

In German usage, the aspect of religious offering or religious-cultic connotations is more seldom connected with sacrifice. Obviously this does occur most clearly in religious contexts: the sacrifice of the Mass and above all in statements of the sacrificial death of Christ. This connotation is to be found marginally in statements about war victims or about victims of tyranny. A contemporary example of the activation of sacral connotations of sacrificial terms is the term *holocaust* to label the mass murder of European Jews (Spämann 1995:13). The term relates to the Greek or Latin equivalents of the Old Testament burnt-offering (*holocaust*). Because of the term's religious-cultic background, it is not controversial. Fundamentally, however, our everyday usage hardly connotes anything of the religious-cultic reality of sacrificial praxis. One might therefore speak of a "secularization" of sacrifice, or even of its "banalization in everyday language" (Schenk 1995:6), in as much as the original religious frame of reference is no longer of any important. However I would maintain that the modern terms for sacrifice, with their predominant meanings of loss and self-devotedness, imply a frame of reference rooted in economics rather than in religion. An impressive clue to the implied context of this usage is the English phrase, "to sell at a sacrifice." And it is precisely the reflectional moment of sacrifice—self-sacrifice—which connects the victim with a "transformation into subjectivity" that seems to have become a hallmark of the language of sacrifice. From this perspective, the statement of Horkheimer and Adorno (1969:62) makes sense: "The history of civilization is the history of the introversion of sacrifice. In other words, the history of self-renunciation. Self-renouncing persons give more of their life than they get in return, more than the life that they defend. This develops in the context of false society."

The Emphatic Character of Everyday Sacrificial Language.
However this dictum is valid only for modern usage, which is closely tied up with changes relative to ancient sacrificial language in that *discourse about sacrifice is no longer considered to be metaphoric.* It has become part and parcel of actual language. This is particularly evident in the contrast between victim and criminal. The term "victim" in a crime context has only residual figurative or interpretative power. Contrary to the oft-expressed opinion that our sacrificial language is metaphorical (for instance, Spämann 1995:12), I would rather say that "sacrifice" has assumed that characteristic features of a *dead* or contentional metaphor. For example, when we use the expression, "table leg," we no longer reflect on the metaphorical background of the designation. The same is true of the collocation of victim and criminal. And where German and English usage equate victims with loss of human life (in war, fire, flood, storms and the like), the terms function rather synonymously.

Nevertheless, one must recognize that the word-field of sacrifice—for instance when used to describe the voluntary sacrifice on behalf of other persons (e.g. parents for their children)—intends to add a higher significance to the loss in question. Naturally the sacrifice in question connotes something quite beyond those designated as traffic victims or war victims. In this context, sacrifice designates the price persons pay for another, willingly or not, be it for their own children, or for their own country (war victims), or for society as a whole (traffic victims). In this regard, the largely unexpressed yet resonant elements of the word field of sacrifice presuppose distinct frames of reference.

Generally speaking, everyday sacrificial language can bestow higher significance to loss or suffering or self-giving in that sacrifice is made *for others*, for members of one's family, for one's community, or for anonymous society at large. In these cases, sacrificial terms are an interpretative device. Their interpretative power derives from perceptions of sacrifice that have their origin in a long and complicated history. An aspect of the ancient understanding of sacrifice has survived in them. But as will be shown later, in the ancient metaphor of sacrifice (for the most part) the religious frame of reference has remained preserved. To what extent that is the case depends on the fact that unlike ancient sacrificial language (or in contrast with contemporary cultures which are still familiar with the practice of ritual sacrifice), genuine sacrifice no longer belongs to modern experience. This means that in comparison with ancient sacrificial language, modern usage stands independent of religious-cultic behavior and is therefore only in rare instances understood as a transferred mode of expression.

Preliminary Remarks on the Ancient Sacrificial Language
The foregoing brief remarks concerning our standard usage of sacrificial language are important to me since in contrast, the ancient texts lived with the experience of and regard for religious-cultic rites which were performed in contexts of fixed or occasional (that is, at extraordinary occurrences such as at a battle or at a dangerous river crossing) rituals. Sacrifices were offered to certain deities in connection with petitions or thanksgivings. The emotional atmosphere at the ritual activity was rather happy and festive. The idea of deprivation, that something was to be given up, could have been the basis for the sacrifice (gift offering); but it was not at all chiefly bound up with loss. The ancient terms for sacrifice have to be radically distinguished from modern everyday language of sacrifice. An initial reason for such distinction is indicated by the fact that ancient sacrifices were to be as large as possible for those offering them, that is wealthier people offered quantitatively greater sacrifices than poorer persons. Further, emphasis was put on the action of giving something rather than on the passive giving up of something (Daly 1990:191-198). Furthermore, in ancient documents comparisons of human behaviors with sacrifice come from societies in which sacrifice to a deity was a meaningful form of human behavior. Such is not the case with modern usage. The reason for this, again, is that ancient sacrificial metaphors make direct and clear allusion or reference to the religious-cultic activity of sacrifice that all could experience. That would mean that ancient sacrificial metaphors principally possess a *denotative* character, or to use Ricoeur's phrase, such metaphors allow for imagining a "heuristic fiction" of reality (Ricoeur 1986). I would not categorize ancient sacrificial metaphors *per se* as direct or absolute metaphors, like the metaphors found in poetic speech. However it is quite fitting to characterize the compara-

tive usage of sacrificial terms in ancient texts as *semantically motivated emphasis*.

Spiritualizing or Metaphor?

Emphatic or forceful sacrificial metaphors can be found in the Bible (both Testaments), in Second Temple Israelite writings and in early Christian literature as well as in Graeco-Roman documents. It is to these latter that I would like to refer explicitly.

Concerning the Idea of Spiritualizing Sacrifice

Example of sacrificial metaphors in the Bible are discussed mostly under the heading of "spiritualizing." This has been the case in theological scholarship at least since the research of Wenschkewitz. Wenschkewitz used the term "spiritualizing" to designate passages in which cultic terms are applied "to a cultic event that is not ritualism in the strict sense" (Wenschkewitz 1932:228). Subsequently, Hermisson understood spiritualizing as "the detachment (!) of ritual conceptions and language from the cultic phenomenon bound up with or designated by them" (Hermisson 1965:27). What is significant is that the idea of spiritualizing is quite unsuitable here because it is presented as a higher level category, yet in reality, it embraces completely different phenomena. These cover dematerializing as well as rationalizing, and ethicizing or even the substitution of sacrifice. In this way martyrdom as well as an ascetical way of life and almsgiving are designated by the term spiritualizing. So is martyrdom the spiritualizing of animal sacrifice? Is ascetical living a spiritual sacrifice? And almsgiving represents a substitution, but not a spiritualizing, of sacrifice (Track 1996:141-42).

Sacrificial Metaphor

In fact, the idea of sacrificial metaphor makes far more sense to me. It marks off implicitly metaphorical sacrificial language from such linguistic utterances that refer to actual sacrifice. Sacrificial metaphor compares a certain extra-textual referent with actual sacrifice, underscores similarities and thus expresses something new about reality. In other words, the extra-textual referent owes its designation as sacrifice to the author of the text, not to itself. I hope to clarify this point with an example, to which I shall again return. In the *Martyrdom of Polycarp*, Polycarp is "presented as an offering like a festively decorated ram from a great herd, prepared as a burnt-offering well pleasing to God." The historical referent of this statement is the execution of the Christian martyr, Polycarp, according to the regulations of a specific Roman capital punishment, death by fire. The statement cited from the Martyrdom of Polycarp does not describe this commonplace occurrence but obliterates any reference to political or legal procedure by means of metaphorical elements. In this way it discloses and reveals the author's own particular view of the reality of Polycarp's death.

Examples of Ancient Sacrificial Metaphor

In what follows, my chief concern is to illustrate the denotative character of ancient sacrificial metaphor. While there are numerous aspects of sacrifice used metaphorically, I can present only a few examples. I begin with that aspect of sacrifice which for Girard (1987) is its fundamental significance, that is violence (1). Then the relationship between sacrifice and war will be briefly presented (2). The innovative power of the metaphor of sacrifice as a model of a counter world is treated in a further subsection (3). The aspect of sacrifice as self-giving, an aspect quite important in modern usage, will be extensively discussed (4.). Finally, a specific dimension of the ancient understanding of sacrifice, that of exclusivity (setting apart) will conclude this series of examples of ancient sacrificial metaphors (5).

1. Sacrificial Metaphor and Violence

The verb *spházein* (more seldom *immolare*) as well as the noun *sphágion* (originally, immolation, a sacrifice in which the victim is totally destroyed) have been used in a figurative sense. Recourse to *sphágion* (sacrifice of immolation) is significant. I have not found any cases of the noun *thysía* in Graeco-Roman documents that clearly have metaphorical meaning. The word takes on this meaning in Christian texts, both in the New Testament as well as in the Apostolic Fathers and the Fathers of the Church (Eph 5:2; Heb 10:12; 13:15-16; Rom 12:1; Phil 2:17; 4:18; 1 Pet 2:5; *Barn.* 2:10; 7:3; *1 Clem.* 18:17; 52:4; see also the later examples in the Church Fathers). Rarely, however, is the verb *thuein* used metaphorically (Behm 1938:181-182; Examples: Aeschylus, *Ag.*137—in the sense of tear to pieces (wild animals), to butcher, to murder; Euripides, *IphTaur* 621; cf. 1 Macc 7:19; John 1:10); of course it is widely overshadowed by the number of instances for *spházein* ktl. (Burkert 1987:17; some examples: Xenophon, *Anab* 4, 1, 23; *Hell* 4,4,3; Thucydides 7,84; Aeschylus, *Ag* 1433; for *immolare* [to kill as sacrificial victim, to immolate]: Virgil, *Aen* 10,541; 12,949; *Phaedr* 4,6,9; similarly also in the New Testament). Among other things, what is involved semantically is the drastic and vivid linguistic expression of the act of killing itself along with its attendant cruel aggressiveness: for example, to cut a person's throat, or to butcher or slaughter another. Further, murder, political assassination, and fratricide can be described with the term (Cain and Abel: 1 John 3:12; Michel 1964); also the murderer—*ho sphrageús* (Philo, *Legat,* 92). It is especially reprehensible when human beings are slaughtered alongside sacrificial animals (Josephus, *Bell.* 2:30; *Ant.* 17:165, 237, 239). This is probably the background of the remarkable phrasing in Luke 13:1 about the Galileans who blood Pilate mixed with their sacrifice.

No matter how the metaphorical character of individual texts is assessed, one cannot fundamentally refute the fact that sacrificial terms predicate aggressive and murderous violence. And Burkert (1972) and Girard have suggested a fundamental theory that sacrifice, or the sacred itself, has something to do with violence—in any case in animal sacrifice. I find it noteworthy that the metaphorical usage of "to sacrifice/ slaughter" activates the aggressive aspect of sacrifice, but obviously not the religious-ritualistic aspects (the exception perhaps are the tragedies). Succinctly put: those who slaughter human beings do not get halos even if their killings are described in sacrificial terms. If it follows that sacrifice as "pure" violence channels impurely (Girard), it is nevertheless noteworthy that impure violence can be expressed in an inflated way with the terminology of sacrifice. In my opinion, Burkert comes closest to the meaning of the ancient texts when he joins the sacralization of killing in sacrificial ritual with crossing taboo boundaries. But murder and fratricide likewise cross taboo boundaries.

I also think that the metaphorical usage of "slaughter," with its overtones of sacrifice, especially activates the aggressive aspects of sacrifice and boundaries of taboo crossed by killing. It is interesting to compare the use of *spházein* for slaughtering in war (Behm 1938:932- 933) with other war-related sacrificial metaphors, which specifically activate the religious sphere. More about this point shortly. But first, note that in Hebrew there is a difference between *šahat* and *tabah*; *tabah,* which best corresponds with *spházein,* is not a technical term for sacrificial ritual (Michel 1964:929-930, 933). I see this as an indication that violence and sacrificial violence were differentiated. An example:

> For the Lord has a sacrifice (*zebah*) in Bozrah, a great slaughter (*tebah*) in
>   the land of Edom.
> Wild oxen shall fall with them, and young steers with the mighty bulls.
> Their land shall be soaked with blood, and their soil made rich with fat
>   (Isa 34:6b-7).

Here too we find sacrificial metaphor (*zebah*), yet the blood drenched slaughter is not described with a sacrificial term.

The terminology of "slaughter," which alludes to immolation (the victim is totally annihilated), can be employed in the New Testament as well. It is found there without reference to the death of Jesus in the sense of "to massacre" or "to butcher" (Rev 6:4, 9; 13:3; 18:24; 1 John 3:12). The contexts point to violent killing, perhaps even to beheading (Rev 13:3). The death of Jesus, likewise, is described metaphorically with the terminology of slaughter. Thus, for instance, Acts 8:32, where a citation of Isaiah (Isa 53:7) is applied to Jesus. Jesus was led *like* a sheep to the slaughter (*sphagé*). However the figurative usage of "slaughter/sacrifice" relative to Jesus is even more significant in the Apocalypse of John (5:6 ff.). I shall treat of this passage in section three below, since I believe the sacrificial metaphor here is employed in the framework of a model of a counter world.

2. Sacrifice and War

Pindar is already credited with the viewpoint that death for one's country (that is: city-state, *polis*) is a sacrificial death. Plutarch, among others, hands down Pindar's statement:

> Hearken, Alala (personified war cry), daughter of War,
> Thou prelude of clashing spears, thou to whom are offered
> Heroes in the holy sacrifice of death (*Moralia* 349C).

We also find in Plutarch a saying of the Theban military chief, Epaminondas, who was to have comforted his solders by calling death in war a sacrificial death (*Moralia* 192C). Both instances proffer similarities with the death of sacrificial animals, but there are also elements of religious-cultic sacrificial symbolism, in that those dying are consecrated to the deity. In war one sacrifices his life for the rescue of one's homeland; a person dies a God-consecrated death. The exclusivity aspect (*setting apart*) of sacrifice is part and parcel of the event (see only Malina 1993a:166 ff.). By the way, the army of Epaminondas would henceforth never be seized by fear or panic (*thórybos*). Sacrificial metaphors, therefore, have pragmatic significance here as well: Epaminondas removes his men's anxiety with his interpretation of a soldier's death in terms of a sacrificial metaphor.

Special consideration should be given to the Roman *devotio* by which a Roman general consecrated himself or the opposing army to the subterranean beings. Should he die in battle, the gods are obliged to destroy the enemy in the counter-attack. Diodorus Siculus (21,6,1) describes *devotio* in Greek as: *apodidomi heauton eis sphagen*. The phrase clearly brings out the reflexive quality (self-giving) of the behavior. In our context, it is interesting to note that Cicero (*De fin* 2,61) mentions that Decius (one of those Decii concerning whose family *devotio* is actually reported) fell in battle against Pyrrhus and offered himself as sacrifice for the state (*se victimam rei publicae praebuisset*). The person consecrated (*devotus*) was understood to be the equivalent of a sacrificial animal. Further, *devotio* was likewise associated with ritual consecration. In this regard, we might speak of a real sacrifice, to which expiatory function was ascribed by Livy (Livy X, 28). In the passage one of the Decii interprets his *devotio* not only as the family's fate (*familiare fatum*), but understand it as expiatory sacrifice (*piaculum*) for the liberation of the Roman people from danger. Cicero uses *devotio* metaphorically (*De domo* 145), also in connection with *hostia* (sacrificial animal, victim). According to Cicero, P. Clodius was predestined by providence to be a sacrificial victim (*hostia*) for Titus Annius (Milo) (*De harusp* 6). In fact P. Clodius was indicted by Milo and killed. Livy (XXII, 6,3) has a formulation that is comparable; an enemy warrior expresses the intention of offering the Roman consul as sacrifice (*victima*) to the shadows of the dead (*manes*) of his fallen fellow citizens.

Thus a number of instances from antiquity demonstrate the metaphorical usage of sacrificial terminology in the context of war. The ancient passages are undoubtedly to be understood quite more emphatically than the corresponding inflationary usage of modern speech. Generally speaking, one would have to consider that the religious frame of reference remains preserved in sacrificial terminology. The Greek solder or the Roman general sacrifice their lives *for the sake of* the city-state or the *res publica*, and they consecrate their lives to the deity or to the subterranean beings; they thus envision their lives as exclusive gift. In *devotio* the quality of reciprocity is clearly recognizable (on this only Malina 1993:a101-102, 131, 137). The pragmatic function of the process is equally notable: the allaying of anxiety—just as the *sphagion* before battle shifts anxiety to the sacrificial victim, the sacrifice at the same time serves as a sort of practice run for the bloody slaughter of war. Lucan (*BellCiv* 9, 132; 10, 524), in his description of the civil war, employs the term *victima* almost in the sense of our usage, "to fall in war as victim." Compare also the execution of the knight Titus Sabinus by Emperor Tiberius (Tacitus, *Ann* 4,70); as he was about to be killed, Sabinus referred to his death as sacrifice (*victima*) for Sejanus.

3. Sacrificial Metaphor as Model of a Counter-World

In the previously mentioned Martyrdom of Polycarp, the execution of Polycarp by being burned alive was interpreted as a sacrifice (*MartPolyc* 12-14). This cruel and not unusual form of capital punishment is described in the Christian document as follows: Polycarp "was bound, as a noble ram out of a great flock, for an oblation, a whole burnt offering (*holokaútoma*) made ready and acceptable to God." In prayer, then, the Bishop asks God that he "be received among them [martyrs] before Thee, as a rich and acceptable sacrifice (*thysía*)." Thus with quite specific terminology, Polycarp's execution is interpreted as a sacrifice and whole burnt immolation. This is all the more notable in that one of the counts against Polycarp was that he kept the crowd away from sacrifice. Similarly, in his letter to the Romans, Ignatius of Antioch likewise interpreted his approaching execution (*ad bestias*) under the category of sacrifice: "Grant me nothing more than that I be poured out as libation to God, while an altar is still ready, that forming yourselves into a choir of love, you may sing to the Father in Christ Jesus" (Ign. *Rom.* 2:2). And more clearly still: "Beseech Christ on my behalf, that I may be found a sacrifice (*thysía*) through these instruments (the wild beasts)" (Ign. *Rom.* 4:2). The death of Christian martyrs is thus interpreted with sacrificial metaphors, analogously to the sacrificing of animals or to sacrificial libations. With the help of the word-field of sacrifice, cruel Roman capital punishments (being burned alive, being sent *ad bestias*) are ascribed religious-cultic significance, and later, expiatory effectiveness as well.

Origen states (*Comm. Joh.* 6.54.36) that martyrs are persons related to the sacrifice (*thysía*) of Christ, that their blood equally has expiatory effectiveness. In another passage (*Exh. Mart.* 30) he once more interprets martyrdom as remission of sins, and the martyrs as priests who offer themselves as sacrifice. Cyprian (*Ep.* 57,3) likewise describes martyrdom in sacrificial terms. Martyrdom is a priestly function and those who have to face martyrdom are sacrificial offerings (*hostiae*) and sacrificial victims (*victimae*).

The event of martyrdom is thus defined as something extraordinary, as a profound instance of Christian existence. Sacrificial terminology serves to override the significance of the political exercise of power over deviant citizens. What regulates the interpretation of the event is not the penal code of the Roman state, but the religiously oriented vision of the cosmic order of persons subject to Rome. Sacrificial metaphor provides something like a religious-ideological reaction to an experience of crisis. The previously mentioned passage in Revelation

(Rev 5:6 ff.) likewise belongs here. To briefly summarize that passage: The seer views Christ in the sky in the form of a slaughtered lamb (*arníon hos esphagménon*: 5:6; cf. 13:8). Celestial beings pay homage to him by bowing down in the context of a cultic ritual (5:8ff.). The sacrificed lamb is praised for having "bought" with his blood a community of persons for God. These persons come from all tribes and peoples, and they, in turn are made into a "kingdom" and priests to rule over all the land (5:10). Finally the sacrificed lamb is declared to be worthy by a choir of powerful celestial beings.

The passage is metaphorically complex. The first item to note is that it pictures Christ's death as that of a lamb slaughtered in sacrifice. And in verse 9b the sacrificial metaphor seems to activate the symbolic meaning of sacrificial execution (atonement). However upon closer inspection, the passage departs from the sacrifice metaphor at a crucial point, for with the metaphor of "buying" the significance of Christ's sacrifice shifts away from atonement to an act of liberation and election (see notably Rev 1:5). The heuristic function of the sacrificial metaphor has to be sought in the paradoxical contrast between the image of the slaughtered lamb and that of the divine rule or divine veneration (5:12-13). The sacrificial lamb becomes the ruler of the world (together this God). The metaphorical process comes back to the similarity with sacrificial animal. With this is it mainly takes up the aspect of aggressive superiority in sacrifices of annihilation, and yet reverses this aspect. Even more, in identifying with the sacrificed lamb, person despairing under the tyranny of government experience, through an imaginative process, the transformation of their situation into one of superiority. Those presently oppressed (see only Rev 1:9) become a royal and priestly community ruling over the earth. From the perspective of anthropology or text-pragmatics, what is going on is the processing of and the working through of fear (Stegemann 1996:120 ff.; for an explanation of the passage in the context of ancient astrology, see Malina 1995b:101ff.).

I should likewise mention in this context an incident noted by Tacitus (*Annales* 16:34f.) which describes something like a Roman martyrdom. The senator Thrasea Paetus, together with others, got involved in some political intrigue during Nero's reign and was sentenced to death. He was permitted to choose the form of execution. Shortly before his death, the Stoic held a discussion with a Cynic philosopher about the separation of the soul from the body after death. The quaestor then conveyed the decree to him:

> Upon receiving the senatus-consultum, he led Helvidius and Demetrius into his bedchamber. When blood began to flow from the veins of both of his arms, which he had cut open, he called for the quaestor as well and sprinkled his blood on the ground saying: "We offer a libation to Jupiter, the Liberator. Take heed, young man! May the gods prevent it that the end of my life should have a bad omen for you! But you were born at a time when it is good for a man to harden his spirit by the sight of uncompromising determination (*Ann.* 16, 35).

The suicide carried out by order of a senatus-consultum, an upper class variant of the aforementioned inhuman capital punishment of Christians, has two aspects to it. On the one hand it is said to be a heroic act of uncompromising determination, while on the other it is interpreted as a libation sacrifice linked with the possibility of an evil omen. Here too, sacrificial metaphor is used to give meaning to a suicide dictated by the state, endowing the event with the character of an initiatory act of liberation in face of the apparent evidence of definitive defeat.

From the foregoing instances, it is quite clear that sacrificial metaphor is not used randomly. It serves a heuristic function for the reality it describes; it interprets that reality with elements of meaning which allow for a vision of that reality not at all perceivable in the event itself. The texts do not simply state the senatorial decrees or the verdicts of the court, both expressions of a system of more or less legal exercise of government, enforcing the law against deviants. However the (sacrificial) victims of this system are not only victims in our sense of the term, victims of circumstances or victims of political power. We can see how colorless modern sacrificial metaphors are! Rather they are sacrificial victims in a quite emphatic sense. The use of ancient cultic-religious language of sacrifice inserts a hermeneutical concept into those deaths. Presumed powerlessness can become political resistance (Tacitus), or in the case of Christian martyrs, triumph belongs not to the Roman world order, but to God's. Sacrificial metaphor envisions a sort of counter-world consisting of defeated persons. It sets up a set of relations with a superior power, which actual sacrifice always implies inasmuch as it presupposes an offering to a deity of superior status. Here too superior power is set over against inferior power, represented by government officials.

The types of sacrifice to which sacrificial metaphors allude seem rather unimportant. They should not be symbolically deconstructed. Obviously, Polycarp's type of death suggests the *holocaustum*. *Thysía* (Ignatius), while not used especially for food offerings, is rather a more general term for sacrifice. The libation (Tacitus, Ignatius) is even an unbloody sacrifice. Interpretations of martyrdom as human sacrifice would be quite inappropriate. Although this is not the place to discuss the point, martyrdom might be compared with the human sacrifice described by Plutarch at the battle of Salamis (*Themosticles* 13,2-5; human sacrifice as whole-burnt offering. Israelite martyrdom would also belong to this context).

4. Sacrifice and Self-giving (Virtuous Living or Asceticism)

The use of sacrificial terms in the context of an ascetic way of living seems to be a particularly Christian phenomenon. Origen presupposes *continual* chastity as a personal requirement of Old Testament sacrifice, and hence can, in turn, understand that a person who lives in *castitas* is one who consecrates his body (*corpus*) to God (*Hom. Num.* 23,3; 24,2). Tertullian ranks fasting and celibacy with sacrifices please to God (*sacrificia Deo grata, De res carn.* 8). Methodius too interprets chastity and celibacy in sacrificial categories (*Symp.* 5,4): virgins and widows are the unbloody altar of God, whose love and prayer ascend to God like the sweet odor of sacrifice (5.6.8; see Ferguson 1980:1187). In these texts we already find that sacrificial motif that Horkheimer and Adorno have called the "introversion" of sacrifice. These specific sacrificial metaphors have antecedents in the New Testament. One gets the strong impression that sacrificial metaphoric overrating of renunciation is an *interpretatio Christiana.* I would like to note that the connection is rather complicated.

Let us begin with two New Testament passages. The best known is doubtlessly Rom 12:1: "Present your bodies as a living sacrifice (*thysia*), holy and acceptable to God, which is your rational worship." The statement contains specific sacrificial terms and refers sacrifice to sacrificial cult as the quintessential feature of Graeco-Roman as well as Israelite worship. The passage, of course, is quite odd in face of our everyday experience since what is to be presented as sacrificial victims are the addressees themselves, not animals, and this as a living (*zōsan*) sacrifice, not dead victims. Finally the cult is described as rational or reasons worship (*logiké latreía*). This too underscores a difference from contemporary sacrificial practice since it points up a characteristic distinctive of human beings (*logikós*) not shared with animals. Let us leave aside the problem of "rational worship" and concentrate on Paul's demand in general. I take the meaning of body (*sōma*) in the sense of "self" with emphasis on the physical quality of the person, that is, the self in its concrete relationships in the world (Dunn 1988:709). Because the person is body, one can experience the world and relate to others. With this assumption, the Pauline demand can therefore be understood in the sense that the addressees of Romans are to offer themselves as sacrifice to God in their daily living. However I would not say that they are to offer their total being but rather themselves in their everyday living. The following parenetic comments suggest that the reference here is basically ethical behavior. *There is no particular allusion to an ascetical way of life.*

I also would note Eph 5:2-3: "And walk in love, as Christ loved us and gave himself up for us, a fragrant offering and sacrifice to God. But fornication and all impurity or covetousness must not even be named among you, as is fitting among the saints." The passage calls for the *imitatio Christi*. The point of comparison is Christ's self-giving in his sacrificial death. It is noteworthy that the sacrificial metaphor is applied quite liberally, with different types of sacrifice directly mentioned in one breath: there is the sacrificial gift (*prosphorá*) and food sacrifice proper (*thysía*). Eph 5:2 evidences an abstract usage of sacrificial terms with regard to Christ. Of course there is nothing about atonement here. Rather, just as Christ's sacrificial death accentuates his love for Christians, so too Christians are to offer sacrifice, namely their love for one another and certain ethical renunciation consisting in abstaining from various vices. Here too there is no explicit allusion to an ascetical way of living, but to certain ethical demands or abstentions (see also 1 Pet 2:5). Thus Rom 12:1 and Eph 5:2-3 differ form the aforementioned early Fathers of the Church. Both passages, Eph 5 even more clearly than Rom 12, represent the reflexive type of sacrifice, self-offering. The prototype is the self-sacrifice of Christ which, as in Eph 5, becomes a model of Christian self-offering. From here it is not far to self-sacrifice as asceticism as found in the Church Fathers.

It is noteworthy enough to indicate that the peculiarity of Christian sacrificial language did not fall from haven. It has Graeco-Roman and Israelite precedents, partially true even of sexual asceticism. In an epigram, Martial (XI 104) says of a wife's sexual behavior: "You lay there without moving, neither by words, speech or fingers, do you deign to accommodate me (sexually), just as if you were getting ready (to sacrifice) incense and wine (*tanquam tura merumque pares*)." The translation is a bit periphrastic, but quite to the point. What is obviously presumed is sexual abstinence in preparation for sacrifice on the following day. The point of comparison, then, is ritually required chastity before burning sacrificial incense (*tus*), the offering of wine as libation or of sacrifice in general. Burkert refers to the fact that sacrifice entailed certain preparations ("bathing and dressing up in clean clothes, ornaments and wreaths ... and often sexual abstinence as well," Burkert 1972:10-14). Recall that for Origen, (*permanent*) chastity of the priest is bound up with the sacrificial metaphorical interpretation of the chaste life. It can be assumed, therefore, that the particular metaphorical interpretation of the ascetical life as sacrifice establishes a similarity with the personal disposition of a person who offers sacrifice. What is involved, ultimately, is the specific conditioning of the person who sacrifices.

In this regard as well, the *interpretatio Christiana* is based upon a set of presuppositions and is part of a far-reaching ancient tradition. For there exists a whole range of texts in which virtuous or disciplined living focused on certain values is set forth as a theme not only as prerequisite for true sacrifice but even as replacement for sacrifice itself. Early on, for example, the opinion that the gods have greatest pleasure in the gifts of the "most pious" is attributed to Socrates (Xenophon, *Mem.* 1.3.3). According to Plato, only the *agathós* can expect get credit for gifts offered to the gods (Plato, *Leg.* 4,716D-E). Seneca, too, places special value on the sacrificer's personal predispositions, which are more important than the sacrificial victim: *recta ac pia voluntate* (Seneca, *De ben.* 1.6.3). That is why vegetable sacrifices suffice for the *boni*, while rivulets of blood cannot outrun *impietas*. Epictetus (*Ench.* 31,5) name purity on the part of the one offering sacrifice as prerequisite. The Hebrew Bible and early Judaism likewise attest to the ethical and cultic condition of the sacrificer. There are countless example (Prov 15:8; 21:27; cf. Philo, *Mos.* 2,279; Mal 3:3ff; Jer 6:19f; cf. Sir 34:19 [34:18-26]; 35:1-6; Philo, *Spec.* 1,253.277.290; 1.277; *Plant.* 1,107f). Requisite virtues can even be understood as better than sacrifice (Prov 21:3; Hos 6:6; Isa 1:10ff; Jer 7:21ff; 1 Sam 15:22; Ps 49:7ff; cf. Jud 16:16; *Ep.Arist.* 234; *1 En* 45:3). Indeed, it is even explicitly stated that God is pleased by certain virtues instead of by sacrifice (Ps 51:18ff; cf. also Sir 35:2f; *Jub.* 2:22; *T. Levi* 3:5f; Dan 3:38-40 LXX; Tob 4:10f; 4 Macc 6:29; 17:22; 1QS 9:4f; Philo, *Migr.* 89-93). In this context, Philo deserves special notice. For him, the best sacrifice is that in which sacrificers offer themselves as perfect fulfillment of virtue (Philo, *Spec.* 1,272). Concerning the Therapeutes, he states that they do not sacrifice animals, but rather sanctify their minds (Philo, *Quod omnis probus liber sit* 75).

Result: I therefore suppose a rather broad Graeco-Roman as well as Israelite-Christian stream of tradition made the "introversion" of sacrifice possible. This was not as such a Christian "discovery." To be sure, Christian tradition did play a sort of pivotal role in the further handing down of the motif of renunciation well up to modern times. But in my opinion, only the Christian tradition explicitly connects this feature with asceticism.

5. Sacrificial Metaphor and Exclusivity

Since in the limits of this essay I can mention only a few aspects of sacrificial metaphors, under this heading I offer but one example: Romans 15:16. The passage specifically looks to the idea of exclusivity, to *setting apart*: "... because of the grace given me by God to be a (priestly) minister of Christ Jesus to the Gentiles in the priestly service of the gospel of God, so that the offering (*prosphorá*) of the Gentiles may be acceptable, sanctified by the Holy Spirit." In this verse we encounter several cultic terms; Paul describes his proclamation among Gentiles as a priestly service in the Graeco-Roman world, and calls his Graeco-Roman converts a sacrificial offering. The word *hierourgein* (to do priestly service) can be used metaphorically, as we learn from a variant reading of 4 Macc 7:8 (cf. also *Odes Sol.* 20:1-5: "those who render priestly service to the Torah"). The noteworthy difference in Paul's usage is that he does priestly service to the gospel of God, not the Torah! That it is in fact the priestly service of sacrifice here is indicated by the description of the Graeco-Roman converts as "offering" or the purpose of the offering process, that is the expected acceptance by God, indicated by the adjective *euprósdektos*. Paul thus compares the Graeco-Romans acquired for Christ with a sacrificial offering. A parallel from the Old Testament is instructive—Isa 66:20: "And they shall bring all your brethren from all the nations as an offering to the Lord, upon horses, and in chariots, and in litters, and upon mules, and upon dromedaries, to my holy mountain Jerusalem, says the Lord, just as the Israelites bring their cereal offering in a clean vessel to the house of the Lord." For Isaiah, it is Israel of the Diaspora that is presented as an offering to God, while for Paul it is the Gentiles! Finally, the verb *hagiázein* (to sanctify), only attested in the Bible, expresses the act of *setting apart*, of making exclusive to God. In this sense Israel can be called a people set apart or sanctified (see only Exod 19:14; Lev 11:44; 20:8).

In sum, then, the metaphorical usage of ritual/cultic terminology in Rom 15:16 would express in cultic terminology, the apostolic service of Paul among the Gentiles as priestly service, on the one hand, and the conversion of Gentiles as their being set apart for God, on the other. Sacrificial metaphors have interpretative power; they state the particular features of Pauline theology and preaching activity—the inclusion of Gentiles in Israel's salvation—a hermeneutical horizon within Israel's self-understanding. Just as Israel, those called among the nations are a people sanctified to God (see Rom 9:25 f.).

A Summary Comparison of Modern and Ancient Sacrificial Metaphors

The modern usage of sacrificial language is (largely) unmetaphorical. In comparison with ancient usage, it is striking that semantically what dominates is analogy with the passive sacrificial role, that of the sacrificial victim. Bound up with this victim-oriented sacrificial logic are such features as loss, suffering, and self-offering, among others. Where terms for sacrifice still have denotative force, they largely bear reference to loss, suffering or self-devotedness, for the most part in a context of a community's system of interrelations (family, nation) that transcends the individual or some higher level goals for which one undergoes sacrifice and within which the accompanying negative effects make sense. Comparable in this respect is the ancient usage of sacrificial metaphors in the context of dying in war (2 above). Even more noteworthy is the fact that ancient usage witnesses to analogy with the role of a sacrificial animal, the victim, and even give emphatic attention to it. Furthermore, in some ancient documents there are instances of clear allusions to exclusivity as a quality of sacrifice, the *setting apart* of the victim, that is sacrifice is understood implicitly or explicitly within its original religious frame of reference. Sacrificial death on behalf of the community (*res publica* or *pólis*) takes on its exclusivistic significance not from the community context, but rather from the religious frame of reference. The fact of being set apart can, of course, be transferred to the group or community in question (cf. 5 above), hence it can have the function of establishing a community. Yet here too, the religious frame of reference of actual sacrifice is retained in as much as the community, compared to a sacrificial gift, as well as the sacrifice itself are conceived in terms of an exclusive relationship to God (sacred). Thus it is a sacrificial gift metaphorically, but in a very real sense, sacred.

In modern language usage, terms for sacrifice are also employed for the process of being subject to power, to playing the passive role in a power structure. This occurs quite distinctively in the contrast of criminal and victim. To some extent this language usage is also found in ancient documents (see Lucan, *Bell.Civ.* 9,132; 10,524). But this usage differs from the modern in two respects: on the one hand, with the connotation of violence and an active sense of slaughter, aggressive superiority or the cruelty of the killing process predominates. It seems that the crossing of taboo boundaries is involved (cf. 1 above). On the other hand, the word sacrifice suggests an emphatic interpretation of subjection to violent force, that is, the "victims" are representatives of a counter world legitimated by God (cf. 3 above). Those subject to force are, as victims, no longer merely passive objects of an earthly power (actually) superior to them. They are victims in an emphatic sense, insofar by the interpretation of their death as that of sacrificial victims, present power relations are reversed and the religious frame of reference is not only retained, but factual powerlessness is turned into an attitude of superiority.

Self-giving is also known among ancient sacrificial metaphors (cf. 4 above). Its specific and heightened focus in asceticism is, in my opinion, not biblically documented. In the New Testament, the self-giving of Christ *qua* sacrificial victim is a model of ethical behavior that is conceived as something all-embracing (Rom 12:1), but probably not in an ascetical form. Self-sacrifice *qua* asceticism seems first attested in the early church; it was an idea prepared for through the biblical tradition. Of course, there are comparable viewpoints in Greco-Roman (as well as in Second Temple Israelite) tradition. On the one hand, there was the worthiness of the person sacrificing, prepared by conditioning in specific, virtuous conduct, that also (!) included sexual abstinence, and on the other the worthiness of the victim to be sacrificed. Briefly stated, the act of self-giving involved a shifting and mixing of the roles of sacrificer and of victim in the interest of the worthiness of the sacrifice. In its ultimate form, self-giving is raised to the level of self-sacrifice. However for completeness' sake, I note once more that here too, instances from the ancient world always preserved a religious frame of reference.

13

Soldiers in the Gospels: a Neglected Agent

T.R. Hobbs, *Hamilton, Ontario, Canada*

Introduction

Speaking out of personal interest, this is an absorbing topic for study. In my opinion, it has been a subject of neglect in Gospel studies, and on the surface this might seem trivial. But I think a study of it adds to our knowledge of the meaning of the Gospels, if in a small way. My current interest in the topic stems in part from my near-obsession with things military, ancient and modern, but also from my own suggestion, made a few years ago, that one needed to look at the role of soldiers in the Gospels (and Acts) to form a more complete understanding of the language of warfare in the New Testament (Hobbs 1995:261).

Bruce Malina has suggested to me on more than one occasion that the military needs to be understood as an institution of the first century Mediterranean world. This essay is prelude to pulling together something on the military as an institution at the time of the New Testament. This kind of enterprise is very important, and something I have attempted to do in numerous other publications when dealing with the Old Testament. But I suggest that it has yet to be done in terms of the Christian literature both within the canon and outside. The ninety-two year old work of Adolph Harnack still remains a classic, if now somewhat outdated, treatment of the topic of the New Testament and its relationship to military language (Harnack 1905).

What I offer in this paper is just one piece of the giant puzzle that must be put together for this task It is by no means a complete picture, in fact, it is an exploration into the subject, but I trust it will be found useful and a spur to further reflection and study.

First of all, the title deserves some comment. As will be seen below, the issues which concern most Gospel commentators are not those I share, hence the sense of neglect. Commentators on the whole play with the same limited historical evidence and mull over the same historical questions without much of a wider angle of vision. It is this angle of vision I hope to enlarge. The second part of the title deals with agency, and it is fair to ask, Of what? It is at this point that social scientific material, such as it is, will prove helpful. Here not only do we enter a study of historical roles, which are reasonably covered, but also of perceptions of the soldiers' activity in the world created by the Gospel writers in their narratives. The language used, the context—literary and social—in which it is used, move us into areas of social science.

My intention is (1) to sketch the occurrences in the Gospels of military personnel pointing out some anomalies. I will then (2) offer a sample of traditional interpretations of these phenomena. Following this I will (3) expound some social scientific concepts relevant to the subject, paying attention to the understanding of military and society, and the military as an institution. My concluding section will (4) return to the Gospels, reacting to, and modifying some already existing studies for a deeper analysis of the subject. This study is perhaps more theoretical and programmatic than I would have liked, but it does provide a necessary *prolegomenon* to a larger work. But first a statement of the obvious.

Occurrences of Roles and Activities of Soldiers

Language
Military personnel figure frequently in the Gospels and the Book of Acts. The terms used of them are typical and unremarkable. The common soldier is the *stratiotes* (less common is the use of the word *strategos*, a Lukan term, which is reserved in translation for the temple police). There are occasional references to a centurion (*hekatonarkos*), and one of higher rank, a tribune (*chiliarkos*). The first of these is the equivalent of the Roman *miles*, the citizen soldier, although is not immediately clear whether the soldiers referred to in the Gospels are Romans or auxiliary troops. The distinction is a fine one and of no great consequence. The centurion commanded between eighty and a hundred men, depending on length of service, and priority of the century within the legion's structure. The tribune commanded one thousand men, and was a man of equestrian rank and from a wealthy background. Although the Roman army was a citizen army, an imposition of modern anachronistic notions of the term is to be avoided.

There should be no doubt that the Roman army represented the imperium.

Distribution of characters

All Gospels feature references to at least the first two of these (*stratiotes, hekatonarkos*), the third (*chiliarkos*) being restricted to the Book of Acts, with the exception of Mark 6:21 and John 18:12. For the most part the soldiers are found in the cluster of stories related to the betrayal, arrest, trial and crucifixion of Jesus. They also assume some similar role in the death of the Baptizer, at least in Mark's account (Mark 6:17-29). One should note here also the role of the tribune (*chiliarkos*) in the account of the death of the Baptizer. The following chart provides a brief breakdown of these occurrences in the Gospels. The weight of their activity in the final days of Jesus is obvious.

	Military Personnel in the Gospels			
		Matt	Mark	Luke	John
1.	The Baptizer's teaching			3:10-14	
2.	The centurion's servant	8:5-13		7:1-10	
3.	Death of the Baptizer	*(14:3-12)*	6:17-29	*(3:19-20)*	
4.	Betrayal by Judas	*(26:14-16)*	*(14:10-11)*	22:3-6	18:3
5.	Jesus taken captive	*(26:47-56)*	*(14:43-52)*	22:47-53	18:12
6.	Jesus before Herod			23:6-16	
7.	Mocking by soldiers	27:27-31	15:16-20		19:2
8.	Crucifixion	27:33-44	15:22-32	23:33-43	19:23-25
9.	Burial of Jesus	*(27:57-61)*	15:42-47	23:50-56	
10.	Breaking of legs, piercing side				19:32-34
11.	Guard at tomb	27:62-66			
12.	Bribery of soldiers	28:11-15			

Figure 1

The following may be noted:

a. Citations in italics are parallel accounts, but contain no reference to soldiers

b. In #6 Luke has the mocking done by Herod's soldiers, Matthew and Mark have it done by Pilate's soldiers.

c. In Luke 22:3-6, and 22:47-53 the Gospel writer uses the term *straps*, and clearly indicates that these officers are in the service of the temple (see. v. 52).

Anomalous feature

Yet, there is an apparent anomaly when one looks at the activity of the military personnel in the Gospels. While "soldiers" are almost always cast in a negative role in the Gospels, there are some military personnel who are cast in a very positive light. In Matt 8:5-13 and Luke 7:1-10 the centurion with a sick child/servant is favorably compared with the lack of "faith", i.e. loyalty, trustworthiness (see Pilch and Malina 1993: 67-70) in Israel. This is a common theme in prophecy (Jer 2:13 etc.). The inspiration for this presentation is most probably the story of Naaman in 2 Kings 5. In that story, the infirm foreign commander is presented as a man of somewhat reluctant faith, but a faith far surpassing that of his Israelite contemporaries. In 2 Kings there is a constant theme of a "prophet/God in Israel" to whom gentiles come in contrast with Israelites (see 2 Kings 1; 3; 5; 8).

Military Personnel and Attitudes in the Gospels					
Text	Positive	Object	Negative	Object	Rank
stratiotes, hekantoontarchos, chiliarchos					
Mt. 8:8-13	X	Jesus			Centurion
27:27			X	Jesus	Soldiers
27:54	X	Jesus			Centurion
28:12			X	Jesus	Soldiers
Mk 6:27			X	Baptizer	Soldiers
15:16			X	Jesus	Soldiers
15:39	X	Jesus			Centurion
15:44-45		*Testimony concerning Jesus' death*			*Centurion*
Lk. *3.14*		*Objects of the Baptizer's teaching*			*Soldiers*
7:8	X	Jesus			Centurion
23:11			X	Jesus	Soldiers
23:36			X	Jesus	Soldiers
23:47	X	Jesus			Centurion
Jn 18:3	("detachment"= *speira*)		X	Jesus	Soldiers
18:12	(*speira*)		X	Jesus	Tribune/ Soldiers
19:2			X	Jesus	Soldiers
19:23			X	Jesus	Soldiers
19:25			X	Jesus	Soldiers
19:32			X	Jesus	Soldiers
19:34			X	Jesus	Soldiers

Figure 2

All three synoptics place into the mouth of a centurion a form of confession at the crucifixion (Matt 27:54; Mark 15:39; Luke 23:47). In John's Gospel no such confession from any soldier is forthcoming, but a similar confession is found on the lips of Thomas (John 20:28). In contrast to Luke especially, the only such of officer mentioned in John is found leading the detachment that arrested Jesus (John 18:12). The figure opposite presents these characteristics in graphic form.

Again, the following may be noted:

1. In the Gospels the "soldiers" are almost always anonymous followers of orders. The exception to this is Luke 3:14 where they, by a question, elicit a response from the Baptizer.

2. The officers depicted, centurions, are active participants in the narrative, take a decisive role themselves, and contribute to the discourse of the narrative, by asking questions, making confessions, and demonstrating faith.

Traditional Treatments

Biblical studies—Nice Guys and Bullies

In studies on the Gospels, when texts dealing with soldiers are discussed, it is the "literary" and historical matters that dominate the discussion. Most commentators on the passages listed indulge in redactional analyses of the stories at various levels of detail. Davies and Allison (17-18) commenting on Matthew 8 will serve as typical of many. Set within the triadic structure of miracle stories the structure of this encounter with the centurion in Matt 8 is analyzed as: introduction and setting (v. 5), speech of the centurion (v. 6), speech of Jesus (v. 7), speech of the centurion (vv. 8-9), speech of Jesus (vv. 10-13a) and conclusion. But, they suggest that, in spite of its setting, the story is better understood not as a miracle story but as a "pronouncement story". This analysis imposes an anachronistic form on to the story which clearly detracts from its own inner drama and the roles of the dramatis personae. In modern analysis, the story is a discourse (conversation), with its own coherence, and its own set of presuppositions about what Jesus and the centurion, and indeed the other characters in the story mean when they speak. The path to this meaning is lost by making Jesus into a mouther of theological platitudes. The centurion who comes to Jesus for healing in Matthew 8 and Luke 7 is also a prime candidate for western-style character analysis. Is he Roman (Davies–Allenson 20), or Syrian (Gnilka 1986:I, 296-298)? If the former, he was seconded to Herod Antipas' army, and if the second, he was in the tradition of the heteroglot character of the Herodian army which, though fashioned on the Roman mode, was replete with Thracians, Gauls, Germans and others. But, the centurion is generally depicted as a "nice man". Whatever his background, Filson feels confident enough to determine his character as "a humane and responsible Gentile." (Filson 110-111), a judgment based presumably on his generosity to the local population. But although Filson is writing a commentary on the Gospel of Matthew, this generosity is mentioned not in Matthew, but only in Luke (see Luke 7:1-10). Further, the purpose of this generosity needs to be interpreted not according to western standards of "niceness", "humanity", nor "responsibility", but in the context of gift-giving, patronage and honor, all concepts either implied or mentioned in the Lukan account. The language of "worthiness", "love", and the act of gift-giving, all mentioned in Luke's account by the elders of the village, his clients, befit the model of patron-client relationships so common in the first century Mediterranean world (Gellner and Waterbury 1977; Lemche 1965; Mitchell 1996).

Similarly, others offer insight into the character of the soldiers who molest Jesus during the trial and crucifixion. They were, states Hagner, "rough men" and "immature" (Hagner 2.829-832). Similarly Lane (Lane 559) characterizes this whole episode as an "impious masquerade", reflecting a "perverted sense of humor" on the part of the soldiers. The presuppositions of these judgments are, of course, modern and western. Such roughness and "immaturity" is expected of soldiers, and quite common in their acknowledged roles in first century politics (see Tacitus, *Histories*). Soldiers in all societies are trained to do harm to others, and nowhere was this clearer than in the Roman army (Watson 1969). It should come as no surprise then that soldiers inflict harm in the story of the crucifixion.

An additional puzzle to many commentators is the nature and identity of the cohort mentioned in Matt 27:27 and parallels. Five cohorts were known to have been stationed in Judaea at some time during the first century (Broughton). But many wonder over the statement of the "whole" cohort witnessing the mocking of Jesus (Hagner 2.282). One should be aware, of course, that this Gospel also speaks of "all Judaea" coming to see the Baptizer (Matt 3:3). The use of the term *speira* may be taken literally as referring to a unit of five hundred men, or as the equivalent of the German military term *Abteilung*, which is used of units from company to regiment. Similar concern is expressed over the specific use of the transliterated Latin term speculator in Mark 6:27, as the agent of the execution of the Baptizer (see Lane 222). Of course, these historical issues are not without importance, but evidence often escapes the investigator.

Historical Studies

1. Roman Army in the East

The precise nature of the make-up of the army stationed in Judaea in the early part of the first century is a matter of some dispute. One must, I firmly believe, put away the notions, perpetuated in novels and films like "Ben Hur" that early first century Palestine was infested with Roman legions. As far as the evidence will allow, we can conclude that at this time before the Jewish war there were probably four legions stationed in the east, all in Syria, one of which occasionally ventured into Judaea to strengthen garrison forces there. The Judaean garrison was relatively small and supported by numerous local auxiliary troops which made up the bulk of the occupying force. In Judaea there were five Roman cohorts, only one stationed in Jerusalem, presumably at the Antonia.

Many studies of the Roman-Hellenistic social world of the New Testament offer a strange silence on things military, except as an unexplored background to "politics". Meeks (1983) and Malherbe (1983) are silent on the matter, and even the exhaustive study by Koester (1984) offers no section on the make-up of the military, its relations to Roman and local society. In spite of numerous references to "soldiers" listed in the index, the work of Stambaugh and Balch offers nothing close to what is needed, except two paragraphs on "Police", which consists of generalizations drawn from existing Biblical data (Stambaugh and Balch 1986:35-36).

Yet, it is difficult to conceive of life in first century Palestine without some acknowledgment of the presence of the military. It was an ever-present reality, and, the evidence clearly demonstrates that warfare—the extension of politics by others means—to cite a nineteenth century writer on the topic (van Clausewitz 1832), was a commonplace in the classical world. Finley's excellent chapter on "War and Empire" makes the important point that we cannot judge this period by the niceties of modern liberalism (Finley 1985:67-87, see also Howard 1981). This, after all, was the period which Tacitus so graphically described as "rich in disasters, frightful in its wars, torn by civil strife, and even in peace full of horrors ... there was profligacy in the highest ranks: the sea was crowded with exiles, and its rocks polluted with bloody deeds. In the capital there were yet worse horrors" (Tacitus, *Histories*). Finley suggests that this was the norm, rather than exception (1985). The imperial paranoia that such a state of affairs engendered must have affected Judaea. The army was a constant feature of political and civic life, as is demonstrated by the role of the army in the removal and replacement of emperors during the late first century. Whether it was composed of Romans or locals, it served mainly as a symbol of power over the populace. I would suggest that it was the most common channel through which power was exercised upon the people.

It is a moot point whether that the writers of the Gospels themselves were fully aware of the details of the military situation, nor of the niceties of Roman military protocol. In true artistic fashion, the Gospels writers create their literary worlds through the narratives they construct, and the characters that occupy these worlds. Schnackenburg, in dealing with Johannine crucifixion narrative, in which the soldiers play their most negative role, comes close to arguing this with his comment that "John has arranged the facts in such a way, that the succession of the scenes successfully builds up to the pronouncement of judgment, and Jesus' hidden kingship comes ever more clear to the fore in the contradiction of his enemies" (Schnackenburg 198:255).

Nevertheless, there is a body of "background knowledge", presupposed by all the Gospel writers, which the mere mention of the word "soldier" evokes. In his valuable text on the nature of social science criticism on the New Testament, Jack Elliott suggests an inventory on military systems and institutions and the endowment of law in the first century world (Elliott 1994:111). But there are few, if any, existing examples of such work. Many historical studies exist, but within these studies, the east tends to be neglected There are some exceptions to this, such as Dabrowa (1994), Isaac (1994), Miller (1994), and Kennedy (1996), but they are few and far between.

2. Roman Army and Society
More disturbing is the almost complete lack of studies which deal with the twin concepts of military and society in the first century world. If it is true, as Michael Howard has argued, that "The roots of victory and defeat often have to be sought far from the battlefield, in political, social and economic factors which explain why armies are constituted the way they are, and why their leaders conduct them in the way they do" (Howard 1983:196-197), then it is surprising that there are few studies on the specific relationships between war and society in the Roman world, comparable to Hale's study on Renaissance Europe (Hale 1985). The collection of essays edited by Rich and Shipley

(1993) is one of the few. Within Roman society, the recruitment, training, and expectations of the citizen-soldier were all important reflections (one might almost say, extensions) of that society. the roles of the auxilia were more circumscribed. One of the most refreshing, but brief, studies is that of Moses Finley, "War and Empires (Finley 1983:67-8;. see also A. Goldsworthy, *The Roman Army at War; 100 BC—AD 200* [Oxford: the Clarendon Press, 1996]). The precise role of the Roman army in occupied society is difficult to determine, especially in the period before the Jewish revolts. It did, nevertheless, wield considerable power in daily life.

Classical historians have had a strong antipathy to the use of models of social and cultural analysis on historical material, and this is a battle which Carney fought over twenty years ago. The tide is slowly swinging, thanks to the powerful work of Momigliano and Finley, and others, but has yet to affect the study of the military institutions of ancient Rome (see Finley 1986). I would suggest also that the distaste for many things military in recent years has aided this benign neglect.

The Military as an Institution

There is a modern distinction between the military as "institution" and as "occupation" and is becoming common in studies of modern military organizations. The notion of the modern army as "occupational" is viewed both positively (Janowitz) and negatively (Creveld), especially when it relates to matters of leadership. However, the distinction does throw into sharp focus the elements of the older type of institution, with its distinctive characteristics. These are characteristics which the Army of the first century would certainly have shared.

In trying to reconstruct meaningful background knowledge (scenarios) for the understanding of soldiers in the Gospels, it would be a mistake to ignore the notion of the military as an *institution*. In the light of the more recent shift of the military to "occupation", i.e. an all-volunteer army set against the background of modern individualism, this omission would be even more of an error. The assumed parallels are disappearing, and the possibility of error is increasing if one does not do a careful comparative historical study. The modern all-volunteer army is a brainchild of Jean Jacques Rousseau, who envisaged a perfect parallel between his concept of society (an aggregation of individual wills) and the defense of that society by the same citizens (Rousseau 1762). This is, in fact, a far cry from the "Citizen armies" of the Roman imperium.

There is a growing amount of literature on the military as an *organization*, with an extremely complex bureaucracy. This was as true in antiquity as ever. This organization absorbs the lion's share of the society's interests, goods and resources, and is paid for in part by the accumulation of goods by means of forcible exchange (tribute) and in the form of slaves, and plunder. The military itself, develops an ideology which appears to reflect the ideology of the "host society", but this organizational ideology is not without its flaws (see Janis 1774; Dixon 1976). But, added to this notion of the military as an institution with all-absorbing tendencies is the military as the bearer (at least in traditional propaganda) of the fundamental traditional values of the society. The military, as organization, stands for stability, continuity and the homogeneity of these societies and their traditions. Experience in Latin America in the 1970s and 1980s would suggest this is a sound picture.

Thus, the relationship of the military power (the occupying power, whether Roman or Herodian) to the host society is one of necessary symbiosis, and the two cannot be separated, especially in the first century Roman-Hellenistic world. The values espoused by both, yet exemplified predominantly by the military, and legitimating both are "values and norms ... a purpose transcending the individual self-interest in favor of a presumed higher good. Members are seen as following a calling identified with words such as duty. honor and country" (Harries-Jenkins 1977). Within the Roman army such values are embodied in the sacramentum, the chief characteristic of which is "faith" (fides) (see Hobbs 1995:273). The identity of a person as a "soldier" in the first century Roman-Hellenistic world, I contend, implied such expectations and commitment. In Tacitus, approbation is reserved for those (frequent) times when such qualities and characteristics are lacking in the scattered imperial armies. The same is found in Josephus.

Towards a Social Science Perspective

Soldiers as Anonymous "Persons"

In looking at "the soldiers" and other military personnel in the Gospels we are not really dealing with "personality" in the modern sense, and even the traditional Mediterranean notion of person surfaces only rarely. By this, I mean the understanding of visible individuals within the narrative (so ably expound by Malina and Neyrey 1997). The individual soldier, with few exceptions, rarely appears in the Gospel. Rather the "soldier appears as a stereotype". The soldiers are an anonymous group, parallel in status in the Gospels to the *ochlos*. This is something our western obsession with individuals clouds over. These soldiers are seen as a unit, not even a collective, which implies a Rousseau-like aggregation of individuals. This kind of unified view of social segments is typical of biblical and other contemporary literature. The Old Testament speaks often of the "-ites" who oppose Israel and Judah, the New Testament allows that "Cretans are liars", and Tacitus (*Histories* passim) continually speaks "the military" as a group with a single will and purpose. Josephus (*Bell.*, passim) almost follows suit with his references to countless, anonymous soldiers on both sides who do their commanders' wills often to their own peril. It is only in the age of the literate soldier do we get the notion of the individual fighter or man in uniform who is worthy of our interest. This is a phenomenon fully exploited by modern authors (see Holmes 1986, 1991; Macdonald 1983, 1988a, 1988b). But the rise of the literate soldier in the eighteenth and early nineteenth centuries corresponds to the rise in education focused on the individual *qua* individual. For many of us it is a truism, but one that is ignored by many others, that "if we wish to come to understand the persons of the ancient Mediterranean world, we should be prepared to learn entirely new ways of perceiving so as to assess those persons on their own terms", that is, as members of a group (Malina and Neyrey 1996:4).

Existing Models
Our second task at this stage is to look at existing models of social organization, particularly those that can help us understand the role and perception of the military. There are some models of social groups and societies which might aid us in our quest, and they are models most familiar with this group of scholars. I mentioned above Tom Carney's important study "How Military Institutions Affect their Host Societies". I turn to a brief presentation of it now. (See Figure 3.)

Carney's model was intended to examine an historical problem in classical history, namely the social and political changes that emerged with the rise of the new military invention of the "hoplite" in the ancient Hellenic army (Carney 1974). It demonstrates quite well the pervasive effect of a dominant military institution in a society, and the widespread effect it had on all aspects of that society. In an earlier essay "An Experiment in Militarism" (Hobbs 1988), I attempted a similar analysis of the rise of a standing army under the United monarchy in Israel. (See also Finley 1986.) Within Carney's model, technology, population structure, distribution of natural resources (and goods and

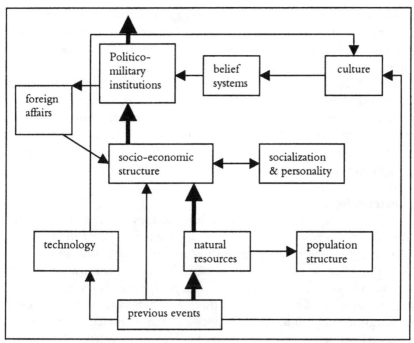

Figure 3. How Military Institutions Affect Their Host Societies

From T.F. Carney, *The Shape of the Past: Models in Antiquity*, Kansas City: Colorado Press, 1977: 246.

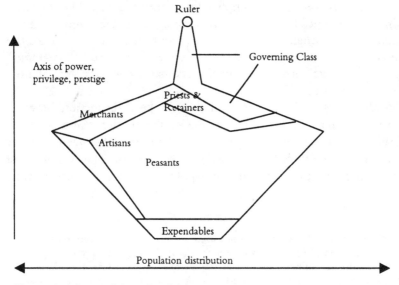

Figure 4. Advanced Agrarian Society

services) socialization, economics, foreign affairs, culture and belief systems are all related to and influenced by the institutional military organization. In a real sense one can speak of the "militarization" of such a society.

The model of an advanced agrarian society, developed by Lenski and Lenski has decorated the pages of BTB on more than one occasion, and to good effect. It depicts the general structure of society thought to be behind the writings of the first and early second centuries BCE. It is reproduced in Figure 4 and there is no need for me to expand on something that is so familiar.

Shortcomings

But while both of these models are helpful, they are so only to a certain extent. Carney's especially provides a good understanding of the relationship of the military institution to the society as a whole, and Lenski and Lenski offer a more detailed picture of the nature of that society. However, being analyses of large systems (with a deceptive impression of stability) neither of them accommodates either dissident or marginalized groups, and their views of the dominant military presence and influence in those societies.[1] The same is true of the later studies of M. Janowitz on modern European and Latin American military systems (Janowitz 1977, 1981). M. Feld (Feld 1977) has provided an excellent model of the relationships of a military organization to its "host" society. Not only does this model supplement Carney, but it also provides a more complete taxonomy of armies like the army of imperial Rome. It also helps us to understand the complex set of relationships between imperial structures and ideology, the role of the military in these structures, and the presence of so called "client-kings" and their "native" armies within the Roman imperial system. I now turn to a summary of Feld's thesis.

While military history has tended to make a distinction between "normal" civilian society and the role of the soldier, there is an increasing awareness of the symbiotic relationship between military organizations and their "host societies." Feld states, "The commitment to and the support of a specific social-political system is inherent in the

---

[1] By "marginalized" groups I am not using the term in the modern sense of "minorities". In the ancient world the largest part of the population was marginalized because it had no political power, and was permanently fixed on the edges of the decision-making processes, or excluded altogether. The model assumed here is that of E. Shil's "Center and Periphery" (Shils 1988:90-100).

nature of military organization." (32). But these relationships are not uniform.

Further, in contrast to the civilian organization on which the military organization relies, the latter demands a much more advanced sense of solidarity, in which individualism and individual initiative tends to be muted, if not suppressed. Being "institutional" in its make-up and ethos, the military organization displays the basic characteristics of the organization, so well described by Douglas and Wildavsky (1986:) and Bailey (1988:). To help define the role of armies within the overall social structure, Feld develops a model of five "ideal types" of military organization and culture. He states them as follows:

> military elites that maintain themselves as an alien body superimposed on a conquered society: military elites that maintain themselves as an alien body distributed within the conquered society; military elites which make their place in society as members of a native and politically oriented aristocracy; military elites which qualify themselves in terms of some socially oriented scale of aptitudes; and, finally, military elites whose composition corresponds to the overall structure of power within the nation in arms. (34)

Our concern will be with the first two of these types, which he depicts as (1) External dominance—imperial; and (2) Internal dominance —feudal. The two types broadly reflect the historical shift between the pre- and post-revolutionary Palestine at the end of the first century, and are possibly reflected in the wide ranging changes introduced into the imperial military establishment by Vespasian and his successors (Grant 1974:209ff.). One characteristic of the latter period is the growth of veterans' settlements (Legio [Lejjun], Colonia [Qaluniya]). The profiles of Miller (1995) and the list of Isaac (1990: 426-435) are based on the archaeological evidence of the latter period. A parallel development is found in Egypt, and is well depicted in Alston (1995:37ff.). The typology is further expounded by Feld in the following diagram:

Structure	Policy base	Self-image	Policy role	Social model	Control	Indoctrin.
External dominance	Imperial	Civilization	Aggrandize	Three-class	Flow of officers	Officer-enlisted man emulation
Internal dominance	Feudal	Blood élite	Legitimize	Two-class	Flow of status	Officer-officer emulation

Figure 5

The external dominance type, whose policy-base is imperial conquest, entails several other characteristics. They are:

1. A rigid separation between the military organization and the "host" (i.e. conquered) society.
2. The military elite are absorbed into the structure of the military organization.
3. The political form is that of empire, and external dominance a vocational ideal. There is a rigid adherence to organizational boundaries.
4. The self-image of the imperial soldier "... is not that of a man who is fleeing his society but one dedicated to its institutions and virtues, those of civilization" (36).
5. The primary value of the external dominance organization is the propagation of civilization.
6. The dominant policy of empire is of self-aggrandizement, "while the conquests of an external dominant army may eventually result in an increase in the commerce and security of its parent state. The mission which colors the actions of such a force is that of spreading civilization over a wider area. Economic exploitation is the function and the rewards of groups other than the military" (36).
7. The involvement of the person involved in military life is all-absorbing.
8. This results in the creation of a third class between conqueror and conquered, a stratum of administrators and middlemen, who may consist of one or more of several groups—lower-caste members of parent society, local collaborators, or migrant adventurers. "The three classes thus created represent three worlds, authority at the top, privilege in the middle, and subservience below" (37).
9. The relationship between conqueror and conquered is one of antagonism. The "martial" spirit, so carefully constructed as an ideological inspiration to the actions of the soldiers, must continue to be turned outward. Turned inward it becomes "self-destructive, an instrument for razing the platform on which it stands" (32).

Because of this, the positions of military leadership in the imperial organization are barred to the conquered. If it is admitted that they are capable of military responsibility (except as controlled client-leaders) then it has to be admitted that they can manage the rest of their affairs.

I offer no suggestion that the communities which produced the Gospels understood the social, cultural and political dynamics of the Imperial occupation in such a sophisticated way. It would have been completely beyond the purview of the Christian community to understand the political and economic niceties of the occupation. However, the above sketch offers a scenario, an assumed context, in which "soldiers" are understood in the Gospels. Further, these Gospel communities would certainly have felt the effects of such a system on their daily lives.

With New Testament material we are dealing an "outgroup" which extends beyond these available systemic models of Carney and Lenski and Lenski. By outgroup I mean a faction/sect which is removing itself from the value-system and indeed the social system of the dominant group. In Halliday's words, it can be an "anti-society", whose language ("anti-language") encodes the group's values, not those of the dominant ones (Halliday 1978:164-182). In Halliday's understanding, such "anti-language" relexicalizes existent language, and resocializes the members of the anti-society into an alternate reality. In its language, stories and texts the anti-society betrays its own social positioning and social values. In Halliday's words:

> An antilanguage is the means of realization of a subjective reality: not merely expressing it, but actively creating and maintaining it ... the reality is a counter-reality, and this has certain special implications. It implies the foregrounding of the social structure and the social hierarchy. It implies a preoccupation with the definition and defense of identity through the ritual functioning of the social hierarchy. It implies a special conception of information and knowledge. (Halliday 1978:172)

This special conception Halliday identifies as secrecy. In such an anti-society, "... social meaning will be seen as oppositions: values will be defined by what they are not." (172)

Soldiers in the Gospels

I now return to a look at the Gospels and their treatment of "soldiers" and their officers, and do this by reflecting on some recent studies which, if they do not deal directly with the role of soldiers, certainly aid in an analysis of the topic. It is impossible to conduct a thorough analysis here of each text. I am still thinking in general, theoretical terms. It is unnecessary for this audience for me to sketch the kind of social and cultural and context within these writers wrote. Nor do I think is it necessary to say much on the accepted premise that they wrote for specific groups within the Christian movement. Their documents (texts) embody strategies for these grows living in their varied circumstances.

I shall deal with four studies, rather than a whole range of literature. These studies are at least sympathetic to the general approach I have taken. I shall take each in turn as they deal with individual Gospels.

Luke

Among the studies which comes close to a social science analysis of the role of soldiers in the Gospels is the essay by Vernon Robbins in the collection *Images of Empire* (Robbins 1991b). Using a broader framework of the two volumes of Luke-Acts as a "narrative map of territoriality for the development of Christian alliances throughout the eastern Roman Empire" (Robbins 1991b:203), Robbins analyses the two stories of centurions in the work (Luke 7:1-10; Acts 10). For him they represent a deferential treatment of "the upper levels of [the] power structure" (204). The purpose of which was to demonstrate a mutual means of communication between the primitive Christian community (i.e. Luke's community) and the Roman powers. This was done, it would seem, at the expense of the Judaeans and the local client-leaders. Robbins claims that "From the perspective of Luke and Acts" the power structure of Christianity [sic!] works symbiotically with the power structure of Rome" (207). Further, the centurion is depicted as "a broker between the emperor and the Jewish people, successfully negotiating with Jesus who is a broker between God and people" (209). Much of analysis of these stories is perceptive. I especially admire Robbins' mirror identification of the Roman soldier and the follower of Jesus as evangelist (218-219). But the whole only works if the centurion, a military rank, is transformed into a decurion (retired centurion) who now functions as a magistrate, a civilian rank, in the eastern part of the empire. To suggest that this officer, who would be the equivalent of the modern staff-sergeant, is the broker between emperor and people, is pure hyperbole. The role of the tribune (*chiliarkos*), a much higher rank than the centurion, throughout Acts is ignored, although he is generally viewed positively. But the great lack in the study is the extremely negative presentation of the activity of the "soldier" (*stratiotes*) in both the Gospels which even Luke adopts (Luke 23:11, 36). Since Roman soldiers are representatives of Roman power, as much as are centurions and tribunes, this is a strange omission, and if this positive view of a Roman soldier is intended to be taken at face-value, it is the exception rather than the rule. Robbins also overlooks the fact that the ones over whom the centurion in the Gospel of Luke has authority, those who come and go at his command, are colleagues of the very anonymous group who later take part in the crucifixion of Jesus, and they, together with the centurion in the Gospel, represent the imperium

Mark

The other study is Richard Rohrbaugh's essay on the social location of the audience of Mark's Gospel (Rohrbaugh 1993). He adopts a south Syrian, Upper Transjordan, possibly Galilean origin for the Gospel. But more important than this he argues persuasively for the population among which the audience found itself as rural, therefore illiterate (though not unintelligent). The Gospel, he suggests, was written to be read aloud among such people.[2] In the social stratification he adopts, based on the model by Lenski and Lenski, the soldiers and the centurions mentioned in the Gospels are to be found among the retainers. These, by virtue of who they are carry out the will of their overlords. In Rohrbaugh's words,

> They worked primarily in the service of the elite and served to mediate both governmental and religious functions to the lower classes and to the village areas. This group did not wield much power independently, however, but depended for its position on its relation to the urban elite (Rohrbaugh 119).

It is significant that of those mentioned as retainers in Rohrbaugh's study, most are seen only as anonymous groups. They include Pharisees, people from Jairus's house, men arresting the Baptizer, sellers in the temple, crowds sent by the priests and elders, courtiers, tax collectors, slaves, and, of course the soldiers. If one appeals, as he does, to the notion of territoriality (Sack 1986; Malmberg 1978), which I believe is a legitimate appeal, then some fine-tuning is needed, especially where it concerns soldiers. Elements of territoriality, according to Sack and Malmberg are, control, space as a social construction, boundary and markings. Presumably, the village dwellers, dependent upon, and often at the mercy of the urban elites, find these elements difficult to implement. Yet in the Gospel of Mark, Jesus does provide elements of

---

[2] At this stage it is impossible to develop the implications of this suggestion. In the light of Goody's thesis that the transfer of words from oral (contextualized) to written (decontextualized) settings represents a move towards power, control of information and resources (See J. Goody 1986, 1987), this reversal of the trend to the community listening to oral presentations of written documents is a fascinating thought to develop—elsewhere!

each. But it is also significant that, in distinction from the Pharisees, whose activity is divided between village and city in Mark, the soldiers are always seen in the city, or in centers of elite power. They never venture into the villages to enforce the will of the elites. Thus in Mark's presentation of soldiers, one could argue that the sphere of influence of the imperium is limited.

If Mark's audience is correctly identified by its social location in a rural village context, then soldiers represent a threat of the urban elite, who conspire in the death of Baptizer, and finally of Jesus. Such a so-cio-political dynamic is by no means uncommon in village/peasant societies. The strategies for dealing with this, however, vary. They include not only outright rebellion -almost a fetish with US scholars (see Horsley)—but also what appears to be apathetic non-involvement (Adas 1981; Scott 1985), a kind collective "Sveijkism", or "disen-gagement" as Bailey calls it (Bailey 1993). One such extreme strategy is withdrawal, and protection, as far as possible, of their own territory. On their own territory, the rural landscape and village, they are rea-sonably safe. In the give and take of the honor-shame game, so clearly depicted in the early chapters of the Gospel, there Jesus, and thereby the community, win. But in the centers of power, Herod's palace (ch. 6) and the city of Jerusalem (ch. 15), they are opposed, and on the surface, lose. As representatives of an "urban-military complex" the soldiers are antithetical to Mark, his audience and to his Jesus. F.G. Bailey's description of the village peasants among whom he worked is appropriate here:

> Beyond this category are people whose culture—the way they speak the way they dress, their deportment, the things they speak about as valuable and important—places them unambiguously beyond the moral commu-nity of the peasant; revenue inspectors, policemen, development officers, health inspectors, veterinary officials and so on; men in bush shirts and trousers, men who are either arrogant or distant or who exhibit a cama-raderie which, if the villager reciprocates. is immediately switched off; men who come on bicycles or in jeeps, but never on their feet. These are the people to be outwitted: these are the people whose apparent gifts are by definition, the bait for some hidden trap (Bailey 1971:303).

Matthew

Dennis Duling's article on the use of the "Son of David" in Matthew's Gospel (Duling 1992) is a useful place to begin in discussing this Gos-pel. For him, the title "Son of David" is part of a strategy by "Matthew", the urban scribe, against the Pharisees and Sadducees, and especially post-70 CE developments within "Judaism". The title is a device which invests Jesus with "power, privilege [and] prestige for ascribed honor" (113), as a mirror image of the rulers of Judaism. With this I can concur, and countless interpreters have placed Matthew within the struggle of the Jesus movement against Pharisaism. But this I would add.

In the account of the arrest of Jesus, Matthew, unlike the others, includes no reference to soldiers (Matt 26:47-56). But, in the face of violence, Jesus urges non-resistance (vv. 51-52). Later in the Gospel the soldiers who mock Jesus become what they are always trained to be, followers of orders, even to the point of accepting bribery in falsifying the account of the empty tomb (Matt 28:11-15).

I am not sure whether Matthew is, like Luke, using soldiers and enemies of the Christian movement as shadow images of the followers of Jesus, but it is important in his Gospel that false witness is condemned and truthfulness praised (Matt 5.33-37). This is a section of the "Sermon on the Mount/Plain" omitted by Luke. If it is true that by so portraying Jesus as "Son of David" "Matthew, a disciple and a scribe trained for the Kingdom makes a claim of honor for himself against the Pharisees of his own day" (Duling 114), then Matthew also presents for himself and his readers the ideal of non-violent truth-sayer, against forceful liars, represented by the servants of the imperium.

John

For John one of the most helpful recent studies is Bruce Malina's provocative article on John's "Maverick Christian Group" (Malina 1994b). Again the details need not concern this audience. When dealing with soldiers in John I am restricted, of course, to the Passion story which is the only place they appear. Malina's use of notions of speech accommodation and antilanguage unveil a group which seeks to live within the existing social system, but on its own terms. The language it uses encodes its own values (174), and the group for which John wrote represents an ideal of an alternative reality to what exists and is seen.

Within this vision of the alternative reality the soldiers appear at the climax of the story John tells. Of all the Gospels, John portrays the soldiers, including their officers, most negatively. In a parody of the ascension ritual of the Caesars, they unknowingly crown Jesus King. Their activity is most meticulous, abusing even the body of Jesus after his death. They have no redeeming features and are clearly presented as part of the all-powerful system represented by Pilate. Yet they, unwittingly fulfil God's will and confirm the destiny of Jesus in their activities, the very powers intended to destroy, testify to the truth of the Gospel which John proclaims, the claims of his Jesus to be light, truth. The servants of the imperium become, unwittingly, the servants of the Kingdom. Modern writers label such a device "ironic" (see Fusi 1997).

Concluding Comments

In concluding this survey, there are two things left to say. The first concerns the positive view of the officers (particularly centurions) which I have outlined. What can be made of this, in the light of the negative portrayal of the mob of soldiers? Davies and Allison are correct in their assertion that such a portrayal is "typical of the New Testament. Roman centurions not only merit respect but are also pious This is somewhat surprising given the hostility many first century Jews [sic!] felt towards the invincible Roman army" (19). There are features of the presentation of these officers which are worth commenting upon.

Wherever they appear, they speak, either in conversation with Jesus (Matt 8, Luke 7), or in utterances at the cross (Matt, Mark, Luke). Conversations, of course, are not mere "chats", but are meaningful forms of social communication. In the story of the centurion with a sick slave, the conversation between Jesus and the Roman is not one between equals. The centurion denies his worthiness (honor) to speak to Jesus and to entertain him in his house. In Luke's version he is aided in this by intermediaries. He comes as supplicant, as client to a patron, and receives the gift of the healing only on Jesus' terms.

The differently worded utterances at the cross are no small thing, because here, the symbol of power—who commands to one go, and he goes, and to another come, and he comes—acknowledges the power of weakness. Whether this be hope for the submission of that power to that of the Risen Christ, or demand, takes us beyond the scope of this paper. But, as always, it is worth pursuing.

14

Prayer, in Other Words:
New Testament Prayers in Social-Science Perspective

Jerome H. Neyrey, *University of Notre Dame, IN*

Introduction: Status Quaestionis and Proposal

What is prayer? How do we interpret individual prayers? Biblical interpreters are grateful heirs of Gunkel's description of the psalms.[1] His
work and that of his followers provides us with analyses of various
types of psalms, identification of their formal elements and indication
of their respective purposes. In addition, productive attention has been
given both in antiquity and in modern criticism to understanding the
premier Christian prayer, the Our Father. Scholars have also examined
topics related to prayer, such as the Israelite roots of Christian prayer,[2]

---

[1] Herman Gunkel, *The Psalms. A Form-Critical Introduction* (Philadelphia: Fortress
Press, 1967); B. W. Anderson, *Out of the Depths. The Psalms Speak for Us Today* (Phila-
delphia: Westminster, 1983); Claus Westermann, *Praise and Lament in the Psalms*
(Atlanta: John Knox Press, 1981); Hans-Joachim.Kraus, *Psalms 1-59: A Commentary*
(Minneapolis: Augsburg Pub. House, 1988); see also Patrick Miller, *They Cried to the
Lord. The Form and Theology of Biblical Prayer* (Minneapolis: Fortress, 1994).

[2] Roger T. Beckwith, "The Daily and Weekly Worship of the Primitive Church
in Relation to its Jewish Antecedents. Pt 1," *EvQ* 56 (1984) 65-80. James H. Charlesworth, "A Prolegomenon to the Study of the Jewish Background of the Hymns and
Prayers in the New Testament," *Journal of Jewish Studies* 33 (1982) 264-85; "Prayer in
the New Testament in Light of Contemporary Jewish Prayers." *SBLSP* 1993: 773-86,
"Jewish Hymns, Odes, and Prayers (ca. 167 b.c.e—135 c.e.)," *Early Judaism and Its
Modern Interpreters*. R.A. Kraft and G.W.E. Nickelsburg, eds. (Atlanta: Scholars Press,
1996), 411-36. See also Michael Wyschogrod, "The 'Shema Israel' in Judaism and the
New Testament (Deut 6:4-9; 11:13-21; Num 15: 37-41)." Pp. 23-32 in H. G. Link,
ed., *The Roots of our Common Faith* (1984); T. Zahavy, "Three Stages in the Development of Early Rabbinic Prayer," in Jacob Neusner, Ernest Frerichs, and Nahum Sarna,
eds., *From Ancient Israel to Modern Judaism: Essays in Honor of Marvin Fox*. Vol. 1 (Atlanta: Scholars Press, 1989).

the prayers of Jesus,[3] prayer in the Pauline letters,[4] the function of prayer in Luke's gospel,[5] and the shape of New Testament doxologies.[6] Of course there are many fine works examining prayer in the Bible,[7] the Greco-Roman world,[8] as well as the early church.[9] Recently, a working group in the Society of Biblical Literature undertook to study "Prayer in the Greco-Roman Period" (1989-92), the results of which appeared in *The Lord's Prayer and Other Prayer Texts from the Greco-Roman Era*.[10] While this volume contains seven articles on different ancient authors and their prayers, its major contribution lies in the rich bibliography of the text and history of interpretation of these select prayers. Yet it is fair to say that in terms of methods of interpreting prayer, even this latest effort prayer brings little new to the table. Current scholarship on biblical prayer operates from the perspective of form criticism and history-of-religions examination of background, but not necessarily from the perspective of interpretation, since its aim continues to be some form of history, not interpretation.

Yet there are available to scholars fresh and productive ways of interpreting prayers, namely the resources of cultural anthropology. Bruce Malina in particular has digested and made available to biblical scholars many of the basic, reliable models from the social sciences for

---

[3] For example, Joachim Jeremias, *The Prayers of Jesus* (Philadelphia: Fortress Press, 1978) and *The Lord's Prayer* (Philadelphia: Fortress Press, 1980).

[4] Gordon P. Wiles, *Paul's Intercessory Prayers: The Significance of the Intercessory Prayer Passages in Paul's Letters*. Cambridge: Cambridge University Press, 1974).

[5] Gerald F. Downing, "The Ambiguity of 'The Pharisee and the Toll-Collector' (Luke 18:9-14) in the Greco-Roman World of Late Antiquity," *CBQ* 54 (1992) 80-99; Allison A. Trites, "The Prayer Motif in Luke-Acts." *Perspectives on Luke-Acts*. Charles H. Talbert, ed. (Danville, VA: Association of Baptist Professors of Religion, 1978), 168-86; and Steven F. Plymale, *The Prayer Texts of Luke-Acts*. (New York: Peter Lang, 1991).

[6] Reinhart Deichgräber, *Gotteshymnus und Christushymnus in der frühen Christenheit* (Göttingen: Vandenhoeck & Ruprecht, 1969), 25-40, 97-102; Matthew Black, "The Doxology to the *Pater Noster* with a Note on Matthew 6:13b, "*A Tribute to Geza Vermes* (Philip Davies and Richard White, eds.; Sheffield: JSOT Press, 1991) 327-38.

[7] Samuel E. Balentine, *Prayer in the Hebrew Bible* (Minneapolis: Fortress Press, 1993) and Patrick Miller, *They Cried to the Lord*.

[8] Pieter van der Horst and Gregory Sterling, *Prayers in Antiquity: Greco-Roman, Jewish and Christian Prayers* (Notre Dame, IN: University of Notre Dame Press, 1992); and Simon Pulleyn, *Prayer in Greek Religion* (Oxford: Clarendon, 1997).

[9] See Carl A. Volz, "Prayer in the Early Church., *A Primer on Prayer*. Paul R. Sponheim, ed. (Philadelphia: Fortress, 1988), 36-50.

[10] This volume was edited by James H. Charlesworth with Mark Harding and Mark Kiley (Trinity Press International: Valley Forge, PA, 1994). See also Mark Kiley, ed., *Prayer from Alexander to Constantine. A Critical Anthology* (New York: Routledge, 1997).

understanding the communication which is prayer and the social exchange which occurs during it. Hence, if imitation is the sincerest form of praise, then the use of the materials which Bruce Malina has introduced to scholars is the sincerest form of praise I know. Other scholars have employed social science models for interpretation, whose suggestions will be considered as well.[11] This article, then, aims systematically to introduce readers to these cultural ways of interpreting prayers by providing an appropriate set of social and cultural lenses.

Prayer as Communication

Twenty years ago in an article much too large for the journal in which it was printed,[12] Bruce Malina analyzed prayer as an act of communication. Typical of Malina, but unlike most commentators, he offered a definition of prayer:

Prayer is a socially meaningful symbolic act of communication, bearing directly upon persons perceived as somehow supporting, maintaining, and controlling the order of existence of the one praying, and performed with the purpose of getting results from or in the interaction of communication.[13]

This definition identifies the nature of the activity, its object and its purpose. Prayer may take the form of petition, adoration, contrition or thanksgiving, but it is always a communication. Since prayer always addresses the person perceived as supporting, maintaining and controlling the order of existence of the one praying, it presupposes a superior/subordinate relationship. Finally prayer aims to have some effect on the person with whom the pray-er communicates, that is, it seeks results.

Malina next classified prayers in terms of their purposes, identifying seven results or aims the pray-er desires through the communication which is prayer:

1. *Instrumental* ("I want ..."): petitionary prayers to obtain goods and services for individual and social needs.

[11] Jerome H. Neyrey, *2 Peter, Jude* (AnB 37C; New York: Doubleday, 1993) 94-101; Douglas E. Oakman, "The Lord's Prayer in Social Perspective." Pp. 137-86 in *Authenticating the Words of Jesus.* Edited by Bruce Chilton and Craig Evans. Leiden: Brill, 1999; John J. Pilch, "Prayer in Luke," *The Bible Today* 18 (1980) 221-225.

[12] Bruce J. Malina, "What Is Prayer?" *The Bible Today* 18 (1980) 214-220.

[13] Malina, "What Is Prayer?" 215.

2. *Regulatory* ("Do as I tell you ..."): prayers to control the activity of God, to command God to order people and things about on behalf of the one praying.[14]

3. *Interactional* ("me and you ..."): prayer to maintain emotional ties with God; prayer of simple presence.

4. *Self-focused* ("Here I come ...; here I am ..."): prayers that identify the self—individual and social—to God; prayers of contrition and humility, as well as boasting and superiority.

5. *Heuristic* ("Tell me why...?"): prayer that explores the world of God and God's workings within us individually and collectively; meditative prayers, perceptions of the spirit in prayer.

6. *Imaginative* ("Let's pretend..."): prayer to create an environment of one's own with God; prayers in tongues and those recited in languages unknown to the pray-er.

7. *Informative* ("I have something to tell you"): prayers that communicate new information: prayers of acknowledgment, praise and thanksgiving.[15]

This taxonomy differs in many ways from the standard classification of psalms, and the differences are worthy of note. On the one hand, psalms are said to be either lament (complaint + petition) or praise and thanksgiving. But "prayer" is a more complex phenomenon than psalms, and needs a more discriminating classification. The lament and praise categories are further broken down by form critics of the psalms into six or seven types of psalms: 1) praise, 2) petition, 3) royal psalms, 4) songs of Zion, 5) didactic poetry, 6) festival psalms and liturgies.[16]

This classification is based on several criteria: 1) instructions to the pray-er ("Praise the Lord!"), 2) repetitive formal characteristics, 3) differing *Sitze-im-Leben* (royal wedding, coronation of the king, festivals), 4) wisdom instructions, and the like. While such criteria are useful in classifying *psalms*, they prove less reliable in sorting out the communication which is *prayer*. Malina's taxonomy, however, builds

[14] Included here are curses, spells, incantations and the like. See Christopher A. Faraone and Dirk Obgink, eds., *Magika Hiera. Ancient Greek Magic and Religion* (New York: Oxford University Press, 1991); Hans Dieter Betz, ed., *The Greek Magical Papyri in Translation*, 2nd edition (Chicago: University of Chicago Press, 1986); Martin Meyer and Richard Smith, eds., *Ancient Christian Magic. Coptic Texts of Ritual Power* (San Francisco: Harper, 1994).

[15] Malina, "What Is Prayer?" 217-218.

[16] Kraus, *Psalms 1-59. A Commentary*, 38-62. See Claus Westermann, *The Praise of God in the Psalms* (Richmond, VA: John Knox, 1961) and *The Psalms, Structure, Content, and Message* (Minneapolis: Augsburg, 1980); Patrick D. Miller, *Interpreting the Psalms*, passim.

on previous form-critical insights and provides a more discriminating classificatory system which focuses on the desired results of the communication and the social relationship between pray-er and deity.

Whereas psalm critics speak of psalms of lament, Malina's taxonomy more critically distinguishes the "lament" as *interactive* prayer and the petition as *instrumental* prayer. Psalms of "praise," "thanksgiving" and "trust" are *informative* prayers, a category which includes acknowledgment, blessing, honor, glory and the like. Communication classification aids greatly in appreciating prayers such as Ps 84 ("How lovely is your dwelling place, Lord, God of hosts!") as both *heuristic* meditation which explores the world of God and *imaginative* construction of a personal environment with God.

In regard to prayers which are not psalms, the taxonomy based on communication theory allows those who read biblical prayers to analyze and classify them in more accurate and informative ways. For example, *instrumental* prayer describes the petitions in the Our Father for bread, debt remission and deliverance (Matt 6:13), as well as the charge of Jesus to his disciples in Mark 14:36 that they "pray" to escape the coming crisis. But the first part of the Our Father contains *interactional* prayer of praise and benediction. *Interactional* prayer captures Mary's sentiments of blessedness, as well as her *informative* thanksgiving to God (Luke 1:46-55). *Self-focused* prayer describes both the Pharisee and the publican in Luke 18:10-13.[17] *Heuristic* prayer identifies well Job's many requests to God to know the reason for his suffering. Speaking in tongues provides an example of *imaginative* prayer (1 Cor 14:6-26); and *informative* communication describes thanksgivings offered to God,[18] doxologies proclaimed,[19] and praise extended to Him.[20] Communication taxonomy also aids in interpreting prayers such as Simeon's address to God in Luke 2:29-32 (*informative and interactional*), Jesus' "acknowledgment" of God in Matt 11:25-26 (*informative*), and Zechariah's canticle extolling God's faithfulness in Luke 1:68-79 (*informational*).

---

[17] In a careful study of Luke 18:9-14, F. Gerald Downing carefully analyzed the prayers of pharisee and tax collector against the background of prayers in the Israelite and Greco-Roman world ("The Ambiguity of 'The Pharisee and the Toll-Collector'". One of Downing's conclusions was that both prayers were "self-absorbed," but he had no broader classification system to sort out the prayers.

[18] For example, both Psalms of thanksgivings (Ps 116) and epistolary prayers of thanksgiving (Rom 1:8-15; 1 Cor 1:4-9; Phil 1:3-11; Col 1:3-8; 1 Thess 1:3-10) and blessings of God (2 Cor 1:3-7; Eph 1:3-10; 1 Peter 1:3-9).

[19] For example, Rom 16:25-27; Phil 4:20; Jude 24-25.

[20] Ps 118 is the clearest example of this, but see also Pss 30 and136.

The Value System of Addresser and Addressee

In his work on the anthropology of illness and wellness in antiquity, John Pilch introduced to biblical scholarship a cross-cultural model which aids in the discovery of different configurations of values which characterize social groups.[21] Anthropologists originally developed this model to differentiate and understand the four different cultures found in New Mexico (Native American, Spanish, Mexican-American, and Anglo). Health-care deliverers then successfully utilized it for understanding the cultural variations among a host of immigrant groups in America in regard to illness and health care.[22] Recently John Pilch and Bruce Malina edited a volume entitled *Biblical Social Values*, to whose introduction we turn for a mature elaboration of a model of differing cultural values applicable to biblical literature. They define "value" as: "... some general quality and direction of life that human beings are expected to embody in their behavior. A value is a general, normative orientation of action in a social system."[23] Just as Americans consider money or wealth a "value," so early Christians held kinship and honor to be paramount values.[24] What, then, is value comparison all about?

The following diagram provides a productive way of discovering the value preferences of a group. In a given context and faced with a

[21] John J. Pilch, "Healing in Mark: A Social-Science Analysis," *BTB* 15 (1985) 142-50; "The Health Care System in Matthew," *BTB* 16 (1986) 102-106; "Understanding Biblical Healing: Selecting the Appropriate Model," 18 (1988) 60-66; "Sickness and Healing in Luke-Acts," *The Social World of Luke-Acts. Models for Interpretation* (Jerome H. Neyrey, ed.; Peabody, MA: Hendrickson, 1991) 181-210; "Understanding Healing in the Social World of Early Christianity," *BTB* 22 (1992) 26-33; "Insights and Models for Understanding the Healing Activity of the Historical Jesus," *SBLSP* 1993: 154-77. For an updated version of these articles, see John J. Pilch, *Healing in the New Testament: Insights from Medical and Mediterranean Anthropology.* Minneapolis: Fortress, 1999.

[22] F. R. Kluckhorn and F. L. Strodbeck, *Variations in Value Orientations.* (New York: Harper and Row, 1961); Arthur Kleinman, *Patients and Healers in the Context of Culture* (Berkeley: University of California Press, 1980); Monica McGoldrick John K. Pearce, and Joseph Giordano, eds., *Ethnicity and Family Therapy* (New York: The Guilford Press, 1982).

[23] John J. Pilch and Bruce J. Malina, *Biblical Social Values and Their Meanings* (Peabody MA: Hendrickson, 1993), xiii.

[24] Time and again in their efforts to sensitive Euro-American readers to the differences between us moderns and them ancients, Bruce Malina in particular has provided a detailed series of contrasts between modern first-world countries and the ancient world. See, for example, Bruce J. Malina and Jerome H. Neyrey, *Calling Jesus Names. The Social Value of Labels in Matthew* (Sonoma, CA: Polebridge, 1988) 145-51; Bruce Malina, *Windows on the World of Jesus. Time Travels to Ancient Judea* (Louisville: Westminster/John Knox, 1993); Bruce Malina and Jerome Neyrey, *Portraits of Paul. An Archeology of Ancient Personality* (Louisville: Westminster/John Knox, 1996), 226-31.

specific task, individuals prefer to act in certain predictable ways which would be recognized and approved by their peers; all three options are theoretically available, but generally one or two are more prevalent.[25]

PROBLEM	RANGE OF SOLUTIONS		
Principal Mode of **Human Activity**	Being	Being-in-Becoming	Doing
Interpersonal Relationships	Collateral	Hierarchical	Individual
Time Orientation	Present	Past	Future
Relationship of humans to **Nature**	Be subject to it	Live in harmony with it	Master it
View of Human Nature	Mixture of good and evil	Evil	Good

In applying this to prayers in antiquity, one must distinguish the values of those praying from those attributed to the Deity, the object of prayer. 1. *Activity.* Whereas the ancients themselves may be described as valuing "being," God is almost always described as "doing," whether creating and maintaining the universe or rising up to fight Israel's enemies (Acts 4:24-30).[26] All prayers of petition, then, ask God to "do something," that is, "be active" on behalf of the pray-er. 2. *Relationships* among mortals are both collateral and hierarchical; for, in addition to the vertical relationships people find themselves in (father/son; landlord/peasant; sovereign/subject), they also enjoy collateral relationships with friends and relatives. God, however, is generally addressed in terms of some hierarchical relationship, "Father,"[27] "Lord," "God of Israel," "Sovereign," and the like. The sense of social

[25] This adaptation of the value map appeared first in Pilch's *Introducing the Cultural Context of the New Testament* (New York/Mahwah: Paulist Press, 1991), 244; the version in our text is that of Pilch and Malina, *Biblical Social Values*, xxiii.

[26] Especially in the holy war tradition, Israel is told to "be still" while God battles on their behalf (Exod 14:4; Ps 37:7 and 46:10).

[27] In response to the work of Joachim Jeremias, James Barr ("Abba Isn't Daddy," *JTS* 39 [1988] 28-47) examined the linguistic evidence concerning interpretation of the Abba in Jesus' own prayer; it does not mean "Daddy."

distance separating a pray-er and God is never made clearer than in prayers of petition, where the pray-ers confess that God alone controls the universe or at least their enemies, or the rain in their valley. Therefore God will be addressed and treated like the various patrons or sovereigns in the life of the pray-er. 3. In regards to *time*, ancient Judeans both appealed to the past (Israel's legal and wisdom traditions embodied in Scripture) and focused on the present. In contrast, the God of Israel enjoys an eternity which temporally reaches back and forward without limit: It is God alone "who is, who was, and who will be."[28] Unlike mortals who come into being and inevitably die, God—the immortal one—has no beginning and no end. Yet pray-ers ask God to act in the present; or, they call upon God to remember his actions "as of old" and to perform them now again. The future, however, belongs to God alone and it is sacrilegious to try and discover it; God alone knows the future, and those to whom it pleases God to disclosed it.[29] 4. *Nature*. Native Americans are reputed to live in harmony with nature, whereas mainstream Americans consider themselves superior to it. Hence they dam rivers, tunnel under the seas, and make deserts bloom. But the ancients thought of themselves as subject to nature: storms wreck their vessels,[30] droughts cause terrible famines,[31] and the like. Yet God the all-powerful rules sky, sea and earth; God can send rain as well as rescue people from shipwreck. God, who is both pantocrator and sovereign of the universe, can providentially aid pray-ers on land or at sea.[32] 5. *Human nature*. Whereas Euro-Americans are socialized to view their children as innocent and good, Sirach ad-

---

[28] See Isa 41:4; Rev 1:4, 8; 4:8; see also Jerome H. Neyrey, "'Without Beginning of Days or End of Life' (Hebrews 7:3): Topos for a True Deity," *CBQ* 53 (1991) 439-55.

[29] Bruce Malina ("Christ and Time: Swiss or Mediterranean?" *CBQ* 51 [1989] 1-31) provided the biblical guild with an excellent anthropological study on the meaning of time as it applies to the Bible. Of the future he writes: "The past and the future as the possible cannot belong and never will belong to human beings. To glimpse the world of the distant past, or of the future, the world of the possible, is to assume divine prerogatives. In Israel such insolence was idolatry, while for Greeks it was hubris. The possible past and the possible future are simply closed to human beings" (p. 15).

[30] Jonah 1:4-16, Mark 4:35-41, Acts 27:13-44; storms themselves were thought to be caused by some heavenly being, either the God of Israel or a hostile spirit. Nevertheless, those caught in storms were powerless against them. See Vernon Robbins, "'By Land and by Sea': The We-Passages and Ancient Sea Voyages," *Perspectives on Luke-Acts* (Charles H. Talbert, ed.; Macon, GA: Mercer University Press, 1978), 215-42.

[31] In addition to the seven-year famine at the end of Genesis, see 1 Kings 17:1-16; Acts 11:27-30.

[32] See Wilhelm Michaelis, "παντοκρατωρ" *TDNT* 3.914-15.

vises the wise of ancient Israel in regard to their sons, "Beat his ribs."[33] Yet certain strains of Christianity likewise believe that children are born in sin, and so must be treated accordingly. Ancient Israel in general seemed to consider human nature as a mixture of good and evil. In petitionary prayer, pray-ers regularly describe their oppressors as evil; yet pray-ers themselves on occasion seek forgiveness and reconciliation and so confess their own sinfulness, error or failure. Human nature for the ancients was, at best, a mixture of good and evil.

From this value map, we draw the following conclusions. (1) In both prayers of thanksgiving and petition God is always thought of as "doing" something, either in the past, present or future. Many prayers refer to past actions of God as warrants and proof of what God should presently do. (2) The vertical relationship between God and Israel or the disciples of Jesus expresses the transcendent distance between the Immortal One and His mortal subjects. In contrast, humans characteristically look laterally to their friends and relatives for aid, as well as hierarchically to their covenant Lord and Patron. (3) In terms of time, pray-ers in the Bible regularly looked to the past to clarify the present: i.e., reflection on God's faithfulness in the covenants with Abraham and David, the endurance of their ancestral law and the ancient system of worship as evidence of what God has done and should continue doing.[34] Yet if the roots of hope exist back in God's past actions, pray-ers expect God's assistance today ("Give us this day our today bread," Matt 6:11; Luke 11:3) or stand under God's judgment today ("Today if you hear his voice ..." Ps 95:7-11/Heb 3:7-4:13). They might also rejoice today that ancient prophecies or promises are now fulfilled (Luke 2:28; 4:21).[35] (4) All prayers of praise and petition celebrate God's omnipotence over nature, that is, divine power to make the rains fall (or not fall), to multiply food and to still storms. (5) With the

---

[33] Particularly helpful here is the study by John Pilch, "'Beat His Ribs While He Is Still Young' (Sirach 30:12): A Window on the Mediterranean World," *BTB* 1993: 101-13.

[34] In Phil 1:6 Paul states his hope in God relative to past and present: "And I am sure that He who began a good work in you will bring it to completion at the day of Jesus Christ."

[35] On the motif of prophecy-fulfilment, see R. H. Gundry, *The Use of the Old Testament in St. Matthew's Gospel* (NovTSupp 18; Leiden: Brill, 1967); G. M. Soares-Prabhu, *The Formula Quotations in the Infancy of Matthew* (Analecta Biblica 63; Rome: Pontifical Biblical Institute, 1976); on Luke's gospel, see David L. Tiede, *Prophecy and History in Luke-Acts* (Philadelphia: Fortress, 1980) and Charles H. Talbert, "Prophecy and Fulfillment in Lucan Theology," *Luke-Acts. New Perspectives from the Society of Biblical Literature Seminar* (Charles H. Talbert, ed.; New York: Crossroads, 1984), 91-103.

story of Adam's sin, Israelites and early Christians thought of human nature as evil or a mixture of good and evil. In Romans Paul declared that "all have sinned and fallen short of the glory of God" (Rom 3:22-23).[36] But God of course is holy beyond measure, who forgives humans their sins and sends Jesus as their savior. God will also transform corruptible humankind and make them incorruptible, and have their mortality changed to immortality so that they may worthily enter the presence of God (1 Cor 15:53-54).

Honor and Shame and Prayer

To my knowledge, Bruce Malina pioneered New Testament research on the importance of honor and shame for biblical interpretation.[37] His synthesis of various field studies from countries bordering on the Mediterranean led him to develop a model of this "pivotal value." Honor refers to the *claim* of worth, value and respect which must be publicly *acknowledged*.[38] The *claim* may be made either by the person demanding respect or by others on his behalf, usually family or fictive-kin (co-citizens, co-members of the army); and the *acknowledgment* must always be public approval of this claim. The ancients used many different verbs to express this *acknowledgment*, such as to glorify, praise, acclaim, exalt, magnify, celebrate, make famous, declare the name of the Lord, know the Lord, and the like.[39]

---

[36] On Romans 5:12-21, see the sage remarks of Joseph A. Fitzmyer, *Romans* (AnB 33; New York: Doubleday, 1993), 405-28.

[37] Bruce J. Malina, *The New Testament World. Insights from Cultural Anthropology* (Rev. ed.; Louisville: Westminster/John Knox, 1993), 28-62. See also Bruce J. Malina and Jerome H. Neyrey, "Honor and Shame in Luke-Acts: Pivotal Values of the Mediterranean World," *The Social World of Luke-Acts. Models for Interpretation* (Jerome H. Neyrey, ed.; Peabody, MA: Hendrickson, 1991), 97-124. See also Johannes Pedersen, *Israel: Its Life and Culture*, vol 1 (Atlanta: Scholars Press, 1991), 213-44.

[38] Julian Pitt-Rivers, "Honour and Social Status," *Honour and Shame: The Values of Mediterranean Society* (J. G. Peristiany, ed.; London: Weidenfeld and Nicolson, 1965), 19-78; "Honor." *IESS* 6.503-11 (1968); *The Fate of Shechem or The Politics of Sex: Essays in the Anthropology of the Mediterranean* (Cambridge Studies in Social Anthropology 19; Cambridge University Press, 1977), 1.

[39] Malina, *New Testament World*, 59. The study of "honor" by Johannes Schneider ("τιμή") *TDNT* 8.169-80) presents the various meanings of τιμή; but "honor" is expressed by other terms, hence semantic word field studies are needed, such as A. Klose, "Altrömische Wertbegriffe (*honos* und *dignitas*)," *Neue Jahrbücher für Antike und deutsche Bildung* 1 (1938), 268-78 and Emile Benveniste, *Indo-European Language and Society* (Coral Gables, FL: University of Miami Press, 1969), 334-45.

Sources of Honor

A person acquires honor in two basic ways: *ascription* by another or *achievement* by the claimant. Most people in antiquity have honor ascribed to them first and foremost by the parents, family and clan into which they were born.[40] If the family belongs to the elite strata and ruling class, the offspring—primarily the male ones—are born with high honor manifested in the family's power, wealth, reputation and worth. Conversely, offspring born of peasants share in their relative honor, symbolized by modest land holdings or modest flocks. We observe constantly that most people are introduced as the "son of so-and-so" or the "wife of so-and-so." Thus children inherit the social worth or honor of their parents. Adoption into a family provides a comparable process, as would commissioning as ambassador or assignment as procurator. On the other hand, individuals may acquire fame, glory and renown through military, athletic or aesthetic prowess. A city's benefactor may earn the its praise for gift of an aqueduct or theater. Or individuals may engage in the ubiquitous game of challenge and riposte.

Honor and Virtue

Honor in antiquity dealt with "excellence" of some sort, either the prowesses mentioned above or some socially-sanctioned virtue or uniqueness. The most common virtues meriting respect and honor are courage (military and athletic prowess) and justice. Because of its importance for assessing behavior in prayer, we take a closer look at what the ancients understood by "justice." Since discourse on virtue was taught by ancient rhetoricians, we take the remarks of a Roman writer close in time to the New Testament to illustrate the traditional understanding of justice. This author represents the utterly conventional, ancient discourse stretching back to Aristotle and forward into Byzantine times.

> We will be using the *topics of justice* if we say that we ought to *pity* innocent persons and suppliants; if we show that it is proper to *repay* the well-deserving with *gratitude*; if we explain that we ought to *punish the guilty*; if we urge that *faith* ought zealously to be *kept*; if we say that the *laws and customs* of the state ought especially to be *preserved*; if we contend that *alliances and friendships* should scrupulously be *honored*; if we make it clear that the *duty* imposed by nature *towards parents, gods, and fatherland* must be religiously *observed*; if we maintain that *ties of hospitality, clientage, kin-*

---

[40] See Malina, *New Testament World*, 33-34; see also Bruce J. Malina and Jerome H. Neyrey; *Portraits of Paul*, 16-17, 92-93, 202-205.

ship, and *relationship by marriage* must inviolably be *cherished* (*Herennium.* 3.3.4, italics added).[41]

This rhetorician flags as marks of justice: (1) gratitude, (2) fair judgment, (3) fidelity, (4) duty to gods, parents, and fatherland, and (5) maintenance of important social ties. Thus pray-ers are just when they offer thanks for benefaction, keep covenant fidelity with God, fulfil their duty to God by obeying His commandments, and maintain their ties of clientage with their heavenly Patron. Similarly, God will be shown in prayer to be just and worthy of praise when God judges the wicked and rewards the faithful, when God's faithfulness is acknowledged, when God's patronage is seen as reliable and everlasting. Thus the psalmist praises God: "The Lord is faithful in all his words, and gracious in all his deeds" (Ps 145:13).

Honor and Benefaction

Benefaction may be one of the most productive concepts in assessing God's honor in the social structure of prayers. The custom whereby powerful and wealthy people in the ancient world provided important public services is well known.[42] Wealthy aristocrats and monarchs were expected to provide public festivals, fund war ships, and build aqueducts and theaters and the like for their cities or kingdoms.[43] Josephus

---

[41] The definition given by Ps. Aristotle goes as follows: "To **righteousness** (δι-καιοσύνη) it belongs to be ready to distribute according to desert, and to preserve ancestral customs and institutions and the established laws, and to tell the truth when interest is at stake, and to keep agreements. First among the claims of righteousness are our *duties to the gods, then our duties to the spirits, then those to country and parents, then those to the departed*; among these claims is *piety* (εὐσεβεία), which is either a part of righteousness or a concomitant of it. Righteousness is also accompanied by *holiness* (ὁσιοτης) and *truth and loyalty* (πίστις) and hatred of wickedness" (*Virtues and Vices*, V.2-3, italics added). See also Cicero, *Inv.* 2.160-161; Menander Rhetor I.361.17-25.

[42] The premier collection of benefaction inscriptions for biblical study is that of Frederick C. Danker, *Benefactor. Epigraphic Study of a Graeco-Roman and New Testament Semantic Field* (St. Louis: Clayton Publishing House, 1982); see also A. R. Hands, *Charities and Social Aid in Greece and Rome* (Ithaca: Cornell University Press, 1968), 175-209. See also S. R. Llewellyn, "The Development of Systems of Liturgies," *NDIEC* 7 (1994) 93-111; Stephen C. Mott, "The Power of Giving and Receiving: Reciprocity in Hellenistic Benevolence," *Current Issues in Biblical and Patristic Interpretation* (Gerald Hawthorne, ed.; Grand Rapids: W.B. Eerdmans, 1975), 60-72.

[43] Isaeus provides an excellent example of this: "Our forefathers ... performed every kind of choregic office, contributed large sums for your expenses in war, and never ceased acting as trierarchs. As evidence of all these services, they set up in the temples out of the remainder of their property, as a memorial of their civic worth, dedications, such as tripods which they had received as prizes for choregic victories in the temple of Dionysus, or in the shrine of Pythian Apollo. Furthermore, by dedicating on the Acropolis the first-fruits of their wealth, they have adorned the shrine with

provides the following record of how Athens honored the Judean king, Hyrcanus for his benefaction. In it we note the balance between Hyrcanus' benefaction and Athenian public acknowledgment of his noble deed. The acknowledgment took the form of a golden crown, a statue, and heralding of the Judean king's worth at the most important public events in the city's calendar—both its dramatic and athletic festivals. Finally, Athens's leaders make their continued praise and honor contingent upon future benefaction from the king. But in general this proclamation registers their "reward of merit," the acknowledgment of Hyrcanus as a worthy benefactor.

> Inasmuch as Hyrcanus, son of Alexander, the high priest and ethnarch of the Jews, has continued to show his goodwill to our people as a whole and to every individual citizen, and to manifest the greatest zeal on their behalf ... it has therefore now been decreed to honor this man with a golden crown as the reward of merit fixed by law, and to set up his statue in bronze in the precincts of the temple of Demos and the Graces, and to announce the award of the crown in the theater at the Dionysian festival when the new tragedies are performed, and at the Panathenaean and Eleusinian festivals and at the gymnastic games; and that the magistrates shall take care that so long as he continues to maintain his good will toward us, everything which we can devise shall be done to show honor and gratitude to this man for his zeal and generosity (Josephus, *Ant.* 14.149-55).

This proclamation describes the gifts of a Judean monarch to a Greek city, a relationship in which no "duty" was involved. The same would not be true of elites and populations of the same city-state or region. For them the virtue of justice would indicate a duty to benefit one's own and a corresponding duty by those benefitted to acknowledge the gift.[44] In this convention the worthy person might well be addressed as "Benefactor" (εὐεργητής), "Father," "Friend," or "Savior," names which evoke a kinship relationship even as they mask its harsher aspects.

Honor from Conflict

Another way of acquiring honor and respect deserves closer attention, namely, the game of challenge and riposte. It is regularly observed in Greco-Roman as well as early Christian literature that social games are

---

bronze and marble statues, numerous, indeed, to have been provided out of a private fortune" (*On the Estate of Dicaeogenes* 5.41-42).

[44] For a clearer sense of the *do ut des* character of benefactions, see Josephus, *Ant.* 14.212.

played in public in which challenges are made to another, the purpose of which is to diminish the one challenged and so garner the esteem in which the challenged person basks.[45] These challenges are easily recognized in the rhetorical *chreiai* in which a philosopher or sage is asked a question intended to stump him.[46] A witty riposte dismisses the challenger and confirms the reputation of the wise man.

This ubiquitous social game of push-and-shove also serves as background for appreciating many prayers. A petitioner might complain to God that he, the petitioner, has been faithful and loyal to God, but is now hard pressed. He does not now experience God's beneficent generosity,[47] and his complaint puts God on the spot, so to speak. The pray-er has transformed the challenge from his enemy into a challenge to God. One thinks immediately of Jesus' dying words, which are formally a prayer, i.e. Ps 22:1, "My God, my God, why have you forsaken me?"[48] God, then, is challenged to honor his loyal benefaction to Jesus. Similarly, if the Davidic monarch, the Temple, or Jerusalem were threatened, the pray-er might remind God of God's ancient promises and thus petition the Deity to defend His own interests. God, then, is put on the spot; and the pray-er petitions God to deliver the fitting riposte to the foreign monarch and the threatening army, thus fulfilling the divine promise to Israel. God, therefore, is perceived as engaged in a challenge/riposte situation. Divine failure to respond to such challenges might be considered a loss of divine honor as well as a lack of virtue (faithfulness) on God's part.

What do we know if we know all this? First, we recognize that many prayers acknowledge God's worth as the pray-er exclaims "praise to," "glory be to …," "honor be to …" and "alleluia!" Mortals give God nothing which God lacks, rather they acknowledge the deity's claims. Second, God's honor is never ascribed; for no one in the uni-

---

[45] One is reminded of the practice of victorious kings putting atop their already crowned head the crown of the monarch just vanquished. Thus the honor taken from the defeated directly increased that of the victor. The same would be true of the spoils of war.

[46] See Ronald F. Hock and Edward N. O'Neil, *The Chreia in Ancient Rhetoric. Volume I. The Progymnasmata* (Atlanta: Scholars Press, 1986); Jerome H. Neyrey, "Questions, *Chreiai*, and Challenges to Honor: The Interface of Rhetoric and Culture in Mark's Gospel," *CBQ* 60 (1998), 657-81.

[47] For an enlightened exposition of these psalms of complaint or lament, see Patrick Miller, *They Cried to the Lord*, 68-86.

[48] For a fuller exposition of Ps 22 as Jesus' dying prayer, see my *Honor and Shame in the Gospel of Matthew* (Louisville: Westminster John Knox, 1998), 156-60. The aggressive nature of questions such as "Where is …? Why have you …?" has been splendidly analyzed by Patrick Miller, *They Cried to the Lord*, 68-79, 99-100.

verse can be found higher than God to bestow it (see Heb 7:7).[49] Third, one finds in prayers a sense that there is a "more" and "less" to God's honor. For example, the Bible states that God acts so as to win Himself glory,[50] which suggests that pray-ers thought that God could increase in majesty in some way.[51] Similarly, pray-ers state that should the nation be destroyed or should the pious come to ruin, who then would praise God?[52] Fourth, the virtue of "justice" in its many aspects frequently appears in prayer, and praise is regularly awarded for virtue. God is acclaimed as "faithful" or "faithful and true"[53] and God's stead-fast loyalty to the nation often serves as the reason for or basis of relationship in petitioning God. God's just judgment, especially of foreigners and sinners, redounds to God's honor, for it belongs to jus-tice to judge justly. Fifth, God is frequently understood in prayers as the benefactor par excellence. Hence a rehearsal of God's deeds often precedes acknowledgment of God's honor in statements of praise and glory. Sixth, the psalmist occasionally challenges God by calling into question God's loyalty and faithfulness; such challenging questions beginning with "How long, O Lord ...?"[54] or "Why have you ...?"[55] or "Where is our God?"[56] Thus in terms of this human logic, God is expected to act vigorously to defend God's honor or be shamed as unfaithful or powerless.

---

[49] Yet Harold Attridge (*The Epistle to the Hebrews* [Philadelphia: Fortress, 1989], 196), cites biblical examples of lesser people blessing greater ones. Yet his discussion seems innocent of social-science concepts such as ascribed and achieved honor.

[50] The premier example is the boast God makes before destroying the Egyptian army at the Exodus: "And I will get glory over Pharaoh and all his host" (Exod 14:4; see also vv 17-18; Ezek 28:22).

[51] In a henotheistic world, Yahweh competes with the gods of the nations for glory and honor; therefore God is in conflict with the gods of the nations as these peoples fight against Israel. In a monotheistic world, Yahweh as the only deity in the universe does not need to battle other deities. Hence, it would seem that notions such as God "getting glory" would belong to henotheistic times and would have little meaning in a monotheistic world.

[52] God is regularly reminded that "The dead do not praise the Lord, nor do any that go down into silence" (Ps 115:17; see also Isa 38:18-19). The same sentiment appears also at Qumran: "Surely a maggot cannot praise thee nor a grave-worm re-count thy lovingkindness, but the living can praise thee" (11QPs-a XIX. 1-2). Thus pray-ers, at least, see God as gaining more or less honor in proportion to the number of the living who acknowledge the Lord.

[53] See Deut 7:9; Pss 31:5; 69:13; 97:10; 111:7; 145:13; Isa 49:7; 1 Cor 1:9; 10:13; 2 Cor 1:18; 1 Thess 5:24; 2 Thess 3:3; 2 Tim 2:13; Heb 10:23 and 1 John 1:9.

[54] Pss 13:1-2; 35:17; 74:10; 79:5; 80:4; 89:46; 90:13; 94:3.

[55] Pss 10:1; 22:1; 42:9; 44:23-24; 74:1, 11; 88:14.

[56] Pss 79:10; 115:2; as mentioned above, an excellent treatment of this questioning material can be found in Miller, *They Cried to the Lord*, 71-74.

Prayer and Exchange

We saw earlier how Malina brought to our understanding of prayer a model of communication, consisting of sender—channel—receiver. Later he digested and adapted another model of communication from Talcott Parsons, this time paying attention to the "channel" by means of which a source presents a receiver "with goods, services, actions or a range of words."[57]

Power, Commitment, Inducement and Influence

Talcott Parsons identifies four basic media of communication, which result from his efforts to find meaningful ways to gather and classify diverse social phenomena.[58] He identified four basic media: *power, commitment, inducement* and *influence*, abstract categories which distinguish the means by which senders seek to have an impact on receivers. 1. *Power* refers to collective effectiveness systems such as government (king, president, ruler, judge); power means the ability to make others act in certain ways. 2. *Commitment* refers to the belonging system— family, extended family, and groups of friends. 3. *Inducement* touches on the economic system, that is, the exchange of things of value (agricultural produce, clothing, money and the like). 4. Finally *influence* refers to the meaning system, the reasons for something or the learning amassed in a culture. In his characteristic way, Malina explains how even Euro-American audiences can quickly grasp these four categories:

> Consider the following sentence and insert the roles of the persons who asked or told you to do or not to do something that in fact you did or did not do: "I did it because he or she was: my mother, father, sister, brother, friend, relative (= commitment); a doctor, lawyer, clergy person, teacher (= influence); the police, mayor, president of the U.S. (= power); my boss at work, employer, foreman, customer, client (= inducement)."[59]

Broadly speaking, the Deity addressed in ancient prayers possesses all four of the media of communication, but not the pray-ers. It is unthinkable that mere mortals would offer God *power*, especially as many prayers acclaim God as "omnipotent," "creator," and "mighty war-

---

[57] Bruce J. Malina, *Christian Origins and Cultural Anthropology. Practical Models for Biblical Interpretation* (Atlanta: John Knox Press, 1986), 75-76; he is digesting Talcott Parsons, *Politics and Social Structure* (New York: Free Press, 1969), 352-429.

[58] Talcott Parsons, *Politics and Social Structure* (New York: Free Press, 1969), 352-437; see also his earlier article, "On the Concept of Influence," *Public Opinion Quarterly* 27 (1963) 37-62.

[59] Malina, *Christian Origins and Cultural Anthropology*, 77.

rior." Pray-ers on the contrary pray to God to defeat their enemy, stop a drought, or deliver them from war: all petitions for God's unique *power*. Similarly, mortals have no *influence*, that is, knowledge, wisdom or secret, that they can bring to the "omniscient"[60] Deity. They may, however, inform God of sorrow for sin (Ps 51) or like Job petition to know the cause misfortune. God alone knows all things, especially the secrets of the human heart. Concerning *inducement*, although people have on occasion promised God wealth or vowed offerings to temples if their prayers are heard, this attempt at plying God with *inducement* received mixed reactions in antiquity.[61] On the one hand, Israel's temple system offered *inducement* to God in its vast array of sacrifices (holocausts and thanksgiving sacrifices; grain and wine offerings).[62] We also read of many prophetic denunciations of the temple system as a form of bribery.[63] No, God is the source of *inducement*, hence pray-ers petition that God send them food in due season, rain in time of drought or wealth to deliver them from debt. It is God from whom all goods flow. Finally, *commitment* seems to be the premier expectation of God by pray-ers as well as their unique manner of communicating with God. *Commitment* may express any or all of the following sentiments: obedience, faithfulness, thanksgiving, blessing, praise, acknowledgment, honor, glory, respect, and the like. When we read of relationships expressed as "God and the people He has chosen," "as a Father carries his infant …" and similar expressions, we recognize that commitment is being appealed to. Similarly, when pray-ers appeal to God's covenantal faithfulness and beg God to act once more as loyal Patron, they express their own *commitment* and seek to activate God's *commitment*. Moreover, many prayers consist of blessing and thanksgiving to God for benefaction received, thanksgiving being another example of commitment; other prayers may pledge faithfulness and loyalty. Therefore, biblical pray-ers primarily use *commitment* as their

---

[60] Earlier we described one of the types of prayer as "informative," in which senders make known sentiments such as sorrow for sins as well as thanksgiving. The prayer may consider this secret information, yet some Psalms indicate that God knows the hearts of all (Ps 139 "O Lord, you have searched me and know me").

[61] In the case of Saul, "to obey (*commitment*) is better than sacrifice (*inducement*)" (1 Sam 15:10-23); see Ps 40:6-8 LXX.

[62] On sacrifice as a form of *inducement*, Bruce J. Malina ("Mediterranean Sacrifice: Dimensions of Domestic and Political Religion," *BTB* 26 [1996] 37) defined sacrifice as, "a ritual in which a deity or deities is/are offered some form of inducement, rendered humanly irretrievable, with a view to some life-effect for the offerer(s)."

[63] See Isa 1:11-16; Jer 6:20; 7:3-29; Hos 6:6; 8:11-13; Amos 5:21-24; Micah 6:6-8; Malachi 1:6-14.

medium of communication with God, along with sacrificial *inducement*, but never *power* and *influence*. God, on the other hand, is perceived as having all four of the media at His disposal and in great supply.

Reciprocity

Discussion of the media of communication leads to an inquiry about the kind of exchange in which the participants engage. Malina has digested the relevant theory of exchange which identifies three kinds: *generalized, balanced* or *negative* reciprocity.[64] 1. *Generalized* reciprocity refers to the altruistic, asymmetrical attention payed to the wants and needs of another. Characteristic of kinship, it includes hospitality, gifts, and assistance to kin. 2. *Balanced* reciprocity focuses on the mutual interests of both parties in a symmetrical way. This type of reciprocity characterizes the communication between neighbors, not kin; and its typical forms are trade agreements, fees payed for services and exchange or barter. 3. Finally *negative* reciprocity describes the attempt in an exchange to get as much as possible for oneself, while giving as little as possible in return. Examples of negative reciprocity include use of fraudulent weights in commerce, as well as devaluation of coinage and theft. Obviously one does not treat either kin or neighbors in this way, but rather strangers or enemies.

What forms of reciprocity do the pray-ers use in communicating with God and what forms do pray-ers think characterize God's dealing with them? Most frequently in prayers of petition and praise/thanksgiving, God's creatures, whose being, life and happiness are in God's hands, acknowledge the Deity as Creator, Father, Savior and Benefactor to whom they turn "to give them their food in due season." As clients in a patron-client relationship with the deity, they depend on God's election of them (*generalized* reciprocity) and faithful maintenance of the covenant bond. They appreciate the gratuity of God's benefaction of all four symbolic media (power, commitment, inducement and influence), but indicate that their commitment (loyalty, obedience, praise, thanks and honor) in no way balances the scales of reciprocity. Pray-ers do not engage God in terms of *generalized* reciprocity; on the contrary they are recipients of God's altruism.

When pray-ers communicate with God or the gods, even the ancients agree that *negative* reciprocity is blasphemous, for mortals are shameful who attempt to despoil God by lying, deceiving, cheating or

---

[64] Malina, *Christian Origins and Cultural Anthropology*, 98-106; he drawing on the work of Marshall Sahlin, *Stone Age Economics* (Chicago: Aldine-Atherton, 1972).

stealing from Him.[65] Yet their criticism of superstition acknowledges that indeed some pray-ers do just this, even though such prayers are recognized as shallow and self-serving.[66]

Although some ancients described the petitionary relationship between Deity and pray-er as a *balanced* exchange (*do ut des* or "give so as to get"). Lucian's famous satire of ancient sacrifice describes sacrifice and prayer by some as *negative* reciprocity.

> So nothing, it seems, that they [the gods] do is done without compensation. They sell men their blessings, and one can buy from them health, it may be, for a calf, wealth for four oxen, a royal throne for a hundred, a safe return from Troy to Pylos for nine bulls, and a fair voyage from Aulis to Troy for a king's daughter! Hecuba, you know, purchased temporary immunity for Troy from Athena for twelve oxen and a frock. One may imagine, too, that they have many things on sale for the price of a cock or a wreath or nothing more than incense (Lucian, *On Sacrifices* 2).

At first glance Lucian seems to mock the exchange of sacrificial petitions from mortals with benefactions provided by the gods. This is by no means a *balanced* exchange, but tends rather toward *negative* reciprocity. Mortals give as little as possible for indescribable results: health, wealth and royal rule can be had for a mere calf or four oxen or a hundred oxen. Although bad enough to imagine that one could engage in a balanced exchange of the general symbolic media with God, it is shameful to think that one could trick a deity into bestowing superior goods for a meager offering.

Yet, some pray-ers on occasion imply that their communication with God has an element of *balanced* reciprocity. In some cases we read of complaints against the deity, which express the pray-ers' commitment and even sacrificial inducement to God *which is not now being reciprocated.*[67] At least for the moment, such complaints testify both to the pray-er's commitment to God (faithfulness, constant prayer; sacri-

---

[65] One might profitably think of "regulatory" prayer as in some way being an example of negative reciprocity; the pray-er performs perfunctory rites, bringing as little as is needed to secure a powerful result. God is shamed both by the assertion of the pray-er's power or control and by the desire to reduce contact with the deity to the most minimal level. God loses all around.

[66] See James 1:5-8; on the traditions reflected here, see Luke T. Johnson, *The Letter of James* (AnB 37A; New York: Doubleday, 1995), 179-81.

[67] See Claus Westermann, *Praise and Lament in the Psalms*, 176ff; Samuel Balentine, *The Hidden God: The Hiding of the Face of God in the Old Testament* (New York: Oxford University Press, 1983), 116-35; Craig Broyles, *The Conflict of Faith and Experience in the Psalms* (JSOTSup 52.; Sheffield: Sheffield Academic Press, 1989), 80-82; Patrick Miller, *They Cried to the Lord*, 70-76.

fice), but also to the experience of shame, mockery and humiliation. An imbalance is perceived and so God is faulted for failing to respond with divine benefaction to the pray-er's commitment to God. Moreover, although in some situations pray-ers seem to engage in a sort of *balanced* reciprocity when they make promises and vows to God[68] to be fulfilled upon receipt of God's grant of deliverance or health, the psalmist declares that nothing that could be offered would be a sufficient repayment: "What shall I render to the Lord for all of his bounty to me?" (Ps 116:12). The best that can be done is "to pay my vows to the Lord," a remark which I suggest is but acknowledging God's honorable benefaction, not balancing it with anything. In the main, pray-ers receive God's *generalized* reciprocity, and their public praise only acknowledges God's claims of honor. *Balanced* reciprocity, at best, is but an occasional and illusory suggestion. *Negative* reciprocity, such as Lucian described, is shameful.

According to the definition of justice noted earlier, we often read of virtuous people who fulfil their duties to God, country and family. Does God have duties and obligations to the world He created and the people God has made His own? Does justice contain an element of *balanced* reciprocity? Just worshipers owe God the fulfilment of their vows, even as justice dictates that benefactions received are to be acknowledged. Commitment, as we saw, is what pray-ers owe the Deity, whether this be hymns of thanksgiving and praise or sacrifices, which acknowledge God's benefaction. Yet this relationship is hardly *balanced*, nor were ancient pray-ers bold enough to say that they had satisfied for all time the debt of benefaction from the Creator-Parent, which is implied in *balanced* reciprocity. Mortals can never repay the Lord or balance the scales, but live forever with the duty to praise and thank God. Josephus describes just this sort of piety:

> Twice every day, at the dawn thereof, and when the hour comes for turning to repose, let all acknowledge before God the bounties which he has bestowed on them through their deliverance from the land of Egypt: *thanksgiving is a natural duty*, and is rendered alike in gratitude for past mercies and to incline the giver to others yet to come (*Ant.* 14.212, italics added).

"Duty," the emic term describing what mortals express in prayer of thanksgiving, encodes a sense of obligation to acknowledge God's benefaction. While it may be viewed by some as reciprocity (see Ath-

---

[68] See Num 21:2; 30:2-3; Deut 23:18, 21; Pss 22:25; 50:14; 56:12; 61:5, 8; 66:13; 116:14, 18.

ens' honoring of Hyrcanus earlier), it looks more to the protocols of honor claims which are acknowledged, than to balanced reciprocity which seeks to equalize the scales of the exchange and thus terminate a particular act of barter. To render God His due, then, is not to engage in balanced reciprocity, but to send a response of commitment in view of altruistic benefactions received.

What do we know if we know this? First, we become aware of the four media of exchange (power, commitment, inducement and influence), which aid us in appreciating what a sender might communicate to a receiver. In general, mortal pray-ers communicate with God in terms of commitment, but also inducement-as-sacrifice; God may respond with all four forms of symbolic media. Second, if exchange appropriately describes the communication between pray-er and Deity, it seems best to describe God as exercising *generalized* reciprocity or altruism in bestowing divine benefaction in the form of power, commitment, inducement or influence. The pray-er's petition for or praise of divine benefaction does not seem to be a form of reciprocity of any kind. Pray-ers, we saw, approach God either as needy or grateful; but they are not exercising any power over God, nor bribing Him, nor bringing God anything God lacks. Unless by magical prayers they bind God (superstition) or think to extract resources from God through sacrifice (*negative* reciprocity). They engage in no reciprocity with God; pray-ers are the recipients of divine benefaction, that is, of divine favoritism or election. As recipients they are thereby indebted to God and have an obligation in justice to offer praise and thanksgiving. But this is hardly what was meant by *balanced* reciprocity, for there is no commensurability between gift and thanksgiving. The commitment of pray-ers is balanced by God's commitment, so to speak, but the Deity's eternal faithfulness and loyalty greatly surpass that of the pray-ers; hence there is no balance here.[69]

Patron-Client Relationships

Classicists have long appreciated the importance of the patron-client relationship in antiquity.[70] Frederick Danker brought to the attention

---

[69] The Sacramentary of the Roman Catholic Church contains a preface prayer for use on weekdays: "You have no need of our praise, yet our desire to thank you is itself your gift. Our prayer of thanksgiving adds nothing to your greatness, but makes us grow in your grace" (Weekdays IV P40).

[70] For example, Richard P. Saller, *Personal Patronage Under the Early Empire* (Cambridge: Cambridge University Press, 1982); Paul Veyne, *Bread and Circuses. Historical Sociology and Political Pluralism* (London: Penguin Press, 1990); Andrew Wallace-Hadrill, ed., *Patronage in Ancient Society* (London: Routledge, 1989).

of New Testament interpreters the grand tradition of honoring benefactors, a form of patron-client relations characteristic of the eastern
Mediterranean.[71] Bruce Malina, however, pioneered the formal use of
the anthropology of patron-client relations for interpreting early
Christian literature.[72] His adapted model[73] of patron-client relations
describes those that arise among peoples of unequal status and resources: landlord/vassal, aristocrat/peasant, king/subject, father/son,
and God/Israel. Thus patron-client relationships describe the vertical
dimension of exchange between higher-status and lower-status persons. A full inventory of the standard features of patron-client
relationships is found in the following note,[74] but we highlight those
pertinent to this discussion.

First, patron-client relations all contain an element of ex-
change/benefit in them; otherwise, it would be difficult to know why
patron and client engaged in a relationship at all. Malina noted: "Pa-

---

[71] Frederick W. Danker, *Benefactor. Epigraphical Study of a Graeco-Roman and New
Testament Semantic Field*, mentioned above in note 43. 1982.

[72] The initial study is Bruce J. Malina, "Patron and Client: The Analogy Behind
Synoptic Theology," *Forum* 4,1 (1988) 2-32; this article was made more widely available in Malina's *The Social World of Jesus and the Gospels* (London: Routledge, 1996)
143-75. See also John H. Elliott, 1987.

[73] The important anthropological literature includes Steffen Schmidt, James Scott,
Carl Landé, and Laura Guasti, *Friends, Followers and Factions: A Reader in Political Clien-
talism* (Berkeley, CA: University of California Press, 1977); Jeremy Boissevain, *Friends
of Friends: Networks, Manipulators and Coalitions* (New York: St. Martin's Press, 1974);
Shlomo Eisenstadt and Louis Rhoniger, *Patrons, Clients, and Friends: Interpersonal Relations and the Structure of Trust in Society* (Cambridge: Cambridge University Press,
1984).

[74] The following features of patron-client relations as described in anthropological
literature include: 1. patron-client relations are particularistic; 2. patron-client interaction involves the exchange of a whole range of generalized symbolic media: power,
influence, inducement and commitment; 3. the exchange entails a package deal, so
that the generalized symbolic media cannot be given separately (i.e., concretely useful
goods must go along with loyalty, solidarity); 4. solidarity here entails a strong element
of unconditionality and long-range social credit; 5. hence, patron-client relations
involve a strong element of personal obligation, ranging from high to low salience,
even if relations are often ambivalent; 6. these relations are not fully legal or contrac-
tual, but very strongly binding, i.e., they are informal and often opposed to official
laws of the country; 7. in principle, patron-client relations entered into voluntarily can
be abandoned voluntarily, although always proclaimed to be life-long, long-range,
forever, etc. 8. patron-client relations are vertical and dyadic (between individuals or
networks of individuals) and, thus, they undermine the horizontal group organization
and solidarity of clients and other patrons. 9. patron-client relations are based on
strong inequality and difference between patrons and clients. Patrons monopolize
certain positions of crucial importance to clients, especially access to means of production, major markets, and centers of society (Malina, "Patron and Client," 3-4).

tron-client relations are based on strong inequality and difference between patrons and clients. Patrons monopolize certain positions of crucial importance to clients, especially access to means of production, major markets, and centers of society."[75] What, then, do patrons bestow on clients and what do clients render in return? Patrons are usually wealthy and powerful people, who have first-order goods, that is: (1) *power* to stop agonistic behavior threatening the life and livelihood of a client; (2) *commitment* to support clients by giving them a sense of kinship, albeit fictive, with the patron; (3) *inducement*, such as a dowry for the client's daughter, seed for his fields, or a daily ration of bread or money[76]; and (4) *influence,* passing on a favorable word to the client's creditor or putting the client in touch with the right person to solve the client's problems. As Malina has shown, God is regularly understood as the patron-benefactor who bestows "grace" or favor,[77] that is altruistic benefaction. God's patronage, similar to that of earthly patrons, consists of first-order goods: (1) *power*: ability to create, to defeat Egyptian, Assyrian, and Seleucid armies, and to subdue the heavenly spirits who attack God's clients; (2) *commitment*: pledges of eternal loyalty and fidelity in a covenant of steadfast love with Abraham, David and their descendants; (3) *inducement*: bestowal of rain and sunshine for crops, increase of herds, and many children; (4) *influence*: knowledge of God's law and prophetic information of God's plans. Clients, as we saw above, cannot give *power* to this Patron for God is omnipotent, or provide God with information for God is omniscient. But clients can bring *inducement*, a material gift such as a sacrifice, and offer *commitment*, public praise of and loyalty to Him.

Second, although we identified earlier four distinct symbolic media of exchange, the patron-client relationship does not seem to function in a one-for-one exchange: i.e., clients petition for *inducement* to pay taxes, in return for which they offer *commitment*. Rather, the symbolic media are exchanged as a package. With *commitment* from God the Patron comes *power* and/or *inducement*. In prayer, however, it becomes clear that the pray-er best brings God only *commitment;* for, as many

[75] Malina, "Patron and Client," 4.

[76] Duncan Cloud ("The Patron-Client Relationship: Emblem and Reality in Juvenal's First Book," *Patronage in Ancient Society*, 210) notes that Pliny, Martial and Perseus all describe Roman patrons bestowing 25 asses on each client at the morning *salutatio*.

[77] In a lengthy note, Malina ("Patron and Client," 171-172) describes the various meanings of χάρις, χαρίζομαι, and χάρισμα which express patronage.

biblical instances note, sacrifices and holocausts do not move the De-ity, but rather faithfulness, obedience and loyalty, i.e., commitment.[78]

Third, anthropologists describe the relation between patron and cli-ent as particularistic, in that the patron does not treat all real or potential clients the same. Some individuals or groups are "chosen" favorites, singled out from the rest, and most favored.[79] Thus favorit-ism, so offensive to modern democratic ears and their notions of egalitarianism, thrives in a patron-client world. The Bible knows of many favorites of God:[80] Abraham (Gen 12:1-3; 15:13-16), David (2 Sam 7:8-16), and Israel: "The Lord your God has chosen you to be a people for his own possession, out of all the people that are on the face of the earth. It is not because you were more in number than any other people that the Lord set his love on you and chose you, for you were the fewest of all peoples" (Deut 7:6-7).

Fourth, patron-client relations purport to endure for a long time, either the lifetime of the patron and client or, in the case of God's covenant with Israel, forever. An important corollary of this suggests that the virtues of loyalty and faithfulness, which are parts of the virtue of justice, will then become important in prayer relationships with the Deity.[81] As Deuteronomy said above about God's covenant with Israel, the Deity "keeps covenant and steadfast love ... to a thousand genera-tions." Similarly, the promise to David came to be interpreted as the

[78] The more notable examples are 1 Sam 15:22; Pss 40:6-8; 50:8-15; 51:16, 17; Isa 1:10-17; Jer 7:21-26; Hosea 6:6; Amos 5:21-24.

[79] Mary, the mother of Jesus, is declared "favored" by God (Luke 1:28, 30), a fa-voritism which forms part of her canticle (1:47-49). In ancient Israel, David, his successors in his dynasty, and also the people Israel are all declared "chosen" or "elected" by God. The psalmist prays "I know that the Lord has set apart the godly for himself" (Ps 4:3); and in another place, "Thou art the glory of their strength; by thy favor is their horn exalted" (Ps 89:17); "He led forth his people with joy, his chosen ones with singing" (Ps 105:43). In the Christian scriptures, Jesus himself is "that living stone, rejected by men but in God's sight chosen and precious" (1 Peter 2:4); and the followers of Jesus are called "a chosen race, a royal priesthood, a holy nation, God's own people" (1 Peter 2:9). On this theme of favoritism, see G. Quell, "ἐκλέγομαι," *TDNT* 4.145-68.

[80] For example, it seems to be a pattern that God chooses the younger son over his older brother, a clear mark of favoritism: Abel over Cain, Isaac or Ishmael, Jacob over Esau, Joseph over his brothers. The same argument is used by Paul in his explanation of the choosing of the gentiles (Rom 9:6-29).

[81] Paul's "thanksgiving" prayer which opens 1 Corinthians contains an inventory of God's blessings past and future; it concludes appropriately with confession of God's faithfulness: "God is faithful (πιστός) by whom you were called into the fellowship of his Son" (1:9; see 10:13). And the doxology which concludes 1 Thessalonians also expresses the same idea: "He who calls you is faithful (πιστός) and he will do it" (5:24; see 2 Thess 3:3).

patron's pledge of an eternal dynasty: "Your house and your kingdom shall be made sure forever before me; your throne shall be established forever" (2 Sam 7:13). Mortal clients, on the other hand, may pledge the same undying loyalty but be unable to maintain the commitment. Nevertheless mutual pledges are frequent characteristics of patron-client relations, especially in prayers. In this context we recall the Athenian benefaction proclamation to Hyrcanus, in which they made it painfully clear that the client's duty to acknowledge the patron's worth entirely depends on Hyrcanus' continued patronage to them. Ideally, then, faithfulness and loyalty are core elements of a patron-client relationship.

What do we know as a result of this? The ubiquitous and ancient pattern of benefactor and patron-client relations greatly aids our interpretation of prayer. First, in prayer God and the pray-er are hierarchically or vertically positioned. God, who is Sovereign, Father, Lord and Savior, is also the Most High and vastly removed in status from mortals; nevertheless, there is a personal relationship expressed in these patron-client relationships. Second, in terms of the commerce of this relationship, God possesses and bestows all four media of exchange; but mortals, always the recipients of patronage, have only their *commitment* with which to acknowledge divine benefaction, and frail commitment at that. Prayer, then, is not an exchange of heavenly patronage for clients' earthly gifts. Rather, divine patronage is honorably acknowledged (i.e., commitment) with the sense that nothing else is suitable to bring to God. Finally, favoritism emerges as a significant element in patron-client relationships. Only some individuals or some peoples enjoy the patron's attention.

Prayer and Ritual

Bruce Malina conveniently summarized for us the anthropological understanding of ritual, an essential element for appreciating the social dynamics called prayer. Gathering the insights of those who study ritual, Malina articulated a basic distinction between *status-transformation ritual* and *ceremony*.[82] By *status-transformation ritual*, he means the process

---

[82] Malina, *Christian Origins and Cultural Anthropology*, 139-65. Victor Turner makes this distinction clear: "I consider the term 'ritual' to be more fittingly applied to forms of religious behavior associated with social *transitions*, while the term 'ceremony' has a closer bearing on religious behavior associated with religious *states* ... Ritual is transformative, ceremony confirmative" (*The Forest of Symbols. Aspects of Ndembu Ritual* [Ithaca, NY: Cornell University Press, 1967], 95). See also Raymond Firth and John

where persons assume a new role or status, hence a transformation of their status. For example, two people who marry move from single to exclusive status; and should the female in this marriage bear a child, she assumes a new role, namely, mother. Similarly, in the transformation which is baptism, people enter a Christian church, changing status from outsider to insider and from unclean to washed clean in the blood of the Lamb. Other status-transformation rituals include: birth and death (entering and leaving the land of the living), trial and imprisonment (unfit for society); graduation (from unskilled or ignorant status to that of a skilled and trained professional), and the like. Conversely, *ceremonies* serve to confirm institutions as well as roles and statuses within them. For example, a school or business or municipality may at a picnic or dinner host people employed by it or who are benefactors of it. The institution experiences confirmation of loyalty and support from those who attend the fete. Ceremonies include all memorials, anniversaries and birthdays at which the roles and statuses of those honored are re-burnished and thus confirmed. The entire liturgical calendar of the Christian church consists of a series of ceremonies.

The following diagram aims at sharpening the differences between status-transformation rituals and ceremonies so to make salient the social functioning of each.

Elements of a Ritual	Category	Elements of a Ceremony
1. irregular pauses	Frequency	1. regular pauses
2. unpredictable, when needed	Schedule/ Calendar	2. predictable, planned
3. present-to-future	Temporal Focus	3. past-to-present
4. professionals	Presided Over By	4. officials
5. status reversal status transformation	Purpose/ Function	5. confirmation of roles and statuses in institutions

1. It is evident that transformation rituals are irregular, since no one plans to be ill or unclean or guilty or dead. Ceremonies such as meals, anniversaries or festivals, on the other hand, occur regularly, either daily, weekly, monthly or annually. 2. Thus transformation rituals,

Skorupski, *Symbol and Theory. A Philosophical Study of Theories of Religion in Social Anthropology* (Cambridge: Cambridge University Press, 1976), 164.

which focus on the change from sickness to health, sinfulness to holiness or life to death, do not fit into a calendar or schedule, since they occur unpredictably. Yet ceremonies are anticipated and planned for: the civic calendar marks the founding of the city, the birthday of the emperor and the feasts of the city's patron deities. 3. Transformation rituals all begin with the present, current situation (illness, sinfulness) and look to the future when that status will be changed. On the contrary, ceremonies look to some past event, historical or mythical, and affirm its significance in the present, as do national holidays such as July 4th or Memorial Day. 4. Transformation rituals are presided over by people deemed competent to deal with the situation; police deal with criminals, doctors treat the sick, firemen control blazes, ministers and priests counsel and forgive, and sanitation engineers dispose of our waste. On the other hand, the officials in our various national, state or local political institutions conduct ceremonies such as anniversaries and memorials (politics); priests and ministers officiate at liturgies (church), and parents prepare daily as well as birthday festivities for their children (kinship). 5. Finally, rituals of transformation do just that, ritualize either elevation or demotion in role and status. The person undergoing a transformation ritual experiences social change which is noted by a public: in marriage two people "become one flesh," a new social entity; in criminal proceedings the accused may be convicted and thus incarcerated or acquitted and set free; in illness the sick may either recover and return to family or worsen, die and be buried. Ceremonies, however, function to confirm role and status in a given institution. Anniversaries and birthdays bring to mind the king's birthday (Mark 6:21) or deliverance from bondage (Exod 12) or the Temple's purification (2 Macc 10:7-8; John 10:22). In the realm of sacrifice, those who participate in the consumption of the meat of the offering indicate their status as members of a clan or family or fictive-family.[83] Thus Antipas' powerful status is acknowledged both by the feast he prepares and by the attendance of his courtiers.[84] Participation with Jesus at the Passover meal on the night before he died confirms for all time the identity and status of Jesus' select disciples (Luke 22:14-34).

---

[83] Nancy Jay, *Throughout Your Generations Forever* (Chicago: University of Chicago Press, 1991), 41-60; see Marcel Detienne, "Culinary Practices and the Spirit of Sacrifice," *The Cuisine of Sacrifice among the Greeks* (Marcel Detienne and Jean-Pierre Vernant, eds.; Chicago: University of Chicago Press, 1989), 4-14.

[84] Matt 22:3-4 and Luke 14:17-20, 24. See Richard L. Rohrbaugh, "The Pre-Industrial City in Luke-Acts," *The Social World of Luke-Acts* (Jerome H. Neyrey, ed.; Peabody, MA: Hendrickson, 1991), 137-46.

When we interface this information on prayer as either status transformation or confirmation with the earlier classification of prayer as communication, we further appreciate the character of those seven types of prayer.

Type of Communication	Status Transformation or Ceremony	Distinguishing Aim
1. instrumental	status transformation	petition for what is lacking
2. regulatory	status transformation	petition to change self or other
3. interactional	ceremony	contentment with current relationships
4. self-focused	ceremony	contentment with current status
5. heuristic	status transformation	seeking information which is currently lacking
6. imaginative	ceremony	status transformation when newcomer participates; ceremony in repeated performances
7. informational	ceremony	confirmation of relationship

Instrumental or petitionary prayer, then, implies status transformation situation. Sinners beg for mercy so as to be changed into a state of blamelessness and holiness once more (Pss 38, 51); those overwhelmed by trials or attacked by enemies ask to be elevated from the current negative status to one of peace and harmony (Pss 56, 59). Regulatory prayers look to changes in status, either the rise in the pray-er's status or the lowering of some one else's. Interactional prayer ceremonially confirms roles and statuses in the institution of the House of Israel. The pray-er who prays Ps 84 ("How lovely is your dwelling place") is a member of the House of Israel who finds contentment and fulfilment in the temple of Israel's God; and the Deity addressed in this way is confirmed as the Patron of the people. Far from asking for change, the pray-er expresses satisfaction in his current status and wishes it to continue. Self-focused prayer confirms the status of the prayer, who may even boast in his present situation. Heuristic prayer seeks a status transformation from not knowing to knowing the mind and plans of God. Imaginative prayer, such as speaking in tongues, seems to have functioned at Corinth initially as status transformation but subsequently as ceremony. Those speaking in tongues initially experienced a transformation from non-elite to elite status, but every subsequent prayer in tongues confirmed them as special elite members of the Corinthian church. The informational type of prayer would seem to reflect what was said about ceremonies; namely, it serves to confirm roles and statuses in a given institution. Hence prayers of praise, thanks, honor and glory to God do not change the status of the pray-er or the Deity so honored; on the contrary, such prayers confirm God's role and status as Creator or Patron, while at the same time confirming the status of the pray-er as client of this heavenly Patron and worshiper of this particular Deity, all within the House of Israel. For example, the rubrics for Passover specify that Israel pray the Hillel psalms, Pss 113-114 after the third cup and Pss 115-116 at the very end of the meal (Mark 14:26). Those who pray these psalms confirm their membership in the people whom God rescued from slavery in Egypt. God, moreover, is confirmed as the Deity who works mighty works for his chosen people. Finally, prayers and psalms which became attached to certain festivals serve to confirm the roles and statuses of the pray-ers and the Deity addressed; they commemorate and thus bring a past event to present consciousness, thus renewing and strengthening the relationship of the clients with their Patron.[85]

Summary, Conclusions and Further Questions

Summary and Conclusions

This article aimed to introduce into the scholarly conversation about biblical prayer other ways of interpreting prayer texts, one that should take its place alongside of and in conversation with more conventional form-critical and history-of-religion studies. We do not find this approach in conflict with other methods of interpretation, rather it is a

---

[85] The traditional classification of certain types of psalms are best seen as ceremonies: 1) royal psalms (Pss. 2; 20; 21; 45; 72; 89; 101; 110; 132; 141:1-11); 2) songs of Zion (Pss (46); 48: 76; 84; 87; 122; (132); 3) festival psalms and liturgies (Pss 50; 81; 95).

new player drafted into the team. This article has presented a systematic approach to understanding prayer in terms of cultural patterns which make up the social and political lives of the pray-ers. It began with a taxonomy of prayer based on a communications model, followed by a model for uncovering the complex value systems of both pray-er and God. Then it brought into conversation cultural and rhetorical notions of honor and shame, highlighting how honor is acquired [virtue, prowess, benefaction, conflict] and how this material relates to God as described in Israelite and Christian prayers. The system of exchange and modes of reciprocity served to clarify what pray-ers think they are offering and receiving from God. Most importantly, this material sharpened the ancient criticism of ritual and sacrifice, offering a coherent way of appreciating the frequent critique of formal religion by ancient reformers. Finally, the theory of ritual allowed us to examine more closely the process (transformation or confirmation) and players (prophet or priest) involved in the various types of prayer classified by the communications taxonomy. Thus we see that the various models used in this study overlap and often replicate one another.

The scope of this paper allowed no space for a lengthy interpretation of this or that prayer to test the model so as to draw any conclusions about its suitability for ancient prayers and pray-ers or the worth of a cultural analysis of ancient prayers. And this is unfortunate, because the proof of the pudding is in the eating. Hence, what is needed now is detailed analysis of certain prayers in Luke-Acts, the Letters of Paul, and Revelation to see what is gained or lost by using such modeling. Moreover, the use of the exchange and reciprocity models raises sensitive questions about the understanding of one's relationship to God, whether one can be said to add to God's honor or in any way obligate God. It may be that the answers in the biblical literature are many, not uniform; and further study is warranted which may involve philosophical and theological discussions of religion in antiquity. As far as I am concerned, this question remains open and troublesome.

Further Questions
What other cultural models for interpreting prayers might be added to those developed here? The following four perspectives seem like fresh questions to ask about prayers.

1. The conversation on prayer would benefit by the use of the model of social stratification articulated by Lenski and Lenski.[86] This allows a reader to plot the pray-er as well as others mentioned in the psalm in terms of social location and social status. Thus the pray-er may be immediately in communication with God, or be employing priests and liturgy as intermediaries. The pray-er may be asking God to turn the world upside down, raising the lowly and humbling the mighty. Hence, the presence and performance of mediating figures is at stake, as well as a petition for reform of the social order.

2. Many biblical prayers employ language reflecting both the vocabulary of purity and pollution and the social function of this language. Strong boundary making and identity confirming is often noticed by scholars, which can be brought into conversation with the treatment above concerning status transformation rituals and ceremonies, which move people across social lines or confirm social lines in and around a group.

3. Models of ancient personality should be brought into the conversation on prayer.[87] For, if the ancients are group-oriented persons, not individualists as modern Westerners are, then the ego of the pray-er must be assessed in terms of that construct, lest we engage in ethnocentrism. By group-oriented person, we refer to the type of individual Josephus describes:

> Our sacrifices are not occasions for drunken self-indulgence—such practices are abhorrent to God—but for sobriety. At these sacrifices prayers offered for the welfare of the community take precedence of those for ourselves; for we are born for fellowship, and he who sets its claims above his private interests is especially acceptable to God (*Against Apion* 2.195-96).

4. Finally, since so many psalms and prayers contain references to body parts, lifting of hands, falling to one's knees, God's right hand, eyes, ears, and heart, it would be worthwhile to bring the description

---

[86] Gerhard Lenski and Jean Lenski, *Human Societies. An Introduction to Macro-sociology* (New York: McGraw Hill, 1987). For excellent use of this model, see Dennis C. Duling, "Matthew's Plurisignificant 'Son of David' in Social Science Perspective: Kinship, Kingship, Magic and Miracle," *BTB* 22: 99-116; Richard L. Rohrbaugh, 1993a"The Social Location of the Marcan Audience," *BTB* 23: 114-27.

[87] Bruce Malina and Jerome Neyrey, "First-Century Personality: Dyadic, Not Individual" (Jerome H. Neyrey, ed., *The Social World of Luke-Acts. Models for Interpretation.* Peabody, MA: Hendrickson, 1991), 67-96; *Portraits of Paul. An Archaeology of Ancient Personality* (Louisville: Westminster/John Knox Press, 1996).

of the three body zones into the conversation on prayer.[88] This model might be particularly useful in assessing the degree of personal involvement in either sin (many zones) and repentance or praise. Moreover it provides a way of assessing the tension that might arise in prayer between the external rituals of some (hands and feet) and the internal processes of reformers (heart).

---

[88] Bernard De Geradon, O.S.B., "L'homme à l'image de Dieu," *NRT* 80 (1958) 683-95.

Publications of Bruce J. Malina

Books

1968
The Palestinian Manna Tradition. Arbeiten zur Geschichte des späteren Judentums und des Urchristentums 7. Leiden: E.J. Brill.

1976
Translation of Gerhard Lohfink, *Paulus vor Damaskus,* under the title: *The Conversion of St. Paul.* Chicago: Franciscan Herald Press.

1981
The New Testament World: Insights from Cultural Anthropology. Atlanta: John Knox.

1985
The Gospel of John in Sociolinguistic Perspective. 48th Colloquy of the Center for Hermeneutical Studies, ed. Herman Waetjen. Berkeley: Center for Hermeneutical Studies.

1986
Christian Origins and Cultural Anthropology: Practical Models for Biblical Interpretation. Atlanta: John Knox.

1988
—— with Jerome H. Neyrey. *Calling Jesus Names: The Social Value of Labels in Matthew.* Sonoma, CA: Polebridge Press.

1992
—— with Richard L. Rohrbaugh, *Social Science Commentary on the Synoptic Gospels.* Minneapolis: Fortress.

1993
Windows on the World of Jesus: Scenarios for New Testament Interpretation. Louisville: Westminster John Knox.

The New Testament World: Insights from Cultural Anthropology. 2nd rev. ed. Louisville: Westminster John Knox.

Die Welt des Neuen Testaments: Kulturanthropologische Einsichten. Translated by Wolfgang Stegemann. Stuttgart: Kohlhammer.

—— co-editor and contributor with John J. Pilch. *Biblical Social Values and Their Meanings: A Handbook..* Peabody, Mass: Hendrickson.

1995
On the Genre and Message of Revelation: Star Visions and Sky Journeys. Peabody, Mass: Hendrickson.

El mundo del Nuevo Testamento: Perspectivas desde la antropología cultural. Translated by Víctor Morla Asensio. (Agora 1) Estella (Navarra): Verbo Divino.

—— with Stephan Joubert and Jan G. van der Watt. *Vensters wat die Woord laat oopgan.* Johannesburg: Orion.

1996
—— with Jerome H. Neyrey. *Portraits of Paul: An Archaeology of Ancient Personality.* Louisville: Westminster John Knox.

—— with Richard L. Rohrbaugh. *Los evangelios sinopticos y la cultura mediterránea del siglo I. Comentario desde las ciencias sociales.* Estella (Navarra): Verbo Divino.

The Social World of Jesus and the Gospels. London/New York: Routledge.

—— with Stephan Joubert and Jan G. van der Watt, *A Time Travel to the World of Jesus: A Modern Reflection of Ancient Judea.* Johannesburg: Orion.

1998
—— with Richard L. Rohrbaugh. *Social-Science Commentary on the Gospel of John.* Minneapolis: Fortress .

—— coeditor and contributor with John J. Pilch, *Handbook of Biblical Social Values.* Rev. ed. Peabody, MA: Hendrickson.

—— Korean translation of the above: *Sungseh Unuhwah Sahhehjuhk Wahmi.* Seoul: The Presbyterian Church Publishing House.

2000
The New Jerusalem in the Revelation of John: The City as Symbol of Life with God. Zacchaeus Studies. Collegeville: The Liturgical Press.

—— with John J. Pilch. *Social-Science Commentary on the Book of Revelation.* Minneapolis: Fortress.

The Social Gospel of Jesus: The Reign of God in Mediterranean Perspective. Minneapolis: Fortress.

Articles

1967
"Matthew 2 and Is 41,2-3, A Possible Relationship?" *Studii Biblici Franciscani Liber Annuus* 17 (1967): 260-302.

1969
"Some Observations on the Origin of Sin in Judaism and in St. Paul." *Catholic Biblical Quarterly* 31 (1969): 18-34.

1970
"The Nature of Sin in Paul: A Modern Equivalent." *Australasian Catholic Record* 47 (1970): 34-36.

1971
"The Literary Structure and Form of Mt XXVIII.16-20." *New Testament Studies* 17 (1971): 87-103.

1972
"Does Porneia Mean Fornication?" *Novum Testamentum* 14 (1972): 10-17.

1973
"Jewish Christianity: A Select Bibliography." *Australian Journal of Biblical Archaeology* 6 (1973): 60-65.

—— with Thomas O. Nitsch, *Toward Human Economy.* (Faculty Working Paper, Dec. 25, 1973) Omaha: Creighton University College of Business Administration.

1975
"Peter's Confession (!) and True Discipleship (Mk 8:27-33)." *The Bible Today* 13 (1975): 233-240.

1976
"Jewish Christianity or Christian Judaism: Toward a Hypothetical Definition." *Journal for the Study of Judaism* 7 (197 6): 46-57.

1977
"First Century Miracles and Contemporary Paradigms." *The Bible Today* 15 (1977): 1199-1206.

"Dimensions of Christian Discernment." *The Bible Today* 15 (1977): 1262-1267.

1978

"Freedom: The Theological Dimensions of a Symbol." *Biblical Theology Bulletin* 8 (1978): 62-76.

"The Social World Implied in the Letters of the Christian Bishop-Martyr (Named Ignatius of Antioch)." Pages 71-119 in *Society of Biblical Literature Seminar Papers, Vol. II.* Edited by Paul J. Achtemeier. Missoula: Scholars Press, 1978.

"Limited Good and the Social World of Early Christianity." *Biblical Theology Bulletin* 8 (1978): 162-176.

"What Are the Humanities: A Perspective for the Scientific American." Pages 33-47 in *The Humanities and Public Life.* Edited by William L. Blizek. Lincoln: Pied Publications, 1978.

1979

"The Individual and the Community: Personality in the Social World of Early Christianity." *Biblical Theology Bulletin* 9 (1979): 126-138.

1980

"What is Prayer?" *The Bible Today* 18 (1980): 214-220.

1981

"The Apostle Paul and Law: Prolegomena for an Hermeneutic." *Creighton Law Review* 14 (1981): 1305-1339.

1982

"The Social Sciences and Biblical Interpretation." *Interpretation* 37 (1982): 229-242. Reprinted in *The Bible and Liberation.* Edited by Norman K. Gottwald. Maryknoll: Orbis, 1982. Pages 11-25.

1983

"Why Interpret the Bible with the Social Sciences." *American Baptist Quarterly* 2 (1983): 119-133.

1984

"Jesus as Charismatic Leader?" *Biblical Theology Bulletin* 14 (1984): 55-62.

—— with Thomas O. Nitsch, *On the Role of A Transcendent in Human Economy: Toward A New Synthesis.*(Faculty Working Paper, June 24, 1984) Omaha: Creighton University College of Business Administration.

1985
"Banquet," Cup," "Hospitality," "Humility," "Laying on of Hands," "Pity," "Service," in *Harper's Bible Dictionary*. Edited by Paul J. Achtemeier. San Francisco: Harper and Row, 1985.

—— with Thomas O. Nitsch, "On the Role of a Transcendent in Human Economy: Toward a New Synthesis." *Humanomics* 1/3 (1985): 55-87.

"Normative Dissonance and Christian Origins." Pages 35-39 in *Social-scientific Criticism of the New Testament and Its Social World*. Edited by John H. Elliott. Semeia 35 (1986).

"The Received View and What It Cannot Do: III John and Hospitality." Pages 171-194 in *Social-scientific Criticism of the New Testament and Its Social World*. Edited by John H. Elliott. Semeia 35 (1986).

"Reader Response Theory: Discovery or Redundancy." *Creighton University Faculty Journal* 5 (1986): 55-66.

"Interpreting the Bible with Anthropology: The Question of Poor and Rich." *Listening* 21 (1986): 148-159.

"Religion in the World of Paul: A Preliminary Sketch." *Biblical Theology Bulletin* 16 (1986): 92-101.

"Miracles or Magic II." *Religious Studies Review* 12 (1986): 35-39.

1987
"Wealth and Poverty in the New Testament and Its World." *Interpretation* 41: 354-367. This is an abridged version of "Wealth and Poverty in the New Testament." In *Urkristendommen: Prosjekthefter 1-2*. Edited by H. Moxnes. Oslo: Universitet I Oslo, 1987.

"Patron and Client: The Analogy behind Synoptic Theology." *Forum* 4/1 (1987): 2-32.

"Mark 7: A Conflict Approach." *Forum* 4/3 (1987): 3-30.

1989
"Christ and Time: Swiss or Mediterranean." *Catholic Biblical Quarterly* 51 (1989): 1-31.

"Dealing with Biblical (Mediterranean) Characters: A Guide for U.S. Consumers." *Biblical Theology Bulletin* 19 (1989): 127-141.

—— with Thomas O. Nitsch, "On the Role of a Transcendent in Human Economy: Toward a New Synthesis." *Humanomics* 5 (1989): 33-59.
1990
"Theological Reflections for Fifth Sunday of Lent." *Lectionary Homiletics* 1/5 (1990): 2-3.

"Theological Reflections for Palm Sunday." *Lectionary Homiletics* 1/5 (1990): 8-9.

"Does the Bible Mean What It Says." *Window.* (Creighton University Public Relation Department) 6/2 (1989/90): 10-13.

"Mary—Woman of the Mediterranean: Mother and Son." *Biblical Theology Bulletin* 20 (1990): 54-64.

"Mary—Woman of the Mediterranean: From Isis to Medjugorje: Why Apparitions." *Biblical Theology Bulletin* 20 (1990): 76-84

1991
"Reading Theory Perspective: Reading Luke-Acts." Pages 3-23 in *The Social World of Luke-Acts: Models for Interpretation.* Edited by Jerome H. Neyrey. Peabody, Mass: Hendrickson, 1991.

—— with Jerome H. Neyrey. "Honor and Shame in Luke-Acts: Pivotal Values of the Mediterranean World." Pages 25-65 in *The Social World of Luke-Acts: Models for Interpretation.* Edited by Jerome H. Neyrey. Peabody, Mass: Hendrickson, 1991.

—— with Jerome H. Neyrey. "First-Century Personality: Dyadic, Not Individual." Pages 67-96 in *The Social World of Luke-Acts: Models for Interpretation.* Edited by Jerome H. Neyrey. Peabody, Mass: Hendrickson, 1991.

—— with Jerome H. Neyrey. "Conflict in Luke-Acts: A Labelling–Deviance Model." Pages 97-122 in *The Social World of Luke-Acts: Models for Interpretation.* Edited by Jerome H. Neyrey. Peabody, Mass: Hendrickson, 1991.

"Interpretation: Reading, Abduction, Metaphor." Pages 253-266 in *The Bible and the Politics of Exegesis: Essays in Honor of Norman K. Gottwald on His Sixty-Fifth Birthday.* Edited by David Jobling, Peggy L. Day and Gerald T. Sheppard. Cleveland: Pilgrim Press, 1991.

"Scienze sociali e interpretazione storica: La questione della retrodizione." *Rivista Biblica* 39 (1991): 305-323.

"Theological Reflections for First-Fourth Sundays of Advent." *Lectionary Homiletics* 2/5 (1991): 1-2; 8-9; 15-16; 23-24.

"Theological Reflections for First Sunday after Christmas." *Lectionary Homiletics* 2/5 (1991): 30-31.

—— with Thomas O. Nitsch. "The Bishops' Pastoral Letter and the Poverty Problem: Early vs. Contemporary Concerns and Doctrines." *Humanomics* 7 (1991): 40-70.

1992
"Is There a Circum-Mediterranean Person: Looking for Stereotypes." *Biblical Theology Bulletin* 22 (1992): 66-87.

1993
"Apocalyptic and Territoriality." Pages 369-380 in *Early Christianity in Context: Monuments and Documents. Essays in Honour of Emmanuel Testa.* Edited by Frederic Manns and Eugenio Alliata. Jerusalem: Franciscan Printing Press, 1993.

1994
"Let Him Deny Himself" (Mark 8:34//): A Social Psychological Model of Self-Denial." *Biblical Theology Bulletin* 24 (1994): 106-119.

"Religion in the Imagined New Testament World: More Social Science Lenses." *Scriptura* 51 (1994): 1-26.

"The Book of Revelation and Religion: How did the Book of Revelation Persuade." *Scriptura* 51 (1994): 27-50.

"Establishment Violence in the New Testament World." *Scriptura* 51 (1994): 51-78.

"John's: The Maverick Christian Group: The Evidence of Sociolinguistics." *Biblical Theology Bulletin* 24 (1994): 167-182.

1995
"Power, Pain and Personhood: Asceticism in the Ancient Mediterranean World." Pages 162-177 in *Asceticism.* Edited by Vincent L. Wimbush and Richard Valantasis. New York: Oxford University Press, 1995.

"Thinking About the Bible." *Bulletin Dei Verbum* (Catholic Biblical Federation) No. 34 (1/1995) 6-8. Also "Zur Reflexion über das Bibellesen." *Bulletin Dei Verbum* (Katholische Bibelföderation) Nr. 34 (1/1995) 6-8; "Distintos marcos desde donde se lee la Biblia." *Boletín Dei Verbum* (Federación Bíblica Católica) No. 34 (1/1995) 6-8; "Lire la Bible." *Bulletin Dei Verbum* (Fédération Biblique Catholique) No. 34 (1/1995) 6-8.

"Maria, Doncella y Madre Mediterranea: Mundo mediterráneo: trasfondo mítico de los siglos I-IV." *Ephemerides Mariologicae* 45 (1995): 69-91.

"Early Christian Groups: Using Small Group Formation Theory to Explain Christian Organizations." Pages 96-113 in *Modelling Early Christianity: Social-Scientific Studies of the New Testament in its Context*. Edited by Philip F. Esler. London: Routledge, 1995.

"Wealth and Poverty in the New Testament World." Pages 88-93 in *On Moral Business: Classical and Contemporary Resources for Ethics in Economic Life*. Edited by Max L. Stackhouse, Dennis P. McCann, Shirley J. Roels and Preson N. Williams. Grand Rapids: Eerdmans, 1995.

"Social Scientific Criticism and Rhetorical Criticism: Why Won't Romanticism Leave Us Alone." Pages 71-101 in *Rhetoric, Scripture and Theology: Essays from the 1994 Pretoria Conference*. Journal for the Study of the New Testament Supplement. Edited by Stanley E. Porter and Thomas H. Olbricht. Sheffield: Sheffield Academic Press, 1995.

1996
"Mediterranean Sacrifice: Dimensions of Domestic and Political Religion." *Biblical Theology Bulletin* 26 (1996): 26-44.

"Review Essay: The Bible—Witness or Warrant. Reflections on Daniel Patte's *Ethics of Biblical Interpretation*." *Biblical Theology Bulletin* 26 (1996): 82-87.

"Understanding New Testament Persons: A Reader's Guide." Pages 41-61 in *Using the Social Sciences in New Testament Interpretation*. Edited by Richard L. Rohrbaugh. Peabody, Mass.: Hendrickson, 1996.

1997
"Embedded Economics: The Irrelevance of Christian Fictive Domestic Economy." *Forum for Social Economics* 26/2 (1997): 1-20.

"Jesus as Astral Prophet." *Biblical Theology Bulletin* 27 (1997): 83-98.

"Mediterranean Cultural Anthropology and the New Testament." Pages 151-178 in *La Bíblia I el Mediterrani—La Biblia y el Mediterráneo—La Bible et la Méditerranée—La Bibbia e il Mediterraneo*. Actes del Congrés de Barcelona 18-22 de setembre de 1995. Vol. 1. Edited by Augustí Borrell, Alfonson de la Fuente and Armand Puig. Abadia de Montserrat: Associació Bíblica de Catalunya, 1997.

1998
"How a Cosmic Lamb Marries: The Image of the Wedding of the Lamb (Rev 19:7 ff.)," *Biblical Theology Bulletin* 28 (1998): 75-83

1999

"Criteria for Assessing the Authentic Words of Jesus: Some Specifications." Pages 27-45 in *Authenticating the Words of Jesus*. New Testament Tools and Studies 28/1. Edited by Craig A. Evans and Bruce Chilton. Leiden: Brill, 1999.

"Assessing the Historicity of Jesus' Walking on the Sea: Insights from Cross-Cultural Social Psychology." Pages 351-371 in *Authenticating the Activities of Jesus*. New Testament Tools and Studies 28.2. Edited by Craig A. Evans and Bruce Chilton. Leiden: Brill, 1999.

"Three Theses for a More Adequate Reading of the New Testament," in Michael G. Lawler (ed.) Forthcoming.

"Rituale der Lebensexklusivität: Zu einer Definition des Opfers." Pp. XXX in *Opfer—theologische und kulturelle Kontexte* (Internationales Wisseschaftsforum der Universität Heidelberg: Internationales Symposion 19.–21. Oktober, 1995) Suhrkamp Verlag (forthcoming)

Book Reviews

1972

Sin, Redemption and Sacrifice: A Biblical and Patristic Study, by S. Lyonnet and L. Sabourin (AnBib 48, Rome: PIB, 1970) in *Journal of Biblical Literature* 91: 274-275.

—— *The Several Israels and an Essay: Religion and Modern Man*, by Samuel Sandmel (The James Gray Lectures 1968, N.Y.: Ktav, 1971) in *Catholic Biblical Quarterly* 34: 388.

—— *Das Koranische Jesusbild: Ein Beitrag zur Theologie des Korans*, by Heikki Räisänen (Finnische Gesellschaft für Missiologie und Oekumenik 20, Helsinki: Missiologian ja Ekumeniikan Seura R.V., 1971) in *Catholic Biblical Quarterly* 34: 529.

1973

Pharisaism in the Making: Selected Essays, by Louis Finkelstein (New York: Ktav, 1972) in *Catholic Biblical Quarterly* 35: 381-382.

1974

The Idea of Divine Hardening: A Comparative Study of the Notion of Divine Hardening, Leading Astray and Inciting to Evil in the Bible and the Qur'an, by Heikki Räisänen (Helsinki: Finnish Exegetical Society, 1972) in *Catholic Biblical Quarterly* 36: 136-137.

—— *Rabbinic Essays*, by Jacob Z. Lauterbach (New York: Ktav, 1973) in *Catholic Biblical Quarterly* 36: 413-414.

1975
The Hebrew Fragments of Pseudo-Philo's Liber Antiquitatum Preserved in the Chronicles of Jerahmeel, ed. by Daniel Harrington (Texts and Translations 3, Pseudepigrapha Series 3, Missoula: Society of Biblical Literature, 1974) in *Catholic Biblical Quarterly* 37: 261-262.

1976
The Testament of Job, ed. by Robert Kraft (Texts and Translations 4, Pseudepigrapha Series 4, Missoula: Society of Biblical Literature, 1974) in *Catholic Biblical Quarterly* 38: 112.

—— *Early Rabbinic Judaism: Historical Studies in Religion*, by Jacob Neusner (Studies in Judaism in Late Antiquity 13, Leiden: Brill, 1975) in *Catholic Biblical Quarterly* 38: 250-252.

1977
Aspects of Religious Propaganda in Judaism and Early Christianity, ed. Elisabeth S. Fiorenza (University of Notre Dame Center for the Study of Judaism and Early Christianity in Antiquity 2, South Bend: University of Notre Dame Press, 1976) in *Catholic Biblical Quarterly* 39: 150-151.

—— *Matthew, Luke and Mark*, by Bernard Orchard, O.S.B. (Griesbach Solution to the Synoptic Question 1, Manchester, Eng.: Koinonia Press, 1976) in *Catholic Biblical Quarterly* 39: 443-444.

—— *Pseudo-Philon. Les antiquités bibliques. Tome 1: Introduction et textes critiques*, by Daniel J. Harrington; *Tome 2: Introduction litteraire, commentaire et index*, by Charles Perrot and Pierre Maurice Bogaert (SC 229 & 230, Paris: Éditions du Cerf, 1976) in *Catholic Biblical Quarterly* 39: 598-600.

1978
Variant Versions of Targumic Traditions within Codex Neofiti I, by Shirley Lund and Julia A. Foster (SBL Aramaic Studies 2, Missoula: Scholars Press, 1977) in *Catholic Biblical Quarterly* 40: 409-410.

—— *Paul and Palestinian Judaism: A Comparison of Patterns in Religion*, by E. P. Sanders (London: SCM Press, 1977) in *Biblical Theology Bulletin* 8: 190-191.

1979
Sociology of Early Palestinian Christianity, by Gerd Theissen (Philadelphia: Fortress Press, 1978) in *Catholic Biblical Quarterly* 41: 176-178.

—— *The Tosefta Translated from the Hebrew: Sixth Division: Tohorot (The Order of Purities)*, by Jacob Neusner (N.Y.: Ktav), in *Biblical Theology Bulletin* 9: 44.

—— *The Lord's Prayer and Jewish Liturgy*, edited by J. J. Petuchowski and M. Brocke (N.Y.: Seabury, 1979) in *Biblical Theology Bulletin* 9: 89.

—— *Conversion to Judaism: From the Biblical Period to the Present*, by Joseph R. Rosenbloom (Cincinnati: Hebrew University College Press, 1978) in *Biblical Theology Bulletin* 9: 92-93.

1980

Wesen und Wirklichkeit der Wunder Jesu: Heilungen—Rettungen—Zeichen—Aufleuchtungen, by Otto Betz and Werner Grimm (Arbeiten zum Neuen Testament und Judentum, 2, Frankfurt a.M./Bern/Las Vegas: Lang, 1977) in *Journal of Biblical Literature* 99: 310-312.

—— *Targum y Resurreccion: Estudio de los textos del Targum Palestinense sobre la resurreccion*, by Antonio Rodriguez Carmona (Biblioteca teologica granadina, 18, Granada: Facultad de Teologia, 1978) in *Catholic Biblical Quarterly* 42: 419-420.

—— *Donum gentilicium: New Testament Studies in Honour of David Daube*, edited by E. Bammel, C.K. Barrett and W.D. Davies (Oxford: Oxford University Press, 1978) in *Catholic Biblical Quarterly* 42: 586-588.

1981

Jesus and His Adversaries: The Form and Function of the Conflict Stories in the Synoptic Tradition, by Arland J. Hultgren (Minneapolis: Augsburg, 1979) in *Catholic Biblical Quarterly* 43: 131-133.

—— *Anti-Judaism in Christian Theology*, by Charlotte Klein, trans. Edward Quinn (Philadelphia: Fortress, 1978) in *Biblical Theology Bulletin* 11: 31.

—— *The Tribes of Yahweh: A Sociology of Religion of Liberated Israel 1250–1050 B.C.E.*, by Norman K. Gottwald (Maryknoll: Orbis, 1979) in *Biblical Theology Bulletin* 11: 60.

—— *The Bible in its Literary Milieu*, edited by John Maier and Vincent Tollers (Grand Rapids: Eerdmans, 1979) in *Biblical Theology Bulletin* 11: 61-62.

—— *Christian Origins in Sociological Perspective: Methods, Resources*, by Howard Clark Kee (Philadelphia: Westminster, 1980) *Catholic Biblical Quarterly* 43: 470-472.

—— *Die Oden Salomos in ihrer Bedeutung für Neues Testament und Gnosis*, by Michael Lattke (Orbis Biblicus et Orientalis 25/1 and 25/2, Fribourg: Éditions

Universitaires, and Gottingen: Vandenhoeck & Ruprecht, 1979) in *Biblical Theology Bulletin* 11: 93.

1982
The Fragment-Targums of the Pentateuch According to their Extant Sources: Vol. 1, Texts, Indices, and Introductory Essays; Vol. 2, Translation, by Michael L. Klein (AnBib 76; Rome: PIB, 1980) in *Catholic Biblical Quarterly* 44: 651-652.

—— *Ideal Figures in Ancient Judaism: Profiles and Paradigms*, edited by John J. Collins and George W. E. Nickelsburg (Society of Biblical Literature Septuagint and Cognate Studies 12, Chico: Scholars Press, 1980) in *Catholic Biblical Quarterly* 44: 700-701.

1983
Mark as Story: An Introduction to the Narrative of a Gospel, by David Rhoads and Donald Michie (Philadelphia: Fortress, in *Biblical Theology Bulletin* 13: 102.

—— *Shirley Jackson Case and the Chicago School: The Socio-Historical Method*, by William J. Hynes (Society of Biblical Literature Biblical Scholarship in North America 5, Chico: Scholars Press, 1981) in *Interpretation* 37: 422-424.

—— *Questioning Christian Origins*, by J. K. Elliott (London: SCM Press, 1982) in *Religious Studies Review* 9: 272.

—— *Zum Regierungstil des römischen Kaisers: eine Antwort auf Fergus Millar*, by Jochen Bleicken (Sitzungberichte der wissenschaftlichen Gesellschaft an der Johann Wolfgang Goethe-Universität Frankfurt am Main 18/5, Wiesbaden: Steiner Verlag, 1982) in *Religious Studies Review* 9: 275.

—— *Foi et justification à Antioche: Interprétation d'un conflit (Ga 2,14-21)*, by René Kiefer (Lectio Divina 111, Paris: Cerf, 1982) in *Catholic Biblical Quarterly* 45: 691-692.

1984
Targum Onkelos to Genesis: A Critical Analysis Together with an English Translation (Based on A. Sperber's Edition), by Moses Aberbach and Bernard Grossfeld (New York: Ktav; Denver: Denver University/Center for Judaic Studies, 1982) in *Catholic Biblical Quarterly* 46: 300-301.

—— *In Memory of Her: A Feminist Theological Reconstruction of Christian Origins*, by Elisabeth Schüssler Fiorenza (New York: Crossroad, 1983), in *Religious Studies Review* 10: 179.

—— *Between Athens and Jerusalem: Jewish Identity in the Hellenistic Diaspora*, by John J. Collins (New York: Crossroad, 1983), in *Biblical Theology Bulletin* 14: 157.

1985

The New Testament and Homosexuality: Contextual Background for Contemporary Debate, by Robin Scroggs (Philadelphia: Fortress, 1983), in *Catholic Biblical Quarterly* 47: 173-174.

—— *Prophecy in Early Christianity and the Ancient Mediterranean World*, by David E. Aune (Grand Rapids: Eerdmans, 1983) in *Biblical Theology Bulletin* 15: 81.

—— *The Gospel and the Poor*, by Wolfgang Stegemann, trans. Dietlinde Elliott (Philadelphia: Fortress, 1984) in *Biblical Theology Bulletin* 15: 83-84.

—— *Targum Onkelos to Deuteronomy. An English Translation of the Text with Analysis and Commentary (Based on A. Sperber's Edition)*, by Israel Drazin (New York: Ktav, 1982) in *Catholic Biblical Quarterly* 47: 515-516.

—— *The First Urban Christians: The Social World of the Apostle Paul*, by Wayne A. Meeks (New Haven/London: Yale University Press, 1983), in *Journal of Biblical Literature* 104: 346-349.

—— *The Commerce of the Sacred: Mediation of the Divine among Jews in the Graeco-Roman Diaspora*, by Jack N. Lightstone (Brown Judaic Studies 59; Chico, CA: Scholars, 1984), in *Catholic Biblical Quarterly* 47: 731-732.

1986

Naming the Powers: The Language of Power in the New Testament (The Power: Volume I), by Walter Wink (Philadelphia: Fortress Press, 1984) in *Union Seminary Quarterly Review* 40 (1985) 73-76.

1987

The New Testament in Its Social Environment, by John E. Stambaugh and David L. Balch (Philadelphia: Westminster, 1986) in *Theology Today* 43/4: 601-602.

—— *Status und Rollen in den Paulusbriefen: Eine inhaltsanalytische Untersuchung zur Religionssoziologie*, by Aloys Funk (Innsbrucker Theologische Studien 7; Innsbruck/Vienna/Munich: Tyrolia, 1981) in *Catholic Biblical Quarterly* 49: 143-144.

—— *Bandits, Prophets, and Messiahs: Popular Movements at the Time of Jesus*, by Richard Horsley and John Hanson (Minneapolis: Winston Press, 1986) in *The Journal of Religion* 67: 537-538.

1988

Medicine, Miracle and Magic in New Testament Times, by Howard Clark Kee (SNTSMS 55; Cambridge/London/New York: Cambridge University Press, 1986) in *Catholic Biblical Quarterly* 50: 330-331.

—— *The Illegitimacy of Jesus: A Feminist Theological Interpretation of the Infancy Narratives*, by Jane Schaberg (San Francisco: Harper & Row, 1987) in *Biblical Theology Bulletin* 18: 118-119.

—— *Extraordinary Groups: An Examination of Unconventional Life-Styles*, by William M. Kephart (3rd ed., New York: St. Martin's Press, 1987) in *Religious Educator* 83: 144-145.

1989
Psychological Aspects of Pauline Theology, by Gerd Theissen (Philadelphia: Fortress Press, 1987) in *Catholic Biblical Quarterly* 51: 165-167.

—— *Das Charisma des Gekreuzigten: Zur Soziologie der Jesusbewegung*, by Michael N. Ebertz (WUNT 45; Tübingen: Mohr [Siebeck], 1987) in *Catholic Biblical Quarterly* 51: 741-743.

1990
The Creed as Symbol, by Nicholas Ayo (Notre Dame: University Press of Notre Dame, 1989) in *Religious Studies Review* 16: 246.

—— *The Social Structure of the Early Christian Communities*, by Dimitris J. Kyrtatas (London/N.Y.: Verson, 1987) in *Biblical Theology Bulletin* 20: 128-129.

—— *The Social and Ethnic Dimensions of Matthean Social History: "Go nowhere among the Gentiles ..." (Matt 10:5b)*, by Amy-Jill Levine (Lewiston: Mellen, 1988) in *Biblical Theology Bulletin* 20: 129-180.

—— *Christianity as a Social Movement*, by Anthony J. Blasi (New York: Peter Lang, 1989) in *Biblical Theology Bulletin* 20: 169.

1991
Giudaismo e nuovo testament: Il Caso delle decime, by Marcello del Verme (Naples: M. D'Auria, 1989) in *Biblical Theology Bulletin* 21: 79-80.

—— *Adults and Children in the Roman Empire*, by Thomas Wiederman (New Haven: Yale, 1989) in *Religious Studies Review* 17: 66.

1992
Discovering the Roman Family: Studies in Roman Social History, by Keith R. Bradley. (New York: Oxford University Press, 1991) in *Religious Studies Review* 18: 326.
—— *The Social History of Palestine in the Herodian Period: The Land is Mine*, by David A. Fiensy. (Lewiston: The Edwin Mellen Press, 1991) in *Journal for the Study of Judaism* 23/2 255-256.

1993

The Roman Family, by Suzanne Dixon (Baltimore: Johns Hopkins University Press, 1992) in *Religious Studies Review* 19: 258.

—— *Anthropology and Roman Culture: Kinship, Time, Images of the Soul*, by Maurizio Bettini. Trans. John Van Sickle. (Baltimore and London: Johns Hopkins University Press, 1991) *Biblical Theology Bulletin* 23: 181-182.

1994

Death-Ritual and Social Structure in Classical Antiquity, by Ian Morris. (Cambridge: Cambridge University Press, 1993) in *Religious Studies Review* 20: 54.

—— *A View from Rome: On the Eve of the Modernist Crisis*, by David G. Schultenover, S.J. (New York: Fordham University Press, 1993). *Bulletin of the Center for Religion and Society* 2:3-4.

—— *The Family, Women and Death: Comparative Studies* 2nd. ed., by S. C. Humphreys. (Ann Arbor: University of Michigan Press, 1993). *Religious Studies Review* 20: 331.

—— *The Victim: The Johannine Passion Narrative Reconsidered*, by J. Duncan M. Derrett. (Shipston-on-Stour, Warwickshire, England: Peter I. Drinkwater, 1993). *Biblical Theology Bulletin* 24: 198-199.

—— *Law, Politics and Society in the Ancient Mediterranean World*, eds. Baruch Halpern and Deborah W. Hobson (Sheffield: Sheffield Academic Press, 1993). *Catholic Biblical Quarterly* 56: 828-829.

1995

The Demography of Roman Egypt, by Roger S. Bagnall and Bruce W. Frier. (New York, NY: Cambridge University Press, 1994). *Religious Studies Review* 230.

—— *Scripture: The Soul of Theology*, by Joseph A. Fitzmyer (New York/Mahwah: Paulist Press, 1994). *Biblical Theology Bulletin* 25: 92.

—— *The Lord's Table: The Meaning of Food in Early Judaism and Christianity*, by Gillian Feeley-Harnick (Washington: Smithsonian, 1994). *Bible Review* 11/5: 14.

—— *The Origins of Christian Morality*, by Wayne A. Meeks. (New Haven: Yale University Press, 1993). *Theology Today* 52: 269-270.

Editing
——Board editor for *Transformations, Passages and Processes: Ritual Approaches to Biblical Texts* ed. by. Mark McVann. Semeia 67 (1994). Published 1995.

1996

La mesa compartida: Estudios del NT desde las ciencias sociales, by Rafael Aguirre.
(Presencia teológica 77; Santander: Editorial Sal Terrae, 1994). *Catholic Biblical
Quarterly*

—— *Birth, Death, and Motherhood in Classical Greece,* by Nancy Demand (Baltimore: Johns Hopkins University Press, 1994) *Religious Studies Review* 22/2:
153.

1997

A Feast of Meanings: Eucharistic Theologies from Jesus through Johannine Circles, by
Bruce Chilton. (Supplements to Novum Testamentum, 72. Leiden: Brill,
1994) *Biblical Interpretation* 5: 220.

—— *Crossing the Boundaries: Essays in Biblical Interpretation in Honor of Michael
D. Goulder,* ed. by Stanley E. Porter, Paul Joyce, and David E. Orton. (Biblical
Interpretation Series, 8. Leiden: E. J. Brill, 1994) *Biblical Interpretation* 5: 219.

—— *The Gospel Behind the Gospels: Current Studies on Q,* ed. by Ronald A.
Piper (Supplements to Novum Testamentum, 75. Leiden: E. J. Brill, 1995)
Biblical Interpretation 5: 220-21

—— *Despising Shame: Honor Discourse and Community Maintenance in the Epistle
to the Hebrews,* by David Arthur deSilva. SBLDS 152. Atlanta: Scholars Press,
1995. *Journal of Biblical Literature* 116 (1997) 378-80.

—— *The Rise of Christianity: A Sociologist Reconsiders History,* by Rodney Stark.
(Princeton: Princeton University Press, 1996). *Catholic Biblical Quarterly* 59:
593-95.

1998

Origins of Narrative: The Romantic Appropriation of the Bible, by Stephen Prickett.
Cambridge: Cambridge University Press, 1996. *Biblical Theology Bulletin* 28
(1998) 35-37.

—— *The Sign of Jonah Reconsidered: A Study of Its Meaning in the Gospel Traditions,* by Simon Chow. Coniectanea Biblica NT Series 27. Stockholm:
Almqvist & Wiksell International, 1995. *Biblical Interpretation* 6: 117-18.

—— *L'Église à l'âge apostolique,* by Hermann Hauser. Lectio Divina 164. Paris:
Cerf, 1996. *Biblical Interpretation* 6: 115-16.

—— *Moral Codes and Social Structure in Ancient Greece: A Sociology of Greek
Ethics from Homer to the Epicureans and Stoics,* by Joseph M. Bryant. Albany:
State University of New York Press, 1996. *Religious Studies Review* 24:291-
292.

——*Urchristliche Sozialgeschichte: Die Anfänge im Judentum und die Christusgemeinden in der Mediterraneen Welt.* By E. W. Stegemann and W. Stegemann. Stuttgart/Berlin/Cologne: Kohlhammer, 1995. *Religious Studies Review* 24: 301.

—— *Ancestor Masks and Aristocratic Power in Roman Culture.* By Harriet I. Flower. Oxford: Clarendon, 1996. *Religious Studies Review* 24: 416.

—— *The Birth of Christianity: Discovering What Happened in the Years Immediately after the Execution of Jesus.* By John Dominic Crossan. San Francisco: HarperSanFrancisco, 1998. *Religious Studies Review* 25:

—— *Conflict in the Miracle Stories: A Socio-Exegetical Study of Matthew 8 and 9.* By Evert-Jan Vledder. JSNT Supplement Series, 152; Sheffield, UK: Sheffield Academic Press, 1995. *Biblical Theology Bulletin* 29:45-46.

—— *A Postmodern Revelation: Signs of Astrology and the Apocalypse.* By Jacques M. Chevalier. Toronto, Buffalo, London: University of Toronto Press. 1997. *Journal of Religion* 79: 122-23.

—— *Greeks Bearing Gifts: The Public Use of Private Relationships in the Greek World, 435–323 BC.* By Lynette G. Mitchell. New York: Cambridge University Press, 1997. *Religious Studies Review* 25: 84-85.

1999
The Three Worlds of Paul of Tarsus. By Richard Wallace and Wynne Williams. New York/London: Routledge, 1998. *Biblical Theology Bulletin* 29: 47-48.

Bibliography

Abrahams, Roger D. 1970. A Performance-Centered Approach to Gossip. *Man* 5/2:232-254

Adan-Bayewitz, David and I. Perlman. 1990. The Local Trade of Sepphoris in the Roman Period. *IEJ* 40:153-172.

Adas, M. 1981. From Avoidance to Confrontation: Peasant Protest in Pre-colonial and Colonial South-East Asia. *Comparative Studies in Society and History* 23:217-247.

Alonso-Schökel, Luis. 1974. Narrative Structures in the Book of Judith. *Protocol Series of the Colloquies of the Center for Hermeneutical Studies in Hellenistic and Modern Culture.* 12/17: 1-20.

Alston, R. 1995. *Soldier and Society in Roman Egypt.* London: Routledge.

Appelbaum, Shimon. 1978. Judaea as a Roman Province: the Countryside as a Political and Economic Factors. *ANRW* II 8:355-396.

Applebaum, Shimon et al. 1978. The Towers of Samaria. *PEQ* 110:91-100.

Arav, Rami. 1988. Bethsaida. *IEJ* 38:187-88.

———. 1989. Bethsaida. *IEJ* 39:99-100.

———. 1991. Bethsaida. *IEJ* 41:184-85.

———. 1992. Bethsaida. *IEJ* 42:252-254.

Arendt, H. 1958. What was authority. Pages 81-112 in *Nomos I: Authority.* Edited by C.J. Friedrich. Cambridge, MA: Harvard University Press.

Arno, Andrew. 1980. Fijian Gossip as Adjudication: A Communication Model of Informal Social Control. *Journal of Anthropological Research* 36 3:343-360.

Ashton, John. 1991. *Understanding the Fourth Gospel.* Oxford: Clarendon.

Atkins, Robert A., Jr. 1991. *Egalitarian Community: Ethnography and Exegesis.* Tuscaloosa: University of Alabama Press.

Aune, David Edward. 1987. *The New Testament in Its Literary Environment.* Philadelphia: Westminster.

———. 1991. Romans as a Logos Protreptikos. Pages 278-296 in *The Romans Debate.* Edited by Karl P. Donfried. Rev. ed. Peabody, MA: Hendrickson.

Aviam, Mordechai. 1993. Galilee: The Hellenistic to Byzantine Periods. Pages 453-458 in vol. 2 of *The New Encyclopedia of Archaeological Excavations in The Holy Land.* Edited by Ephraim Stern. 4 vols. New York: Simon & Schuster 1993.

Avigad, Nahman. 1976. How the Wealthy Lived in Herodian Jerusalem. *BAR* 2,4:22-35.

Bader, Chris, and Alfred Demaris. 1996. A Test of the Stark-Bainbridge Theory of Affiliation with Religious Cults and Sects. *JSSR* 35:285-303.

Bader, G. 1988. *Symbolik des Todes Jesu.* Tübingen: Mohr.

Bagatti, Bellarmino and V. Tzaferis. 1993. Nazareth. Pages 1103-1106 in vol. 3 of *The New Encyclopedia of Archaeological Excavations in The Holy Land.* Edited by Ephraim Stern. 4 vols. New York: Simon & Schuster 1993.

Bagatti, Bellarmino. 1969. *Excavations in Nazareth, Vol. 1: From the Beginning till the XII Century.* Studium Biblicum Franciscanum, 17. Jerusalem: Franciscan Printing Press.

Bailey, F.G., ed. 1971. *Gifts and Poisons: The Politics of Reputation.* Oxford: Blackwell.

Bailey, F.G. 1971 [1966]. The Peasant View of the Bad Life. Pages 299-321 in *Peasants and Peasant Societies.* Edited by T. Shanin. Harmondsworth: Penguin Books.

Bailey, F.G. 1991. *The Prevalence of Deceit.* Ithaca and London: Cornell University Press.

Bailey, F.G. 1993. *The Kingdom of Individuals: an Essay on Self-respect and Social Obligation.* Ithaca: Cornell University Press.

Bailey, K.E. 1983. *Through Peasant Eyes: A Literary Cultural Approach to the Parables of Luke.* Grand Rapids, Mich.: Eerdmans.

Bainbridge, William Sims. 1978. *Satan's Power: a Deviant Psychotherapy Cult.* Los Angeles: Univ of California Press.

Bal, Mieke. 1995. *Head Hunting: Judith on the Cutting Edge of Knowledge* . Pages 253-285 in Brenner 1995.

Balch, Robert W. 1985. What's Wrong with the Study of New Religions and What We Can Do about It. Pages 24-39 in *Scientific Research of New Religions: Divergent Perspectives.* Proceedings of the Annual Meeting of the Pacific Division of the American Association for the Advancement of Science, and the 59th Meeting of the Rocky Mountain Division. Edited by Brock K. Kilbourne. San Francisco: AAAS.

Balch, Robert W. 1980. Looking Behind the Scenes in a Religious Cult: Implications for the Study of Conversion. *Sociological Analysis* 41:137-43.

Barker, Eileen. 1981. Who'd Be a Moonie?: A Comparative Study of Those Who Join the Unification Church in Britain. Pages 59-96 in *The Social Impact of New Religious Movements.* Edited by Bryan Wilson. New York: Rose of Sharon.

Barnes, John A. 1954. Class and Committees in a Norwegian Island Parish. *Human Relations* 7/1:39-58.

———. 1969. Networks and Political Process. Pages 51-76 in *Social Networks in Urban Situations: Analyses of Personal Relationships in Central African Towns.* Edited by J. C. Mitchell. Manchester: Manchester University Press.

Barrett, Charles Kingsley. 1978. *The Gospel According to St John.* Second ed. London: SPCK.

Barth, F. 1971. Role Dilemmas and Father-Son Dominance in Middle Eastern Kinship Systems. Pages 87-95 in *Kinship and Structure.* Edited by L. K. Hsu. Chicago: Universityof Chicago Press.

Barton, S. C. 1994. *Discipleship and Family Ties in Mark and Matthew.* Society for New Testament studies Monograph Series 80. Cambridge: Cambridge University Press.

Bauckham, Richard J., ed. 1998. *The Gospels for All Christians: Rethinking the Gospel Audiences*. Edinburgh: T. & T. Clark.

Beasley-Murray, George R. 1987. *John*. Word Biblical Commentary 36. Waco, Tex.: Word Publishers.

Beckford, James A. 1973. Religious Organisation: A Trend Report and Bibliography. *Current Sociology* 212:7-170.

———. 1978. Accounting for Conversion. *British Journal of Sociology* 29:249-61.

Behm, Johannes. 1938. θύω κτλ. *TWNT* III:180–223.

———. 1965. κλάω κτλ. *TDNT* 3:726-43.

Bellah, Robert N. 1970. Religious Evolution. Pages 20-50 in *Beyond Belief: Essays on Religion in a Post-traditional World*. New York: Harper & Row.

Ben-Tor, Amnon. 1993. Qiri, Tel. Pages 1228-1229 in vol. 4 of *The New Encyclopedia of Archaeological Excavations in the Holy Land*. Edited by Ephraim Stern. 4 vols. New York: Simon & Schuster, 1993.

Berger, P. L. 1954. The Sociological Study of Sectarianism. *Social Research* 21:467-485.

Best, E. 1981. *Following Jesus. Discipleship in the Gospel of Mark*. Journal for the Study of the New Testament Supplement Series 4. Sheffield: Sheffield Academic.

Betlyon, John W. 1992. Coinage. *ABD* 1:1085-89.

Blau, Peter M. 1964. *Exchange and Power in Social Life*. London: John Wiley.

Bloch, R.1977. La religión romana. *Historia de las Religiones* III:224-257.

Blok, A. 1969. Variations in Patronage. *Sociologische Gids* 16:365-378.

Blumenthal, A. 1937. The Nature of Gossip. *Sociology and Social Research* 22:31-37.

Boissevain, Jeremy. 1966. Patronage in Sicily. *Man* 1:18-33.

———. 1968. The Place of Non-groups in the Social Sciences. *Man* 3:542-56.

———. 1974. *Friends of Friends: Networks, Manipulators and Coalitions*. Oxford: Blackwell.

———. 1979. Network Analysis: A Reappraisal. *Current Anthropology* 20:392-94.

———. 1985. Networks. *The Social Science Encyclopedia*. Edited by A. Kuper and J. Kuper. London: Routledge.

Boissevain, Jeremy, and J. Clyde Mitchell, eds. 1973. *Network Analysis: Studies in Human Interaction*. The Hague: Mouton.

Bokser, Baruch M. 1992. Unleavened Bread and Passover, Feasts of. *ABD* 6:755-765.

Bolchazy, Ladislaus J. 1977. *Hospitality in Antiquity: Livy's Concept of its Humanizing Force*. Chicago: University of Chicago Press.

Bolle, Kees W., ed. 1987. *Secrecy in Religions*. Leiden: E. J. Brill.

Borg, Marcus J. 1984. *Conflict, Holiness and Politics in the Teachings of Jesus*. New York and Toronto: Edwin Mellen.

———. 1987. *Jesus. A New Vision*. San Francisco: Harper & Row.

———. 1991. Portraits of Jesus in Contemporary North American Scholarship. *HTR* 84:1-22.

Boring, M. Eugene. 1985. Criteria of Authenticity. The Lukan Beatitudes as a Test Case. *Forum* 1/4:3-38.

Bormann, Lukas 1995. *Stadt und Christengemeinde zur Zeit des Paulus*. Leiden: E. J. Brill.

Bosetti, E. – Nicacci, A. 1993. Lindemoniato e il festaiolo. Lc 7:34-35 Mt 11:18-19 sullo sfondo della tradizione sapienziale biblico-giudaica. Pages 381-394 in *Early Christianity in Context*. Monuments and Documents. Edited by F. Manns and E. Alliata. Jerusalem: Franciscan Printing Press.

Bott, E. 1957. *Family and Social Network*. London: Tavistock Publications.

Bourdieu, Pierre. 1965. The Sentiment of Honour in Kabyle Society. Pages 191-241 in *Honour and Shame: The Values of Mediterranean Society*. Edited by J. G. Peristiany. London: Weidenfeld & Nicolson.

Brandon, S. G. F. 1967. *Jesus and the Zealots: a Study of the Political Factor in Primitive Christianity*. New York: Scribners.

Braund, David. 1989. Function and Dysfunction: Personal Patronage in Roman Imperialism. Pages 137-52 in *Patronage in Ancient Society*. Edited by Andrew Wallace-Hadrill. London/New York: Routledge.

Brenner, Athalya, ed. 1995. *A Feminist Companion to Esther, Judith and Susannah*. The Feminist Companion to the Bible. Volume 7. Sheffield: Sheffield Academic Press.

Bromley, David G., and Phillip E. Hammond.1987. *The Future of New Religious Movements*. Macon, GA: Mercer.

Bromley, David G., and Anson D. Shupe. 1979. *Moonies in America: Cult, Church, and Crusade*. Beverly Hills: Sage Publications.

Brooke, George J. 1994. Isaiah 40:3 and the Wilderness Community. Pages 117-1132 in *New Qumran Texts and Studies: Proceedings of the First International Organization for Qumran Studies*. Edited by George J. Brooke and Florentino García Martínez. Paris, 1994. Studies on the Texts of the Desert of Judah 15. Leiden: E.J. Brill.

Broughton, T.R.S. 1933. The Roman Army. Pages. 427-445 in *The Beginnings of Christianity, Part I The Acts of the Apostles*. Edited by F.J. Foakes Jackson. London: Macmillan.

Brown, John Pairman. 1991. Prometheus, the Servant of Yahweh, Jesus: Legitimation and Repression in the Heritage of Persian Imperialism. Pages 109-125 in *The Bible and the Politics of Exegesis*. Edited by David Jobling, et al. Cleveland: Pilgrim.

Brown, Raymond E. 1966. *The Gospel According to John I-XII*. Anchor Bible 29A. Garden City, NY: Doubleday.

Brown, Raymond E.1972. The Gospel According to John XIII-XXI. Anchor Bible 29B. London: Geoffrey Chapman.

Brown, Raymond E. 1979. *The Community of the Beloved Disciple*. London: Geoffrey Chapman.

Brown, Raymond E., Joseph A Fitzmyer, and Roland E. Murphy, Roland E., eds. 1968. *Jerome Biblical Commentary*. Englewood Cliffs, N.J.: Prentice-Hall.

Bruns, Edgar J. 1954. Judith or Jael? *CBQ* 16:12-14.

——. 1956. The Genealogy of Judith. *CBQ* 18:19-22.

Buechler, Steven M. 1993. Beyond Resource Mobilization? Emerging Trends in Social Movement Theory. *The Sociological Quarterly* 34: 217-35.

Bultmann, R. 1963. *The History of the Synoptic Tradition.* Oxford: Clarendon.

——. 1968. *The History of the Synoptic Tradition.* Trans. John Marsh. Oxford: Basil Blackwell.

——. 1971. *The Gospel of John. A Commentary.* Trans. by G. R. Beasley-Murray, R.W.N. Hoare & J.K. Riches. Philadelphia: Westminster.

Burkert, Walter. 1972. *Homo Necans. Interpretation altgriechischer Opferriten und Mythen,* Berlin–New York: De Gruyter.

——. 1987. *Anthropologie des Religiösen Opfers. Die Sakralisierung der Gewalt.* Second Edition. Munich: Carl Friederich von Siemens Stiftung.

——. 1990. Griechische Tragödie und Opferritual. In *Wilder Ursprung.* Berlin: K. Wachenbach

Burt, Ronald S., and M. J. Minor, eds. 1983. *Applied Network Analysis: A Methodological Introduction.* Beverly Hills, CA: Sage.

Cameron, P.S. 1990. The Structure of Ephesians. *Filología Neotestamentaria* 5:3-17.

Campbell, J.K. 1964. *Honour, Family and Patronage: a Study of Institutions and Moral Values in a Greek Mountain Community.* Oxford: Clarendon.

Caponigro, Mark Stephen. 1992. Judith, Holding the Tale of Herodotus. Pages 47-59 in VanderKam 1992.

Carney, T.F. 1975. *The Shape of the Past: Models in Antiquity.* Lawrence, Kans.: Coronado.

Carson, D. A. 1988. John and the Johannine Epistles. Pages 245-264 *It Is Written: Scripture Citing Scripture. Essays in Honour of Barnabas Lindars.* Edited by D. A. Carson and H. G. M. Williamson. Cambridge: Cambridge University Press.

——. 1991. *The Gospel According to John.* Leicester, U.K.: Inter-Varsity Press and Grand Rapids, Mich.: W. B. Eerdmans.

Chenol, Rafael. 1996. Sol Invictus: un modelo religioso de integración imperial. Pages 81-109 in *La Religión como factor de integración y conflicto en el Mediterráneo.* Edited by A. Pérez and G. Cruz.

Chilton, Bruce. 1994. The Kingdom of God in Recent Discussion. Pages 254-280 in *Studying the Historical Jesus.* Edited by Bruce Chilton and Craig A. Evans. Leiden: Brill.

Clark, Elizabeth A. 1992. Elite Networks and Heresy Accusations: Towards a Social Description of the Origenist Controversy. *Semeia* 56:79-117.

Cohn, Norman. 1961. *The Pursuit of the Millennium.* 2nd ed. New York: Harper.

Collins, Randall. 1988. *Theoretical Sociology.* San Diego: Harcourt Brace Jovanovitch.

Conzelmann, H. 1954. *Die Mitte der Zeit. Studien dur Theologie des Lukas.* Tübingen: Mohr.

Cotter, Wendy 1996. The Collegia and Roman Law. State Restrictions on Voluntary Associations, 64 BCE–200 CE. Pages 74-89 in *Voluntary Asso-*

ciations in the Graeco-Roman World. Edited by John S. Kloppenborg and Stephen G. Wilson. London and New York: Routledge.

Cowley, A. E. 1913. The Book of Judith. Pp. 242-267 in *The Apocrypha and the Pseudepigrapha of the Old Testament in English: With Introductions and Critical and Explanatory Notes to the Several Books*. Volume 1: Apocrypha. Edited by C. H. Charles Oxford: Clarendon.

Cox, Bruce A. 1970. What is Hopi Gossip About? Information Management and Hopi Factions. *Man* 5:88-98.

Craffert, P. F. 1992. More on Models and Muddles in the Social-scientific Interpretation of the New Testament: The Sociological Fallacy Reconsidered. *Neotestamentica* 261:217-239.

———. 1993. The Pauline Movement and First-century Judaism: A Framework for Transforming the Issues. *Neotestamentica* 272:233-262.

Craven, Toni, 1977. Artistry and Faith in the Book of Judith. *Semeia* 8:75-101.

———. 1983. *Artistry and Faith in the Book of Judith*. Society of Biblical Literature Dissertation Series 70. Chico, CA: Scholars Press.

Crawshaw, R. 1974. Gossip Wears a Thousand Masks. *Prism* 2:45-47.

Creveld, M. van 1985. *Command in War*. London: Oxford University Press.

Crossan, John Dominic. 1991. *The Historical Jesus: The Life of a Mediterranean Jewish Peasant*. San Francisco: Harper.

———. 1993. *Jesus: a Revolutionary Biography*. San Francisco: Harper.

Dabrowa, E. ed. 1994. *The Roman and Byzantine Army in the East*. Krakow, Poland: Jagiellonian University Press.

Daly, Robert J., S.J. 1990. The Power of Sacrifice in Ancient Judaism and Christianity. *Journal of Ritual Studies* 4:191-198.

Dancy, J. C. 1972. *The Shorter Books of the Apocrypha*. Cambridge: Cambridge University Press.

Danker, Frederick W. 1972. *Jesus and the New Age*. St. Louis: Clayton Publishing House.

———. 1982. *Benefactor: Epigraphic Study of a Graeco-Roman and New Testament Semantic Field*. St. Louis, MI: Clayton Publishing House.

Dar, Shimon 1986. *Landscape and Pattern*. Oxford: BAR.

Davies, W.D. 1990. *The Gospel and the Land*. Berkeley: University of California Press.

Davies, W.D., and D.C. Allison 1988. *A Critical and Exegetical Commentary on the Gospel According to St. Matthew*. International Critical Commentary, vols. 1 & 2. Edinburgh: T & T Clark.

Deissmann, Adolf. 1965. *Light from the Ancient East*. Trans. Lionel R. M. Strachan. 4th ed. Grand Rapids, Mich.: Eerdmans. Original German 1908.

Delcor, Matthias. 1967. Le livre de Judith et l'époque grecque. *KLIO* 49: 151-179.

Dibelius, Martin. 1934. *From Tradition to Gospel*. Trans. Bertram Lee Wolf. New York: Charles Scribners Sons.

Dixon, N.F. 1976. *On The Psychology of Military Incompetence*. London: Futura Macdonald.

Dixon, S., 1992. *The Roman Family*. Baltimore: Johns Hopkins University Press.

Dodd, C. H. 1978. *The Interpretation of the Fourth Gospel*. Cambridge, etc: Cambridge University Press.

Dorn, Pamela. 1986. Gender and Personhood: Turkish Jewish Proverbs and the Politics of Reputation. *Womens Studies International Forum* 9/3: 295-301.

Douglas, Mary. 1990. Foreword to *The Gift. The Form and Reason for Exchange in Archaic Societies*, by Marcel Mauss. London: W. W. Norton.

Downing, F. Gerald. 1992. The Ambiguity of "The Pharisee and the Taxcollector" in the Greco-Roman world of Late Antiquity. *CBQ* 54: 80-99

Droge, Arthur J. 1983. Call Stories in Greek Biography and the Gospels. SBLSP 22:245-257.

Drummond, Andrew. 1989. Early Roman *clientes*. Pages 89-115 in *Patronage in Ancient Society*. Edited by Andrew Wallace-Hadrill. London/New York: Routledge.

du Boulay, Juliet. 1974. *Portrait of a Greek Mountain Village*. Oxford: Clarendon.

———. 1976. Lies, Mockery and Family Integrity. Pages 389-406 in *Mediterranean Family Structures*. Edited by J. G. Peristiany. Cambridge: Cambridge University Press.

Dubarle, A. M. 1959. La Mention de Judith dans la littérature ancienne, juive et chrétienne. *RB* 66:514-549.

Duling, Dennis C. 1979. *Jesus Christ through History*. New York: Harcourt, Brace, Jovanovich.

———. 1990. Binding and Loosing Matt 16:19; 18:18; John 20:23. *Forum* 3/4:3-31.

———. 1992a. Matthew's Plurisignificant Son of David in Social Science Perspective: Kinship, Kingship, Magic, and Miracle. *BTB* 22:99-116.

———. 1992b. Matthew Disciple. *ABD* 4:618-22.

———. 1993. Matthew and Marginality. *SBLSP* 32: 642-671.

———. 1995a. Small Groups: Social Science Research Applied to Second Testament Study. *BTB* 25:179-93.

———. 1995b. The Matthean Brotherhood and Marginal Scribal Leadership. Pages159-182 in Esler 1995.

———. 1997. Egalitarian Ideology, Leadership, and Factional Conflict in the Matthean Group. *BTB* 27:124-137.

Duling, Dennis C., and Norman Perrin. 1994. *The New Testament. Proclamation and Parenesis, Myth and History*. 3rd ed. Fort Worth: Harcourt Brace.

Duncan, J. and D. Ley, eds. 1993. *Place, Culture, Representation*. London: Routledge.

Dunn, J.D.G. 1988. *Romans 9–16*. Word Biblical Commentary. Dallas: Word.

Dyson, S.L. 1971. Native Revolt Patterns in the Roman Empire. *ANRW* II.3, 138-75.

Ebaugh, Helen Rose Fuchs, and Sharron Lee Vaughn. 1984. Ideology and Recruitment in Religious Groups. *Review of Religious Research* 26:148-57.

Edwards, Douglas. 1988. First Century Urban/Rural Relations in Lower Galilee. *SBLSP* 27: 169-82.

———. 1991. Surviving the Web of Roman Power: Religion and Politics in the Acts of the Apostles, Josephus, and Chariton's Chaereas and Callirhoe. Pages 179-201 in *Images of Empire*. Edited by L. Alexander. Sheffield: Sheffield Academic Press.

———. 1992. The Socio-Economic and Cultural Ethos of the Lower Galilee in the First Century: Implications for the Nascent Jesus Movement. Pages 53-73 in Levine 1992.

Eisenstadt, S. N. and Louis Roniger. 1980. Patron-Client Relations as a Model of Structuring Social Exchange. *Comparative Studies in Society and History* 22:42-77.

———. 1984. *Patrons, Clients and Friends: Interpersonal Relations and the Structure of Trust in Society.* Cambridge: Cambridge University Press.

Elliott, John H. 1966. *The Elect and the Holy.* Supplements to Novum Testamentum 12. Leiden: E.J. Brill.

———. 1981; 1990. *A Home For The Homeless. A Sociological Exegesis of I Peter, Its Situation and Strategy.* Philadelphia: Fortress. Second expanded edition with with a New Introduction (1990).

———. 1986. Social-Scientific criticism of the New Testament: More on Methods and Models. *Semeia* 35:1-33.

———. 1987. Patronage and Clientism in Early Christian Society: A Short Reading Guide. *Forum* 3/4:39-48.

———. 1990. Stages of the Jesus Movement: From Faction to Sect. Unpublished Paper read at the University of Pretoria.

———. 1991. Temple versus Household in Luke-Acts. Pages 211-240 in Neyrey ed.1991.

———. 1991a. The Evil Eye in the First Testament: The Ecology and Culture of a Pervasive Belief. Pp. 147-159 in *The Bible and the Politics of Exegesis*. Edited by David Jobling et al. Cleveland, Oh.: Pilgrim.

———. 1993. *What Is Social-scientific Criticism? Guides to Biblical Scholarship.* New Testament Series. Minneapolis: Fortress. British ed: *Social-scientific Criticism of the New Testament. An Introduction.* London: SPCK, 1995.

———. 1995. The Jewish Messianic Movement: From faction to sect. Pages 75-95 in Esler 1995.

———. 1996. Patronage and Clientage. Pages 144-156 in *The Social Sciences and New Testament Interpretation*. Edited by Richard L. Rohrbaugh. Peabody, Mass.: Hendrickson Publishers.

Ellwood, Robert S. 1988. *Religious and Spiritual Groups in Modern America.* 2nd ed. Englewood Cliffs, NJ: Prentice Hall.

Engberg-Pedersen, G. 1990. *The Stoic Theory of Oikeiôsis.* Denmark: Ahrrus University Press.

Esler, Philip F. 1998a. The Madness of Saul: A Cultural Reading of 1 Samuel 8-31. In *Biblical Studies/cultural Studies*. Edited by J. Cheryl Exum and Stephen D. Moore. Sheffield: Sheffield Academic Press.

——. 1998b. Community and Gospel in Early Christianity: A Response to Richard Bauckhams Gospels for All Christians. *Scottish Journal of Theology* 51:235-248.

——. 1998c. The David and Goliath Tradition in Mediterranean Perspective. Presented at the annual meeting of The Context Group, Portland, Oregon. March 20,1998.

——. 1998d. *Galatians.* London and New York: Routledge.

——. 1989. *Community and Gospel in Luke-Acts: The Social and Political Motivations of Lucan Theology.* Cambridge: Cambridge University Press.

——. 1994. The First Christians in Their Social Worlds: Social-scientific Approaches to New Testament Interpretation. London and New York: Routledge.

Esler, Philip F., ed. 1995. *Modelling Early Christianity: Social-scientific Studies of the New Testament in Its Context.* London and New York: Routledge.

Evans, Craig A. 1989. Jesus Action in the Temple and Evidence of Corruption in the First-Century Temple. *SBLSP* 28:522-39.

——. 1993. From Public Ministry to the Passion: Can a Link Be Found between the Galilean Life and the Judean Death of Jesus. *SBLSP* 32:460-74.

Evans Pritchard, E. E. 1976. Some Reminiscences and Reflections on Fieldwork. Pages 240-254 in *Witchcraft Oracles and Magic among the Azande.* Abridged with an Introduction by Eva Gillies. Oxford: Clarendon.

Feld, M.D. 1977. A Typology of Military Organization. Pages 31-69 in *The Structures of Violence: Armed Forces and Social Systems.* Beverly Hills, CA: Sage Publications.

Ferguson, E. 1980. Spiritual Sacrifice in Early Christianity and its Environment. *ANRW* II 23/2: 1151-1187.

Ferree, Myra Marx. 1992. The Political Context of Rationality: Rational Choice Theory and Resource Mobilization. Pages 29-52 in Morris and Mueller.

Festinger, Leon. 1954. A Theory of Social Comparison Processes. *Human Relations* 7:117-140.

Fiensy, David. 1991. *The Social History of Palestine in the Herodian Period.* Studies in the Bible and Early Christianity 20. Lewiston, N.Y.: Edwin Mellen.

——. 1994. Craftsmen as Brokers. Pages 57-68 in *Proceedings XIV. Eastern Great Lakes and Midwest Biblical Societies.*

Filson, F.V. 1960. *A Commentary on the Gospel According to St. Matthew.* Blacks New Testament Commentary. London: A & C Black.

Finegan, Jack. 1992. *The Archeology of the New Testament.* Revised edition. Princeton: Princeton University Press.

Finkelstein, Louis. 1938. The Oldest Midrash: Pre-Rabbinic Ideals and Teachings in the Passover Haggadah. *HTR* 31:291-317.

——. 1942. Pre-Maccabean Documents in the Passover Haggadah. *HTR* 35:291-332.

——. 1943. Pre-Maccabean Documents in the Passover Haggadah. *HTR* 36:1-38.

Finley, Moses I. 1985. War and Empire. Pages 67-87 in *Ancient History: Evidence and Models*. New York: Viking.

———. 1986. Anthropology and the Classics. Pages 102-119 in *Uses and Abuses of History*. London: Hogarth.

Firth, Raymond. 1956. Rumor in a Primitive Society. *Journal of Abnormal and Social Psychology* 53:122-32.

Fitzmyer, Joseph A. 1972. David, Being Therefore a Prophet... *Catholic Biblical Quarterly* 34:332-39.

———. 1974. The Story of the Dishonest Manager Luke 16:1-13. Pages 161-184 in *Essays on the Semitic Background of the New Testament*. Sources for Biblical Study 5. Missoula, Mont.: Scholars Press.

Fleddermann, H. 1992. The Demands of Discipleship. Mt 8:19-20 par. Lk 9:57-62. Pages 541-561 in *The Four Gospels*. Edited by F. van Segbroeck. Louvain: Louvain University Press.

Ford, Stephen. 1672. *The Evil Tongue Tryed and Found Guilty, Or, The Hainousness and Exceeding Sinfulness of Defaming and Back-biting Opened and Declared*. Microfilm. Ann Arbor, Mich.: University Microfilms 1982.

Foster, George M. 1967. Peasant Society and the Image of Limited Good. Pages 300-333 in *Peasant Society. A Reader*. Edited by Jack M. Potter, May N. Diaz and George M. Foster, Boston: Little, Brown and Company.

Fowler, Robert M. 1981. *Loaves and Fishes. The Function of the Feeding Stories in the Gospel of Mark*. Chico, Calif.: Scholars Press.

Frankel, Rafael. 1992. Some Oil Presses from Western Galilee. *BASOR* 286:39-71.

Freund, Richard A. 1991. Lying and Deception in the Biblical and Post-Biblical Judaic Tradition. *Scandinavian Journal of the Old Testament* 1:45-61.

Freyne, Sean. 1980. *Galilee from Alexander the Great to Hadrian 323 B.c.e. to 135 C.e.: a Study of Second Temple Judaism*. University of Notre Dame Center for the Study of Judaism and Christianity in Antiquity 5. Wilmington, Del.: Michael Glazier, Inc. and South Bend, Ind.: University of Notre Dame Press.

———. 1988. *Galilee, Jesus and the Gospels: Literary Approaches and Historical Investigations*. Philadelphia: Fortress.

———. 1992. Hellenistic/Roman Galilee. *ABD* 2:895-99.

Frischer, Bernard.1982. *The Sculpted Word. Epicureanism and Philosophical Recruitment in Ancient Greece*. Berkeley: University of California Press.

Funk, Robert W. 1959. The Wilderness. *JBL* 78:205-214.

Fürst, H. 1977. Verlust der Familie—Gewinn einer neuen Familie Mk 10:29-30 par. Pages 17-46 in *Studia Historico-ecclesiastica. Festgabe für L. G. Spätling*. Edited by I. Vázquez. Roma.

Fusco, V. 1991. *Povertá e Sequela*. Studia Biblica 94. Brescia: Paideia.

Fusi, A. 1997. *Inside and Outside the Praetorium: Jesus and Pilate in John*. Unpublished Th.M. Thesis. Prague: International Baptist Theological Seminary.

Fustel de Coulanges, N. D. 1864, *La Ciudad antigua*. Barcelona: Ediciones Península, 1984.

Gamson, William A. 1992. The Social Psychology of Collective Action. Pages 53-76 in Morris and Mueller 1992.

Garrett, Susan. 1989. *The Demise of the Devil. Magic and the Demonic in Luke's Writings.* Minneapolis: Fortress.

———. 1990. Sociology and New Testament Studies: A Critical Evaluation of Rodney Stark's Contribution. *JSSR* 29:377-84.

Gauthier, P. 1973. Notes sur l'étranger et l'hospitalité en Grèce et à Rome. *Ancient Society* 4:1-21.

———. 1985. *Les Cités grecques et leurs bienfaiteurs. Contribution à l'histoire des institutions.* Paris: Supplément XII des Bulletins de Correspondance Hellénique.

Geertz, Clifford. 1966. Religion as cultural system. In *Anthropological Approaches to the Study of Religion.* Edited by M. Banton. New York: Praeger.

———. 1973. Thick Description: Toward an Interpretive Theory of Culture. Pages 3-30 in *The Interpretation of Cultures.* San Francisco: HarperCollins.

Gellner, E. Waterbury, J. 1977. *Patrons and Clients in Mediterranean Societies.* London: Duckworth.

Gilmore, David D. 1978. Varieties of Gossip in a Spanish Rural Community. *Ethnology* 17/1:89-99.

———. 1982. Anthropology of the Mediterranean Area. *Annual Review of Anthropology* 11:175-205.

———. 1987a. *Honor and Shame and the Unity of the Mediterranean.* Special Publication 22. Washington: American Anthropological Association.

———. 1987b. *Aggression and Community: Paradoxes of Andalusian Culture.* New Haven: Yale University Press.

Gilsenan, Michael. 1976. Lying, Honor, and Contradiction. Pages 191-219 in *Transaction and Meaning: Directions in the Anthropology of Exchange and Symbolic Behaviour.* Edited by Bruce Kapferer. Philadelphia: Institute for the Study of Human Issues.

Girard, R. 1987. *Das Heilige und die Gewalt,* Zürich.

Glaser, Barney G. 1967. Awareness Contexts and Social Interaction. In *Symbolic Interaction: A Reader in Social Psychology.* Edited by J.G. Manis and B.N. Meltzer. Boston: Allyn & Bacon.

Glatzer, Nahum ed. 1979. *The Passover Haggadah.* With English Translation, Introduction, and Commentary. Based on the commentaries of E. D. Goldschmidt. New York: Schocken.

Gluckman, Max. 1963. Gossip and Scandal. *Current Anthropology* 4:307-16.

———. 1968. Psychological, Sociological and Anthropological Explanations of Witchcraft and Gossip. *Man* 3:20-34.

Gnilka, J. 1986. *Das Matthäusevangelium Teil 1.* Freiburg: Herder.

Goitein, S.D. 1988. *A Mediterranean Society.* Vol. 5: The Individual. Berkeley, Calif.: University of California Press.

Goldschmidt, Walter. 1972. An Ethnography of Encounters: A Methodology for Enquiry into the Relationship between the Individual and Society. *Current Anthropology* 13:59-78.

Goldsmith, Daena. 1989. Gossip from the Natives Point of View. *Research on Language and Social Interaction* 23:163-193.

Goldsworthy, A. 1996. *The Roman Army at War 100 BC–AD 200.* Oxford: Clarendon.

Good, Edwin M. 1965. *Irony in the Old Testament.* Philadelphia: Westminster.

Goody, J. 1968. Kinship: II. Descent Groups. Pages 401-408. In *International Encyclopedia of The Social Sciences.* Vol. 3. Edited by D. L. Sills. New York: Macmillan and Free Press.

Gottwald, Norman K. *The Tribes of Yahweh. A Sociology of the Religion of Liberated Israel 1250-1050 B.C.E.* Maryknoll, N.Y.: Orbis, 1979.

———. 1985. *The Hebrew Bible: A Socio-literary Introduction.* Philadelphia: Fortress.

Green, Joel B. 1997. *The Theology of the Gospel of Luke.* Cambridge: Cambridge University Press.

Greenspahn, Frederick E. 1994. *When Brothers Dwell Together: The Preeminence of Younger Siblings in the Hebrew Bible.* New York and Oxford: Oxford University Press.

Greil, Arthur L., and David R. Rudy 1984. What Have We Learned from Process Models of Conversion? An Examination of Ten Case Studies. *Sociological Analysis* 17:305-23.

Greil, Arthur L. 1977. Previous Dispositions and Conversion to Perspectives of Social and Religious Movements. *Sociological Analysis* 38:115-25.

Guépin, J.-P. 1968. *The Tragic Paradox. Myth and Ritual in Greek Tragedy.* Amsterdam: A.M. Hakkert.

Guijarro, S. 1997. The Family in First Century Galilee. Pages 42-65. In *Constructing Early Christian Families.* Edited by Halvor Moxnes. New York/London: Routledge.

Guillen, J. 1985. *Urbs Roma. Vida y costumbres de los Romanos III. Religión y ejército.* Salamanca: Ediciones Sigueme.

Gumerman, G. J., and D. A. Phillips 1978. Archaeology beyond Anthropology. *American Antiquity* 432:184-191.

Guss, David M. 1982. The Enculturation of Makiritare Women. *Ethnology* 21/3:259-269.

Gutman, Shmaryahu 1993. Gamala. Pages 459-463 in vol. 2 of *The New Encyclopedia of Archaeological Excavations in the Holy Land.* Edited by Ephraim Stern. 4 vols. New York: Simon & Schuster 1993.

Haenchen, E. 1984. *John 2: a Commentary on the Gospel of John 7-21.* Hermeneia. Philadelphia: Fortress.

Hagner, D.A. 1993. *Matthew 1-13.* Word Biblical Commentary 33A. Dallas, Tex.: Word Books.

Hale, J. R. 1985. *Warfare and Society in Renaissance Europe* 1450–1620. Ithaca: Cornell University Press.

Hall, Edward T. 1976. *Beyond Culture.* Garden City, N.Y.: Doubleday Anchor.

———. 1983. *The Dance of Life.* Garden City, N.Y.: Doubleday Anchor.

Halliday, M.A.K. 1978. *Language as Social Semiotic. The Social Interpretation of Language and Meaning.* London: Arnold.

Hames-Jenkins, G. and C.C. Moskos. 1981. The Armed Forces and Society. *Current Sociology* 291-170.

Handelman, Don. 1973. Gossip in Encounters: The Transmission of Information in a Bounded Social Setting. *Man* 8/2:210-227.

Hands, A. R. 1968. *Charities and Social Aid in Greece and Rome*. Ithaca, NY: Cornell University Press.

Hannerz, Ulf.1967. Gossip, Networks and Culture in a Black American Ghetto. *Ethnos* 32:35-60.

Hannigan, John A. 1990. Apples and Oranges or Varieties of the Same Fruit? The New Religious Movements and the New Social Movements Compared. *Review of Religious Research* 31:246-58.

1991. Social Movement Theory and the Sociology of Religion: Toward a New Synthesis. *Sociological Analysis* 52: 311-331.

Hanson, K.C. 1996. Networks: An Annotated Bibliography. Unpublished paper for the Social Sciences Section, Catholic Biblical Association, 1996.

——. 1997. The Galilean Fishing Economy and the Jesus Tradition. BTB 27:99-111.

Hanson, K.C. and Douglas E. Oakman. 1998. *Palestine in the Time of Jesus: Social Structures and Social Conflicts*. Minneapolis: Fortress Press. <www. stolaf.edu/people/kchanson/ptj.html>

Harmon, D.P., 1978. The Family Festivals of Rome. *ANRW* II 16/2:1592-1603.

Harnack, A. 1905. *Militia Christi: the Christian Religion and the Military in the First Three Centuries* Transl. D.I. Gracie. Philadelphia: Fortress.1981.

Harries-Jenkins, G. 1977. *The Army in Victorian Society*. London: Routledge and Kegan Paul.

Harvey, David.1990. *The Condition of Postmodernity*. Oxford: Blackwell.

Haviland, John B.1977a. *Gossip, Reputation and Knowledge in Zinacantan*. Chicago: University of Chicago Press.

——. 1977b. Gossip as Competition in Zinacantan. *Journal of Communication* 27/1:186-191.

Headland, Thomas N., Kenneth L. Pike, and Marvin Hams 1990. *Emics and Etics. The Insider/Outsider Debate*. New York: Sage Publications.

Heichelheim, Fritz, 1959. Roman Syria. *An Economic Survey of Ancient Rome*. Vol. 4:121-257. General editor, Frank Tenney. Paterson, N.J.: Pageant Books Reprint.

Helgeland, J. 1980, Time and Space: Christian and Roman. *ANRW* II 23.2, 1285-1305.

Hellmann, Monika. 1992. *Judith—eine Frau im Spannungsfeld von Autonomie und göttlicher Führung*. Europäische Hochsschulshriften 23/444. Frankfurt am Main: Lang.

Hendin, David. 1976. *Guide to Ancient Jewish Coins* with values by Herbert Kreindler. New York: Attic Books.

Hengel, Martin. 1974. *Judaism and Hellenism*. 2 vols. Translated by John Bowden. Philadelphia: Fortress.

——. 1981a. *The Charismatic Leader and His Followers*. Trans. J. Greig. New York: Crossroad. [original ed. 1968]

——. 1981b. *Seguimiento y carisma. La radicalidad de la llamada de Jesús*. Santander: Sal Terrae.

——. 1989a. *The Zealots: Investigations into the Jewish Freedom Movement in the Period from Herod I until 70. A.D.* Edinburgh: T. & T. Clark.

——. 1989b. *The Johannine Question*. Translated by John Bowden. London: SCM Press and Philadelphia: Trinity.

Henten, Jan Willem van. 1995. Judith as Alternative Leader: A Rereading of Judith 7-13. Pages 224-252 in Brenner 1995.

Herzog, William R. 1994. *Parables as Subversive Speech: Jesus as Pedagogue of the Oppressed*. Louisville: Westminster John Knox.

Hobbs, T.R. 1988. An Experiment in Militarism. In *Ascribe to the Lord: Essays in Memory of Peter Campbell Craigie*. Edited by L. Eslinger et al. Sheffield: Sheffield Academic Press.

——. 1989 *a Time for War: a Study of Warfare in the Old Testament* Wilmington, Del.: Michael Glazier.

——. 1995. The Language of Warfare in the New Testament. Pages 259-273 in *Modelling Early Christianity: Social Scientific Studies of the New Testament and its Context*. Edited by Philip F. Esler. London: Routledge.

——. 1997. Reflections on Honor, Shame, and Covenant Relations. *JBL* 116:501-503.

Hobsbawn, Eric. 1959. *Primitive Rebels*. Manchester: Manchester University Press.

Hock, Ronald E. 1991. By the Gods, it's my one desire to see an actual Stoic: Epictetus Relations with Students and Visitors in His Personal Network. *Semeia* 56:121-142.

Hofstede, Geert. 1980. *Cultures Consequences: International Differences in Work-related Values*. Beverly Hills, CA: Sage Publications.

——. 1994. *Cultures and Organizations: Software of the Mind: Intercultural Cooperation and its Importance for Survival*. London: Harper Collins Publishers.

Hollenbach, Paul. 1993. Review of Jerome H. Neyrey ed. 1991. *CBQ* 55:175-76.

Holmberg, B. 1990. *Sociology and the New Testament: an Appraisal*. Minneapolis: Fortress.

Holmes, R. 1985. *Acts of War: The Behavior of Men in Battle*. New York: Free Press.

——. 1991. *Nuclear Warriors: Soldiers, Combat and Glasnost*. London: Jonathan Cape.

Horkheimer, M. – Adorno, Th.W. 1969. *Dialektik der Aufklärung*. Frankfurt am Main: Fischer.

Horsley, Richard A. 1988. *Jesus and the Spiral of Violence: Popular Jewish Resistance in Roman Palestine*. San Francisco: Harper.

——. 1989. *Sociology and the Jesus Movement*. New York: Crossroad.

Horsley, Richard A., and Hanson, John S. 1985. *Bandits, Prophets, and Messiahs: Popular Movements in the Time of Jesus*. Minneapolis: Winston.

Howard, M. 1981. *War and the Liberal Conscience*. London: Oxford University Press.

———. 1983. *The Causes of War and Other Essays*. Cambridge, Mass.: Harvard University Press.

Hughes, H. M. 1909. *The Ethics of Jewish Apocryphal Literature*. London: Robert Culley.

Humphreys, S.C. 1983. *The Family, Women and Death. Comparative Studies*. London: Routledge and Kegan Paul

Inwood, B. 1995. Politics and Paradox in Seneca's De beneficiis. In *Justice and Generosity. Studies in Hellenistic Social and Political Philosophy*. Edited by A. Laks and M. Schofield. Cambridge: Cambridge University Press.

Isaac, B. 1990. *The Limits of Empire*. Oxford: Clarendon.

Jacobson, A. D. 1995. Divided Families and Christian Origins. Pages 361-380 in *The Gospel behind the Gospels. Current Studies on Q*. Edited by R. A. Piper. Novum Testament Supplements 75. Leiden: E.J. Brill.

James, P. 1992. Forms of Abstract 'Community': From Tribe to Nation and State. *Philosophy of the Social Sciences* 22:313-336.

Janis, I.L. 1974. *The Victims of Groupthink*. Boston, Mass: Houghton and Mifflin.

Janowitz, M. ed. 1981. *Civil-military Relations: Regional Perspectives*. Beverley Hills, CA: Sage Publications.

Janowitz, M., and R.W. Little. 1975. Primary Groups and Military Effectiveness. Pages 93-115 in *Sociology and the Military Establishment*. Edited by M. Janowitz and. R.W. Little. Berkeley, Calif.: Sage Publications.

Jay, N. 1992. *Throughout Your Generations Forever. Sacrifice, Religion, and Paternity*. Chicago: University of Chicago Press

Jeremias, J. 1968. Poimên, etc. *TDNT* 6:485-502.

Jeremias, Joachim 1963. *The Parables of Jesus*. Second revised edition. New York: Scribners.

———.1966. *The Eucharistic Words of Jesus*. London: SCM.

Jervell, Jacob. 1972. *Luke and the People of God*. Minneapolis: Fortress.

———. 1991. Retrospect and Prospect in Luke-Acts Interpretation. *SBLSP* 30:383-404.

Johnson, B. 1963. On Church and Sect. *American Sociological Review* 28: 539-549.

———. 1987. A Sociologist of Religion Looks at the Future of New Religious Movements. Pages. 251-260. In Bromley and Hammond.

———. 1992. On Founders and Followers: Some Factors in the Development of New Religious Movements. *Sociological Analysis* 53: S1-S13.

Johnson, Jeffrey C. 1994. Anthropological Contributions to the Study of Social Networks: A Review. Pages 113-151. In *Advances in Social Network Analysis. Research in the Social and Behavioral Sciences*. Edited by Stanley Wasserman and Joseph Galaskiewicz. Thousand Oaks, Calif.: Sage Publications, Inc.

Johnson, Luke T. 1991. *The Gospel of Luke*. Collegeville, Minn.: The Liturgical Press.

Johnson, Robert A. 1977. Introduction. Pages 1-18 in *Psychohistory and Religion*. Edited by Roger A. Johnson. Philadelphia: Fortress.

Johnson, S.E. 1960. *The Gospel According to St. Mark. Black's New Testament Commentary*. London: A & C Black.

Johnson, Terry and Christopher Dandeker. 1989. Patronage: Relation and System. Pages 219-242 in *Patronage in Ancient Society*. Edited by Andrew Wallace-Hadrill. London and New York: Routledge.

Jones, Deborah. 1980. Gossip: Notes on Women's Oral Culture. *Women's Studies International Quarterly* 3/2-3:193-198.

Jordan, Mark D. 1986. Ancient Philosophic Protreptic and the Problem of Persuasive Genres. *Rhetorica* 4:309-33.

Joubert, Stephan J. 1994. A Kaleidoscope of Approaches: Paradigms, Paradigm-Changes and the *Umwelt* of the New Testament. *Neotestamentica* 28/1:23-40.

Kant, Laurence H. 1994. *The Interpretation of Religious Symbols in The Graeco-Roman World*. 3 vols. Dissertation. New Haven, Conn.: Yale University.

Käsemann, Ernst. 1968. *The Testament of Jesus. A Study of The Gospel of John in The Light of Chapter 17*. Translated by G. Krodel. London: SCM.

Kato, Takashi. 1997. *La Pensée sociale de Luc-Actes*. Paris: Presses Universitaires de France.

Kautsky, John H. 1982. *The Politics of Aristocratic Empires*. Chapel Hill, N.C.: University of North Carolina.

Kennedy, D.L 1996. *The Rome Army in the East*. JRA Supplement 18. Ann Arbor, Mich.: JRA.

Keppler, Angela. 1987. Der Verlauf von Klatschgesprächen. *Zeitschrift für Soziologie* 16/4:288-302.

Kidd, Reggie M. 1990. *Wealth and Beneficence in the Pastoral Epistles*. Atlanta, Ga.: Scholars Press.

Kindler, Arie. 1974. *Coins of the Land of Israel: Collection of the Bank of Israel: a Catalogue*. Translation edited by Gabriel Sivan. Jerusalem: Keter Publishing House Jerusalem Ltd.

Kingsbury, Jack D. 1978. The Verb ἀκολουθεῖν to follow as an Index of Matthew's View of His Community. *JBL* 97:56-73.

Kittel, G. 1964. ἀκολουθέω κτλ. *TDNT* 1:210-16.

Klandermans, Bert, and Dirk Oegema. 1987. Potentials, Networks, Motivations, and Barriers: Steps Towards Participation in Social Movements. *American Sociological Review* 52:519-31.

Klauck, Hans-Josef. 1996. *Die Religiöse Umwelt des Urchristentums II. Herrscher- und Kaiserkult, Philosophie, Gnosis*. Stuttgart: Kohlhammer Verlag.

Klausner, J. 1972. Queen Salome Alexandra. In Schalit 1972a:242-254.

Kloppenborg, John S. 1987. *The Formation of Q. Trajectories in Ancient Wisdom Collections*. Philadelphia: Fortress.

——. 1988. *Q Parallels. Synopsis, Critical Notes, and Concordance*. Sonoma, Calif.: Polebridge.

——.John S. 1989. The Dishonoured Master Luke 16,1-8a. *Bib* 70:474-95.

Kloppenborg, John S., and Stephen G. Wilson, eds. 1996. *Voluntary Associations in the Graeco-Roman World*. London and New York: Routledge.

Koepping, K-P. 1977. Ideologies and New Religious Movements: The Case of Shinreikyo and Its Doctrines in Comparative Perspective. *Japanese Journal of Religious Studies* 42-3:103-149.

Koester, H. 1982. *History Culture and Religion of the Hellenistic Age*. Philadelphia, PA: Fortress.

———. 1990. *Ancient Christian Gospels. Their History and Development*. Philadelphia: Trinity.

Kraabel, A. T. 1987. Unity and Diversity among Diaspora Synagogues. Pages 49-60 in *The Synagogue in Late Antiquity*. Edited by L. I. Levine. Philadelphia: American School of Oriental Research.

Kristen, P. 1995. *Familie, Kreuz und Leben. Nachfolge Jesu nach Q und dem Markusevangelium* MThS 42. Marburg.

Kuhn, Thomas S. 1970. *The Structure of Scientific Revolutions*. Chicago, Il.: University of Chicago Press.

Kuhrt, A. 1987. Usurpation, Conquest and Ceremonial from Babylon to Persia. Pages 20-55 in *Rituals of Royalty: Power and Ceremonial in Traditional Societies*. Edited by D. Cannadine and S. R. Price eds. Cambridge: Cambridge University Press.

Kühschelm, R. 1983. *Jüngerverfolgung und Geschick Jesu. Eine Exegetisch- bibeltheologische Untersuchung der Synoptischen Verfolgunsankündigen Mk 13,9-13 par und Mt 23,29-26 par*. Klosterneuburg: Katholisches Bibelwerk.

La Sor, William.1987. Discovering What Jewish Miqvaot Can Tell Us about Christian Baptism. *BAR* 13/1:52-59.

LaCapra, Dominick.1983. *Rethinking Intellectual History: Texts, Contexts, Language*. Ithaca and London: Cornell University Press.

Lacey, W. K. 1968. *The Family in Classical Greece*. Ithaca and London: Cornell University Press.

Lane, W.L 1974. *The Gospel According to St. Mark*. New International Commentary on the New Testament. Grand Rapids, Mich.: Eerdmans.

Lefebvre, Henri. 1991. *The Production of Space*. French orig. *La Production de l'espace*.1974. Oxford: Blackwell.

Lemche, N.P. 1995. Of Kings and Clients: On Loyalty between the Ruler and the Ruled in Ancient Israel. *Semeia* 66:119-132 .

Lenski, Gerhard, and Jean Lenski. 1987. *Human Societies. An Introduction to Macrosociology*. 5th ed. New York: McGraw-Hill.

Lenski, Gerhard. 1984. *Power and Privilege: A Theory of Social Stratification*. Chapel Hill: University of North Carolina Press.

Lévi-Strauss, Claude. 1957. The Principle of Reciprocity. In *Sociological Theory*. Edited by Lewis A. Coser and B. Rosenberg. New York: MacMillan.

Levine, Amy-Jill. 1992. Sacrifice and Salvation: Otherness and Domestication in the Book of Judith. Pages 17-30 in VanderKam 1992.

Levine, Lee ed. 1992. *The Galilee in Late Antiquity*. New York and Jerusalem: The Jewish Theological Seminary of America.

Lewis, Naphtali, and M. Reinhold. 1955. *Roman Civilization*. Vol. 2: The Empire. New York: Columbia University Press.

Lightstone, J. N. 1984. *The Commerce of the Sacred: Mediation of the Divine among Jews in the Graeco-Roman Diaspora*. Chico, Ca.: Scholars Press.

Lincoln, A.T., and A.J. Wedderburn. 1993, *The Theology of the Later Pauline Letters*. Cambridge: Cambridge University Press

Lindars, Barnabas. 1972. *The Gospel of John*. New Century Bible. London: Oliphants.

Link, J. 1990. *Literaturwissenschaftliche Grundbegriffe*. 4th ed. Munich: W. Fink

Linton, Ralph. 1943. *Nativistic Movements*. Indianapolis: Bobbs-Merrill.

Liverani, M. 1979. The Ideology of the Assyrian Empire. Pages 297-312 in *Power and Propaganda: A Symposium on Ancient Empires*. Edited by M. T. Larsen. Copenhagen: Akademisk Vorlag.

Lofland, John, and Norman Skonovd. 1981. Conversion Motifs. *JSSR* 20: 373-85.

Lofland, John, and Rodney Stark. 1965. Becoming a World Saver: A Theory of Conversion to a Deviant Perspective. *American Sociological Review* 30:862-75.

Lofland, John. 1977. Becoming a World-Saver Revisited. *American Behavior Scientist* 20:805-18. Reprinted as pages 10-23 in *Conversion Careers: In and Out of the New Religions*. Edited by J. Richardson. Beverly Hills: Sage, 1978.

Lohfink, Gerhard. 1996. *La Iglesia que Jesús quería*. Bilbao: Desclée de Brouwer.

Louw, Johannes P., and Eugene A. Nida, eds. 1988. *Greek-English Lexicon of The New Testament Based on Semantic Domains*. Vol. 1: Introduction and Domains. New York, N.Y.: United Bible Societies.

Luz, Ulrich. 1990. *Das Evangelium Nach Matthäus. Mtt. 8–17.* (EKK NT 1.2). Zürich: Benziger Verlag.

Ma'oz, Zvi Uri 1993. Golan: Hellenistic Period to the Middle Ages. Pages 534-546 in vol. 2 of *The New Encyclopedia of Archaeological Excavations in The Holy Land*. Edited by Ephraim Stern. 4 vols. New York: Simon & Schuster 1993.

Macdonald, L. 1983. *Somme*. London: Athenaeum.

———. 1988a. *1914*. London: Athenaeum.

———. 1988b *1914-1918: Voices and Images of the Great War*. Harmondsworth: Penguin Books.

MacDonald, M.Y. 1988. *The Pauline Churches: A Socio-historical Study of Institutionalization in the Pauline and Deutero-pauline Writings*. Cambridge: Cambridge University Press.

Mack, Burton L. 1988. *A Myth of Innocence: Mark and Christian Origins*. Philadelphia: Fortress.

———. 1993. *The Lost Gospel: The Book of Q and Christian Origins*. San Francisco: Harper.

MacMullen, Ramsay.1974, *Roman Social Relations*, London: Yale University Press.

——. 1970. Market-Days in the Roman Empire. *Phoenix* 24:333-41.

Malherbe, Abraham.1977. *The Cynic Epistles: a Study Edition*. Missoula, Mont.: Scholars Press.

——. 1983. *Social Aspects of Early Christianity*. Second ed. Philadelphia: Fortress.

Malina, Bruce J. 1980. What is Prayer? *The Bible Today* 18: 214-220.

——. 1981. *The New Testament World: Insights from Cultural Anthropology*. Atlanta: John Knox; London: SCM.

——. 1983. Why Interpret the Bible with the Social Sciences. *American Baptist Quarterly* 2:119-133.

——. 1984. Jesus as Charismatic Leader? *BTB* 14: 55-62.

——. 1986a *Christian Origins and Cultural Anthropology. Practical Models for Biblical Interpretation*. Atlanta: John Knox.

——. 1986b. Religion in the World of Paul. *BTB* 163:92-102.

——. 1986c. The Received View and What It Cannot Do: III John and Hospitality. *Semeia* 35:171-94.

——. 1987. Wealth and Poverty in the New Testament and Its World. *Interpretation* 41: 354-367.

——. 1988a Patron and Client. The Analogy behind Synoptic Theology. *Forum* 4/1:2-32.

——. 1988b A Conflict Approach to Mark 7. *Forum* 4/3:3-30.

——. 1990. Mother and Son. *BTB* 20:54-64.

——. 1991a. Reading Theory Perspective. Reading Luke-Acts. Pages 3-23 in Neyrey ed.1991.

——. 1991b. Interpretation: Reading, Abduction, Metaphor. Pages 253-266 in *The Bible and the Politics of Exegesis*. Edited by David Jobling, et al. Cleveland, Oh: Pilgrim Press.

——. 1993a. *The New Testament World. Insights from Cultural Anthropology*. Second Revised Ed. Louisville: Westminster John Knox.

——. 1993b. Apocalyptic and Territoriality. Pp. 369-380 in *Early Christianity in Context. Monuments and Documents*. Edited by F. Manns and E. Alliata. Jerusalem: Franciscan Printing Press.

——. 1994a. Religion in the imagined New Testament World: More Social Science Lenses. *Scriptura* 51:1-26.

——. 1994b. John's: The Maverick Christian Group—The Evidence of Sociolinguistics. *BTB* 24:167-182.

——. 1995a. *On the Genre and Message of Revelation. Star Visions and Sky Journeys*. Peabody, Mass.: Hendrickson Publishers.

——. 1995b. Early Christian Groups: Using Small Group Formation Theory to Explain Christian Organizations. Pages 96-113 in Esler 1995.

——.1995c. *El Mundo del Nuevo Testamento*. Estella: Verbo Divino.

——. 1996a. Mediterranean Sacrifice: Dimensions of Domestic and Political Religion. *BTB* 261:26-44.

——. 1996b Rhetorical Criticism and Social Scientific Criticism: Why Won't Romanticism Leave Us Alone? Pages 72-101in *Rhetoric, Scripture and Theology: Essays from the 1994 Pretoria Conference*. Journal for the Study of the

New Testament Supplement 131. Edited by S. E. Porter and T. H. Ol-
bright. Sheffield: Academic Press.

———. 1996c. *The Social World of Jesus and the Gospels.* London and New York:
Routledge.

———. 1996d. Mediterranean Sacrifice: Dimensions of Domestic and Political
Religion. *BTB* 26: 26-44.

Malina, Bruce J., and Jerome H. Neyrey. 1988. *Calling Jesus Names. The Social
Value of Labels in Matthew.* Foundations and Facets, Social Facets. Sonoma,
Calif.: Polebridge Press.

———. 1991a. Honor and Shame in Luke-Acts: Pivotal Values of the Mediterranean World. Pages 25-65 in Neyrey ed. 1991.

———. 1991b. Conflict in Luke-Acts. Labelling and Deviance Theory. Pp. 97-
122. In Neyrey ed.1991.

———. 1996. *Portraits of Paul: An Archaeology of Ancient Personality.* Louisville,
KY: Westminster John Knox.

Malina, Bruce J. and Richard L. Rohrbaugh. 1992. *Social-science Commentary
on the Synoptic Gospels.* Minneapolis: Fortress.

———. 1998. *Social-science Commentary on the Gospel of John.* Minneapolis: Fortress.

Malmberg, T. 1980. *Human Territoriality: Survey of Behavioural Territories in Man
with Preliminary Analysis and Discussion of Meaning.* The Hague: Mouton.

Marco Perez, A. 1993. El concepto de xeinos en Homero y en el N.T. Pages
293-300 in *IV Simposio Bíblico Español I. Biblia y culturas.* Valencia-Granada.

Marrou, H. I. 1956. *A History of Education in Antiquity.* Madison: University of
Wisconsin Press.

Marsden, Peter V. 1992. Social Network Theory. Pages 1887-1894 in vol. 4
Encyclopedia of Sociology. Edited by E. F. Borgatta and M. L. Borgatta. Five
vols. New York: Macmillan.

Marshall, I. H. 1978. *The Gospel of Luke. A Commentary on the Greek Text.*
Exeter: Paternoster.

Marshall, Peter. 1987. *Enmity in Corinth: Social Conventions in Paul's Relations
with the Corinthians.* Tübingen: J. C. B. Mohr [Paul Siebeck].

Martyn, J. Louis. 1968. *History and Theology in the Fourth Gospel.* New York:
Harper & Row.

Marxsen, W. 1981. *El Evangelista Marcos.* Salamanca: Ediciones Sígueme.

Mason, Steve. 1996. Philosophiai. Graeco-Roman, Judean and Christian.
Pages 31-58 in *Voluntary Associations in the Graeco-Roman World.* Edited by
John S. Kloppenborg and Stephen G. Wilson. London and New York:
Routledge.

Maurach, G. 1991. *Seneca. Leben und Werk.* Darmstadt: Wissenschaftliche Buch-
gesellschaft.

Mazar, Benjamin. 1980. Excavations near Temple Mount Reveal Splendors of
Herodian Jerusalem. *BAR* 6/4:44-59.

Mazzolani, L. 1972. *The Idea of the City in Roman Thought.* Bloomington, Ind.:
Indiana University Press. First ed.1970.

McCarthy, John D., and Mayer Zald. 1973. *The Trend of Social Movements in America: Professionalization and Resource Mobilization.* Morristown, N.J.: General Learning.

McVann, Mark, ed. 1993. The Apocalypse of John in Social-Scientific Perspective. The focus of the Fall 1993 issue of *Listening: Journal of Religion and Culture* 28/3.

Meeks, Wayne A. 1972. The Man from Heaven and Johannine Sectarianism. *JBL* 91:44-72

———. 1983. *The First Urban Christians: The Social World of the Apostle Paul.* New Haven: Yale University Press.

———. 1986. *The Moral World of The First Christians.* London: SPCK.

Meier, John P. 1994. *A Marginal Jew. Rethinking the Historical Jesus.* Vol. 2. New York: Doubleday.

Melton, J. Gordon. 1993. Another Look at New Religions. *The Annals of the American Academy of Political and Social Science.* London: Sage.

Merideth, Betsy. 1989. Desire and Danger: The Drama of Betrayal in Judges and Judith. In *Anti-covenant: Counter-reading Women's Lives in the Hebrew Bible.* Edited by M. Bal. Sheffield: Almond Press.

Meshorer, Yaakov. 1982. *Ancient Jewish Coinage. Volume 1: Persian Period through Hasmoneans.* New York: Amphora Books.

Meyers, Eric M. 1992a. Roman Sepphoris in Light of New Archeological Evidence. Pages 321-338 in Levine 1992.

———. 1992b. The Challenge of Hellenism for Early Judaism and Christianity. *BA* 55:84-91.

Meyers, Eric M., and J. F. Strange. 1981. *Archaeology, the Rabbis, and Early Christianity.* Nashville: Abingdon.

Michel, O. 1964. *spházo, sphagé, TWNT* VII:925.

Millar, F. 1993. *The Roman Near East, 32 BC–AD 337.* Cambridge, Mass.: Harvard University Press.

Miller, D. E. 1979. Sectarianism and Secularization: The Work of Bryan Wilson. *Religious Studies Review* 53:161-174.

Miller, Patrick. 1999. *They Cried to the Lord. The Form and Theology of Biblical Prayer.* Minneapolis: Fortress.

Miller, Robert J. 1991. The Ahistoricity of Jesus' Temple Demonstration: A Test Case in Methodology. *SBLSP* 30:235-52.

Mitchell, J. Clyde. 1969. The Concept and Use of Social Networks. Pages 1-50 in *Social Networks in Urban Situations: Analyses of Personal Relationships in Central African Towns.* Edited by J. Clyde Mitchell. Manchester: Manchester University Press.

———. 1973. Network Analysis: Studies in Human Interaction. Pages 14-38 in Boissevain and Mitchell 1973.

———. 1974. Social Networks. *Annual Review of Anthropology* 3:279-99.

Mitchell, J.P. 1996. Patrons and Clients. Pages 416-417 in *Encyclopedia of Social and Cultural Anthropology.* Edited by A. Barndard and J. Spencer. London: Routledge.

Moessner, David P. 1988. The Ironic Fulfillment of Israel's Glory. Pages 35–50 in *Luke–Acts and the Jewish People*. Edited by Joseph B. Tyson. Minneapolis: Fortress.

Moore, Carey A. 1985. *Judith: A New Translation with Introduction and Commentary*. The Anchor Bible 7. Garden City, NY: Doubleday.

Moore, Carey A. 1992b Why Wasn't the Book of Judith Included in the Hebrew Bible? Pages 61–71 in VanderKam 1992.

Moore, Carey A. 1992a Judith. ABD Vol. 3: 1117–1125.

Moorey, P. R. S. 1991. *A Century of Biblical Archaeology*. Louisville: Westminster John Knox.

Morris, Aldon D., and Carol McClurg Mueller, eds. 1992. *Frontiers in Social Movement Theory*. New Haven: Yale University Press.

Mott, Stephen C. 1975. The Power of Giving and Receiving: Reciprocity in Hellenistic Benevolence. In *Current Issues in Biblical and Patristic Interpretation. In Honor of M. Tenney*, Edited by Gerald Hawthorne. Grand Rapids, Mich.: Eerdmans.

Moxnes, Halvor. 1986. Meals and the New Community in Luke. *SEA* 51:158-67.

———. 1988. *The Economy of the Kingdom. Social Conflict and Economic Relations in Luke's Gospel*. Philadelphia: Fortress.

———. 1991. Patron-Client Relations and the New Community in Luke-Acts. Pages 241-268 in Neyrey ed. 1991.

———. 1995. He saw that the city was full of idols Acts 17:16. Visualizing the world of the First Christians. Pages 107-131 in *Mighty Minorities? Minorities in Early Christianity—Positions and Strategies*. Edited by D. Hellholm, H. Moxnes, and T. Karlsen Seim. Oslo: Scandinavian University Press.

Mueller, Carol McClurg. 1992. Building Social Movement Theory. Pages 3-25 in Morris and Mueller 1992.

Muilenburg, James. 1969. Form Criticism and Beyond. *JBL* 88:1-18.

Müller, Klaus W. 1991. König und Vater. Pages 21-43 in *Königsherrschaft Gottes und himmlischer Kult*. Wissenschaftliche Untersuchungen zum Neuen Testament 55. Edited by M. Hengel and A.M. Schwemer. Tübingen: J.C. Mohr.

Netzer, Ehud. 1993. Masada. Pages 973-985 in vol. 3 of *The New Encyclopedia of Archaeological Excavations in the Holy Land*. Edited by Ephraim Stern. 4 vols. New York: Simon and Schuster, 1993.

Neyrey , Jerome H. 1998. *Honor and Shame in the Gospel of Matthew*. Louisville, Ky.: Westminster John Knox Press.

———. 1985. *The Passion According to Luke*. New York: Paulist.

———. 1991. Ceremonies in Luke-Acts: The Case of Meals and Table-Fellowship. Pages 361-387 in Neyrey ed. 1991.

———. 1995. Loss of Wealth, Loss of Family and Loss of Honour. The Cultural Context of the Original Makarisms in Q. Pages 139-158 in Esler 1995.

———. 1997. Male and Female Space Terms. *Personal Correspondence*.

Neyrey, Jerome H., ed. 1991. *The Social World of Luke-Acts: Models for Interpretation*. Peabody, Mass.: Hendrickson Publishers.

Nillson, M.P. 1954. Roman and Greek Domestic Cult. Pages 77-85 in *Opuscula Romana*. Vol. 1. Lund: Skrifter Utgivna Svenska Institute i Rom.

Nun, M. 1990. *El Mar de Galilea y sus pescadores*. Kibbutz Ein Gev.

Oakman, Douglas E. 1986. *Jesus and the Economic Questions of His Day*. Studies in the Bible and Early Christianity 8. Lewiston, N.Y.: Mellen Press.

———. 1992. Was Jesus a Peasant? Implications for Reading the Samaritan Story Luke 10:30-35. *BTB* 22:117-25.

———. 1993. The Ancient Economy and St. John's Apocalypse. *Listening: Journal of Religion and Culture* 28:200-14.

———. 1996. *After Ten Years. A Draft History of the Context Group: Project on the Bible in Its Cultural Context*. Unpublished.

Ore, Oystein.1990. *Graphs and Their Uses*. Revised and updated by Robin J. Wilson. The Mathematical Association of America.

Orr, D.G. 1978. Roman Domestic Religion: the Evidence of the Household Shrines. *ANRW* II 16/2:1557-1591.

Osiek, Carolyn, and David Balch. 1997. *Families in the New Testament World: Households and House Churches*. Louisville, Ky.: Westminster John Knox.

OToole, R. 1976. Underground Traditions in the Study of Sectarianism: Non-religious Uses of the Concept "Sect." *JSSR* 152:145-156.

———. 1987. The Kingdom of God in Luke-Acts. Pages 147-162 in *The Kingdom of God in 20th-Century Interpretation*. Edited by W. Willis. Peabody, Mass.: Hendrickson Publishers.

Overman, J. Andrew. 1988. Who Were the First Urban Christians? *SBLSP* 27:160-68.

Paine, Robert 1967. What is Gossip? An Alternative Hypothesis. *Man* 2:278-285.

———. 1968. Gossip and Transaction. *Man* 3:305-308.

———. 1970. Informal Communication and Information Management. *Canadian Review Social Anthropology* 7:172-188.

Pamment, Margaret. 1982. John 17:20-23. *Novum Testamentum* 24:383-384.

Parsons, Talcott 1937. *The Structure of Social Action*. New York: McGraw-Hill.

———. 1969. *Politics and Social Structure*. Glencoe, Il.: Free Press.

———. 1971. *The System of Modern Societies*. Foundations of Modern Sociology Series. Englewood Cliffs, N.J.: Prentice-Hall.

Patterson, Stephen J. 1989. Fire and Dissension. Ipsisima Vox Jesu in Q 12:49, 51-53. *Forum* 5/2:121-139.

———. 1993. *The Gospel of Thomas and Jesus*. Sonoma, Calif.: Polbridge Press.

Peristiany, J. G., ed. 1965. *Honour and Shame: The Values of Mediterranean Society*. London: Weidenfeld & Nicholson.

Pesce, M. 1984. Discepolato gesuano e discepolato rabbinico. Problemi e prospettive della comparazione. *ANRW* II 25/1:351-89.

Pesch, R. 1969. Berufung und Sendung, Nachfolge und Mission. Eine Studie zu Mk 1, 16-20. *ZKT* 91: 1-31.

Peterman, G. W. 1997. *Paul's Gift from Philippi. Conventions of Gift Exchange and Christian Giving*. Cambridge: Cambridge University Press.

Pike, Kenneth L. 1966. Etic and Emic Standpoints for the Description of Behavior. Pages 152-163 in *Communication and Culture. Readings in the Codes of Human Interaction*. Edited by Alfred G. Smith. New York: Holt, Rinehart and Winston.

Pilch, John J. 1985. Healing in Mark: A Social Science Analysis. *BTB* 15: 142-150.

———. 1986. The Health Care System in Matthew. *BTB* 16 : 102-106.

———. 1988. Understanding Biblical Healing: Selecting the Appropriate Model. *BTB* 18: 60-66.

———. 1991. Sickness and Healing in Luke-Acts. Pages 181-209 in Neyrey ed.1991.

———. 1991a. *Introducing The Cultural Context of the Old Testament*. Hear the Word Vol. 1. New York/Mahwah, N.J.: Paulist.

———. 1991b. *Introducing the Cultural Context of the New Testament*. Hear the Word Vol. 2. New York/Mahwah, N. J.: Paulist Press.

———. 1992a. Lying and Deceit in the Letters to the Seven Churches: Perspectives in Cultural Anthropology. *BTB* 22: 126-157.

———. 1992b. Understanding Healing in the Social World of Early Christianity. *BTB* 22: 26-33

———. 1993a. Beat His Ribs While He is Young. Sir 30:12: A Window on the Mediterranean World. *BTB* 23:101-113.

———. 1993b. Insights and Models for Understanding the Healing Activity of the Historical Jesus. *SBLSP* 32: 154-177.

———. 1994. "Secrecy in the Mediterranean World: An Anthropological Perspective," *BTB* 24: 151-157.

———. 1997. BTB Readers' Guide: Psychological and Psychoanalytical Approaches to Interpreting the Bible in Social-Scientific Context. *BTB* 27:112-116

Pilch, John J., and Bruce J. Malina eds. 1998. *Handbook of Biblical Social Values*. Peabody, Mass.: Hendrickson Publishers. Updated and revised edition of 1993.

Pitt-Rivers, J. 1965. Honour and Social Status. Pages 19-78 in *Honour and Shame: The Values of Mediterranean Society*. Edited by J. G. Peristiany. London: Weidenfeld and Nicolson.

———. 1968a. Honor. Pages 503-511 in the *International Encyclopedia of the Social Sciences*. Vol 6. Edited by D.L. Sills. New York: MacMillan and Free Press.

———. 1968b. Pseudo-Kinship. Pages 408-413 in the *International Encyclopedia of the Social Sciences*. Vol 8. Edited by D.L. Sills. New York: MacMillan and Free Press.

———. 1977. *The Fate of Shechem or The Politics of Sex: Essays in the Anthropology of the Mediterranean*. Cambridge: Cambridge University Press.

Polag, A. 1982. *Fragmenta Q*. Neukirchen: Vluyn.

Polanyi, Karl 1977. *The Livelihood of Man*. Edited by H. W. Pearson. New York: Academic Press.

Polanyi, Karl, C. M. Arensberg, and H. W. Pearson eds. 1957. *Trade and Market in the Early Empires.* Glencoe, Il.: Free Press.

Prell, Marcus. 1997. *Armut im Antiken Rom. Von den Graecchen bis Kaiser Diokletian.* Stuttgart: Steiner Verlag.

Price, Jonathan. 1992. *Jerusalem under Siege: The Collapse of the Jewish State, 66–70 C.E.* Leiden: E. J. Brill.

Price, S.R.F. 1984. *Rituals and Power: The Roman Imperial Cult in Asia Minor.* Cambridge: Cambridge University Press

Prieur, Alexander. 1996. *Die Verkündigung der Gottesherrschaft.* Wissenschaftlichen Utersuchungen des Neuen Testament. Zweite Reihe. 89. Tübingen: J.C.B. Mohr.

Quass, Friedemann. 1993. *Die Honoratiorenschicht in den Städten des griechischen Ostens. Untersuchungen zur politischen und sozialen Entwicklung in hellenistischer und römischer Zeit.* Stuttgart: Steiner Verlag.

Quast, Kevin. 1989. *Peter and the Beloved Disciple: Figures for a Community in Crisis.* Journal for the Study of the New Testament Supplement Series 32. Sheffield: Academic Press.

Raadt, J. D. R. de. 1991. *Information and Managerial Wisdom.* Idaho: Paradigm Publications.

Rajak, Tessa. 1996. Benefactors in the Greco-Jewish Diaspora. In *Geschichte—Tradition—Reflexion. Band I: Judentum. Festschrift für Martin Hengel.* Edited by Peter Schäfer. Tübingen: J. C. B. Mohr [Paul Siebeck].

Rasmussen, Susan J. 1991. Modes of Persuasion: Gossip, Song and Divination in Tuareg Conflict Resolution. *Anthropological Quarterly* 64/1:30-46.

Reich, Ronny. 1987. More on Miqvaot. *BAR* 13,6:59-60.

———. 1993. The Great Mikveh Debate. *BAR* 19,2:52-53.

Reinhartz, A. 1993. Parents and Children: A Philonic Perspective. Pages 61-88 in *The Jewish Family in Antiquity.* Edited by Shaye J. D. Cohen. BJS 289. Atlanta: Scholars Press.

Rendsburg, Gary 1992. The Galilean Background of Mishnaic Hebrew. Pages 225-237 in Levine 1992.

Rich, J., and G. Shipley, eds. 1993. *War and Society in the Roman World.* London: Oxford University Press.

Rich, John. 1989. Patronage and Interstate Relations in the Roman Republic. Pages 117-135 in *Patronage in Ancient Society.* Edited by Andrew Wallace-Hadrill. London and New York: Routledge.

Richardson, James T. 1985. The Active vs. Passive Convert: Paradigm Conflict in Conversion/Recruitment Research. *JSSR* 24:163-79.

Richardson, Peter 1992. Why Turn the Tables? Jesus Protest in the Temple Precincts. *SBLSP* 31:507-23.

Ricoeur, P. 1986. *Die lebendige Metapher.* Munich. W. Fink.

Robbins, Thomas 1988. *Cults, Converts and Charisma: The Sociology of New Religious Movements.* London: Sage.

Robbins, Vernon K. 1982. Mark I.14-20: An Interpretation at the Intersection of Jewish and Graeco-Roman Traditions. *NTS* 28:220-36.

———. 1984. *Jesus the Teacher.* Philadelphia: Fortress. Second edition 1992.

——. 1989. Foxes, Birds, Burials, and Furrows. Pages 69-84 in *Patterns of Persuasion in the Gospels*. Burton L. Mack and Vernon K. Robbins. Sonoma, Calif.: Polebridge Press.

——. 1991a. The Social Location of the Implied Author of Luke-Acts. Pages 305-332 in Neyrey ed. 1991.

——. 1991b. Luke-Acts: A Mixed Population Seeks a Home in the Roman Empire. Pages 202-221 in *Images of Empire*. Edited by L. Alexander. Sheffield: Sheffield Academic Press.

——. 1996a. *The Tapestry of Early Christian Discourse: Rhetoric, Society and Ideology*. London: Routledge.

——. 1996b. *Exploring The Texture of Texts: A Guide to Socio-rhetorical Interpretation*. Valley Forge, Penn.: Trinity.

Rohrbaugh, Richard L.1991. The Pre-industrial city in Luke-Acts: Urban Social Relations. Pages 125-149 in Neyrey ed. 1991.

Rohrbaugh, Richard L., ed. 1996. *The Social Sciences and New Testament Interpretation*. Peabody, Mass.: Hendrickson Publishers.

Roitman, Adolfo D. 1992. Achior in the Book of Judith: His Role and Significance. Pages 31-45 in VanderKam 1992.

Roniger, Luis. 1983. Modern Patron-Client Relations and Historical Clientelism: Some Clues from Ancient Republican Rome. *Archives Européennes de Sociologie* 24:63-95.

Rose, H.J. 1957. The Religion of a Greek Household. *Euphrosyne* 1:95-116

Rosnow, Ralph, and Gary A. Fine. 1976. *Rumor and Gossip: The Social Psychology of Hearsay*. New York: Elsevier.

Roth, S. John. 1997. *The Blind, the Lame and the Poor. Character Types in Luke-Acts*. Sheffield: Sheffield Academic Press.

Rousseau, Jean Jacques. 1762. The Social Contract. Pages 3-158 in *Rousseau: Political Writings*. Edited by F. Watkins. London: Nelson, 1953.

Rousseau, John J., and Rami Arav. 1995. Fishing, Nets. Pages 93-97 in *Jesus and His World*. Minneapolis: Fortress.

Rysman, Alexander. 1977. How the Gossip Became a Woman. *Journal of Communication* 27/1 :160-163.

Sack, R.D. 1986. *Human Territoriality: Its Theory and History. Cambridge Studies in Historical Geography*. Cambridge: Cambridge University Press.

Sahlins, Marshall. 1966. *Tribesmen*. Englewood-Cliffs, N.J.: Prentice-Hall.

Saldarini, Anthony J. 1984. *Jesus and Passover*. New York: Paulist Press.

——. 1988a. *Pharisees, Scribes, and Sadducees in Palestinian Society. A Sociological Approach*. Wilmington, Del.: Michael Glazier.

——. 1988b Political and Social Roles of the Pharisees and Scribes in Galilee. *SBLSP* 27: 200-09.

——, 1988c. The Social Class of the Pharisees in Mark. Pages 69-77 in *The Social World of Formative Christianity and Judaism*. Edited by J. Neusner et al. Philadelphia: Fortress.

Saller, Richard P. 1982. *Personal Patronage under the Early Empire*. Cambridge: Cambridge University Press.

——. 1984. Familia, Domus and the Roman Conception of the Family. *Phoenix* 38:336-55.

——. 1989. Patronage and Friendship in Early Imperial Rome: Drawing the Distinction. Pages 49-62 in *Patronage in Ancient Society*. Edited by Andrew Wallace-Hadrill. London and New York: Routledge.

Sanders, E. P. 1985. *Jesus and Judaism*. Philadelphia: Fortress.

——. 1993. Jesus in Historical Context. *Theology Today* 50:429-48.

Sanders, J.A. 1975. From Isaiah 61 to Luke 4. Pages 75-106 in *Christianity, Judaism and Other Greco-Roman Cults. I*. Edited by J. Neusner. Leiden: E.J. Brill.

Schalit, Abraham, ed. 1972a. *The World History of the Jewish People: First Series: Ancient Times. Volume 6: The Hellenistic Age: Political History of Jewish Palestine from 332 B.C.E. to 67 B.C.E.* Jerusalem: Massada Publishing Co.

——. 1972b. The Political and Legal Instutions of the Hasmonean State. Pages 256-265 in Schalit 1972a.

Schenk, R. 1995. Einleitung in die Thematik. Zur Theorie des Opfers. Pages 1ff in *Zur Theorie des Opfers. Ein interdisziplinäres Gespräch*. Edited by R. Schenk. Stuttgart-Bad Cannstadt: Fromman-Holzboog.

Schmidt, K.L. 1965. καλέω. *TDNT* 3:487-501.

Schmidt, Steffen W. et al., ed. 1977. *Friends, Followers, and Factions*. Berkeley, Calif.: University of California Press.

Schnackenburg, Rudolf. 1982. *The Gospel according to St John*. Vol. 3: Commentary on Chapters 13-21. Translated by David Smith & G. A. Kon. London/Tunbridge Wells: Burns & Oates.

——. 1989. *El Evangelio según San Juan*. Vol I. Barcelona: Herder.

Schüssler Fiorenza, E. 1989. *En Memoria de Ella*. Bilbao: Desclée de Brouwer.

Schwankl, Otto. 1997. Lauft so, daß ihr gewinnt. Zur Wettkampfmetaphorik in 1 Kor 9. *Biblische Zeitschrift* 41/2:174-191.

Scott, Bernard Brandon. 1986. Essaying the Rock: The Authenticity of the Jesus Parable Tradition. *Forum* 2/1:3-53.

——. 1989. *Hear Then the Parable: A Commentary on the Parables of Jesus*. Minneapolis: Fortress.

Scott, J. 1985. *Weapons of the Weak: Everyday Forms of Peasant Resistance*. New Haven: Yale University Press.

——. 1996. Networks. Pages 794-795 in *The Social Science Encyclopedia*. Edited by Adam Kuper and Jessica Kuper. Second edition. London: Routledge.

Scroggs, R. 1975. The Earliest Christian Communities as Sectarian Movement. Pages 1-23 in *Christianity, Judaism and Other Greco-Roman Cults*. Vol 12. Part 2. Edited by J. Neusner. Leiden: E.J. Brill.

——. 1980. The Sociological Interpretation of the New Testament: The Present State of Research. *NTS* 26:164-79.

Seeley, David. 1993. Jesus' Temple Act. *CBQ* 55:263-83.

Seeman, Christopher. 1993. *The Urbanization of Herodian Galilee as an Historical Factor Contributing to the Emergence of the Jesus Movement*. Unpublished M.A. Thesis. Berkeley: Graduate Theological Union.

Segal, J. B. 1963. *The Hebrew Passover: from the Earliest Times to A.D. 70.* London Oriental Series 12. London: Oxford Univiversity Press.

Seim, Turid Karlsen, 1994. *The Double Message. Patterns of Gender in Luke-Acts.* Edinburgh: T & T Clark.

Seland, T. 1987. Jesus as Faction Leader: On the Exit of the Category "Sect". Pages 197-211 in *Context: Essays in Honour of Peder Johan Borgen.* Edited by W. Bøckman and R. E. Kristiansen. Trondheim: Tapir.

Selew, Philip. 1987. Reconstruction of Q 12:35-59. *SBLSP* 26:617-68.

Shanin, T. 1971 [1966]. The Peasantry as a Political Factor. Pages 238-263 in *Peasants and Peasant Societies.* Edited by T. Shanin. Harmondsworth: Penguin Books.

Shanks, Hershel. 1987. Devers' Sermon on the Mound. *BAR* 13,2:54-57.

Sharples, R. W. 1996. *Stoics, Epicureans and Sceptics. An Introduction to Hellenistic Philosophy.* London: Routledge.

Simmel, G. 1908. The Stranger. Pages 91-105. In G. Simmel, *On Individuality and Social Forms.* Edited by D.N. Levine. Repr. Chicago: University of Chicago Press, 1971.

Simpson, John H. 1990. The Stark-Bainbridge Theory of Religion. *JSSR* 29:367-71

Sjoberg, G. 1960. *The Preindustrial City.* New York: Free Press.

Skehan, Patrick W. 1962. Why Leave Out Judith? *CBQ* 24:147-154.

———. 1963. The Hand of Judith. *CBQ* 25:94-110.

Smith, Jonathan Z. 1989. *To Take Place. Toward a Theory in Ritual.* Chicago: University of Chicago Press.

Snow, David A., and Cynthia L. Phillips. 1980. The Lofland-Stark Conversion Model: A Critical Reassessment. *Social Problems* 27:430-47.

Snow, David A., Louis A. Zurcher, and Sheldon Ekland-Olson. 1980. Social Networks and Social Movements: A Microstructural Approach to Differential Recruitment. *American Sociological Review* 45:787-801.

Snow, David A., and Richard Machalek. 1984. The Sociology of Conversion. *Annual Review of Sociology* 10:167-90.

Sørensen, V. 1985. *Seneca. Ein Humanist an Neros Hof.* Second ed. München: C. H. Beck.

Spämann, R. 1995. Einleitende Bemerkungen zum Opferbegriff. Pp. 11 ff. in *Zur Theorie des Opfers. Ein interdisziplinäres Gespräch.* Edited by R. Schenk. Stuttgart-Bad Cannstadt: Fromman-Holzboog.

Spencer, J. 1996. Peasants. Pages 418-419 in *Encyclopedia of Social and Cultural Anthropology.* Edited by A. Barnard and J. Spencer. London: Routledge.

Spicq, C. 1994. εὐεργεθία. *Theological Lexicon of the New Testament,* Vol. 2. Peabody, Mass.: Hendrickson Publishers.

St. Croix, G. E. M. de. 1981. *The Class Struggle in the Ancient Greek World.* Ithaca, N.Y.: Cornell University Press.

Stählin, G., *xeinos. Grande Lessico del Nuovo Testamento* VIII:6-102.

Stambaugh, J. E., and David L. Balch. 1983. *The New Testament in Its Social Environment.* Philadelphia: Westminster.

Stanley, J. E. 1986. The Apocalypse and Contemporary Sect Analysis. *SBLSP* 25:412-421.

Stark, Rodney. 1980. Networks of Faith: Interpersonal Bonds and Recruitment to Cults and Sects. *American Journal of Sociology* 85:1376-1395.

———. 1987a. *A Theory of Religion*. New York: Peter Lang.

———. 1987b. How New Religions Succeed: A Theoretical Model. Pages 11-29 in Bromley and Hammond.

———. 1990. Response. *JSSR* 29:385-86.

———. 1996. *The Rise of Christianity. A Sociologist Reconsiders History*. Princeton: Princeton University Press.

Stark, R. &. Bainbridge, W. S. 1979. Of Churches, Sects, and Cults: Preliminary Concepts for a Theory of Religious Movements. *JSSR* 182:117-133.

Stark, Rodney, and Lynne Roberts. 1987. The Arithmetic of Social Movements: Theoretical Implications. Pages 346-365 in Bromley and Hammond 1987.

Stegemann, W. 1996. Der Tod Jesu als Opfer? Anthropologische Aspekte seiner Deutung im Neuen Testament. Pages 120ff in *Abschied von der Schuld: Zur Anthropologie und Theologie von Schuldbewusstsein, Opfer und Versöhnung*. Edited by R. Riess. Stuttgart: Kohlhammer.

Stein, R. H. 1989. Luke 14:26 and the Question of Authenticity. *Forum* 5/2:187-192.

Steinhauser, M. G. 1989. Putting One's Hand to the Plough. The Authenticity of Q 9: 61-62. *Forum* 5/2:151-158.

Stendahl, Krister. 1963. The Apostle Paul and the Introspective Conscience of the West. *HTR* 56:199-215.

Stern, M. 1974a The Reign of Herod and the Herodian Dynasty. Pages 216-307 in *The Jewish People in the First Century. Vol. One*. Edited by S. Safrai et al. Compendia Rerum Iudaicarum ad Novum Testamentum. Section One. Assen: Van Gorcum.

Stevenson, T. R. 1992. The Ideal Benefactor and the Father Analogy in Greek and Roman Thought. *Classical Quarterly* 42/2:421-436

Stone, Nira. 1992. Judith and Holofernes: Some Observations on the Development of the Scene in Art. Pages 73-93 in VanderKam 1992.

Strange, James F. 1992. Some Implications of Archaeology for New Testament Studies. What has Archaeology to do with Faith? Pages 23-59 in *Faith and Scholarship Colloquies*. Edited by James H. Charlesworth. Philadelphia: Trinity.

Stuehrenberg, Paul F.1992. Proselyte. *ABD* 5:503-505

Suggit, J. 1984. John XVII.17: *Ho Logos ho sos aletheia estin*. *JTS* n.s. 35: 104-117.

Suls, Jerry M. 1977. Gossip as Social Comparison. *Journal of Communication* 27/1:164-168.

Swatos, W. H. 1976. Weber or Troeltsch?: Methodology, Syndrome, and the Development of Church-Sect Theory. *JSSR* 152:129-144.

Tefft, Stanton K., ed. 1980a. *Secrecy: A Cross-cultural Perspective*. New York and London: Human Sciences.

Tefft, Stanton K. 1980b. Secrecy, Disclosure and Social Theory. Pages 35-72 In Tefft 1980a.

Theissen, Gerd. 1976. Die Tempelweissagung Jesu: Prophetie im Spannungsfeld von Stadt und Land. *TZ* 32:144-58.

———. 1978. *Sociology of Early Palestinian Christianity*. Philadelphia: Fortress. ET of *Soziologie der Jesusbewegung*. = 1977. *The First Followers of Jesus*. London: SCM, 1978. = *Sociología del Movimiento de Jesús*. Santander: Sal Terrae, 1979.

———. 1985. Nosotros lo hemos dejado todo y te hemos seguido Mc 10, 28. Seguimiento y desarraigo social en la sociedad judeo-palestina del siglo I d. C. Pages 41-78 in *Estudios de sociología del cristianismo primitivo*. Edited by G. Theissen. Salamanca: Ediciones Sígueme.

Theissen, G., and A. Mertz. 1996. *Der Historische Jesus*. Göttingen: Vandenhoeck and Ruprecht.

Theron, S. W. 1987. *Hina ôsin hen*. A Multifaceted Approach to an Important Thrust in the Prayer of Jesus in John 17. *Neotestamentica* 21:77-94.

Tidball, Derek J. 1985. On Wooing a Crocodile: An Historical Survey of the Relationship between Sociology and New Testament Studies. *Vox Evangelica* 15:95-109.

Tov, Emanuel. 1985. The Composition of 1 Samuel 16-18 in the Light of the Septuagintal Version. Pages 93-130 in *Empirical Models of Biblical Criticism*. Edited by Jeffrey H. Tigay. Philadelphia: University of Pennsylvania Press.

———. 1986. The Nature of the Differences between MT and the LXX in 1 Sam 17-18. Pages 19-46 in *The Story of David and Goliath: Textual and Literary Criticism*. Dominique Barthélemy, David W. Gooding, Johan Lust, and Emanuel Tov. Göttingen: Vandenhoeck & Ruprecht.

Track, J. 1996. Das Opfer am Ende. Pages 140 ff in *Abschied von der Schuld? Zur Anthropologie und Theologie von Schuldbewusstsein, Opfer und Versöhnung*. Edited by R. Riess. Stuttgart: Kohlhammer.

Troeltsch, Ernst. 1912. *Die Soziallehren der Christlichen Kirchen und Gruppen*. *Gesammelte Schriften* 1. Tübingen: Mohr Siebeck. Second ed. 1919. ET: *The Social Teaching of the Christian Churches*. 2 vols. New York: Harper & Brothers, 1960 first ET 1931.

Turner, Jonathan H. 1984. *Societal Stratification. A Theoretical Analysis*. New York: Columbia University Press.

Vaage, Leif E. 1989. Q1 and the Historical Jesus: Some Peculiar Sayings. *Forum* 5/2:159-176.

———. 1994. *Galilean Upstarts: Jesus' First Followers According to Q*. Valley Forge, Penn.: Trinity.

Van Iersel, B. M. F. 1996. Failed Followers in Mark: Mark 13:12 as a Key for the Identification of the Intended Readers. *CBQ* 58:244-263.

VanderKam, James C., ed. 1992. *No One Spoke Ill of Her: Essays on Judith*. Atlanta, Ga.: Scholars Press.

Vermes, Geza. 1993. *The Religion of Jesus the Jew*. Minneapolis: Fortress.

Veyne, P. 1990. *Bread and Circuses. Historical Sociology and Political Pluralism*. London: Penguin Books.

Von Clausewitz, K. 1832. *On War*. With an Introduction by A. Rapaport. Harmondsworth: Penguin Books, 1968.

Wallace-Hadrill, Andrew. 1989. *Patronage in Ancient Society*. London and New York: Routledge.

———. 1989. Patronage in Roman Society. Pages 91-87 Wallace-Hadrill.

Walsh, J. P. M. 1987. *The Mighty from Their Thrones: Power in the Biblical Tradition*. Philadelphia: Fortress.

Walzer, M. 1992. Les deux universalismes. *Esprit* 187:114-133.

Watson, F. 1986. *Paul, Judaism and the Gentiles: A Sociological Approach*. Cambridge: Cambridge University Press.

Watson, G.R. 1969. *The Roman Soldier*. London: Oxford University Press.

Weiser, A. 1991. Reich Gottes in der Apostelgeschichte. Pages 127-135 in *Der Treue Gottes Trauen. Beiträge zum Werk des Lukas*. Edited by C. Bussmann and W. Radl. Freiburg.

Wenschkewitz, H. 1932. *Die Spiritualisierung der Kultusbegriff Tempel, Priester und Opfer im Neuen Testament*. Angelos Beih. 4. Leipzig: E. Pfeiffer.

———. 1974. The Province of Judaea. Pages 308-376 in *The Jewish People in the First Century*. Vol. One . Edited by S. Safrai et al. Compendia Rerum Iudaicarum ad Novum Testamentum. Section One. Assen: Van Gorcum.

———. 1975. The Reign of Herod. Pages 71-123 in *The World History of the Jewish People*. Vol. VII, The Herodian Period. Edited by M. Avi-Yonah. London: W.H. Allen.

White, John M. 1997. The Glory of Christ. *ET* 108:179-180.

White, L. Michael. 1988. Shifting Sectarian Boundaries in Early Christianity. *BJRL* 703:7-24.

———. 1990. Morality Between Two Worlds: A Paradigm of Friendship in Philippians. In *Greeks, Romans and Christians, Essays in Honor of Abraham. J. Malherbe*. Edited by David L. Balch, Everett Fergusson and Wayne A. Meeks. Minneapolis: Fortress.

White, L Michael, ed. 1991. Social Networks in the Early Christian Environment: Issues and Methods for Social History. *Semeia* 56:1-202.

White, Sidnie Ann. 1992. In the Steps of Jael and Deborah: Judith as Heroine. Pages 5-16 in VanderKam 1992.

Whitten, N., Jr., and A. Wolfe. 1973. Network Analysis. Pages 717-746 in *Handbook of Social and Cultural Anthropology*. Edited by J. Honigmann. Chicago, Il: Rand McNally.

Wilde, J. A. 1974. *A Social Description of the Community Reflected in the Gospel of Mark*. Madison, N.J.: Drew University.

———. 1978. The Social World of Marks Gospel: A Word about Method. *SBLSP* 17/2:47-70.

Wilder, Amos 1987. Foreword. Pages vii-x in *The Kingdom of God in 20th-Century Interpretation*. Edited by W. Willis. Peabody, Mass.: Hendrickson Publishers.

Wilken, Robert L. 1992. *The Land Called Holy*. New Haven: Yale University Press.

Willis, W., ed. 1987. *The Kingdom of God in 20th-Century Interpretation*. Peabody, Mass.: Hendrickson Publishers.

Wilson, Bryan R. 1959a. An Analysis of Sect Development. *American Sociological Review* 241:3-15.

———. 1959b. *Sects and Society*. Berkeley: University of California Press.

———. 1973. *Magic and the Millennium. A Sociological Study of Religious Movements of Protest among Tribal and Third World Peoples*. New York: Harper & Row.

———. 1982. Religion in Sociological Perspective. Pages 89-120 in *The Sociology of Sects*. Edited by B. R. Wilson. Oxford: Oxford University Press.

———. 1988. Methodological Perspectives in the Study of Religious Minorities. *BJRL* 703:225-240.

Wilson, Peter J. 1974. Filcher of Good Names. *Man* 9:93-102.

Wilson, S.G. 1985. *Luke and the Law*. Cambridge: Cambridge University Press.

Winter, Bruce W. 1994. *Seek the Welfare of the City. Christians as Benefactors and Citizens*. Grand Rapids, Mich.: Eerdmans.

Witherington, Ben. 1995. *John's Wisdom. A Commentary on the Fourth Gospel*. Cambridge: Lutterworth.

Wolf, Eric.1966. Kinship, Friendship, and Patron-Client Relations in Complex Societies. Pages 1-22 in *The Social Anthropology of Complex Societies*. Edited by M. Banton. New York: Praeger.

Wright, C. J. H. 1990. *God's People in God's Land: Family and Property in the Old Testament*. Grand Rapids, Mich.: Eerdmans.

Wright, C.H.J. 1992. Jubilee, Year of. *ADB* 3:1025-1030

Wuellner, Wilhelm. 1967. *The Meaning of Fishers of Men*. Philadelphia: Fortress.

Yadin, Yagael 1966. *Masada: Herod's Fortress and the Zealots' Last Stand*. Translated by M. Pearlman. New York: Random House.

Yarbrough, O. L. 1993. Parents and Children in the Jewish Family of Antiquity. Pages 39-59 in *The Jewish Family in Antiquity*. Edited by Shaye J. D. Cohen. BJS 289. Atlanta: Scholars Press.

Yeivin, Zeev 1993. Chorazin. Pages 301-304 in vol. 1 of *The New Encyclopedia of Archaeological Excavations in the Holy Land*. Edited by Ephraim Stern. 4 vols. New York: Simon & Schuster. 1993.

Yerkovich, Sally. 1977. Gossiping as a Way of Speaking. *Journal of Communication* 27/1:192-197.

Zald, Mayer N. 1992. Looking Backward to Look Forward. Pages 326-348 in Morris and Mueller 1992.

Zinovieff, Sofka. 1991. Inside Out and Outside In: Gossip, Hospitality and the Greek Character. *Journal of Mediterranean Studies* 1/1:120-134.

Index of Modern Authors

Biblical Index

Old Testament

Errata

The author of chapter 8 of this volume is identified as Santiago Guijarro Oporto. It should be noted that this author has also published under the name Santiago Guijarro.

CPSIA information can be obtained
at www.ICGtesting.com
Printed in the USA
BVHW031915021220
594706BV00012B/84

9 781589 832879